CFA Institute

MW01714259

FINANCIAL STATEMENT ANALYSIS

CFA® Program Curriculum

2026 • LEVEL I • VOLUME 4

WILEY

ISBN 978-1-961409-86-6

May 2025

Please visit our website at
www.WileyGlobalFinance.com.

WILEY

SKYE995CAF0-BD18-4B95-9F18-391C10FF7647_022725

CONTENTS

How to Use the CFA Program Curriculum

The CFA® Program exams measure your mastery of the core knowledge, skills, and abilities required to succeed as an investment professional. These core competencies are the basis for the Candidate Body of Knowledge (CBOK™). The CBOK consists of four components:

A broad outline that lists the major CFA Program topic areas (www.cfainstitute.org/programs/cfa/curriculum/cbok/cbok)

Topic area weights that indicate the relative exam weightings of the top-level topic areas (www.cfainstitute.org/en/programs/cfa/curriculum)

Learning outcome statements (LOS) that tell you the specific knowledge, skills, and abilities you should gain from each curriculum topic area. You will find these statements at the start of each learning module and lesson. We encourage you to review the information about the LOS on our website (www.cfainstitute.org/programs/cfa/curriculum/study-sessions), including the descriptions of LOS "command words" on the candidate resources page at www.cfainstitute.org/-/media/documents/support/programs/cfa-and-cipm-los-command-words.ashx.

The CFA Program curriculum that candidates receive access to upon exam registration.

Therefore, the key to your success on the CFA exams is studying and understanding the CBOK. You can learn more about the CBOK on our website: www.cfainstitute.org/programs/cfa/curriculum/cbok.

The curriculum, including the practice questions, is the basis for all exam questions. The curriculum is selected/developed specifically to provide candidates with the knowledge, skills, and abilities reflected in the CBOK.

CFA INSTITUTE LEARNING ECOSYSTEM (LES)

Your exam registration fee includes access to the CFA Institute Learning Ecosystem (LES). This digital learning platform provides access to all the curriculum content and practice questions. The LES is organized as a series of learning modules consisting of short online lessons and associated practice questions. This tool is your source for all study materials, including practice questions and mock exams. The LES is the primary method by which CFA Institute delivers your curriculum experience. Here, you will find additional practice questions to test your knowledge, including some interactive questions.

DESIGNING YOUR PERSONAL STUDY PROGRAM

An orderly, systematic approach to exam preparation is critical. You should dedicate a consistent block of time every week to reading and studying. Review the LOS both before and after you study curriculum content to ensure you can demonstrate the knowledge, skills, and abilities described by the LOS and the assigned learning module. Use the LOS as a self-check to track your progress and highlight areas of weakness for later review.

Successful candidates report an average of more than 300 hours preparing for each exam. Your preparation time will vary based on your prior education and experience, and you will likely spend more time on some topics than on others.

ERRATA

The curriculum development process is rigorous and involves multiple rounds of reviews by content experts. Despite our efforts to produce a curriculum that is free of errors, we must make corrections in some instances. Curriculum errata are periodically updated and posted by exam level and test date on the Curriculum Errata webpage (www.cfainstitute.org/en/programs/submit-errata). If you believe you have found an error in the curriculum, you can submit your concerns through our curriculum errata reporting process found at the bottom of the Curriculum Errata webpage.

OTHER FEEDBACK

Please send any comments or suggestions to info@cfainstitute.org, and we will review your feedback thoughtfully.

Financial Statement Analysis

LEARNING MODULE

1

Introduction to Financial Statement Analysis

by Elaine Henry, PhD, CFA, J. Hennie van Greuning, DCom, CFA, and Thomas R Robinson, PhD, CFA, CAIA.

Elaine Henry, PhD, CFA, is at Stevens Institute of Technology (USA). J. Hennie van Greuning, DCom, CFA, is at BIBD (Brunei). Thomas R. Robinson, PhD, CFA, CAIA, Robinson Global Investment Management LLC, (USA).

LEARNING OUTCOMES

Mastery	*The candidate should be able to:*
☐	describe the steps in the financial statement analysis framework
☐	describe the roles of financial statement analysis
☐	describe the importance of regulatory filings, financial statement notes and supplementary information, management's commentary, and audit reports
☐	describe implications for financial analysis of alternative financial reporting systems and the importance of monitoring developments in financial reporting standards
☐	describe information sources that analysts use in financial statement analysis besides annual and interim financial reports

The two major accounting standard setters are as follows: 1) the International Accounting Standards Board (IASB) who establishes International Financial Reporting Standards (IFRS) and 2) the Financial Accounting Standards Board (FASB) who establishes US GAAP. Throughout this learning module both standards are referred to and many, but not all, of these two sets of accounting rules are identified. Note: changes in accounting standards as well as new rulings and/or pronouncements issued after the publication of this learning module may cause some of the information to become dated.

1 INTRODUCTION

Financial analysis is the process of interpreting and evaluating a company's performance and position in the context of its economic environment. Financial analysis is used by analysts to make decisions and recommendations such as whether to invest in a company's debt or equity securities and at what price. A debt investor is concerned about a company's ability to pay interest and to repay the principal lent, while an equity investor is interested in a company's profitability and per-share value. Overall, a central focus of financial analysis is evaluating the company's ability to earn a return on its capital that is at least equal to the cost of that capital, to profitably grow its operations, and to generate enough cash to meet obligations and pursue opportunities.

Financial analysis starts with the information found in a company's financial reports. These financial reports include audited financial statements, additional disclosures required by regulatory authorities, and any accompanying (unaudited) commentary by management. Analysts supplement their analysis of a company's financial statements with industry and company research.

LEARNING MODULE OVERVIEW

- Financial analysis for a company often includes obtaining an understanding of the target company's business model, financial performance, financial position, and broader information about the economic environment and the industry in which the company operates. When analytical tasks are not well defined, the analyst may need to make decisions about the approach, the tools, the data sources, the format for reporting the results, and the relative importance of different aspects of the analysis.
- Financial analysis will include evaluating financial results, and structuring and scaling data to facilitate comparisons by calculating percentages, changes, and ratios. Answers to analytical questions often rely not just on numerical results but also on the analyst's interpretation of the numerical results to support a conclusion or recommendation.
- The role of financial statement analysis is to form expectations about a company's future performance, financial position, and risk factors for the purpose of making investment, credit, and other economic decisions.
- · Regulatory authorities require publicly traded companies to prepare financial reports in accordance with specified accounting standards and other securities laws and regulations. An example of such a regulatory authority is the Securities and Exchange Commission in the United States.
- Other organizations exist without explicit regulatory authority and develop reporting standards, facilitate cooperation, and advise governments. Examples include the International Organization of Securities Commissions, the European Securities Committee, and the European Securities and Market Authority.
- Sources of information for analysts and investors include standardized forms that are filed with regulatory authorities, disclosures made in notes, supplementary schedules, and management commentary that accompany financial statements, and audit reports. In an audit report, an independent auditor expresses an opinion on whether the

information in the audited financial statements fairly presents the financial position, performance, and cash flows of the company in accordance with a specified set of accounting standards.

- Despite increasing convergence over time, differences still exist between IFRS (International Financial Reporting Standards) and US GAAP (Generally Accepted Accounting Principles) that affect financial reporting. Analysts must be aware of areas where accounting standards have not converged.
- In addition to information required by regulatory authorities, issuers also communicate through earnings calls, investor day events, press releases, company websites, and company visits. Analysts may also get information by speaking with management, investor relations, and other company personnel.
- Third-party sources for additional information include industry whitepapers, analyst reports, economic information from governments, general and industry-specific news outlets, and electronic data platforms. Analysts also use surveys, conversations, and product evaluations to generate their own information.

FINANCIAL STATEMENT ANALYSIS FRAMEWORK 2

☐ describe the steps in the financial statement analysis framework

Analysts work in a variety of positions within the investment management industry. Some are equity analysts whose main objective is to evaluate potential investments in a company's equity securities as a basis for deciding whether a prospective investment is attractive and what an appropriate purchase price might be. Others are credit analysts who evaluate the creditworthiness of a company to decide whether (and on what terms) a debt investment should be made or what credit rating should be assigned. Analysts may also be involved in a variety of other tasks, such as evaluating the performance of a subsidiary company, evaluating a private equity investment, or finding stocks that are overvalued for purposes of taking a short position.

Exhibit 1 presents a generic framework for financial statement analysis used in these various roles.

Exhibit 1: Financial Statement Analysis Framework

Phase	Sources of Information	Output
Articulate the purpose and context of the analysis.	▪ The nature of the analyst's function, such as evaluating an equity or debt investment or issuing a credit rating. ▪ Communication with client or supervisor on specific needs and concerns. ▪ Institutional guidelines related to developing specific work product.	▪ Statement of the purpose or objective of analysis. ▪ A list (written or unwritten) of specific questions to be answered by the analysis. ▪ Nature and content of report to be provided. ▪ Timetable and budgeted resources for completion.
Collect data.	▪ Financial statements, other financial data, questionnaires, and industry/economic data. ▪ Discussions with issuer investor relations, management, suppliers, customers, competitors, and company or industry experts. ▪ Company site visits (e.g., to production facilities or retail stores).	▪ Financial statements and other quantitative data in a usable form, such as a spreadsheet. ▪ Completed questionnaires, if applicable.
Process data.	Data from the previous phase.	▪ Adjusted financial statements. ▪ Common-size statements. ▪ Ratios and graphs.
Analyze/interpret the data.	Input data as well as processed data.	▪ Analytical results. ▪ Forecasts. ▪ Valuations.
Develop and communicate conclusions and recommendations (e.g., with an analysis report).	▪ Analytical results and previous reports. ▪ Institutional guidelines for published reports.	▪ Analytical report answering questions posed in Phase 1. ▪ Recommendation regarding the purpose of the analysis, such as whether to make an investment or extend credit.
Follow-up.	Information gathered by periodically repeating the previous steps as necessary to determine whether changes to holdings or recommendations are necessary.	▪ Comparison of actual to expected results ▪ Revised forecasts ▪ Updated reports and recommendations.

The following sections discuss the individual phases of financial statement analysis.

Articulate the Purpose and Context of the Analysis

Before undertaking any analysis, it is essential to understand the purpose of the analysis. An understanding of the purpose is particularly important in financial statement analysis because of the numerous available techniques and the substantial amount of data.

Some analytical tasks are well defined, in which case articulating the purpose of the analysis requires little decision making by the analyst. For example, a periodic credit review of an investment-grade debt portfolio or an equity analyst's quarterly report on a particular company may be guided by institutional norms such that the purpose of the analysis is given. Furthermore, the format, procedures, or sources of information may also be given.

For other analytical tasks, articulating the purpose of the analysis requires the analyst to make decisions about the approach, the tools, the data sources, the format in which to report the results of the analysis, and the relative importance of different aspects of the analysis.

When facing a substantial amount of data, a less experienced analyst may be tempted to start calculating ratios without considering what is relevant for the decision at hand. It is generally advisable to resist this temptation and thus avoid unnecessary or pointless efforts. Consider the questions: If you could have all the calculations and ratios completed instantly, what question would you be able to answer? What decision would your answer support?

The analyst should also define the context at this stage. Who is the intended audience? What is the deliverable—for example, a final report explaining conclusions and recommendations? What is the time frame (i.e., when is the report due)? What resources and resource constraints are relevant to completion of the analysis? Again, the context may be predefined (i.e., standard and guided by institutional norms).

Having clarified the purpose and context of the financial statement analysis, the analyst should next compile the specific questions to be answered by the analysis. For example, if the purpose of the financial statement analysis (or, more likely, a stage of a larger analysis) is to compare the historical performance of three companies operating in a particular industry, specific questions would include the following: What has been the relative growth rate of the companies, and what has been their relative profitability?

Collect Data

Next, the analyst obtains information required to answer the specific questions. A key part of this step is obtaining an understanding of the target company's business model, financial performance, and financial position (including trends over time and relative to peer companies). Financial statement data alone may be adequate in some cases. For example, to screen a large number of companies to find those with a minimum level of historical profitability or sales growth, financial statement data alone would be adequate. But to address more in-depth questions, such as why and how one company performed better or worse than its competitors, additional information would be required.

Furthermore, information on the economy and industry is necessary to understand the environment in which the company operates. Analysts often take a top-down approach whereby they (1) gain an understanding of an issuer's macroeconomic environment, such as prospects for growth in the economy and inflation; (2) analyze the prospects of the industry in which the company operates, based on the expected macroeconomic environment; and (3) determine the prospects for the company given the expected industry and macroeconomic environments. For example, an analyst may need to forecast future growth in earnings for a company. Past company data provide the platform for statistical forecasting; however, an understanding of economic and industry conditions and an outlook for them can improve the analyst's ability to make forecasts.

Process Data

After obtaining the requisite financial and other information, the analyst processes these data using appropriate analytical tools. For example, processing the data may involve computing ratios or growth rates; preparing common-size financial statements; creating charts; performing statistical analyses, such as regressions or Monte Carlo simulations; making forecasts; performing valuations; performing sensitivity analyses; or using any other analytical tools or combination of tools that are available and appropriate for the task. A comprehensive financial analysis at this stage may include the following:

- Reading and evaluating financial results for each company being analyzed. This includes understanding any factors that may affect comparability between companies, such as differences in business models, operating decisions (e.g., leasing versus purchasing fixed assets), accounting policies (e.g., when to report revenue on the income statement), and tax jurisdictions.
- Making any needed adjustments to the financial statements or using alternative measures to facilitate comparison. Note that commonly used databases do not always make such analyst adjustments.
- Preparing or collecting common-size financial statement data (which scale data to directly reflect percentages [e.g., of sales] or changes [e.g., from the prior year]) and financial ratios (which are measures of various aspects of corporate performance based on financial statement elements. Analysts can use these to evaluate a company's relative profitability, liquidity, leverage, efficiency, and valuation in relation to past results or peers.

Analyze/Interpret the Data

Once the data have been processed, the next step—critical to any analysis—is to interpret the output. The answer to a specific question is seldom the numerical answer alone. Rather, the answer relies on the analyst's interpretation of the output, and the use of this interpreted output to support a conclusion or recommendation. The answers to the specific analytical questions may themselves achieve the underlying purpose of the analysis, but usually, a conclusion or recommendation is required. For example, an equity analysis may involve forecasts of earnings, free cash flow, and a range of fair value estimates that would be used to issue a buy, hold, or sell recommendation. A credit analyst may also create forecasts of free cash flow, interest coverage, and leverage in support of an investment decision.

Develop and Communicate Conclusions and Recommendations

Communicating the conclusion or recommendation in an appropriate format is the next step. The appropriate format will vary by analytical task, by institution, or by audience. For example, an equity analyst's report for external distribution would typically include the following components:

- summary and investment conclusion;
- industry overview and competitive analysis;
- financial statement model, potentially with several scenarios;
- valuation; and
- investment risks.

The contents of reports may also be specified by regulatory agencies or professional standards. For example, the CFA Institute *Standards of Practice Handbook* (*Handbook*) dictates standards that must be followed in communicating recommendations. According to the *Handbook*:

> Standard V(B) states that members and candidates should communicate in a recommendation the factors that were instrumental in making the investment recommendation. A critical part of this requirement is to

> distinguish clearly between opinions and facts. In preparing a research report, the member or candidate must present the basic characteristics of the security(ies) being analyzed, which will allow the reader to evaluate the report and incorporate information the reader deems relevant to his or her investment decision making process.[1]

The *Handbook* requires that limitations to the analysis and any risks inherent to the investment be disclosed. Furthermore, it requires that any report include elements important to the analysis and conclusions so that readers can evaluate the conclusions themselves.

Follow-Up

The process does not end with the report. If an equity investment is made or a credit rating is assigned, periodic review is required to revise forecasts and recommendations based on the receipt of new information. In the case of a rejected investment, subsequent analyses may still be required should the security price or business conditions change. Follow-up may involve repeating all the previous steps in the process on a periodic basis.

SCOPE OF FINANCIAL STATEMENT ANALYSIS 3

☐ describe the roles of financial statement analysis

The role of financial statement analysis is to use financial reports prepared by companies, combined with other information, to evaluate the past, current, and potential performance and financial position of a company for the purpose of making investment, credit, and other economic decisions. Managers within a company perform financial analysis to make operating, investing, and financing decisions but do not exclusively rely on analysis of related financial statements because they have access to nonpublic financial information.

In evaluating financial reports, analysts typically have a specific economic decision in mind. Examples of these decisions include the following:

- Evaluating an equity investment for inclusion in a portfolio.
- Valuing a security for making an investment recommendation to others.
- Determining the creditworthiness of a company to decide whether to extend a loan to the company and if so, what terms to offer.
- Assigning a debt rating to a company or bond issue.
- Deciding whether to make a venture capital or other private equity investment.
- Evaluating a merger or acquisition candidate.

These decisions demonstrate certain themes in financial analysis. In general, analysts seek to examine the past and current performance and financial position of a company to form expectations about its future performance and financial position. Analysts are also concerned about factors that affect the risks to a company's future performance and financial position. An examination of performance can include an

1 *Standards of Practice Handbook*, 11th ed. (Charlottesville, VA: CFA Institute, 2014), p. 169.

assessment of a company's profitability (the ability to earn a profit from delivering goods and services) and its ability to generate positive cash flows (cash receipts in excess of cash disbursements).

Exhibit 2 shows how news coverage of corporate earnings announcements places corporate results in the context of analysts' expectations. Panel A shows the earnings announcement, and Panel B shows a sample of the news coverage of the announcement. Earnings are also frequently used by analysts in valuation. For example, an analyst may value shares of a company by comparing its price-to-earnings ratio (P/E) to the P/Es of peer companies or may use forecasted future earnings as direct or indirect inputs into discounted cash flow models of valuation.

Exhibit 2: An Earnings Release and News Media Comparison with Analysts' Expectations

Panel A: Excerpt from Sea Limited's Earnings Release

Singapore, August 16, 2022 – Sea Limited (NYSE: SE) ("Sea" or the "Company") today announced its financial results for the second quarter ended June 30, 2022.

> "As we navigate the current environment of increased macro uncertainty with that same nimble and decisive approach, we believe it is vital to be thoughtful, prudent, and disciplined. While we have strong resources and are well on-track to achieve our self-sufficiency targets, we are nevertheless rapidly prioritizing profitability and cash flow management. We are confident that this focus, combined with our demonstrated ability to execute, our scale and leadership, and our proven business models, will position us for long-term sustained success."

Second Quarter 2022 Highlights:

- Total GAAP revenue was US$2.9 billion, up 29.0% year-on-year.
- Total gross profit was US$1.1 billion, up 17.1% year-on-year.
- Total net income (loss) was US$(931.2) million compared to US$(433.7) million for the second quarter of 2021. Total net loss excluding share-based compensation and impairment of goodwill was US$(569.8) million compared to US$(321.2) million for the second quarter of 2021.
- Total adjusted EBITDA was US$(506.3) million compared to US$(24.1) million for the second quarter of 2021.
- E-commerce Segment:
- GAAP revenue was US$1.7 billion, up 51.4% year-on-year. Based on constant currency assumptions, GAAP revenue was up 56.2% year-on-year.
- Gross orders totaled 2.0 billion, an increase of 41.6% year-on-year.
- Gross profit margin for e-commerce continued to improve sequentially quarter-on-quarter, as we have seen faster growth of transaction-based fees and advertising income, which have higher profit margin compared to product revenue and revenue generated from other value-added services.

E-commerce Full Year 2022 Guidance Update:

In our efforts to adapt to increasing macro uncertainties, we are proactively shifting our strategies to further focus on efficiency and optimization for the long-term strength and profitability of the e-commerce business. Given this strategic shift, we will be suspending e-commerce GAAP revenue guidance for the full year 2022. We believe such efforts will further strengthen our ability to better capture the long-term growth opportunities in our markets, which we remain highly positive about.

Source: Sea Limited, "Sea Limited Reports Second Quarter 2022 Results," accessed 16 August 2022, https://cdn.sea.com/webmain/static/resource/seagroup/website/investornews/2Q2022/uXxGiCr8oTGxOFTPhBUB/2022.08.16%20Sea%20Second%20Quarter%202022%20Results.pdf.

Panel B: Excerpt from News Article: Sea Limited Reports Mixed Results, Suspends Revenue Guidance

Singapore-based Sea Limited (SE) reported second-quarter results early Tuesday that missed on revenue but beat on earnings. The company, however, said it will suspend guidance for its e-commerce unit, which accounts for about 60% of company revenue.

The company reported revenue of $2.9 billion, missing estimates of $2.98 billion. It lost 61 cents a share, better than the estimated loss of $1.14 a share, according to FactSet.

SE stock plunged 14.3% during afternoon action on the stock market today.

Sea has one of the largest e-commerce and digital entertainment platforms in the Southeast Asia region. It also provides financial services.

The company said its decision to suspend revenue guidance was driven by a highly volatile and unpredictable macro environment.

"We think the right thing to do in this time of continuing heightened macro volatility is to prioritize efficiency and self-sufficiency," Chief Executive Forrest Li said in written remarks in the Sea Limited earnings report.

Sea's gaming unit, called Garena, accounts for about 31% of revenue.

"We are in an environment of increased macro uncertainty, with rising inflation, rising interest rates, local currency depreciations against the U.S. dollar, and ongoing reopening trends," said Li. "In this environment, being agile and adaptable is even more crucial to the long-term success of our business."

SE stock is down about 62% this year.

Source: Brian Deagon, "Sea Limited Reports Mixed Results, Suspends Revenue Guidance," 16 August 2022, https://www.investors.com/news/technology/se-stock-drops-on-second-quarter-results-earnings/.

Analysts are also interested in the financial position of a company, particularly for credit analysis, as depicted in Exhibit 3. Panel A of the exhibit is an excerpt from an August 2022 T-Mobile's press release highlighting a series of credit rating upgrades that the company received from the three major rating agencies. Panel B of the exhibit is an excerpt from a July 2022 announcement from Moody's Investor Service about its upgrade of T-Mobile's credit rating.

Exhibit 3: Credit Rating Upgrade for T-Mobile

Panel A: Excerpt from Announcement by T Mobile

T-Mobile Secures First-Ever Full Investment Grade Rating

BELLEVUE, Wash.--(BUSINESS WIRE)-- T-Mobile US, Inc. (NASDAQ: TMUS) today announced that following an investment grade issuer rating from S&P Global Ratings (S&P) – the third it has received from credit rating agencies – the company now has its first-ever full investment grade rating. S&P has assigned the Company a BBB- with positive outlook. This follows the company securing a Baa3 rating with a stable outlook from Moody's and a BBB- rating with a positive outlook from Fitch.

This full investment grade rating comes as a result of T-Mobile's successful operational and financial performance, which is consistently demonstrated through strong subscriber growth and the company's ability to translate that into increasing free cash flow.

"Achieving a full investment grade rating is an important milestone for T-Mobile that reflects the leading credit rating agencies' positive outlook on our Un-carrier leadership strategy that is rooted in an unwavering focus on putting customers first," said Peter Osvaldik, T-Mobile chief financial officer. "This 'clean sweep' in upgrades provides T-Mobile with the ability to unlock full access to the deep investment grade debt markets, which will further fuel our growth and momentum toward our mission of being the very best at connecting customers to their world."

Source: "T-Mobile Secures First-Ever Full Investment Grade Rating," 5 August 2022, https://investor.t-mobile.com/events-and-presentations/news/news-details/2022/T-Mobile-Secures-First-Ever-Full-Investment-Grade-Rating/default.aspx.

Panel B: Excerpt from Moody's Announcement About Rating Action on T-Mobile

Rating Action: Moody's upgrades T-Mobile to Baa3; outlook stable

New York, July 20, 2022 -- Moody's Investors Service (Moody's) upgraded T-Mobile USA, Inc.'s (T-Mobile) senior unsecured debt rating to Baa3 from Ba2 and affirmed the Baa3 rating on the company's existing senior secured notes and senior secured revolving credit facility.

Moody's has also withdrawn T-Mobile's Ba1 corporate family rating, Ba1-PD probability of default rating and SGL-1 speculative grade liquidity rating. With this rating action, Moody's changed T-Mobile's ratings outlook to stable from positive.

The ratings upgrade reflects T-Mobile's accelerated achievement of higher than expected operating cost synergies following its April 2020 merger with Sprint, significant and nearly complete network and operations integration and high visibility into the company's steady path towards sustained debt leverage (Moody's adjusted) below 3.75x. T-Mobile's sizable operating scale, high speed 5G coverage footprint, substantial upside growth potential in historically under-indexed rural and enterprise end market segments, solid incremental revenue growth adjacencies in fixed wireless access, extensive asset base and solid industry market position support continued subscriber growth, EBITDA margin expansion and ramping free cash flow over the next 12-18 months. The company's financial policy, which prudently focuses on network infrastructure investments to support market share growth, remains an important driver of the credit profile going forward. Moody's views network investments, including spectrum investments, as supportive of the business profile.

The stable outlook reflects Moody's expectation for T-Mobile's continued subscriber and service revenue growth, EBITDA margin expansion, debt leverage (Moody's adjusted) declining steadily towards and sustained around 3.75x and rising free cash flow.

Source: "Moody's Upgrades T-Mobile to Baa3; Outlook Stable," 20 July 2022, https://www.moodys.com/research/Moodys-upgrades-T-Mobile-to-Baa3-outlook-stable--PR_468077.

In conducting financial analysis of a company, the analyst will regularly refer to the company's financial statements, financial notes, and supplementary schedules as well as a variety of other information sources. The next lesson introduces commonly used information sources.

REGULATED SOURCES OF INFORMATION

4

☐ describe the importance of regulatory filings, financial statement notes and supplementary information, management's commentary, and audit reports

Regulatory authorities require publicly traded issuers to prepare financial reports in accordance with specified accounting standards and other securities laws and regulations. For example, in Switzerland, Swiss-based companies listed on the main board of the Swiss Exchange must prepare their financial statements in accordance with either IFRS (International Financial Reporting Standards) or US GAAP (Generally Accepted Accounting Principles) if they are multinational. [2] While jurisdictions differ in their approach to securities regulations and corporate reporting standards, regulators of jurisdictions that oversee more than 95 percent of world's financial markets are members of the International Organization of Securities Commissions (IOSCO) and share objectives and principles, thereby creating a degree of global uniformity.

International Organization of Securities Commissions

Although technically not a regulatory authority, IOSCO regulates a significant portion of the world's financial capital markets. This organization was formed in 1983 and consists of ordinary members, associate members, and affiliate members. Ordinary members are the securities commission or similar governmental regulatory authority with primary responsibility for securities regulation in the member country.[3] The members regulate more than 95 percent of the world's financial capital markets in more than 115 jurisdictions, and securities regulators in emerging markets account for 75 percent of its ordinary membership.

IOSCO's comprehensive set of *Objectives and Principles of Securities Regulation* is updated as required and is recognized as an international benchmark for all markets. The principles of securities regulation are based upon three core objectives:[4]

- protecting investors;
- ensuring that markets are fair, efficient, and transparent; and
- reducing systemic risk.

2 "Financial Reporting Framework in Switzerland," Deloitte, https://www.iasplus.com/en/jurisdictions/europe/switzerland.

3 Examples include the China Securities Regulatory Commission, Egyptian Financial Supervisory Authority, Securities and Exchange Board of India, Kingdom of Saudi Arabia Capital Market Authority, and Banco Central del Uruguay.

4 *Objectives and Principles of Securities Regulation*, IOSCO, May 2017.

IOSCO's principles are grouped into 10 categories, including principles for regulators, for enforcement, for auditing, and for issuers, among others. Within the category "Principles for Issuers," two principles relate directly to financial reporting:

- There should be full, accurate, and timely disclosure of financial results, risk, and other information that is material to investors' decisions.
- Accounting standards used by issuers to prepare financial statements should be of a high and internationally acceptable quality.

Historically, regulation and related financial reporting standards were developed within individual countries and were often based on the cultural, economic, and political norms of each country. As financial markets have become more global, it has become desirable to establish comparable financial reporting standards internationally. Ultimately, laws and regulations are established by individual jurisdictions, so this also requires cooperation among regulators. Another IOSCO principle deals with the use of self-regulatory organizations (SROs), which exercise some direct oversight for their areas of competence and should be subject to the oversight of the relevant regulator and observe fairness and confidentiality.[5]

To ensure consistent application of international financial standards (such as the Basel Committee on Banking Supervision's standards and IFRS), it is important to have uniform regulation and enforcement across national boundaries. IOSCO assists in attaining this goal of uniform regulation as well as cross-border cooperation in combating violations of securities and derivatives laws.

US Securities and Exchange Commission

The US SEC has primary responsibility for securities and capital markets regulation in the United States and is an ordinary member of IOSCO. Any company issuing securities within the United States (e.g., on the New York Stock Exchange or NASDAQ), or otherwise involved in US capital markets, is subject to the rules and regulations of the SEC. The SEC, one of the oldest and most developed regulatory authorities, was created by reforms after the stock market crash of 1929 that preceded the Great Depression.

From a financial reporting and analysis perspective, the most significant statutes enforced by the SEC are the Securities Acts of 1933 and 1934 and the Sarbanes–Oxley Act of 2002.

- **Securities Act of 1933** (the 1933 Act): This law specifies the financial and other significant information that investors must receive when securities are sold, prohibits misrepresentations, and requires initial registration of all public issuances of securities.
- **Securities Exchange Act of 1934** (the 1934 Act): This law created the SEC, gave the SEC authority over all aspects of the securities industry, and empowered the SEC to require periodic reporting by companies with publicly traded securities.
- **Sarbanes–Oxley Act of 2002**: This law created the Public Company Accounting Oversight Board (PCAOB) to oversee auditors. The SEC is responsible for carrying out the requirements of the act and overseeing the PCAOB. The act addresses auditor independence (it prohibits auditors from providing certain non-audit services to the companies they audit); strengthens corporate responsibility for financial reports (it requires executive management to certify that the company's financial reports fairly present the company's condition); and requires management to report on

5 *Objectives and Principles of Securities Regulation*, IOSCO, May 2017.

the effectiveness of the company's internal control over financial reporting (including obtaining external auditor confirmation of the effectiveness of internal control).

Companies comply with these acts principally through filing standardized forms created by the SEC and by responding to and complying with specific comments on their filings by the SEC staff. More than 50 different types of SEC forms are used to satisfy reporting requirements; the discussion herein is limited to those forms most relevant for financial analysts.

Most of the SEC filings are required to be made electronically, so filings that an analyst would be interested in can be retrieved online from one of many websites, including an issuer's investor relations website and the SEC's own website. Some filings are required on the initial offering of securities, whereas others are required on a periodic basis thereafter. The following are some of the more common filings used by analysts.

- **Securities Offerings Registration Statement**: The 1933 Act requires companies offering securities to file a registration statement. New issuers as well as previously registered companies that are issuing new securities are required to file these statements. Required information and the precise form vary depending upon the size and nature of the offering. Typically, required information includes (1) disclosures about the securities being offered for sale, (2) the relationship of these new securities to the issuer's other capital securities, (3) the information typically provided in the annual filings, (4) recent audited financial statements, and (5) risk factors involved in the business. Interim unaudited financial statements are also provided if the statement is filed three months or more after a fiscal year end.
- **Forms 10-K, 20-F, and 40-F**: Companies are required to file these forms *annually*. Form 10-K is for US registrants, Form 40-F is for certain Canadian registrants, and Form 20-F is for all other non-US registrants. These forms require a comprehensive overview, including information concerning a company's business, risk factors, financial disclosures, legal proceedings, and information related to management. The financial disclosures include audited financial statements and notes, management discussion and analysis (MD&A) of the company's financial condition and results of operations, and auditors' reports.
- **Annual Report**: In addition to the SEC's annual filings (e.g., Form 10-K), most companies prepare an annual report to shareholders. This is not a requirement of the SEC. The annual report is usually viewed as one of the most significant opportunities for a company to present itself to shareholders and other external parties; accordingly, it is often a highly polished marketing document with photographs, an opening letter from the chief executive officer, financial data, market segment information, research and development activities, and future corporate goals. In contrast, the Form 10-K is a more legal type of document with minimal marketing emphasis. Although the perspectives vary, a company's annual report and its Form 10-K have considerable overlap. Some companies prepare only Form 10-K or publish an annual report that consists of a few pages of material and a copy of the 10-K.
- **Proxy Statement/Form DEF-14A**: The SEC requires that shareholders of a company receive a proxy statement before a shareholder meeting. A proxy is an authorization from the shareholder giving another party the right to cast its vote. Shareholder meetings are held at least once a year, but any special meetings also require a proxy statement. Proxies, especially annual meeting

proxies, contain information that is often useful to financial analysts. Such information typically includes proposals that require a shareholder vote, details of security ownership by management and principal owners, biographical information on directors, and disclosure of executive compensation. Proxy statement information is filed with the SEC as Form DEF-14A.

- **Forms 10-Q and 6-K**: Companies are required to submit these forms for interim periods (quarterly for US companies on Form 10-Q, and semiannually for many non-US companies on Form 6-K). The filing requires certain financial information, including unaudited financial statements and an MD&A for the interim period covered by the report. Additionally, if certain types of non-recurring events—such as the adoption of a significant accounting policy, commencement of significant litigation, or a material limitation on the rights of any holders of any class of registered securities—take place during the period covered by the report, these events must be included in the Form 10-Q report. Companies may provide the 10-Q report to shareholders or may prepare a separate, abbreviated, quarterly report to shareholders.

KNOWLEDGE CHECK

1. In September 2017, Sea Ltd, the Singapore-based technology company, filed a registration statement with the US SEC to register its initial public offering of securities (American Depositary Shares, each representing one Class A Ordinary Share) on the New York Stock Exchange. In addition to a large amount of financial information, the registration statement provided over 50 pages of discussion on Sea Ltd.'s business and industry.

   Which of the following is *most likely* to have been included in Sea's registration statement?

   A. Underwriters' fairness opinion of the offering

   B. Assessment of risk factors involved in the business

   C. Projected cash flows and earnings for the business

   Solution:

   B is correct. Information provided by companies in registration statements typically includes disclosures about the securities being offered for sale; the relationship of these new securities to the issuer's other capital securities; the information typically provided in the annual filings; recent audited financial statements; and risk factors involved in the business. Companies provide information useful in developing projected cash flows and earnings but do not typically include these in the registration statement, nor do they provide opinions of the underwriters.

A company or its officers make other SEC filings—either periodically, or, if significant events or transactions have occurred, in between the periodic reports noted previously. By their nature, these forms sometimes contain timely information that may have significant valuation implications.

- **Form 8-K:** In addition to filing annual and interim reports, SEC registrants must report material corporate events on a more current basis. Form 8-K (6-K for non-US registrants) is the "current report" companies must file with the SEC to announce such major events as acquisitions or disposals of corporate assets, changes in securities and trading markets, matters related to accountants and financial statements, corporate governance and management changes, and Regulation FD disclosures.[6]

- **Forms 3, 4, 5, and 144**: Forms 3, 4, and 5 are required to report beneficial ownership of securities. These filings are required for any director or officer of a registered company as well as beneficial owners of greater than 10 percent of a class of registered equity securities. Form 3 is the initial statement, Form 4 reports changes, and Form 5 is the annual report. Form 144 is notice of the proposed sale of restricted securities or securities held by an affiliate of the issuer. These forms can be used to examine purchases and sales of securities by officers, directors, and other affiliates of the company, who collectively are regarded as corporate insiders.
- **Form 11-K:** This is the annual report of employee stock purchase, savings, and similar plans. It might be of interest to analysts for companies with significant employee benefit plans because it contains more information about these plans than disclosed in the company's financial statements.

In jurisdictions other than the United States, similar legislation exists for the purpose of regulating securities and capital markets. Regulatory authorities are responsible for enforcing regulation, and securities regulation is intended to be consistent with the IOSCO objectives described in the previous section. Within each jurisdiction, regulators will either establish or, more typically, recognize and adopt a specified set or sets of accounting standards. The regulators will also establish reporting and filing requirements. IOSCO members have agreed to cooperate in the development, implementation, and enforcement of internationally recognized and consistent standards of regulation.

Capital Markets Regulation in Europe

Each individual member state of the European Union (EU) regulates capital markets in its jurisdiction. Certain regulations, however, have been adopted at the EU level. Importantly, the EU agreed that from 2005 consolidated accounts of EU-listed companies would use International Financial Reporting Standards. The endorsement process by which newly issued IFRS are adopted by the EU reflects the balance between the individual member state's autonomy and the need for cooperation and convergence. When the IASB issues a new standard, the European Financial Reporting Advisory Group advises the European Commission on the standard, and the Standards Advice Review Group provides the Commission with an opinion about that advice. Based on the input from these two entities, the Commission prepares a draft endorsement regulation. The Accounting Regulatory Committee votes on the proposal; and if the vote is favorable, the proposal proceeds to the European Parliament and the Council of the European Union for approval.[7]

Two bodies related to securities regulation established by the European Commission are the European Securities Committee (ESC) and the European Securities and Market Authority (ESMA). The ESC consists of high-level representatives of member states and advises the European Commission on securities policy issues. ESMA is an EU cross-border supervisor established to coordinate supervision of the EU market. As noted earlier, regulation still rests with the individual member states and, therefore,

6 Regulation Fair Disclosure (FD) provides that when an issuer discloses material non-public information to certain individuals or entities—generally, securities market professionals such as stock analysts or holders of the issuer's securities who may trade on the basis of the information—the issuer must make public disclosure of that information. In this way, the rule aims to promote full and fair disclosure.

7 European Commission, https://www.esma.europa.eu/convergence/ias-regulation#:~:text=The%20objective%20of%20the%20International,the%20European%20Union%20(EU).

requirements for registering shares and filing periodic financial reports vary from country to country. ESMA is one of three European supervisory authorities; the two others supervise the banking and insurance industries.

Financial Notes and Supplementary Schedules

The notes (also sometimes referred to as footnotes) that accompany the financial statements are required and often account for a large percentage of the financial disclosures made in regulatory filings. The notes provide information that is essential to understanding the information provided in the statements. Sea Ltd.'s 2021 financial statements, for example, include more than 60 pages of notes.

The notes disclose the basis of preparation for the financial statements. For example, Sea Ltd. discloses that its fiscal year corresponds to the calendar year; its financial statements are prepared in accordance with US GAAP; the statements are thousands of US dollars unless otherwise specified; and the figures have been rounded, which might give rise to minor discrepancies when they are added. Sea Ltd. also states that its financial statements are on a consolidated basis—that is, aggregating the financial records of all its subsidiaries it controls, after eliminating intercompany balances and transactions.

The notes also disclose information about the accounting policies, methods, and estimates used to prepare the financial statements. Both IFRS and US GAAP allow some flexibility in choosing among alternative policies and methods when accounting for certain items. This flexibility aims to meet the divergent needs of many businesses for reporting a variety of economic transactions. In addition to differences in accounting policies and methods, differences arise as a result of estimates needed to record and measure transactions, events, and financial statement line items.

Overall, flexibility in accounting choices is necessary because, ideally, a company will select those policies, methods, and estimates that are allowable and most relevant and that fairly reflect the unique economic environment of the company's business and industry. Flexibility can, however, create challenges for the analyst because the use of different policies, methods, and estimates reduces comparability across different companies' financial statements.

For example, if a company acquires a piece of equipment to use in its operations, accounting standards require that the cost of the equipment be reported as an expense (depreciation) by allocating its cost, less any residual value, in a systematic manner over the equipment's useful life. Accounting standards permit flexibility, however, in determining the way each year's expense is determined. Two companies may acquire similar equipment but use different methods and assumptions to record the expense over time. An analyst's ability to compare the companies' performance is hindered by the difference. Analysts must understand reporting choices to make appropriate adjustments when comparing companies' financial positions and performance.

For many companies, the financial notes and supplemental schedules provide explanatory information about every line item (or almost every line item) on the balance sheet and income statement. In addition, note disclosures include information about the following (this is not an exhaustive list):

- segment reporting;
- business acquisitions and disposals;
- contractual obligations, including both on- and off-balance sheet debt;
- financial instruments and risks arising from financial instruments;
- legal proceedings;
- related-party transactions; and
- subsequent events (i.e., events that occur after the balance sheet date).

Experience using the disclosures made by a company and its competitors typically enhances an analyst's judgment about the relative importance of different disclosures and the ways in which they can be helpful.

Business and Geographic Segment Reporting

Many companies are composed of several businesses. Although companies are not required to provide disaggregated full financial statements for all of its businesses or subsidiaries, they are required to provide some disaggregated information under both IFRS and US GAAP in the notes to financial statements by **operating segment**. An operating segment is defined as a component of a company that

- engages in activities that may generate revenue and create expenses, including a start-up segment that has yet to earn revenues;
- whose results are regularly reviewed by the company's senior management; and
- for which discrete financial information is available.

A company must disclose separate information about any operating segment that meets certain quantitative criteria—namely, the segment constitutes 10 percent or more of the combined operating segments' revenue, assets, or profit. (For purposes of determining whether a segment constitutes 10 percent or more of combined profits or losses, the criteria is expressed in terms of the absolute value of the segment's profit or loss as a percentage of the greater of (1) the combined profits of all profitable segments and (2) the absolute amount of the combined losses of all loss-making segments.) If, after applying these quantitative criteria, the combined revenue from external customers for all reportable segments combined is less than 75 percent of the total company revenue, the company must identify additional reportable segments until the 75 percent level is reached. Small segments might be combined as one if they share a substantial number of factors that define a business or geographical segment, or they might be combined with a similar significant reportable segment. Information about operating segments and businesses that are not reportable is combined in an "all other segments" category.

Companies must disclose the factors used to identify reportable segments and the types of products and services sold by each reportable segment.

For each reportable segment, the following should also be disclosed in the notes to financial statements:

- revenue, distinguishing between revenue to external customers and revenue from other segments;
- a measure of profit or loss;
- a measure of assets and liabilities (if these amounts are regularly reviewed by the company's chief decision-making officer);
- interest revenue and interest expense;
- cost of property, plant, and equipment, and intangible assets acquired;
- depreciation and amortization expense;
- other non-cash expenses;
- income tax expense or income; and
- share of the net profit or loss of an investment accounted for under the equity method.

Companies also must provide a reconciliation between the information of reportable segments and the consolidated financial statements in terms of segment revenue, profit or loss, assets, and liabilities.

A company's reporting segments can be useful as a means of quickly understanding what a company does and how and where it earns money. The segment data shown in Exhibit 4 appear in the notes to the financial statements for Sea Ltd.

Exhibit 4: Segment Reporting

Excerpts from Note 22 (Segment Reporting) of Sea Ltd.'s 2021 Annual Report on Form 20-F

The Company has three reportable segments, namely digital entertainment, e-commerce and digital financial services. The Chief Operating Decision Maker (CODM) reviews the performance of each segment based on revenue and certain key operating metrics of the operations and uses these results for the purposes of allocating resources to and evaluating financial performance of each segment.

Description of Reportable Segments:

Digital entertainment – Garena's platform offers mobile and PC online games and develops mobile games for the global market. Garena is the global leader in eSports, it also provides access to other entertainment content and social features, such as live streaming of gameplay, user chat and online forums.

E-commerce – Shopee's platform is a mobile-centric, social-focused marketplace. It provides users with a convenient, safe, and trusted shopping environment with integrated payment, logistics infrastructure and comprehensive seller services. Products from manufacturers and third parties are also purchased and sold directly to buyers on Shopee platform.

Digital financial services – SeaMoney provides a variety of payment services and loans to individuals and businesses. It is an important payment infrastructure supporting the Company's digital entertainment and e-commerce businesses. In addition, SeaMoney also integrates with third party merchant partners and covers a broad set of consumption use cases.

A combination of multiple business activities that does not meet the quantitative thresholds to qualify as reportable segments are grouped together as "Other services".

Segment Results for Year Ended 31 December 2021 (000s of USD)

	Digital Entertainment	E-Commerce	Digital Financial Services	Other Services	Unallocated Expenses	Consolidated
Revenue	4,320,013	5,122,959	469,774	42,444	0	9,955,190
Operating income (loss)	2,500,081	(2,766,566)	(640,422)	(177,633)	(498,520)	(1,583,060)
Non-operating loss, net						(132,124)
Income tax expense						(332,865)

Segment Results for Year Ended 31 December 2021 (000s of USD)						
	Digital Entertainment	E-Commerce	Digital Financial Services	Other Services	Unallocated Expenses	Consolidated
Share of results of equity investees						5,019
Net loss						(2,043,030)

Revenue by Geography (000s of USD)			
	Year Ended 31 December		
Revenue:	**2019**	**2020**	**2021**
Southeast Asia	1,378,141	2,791,894	6,316,782
Latin America	282,618	790,308	1,850,861
Rest of Asia	489,291	655,007	1,394,342
Rest of the World	25,328	138,455	393,205
Consolidated revenue	2,175,378	4,375,664	9,955,190

From the data in Exhibit 4, an analyst can quickly see that the e-commerce segment accounted for just over 50 percent of total revenues in 2021 but generated a large operating loss, while the digital entertainment segment accounted for most of the remaining revenues and was the only profitable segment. An analyst would likely spend a majority of their time on examining the past and present, and forecasting the future results of these two segments. Similarly, an analyst would use these disclosures to understand that Southeast Asia and Latin America are the company's most important geographies.

Identifying segments requires significant judgment by management, and companies often change the definition of segments and related disclosures.

Another required disclosure is the company's reliance on any single customer. If any single customer represents 10 percent or more of the company's total revenues, the company must disclose that fact, though not the identity of that customer. From an analysts' perspective, information about a concentrated customer base can be useful in assessing the risks faced by the company.

Management Commentary or Management's Discussion and Analysis

Regulatory filings such as Form 10-K and 10-Q include a section in which management discusses a variety of issues, including the nature of the business, past results, and outlook. This section is referred to by a variety of names, including management report(ing), management commentary, operating and financial review, and MD&A.

The discussion by management is arguably one of the most useful parts of a company's annual report besides the financial statements themselves; however, other than excerpts from the financial statements, information included in the management commentary is typically unaudited. In Germany, management reporting has been required since 1931 and is audited.

To help improve the quality of the discussion by management, the International Accounting Standards Board (IASB) issued an IFRS Practice Statement "Management Commentary" includes a framework for the preparation and presentation of management commentary. The framework provides guidance rather than sets forth requirements in a standard. The framework identifies five content elements of a "decision-useful management commentary": (1) the nature of the business; (2) management's objectives and strategies; (3) the company's significant resources, risks, and relationships; (4) results of operations; and (5) critical performance measures.

In the United States, the SEC requires listed companies to provide an MD&A and specifies the content.[8] Management must highlight any favorable or unfavorable trends and identify significant events and uncertainties that affect the company's liquidity, capital resources, and results of operations. The MD&A must also provide information about the effects of inflation, changing prices, or other material events and uncertainties that may cause the future operating results and financial condition to materially depart from the current reported financial information. In addition, the MD&A must provide information about off-balance-sheet obligations and about contractual commitments, such as purchase obligations. Management should also discuss the critical accounting policies that require them to make subjective judgments and that have a significant impact on reported financial results.

The management commentary, or MD&A, is a good starting place for understanding information in the financial statements. In particular, the forward-looking disclosures, such as those about planned capital expenditures, new store openings, or divestitures, can be useful in projecting a company's future performance. However, the commentary is only one input for the analyst seeking an objective and independent perspective on a company's performance and prospects.

Sea Ltd.'s 2021 annual report on Form 20-F includes much information of potential interest to an analyst. The lengthy report contains sections such as "Information on the Company" and "Operating and Financial Review and Prospects" that discuss the company's history, business model, strategies, key performance indicators, risk factors, relevant laws and regulations, recent financial performance and position, cash flows and working capital, capital expenditures, and key accounting policies.

Auditor's Reports

Financial statements presented in companies' annual reports are generally required to be audited by an independent accounting firm in accordance with specified auditing standards. The independent auditor then provides a written opinion on the financial statements. This opinion is referred to as the audit report. Audit reports may vary in different jurisdictions, but the minimum components, including a specific statement of the auditor's opinion, are similar. Audits of financial statements may be required by contractual arrangement, law, or regulation.

International standards on auditing (ISAs) have been developed by the International Auditing and Assurance Standards Board (IAASB). This body has emerged from the International Federation of Accountants. ISAs have been adopted by many countries and are referenced in audit reports issued in those countries. Other countries, such as the United States, specify their own auditing standards. With the enactment of the Sarbanes–Oxley Act of 2002 in the United States, auditing standards for public companies are promulgated by the PCAOB.

8 Relevant sections of SEC requirements are included for reference in the FASB Accounting Standards Codification (ASC). The FASB ASC does not include sections of SEC requirements that deal with matters outside the basic financial statements, such as the MD&A.

Under ISAs, the overall objectives of an auditor in conducting an audit of financial statements are

- to obtain reasonable assurance about whether the financial statements as a whole are free from material misstatement, whether due to fraud or error, thereby enabling the auditor to express an opinion on whether the financial statements are prepared, in all material respects, in accordance with an applicable financial reporting framework; and
- to report on the financial statements, and communicate as required by the ISAs, in accordance with the auditor's findings.[9]

Publicly traded companies may also have requirements set by regulators or stock exchanges, such as appointing an independent audit committee within its board of directors to oversee the audit process. The audit process provides a basis for the independent auditor to express an opinion on whether the information in the audited financial statements presents fairly the financial position, performance, and cash flows of the company in accordance with a specified set of accounting standards.

Audits are designed and conducted using sampling techniques, and financial statement line items may be based on estimates and assumptions. This means that the auditors cannot express an opinion that provides absolute assurance about the accuracy or precision of the financial statements. Instead, the independent audit report provides *reasonable assurance* that the financial statements are *fairly presented*, meaning that there is a high probability that the audited financial statements are free from *material* error, fraud, or illegal acts that have a direct effect on the financial statements.

The independent audit report expresses the auditor's opinion on the fairness of the audited financial statements, and specifies which financial statements were audited, the reporting entity, and the date. An *unqualified* audit opinion states that the financial statements give a "true and fair view" (international) or are "fairly presented" (international and United States) in accordance with applicable accounting standards. This is also referred to as an "unmodified" or a "clean" opinion and is the one that analysts would like to see in a financial report. There are several other types of modified opinions. A *qualified* audit opinion is one in which there is some scope limitation or exception to accounting standards. Exceptions are described in the audit report with additional explanatory paragraphs so that the analyst can determine the importance of the exception. An *adverse* audit opinion is issued when an auditor determines that the financial statements materially depart from accounting standards and are not fairly presented. Finally, a *disclaimer of opinion* occurs when, for some reason, such as a scope limitation, the auditors are unable to issue an opinion.

The audit report also describes the basis for the auditor's opinion and, for listed companies, includes a discussion of Key Audit Matters (international) and Critical Audit Matters (United States).[10] Key Audit Matters are defined as issues that the auditor considers to be most important, such as those that have a higher risk of misstatement, involve significant management judgment, or report the effects of significant transactions during the period. Critical Audit Matters are defined as issues that involve "especially challenging, subjective, or complex auditor judgment" and similarly include areas with higher risk of misstatement or that involve significant management judgment and estimates. However, Key and Critical Audit Matters are not necessarily the most important factors for analysts and investors.

9 See the International Auditing and Assurance Standards Board (IAASB), *Handbook of International Quality Control, Auditing, Review, Other Assurance, and Related Services Pronouncements* (New York: International Federation of Accountants, 2020).

10 Discussion of Key Audit Matters in the auditor's report is required by the International Standard on Auditing (ISA) ISA 701, effective in 2017, issued by the International Audit and Assurance Standards Board. Discussion of Critical Audit Matters in the auditor's report is required by the Auditor Reporting Standard AS 3101, effective for large filers' fiscal years ending on or after 30 June 2019, issued by the PCAOB.

Exhibit 5 presents excerpts from the independent auditor's report contained in Sea Ltd.'s 2021 annual report. Note that Sea Ltd. received an unqualified audit opinion (i.e., clean or unmodified opinion) from Ernst & Young LLP for the company's fiscal year ended 31 December 2021.

Exhibit 5: Excerpts from Sea Ltd.'s 2021 Independent Audit Report

To the Shareholders and the Board of Directors of Sea Limited

Opinion on the Financial Statements

We have audited the accompanying consolidated balance sheets of Sea Limited (the Company) as of December 31, 2021 and 2020, the related consolidated statements of operations, comprehensive loss, cash flows, and shareholders' equity (deficit) for each of the three years in the period ended December 31, 2021, and the related notes (collectively referred to as the "consolidated financial statements"). In our opinion, the consolidated financial statements present fairly, in all material respects, the financial position of the Company as of December 31, 2021 and 2020, and the results of its operations and its cash flows for each of the three years in the period ended December 31, 2021, in conformity with U.S. generally accepted accounting principles.

We also have audited, in accordance with the standards of the Public Company Accounting Oversight Board (United States) (PCAOB), the Company's internal control over financial reporting as of December 31, 2021, based on criteria established in Internal Control-Integrated Framework issued by the Committee of Sponsoring Organizations of the Treadway Commission (2013 framework), and our report dated April 22, 2022 expressed an unqualified opinion thereon.

Basis for Opinion

These financial statements are the responsibility of the Company's management. Our responsibility is to express an opinion on the Company's financial statements based on our audits. We are a public accounting firm registered with the PCAOB and are required to be independent with respect to the Company in accordance with the U.S. federal securities laws and the applicable rules and regulations of the Securities and Exchange Commission and the PCAOB. We conducted our audits in accordance with the standards of the PCAOB. Those standards require that we plan and perform the audit to obtain reasonable assurance about whether the financial statements are free of material misstatement, whether due to error or fraud.

Our audits included performing procedures to assess the risks of material misstatement of the financial statements, whether due to error or fraud, and performing procedures that respond to those risks. Such procedures included examining, on a test basis, evidence regarding the amounts and disclosures in the financial statements. Our audits also included evaluating the accounting principles used and significant estimates made by management, as well as evaluating the overall presentation of the financial statements. We believe that our audits provide a reasonable basis for our opinion.

Critical Audit Matters

The critical audit matters communicated below are matters arising from the current period audit of the financial statements that were communicated or required to be communicated to the audit committee and that: (1) relate to accounts or disclosures that are material to the financial statements and (2) involved our especially challenging, subjective or complex judgments. The communication of critical audit matters does not alter in any way our opinion on the consolidated financial statements, taken as a whole, and we are not, by communicating the critical audit matters below, providing separate opinions on the critical audit matters or on the accounts or disclosures to which they relate.

Recognition of Digital Entertainment ("DE") Revenue

Description of the Matter:

For the year ended December 31, 2021, the Company's revenue arising from DE was $4,320.0 million.

As outlined in Note 2(o) of the consolidated financial statements, DE revenue is recognized over the performance obligation period. The Company has determined that an implied obligation exists to the paying users to continue providing hosting services and access to the purchased virtual goods within the online games over an estimated service period. Such service period is largely determined in accordance with the estimated average lifespan of the paying users of the said games or similar games.

Auditing the DE revenue recognition process was complex and involved judgement to determine the historical paying users' inactive rate and playing behavior, in estimating the average lifespan of the paying users of the said games or similar games. In addition, the Company utilized various operating systems to process user data and transactions and relied on automated processes and controls over the completeness and accuracy of the historical user and game data, which were key inputs to the above-mentioned estimates.

How We Addressed the Matter in Our Audit:

We obtained an understanding, evaluated the design and tested the operating effectiveness of internal controls over the Company's DE revenue recognition process. For example, we tested the automated controls of the related operating systems. We also tested the effectiveness of management's review controls over assessing the completeness and accuracy of the historical user and game data and the appropriateness of the judgements regarding the most relevant historical user and game data to be applied in their estimates.

To test the recognition of DE revenue, our audit procedures included, among others, testing the completeness and accuracy of the above-mentioned underlying historical user and game data and assessing the reasonableness of the historical data applied in estimating the average lifespan of the paying users of the said games or similar games. We also recalculated the amount of revenue to be deferred based on management's estimated service periods and compared those amounts with the amounts recorded by the Company.

Measurement of long-lived assets in E-commerce ("EC") segment

Description of the Matter:

As at December 31, 2021, the Company's long-lived assets in EC segment amounted to approximately 75.7% of the Company's long-lived assets. The long-lived assets include property and equipment, operating lease right-of-use assets and intangible assets.

As outlined in Note 2(m) to the consolidated financial statements, the Company evaluates its long-lived assets for impairment when there are events or changes in circumstances which indicate that the carrying amounts of the long-lived assets may not be recoverable. Due to the continued losses incurred by EC segment, the Company evaluated the related long-lived assets for impairment at the asset group level by comparing the carrying amount of the asset group to the recoverable value determined by forecasted undiscounted cash flows expected to be generated by this asset group.

Auditing management's long-lived assets impairment test was highly judgmental due to the magnitude of the carrying amount of long-lived assets and management's judgement in estimating the recoverable value (undiscounted cash flows) of the asset group, which were sensitive to key assumptions such as projected revenue and sales and marketing expenses.

How We Addressed the Matter in Our Audit:

We obtained an understanding, evaluated the design and tested the operating effectiveness of controls over the Company's long-lived asset impairment process to determine the recoverable value of the asset group. For example, we tested controls over management's review of the key assumptions used in estimating the recoverable value.

To test the impairment of long-lived assets, our audit procedures included, among others, obtaining an understanding from management regarding the basis of which the undiscounted cash flows were prepared and assessing the reasonableness of the forecasted undiscounted cash flows by comparing them against the Company's business strategies and underlying key assumptions over the forecast periods, taking into consideration current industry and economic trends. We performed sensitivity analyses over the key assumptions described above to evaluate the changes to the estimated recoverable value for the asset group that would result from changes in the assumptions.

/s/ Ernst & Young LLP
We have served as the Company's auditor since 2010.
Singapore
April 22, 2022

Source: Sea Ltd., 2021 *Annual Report*.

In the United States, under the Sarbanes–Oxley Act, the auditors must also express an opinion on the company's internal control systems. This information may be provided in a separate opinion or incorporated as a paragraph in the opinion related to the financial statements. Internal controls are the company's processes, personnel, and systems designed to ensure that the company's process for generating financial reports is sound. Although management has always been responsible for maintaining effective internal control, the Sarbanes–Oxley Act greatly increases management's responsibility for demonstrating that the company's internal controls are effective. Management of publicly traded companies in the United States are now required by securities regulators to explicitly accept responsibility for the effectiveness of internal control, evaluate the effectiveness of internal control using suitable control criteria, support the evaluation with sufficient competent evidence, and provide a report on internal control.

Although these reports and attestations provide some assurances to analysts, they are not infallible. The analyst must always use a degree of healthy skepticism when analyzing financial statements.

COMPARISON OF IFRS WITH ALTERNATIVE FINANCIAL REPORTING SYSTEMS

5

☐ describe implications for financial analysis of alternative financial reporting systems and the importance of monitoring developments in financial reporting standards

The adoption of IFRS as the required financial reporting standard by most countries outside the United States has advanced the goal of global convergence. Nevertheless, there are still significant differences in financial reporting in the global capital markets. Arguably, the most critical are the differences that exist between IFRS and US GAAP as a significant number of the world's listed companies use one of these two reporting standards.

In general, the IASB and FASB work together to coordinate changes to accounting standards and reduce differences between the standards. While convergence of conceptual frameworks and existing standards was put on hold in the late 2000s, new accounting standards have been mostly or entirely converged, resulting in increasing uniformity over time as major new standards have been adopted (e.g., revenue recognition, leasing, credit losses). Maintaining convergence on new standards remains a priority of both standard-setting bodies. Later modules provide a more detailed review of related differences in IFRS and US GAAP, though some major differences are outlined in Exhibit 6.

Exhibit 6: Selected Major Differences between IFRS and US GAAP

Basis for Comparison	US GAAP	IFRS
Developed by	Financial Accounting Standards Board (FASB)	International Accounting Standards Board (IASB)
Based on	Rules	Principles
Interest paid	Cash Flows from Operating Activities	Cash Flows from Financing Activities *or* Cash Flows from Operating Activities
Inventory valuation	First in, First out (FIFO); Last in, First out (LIFO); and Weighted Average Method	FIFO and Weighted Average Method
Development cost	Treated as an expense	Capitalized, only if certain conditions are satisfied
Reversal of Inventory Write-down	Prohibited	Permissible, if specified conditions are met

Because reconciliation disclosures between IFRS and US GAAP are not required, an analyst comparing two companies that use different reporting standards must be aware of areas in which accounting standards have not converged. In many cases, a user of financial statements prepared under different accounting standards does not have enough information to make the specific adjustments required to achieve comparability. Instead, an analyst must maintain caution in interpreting comparative financial measures produced under different accounting standards and monitor significant developments in financial reporting standards, as this can have important implications for comparing the performance of companies and security valuation.

Monitoring Developments in Financial Reporting Standards

Analysts need to monitor ongoing developments in financial reporting and assess their implications for security analysis and valuation. The need to monitor developments in financial reporting standards does not mean that analysts should be accountants. An accountant monitors these developments from a preparer's perspective; an analyst needs to monitor them from a user's perspective. More specifically, analysts need to know how these developments will affect financial reports.

Analysts can remain aware of developments in financial reporting standards by monitoring new products or transactions, actions of standard setters and other groups representing users of financial statements (such as CFA Institute), and company disclosures regarding critical accounting policies and estimates.

New Products or Types of Transactions

New products and new types of transactions can have unusual or unique elements to them such that no explicit guidance in the financial reporting standards exists. New products or transactions typically arise from economic events, such as new businesses (e.g., fintech), or from a newly developed financial instrument or financial structure (e.g. cryptocurrencies and other digital assets). Financial instruments, whether exchange traded or not, are typically designed to enhance a company's business or to mitigate inherent risks. At times, however, financial instruments or structured transactions have been developed primarily for purposes of financial report "window dressing."

Although companies might discuss new products and transactions in their financial reports, the analyst can also monitor business journals and the capital markets to identify such items. Additionally, when one company in an industry develops a new product or transaction, other companies in the industry often do the same. Once new products, financial instruments, or structured transactions are identified, it is helpful to gain an understanding of the business purpose. If necessary, an analyst can obtain further information from a company's management, which should be able to describe the economic purpose, the financial statement reporting, significant estimates, judgments applied in determining the reporting, and future cash flow implications for these items.

Evolving Standards and the Role of CFA Institute

The actions of standard setters and regulators are unlikely to be helpful in identifying new products and transactions, given the lag between new product development and regulatory action. Monitoring the actions of these authorities is nonetheless important for another reason: Changes in regulations can affect companies' financial reports and, thus, valuations. This is particularly true if the financial reporting standards change to require more explicit identification of matters affecting asset/liability valuation or financial performance. For example, one regulatory change required companies to include a provision for expenses associated with the grant and vesting of employee stock option grants as an expense in the income statement. Prior to the required expensing, an analyst could assess the dilutive effect to shareholders associated with stock option grants only by reviewing information disclosed in the notes to the financial statements.

To the extent that some market participants do not examine financial statement details and thus ignore some items when valuing a company's securities, more explicit identification could affect the value of the company's securities. Additionally, it is plausible to believe that management is more attentive to and rigorous in any calculations/estimates of items that appear in the financial statements, compared with items that are disclosed only in the notes.

The IASB (www.iasb.org) and FASB (www.fasb.org) provide a great deal of information on their websites regarding new standards and proposals for future changes in standards. In addition, the IASB and FASB seek input from the financial analyst community—those who regularly use financial statements in making investment and credit decisions. When a new standard is proposed, an exposure draft is made available and users of financial statements can draft comment letters and position papers for submission to the IASB and FASB to evaluate the proposal.

CFA Institute is active in supporting improvements to financial reporting. Volunteer members of CFA Institute serve on several liaison committees that meet regularly to make recommendations to the IASB and FASB on proposed standards and to draft comment letters and position papers. The comment letters and position papers of these groups on financial reporting issues are available at www.cfainstitute.org/advocacy.

In 2007, CFA Institute issued a position paper titled *A Comprehensive Business Reporting Model: Financial Reporting for Investors*, which provides a suggested model for significantly improving financial reporting. The position paper remains relevant in stating:

> Corporate financial statements and their related disclosures are fundamental to sound investment decision making. The well-being of the world's financial markets, and of the millions of investors who entrust their financial present and future to those markets, depends directly on the information financial statements and disclosures provide. Consequently, the quality of the information drives global financial markets. The quality, in turn, depends directly on the principles and standards managers apply when recognizing and measuring the economic activities and events affecting their companies' operations. ...
>
> Investors require timeliness, transparency, comparability, and consistency in financial reporting. Investors have a preference for decision relevance over reliability ... "analysts need to know economic reality—what is really going on—to the greatest extent it can be depicted by accounting numbers." Corporate financial statements that fail to reflect this economic reality undermine the investment decision-making process.[11]

Among other principles, the proposed model stresses the importance of information regarding the current fair value of assets and liabilities, of neutrality in financial reporting, and of providing detailed information on cash flows to investors through the choice of the so-called direct format for the cash flow statement.

In summary, analysts can improve their investment decision making by keeping current on financial reporting standards. In addition, analysts can contribute to improving financial reporting by sharing their perspective as users with standard-setting bodies, which typically invite comments concerning proposed changes.

11 *A Comprehensive Business Reporting Model: Financial Reporting for Investors* (Charlottesville, VA: CFA Institute Centre for Financial Market Integrity, July 2007), p. 1, 2.

6 OTHER SOURCES OF INFORMATION

☐ describe information sources that analysts use in financial statement analysis besides annual and interim financial reports

In addition to regulated information from issuers such as the financial statements and notes in filings, analysts use a variety of other information sources for financial analysis, which we group by origin: issuers, public third-party, proprietary third-party, and proprietary primary research.

- Issuer sources (other than regulatory filings such as annual and quarterly reports and proxy statements)
  - Earnings calls. Earnings calls are webcast or teleconferenced presentations and question-and-answer sessions hosted by issuers' management to discuss financial results. The primary audience for the calls are analysts, investors, and members of the media. While not legally required, most public companies conduct these calls to provide complementary information to their regulatory filings, such as explaining differences in performances from expectations, revisions to forward-looking targets, and explaining corporate actions such as acquisitions and restructurings. Analysts ask probing questions to gain further color from management to understand past results and actions to sharpen their estimates. Platforms such as Bloomberg, Wind, and FactSet transcribe earnings calls and other presentations.
  - Presentations and events, such as investor days. Similar to earnings calls but scheduled on an ad hoc basis, issuers and investment banks sometimes host events during which management teams give in-depth presentations on their business or specific topics and business segments. Like earnings calls, analysts must be aware that management is biased to their perspective, and often need to ask questions for the information they want.
  - Press releases. Press releases are announcements and statements of information (typically in writing but can be videos or graphics) by companies and their management. Common topics include notifications of upcoming events, product releases and changes, management and board of director changes, and M&A or restructuring announcements. Press releases are often distributed not only on issuers' websites but also on third-party news sources.
  - Speaking with management, investor relations, or other company personnel.
  - Company website or properties that the analyst may be able to visit as a customer or an investor. It is often useful to experience an issuer's and competitors' products firsthand, though it is not always possible (e.g., pharmaceuticals).
- Public third-party sources
  - Free industry whitepapers or analyst reports from a consultancy, usually accessed through internet search engines.

    - Economic or industry indicators from governments and other organizations, such as retail sales and price indexes, often released monthly or quarterly.
    - General news outlets.
    - Industry-specific news outlets.
    - Social media, which may be a useful gauge of customer sentiment for a company's products.
- Proprietary third-party sources
    - Analyst reports and communications, including from the sell side or analysts and credit rating agencies.
    - Reports and data from platforms such as Bloomberg, Wind, and FactSet.
    - Reports and data from consultancies, often industry-specific sources, such as Rystad in energy, iQvia and Evaluate in biopharma, and Gartner and IDC in information technology industries.
- Proprietary primary research
    - Surveys, conversations, product comparisons, and other studies commissioned by the analyst or conducted directly.

Information on the economy, industry, and peer companies is useful in putting the company's financial performance and position in perspective and in assessing the company's future. In most cases, information from sources apart from the company is crucial to an analyst's effectiveness. For example, an analyst studying a consumer-oriented company will typically seek direct experience with the products (taste the food or drink, use the shampoo or soap, visit the stores or hotels). An analyst following a highly regulated industry will study the existing and expected relevant regulations. An analyst following a highly technical industry will gain relevant expertise personally or seek input from a technical specialist.

PRACTICE PROBLEMS

1. Ratios are an input into which step in the financial statement analysis framework?

   A. Process data

   B. Collect input data

   C. Analyze/interpret the processed data

2. Which phase in the financial statement analysis framework is *most likely* to involve producing updated reports and recommendations?

   A. Follow-up

   B. Analyze/interpret the processed data

   C. Develop and communicate conclusions and recommendations

3. Which of the following *best* describes the role of financial statement analysis?

   A. To provide information about a company's performance

   B. To provide information about a company's changes in financial position

   C. To form expectations about a company's future performance and financial position

4. The primary role of financial statement analysis is *best* described as:

   A. providing information useful for making investment decisions.

   B. evaluating a company for the purpose of making economic decisions.

   C. using financial reports prepared by analysts to make economic decisions.

5. International Financial Reporting Standards are currently developed by which entity?

   A. IFRS Foundation

   B. International Accounting Standards Board

   C. International Organization of Securities Commissions

6. US GAAP are currently developed by which entity?

   A. Securities and Exchange Commission

   B. Financial Accounting Standards Board

   C. Public Company Accounting Oversight Board

7. A core objective of the International Organization of Securities Commissions is to:

   A. eliminate systemic risk.

   B. protect users of financial statements.

C. ensure that markets are fair, efficient, and transparent.

8. Which of the following *best* describes why the notes that accompany the financial statements are required? The notes:

   A. permit flexibility in statement preparation.

   B. standardize financial reporting across companies.

   C. provide information necessary to understand the financial statements.

9. Accounting policies, methods, and estimates used in preparing financial statements are *most likely* to be found in the:

   A. auditor's report.

   B. management commentary.

   C. notes to the financial statements.

10. Information about management and director compensation is *most likely* to be found in the:

   A. auditor's report.

   B. proxy statement.

   C. earnings release.

11. Information about a company's objectives, strategies, and significant risks are *most likely* to be found in the:

   A. auditor's report.

   B. management commentary.

   C. notes to the financial statements.

12. What type of audit opinion is preferred when analyzing financial statements?

   A. Adverse

   B. Qualified

   C. Unqualified

13. An auditor determines that a company's financial statements are prepared in accordance with applicable accounting standards except with respect to inventory reporting. This exception is *most likely* to result in an audit opinion that is:

   A. adverse.

   B. qualified.

   C. unqualified.

14. An independent audit report is *most likely* to provide:

   A. absolute assurance about the accuracy of the financial statements.

   B. reasonable assurance that the financial statements are fairly presented.

C. a qualified opinion with respect to the transparency of the financial statements.

15. Interim financial reports released by a company are *most likely* to be:

    A. monthly.

    B. unaudited.

    C. unqualified.

16. Which of the following sources of information used by analysts is found outside a company's annual report?

    A. Auditor's report

    B. Peer company analysis

    C. Management discussion and analysis

SOLUTIONS

1. C is correct. Ratios are an output of the process information step but are an input into the analyze/interpret data step.

2. A is correct. The follow-up phase involves gathering information and repeating the analysis to determine whether it is necessary to update reports and recommendations.

3. C is correct. In general, analysts seek to examine the past and current performance and financial position of a company to form expectations about its future performance and financial position.

4. B is correct. The primary role of financial statement analysis is to use financial reports prepared by companies to evaluate their past, current, and potential performance and financial position for the purpose of making investment, credit, and other economic decisions.

5. B is correct. The International Accounting Standards Board (IASB) is currently charged with developing International Financial Reporting Standards.

6. B is correct. US Generally Accepted Accounting Principles are developed by the US Financial Accounting Standards Board (FASB).

7. C is correct. A core objective of IOSCO is to ensure that markets are fair, efficient, and transparent. The other core objectives are to reduce, not eliminate, systemic risk and to protect investors, not all users of financial statements.

8. C is correct. The notes provide information that is essential to understanding the information provided in the primary statements.

9. C is correct. The notes disclose choices in accounting policies, methods, and estimates.

10. B is correct. Disclosure of management compensation is typically included in the proxy statement. An earnings release is about corporate earnings, not what managers earn as compensation.

11. B is correct. These are components of management commentary.

12. C is correct. An unqualified opinion is a "clean" opinion and indicates that the financial statements present the company's performance and financial position fairly in accordance with applicable accounting standards.

13. B is correct. A qualified audit opinion is one in which there is some scope limitation or exception to accounting standards. Exceptions are described in the audit report with additional explanatory paragraphs so that the analyst can determine the importance of the exception.

14. B is correct. The independent audit report provides reasonable assurance that the financial statements are fairly presented, meaning that there is a high probability that the audited financial statements are free from material error, fraud, or illegal acts that have a direct effect on the financial statements.

15. B is correct. Interim reports are typically provided semiannually or quarterly and require certain financial information, including unaudited financial statements

and an MD&A for the interim period covered by the report. Unqualified refers to a type of audit opinion.

16. B is correct. When performing financial statement analysis, analysts should review all company sources of information as well as information from external sources regarding the economy, the industry, the company, and peer (comparable) companies.

LEARNING MODULE

2

Analyzing Income Statements

by Elaine Henry, PhD, CFA, and Thomas R. Robinson, PhD, CAIA, CFA.

Elaine Henry, PhD, CFA, is at Stevens Institute of Technology (USA). Thomas R. Robinson, PhD, CAIA, CFA, is at AACSB International (USA).

LEARNING OUTCOMES

Mastery	*The candidate should be able to:*
☐	describe general principles of revenue recognition, specific revenue recognition applications, and implications of revenue recognition choices for financial analysis
☐	describe general principles of expense recognition, specific expense recognition applications, implications of expense recognition choices for financial analysis and contrast costs that are capitalized versus those that are expensed in the period in which they are incurred
☐	describe the financial reporting treatment and analysis of non-recurring items (including discontinued operations, unusual or infrequent items) and changes in accounting policies
☐	describe how earnings per share is calculated and calculate and interpret a company's basic and diluted earnings per share for companies with simple and complex capital structures including those with antidilutive securities
☐	evaluate a company's financial performance using common-size income statements and financial ratios based on the income statement

The two major accounting standard setters are as follows: 1) the International Accounting Standards Board (IASB) who establishes International Financial Reporting Standards (IFRS) and 2) the Financial Accounting Standards Board (FASB) who establishes US GAAP. Throughout this learning module both standards are referred to and many, but not all, of these two sets of accounting rules are identified. Note: changes in accounting standards as well as new rulings and/or pronouncements issued after the publication of this learning module may cause some of the information to become dated.

1 INTRODUCTION

Income statements and analytical measures derived from them, such as sales growth, operating margin, and earnings per share (EPS), are critical for equity and credit analysis. Investors analyze income statements to evaluate companies' growth, profitability, and risks, and often use income statement figures in valuation. Corporate financial announcements frequently emphasize information reported in income statements, particularly earnings, more than information reported in the other financial statements.

LEARNING MODULE OVERVIEW

- Revenue is recognized in the period it is earned, which may or may not be in the same period as the related cash collection.
- An analyst should identify differences in companies' revenue recognition methods and adjust reported revenue where possible to facilitate comparability. In cases in which the available information does not permit adjustment, an analyst can characterize the revenue recognition as more or less conservative and thus qualitatively assess how differences in policies might affect financial ratios and judgments about profitability.
- As of the beginning of 2018, revenue recognition standards have converged across US GAAP and International Financial Reporting Standards (IFRS). The core principle of the converged standards is that revenue should be recognized to "depict the transfer of promised goods or services to customers in an amount that reflects the consideration to which the entity expects to be entitled in an exchange for those goods or services."
- To achieve the core principle, the standard describes the application of five steps in recognizing revenue. The standard also specifies the treatment of some related contract costs and disclosure requirements.
- The general principles of expense recognition include a process to match expenses to revenue (e.g., cost of goods sold), to the period in which the expenditure occurs (e.g., administrative costs), or to the period of expected benefits of the expenditures (e.g., depreciation and amortization).
- In expense recognition, choice of method (i.e., depreciation method and inventory cost method), as well as estimates (i.e., uncollectible accounts, warranty expenses, assets' useful life, and salvage value) affect a company's reported income. An analyst should identify differences in companies' expense recognition methods and adjust reported financial statements where possible to facilitate comparability. In cases in which the available information does not permit adjustment, an analyst can characterize the policies and estimates as more or less conservative and thus qualitatively assess how differences in policies might affect financial ratios and judgments about companies' performance.
- To assess a company's future earnings, it is helpful to separate those prior years' items of income and expense that are likely to continue in the future from those items that are less likely to continue.

- Under IFRS, a company should present additional line items, headings, and subtotals beyond those specified when such presentation is relevant to an understanding of the entity's financial performance. Some items from prior years clearly are not expected to continue in future periods and are separately disclosed on a company's income statement. Under US GAAP, unusual or infrequently occurring items, which are material, are presented separately within income from continuing operations.
- Non-operating items are reported separately from operating items on the income statement. Under both IFRS and US GAAP, the income statement reports separately the effect of the disposal of a component operation as a "discontinued" operation, net of income taxes.
- Basic EPS is the amount of income available to common shareholders divided by the weighted average number of common shares outstanding over a period. The amount of income available to common shareholders is the amount of net income remaining after preferred dividends (if any) have been paid.
- If a company has a simple capital structure (i.e., one with no potentially dilutive securities), then its basic EPS is equal to its diluted EPS. If, however, a company has dilutive securities, its diluted EPS is no greater than its basic EPS.
- Diluted EPS is calculated using the if-converted method for convertible securities and the treasury stock method for options.
- Common-size analysis of the income statement involves stating each line item on the income statement as a percentage of sales. Common-size statements facilitate comparison across time periods and across companies of different sizes.

REVENUE RECOGNITION 2

☐ describe general principles of revenue recognition, specific revenue recognition applications, and implications of revenue recognition choices for financial analysis

General Principles

A fundamental principle of accrual accounting is that revenue is recognized (reported on the income statement) when it is earned, so the company's financial records reflect revenue from the sale when the risk and reward of ownership is transferred; this is often when the company delivers the goods or services. If the delivery was on credit, a related asset, such as trade or accounts receivable, is created. Later, when cash changes hands, the company's financial records simply reflect that cash has been received to settle an account receivable. Similarly, in some situations, a company receives cash in advance and but delivers the product or service later, perhaps over a period of time. In this case, the company would record a liability for **unearned revenue**, or deferred revenue, when the cash is initially received, and revenue would be recognized over time as products and services are delivered. An example would be a subscription payment received in advance for cloud-based software delivered over a year.

Accounting Standards for Revenue Recognition

The converged accounting standards issued by the IASB and FASB in May 2014 introduced some changes to the basic principles of revenue recognition. The content of the two standards is nearly identical, and this discussion pertains to both, unless specified otherwise. The converged standard aims to provide a principles-based approach to revenue recognition that can be applied to many types of revenue-generating activities.

The core principle of the converged standard is that revenue should be recognized to "depict the transfer of promised goods or services to customers in an amount that reflects the consideration to which the entity expects to be entitled in an exchange for those goods or services." To achieve the core principle, the standard describes the application of the following five steps in recognizing revenue:

1. identify the contract(s) with a customer,
2. identify the separate or distinct performance obligations in the contract,
3. determine the transaction price,
4. allocate the transaction price to the performance obligations in the contract, and
5. recognize revenue when (or as) the entity satisfies a performance obligation.

According to the standard, a contract is an agreement and commitment with commercial substance between the contacting parties. It establishes each party's *obligations* and *rights,* including payment terms. In addition, a contract exists only if collectability is probable. Each standard uses the same wording, but the threshold for probable collectability differs. Under IFRS, probable means more likely than not, and under US GAAP, it means likely to occur. As a result, economically similar contracts may be treated differently under IFRS and US GAAP.

The performance obligations within a contract represent promises to transfer distinct good(s) or service(s). A good or service is distinct if the customer can benefit from it on its own or in combination with readily available resources and if the promise to transfer it can be separated from other promises in the contract. Each identified performance obligation is accounted for separately.

The transaction price is what the seller estimates will be received in exchange for transferring the good(s) or service(s) identified in the contract. The transaction price is then allocated to each identified performance obligation. Revenue is recognized when a performance obligation is fulfilled. Steps three and four address amounts, and step five addresses timing of recognition. The amounts recognized reflect expectations about collectability and (if applicable) an allocation to multiple obligations within the same contract.

Revenue should be recognized only when it is highly probable that it will not be subsequently reversed. If it is likely to be reversed, the seller will record a minimal amount of revenue upon sale and recognize a refund liability and "right to returned goods" asset on the balance sheet based on the carrying amount of inventory less costs of recovery.

The entity will recognize revenue when it is able to satisfy the performance obligation by transferring control of the good or service to the customer. Factors to consider when assessing whether the customer has obtained control of include the following:

- entity has a present right to payment,
- customer has legal title,

- customer has physical possession,
- customer has the significant risks and rewards of ownership, and
- customer has accepted the good or service.

For a simple contract with only one deliverable at a single point in time, completing these five steps is straight-forward. For more complex contracts—such as when the performance obligations are satisfied over time, when the terms of the multiperiod contracts change, or when the performance obligation includes various components of goods and services—accounting choices are less obvious. The steps in the standards are intended to provide guidance that can be generalized to most situations.

If the performance obligation is satisfied at the end of these five steps, and there is no contingency regarding payment, then revenue and accounts receivable are recognized. In cases in which revenue is recognized but the payment by the customer is conditional on some other future performance, a contract asset is initially presented on the balance sheet, until performance obligations are met, and a receivable can be recognized. If consideration is received in advance of transferring good(s) or service(s), the seller records a contract liability.

As an analyst, you will encounter many companies with complex revenue recognition policies, reflecting the diversity of business models in practice. Several examples adapted from real companies are discussed in Example 1.

EXAMPLE 1

Applying the Converged Revenue Recognition Standards

Principal Versus Agent

MegaDigital is an online marketplace that sells goods and delivers them quickly to customers. For some sales, MegaDigital acts as a principal in which it controls the product before the goods are transferred to the customer. In other sales, MegaDigital acts as an agent in which it arranges for the transfer of a product controlled by a third-party seller. In transactions in which MegaDigital is the principal, revenue is recorded as the total amount of considerations received for the transfer of the product. In transactions in which MegaDigital is the agent, it records revenue only for the portion of the considerations, which amounts to its fee or commission. This can have a significant impact on common size and ratio analysis. Revenue is lower but profit margins are higher for sales for which MegaDigital is an agent.

Assume MegaDigital sells a particular product as a principal for USD100 that it purchased for USD70. Additionally, there are USD10 of other selling, general, and administrative costs. The margins would be:

Sales	USD100	100 percent
Cost of Sales	70	70 percent
Gross Profit	30	30 percent
SG&A	10	10 percent
Net Profit	20	20 percent

If MegaDigital acts an agent for the same item with the same retail price, MegaDigital would receive a commission of USD30 and still incurs USD10 of other costs. Margins would be:

Sales	USD30	100 percent
Cost of Sales	0	0 percent
Gross Profit	30	100 percent
SG&A	10	33 percent
Net Profit	20	67 percent

For companies selling both as a principal and agent, such as many e-commerce companies, an analyst would need to evaluate the relative proportion of principal versus agent sales to evaluate and forecast overall margins. This is especially important if the mix of principal and agent sales is expected to change.

Franchising/Licensing

Mahjong Pizza both operates and franchises pizza delivery restaurants around the world. Revenue recognition standards require that the company disaggregate revenue from contracts with customers into categories that depict how the nature, amount, timing, and uncertainty of revenue and cash flows are affected by economic factors. Companies must present revenues disaggregated in consolidated statements of income to satisfy this requirement. Mahjong Pizza presents the following disaggregated revenue items:

- company-owned stores revenues,
- franchise royalties and fees, and
- supply chain revenues.

Company-owned stores revenues are of retail sales of food at stores that Mahjong owns and operates.

Franchise royalties and fees are comprised of fees from third-party franchisees that are licensed to operate Mahjong restaurants. Each franchisee is generally required to pay fees equal to 5.5 percent of restaurant sales. The company recognizes the royalty fee as revenue, not the total sales of the franchisees' restaurants. Upfront fees for opening new units are initially recognized as deferred revenue and subsequently amortized to revenue on a straight-line basis over the term of each respective franchise agreement, typically 10 years.

Supply chain revenues are primarily composed of sales of food, equipment, and supplies to franchisees. Revenues are recognized upon delivery or shipment of the related products to franchisees, based on shipping terms.

Software as a Service or License

CReaM Software and Services is a technology company providing customer relationship management software and services to business, government and not-for-profit organizations. Organizations may purchase a software license and install it on their own systems. Alternatively, they may subscribe to CReaM's cloud services platform through which they can access CReaM's software over the internet for a monthly subscription fee.

Under IFRS 15, if a company provides a license to use software where the company will take possession of the software for installation on their own system, the company will report revenue either over the term of the license or at the time of the transfer of the license. Companies should report the revenue from the license over the term of the license, if under the contract or the company's normal business activities:

- the software provider will continue to undertake activities that significantly affect the software (e.g., upgrades/enhancements),

- the rights expose the customer to positive or negative impacts from those activities, and
- the activities do not result in a transfer of goods or services.

If these criteria are not met, then the revenue is recognized when the license is transferred to the customer. CReaM's annual report footnotes state:

> Software revenues include revenues associated with term and perpetual software licenses that provide the customer with a right to use the software as it exists when made available. Revenues from term and perpetual software licenses are generally recognized at the point in time when the software is made available to the customer. Revenue from software support and updates is recognized as the support and updates are provided, which is generally ratably over the contract term.

Under the terms of CReaM's license, the software is sold "as is" and revenue is recognized at the time of the license transfer. CReaM, however, also provides a support contract for updates for which revenue is recognized over the contract term.

CReaM's cloud clients have access to constantly updated software. CReaM reports:

> Cloud services allow customers to use the Company's software without taking possession of the software. Revenue is generally recognized over the contract term. Substantially all of the Company's subscription service arrangements are non-cancelable and do not contain refund-type provisions.

In the case of CReaM, an analyst must understand the composition of revenue between licensed software in which case revenue is recognized upfront versus software as a service in which case revenue is recognized over time.

Long-Term Contracts

Armored Vehicles Inc. (AVI) manufactures weapons systems and vehicles for military customers. The company enters long-term contracts that generally extend over several years. Performance on the contracts is satisfied over time. Under IFRS 15, a performance obligation is satisfied over time if one of the following criteria is met:

- The customer simultaneously receives and consumes the benefits provided by the entity's performance as the entity performs (e.g., routine service contracts).
- The entity's performance creates or enhances an asset that the customer controls as the asset is created or enhanced (e.g., refurbishment of a factory owned and controlled by the customer or building a road for a governmental agency).
- The entity's performance does not create an asset with alternative use to the entity and the entity has an enforceable right to payment for performance completed to date (e.g., construction of a large unique asset that may not be able to be sold to another customer such as a weapons system).

AVI recognizes long-term contract revenue over the contract term as the work progresses, either as products are produced or as services are rendered because of the continuous transfer of control to the customer. For its military contracts, this continuous transfer of control to the customer is supported by clauses in the contract that allow the customer to unilaterally terminate the contract for convenience, pay for costs incurred plus a reasonable profit, and take control of any work in process.

Under IFRS 15, the extent of progress towards completion may be measured by output methods (e.g., appraisals or units completed) or input methods (e.g., costs incurred relative to estimated total costs). AVI reports that its accounting for long-term contracts involves a judgmental process of estimating total sales, costs and profit for each performance obligation. Cost of sales is recognized as incurred. The amount reported as revenues is determined by adding a proportionate amount of the estimated profit to the amount reported as cost of sales. Recognizing revenue as costs are incurred provides an objective measure of progress on the long-term contract and thereby best depicts the extent of transfer of control to the customer.

As an example, AVI has a contract to produce a weapons system for a total price of USD10 million. The expected total costs to produce the system is USD7 million and the estimated profit is USD3 million. The system will take two years to produce. In Year 1 of the contract, AVI incurs USD4.2 million of costs representing 60 percent of total estimated costs. AVI would recognize revenue of USD6 million and profit of USD1.8 million in Year 1 (both 60 percent of expected revenue and profits).

If in Year 2, the system is completed with actual total cumulative costs of USD7.5 million, the company would report revenue of USD4 million and costs of USD3.3 million for a Year 2 profit of USD0.7 million and cumulative profit of USD2.5 million.

Bill and Hold Arrangements

In addition to the long-term contracts discussed previously, AVI produces custom armored vehicles that some customers may not be able to take possession of immediately (because, for example, a lack of storage space). IFRS 15 provides that in such a "bill and hold" arrangement AVI can determine when it has satisfied its performance obligation based on when a customer obtains control of the product. Under IFRS 15, this is when all the following criteria are met:

- The reason for the bill and hold arrangement must be substantive (e.g., the customer has requested the arrangement).
- The product must be identified separately as belonging to the customer.
- The product currently must be ready for physical transfer to the customer.
- The entity cannot have the ability to use the product or to direct it to another customer.

In AVI's case, each vehicle is identified by a unique vehicle identification number and upon completion, title and risk of loss has passed to the customer. AVI recognizes revenue when the product is ready for delivery to the customer but is directed by the customer to hold delivery.

The disclosure requirements under IFRS 15 are quite extensive to provide sufficient information to financial statement users on the nature, amount, and timing of cash flows from customers. Companies are required to disclose revenue from contracts with customers disaggregated into different categories of contracts. The categories might be based on the type of product, the geographic region, the type of customer or sales channel, the type of contract pricing terms, the contract duration, or the timing of transfers. Companies are also required to disclose balances of any contract-related assets and liabilities and significant changes in those balances, remaining performance obligations and transaction price allocated to those obligations, and any significant judgments and changes in judgments related to revenue recognition. These disclosures are typically provided in a note to the financial statements titled "Revenue" or similar.

EXPENSE RECOGNITION

3

☐ describe general principles of expense recognition, specific expense recognition applications, implications of expense recognition choices for financial analysis and contrast costs that are capitalized versus those that are expensed in the period in which they are incurred

Assume a company purchased inventory for cash and sold the entire inventory in the same period. When the company paid for the inventory, absent indications to the contrary, it is clear that inventory cost was incurred and when that inventory is sold, it should be recognized as an expense (cost of goods sold). Assume also that the company paid all operating and administrative expenses in cash within each accounting period. In such a simple hypothetical scenario, no issues of expense recognition would arise. In practice, however, as with revenue recognition, determining when expenses should be recognized can be somewhat more complex.

General Principles

In general, a company recognizes expenses in the period that it consumes (i.e., uses up) the economic benefits associated with the expenditure, or loses some previously recognized economic benefit. The three common expense recognition models are as follows: the matching principle, expensing as incurred, and capitalization with subsequent depreciation or amortization.

Under matching, a company recognizes expenses (e.g., cost of goods sold) when associated revenues are recognized, and thus, expenses and revenues are matched. Associated revenues and expenses are those that result directly and jointly from the same transactions or events. Unlike the simple scenario in which a company purchases inventory and sells all of the inventory within the same accounting period, in practice, it is more likely that some of the current period's sales are made from inventory purchased in a previous period or previous periods. It is also likely that some of the inventory purchased in the current period will remain unsold at the end of the current period and so will be sold in a following period. Matching requires that a company recognizes cost of goods sold in the same period as revenues from the sale of the goods. Strictly speaking, IFRS do not refer to a "matching principle" but rather to a "matching concept" or to a process resulting in "matching of costs with revenues."

Example 2 demonstrate matching applied to inventory and cost of goods sold.

EXAMPLE 2

The Matching of Inventory Costs with Revenues

Kahn Distribution Limited (KDL), a hypothetical company, purchases inventory items for resale. At the beginning of 20X1, Kahn had no inventory on hand. During 20X1, KDL had the following transactions:

Inventory Purchases		
First quarter	2,000	units at USD40 per unit
Second quarter	1,500	units at USD41 per unit
Third quarter	2,200	units at USD43 per unit
Fourth quarter	1,900	units at USD45 per unit
Total	7,600	units at a total cost of USD321,600

KDL sold 5,600 units of inventory during the year at USD50 per unit and received cash. KDL determines that there were 2,000 remaining units of inventory and specifically identifies that 1,900 were those purchased in the fourth quarter and 100 were purchased in the third quarter.

1. What are the revenue and expense associated with these transactions during 20X1 based on specific identification of inventory items as sold or remaining in inventory? (Assume that the company does not expect any products to be returned.)

Solution:

The revenue for 20X1 would be USD280,000 (5,600 units × USD50 per unit). Initially, the total cost of the goods purchased would be recorded as inventory (an asset) in the amount of USD321,600. During 20X1, the cost of the 5,600 units sold would be expensed (matched against the revenue) while the cost of the 2,000 remaining unsold units would remain in inventory as follows:

Cost of Goods Sold		
From the first quarter	2,000 units at USD40 per unit =	USD80,000
From the second quarter	1,500 units at USD41 per unit =	USD61,500
From the third quarter	2,100 units at USD43 per unit =	USD90,300
Total cost of goods sold		USD231,800

Cost of Goods Remaining in Inventory		
From the third quarter	100 units at USD43 per unit =	USD4,300
From the fourth quarter	1,900 units at USD45 per unit =	USD85,500
Total remaining (or ending) inventory cost		USD89,800

To confirm that total costs are accounted for: USD231,800 + USD89,800 = USD321,600. The cost of the goods sold would be expensed against the revenue of USD280,000 as follows:

Revenue	USD280,000
Cost of Goods Sold	231,800
Gross Profit	48,200

An alternative way to think about this is that the company created an asset (inventory) of USD321,600 as it made its purchases. At the end of the period, the value of the company's inventory on hand is USD89,800. Therefore, the amount of the Cost of goods sold expense recognized for the period should be the difference: USD231,800.

The remaining inventory amount of USD89,800 will be matched against revenue in a future year when the inventory items are sold.

Period costs, expenditures that less directly match revenues, are generally expensed as incurred (i.e., either when the company makes the expenditure in cash or incurs the liability to pay). Costs associated with administrative, managerial, information technology (IT), and research and development activities as well as the maintenance or repair of assets generally fit this model. For most companies, payroll expenses are accounted for this way, excluding employees whose compensation is considered a product cost and recognized as inventory and later cost of goods sold or items like sales commissions, which are capitalized and expensed systematically or with sales.

Capitalization versus Expensing

Finally, certain expenditures are capitalized as assets on the balance sheet and typically appear as an investing cash outflow on the statement of cash flows. After initial recognition, a company expenses the capitalized amount over the asset's useful life as depreciation or amortization expense (except assets that are not depreciated, i.e., land, or amortized, e.g., intangible assets with indefinite lives). This expense reduces net income on the income statement and reduces the value of the asset on the balance sheet. Depreciation and amortization are non-cash expenses and therefore, apart from their effect on taxable income and taxes payable, they have no impact on the cash flow statement.

This model is a form of the matching principle, whereby expenses are recognized on the income statement over the expected useful life of the investment, so the costs and benefits are "matched." Example 3 illustrates the impact on the financial statements of capitalizing versus expensing an expenditure.

EXAMPLE 3

General Financial Statement Impact of Capitalizing versus Expensing

Assume two identical (hypothetical) companies, CAP Inc. (CAP) and NOW Inc. (NOW), start with EUR1,000 cash and EUR1,000 common stock. Each year the companies recognize total revenues of EUR1,500 cash and make cash expenditures, excluding an equipment purchase, of EUR500. At the beginning of operations, each company pays EUR900 to purchase equipment. CAP estimates the equipment will have a useful life of three years and an estimated salvage value of EUR0 at the end of the three years. NOW estimates a much shorter useful life and expenses the equipment immediately. The companies have no other assets and make no other asset purchases during the three-year period. Assume the companies pay no dividends, earn zero interest on cash balances, have a tax rate of 30 percent, and use the same accounting method for financial and tax purposes.

The left side of Exhibit 1 shows CAP's financial statements—that is, with the expenditure capitalized and depreciated at EUR300 per year based on the straight-line method of depreciation (EUR900 cost minus EUR0 salvage value equals EUR900, divided by a three-year life equals EUR300 per year). The right side of the exhibit shows NOW's financial statements, with the entire EUR900 expenditure treated as an expense in the first year. All amounts are in euro.

Exhibit 1: Capitalizing versus Expensing

CAP Inc.				NOW Inc.			
Capitalize EUR900 as Asset and Depreciate				**Expense EUR900 Immediately**			
For Year	**1**	**2**	**3**	**For Year**	**1**	**2**	**3**
Revenue	1,500	1,500	1,500	Revenue	1,500	1,500	1,500
Cash Expenses	500	500	500	Cash expenses	1,400	500	500
Depreciation	300	300	300	Depreciation	0	0	0
Income before Tax	700	700	700	Income before Tax	100	1,000	1,000
Tax at 30%	210	210	210	Tax at 30%	30	300	300
Net Income	490	490	490	Net Income	70	700	700
Cash from Operations	790	790	790	Cash from Operations	70	700	700
Cash Used in Investing	(900)	0	0	Cash Used in Investing	0	0	0
Total Change in Cash	(110)	790	790	Total Change in Cash	70	700	700

As of	Time 0	End of Year 1	End of Year 2	End of Year 3	Time	Time 0	End of Year 1	End of Year 2	End of Year 3
Cash	1,000	890	1,680	2,470	Cash	1,000	1,070	1,770	2,470
PP&E (net)	—	600	300	—	PP & E (net)	—	—	—	—
Total Assets	1,000	1,490	1,980	2,470	Total Assets	1,000	1,070	1,770	2,470
Retained Earnings	0	490	980	1,470	Retained Earnings	0	70	770	1,470
Common Stock	1,000	1,000	1,000	1,000	Common Stock	1,000	1,000	1,000	1,000
Total Shareholders' Equity	1,000	1,490	1,980	2,470	Total Shareholders' Equity	1,000	1,070	1,770	2,470

1. Which company reports higher net income over the three years? Total cash flow? Cash from operations?

   Solution:

   Neither company reports higher total net income or cash flow over the three years. The sum of net income over the three years is identical (EUR1,470 total) whether the EUR900 is capitalized or expensed. Also, the sum of the change in cash (EUR1,470 total) is identical under either scenario. CAP reports higher cash from operations by an amount of EUR900 because, under the capitalization scenario, the EUR900 purchase is treated as an investing cash flow.

   Note: Because the companies use the same accounting method for both financial and taxable income, absent the assumption of zero interest on cash balances, expensing the EUR900 would have resulted in higher income and cash flow for NOW because the lower taxes paid in the first year (EUR30 versus EUR210) would have allowed NOW to earn interest income on the tax savings.

2. Based on ROE and net profit margin, how does the profitability of the two companies compare?

Solution:

In general, Ending shareholders' equity = Beginning shareholders' equity + Net income + Other comprehensive income − Dividends + Net capital contributions from shareholders. Because the companies in this example do not have other comprehensive income, did not pay dividends, and reported no capital contributions from shareholders, Ending retained earnings = Beginning retained earnings + Net income, and Ending shareholders' equity = Beginning shareholders' equity + Net income.

ROE is calculated as Net income divided by Average shareholders' equity, and Net profit margin is calculated as Net income divided by Total revenue. For example, CAP had Year 1 ROE of 39 percent (EUR490/[(EUR1,000 + EUR1,490)/2]), and Year 1 net profit margin of 33 percent (EUR490/EUR1,500).

CAP Inc.				NOW Inc.			
Capitalize EUR900 as Asset and Depreciate				Expense EUR900 Immediately			
For Year	1	2	3	For Year	1	2	3
ROE	39%	28%	22%	ROE	7%	49%	33%
Net Profit Margin	33%	33%	33%	Net Profit Margin	5%	47%	47%

As shown, compared to expensing, capitalizing results in higher profitability ratios (ROE and net profit margin) in the first year, and lower profitability ratios in subsequent years. For example, CAP's Year 1 ROE of 39 percent was higher than NOW's Year 1 ROE of 7 percent, but in Years 2 and 3, NOW reports superior profitability.

Note also that NOW's superior growth in net income between Year 1 and Year 2 is not attributable to superior performance compared to CAP but rather to the accounting decision to recognize the expense sooner than CAP. In general, all else equal, accounting decisions that result in recognizing expenses sooner will give the appearance of greater subsequent growth. Comparison of the growth of the two companies' net incomes without an awareness of the difference in accounting methods would be misleading. As a corollary, NOW's income and profitability exhibit greater volatility across the three years, not because of more volatile performance but rather because of the different accounting decision.

3. Why does NOW report change in cash of EUR70 in Year 1, while CAP reports total change in cash of (EUR110)?

Solution:

NOW reports an increase in cash of EUR70 in Year 1, while CAP reports a decrease in cash of EUR110 because NOW's taxes were EUR180 lower than CAP's taxes (EUR30 versus EUR210).

Note that this problem assumes the accounting method used by each company for its tax purposes is identical to the accounting method used by the company for its financial reporting. In many countries, companies are allowed to use different depreciation methods for financial reporting and taxes, which may give rise to deferred taxes.

As shown, discretion regarding whether to expense or capitalize expenditures can impede comparability across companies. Example 4 assumes the companies purchase a single asset in one year. Because the sum of net income over the three-year period is identical whether the asset is capitalized or expensed, it illustrates that although capitalizing results in higher profitability compared with expensing in the first year, it results in lower profitability in the subsequent years. Conversely, expensing results in lower profitability in the first year but higher profitability in later years, indicating a favorable trend.

Similarly, shareholders' equity for a company that capitalizes the expenditure will be higher in the early years because the initially higher profits result in initially higher retained earnings. Example 4 assumes the companies purchase a single asset in one year and report identical amounts of total net income over the three-year period, so shareholders' equity (and retained earnings) for the firm that expenses will be identical to shareholders' equity (and retained earnings) for the capitalizing firm at the end of the three-year period.

Although Example 3 shows companies purchasing an asset only in the first year, if a company continues to purchase similar or increasing amounts of assets each year, the profitability-enhancing effect of capitalizing continues if the amount of the expenditures in a period continues to be more than the depreciation expense. Example 4 illustrates this point.

EXAMPLE 4

Impact of Capitalizing versus Expensing for Ongoing Purchases

A company buys a GBP300 computer in Year 1 and capitalizes the expenditure. The computer has a useful life of three years and an expected salvage value of GBP0, so the annual depreciation expense using the straight-line method is GBP100 per year. Compared with expensing the entire GBP300 immediately, the company's pre-tax profit in Year 1 is GBP200 greater.

1. Assume that the company continues to buy an identical computer each year at the same price. If the company uses the same accounting treatment for each of the computers, when does the profit-enhancing effect of capitalizing versus expensing end?

   Solution:

   The profit-enhancing effect of capitalizing versus expensing would end in Year 3. In Year 3, the depreciation expense on each of the three computers bought in Years 1, 2, and 3 would total GBP300 (GBP100 + GBP100 + GBP100). Therefore, the total depreciation expense for Year 3 will be exactly equal to the capital expenditure in Year 3. The expense in Year 3 would be GBP300, regardless of whether the company capitalized or expensed the annual computer purchases.

2. If the company buys another identical computer in Year 4, using the same accounting treatment as the prior years, what is the effect on Year 4 profits of capitalizing versus expensing these expenditures?

   Solution:

   There is no impact on Year 4 profits. As in the previous year, the depreciation expense on each of the three computers bought in Years 2, 3, and 4 would total GBP300 (GBP100 + GBP100 + GBP100). Therefore, the total depreciation expense for Year 4 will be exactly equal to the capital expenditure in Year 4. Pre-tax profits would be reduced by GBP300, regardless of whether the company capitalized or expensed the annual computer purchases.

Compared with expensing an expenditure, capitalizing the expenditure typically results in greater amounts reported as cash from operations. Analysts should be alert to evidence of companies manipulating reported cash flow from operations by capitalizing expenditures that should be expensed.

In summary, holding all else constant, capitalizing an expenditure enhances current profitability and increases reported cash flow from operations. The profitability-enhancing effect of capitalizing continues so long as capital expenditures exceed the depreciation expense. Profitability-enhancing motivations for decisions to capitalize should be considered when analyzing performance. For example, a company may choose to capitalize more expenditures (within the allowable bounds of accounting standards) to achieve earnings targets for a given period. Expensing a cost in the period reduces current period profits but enhances future profitability and thus enhances the profit trend. Profit trend-enhancing motivations should also be considered when analyzing performance. If the company is in a reporting environment that requires identical accounting methods for financial reporting and taxes (unlike the United States, which permits companies to use depreciation methods for reporting purposes that differ from the depreciation method required by tax purposes), then expensing will have a more favorable cash flow impact because paying lower taxes in an earlier period creates an opportunity to earn interest income on the cash saved.

In contrast with these relatively simple examples, it is generally neither possible nor desirable to identify individual instances involving discretion about whether to capitalize or expense expenditures. An analyst can, however, typically identify significant items of expenditure treated differently across companies. The items of expenditure giving rise to the most relevant differences across companies will vary by industry. This cross-industry variation is apparent in the following discussion of the capitalization of expenditures.

CAPITALIZATION VERSUS EXPENSING

1. All else equal, in the fiscal year when long-lived equipment is purchased:

   A. depreciation expense increases.

   B. cash from operations decreases.

   C. net income is reduced by the amount of the purchase.

   Solution:

   A is correct. In the fiscal year when long-lived equipment is purchased, the assets on the balance sheet increase and depreciation expense on the income statement increases because of the new long-lived asset.

2. Companies X and Z have the same beginning-of-the-year book value of equity and the same tax rate. The companies have identical transactions throughout the year and report all transactions similarly except for one. Both companies acquire a GBP300,000 printer with a three-year useful life and a salvage value of GBP0 on 1 January of the new year. Company X capitalizes the printer and depreciates it on a straight-line basis, and Company

Z expenses the printer. The year-end information in Exhibit 2 is gathered for Company X.

Exhibit 2: Company X Year-End Information

	Company X as of 31 December
Ending Shareholders' Equity	GBP10,000,000
Tax Rate	25%
Dividends	GBP0.00
Net Income	GBP750,000

Based on the information in Exhibit 2, Company Z's return on equity using year-end equity will be *closest* to:

A. 5.4 percent.

B. 6.1 percent.

C. 7.5 percent.

Solution:

B is correct. Company Z's return on equity based on year-end equity value will be 6.1 percent. Company Z will have an additional GBP200,000 of expenses compared with Company X. Company Z expensed the printer for GBP300,000 rather than capitalizing the printer and having a depreciation expense of GBP100,000 like Company X. Company Z's net income and shareholders' equity will be GBP150,000 lower (= GBP200,000 × 0.75) than that of Company X.

$$\text{ROE} = \left(\frac{\text{Net income}}{\text{Shareholders' Equity}}\right)$$

$$= GBP600{,}00/GBP9{,}850{,}000$$

$$= 0.61 = 6.1\%.$$

The following information relates to questions 3-6.

Melanie Hart, CFA, is a transportation analyst. Hart has been asked to write a research report on Altai Mountain Rail Company (AMRC). Like other companies in the railroad industry, AMRC's operations are capital intensive, with significant investments in such long-lived tangible assets as property, plant, and equipment. In November 2008, AMRC's board of directors hired a new team to manage the company. In reviewing the company's 2009 annual report, Hart is concerned about some of the accounting choices that the new management has made. These choices differ from those of the previous management and from common industry practice. Hart has highlighted the following statements from the company's annual report:

Statement 1 "In 2009, AMRC spent significant amounts on track replacement and similar improvements. AMRC expensed rather than capitalized a significant proportion of these expenditures."

Statement 2 "AMRC uses the straight-line method of depreciation for both financial and tax reporting purposes to account for plant and equipment."

Statement 3 "In 2009, AMRC recognized an impairment loss of EUR50 million on a fleet of locomotives. The impairment loss was reported as 'other income' in the income statement and reduced the carrying amount of the assets on the balance sheet."

Exhibit 3 and 4 contain AMRC's 2009 consolidated income statement and balance sheet. AMRC prepares its financial statements in accordance with International Financial Reporting Standards.

Exhibit 3: Consolidated Statement of Income

	2009		2008	
For the Years Ended 31 December	**Euro Millions**	**Revenues (%)**	**Euro Millions**	**Revenues (%)**
Operating revenues	2,600	100.0	2,300	100.0
Operating expenses				
Depreciation	(200)	(7.7)	(190)	(8.3)
Other operating expense	(1,590)	(61.1)	(1,515)	(65.9)
Total operating expenses	(1,790)	(68.8)	(1,705)	(74.2)
Operating income	810	31.2	595	25.8
Other income	(50)	(1.9)	—	0.0
Interest expense	(73)	(2.8)	(69)	(3.0)
Income before taxes	687	26.5	526	22.8
Income taxes	(272)	(10.5)	(198)	(8.6)
Net income	415	16	328	14.2

Exhibit 4: Consolidated Balance Sheet

As of 31 December	2009		2008	
Assets	**Euro Millions**	**Assets (%)**	**Euro Millions**	
Current assets	500	9.4	450	8.5
Property and equipment:				
Land	700	13.1	700	13.2
Plant and equipment	6,000	112.1	5,800	109.4
Total property and equipment	6,700	125.2	6,500	122.6
Accumulated depreciation	(1,850)	(34.6)	(1,650)	(31.1)
Net property and equipment	4,850	90.6	4,850	91.5
Total assets	5,350	100.0	5,300	100.0
Liabilities and Shareholders' Equity				
Current liabilities	480	9.0	430	8.1
Long-term debt	1,030	19.3	1,080	20.4
Other long-term provisions and liabilities	1,240	23.1	1,440	27.2
Total liabilities	2,750	51.4	2,950	55.7

Liabilities and Shareholders' Equity				
Shareholders' equity				
Common stock and paid-in-surplus	760	14.2	760	14.3
Retained earnings	1,888	35.5	1,600	30.2
Other comprehensive losses	(48)	(0.9)	(10)	(0.2)
Total shareholders' equity	2,600	48.6	2,350	44.3
Total liabilities & shareholders' equity	5,350	100.0	5,300	100.0

3. With respect to Statement 1, which of the following is the *most likely* effect of management's decision to expense rather than capitalize these expenditures?

   A. 2009 net profit margin is higher than if the expenditures had been capitalized.

   B. 2009 total asset turnover is lower than if the expenditures had been capitalized.

   C. Future profit growth will be higher than if the expenditures had been capitalized.

   Solution:

   C is correct. Expensing rather than capitalizing an investment in long-term assets will result in higher expenses and lower net income and net profit margin in the current year. Future years' incomes will not include depreciation expense related to these expenditures. Consequently, year-to-year growth in profitability will be higher. If the expenses had been capitalized, the carrying amount of the assets would have been higher and the 2009 total asset turnover would have been lower.

4. With respect to Statement 2, what would be the *most likely* effect in 2010 if AMRC were to switch to an accelerated depreciation method for both financial and tax reporting?

   A. Net profit margin would increase.

   B. Total asset turnover would decrease.

   C. Cash flow from operating activities would increase.

   Solution:

   C is correct. In 2010, switching to an accelerated depreciation method would increase depreciation expense and decrease income before taxes, taxes payable, and net income. Cash flow from operating activities would increase because of the resulting tax savings.

5. With respect to Statement 3, what is the *most likely* effect of the impairment loss?

   A. Net income in years prior to 2009 was likely understated.

   B. Net profit margins in years after 2009 will likely exceed the 2009 net profit margin.

C. Cash flow from operating activities in 2009 was likely lower due to the impairment loss.

Solution:

B is correct. 2009 net income and net profit margin are lower because of the impairment loss. Consequently, net profit margins in subsequent years are likely to be higher. An impairment loss suggests that insufficient depreciation expense was recognized in prior years, and net income was overstated in prior years. The impairment loss is a non-cash item and will not affect operating cash flows.

6. Based on Exhibit 1 and 2, the *best estimate* of the average remaining useful life of the company's plant and equipment at the end of 2009 is:

A. 20.75 years.

B. 24.25 years.

C. 30.00 years.

Solution:

A is correct. The estimated average remaining useful life is 20.75 years.

Estimate of remaining useful life = Net plant and equipment ÷ Annual depreciation expense

Net plant and equipment = Gross P & E – Accumulated depreciation

= €6000 – €1850 = €4150

Estimate of remaining useful life = Net P & E ÷ Depreciation expense

= €4150 ÷ €200 = 20.75

Capitalization of Interest Costs

Companies generally must capitalize interest costs associated with acquiring or constructing an asset that requires a long period of time to get ready for its intended use

As a consequence of this accounting treatment, a company's interest costs for a period can appear either on the balance sheet (to the extent they are capitalized) or on the income statement (to the extent they are expensed).

If the interest expenditure is incurred in connection with constructing an asset for the company's own use, the capitalized interest appears on the balance sheet as a part of the relevant long-lived asset. The capitalized interest is expensed over time as the property is depreciated—and is thus part of depreciation expense rather than interest expense. If the interest expenditure is incurred in connection with constructing an asset to sell, for example, by a real estate construction company, the capitalized interest appears on the company's balance sheet as part of inventory. The capitalized interest is then expensed as part of the cost of sales when the asset is sold.

The treatment of capitalized interest poses certain issues that analysts should consider. First, capitalized interest appears as part of investing cash outflows, whereas expensed interest typically reduces operating cash flow. US GAAP–reporting companies are required to categorize interest in operating cash flow, and IFRS-reporting companies can categorize expensed interest in operating, or financing cash flows. Although the treatment is consistent with accounting standards, an analyst may want to examine the impact on reported cash flows. Second, interest coverage ratios are solvency indicators measuring the extent to which a company's earnings (or cash flow) in a period covered its interest costs. To provide a true picture of a company's interest coverage, the entire amount of interest expenditure, both the capitalized portion and the expensed portion, should be used to calculate interest coverage ratios. Additionally, if a company is depreciating interest that it capitalized in a previous period, income should be adjusted to eliminate the effect of that depreciation. Example 5 illustrates the calculations.

EXAMPLE 5

Effect of Capitalized Interest Costs on Coverage Ratios and Cash Flow

Melco Resorts & Entertainment Limited (NASDAQ: MLCO), a Hong Kong SAR–based casino company, which is listed on the NASDAQ stock exchange and prepares financial reports under US GAAP, disclosed the following information in one of the footnotes to its 2017 financial statements: "Interest and amortization of deferred financing costs associated with major development and construction projects is capitalized and included in the cost of the project. . . . Total interest expenses incurred amounted to $267,065, $252,600, and $253,168, of which $37,483, $29,033, and $134,838 were capitalized during the years ended December 31, 2017, 2016, and 2015, respectively. Amortization of deferred financing costs of $26,182, $48,345, and $38,511, net of amortization capitalized of nil, nil, and $5,458, were recorded during the years ended December 31, 2017, 2016, and 2015, respectively" (Form 20-F filed 12 April 2018). Cash payments for deferred financing costs were reported in cash flows from financing activities.

Exhibit 5: Melco Resorts and Entertainment Limited Selected Data, as Reported (US dollar thousands)

	2017	2016	2015
EBIT (from income statement)	544,865	298,663	58,553
Interest expense (from income statement)	229,582	223,567	118,330
Capitalized interest (from footnote)	37,483	29,033	134,838
Amortization of deferred financing costs (from footnote)	26,182	48,345	38,511
Net cash provided by operating activities	1,162,500	1,158,128	522,026
Net cash from (used) in investing activities	(410,226)	280,604	(469,656)
Net cash from (used) in financing activities	(1,046,041)	(1,339,717)	(29,688)

Notes: EBIT represents "Income (Loss) Before Income Tax" plus "Interest expenses, net of capitalized interest" from the income statement.

1. Calculate and interpret Melco's interest coverage ratio with and without capitalized interest.

   Solution:

   Interest coverage ratios with and without capitalized interest were as follows:

   For 2017

2.37 (USD544,865 ÷ USD229,582) without adjusting for capitalized interest; and

2.14 [(USD544,865 + USD26,182) ÷ (USD229,582 + USD37,483)], including an adjustment to EBIT for depreciation of previously capitalized interest and an adjustment to interest expense for the amount of interest capitalized in 2017.

For 2016

1.34 (USD298,663÷ USD223,567) without adjusting for capitalized interest; and

1.37 [(USD298,663 + USD48,345) ÷ (USD223,567 + USD29,033)], including an adjustment to EBIT for depreciation of previously capitalized interest and an adjustment to interest expense for the amount of interest capitalized in 2016.

For 2015

0.49 (USD58,533÷ USD118,330) without adjusting for capitalized interest; and

0.38 [(USD58,533 + USD38,511) ÷ (USD118,330+ USD134,838)], including an adjustment to EBIT for depreciation of previously capitalized interest and an adjustment to interest expense for the amount of interest capitalized in 2015.

These calculations indicate that Melco's interest coverage improved in 2017 compared with the previous two years. In both 2017 and 2015, the coverage ratio was lower when adjusted for capitalized interest.

2. Calculate Melco's percentage change in operating cash flow from 2016 to 2017. Assuming the financial reporting does not affect reporting for income taxes, what were the effects of capitalized interest on operating and investing cash flows?

Solution:

If the interest had been expensed rather than capitalized, operating cash flows would have been lower in all three years. On an adjusted basis, but not an unadjusted basis, the company's operating cash flow declined in 2017 compared with 2016. On an unadjusted basis, for 2017 compared with 2016, Melco's operating cash flow increased by 0.4 percent in 2017 [(USD1,162,500 ÷ USD1,158,128) – 1]. Including adjustments to expense all interest costs, Melco's operating cash flow also decreased by 0.4 percent in 2017 {[USD1,162,500 – USD37,483) ÷ (USD1,158,128 – USD29,033)] – 1}. If the interest had been expensed rather than capitalized, financing cash flows would have been higher in all three years.

The treatment of capitalized interest raises issues for consideration by an analyst. First, capitalized interest appears as part of investing cash outflows, whereas expensed interest reduces operating or financing cash flow under IFRS and operating cash flow under US GAAP. An analyst may want to examine the impact on reported cash flows of interest expenditures when comparing companies. Second, interest coverage ratios are solvency indicators measuring the extent to which a company's earnings (or cash flow) in a period covered its interest costs. To provide a true picture of a company's interest coverage, the entire amount of interest, both the capitalized portion and the expensed portion, should be used in calculating interest coverage ratios.

Generally, including capitalized interest in the calculation of interest coverage ratios provides a better assessment of a company's solvency. In assigning credit ratings, rating agencies include capitalized interest in coverage ratios. For example, Standard & Poor's calculates the EBIT interest coverage ratio as EBIT divided by gross interest (defined as interest prior to deductions for capitalized interest or interest income).

Maintaining a minimum interest coverage ratio is a financial covenant often included in lending agreements (e.g., bank loans and bond indentures). The definition of the coverage ratio can be found in the company's credit agreement. The definition is relevant because treatment of capitalized interest in calculating coverage ratios would affect an assessment of how close a company's actual ratios are to the levels specified by its financial covenants and thus the probability of breaching those covenants.

Capitalization of Internal Development Costs

Accounting standards require companies to capitalize software development costs after a product's feasibility is established. Despite this requirement, judgment in determining feasibility means that companies' capitalization practices may differ. For example, as illustrated in Exhibit 6, Microsoft judges product feasibility to be established very shortly before manufacturing begins and, therefore, effectively expenses—rather than capitalizes—research and development costs.

Exhibit 6: Disclosure on Software Development Costs

Excerpt from Management's Discussion and Analysis (MD&A) of Microsoft Corporation, Application of Critical Accounting Policies, Research and Development Costs:

> Costs incurred internally in researching and developing a computer software product are charged to expense until technological feasibility has been established for the product. Once technological feasibility is established, all software costs are capitalized until the product is available for general release to customers. Judgment is required in determining when technological feasibility of a product is established. We have determined that technological feasibility for our software products is reached after all high-risk development issues have been resolved through coding and testing. Generally, this occurs shortly before the products are released to production. The amortization of these costs is included in cost of revenue over the estimated life of the products.

Source: Microsoft Corporation, *2017 Annual Report* on Form 10-K, p. 45.

Expensing rather than capitalizing development costs results in lower net income in the current period. Expensing rather than capitalizing will continue to result in lower net income so long as the amount of the current-period development expenses is higher than the amortization expense that would have resulted from amortizing prior periods' capitalized development costs—the typical situation when a company's development costs are increasing. On the statement of cash flows, expensing rather than capitalizing development costs results in lower net operating cash flows and higher net investing cash flows. This is because the development costs are reflected as operating cash outflows rather than investing cash outflows.

In comparing the financial performance of a company that expenses most or all software development costs, such as Microsoft, with another company that capitalizes software development costs, adjustments can be made to make the two comparable. For the company that capitalizes software development costs, an analyst can adjust (1) the income statement to include software development costs as an expense and to exclude amortization of prior years' software development costs; (2) the balance sheet to exclude capitalized software (decrease assets and equity); and (3) the statement of cash flows to decrease operating cash flows and decrease cash used in investing by the amount of the current period development costs. Any ratios that include income, long-lived assets, or cash flow from operations—such as return on equity—also will be affected.

EXAMPLE 6

Software Development Costs

You are working on a project involving the analysis of JHH Software, a (hypothetical) software development company that established technical feasibility for its first product in 2017. Part of your analysis involves computing certain market-based ratios, which you will use to compare JHH to another company that expenses all of its software development expenditures. Relevant data and excerpts from the company's annual report are included in Exhibit 7.

Exhibit 7: JHH SOFTWARE (US dollar thousands, except per share amounts)

Consolidated Statement of Earnings—Abbreviated

For Year Ended 31 December:	2018	2017	2016
Total revenue	USD91,424	USD91,134	USD96,293
Total operating expenses	78,107	78,908	85,624
Operating income	13,317	12,226	10,669
Provision for income taxes	3,825	4,232	3,172
Net income	USD9,492	USD7,994	USD7,479
Earnings per share (EPS)	USD1.40	USD0.82	USD0.68

Statement of Cash Flows—Abbreviated

For Year Ended 31 December:	2018	2017	2016
Net cash provided by operating activities	USD15,007	USD14,874	USD15,266
Net cash used in investing activities*	(11,549)	(4,423)	(5,346)
Net cash used in financing activities	(8,003)	(7,936)	(7,157)
Net change in cash and cash equivalents	(USD4,545)	USD2,515	USD2,763
**Includes software development expenses of and*	*(USD6,000)*	*(USD4,000)*	*(USD2,000)*
includes capital expenditures of	*(USD2,000)*	*(USD1,600)*	*(USD1,200)*

Additional Information:

For Year Ended 31 December:	2018	2017	2016
Market value of outstanding debt	0	0	0
Amortization of capitalized software development expenses	(USD2,000)	(USD667)	0

Additional Information:

For Year Ended 31 December:	**2018**	**2017**	**2016**
Depreciation expense	(USD2,200)	(USD1,440)	(USD1,320)
Market price per share of common stock	USD42	USD26	USD17
Shares of common stock outstanding (thousands)	6,780	9,765	10,999

Footnote disclosure of accounting policy for software development:
Expenses that are related to the conceptual formulation and design of software products are expensed to research and development as incurred. The company capitalises expenses that are incurred to produce the finished product after technological feasibility has been established.

1. Compute the following ratios for JHH based on the reported financial statements for fiscal year ended 31 December 2018, with no adjustments. Next, determine the approximate impact on these ratios if the company had expensed rather than capitalized its investments in software. (Assume the financial reporting does not affect reporting for income taxes. There would be no change in the effective tax rate.)

   A. P/E: Price/Earnings per share

   B. P/CFO: Price/Operating cash flow per share

   C. EV/EBITDA: Enterprise value/EBITDA, where enterprise value is defined as the total market value of all sources of a company's financing, including equity and debt, and EBITDA is earnings before interest, taxes, depreciation, and amortization.

   Solution:

   (US dollars are in thousands, except per share amounts.) JHH's 2019 ratios are presented in the following table:

	Ratios	As reported	As adjusted
A	P/E ratio	30.0	42.9
B	P/CFO	19.0	31.6
C	EV/EBITDA	16.3	24.7

A. Based on the information as reported, the P/E ratio was 30.0 (USD42 ÷ USD1.40). Based on EPS adjusted to expense software development costs, the P/E ratio was 42.9 (USD42 ÷ USD0.98).

Price: Assuming that the market value of the company's equity is based on its fundamentals, the price per share is USD42, regardless of a difference in accounting.

EPS: As reported, EPS was USD1.40. Adjusted EPS was USD0.98. Expensing software development costs would have reduced JHH's 2018 operating income by USD6,000, but the company would have reported no amortization of prior years' software costs, which would have increased operating income by USD2,000. The net change of USD4,000 would have reduced operating income from the reported USD13,317 to USD9,317. The effective tax rate for 2018 (USD3,825 ÷ USD13,317) is 28.72%, and using this effective tax rate would give an adjusted net income of USD6,641 [USD9,317 × (1 – 0.2872)], compared to USD9,492 before the adjustment. The EPS would therefore be reduced from the reported USD1.40 to USD0.98 (adjusted net income of USD6,641 divided by 6,780 shares).

B. Based on information as reported, the P/CFO was 19.0 (USD42 ÷ USD2.21). Based on CFO adjusted to expense software development costs, the P/CFO was 31.6 (USD42 ÷ USD1.33).

Price: Assuming that the market value of the company's equity is based on its fundamentals, the price per share is USD42, regardless of a difference in accounting.

CFO per share, as reported, was USD2.21 (total operating cash flows USD15,007 ÷ 6,780 shares).

CFO per share, as adjusted, was USD1.33. The company's USD6,000 expenditure on software development costs was reported as a cash outflow from investing activities, so expensing those costs would reduce cash from operating activities by USD6,000, from the reported USD15,007 to USD9,007. Dividing adjusted total operating cash flow of USD9,007 by 6,780 shares results in cash flow per share of USD1.33.

C. Based on information as reported, the EV/EBITDA was 16.3 (USD284,760 ÷ USD17,517). Based on EBITDA adjusted to expense software development costs, the EV/EBITDA was 24.7 (USD284,760 ÷ USD11,517).

Enterprise Value: Enterprise value is the sum of the market value of the company's equity and debt. JHH has no debt, and therefore the enterprise value is equal to the market value of its equity. The market value of its equity is USD284,760 (USD42 per share × 6,780 shares).

EBITDA, as reported, was USD17,517 (earnings before interest and taxes of USD13,317 plus USD2,200 depreciation plus USD2,000 amortization).

EBITDA, adjusted for expensing software development costs by the inclusion of USD6,000 development expense and the exclusion of USD2,000 amortization of prior expense, would be USD11,517 (earnings before interest and taxes of USD9,317 plus USD2,200 depreciation plus USD0 amortization).

2. Interpret the changes in the ratios.

Solution:

Expensing software development costs would decrease historical profits, operating cash flow, and EBITDA, and would thus increase all market multiples. So JHH's stock would appear to be more expensive if it expensed rather than capitalized the software development costs.

If the unadjusted market-based ratios were used in the comparison of JHH to its competitor that expenses all software development expenditures, then JHH might appear to be under-priced when the difference is solely related to accounting factors. JHH's adjusted market-based ratios provide a better basis for comparison.

For the company in Example 6, current period software development expenditures exceed the amortization of prior periods' capitalized software development expenditures. As a result, expensing rather than capitalizing software development costs would have the effect of lowering income. If, however, software development expenditures slowed such that current expenditures were lower than the amortization of prior periods' capitalized software development expenditures, then expensing software development costs would have the effect of increasing income relative to capitalizing it.

This section illustrated how decisions about capitalizing versus expensing affect financial statements and ratios. Earlier expensing lowers current profits but enhances trends, whereas capitalizing now and expensing later enhances current profits. Having described the accounting for acquisition of long-lived assets, we now turn to the topic of measuring long-lived assets in subsequent periods.

Implications for Financial Analysts: Expense Recognition

As with revenue recognition policies, a company's choice of expense recognition can be characterized by its relative conservatism. A policy that results in recognition of expenses later rather than sooner is considered less conservative. In addition, many items of expense require the company to make estimates that can significantly affect net income. Analysis of a company's financial statements, and particularly comparison of one company's financial statements with those of another, requires an understanding of differences in these estimates and their potential impact.

If, for example, a company shows a significant year-to-year change in its estimates of uncollectible accounts as a percentage of sales, warranty expenses as a percentage of sales, or estimated useful lives of assets, the analyst should seek to understand the underlying reasons. Do the changes reflect a change in business operations (e.g., lower estimated warranty expenses reflecting recent experience of fewer warranty claims because of improved product quality)? Or are the changes seemingly unrelated to changes in business operations and thus possibly a signal that a company is manipulating estimates to achieve a particular effect on its reported net income?

As another example, if two companies in the same industry have dramatically different estimates for uncollectible accounts as a percentage of their sales, warranty expenses as a percentage of sales, or estimated useful lives as a percentage of assets, it is important to understand the underlying reasons. Are the differences consistent with differences in the two companies' business operations (e.g., lower uncollectible accounts for one company reflecting a different, more creditworthy customer base or possibly stricter credit policies)? Another difference consistent with differences in business operations would be a difference in estimated useful lives of assets if one of the companies employs newer equipment. Or, alternatively, are the differences seemingly inconsistent with differences in the two companies' business operations, possibly signaling that a company is manipulating estimates?

Information about a company's accounting policies and significant estimates are described in the notes to the financial statements and in the management discussion and analysis section of a company's annual report.

When possible, the monetary effect of differences in expense recognition policies and estimates can facilitate more meaningful comparisons with a single company's historical performance or across a number of companies. An analyst can use the monetary effect to adjust the reported expenses so that they are on a comparable basis.

Even when the monetary effects of differences in policies and estimates cannot be calculated, it is generally possible to characterize the relative conservatism of the policies and estimates and, therefore, to qualitatively assess how such differences might affect reported expenses and thus financial ratios.

NON-RECURRING ITEMS

4

☐ describe the financial reporting treatment and analysis of non-recurring items (including discontinued operations, unusual or infrequent items) and changes in accounting policies

From a company's income statements, we can see its earnings from the year just ended and the previous year. Looking forward, the question is: What will the company earn next year and in the years thereafter?

To assess a company's future earnings, it is helpful to separate those prior years' items of income and expense that are likely to continue in the future from those items that are less likely to continue. Some items from prior years are clearly not expected to continue in the future periods and are separately disclosed on a company's income statement. IFRS describe considerations that enter into the decision to present information other than that explicitly specified by a standard. Both IFRS and US GAAP specify that the results of discontinued operations should be reported separately from continuing operations. Other items that may be reported separately on a company's income statement, such as unusual items, items that occur infrequently, effects due to accounting changes, and non-operating income, require the analyst to make some judgments.

Unusual or Infrequent Items

IFRS require that items of income or expense that are material or relevant to the understanding of the entity's financial performance should be disclosed separately. Unusual or infrequent items are likely to meet these criteria. Under US GAAP, material items that are unusual or infrequent, and that are both as of reporting periods beginning after December 15, 2015, are shown as part of a company's continuing operations but are presented separately. For example, restructuring charges, such as costs to close plants and employee termination costs, are considered part of a company's ordinary activities. As another example, gains and losses arising when a company sells an asset or part of a business, for more or less than its carrying value, are also disclosed separately on the income statement. These sales are considered ordinary business activities.

Highlighting the unusual or infrequent nature of these items assists an analyst in judging the likelihood that such items will reoccur. This meets the IFRS criteria of disclosing items that are relevant to the understanding of an entity's financial performance. In Exhibit 8, the income statement of Danone shows an amount for "Recurring operating income" followed by a separate line item for "other operating income (expense)," which is not included as a component of recurring income. Exhibit 9 presents an excerpt from Danone's additional disclosure about this non-recurring amount.

Exhibit 8: Danone Income Statement

Groupe Danone Consolidated Income Statement (in Millions of Euros) [Excerpt]

	Year Ended 31 December	
	2016	**2017**
Sales	21,944	24,677
Cost of goods sold	(10,744)	(12,459)

Groupe Danone Consolidated Income Statement (in Millions of Euros) [Excerpt]

	Year Ended 31 December	
	2016	**2017**
Selling expense	(5,562)	(5,890)
General and administrative expense	(2,004)	(2,225)
Research and development expense	(333)	(342)
Other income (expense)	(278)	(219)
Recurring operating income	**3,022**	**3,543**
Other operating income (expense)	(99)	192
Operating income	**2,923**	**3,734**
Interest income on cash equivalents and short-term investments	130	151
Interest expense	(276)	(414)
Cost of net debt	(146)	(263)
Other financial income	67	137
Other financial expense	(214)	(312)
Income before tax	**2,630**	**3,296**
Income tax expense	(804)	(842)
Net income from fully consolidated companies	**1,826**	**2,454**
Share of profit of associates	1	109
Net income	1,827	2,563
Net income – Group share	**1,720**	**2,453**
Net income – Non-controlling interests	107	110

Exhibit 9: Highlighting Infrequent Nature of Items—Excerpt from Groupe Danone footnotes to its 2017 financial statements

NOTE 6. Events and Transactions Outside the Group's Ordinary Activities [Excerpt]

Other operating income (expense) is defined under Recommendation 2013-03 of the French CNC relating to the format of consolidated financial statements prepared under international accounting standards, and comprises significant items that, because of their exceptional nature, cannot be viewed as inherent to Danone's current activities. These mainly include capital gains and losses on disposals of fully consolidated companies, impairment charges on goodwill, significant costs related to strategic restructuring and major external growth transactions, and incurred or estimated costs related to major crises and major litigation. Furthermore, in connection with Revised IFRS 3 and Revised IAS 27, Danone also classifies in Other operating income (expense) (i) acquisition costs related to business combinations, (ii) revaluation profit or loss accounted for following a loss of control, and (iii) changes in earn-outs related to business combinations and subsequent to the acquisition date.

In 2017, the net Other operating income of €192 million consisted mainly of the following items:

(Euro Millions)	Related Income (Expense)
Capital gain on disposal of Stonyfield	628
Compensation received following the decision of the Singapore arbitration court in the Fonterra case	105
Territorial risks, mainly in certain countries in the ALMA region	(148)
Costs associated with the integration of WhiteWave	(118)
Impairment of several intangible assets in Waters and Specialized Nutrition Reporting entities	(115)

Remainder of table omitted

In Exhibit 9, Danone provides details on items considered to be "exceptional" items and not "inherent" to the company's current activities. The exceptional items include gains on asset disposals, receipts from a legal case, costs of integrating an acquisition, and impairment of intangible assets, among others. Generally, in forecasting future operations, an analyst would assess whether the items reported are likely to reoccur and also possible implications for future earnings. It is generally not advisable simply to ignore all unusual items.

Discontinued Operations

When a company disposes of or establishes a plan to dispose of one of its component operations and will have no further involvement in the operation, the income statement reports separately the effect of this disposal as a "discontinued" operation under both IFRS and US GAAP. Financial standards provide various criteria for reporting the effect separately, which are generally that the discontinued component must be separable both physically and operationally.

Results of discontinued operations are presented on a net basis at the bottom of the income statement, including on a per share basis. The remaining parts of income statement (e.g., revenue, costs of goods sold, EPS from the remaining businesses) are the results of continuing operations and are disclosed as such. Assets and liabilities related to the discontinued operations are aggregated and recognized on the balance sheet as held for sale. This presentation allows an analyst to clearly evaluate continuing versus discontinued operations.

Because the discontinued operation will no longer provide earnings (or cash flow) to the company once the sale or disposal is complete, an analyst may eliminate discontinued operations in formulating expectations about a company's future financial performance after a certain date.

Changes in Accounting Policy

At times, standard setters issue new standards that require companies to change accounting policies. Depending on the standard, companies may be permitted to adopt the standards prospectively (in the future) or retrospectively (restate financial statements as though the standard existed in the past). In other cases, changes in accounting policies (e.g., from one acceptable inventory costing method to another) are made by management for various reasons, such as providing a better reflection of the company's performance. Changes in accounting policies are reported through retrospective application[1] unless it is impractical to do so.

Retrospective application means that the financial statements for all fiscal years shown in a company's financial report are presented as if the newly adopted accounting principle had been used throughout the entire period. Notes to the financial statements describe the change and explain the justification for the change. Because changes in accounting principles are retrospectively applied, the financial statements that appear within a financial report are comparable.

Example 7 presents an excerpt from Microsoft Corporation's Form 10-K for the fiscal year ended 30 June 2018 describing a change in accounting principle resulting from the new revenue recognition standard. Microsoft elected to adopt the new standard 1 July 2017, earlier than the required adoption date. Microsoft also elected to use the "full retrospective method," which requires companies to restate prior periods' results. On its income statement, both 2016 and 2017 are presented as if the new standard had been used throughout both years. In the footnotes to its financial statements, Microsoft discloses the impact of the new standard.

EXAMPLE 7

Microsoft Corporation—Excerpt from Footnotes to the Financial Statements

The most significant impact of the [new revenue recognition] standard relates to our accounting for software license revenue. Specifically, for Windows 10, we recognize revenue predominantly at the time of billing and delivery rather than ratably over the life of the related device. For certain multi-year commercial software subscriptions that include both distinct software licenses and SA, we recognize license revenue at the time of contract execution rather than over the subscription period. Due to the complexity of certain of our commercial license subscription contracts, the actual revenue recognition treatment required under the standard depends on contract-specific terms and in some instances may vary from recognition at the time of billing. Revenue recognition related to our hardware, cloud offerings (such as Office 365), LinkedIn, and professional services remains substantially unchanged. Refer to Impacts to Previously Reported Results below for the impact of adoption of the standard in our consolidated financial statements.

Exhibit 10: Microsoft Impacts to Previously Reported Results

(US dollar millions, except per share amounts)	As Previously Reported	New Revenue Standard Adjustment	As Restated
Income Statements			
Year Ended 30 June 2017			
Revenue	89,950	6,621	96,571
Provision for income taxes	1,945	2,467	4,412
Net income	21,204	4,285	25,489
Diluted earnings per share	2.71	0.54	3.25

1 IAS No. 8, Accounting Policies, Changes in Accounting Estimates and Errors, and FASB ASC Topic 250 [Accounting Changes and Error Corrections].

(US dollar millions, except per share amounts)	As Previously Reported	New Revenue Standard Adjustment	As Restated
Year Ended 30 June 2016			
Revenue	85,320	5,834	91,154
Provision for income taxes	2,953	2,147	5,100
Net income	16,798	3,741	20,539
Diluted earnings per share	2.1	0.46	2.56

1. Based on Exhibit 10, describe whether Microsoft's results appear better or worse under the new revenue recognition standard.

Solution:

Microsoft's results appear better under the new revenue recognition standard. Revenues and income are higher under the new standard. The net profit margin is higher under the new standard. For 2017, the net profit margin is 26.4 percent (= 25,489/96,571) under the new standard versus 23.6 percent (= 21,204/89,950) under the old standard. Reported revenue grew faster under the new standard. Revenue growth under the new standard was 5.9 percent [= (96,571/91,154) – 1] compared with 5.4 percent [= (89,950/85,320) – 1)] under the old standard.

Microsoft's presentation of the effects of the new revenue recognition enables an analyst to identify the impact of the change in accounting standards.

Note that the new revenue recognition standard also offered companies the option of using a "modified retrospective" method of adoption. Under the modified retrospective approach, companies were not required to revise previously reported financial statements. Instead, they adjusted opening balances of retained earnings (and other applicable accounts) for the cumulative impact of the new standard.

In contrast to changes in accounting policies (such as whether to expense the cost of employee stock options), companies sometimes make *changes in accounting estimates* (such as the useful life of a depreciable asset). Changes in accounting estimates are handled prospectively, with the change affecting the financial statements for the period of change and future periods. No adjustments are made to prior statements, and the adjustment is not shown on the face of the income statement. Significant changes should be disclosed in the notes. Exhibit 11 provides an excerpt from the annual Form 10-K of Catalent Inc., a US-based biotechnology company, that illustrates a change in accounting estimate.

Exhibit 11: Change in Accounting Estimate—Excerpt from Catalent Form 10-K

Catalent Inc. discloses a change in the method it uses to calculate both annual expenses related to its defined benefit pension plans. Rather than use a single, weighted-average discount rate in its calculations, the company will use the spot rates applicable to each projected cash flow.

Post-Retirement and Pension Plans

The measurement of the related benefit obligations and the net periodic benefit costs recorded each year are based upon actuarial computations, which require management's judgment as to certain assumptions. These assumptions include the discount rates used in computing the present value of the benefit obligations and the net periodic benefit costs...

Effective June 30, 2016, the approach used to estimate the service and interest components of net periodic benefit cost for benefit plans was changed to provide a more precise measurement of service and interest costs. Historically, the Company estimated these service and interest components utilizing a single weighted-average discount rate derived from the yield curve used to measure the benefit obligation at the beginning of the period. Going forward, the Company has elected to utilize an approach that discounts the individual expected cash flows using the applicable spot rates derived from the yield curve over the projected cash flow period. The Company has accounted for this change as a change in accounting estimate that is inseparable from a change in accounting principle and accordingly has accounted for it prospectively.

Another possible adjustment is a *correction of an error for a prior period* (e.g., in financial statements issued for an earlier year). This cannot be handled by simply adjusting the current period income statement. Correction of an error for a prior period is handled by restating the financial statements (including the balance sheet, statement of owners' equity, and cash flow statement) for the prior periods presented in the current financial statements. Note that disclosures are required regarding the error. These disclosures should be examined carefully because they may reveal weaknesses in the company's accounting systems and financial controls.

Changes in Scope and Exchange Rates

When an issuer acquires a controlling interest in another company, it consolidates its financial statements as of the closing date. Depending on the size of the target relative to the acquirer, an acquisition can materially affect the comparability of the acquirer's financial results and position from prior periods. Additionally, changes in exchange rates often affect multinational companies' income statements (e.g., a strengthening functional currency against the reporting currency increases reported revenues, while a declining functional currency against the reporting currency decreases reported revenues). Unfortunately, accounting standards do *not* require issuers to disclose the effects of either scope or exchange rate changes on the financial statements or in individual items, although most issuers disclose useful summary information (such as revenue and EPS growth rates excluding scope and exchange rate changes) in management reporting or elsewhere.

The financial statement implications of changes in scope and exchange rates will be discussed in detail later in the curriculum.

EARNINGS PER SHARE

5

☐ describe how earnings per share is calculated and calculate and interpret a company's basic and diluted earnings per share for companies with simple and complex capital structures including those with antidilutive securities

One income statement metric of particular importance to equity investors is earnings per share (EPS). IFRS require the presentation of EPS on the face of the income statement for net profit or loss (net income) and profit or loss (income) from continuing operations and similar presentation is required under US GAAP. This lesson outlines the calculations for EPS and explains how the calculation differs for a simple versus complex capital structure.

Simple versus Complex Capital Structure

A company's capital is composed of its equity and debt. Some types of equity have preference over others, and some debt (and other instruments) may be converted into equity. Under IFRS, the type of equity for which EPS is presented is referred to as ordinary. **Ordinary shares** are those equity shares that are subordinate to all other types of equity. The ordinary shareholders are basically the owners of the company—the equity holders who are paid last in a liquidation of the company and who benefit the most when the company does well. Under US GAAP, this ordinary equity is referred to as **common stock** or **common shares**, reflecting US language usage. The terms "ordinary shares," "common stock," and "common shares" are used interchangeably in the following discussion.

When a company has issued any financial instruments that are potentially convertible into common stock, it is said to have a complex capital structure. Examples of financial instruments that are potentially convertible into common stock include convertible bonds, convertible preferred stock, employee stock options, and warrants (a warrant is essentially an equity call option issued by the company; a warrant holder has the right but not the obligation to purchase newly issued shares at the exercise price). If a company's capital structure does not include such potentially convertible financial instruments, it is said to have a simple capital structure.

The distinction between simple versus complex capital structure is relevant to the calculation of EPS because financial instruments that are potentially convertible into common stock could, as a result of conversion or exercise, potentially dilute (i.e., decrease) EPS. Information about such a potential dilution is valuable to a company's current and potential shareholders; therefore, accounting standards require companies to disclose what their EPS would be if all dilutive financial instruments were converted into common stock. The EPS that would result if all dilutive financial instruments were converted is called **diluted EPS**. In contrast, **basic EPS** is calculated using the reported earnings available to common shareholders of the parent company and the weighted average number of shares outstanding.

Companies are required to report both basic and diluted EPS as well as amounts for continuing operations. Exhibit 12 shows the per share amounts reported by AB InBev at the bottom of its income statement. The company's basic EPS ("before dilution") was USD4.06, and diluted EPS ("after dilution") was USD3.98 for 2017. In addition, in the same way that AB InBev's income statement shows income from continuing operations separately from total income, EPS from continuing operations is also shown separately from total EPS. For 2017, the basic and diluted EPS from continuing operations were USD4.04 and USD3.96, respectively. Across all measures, AB InBev's

EPS was much higher in 2017 than in 2016. An analyst would seek to understand the causes underlying the changes in EPS, a topic we will address following an explanation of the calculations of both basic and diluted EPS.

Exhibit 12: AB InBev's Earnings per Share (USD)

	12 Months Ended 31 December		
	2017	2016	2015
Basic earnings per share	4.06	0.72	5.05
Diluted earnings per share	3.98	0.71	4.96
Basic earnings per share from continuing operations	4.04	0.69	5.05
Diluted earnings per share from continuing operations	3.96	0.68	4.96

Basic EPS

Basic EPS is the amount of income available to common shareholders divided by the weighted average number of common shares outstanding over a period. The amount of income available to common shareholders is the amount of net income remaining after preferred dividends (if any) have been paid. Thus, the formula to calculate basic EPS is as follows:

$$\text{Basic EPS} = \frac{\text{Net income} - \text{Preferred dividends}}{\text{Weighted average number of shares outstanding}}.$$

The weighted average number of shares outstanding is a time weighting of common shares outstanding. For example, assume a company began the year with 2,000,000 common shares outstanding and repurchased 100,000 common shares on 1 July. The weighted average number of common shares outstanding would be the sum of 2,000,000 shares × 1/2 year + 1,900,000 shares × 1/2 year, or 1,950,000 shares. So, the company would use 1,950,000 shares as the weighted average number of shares in calculating its basic EPS.

If the number of shares of common stock increases as a result of a stock dividend or a stock split, the EPS calculation reflects the change retroactively to the beginning of the period.

Example 8, 9, and 10 illustrate the computation of basic EPS.

EXAMPLE 8

A Basic EPS Calculation (1)

1. For the year ended 31 December 2018, Shopalot Company had net income of USD1,950,000. The company had 1,500,000 shares of common stock outstanding, no preferred stock, and no convertible financial instruments. What is Shopalot's basic EPS?

   Solution:

   Shopalot's basic EPS is USD1.30 (USD1,950,000 divided by 1,500,000 shares).

EXAMPLE 9

A Basic EPS Calculation (2)

For the year ended 31 December 2018, Angler Products had net income of USD2,500,000. The company declared and paid USD200,000 of dividends on preferred stock. The company also had the common stock share information shown in Exhibit 13:

Exhibit 13: Angler's Common Stock Shares

Shares outstanding on 1 January 2018	1,000,000
Shares issued on 1 April 2018	200,000
Shares repurchased (treasury shares) on 1 October 2018	(100,000)
Shares outstanding on 31 December 2018	1,100,000

1. What is the company's weighted average number of shares outstanding?

   Solution:

   The weighted average number of shares outstanding is determined by the length of time each quantity of shares was outstanding:

1,000,000 × (3 months/12 months) =	250,000
1,200,000 × (6 months/12 months) =	600,000
1,100,000 × (3 months/12 months) =	275,000
Weighted average number of shares outstanding	1,125,000

2. What is the company's basic EPS?

   Solution:

   Basic EPS = (Net income – Preferred dividends)/Weighted average number of shares = (USD2,500,000 – USD200,000)/1,125,000 = USD2.04

EXAMPLE 10

A Basic EPS Calculation (3)

1. Assume the same facts as Example 9 except that on 1 December 2018, a previously declared 2-for-1 stock split took effect. Each shareholder of record receives two shares in exchange for each current share that he or she owns. What is the company's basic EPS?

   Solution:

   For EPS calculation purposes, a stock split is treated as if it occurred at the beginning of the period. The weighted average number of shares would, therefore, be 2,250,000, and the basic EPS would be USD1.02 [= (USD2,500,000 – USD200,000)/2,250,000].

Diluted EPS: The If-Converted Method

If a company has a simple capital structure (in other words, one that includes no potentially dilutive financial instruments), then its basic EPS is equal to its diluted EPS. If, however, a company has potentially dilutive financial instruments, its diluted EPS may differ from its basic EPS. Diluted EPS, by definition, is always equal to or less than basic EPS. The following sections describe the effects of three types of potentially dilutive financial instruments on diluted EPS: convertible preferred, convertible debt, and employee stock options. The final section explains why not all potentially dilutive financial instruments actually result in a difference between basic and diluted EPS.

Diluted EPS When a Company Has Convertible Preferred Stock Outstanding

When a company has convertible preferred stock outstanding, diluted EPS is calculated using the **if-converted method**. The if-converted method is based on what EPS would have been if the convertible preferred securities had been converted at the beginning of the period. In other words, the method calculates what the effect would have been if the convertible preferred shares converted at the beginning of the period. If the convertible shares had been converted, there would be two effects. First, the convertible preferred securities would no longer be outstanding; instead, additional common stock would be outstanding. Thus, under the if-converted method, the weighted average number of shares outstanding would be higher than in the basic EPS calculation. Second, if such a conversion had taken place, the company would not have paid preferred dividends. Thus, under the if-converted method, the net income available to common shareholders would be higher than in the basic EPS calculation.

Diluted EPS using the if-converted method for convertible preferred stock is equal to net income divided by the weighted average number of shares outstanding from the basic EPS calculation plus the additional shares of common stock that would be issued upon conversion of the preferred. Thus, the formula to calculate diluted EPS using the if-converted method for preferred stock is as follows:

$$\text{Diluted EPS} = \frac{(\text{Net income})}{(\text{Weighted average number of shares outstanding} + \text{New common shares that would have been issued at conversion})}.$$

A diluted EPS calculation using the if-converted method for preferred stock is provided in Example 11.

EXAMPLE 11

A Diluted EPS Calculation Using the If-Converted Method for Preferred Stock

1. For the year ended 31 December 2018, Bright-Warm Utility Company (fictitious) had net income of USD1,750,000. The company had an average of 500,000 shares of common stock outstanding, 20,000 shares of convertible preferred, and no other potentially dilutive securities. Each share of preferred pays a dividend of USD10 per share, and each is convertible into five

shares of the company's common stock. Calculate the company's basic and diluted EPS.

Solution:

If the 20,000 shares of convertible preferred had each converted into five shares of the company's common stock, the company would have had an additional 100,000 shares of common stock (five shares of common for each of the 20,000 shares of preferred). If the conversion had taken place, the company would not have paid preferred dividends of USD200,000 (USD10 per share for each of the 20,000 shares of preferred). As shown in Exhibit 14, the company's basic EPS was USD3.10 and its diluted EPS was USD2.92.

Exhibit 14: Calculation of Diluted EPS for Bright-Warm Utility Company Using the If-Converted Method: Case of Preferred Stock

	Basic EPS	Diluted EPS Using If-Converted Method
Net income	USD1,750,000	USD1,750,000
Preferred dividend	–200,000	0
Numerator	USD1,550,000	USD1,750,000
Weighted average number of shares outstanding	500,000	500,000
Additional shares issued if preferred converted	0	100,000
Denominator	500,000	600,000
EPS	**USD3.10**	**USD2.92**

Diluted EPS When a Company Has Convertible Debt Outstanding

When a company has convertible debt outstanding, the diluted EPS calculation also uses the if-converted method. Diluted EPS is calculated as if the convertible debt had been converted at the beginning of the period. If the convertible debt had been converted, the debt securities would no longer be outstanding; instead, additional shares of common stock would be outstanding. Also, if such a conversion had taken place, the company would not have paid interest on the convertible debt, so the net income available to common shareholders would increase by the after-tax amount of interest expense on the debt converted.

Thus, the formula to calculate diluted EPS using the if-converted method for convertible debt is as follows:

$$\text{Diluted EPS} = \frac{(\text{Net income} + \text{After-tax interest on convertible debt} - \text{Preferred dividends})}{\begin{array}{c}(\text{Weighted average number of shares outstanding} + \text{Additional} \\ \text{common shares that would have been issued at conversion})\end{array}}.$$

A diluted EPS calculation using the if-converted method for convertible debt is provided in Example 12.

EXAMPLE 12

A Diluted EPS Calculation Using the If-Converted Method for Convertible Debt

1. Oppnox Company (fictitious) reported net income of USD750,000 for the year ended 31 December 2018. The company had a weighted average of 690,000 shares of common stock outstanding. In addition, the company has only one potentially dilutive security: USD50,000 of 6 percent convertible bonds, convertible into a total of 10,000 shares. Assuming a tax rate of 30 percent, calculate Oppnox's basic and diluted EPS.

Solution:

If the debt securities had been converted, the debt securities would no longer be outstanding and instead, an additional 10,000 shares of common stock would be outstanding. Also, if the debt securities had been converted, the company would not have paid interest of USD3,000 on the debt, so net income available to common shareholders would have increased by USD2,100 [= USD3,000(1 – 0.30)] on an after-tax basis. Exhibit 15 illustrates the calculation of diluted EPS using the if-converted method for convertible debt.

Exhibit 15: Calculation of Diluted EPS for Oppnox Company Using the If-Converted Method: Case of a Convertible Bond

	Basic EPS	Diluted EPS Using If-Converted Method
Net income	USD750,000	USD750,000
After-tax cost of interest		2,100
Numerator	USD750,000	USD752,100
Weighted average number of shares outstanding	690,000	690,000
If converted	0	10,000
Denominator	690,000	700,000
EPS	**USD1.09**	**USD1.07**

Diluted EPS: The Treasury Stock Method

When a company has stock options, warrants, or their equivalents outstanding, diluted EPS is calculated as if the financial instruments had been exercised and the company had used the proceeds from exercise to repurchase as many shares of common stock as possible at the average market price of common stock during the period. The weighted average number of shares outstanding for diluted EPS is thus increased by the number of shares that would be issued upon exercise minus the number of shares that would have been purchased with the proceeds. This method is called the treasury stock method under US GAAP because companies typically hold repurchased shares as treasury stock. The same method is used under IFRS but is not named.

For the calculation of diluted EPS using this method, the assumed exercise of these financial instruments would have the following effects:

- The company is assumed to receive cash upon exercise and, in exchange, to issue shares.
- The company is assumed to use the cash proceeds to repurchase shares at the weighted average market price during the period.

As a result of these two effects, the number of shares outstanding would increase by the incremental number of shares issued (the difference between the number of shares issued to the holders and the number of shares assumed to be repurchased by the company). For calculating diluted EPS, the incremental number of shares is weighted based upon the length of time the financial instrument was outstanding in the year. If the financial instrument was issued before the beginning of the year, the weighted average number of shares outstanding increases by the incremental number of shares. If the financial instruments were issued during the year, then the incremental shares are weighted by the amount of time the financial instruments were outstanding during the year.

The assumed exercise of these financial instruments would not affect net income. For calculating EPS, therefore, no change is made to the numerator. The formula to calculate diluted EPS using the treasury stock method (same method as used under IFRS but not named) for options is as follows:

$$\text{Diluted EPS} = \frac{(\text{Net income - Preferred dividends})}{\begin{array}{l}[\text{Weighted average number of shares} \\ \text{outstanding + (New shares that would} \\ \text{have been issued at option exercise -} \\ \text{Shares that could have been purchased} \\ \text{with cash received upon exercise)} \times \\ \text{(Proportion of year during which the} \\ \text{financial instruments were outstanding)]}\end{array}}$$

A diluted EPS calculation using the treasury stock method for options is provided in Example 13.

EXAMPLE 13

A Diluted EPS Calculation Using the Treasury Stock Method for Options

1. Hihotech Company (fictitious) reported net income of USD2.3 million for the year ended 30 June 2018 and had a weighted average of 800,000 common shares outstanding. At the beginning of the fiscal year, the company has outstanding 30,000 options with an exercise price of USD35. No other potentially dilutive financial instruments are outstanding. Over the fiscal year, the company's market price has averaged USD55 per share. Calculate the company's basic and diluted EPS.

   Solution:

   Using the treasury stock method, we first calculate that the company would have received USD1,050,000 (USD35 for each of the 30,000 options exercised) if all the options had been exercised. The options would no longer be outstanding; instead, 30,000 shares of common stock would be outstanding. Under the treasury stock method, we assume that shares would be repurchased with the cash received upon exercise of the options. At an average market price of USD55 per share, the USD1,050,000 proceeds from option exercise, the company could have repurchased 19,091 shares. Therefore, the incremental number of shares issued is 10,909 (calculated as 30,000 minus 19,091). For the diluted EPS calculation, no change is made to the numerator. As shown in Exhibit 16, the company's basic EPS was USD2.88 and the diluted EPS was USD2.84.

Exhibit 16: Calculation of Diluted EPS for Hihotech Company Using the Treasury Stock Method: Case of Stock Options

	Basic EPS	Diluted EPS Using Treasury Stock Method
Net income	USD2,300,000	USD2,300,000
Numerator	USD2,300,000	USD2,300,000
Weighted average number of shares outstanding	800,000	800,000
If converted	0	10,909
Denominator	800,000	810,909
EPS	**USD2.88**	**USD2.84**

As noted, IFRS require a similar computation but does not refer to it as the "treasury stock method." The company is required to consider that any assumed proceeds are received from the issuance of new shares at the average market price for the period. These new "inferred" shares would be disregarded in the computation of diluted EPS, but the excess of the new shares that would be issued under options contracts minus the new inferred shares would be added to the weighted average number of shares outstanding. The results are the same as the treasury stock method, as shown in Example 14.

EXAMPLE 14

Diluted EPS for Options under IFRS

1. Assuming the same facts given in Example 13, calculate the weighted average number of shares outstanding for diluted EPS under IFRS.

   Solution:

   If the options had been exercised, the company would have received USD1,050,000. If this amount had been received from the issuance of new shares at the average market price of USD55 per share, the company would have issued 19,091 shares. IFRS refer to the 19,091 shares the company would have issued at market prices as the inferred shares. The number of shares issued under options (30,000) minus the number of inferred shares (19,091) equals 10,909. This amount is added to the weighted average number of shares outstanding of 800,000 to get diluted shares of 810,909. Note that this is the same result as that obtained under US GAAP; it is just derived in a different manner.

Other Issues with Diluted EPS and Changes in EPS

It is possible that some potentially convertible securities could be **antidilutive** (i.e., their inclusion in the computation would result in an EPS higher than the company's basic EPS). Under IFRS and US GAAP, antidilutive securities are not included in the calculation of diluted EPS. Diluted EPS should reflect the maximum potential dilution from conversion or exercise of potentially dilutive financial instruments. Diluted EPS will always be less than or equal to basic EPS. Example 15 provides an illustration of an antidilutive security.

EXAMPLE 15

An Antidilutive Security

1. For the year ended 31 December 2018, Dim-Cool Utility Company (fictitious) had net income of USD1,750,000. The company had an average of 500,000 shares of common stock outstanding, 20,000 shares of convertible preferred, and no other potentially dilutive securities. Each share of preferred pays a dividend of USD10 per share, and each is convertible into three shares of the company's common stock. What was the company's basic and diluted EPS?

   Solution:

   If the 20,000 shares of convertible preferred had each converted into three shares of the company's common stock, the company would have had an additional 60,000 shares of common stock (three shares of common for each of the 20,000 shares of preferred). If the conversion had taken place, the company would not have paid preferred dividends of USD200,000 (USD10 per share for each of the 20,000 shares of preferred). The effect of using the if-converted method would be EPS of USD3.13, as shown in Exhibit 17. Because this is greater than the company's basic EPS of USD3.10, the securities are said to be antidilutive and the effect of their conversion would not be included in diluted EPS. Diluted EPS would be the same as basic EPS (i.e., USD3.10).

Exhibit 17: Calculation for an Antidilutive Security

	Basic EPS	Diluted EPS Using If-Converted Method
Net income	USD1,750,000	USD1,750,000
Preferred dividend	−200,000	0
Numerator	USD1,550,000	USD1,750,000
Weighted average number of shares outstanding	500,000	500,000
If converted	0	60,000

	Basic EPS	Diluted EPS Using If-Converted Method	
Denominator	500,000	560,000	
EPS	**USD3.10**	USD3.13	←Exceeds basic EPS; security is antidilutive and, therefore, **not** included. **Reported diluted EPS= USD3.10**.

Changes in EPS

Having explained the calculations of both basic and diluted EPS, we return to an examination of changes in EPS. As noted in Exhibit 12, AB InBev's fully diluted EPS from continuing operations increased from USD0.68 in 2016 to USD3.96 in 2017. In general, an increase in EPS results from an increase in net income, a decrease in the number of shares outstanding, or a combination of both. In the notes to its financial statements (not shown), AB InBev discloses that the weighted average number of shares for both the basic and fully diluted calculations was greater in 2017 than in 2016. Thus, for AB InBev, the improvement in EPS from 2016 to 2017 was driven by an increase in net income. Changes in the numerator and denominator explain the changes in EPS arithmetically. To understand the business drivers of those changes requires further research. Lesson 5 presents analytical tools that an analyst can use to highlight areas for further examination.

6 INCOME STATEMENT RATIOS AND COMMON-SIZE ANALYSIS

- [ ] evaluate a company's financial performance using common-size income statements and financial ratios based on the income statement

In this lesson, we apply two analytical tools to analyze the income statement: common-size analysis and income statement ratios. The objective of this analysis is to assess over a period of time a company's performance relative to its own past performance or to that of another company.

Common-Size Analysis of the Income Statement

Common-size analysis of the income statement can be performed by stating each line item on the income statement as a percentage of revenue. Common-size statements facilitate comparison across time periods (time series analysis) and across companies (cross-sectional analysis) because the standardization of each line item removes the effect of size.

To illustrate, Panel A of Exhibit 18 presents an income statement for three hypothetical companies in the same industry. Company A and Company B, each with USD10 million in sales, are larger (as measured by sales) than Company C, which has only USD2 million in sales. In addition, Companies A and B both have higher operating profit: USD2 million and USD1.5 million, respectively, compared with Company C's operating profit of only USD400,000.

How can an analyst meaningfully compare the performance of these companies? By preparing a common-size income statement, as illustrated in Panel B, an analyst can readily see that the percentages of Company C's expenses and profit relative to its sales are exactly the same as for Company A. Furthermore, although Company C's operating profit is lower than Company B's in absolute dollars, it is higher in percentage terms (20 percent for Company C compared with only 15 percent for Company B). For each USD100 of sales, Company C generates USD5 more operating profit than Company B. In other words, Company C is relatively more profitable than Company B based on this measure.

The common-size income statement also highlights differences in companies' strategies. Comparing the two larger companies, Company A reports significantly higher gross profit as a percentage of sales than does Company B (70 percent compared with 25 percent). Given that both companies operate in the same industry, why can Company A generate so much higher gross profit? One possible explanation is found by comparing the operating expenses of the two companies. Company A spends significantly more on research and development and on advertising than Company B. Expenditures on research and development likely result in products with superior technology. Expenditures on advertising likely result in greater brand awareness. So, based on these differences, it is likely that Company A is selling technologically superior products with a better brand image. Company B may be selling its products more cheaply (with a lower gross profit as a percentage of sales) but is saving money by not investing in research and development or advertising. In practice, differences across companies are more subtle, but the concept is similar. An analyst, noting significant differences, would do more research and seek to understand the underlying reasons for the differences and their implications for the future performance of the companies.

Exhibit 18: income Statement for Three Hypothetical Companies

Panel A: Income Statements for Companies A, B, and C (US dollars)

	A	B	C
Sales	USD10,000,000	USD10,000,000	USD2,000,000
Cost of sales	3,000,000	7,500,000	600,000
Gross profit	7,000,000	2,500,000	1,400,000
Selling, general, and administrative expenses	1,000,000	1,000,000	200,000
Research and development	2,000,000	—	400,000

Panel A: Income Statements for Companies A, B, and C (US dollars)

	A	B	C
Advertising	2,000,000	—	400,000
Operating profit	2,000,000	1,500,000	400,000

Panel B: Common-Size Income Statements for Companies A, B, and C (%)

	A	B	C
Sales	100%	100%	100%
Cost of sales	30	75	30
Gross profit	70	25	70
Selling, general, and administrative expenses	10	10	10
Research and development	20	0	20
Advertising	20	0	20
Operating profit	20	15	20

Note: Each line item is expressed as a percentage of the company's sales.

For most expenses, comparison to the amount of sales is appropriate. In the case of taxes, however, it is more meaningful to compare the amount of taxes with the amount of pretax income. Using note disclosure, an analyst can then examine the causes for differences in effective tax rates. To project the companies' future net income, an analyst would project the companies' pretax income and apply an estimated effective tax rate determined in part by the historical tax rates.

Vertical common-size analysis of the income statement is particularly useful in cross-sectional analysis—comparing companies with each other for a particular time period or comparing a company with industry or sector data. The analyst could select individual peer companies for comparison, use industry data from published sources, or compile data from databases based on a selection of peer companies or broader industry data. For example, Exhibit 19 presents median common-size income statement data compiled for the components of the S&P 500 classified into the 10 S&P/MSCI Global Industrial Classification System (GICS) sectors using 2017 data. Note that when compiling aggregate data such as this, some level of aggregation is necessary and less detail may be available than from peer company financial statements. The performance of an individual company can be compared with industry or peer company data to evaluate its relative performance.

Exhibit 19: Median Common-Size Income Statement Statistics for the S&P 500 Classified by S&P/MSCI GICS Sector Data for 2017

	Energy	Materials	Industrials	Consumer Discretionary	Consumer Staples	Health Care
Number of observations	34	27	69	81	34	59
Gross Margin	37.7%	33.0%	36.8%	37.6%	43.4%	59.0%

	Energy	Materials	Industrials	Consumer Discretionary	Consumer Staples	Health Care
Operating Margin	6.4%	14.9%	13.5%	11.0%	17.2%	17.4%
Net Profit Margin	4.9%	9.9%	8.8%	6.0%	10.9%	7.2%

	Financials	Information Technology	Telecom-munication Services	Utilities	Real Estate
Number of observations	63	64	4	29	29
Gross Margin	40.5%	62.4%	56.4%	34.3%	39.8%
Operating Margin	36.5%	21.1%	15.4%	21.7%	30.1%
Net Profit Margin	18.5%	11.3%	13.1%	10.1%	21.3%

Source: Based on data from Compustat. Operating margin based on EBIT (earnings before interest and taxes).

Income Statement Ratios

One aspect of financial performance is profitability. One indicator of profitability is **net profit margin**, also known as **profit margin** and **return on sales**, which is calculated as net income divided by revenue (or sales):

$$\text{Net profit margin} = \frac{\text{Net income}}{\text{Revenue}}.$$

Net profit margin measures the amount of income that a company was able to generate for each dollar of revenue. A higher level of net profit margin indicates higher profitability and is thus more desirable. Net profit margin can also be found directly on the common-size income statements.

For AB InBev, net profit margin based on continuing operations for 2017 was 16.2 percent (calculated as profit from continuing operations of USD9,155 million, divided by revenue of USD56,444 million). To judge this ratio, some comparison is needed. AB InBev's profitability can be compared with that of another company or with its own previous performance. Compared with previous years, AB InBev's profitability is higher than in 2016 but lower than 2015. In 2016, net profit margin based on continuing operations was 6.0 percent, and in 2015, it was 22.9 percent.

Another measure of profitability is the gross profit margin. Gross profit (gross margin) is calculated as revenue minus cost of goods sold, and the **gross profit margin** is calculated as the gross profit divided by revenue:

$$\text{Gross profit margin} = \frac{\text{Gross profit}}{\text{Revenue}}.$$

The gross profit margin measures the amount of gross profit that a company has generated for each dollar of revenue. A higher level of gross profit margin indicates higher profitability and thus is generally more desirable, although differences in gross profit margins across companies reflect differences in companies' strategies. For example, consider a company pursuing a strategy of selling a differentiated product (e.g., a product differentiated based on brand name, quality, superior technology, or patent protection). The company would likely be able to sell the differentiated product at a higher price than a similar, but undifferentiated, product and, therefore, would likely show a higher gross profit margin than a company selling an undifferentiated product. Although a company selling a differentiated product would likely show a higher gross profit margin, this may take time. In the initial stage of the strategy, the company would likely incur costs to create a differentiated product, such as advertising or research and development, which would not be reflected in the gross margin calculation.

AB InBev's gross profit was USD35,058 million in 2017, USD27,715 million in 2016, and USD26,467 million in 2015. Expressing gross profit as a percentage of revenues, we see that the gross profit margin was 62.1 percent in 2017, 60.9 percent in 2016, and 60.7 percent in 2015. In absolute terms, AB InBev's gross profit was higher in 2016 than in 2015. However, AB InBev's gross profit *margin* was approximately constant between 2015 and 2016.

Exhibit 20 presents a common-size income statement for AB InBev and highlights certain profitability ratios. The net profit margin and gross profit margin described previously are just two of the many subtotals that can be generated from common-size income statements. Other "margins" used by analysts include the **operating profit margin** (profit from operations divided by revenue) and the **pretax margin** (profit before tax divided by revenue).

Exhibit 20: AB InBev's Margins: Abbreviated Common-Size Income Statement

	12 Months Ended 31 December					
	2017		2016		2015	
	US dollars	%	US dollars	%	US dollars	%
Revenue	56,444	100.0	45,517	100.0	43,604	100.0
Cost of sales	(21,386)	(37.9)	(17,803)	(39.1)	(17,137)	(39.3)
Gross profit	**35,058**	**62.1**	**27,715**	**60.9**	**26,467**	**60.7**
Distribution expenses	(5,876)	(10.4)	(4,543)	(10.0)	(4,259)	(9.8)
Sales and marketing expenses	(8,382)	(14.9)	(7,745)	(17.0)	(6,913)	(15.9)
Administrative expenses	(3,841)	(6.8)	(2,883)	(6.3)	(2,560)	(5.9)
Portions omitted						
Profit from operations	**17,152**	**30.4**	**12,882**	**28.3**	**13,904**	**31.9**
Finance cost	(6,885)	(12.2)	(9,382)	(20.6)	(3,142)	(7.2)
Finance income	378	0.7	818	1.8	1,689	3.9
Net finance income/(cost)	(6,507)	(11.5)	(8,564)	(18.8)	(1,453)	(3.3)
Share of result of associates and joint ventures	430	0.8	16	0.0	10	0.0
Profit before tax	**11,076**	**19.6**	**4,334**	**9.5**	**12,461**	**28.6**
Income tax expense	(1,920)	(3.4)	(1,613)	(3.5)	(2,594)	(5.9)
Profit from continuing operations	**9,155**	**16.2**	**2,721**	**6.0**	**9,867**	**22.6**
Profit from discontinued operations	28	0.0	48	0.1	—	—
Profit of the year	**9,183**	**16.3**	**2,769**	**6.1**	**9,867**	**22.6**

Note: reported total amounts may have slight discrepancies due to rounding

The profitability ratios and the common-size income statement yield quick insights about changes in a company's performance. For example, AB InBev's decrease in profitability in 2016 was not driven by a decrease in gross profit margin. Gross profit margin in 2016 was actually slightly higher than in 2015. The company's decrease in profitability in 2016 was driven in part by higher operating expenses and, in particular, by a significant increase in finance costs. The increased finance costs resulted from the 2016 merger with SABMiller. Valued at more than USD100 billion, the acquisition was one of the largest in history. The combination of AB InBev and SABMiller also explains the increase in revenue from around USD45 billion to over USD56 billion. The profitability ratios and the common-size income statement thus highlight areas about which an analyst might wish to gain further understanding.

PRACTICE PROBLEMS

1. Under IFRS, income includes increases in economic benefits from:

   A. increases in liabilities not related to owners' contributions.

   B. enhancements of assets not related to owners' contributions.

   C. increases in owners' equity related to owners' contributions.

2. Fairplay reported the information shown in Exhibit 1 related to the sale of its products during 2009, which was its first year of business:

Exhibit 1: Fairplay

Revenue	USD1,000,000
Returns of goods sold	USD100,000
Cash collected	USD800,000
Cost of goods sold	USD700,000

   Under the accrual basis of accounting, how much net revenue would be reported on Fairplay's 2009 income statement?

   A. USD200,000

   B. USD900,000

   C. USD1,000,000

3. Apex Consignment sells items over the internet for individuals on a consignment basis. Apex receives the items from the owner, lists them for sale on the internet, and receives a 25 percent commission for any items sold. Apex collects the full amount from the buyer and pays the net amount after commission to the owner. Unsold items are returned to the owner after 90 days. During 2009, Apex had the following information:

   - Total sales price of items sold during 2009 on consignment was EUR2,000,000.
   - Total commissions retained by Apex during 2009 for these items was EUR500,000.

   How much revenue should Apex report on its 2009 income statement?

   A. EUR500,000

   B. EUR2,000,000

   C. EUR1,500,000

4. A company previously expensed the incremental costs of obtaining a contract. All else being equal, adopting the May 2014 IASB and FASB converged accounting standards on revenue recognition makes the company's profitability initially appear:

   A. lower.

B. unchanged.

C. higher.

5. Under IFRS, a loss from the destruction of property in a fire would most likely be classified as:

   A. continuing operations.

   B. discontinued operations.

   C. other comprehensive income.

6. A company chooses to change an accounting policy. This change requires that, if practical, the company restate its financial statements for:

   A. all prior periods.

   B. current and future periods.

   C. prior periods shown in a report.

7. For 2009, Flamingo Products had net income of USD1,000,000. At 1 January 2009, there were 1,000,000 shares outstanding. On 1 July 2009, the company issued 100,000 new shares for USD20 per share. The company paid USD200,000 in dividends to common shareholders. What is Flamingo's basic earnings per share for 2009?

   A. USD0.80

   B. USD0.91

   C. USD0.95

8. A company with no debt or convertible securities issued publicly traded common stock three times during the current fiscal year. Under both IFRS and US GAAP, the company's:

   A. basic EPS equals its diluted EPS.

   B. capital structure is considered complex at year-end.

   C. basic EPS is calculated by using a simple average number of shares outstanding.

9. For its fiscal year-end, Sublyme Corporation reported net income of USD200 million and a weighted average of 50,000,000 common shares outstanding. There are 2,000,000 convertible preferred shares outstanding that paid an annual dividend of USD5. Each preferred share is convertible into two shares of the common stock. The diluted EPS is *closest to*:

   A. USD3.52

   B. USD3.65

   C. USD3.70

10. For its fiscal year-end, Calvan Water Corporation (CWC) reported net income of USD12 million and a weighted average of 2,000,000 common shares outstanding. The company paid USD800,000 in preferred dividends and had 100,000 options

outstanding with an average exercise price of USD20. CWC's market price over the year averaged USD25 per share. CWC's diluted EPS is *closest* to:

A. USD5.33

B. USD5.54

C. USD5.94

11. Laurelli Builders (LB) reported the financial data shown in Exhibit 1 for year-end 31 December:

Exhibit 1: Laurelli Builders

Common shares outstanding, 1 January	2,020,000
Common shares issued as stock dividend, 1 June	380,000
Warrants outstanding, 1 January	500,000
Net income	USD3,350,000
Preferred stock dividends paid	USD430,000
Common stock dividends paid	USD240,000

Which statement about the calculation of LB's EPS is *most* accurate?

A. LB's basic EPS is USD1.12.

B. LB's diluted EPS is equal to or less than its basic EPS.

C. The weighted average number of shares outstanding is 2,210,000.

12. Cell Services Inc. (CSI) had 1,000,000 average shares outstanding during all of 2009. During 2009, CSI also had 10,000 options outstanding with exercise prices of USD10 each. The average stock price of CSI during 2009 was USD15. For purposes of computing diluted earnings per share, how many shares would be used in the denominator?

A. 1,003,333

B. 1,006,667

C. 1,010,000

13. When calculating diluted EPS, which of the following securities in the capital structure increases the weighted average number of common shares outstanding without affecting net income available to common shareholders?

A. Stock options

B. Convertible debt that is dilutive

C. Convertible preferred stock that is dilutive

14. Which statement is *most* accurate? A common size income statement:

A. restates each line item of the income statement as a percentage of net income.

B. allows an analyst to conduct cross-sectional analysis by removing the effect of company size.

C. standardizes each line item of the income statement but fails to help an analyst identify differences in companies' strategies.

SOLUTIONS

1. B is correct. Under IFRS, income includes increases in economic benefits from increases in assets, enhancement of assets, and decreases in liabilities.

2. B is correct. Net revenue is revenue for goods sold during the period less any returns and allowances, or USD1,000,000 minus USD100,000 = USD900,000.

3. A is correct. Apex is not the owner of the goods and should only report its net commission as revenue.

4. C is correct. Under the converged accounting standards, the incremental costs of obtaining a contract and certain costs incurred to fulfill a contract must be capitalized. If a company expensed these incremental costs in the years prior to adopting the converged standards, all else being equal, its profitability will appear higher under the converged standards.

5. A is correct. A fire may be infrequent, but it would still be part of continuing operations and reported in the profit and loss statement. Discontinued operations relate to a decision to dispose of an operating division.

6. C is correct. If a company changes an accounting policy, the financial statements for all fiscal years shown in a company's financial report are presented, if practical, as if the newly adopted accounting policy had been used throughout the entire period; this retrospective application of the change makes the financial results of any prior years included in the report comparable. Notes to the financial statements describe the change and explain the justification for the change.

7. C is correct. The weighted average number of shares outstanding for 2009 is 1,050,000. Basic earnings per share would be USD1,000,000 divided by 1,050,000, or USD0.95.

8. A is correct. Basic and diluted EPS are equal for a company with a simple capital structure. A company that issues only common stock, with no financial instruments that are potentially convertible into common stock has a simple capital structure. Basic EPS is calculated using the weighted average number of shares outstanding.

9. C is correct.

   Diluted EPS

   = (Net income)/(Weighted average number of shares outstanding + New common shares that would have been issued at conversion)

   = USD200,000,000/[50,000,000 + (2,000,000 × 2)]

   = USD3.70

   The diluted EPS assumes that the preferred dividend is not paid and that the shares are converted at the beginning of the period.

10. B is correct. The formula to calculate diluted EPS is as follows:

Diluted EPS

= (Net income – Preferred dividends)/[Weighted average number of shares outstanding + (New shares that would have been issued at option exercise – Shares that could have been purchased with cash received upon exercise) × (Proportion of year during which the financial instruments were outstanding)].

The underlying assumption is that outstanding options are exercised, and then the proceeds from the issuance of new shares are used to repurchase shares already outstanding:

Proceeds from option exercise = 100,000 × USD20 = USD2,000,000

Shares repurchased = USD2,000,000/USD25 = 80,000

The net increase in shares outstanding is thus 100,000 – 80,000 = 20,000. Therefore, the diluted EPS for CWC = (USD12,000,000 – USD800,000)/2,020,000 = USD5.54.

11. B is correct. LB has warrants in its capital structure; if the exercise price is less than the weighted average market price during the year, the effect of their conversion is to increase the weighted average number of common shares outstanding, causing diluted EPS to be lower than basic EPS. If the exercise price is equal to the weighted average market price, the number of shares issued equals the number of shares repurchased. Therefore, the weighted average number of common shares outstanding is not affected and diluted EPS equals basic EPS. If the exercise price is greater than the weighted average market price, the effect of their conversion is anti-dilutive. As such, they are not included in the calculation of basic EPS. LB's basic EPS is USD1.22 [= (USD3,350,000 – USD430,000)/2,400,000]. Stock dividends are treated as having been issued retroactively to the beginning of the period.

12. A is correct. With stock options, the treasury stock method must be used. Under that method, the company would receive USD100,000 (10,000 × USD10) and would repurchase 6,667 shares (USD100,000/USD15). The shares for the denominator would be:

Shares outstanding	1,000,000
Options exercises	10,000
Treasury shares purchased	(6,667)
Denominator	1,003,333

13. A is correct. When a company has stock options outstanding, diluted EPS is calculated as if the financial instruments had been exercised and the company had used the proceeds from the exercise to repurchase as many shares possible at the weighted average market price of common stock during the period. As a result, the conversion of stock options increases the number of common shares outstanding but has no effect on net income available to common shareholders. The conversion of convertible debt increases the net income available to common shareholders by the after-tax amount of interest expense saved. The conversion of convertible preferred shares increases the net income available to common shareholders by the amount of preferred dividends paid; the numerator becomes the net income.

14. B is correct. Common size income statements facilitate comparison across time periods (time-series analysis) and across companies (cross-sectional analysis) by stating each line item of the income statement as a percentage of revenue. The relative performance of different companies can be more easily assessed because

scaling the numbers removes the effect of size. A common size income statement states each line item on the income statement as a percentage of revenue. The standardization of each line item makes a common size income statement useful for identifying differences in companies' strategies.

LEARNING MODULE

3

Analyzing Balance Sheets

LEARNING OUTCOMES

Mastery	The candidate should be able to:
☐	explain the financial reporting and disclosures related to intangible assets
☐	explain the financial reporting and disclosures related to goodwill
☐	explain the financial reporting and disclosures related to financial instruments
☐	explain the financial reporting and disclosures related to non-current liabilities
☐	calculate and interpret common-size balance sheets and related financial ratios

The two major accounting standard setters are as follows: 1) the International Accounting Standards Board (IASB) who establishes International Financial Reporting Standards (IFRS) and 2) the Financial Accounting Standards Board (FASB) who establishes US GAAP. Throughout this learning module both standards are referred to and many, but not all, of these two sets of accounting rules are identified. Note: changes in accounting standards as well as new rulings and/or pronouncements issued after the publication of this learning module may cause some of the information to become dated.

1 INTRODUCTION

The balance sheet discloses what an entity owns (assets), what an entity owes (liabilities), and the owners' interest in the net assets of a company (equity) at a specific point in time. While many balance sheet items are reported at historical cost, some items are measured differently, such as at fair value, and some events and transactions—perhaps contrary to analyst's expectations—are not recognized at all. Analysts must be familiar with the different rules and practices for recognition, measurement, and disclosure of balance sheet items to evaluate the liquidity, solvency, and overall financial position of companies. To do so, analysts often compute ratios involving the balance sheet and other financial statements, such as the ratio of debt to operating income or cash flows, which can be compared to other companies and over time.

LEARNING MODULE OVERVIEW

- Some assets and liabilities are measured at fair value and some are measured at amortized or historical cost. Notes to the financial statements provide information that is helpful in assessing the comparability of measurement bases across companies.
- Intangible assets refer to identifiable non-monetary assets without physical substance. Examples include patents, licenses, and trademarks. For each intangible asset, a company assesses whether its useful life is finite or indefinite.
- An intangible asset with a finite useful life is amortized on a systematic basis over the best estimate of its useful life, with the amortization method and useful life estimate reviewed at least annually. Intangibles are subject to impairment as well, in a similar manner to tangible assets like property, plant, and equipment.
- An intangible asset with an indefinite useful life is not amortized. Instead, it is tested for impairment at least annually.
- For internally generated intangible assets, the International Financial Reporting Standards (IFRS) require that costs incurred during the research phase must be expensed. Costs incurred in the development stage can be capitalized as intangible assets if certain criteria are met, including technological feasibility, the ability to use or sell the resulting asset, and the ability to complete the project.
- The most common intangible asset that is not a separately identifiable asset is goodwill, which arises in business combinations. Goodwill is not amortized; instead it is tested for impairment at least annually.
- Financial instruments are contracts that give rise to both a financial asset of one entity and a financial liability or equity instrument of another entity. In general, financial instruments are measured in two ways: fair value or amortized cost. For financial instruments measured at fair value, the two basic alternatives in how net changes in fair value are recognized are (1) as profit or loss on the income statement, or (2) as other comprehensive income (loss) that bypasses the income statement.
- Common long-term liabilities include loans (i.e., borrowings from banks), notes or bonds payable (i.e., fixed-income securities issued to investors), leases, and post-employment liabilities. Liabilities are usually reported at amortized cost or fair value on the balance sheet.

- Vertical common-size analysis of the balance sheet involves expressing each balance sheet item as a percentage of total assets.
- Balance sheet ratios include liquidity ratios (measuring the company's ability to meet its short-term obligations) and solvency ratios (measuring the company's ability to meet long-term and other obligations).

INTANGIBLE ASSETS

2

□ explain the financial reporting and disclosures related to intangible assets

Intangible assets are identifiable non-monetary assets without physical substance.[1] An identifiable asset can be acquired on a standalone basis (i.e., can be separated from the entity) or arises from contractual or legal rights and privileges. Common examples include patents, licenses, trademarks, and customer lists. The most common intangible that is *not* separately identifiable is goodwill, which arises in business combinations and is discussed further in the next lesson.

IFRS permits companies to report intangible assets using either a cost model or a revaluation model. The revaluation model can be selected only when there is an active market for an intangible asset. Both measurement models are essentially the same as described for property, plant, and equipment (PP&E). US GAAP permits only the cost model.

For each intangible asset, a company assesses whether the useful life of the asset is finite or indefinite. Amortization and impairment principles apply as follows:

- An intangible asset with a finite useful life is amortized on a systematic basis over the best estimate of its useful life, with the amortization method and useful life estimate reviewed at least annually.
- Impairment principles for an intangible asset with a finite useful life are the same as for PP&E.
- An intangible asset with an indefinite useful life is not amortized. Instead, at least annually, the reasonableness of assuming an indefinite useful life for the asset is reviewed and the asset is tested for impairment.

Financial analysts traditionally view reported values of intangible assets - particularly goodwill - with caution. Consequently, in assessing financial statements, some analysts exclude the book value assigned to intangibles, reducing net equity by an equal amount (obtaining a "tangible book value") and increasing pretax income by any amortization expense or impairment associated with the intangibles. An arbitrary assignment of zero value to intangibles is not advisable; instead, an analyst should examine each listed intangible and assess whether an adjustment should be made. Note disclosures about intangible assets may provide useful information to the analyst. These disclosures include information about useful lives, amortization rates and methods, and impairment losses recognized or reversed.

Further, a company may have developed intangible assets internally that can be recognized only in certain circumstances. Companies may also have assets that are never recorded on a balance sheet because they are non-identifiable and the company

1 International Accounting Standard 38, *Intangible Assets*, paragraph 8.

does not have sufficient control over their future economic benefits. These assets might include management and technical skills of employees, market share, name recognition, a good reputation among customers, and so forth. Such assets are valuable and are reflected, in theory, in the price at which the company's equity securities trade in the market (and the price at which the entirety of the company's equity would be sold in an acquisition transaction). Such assets may be recognized as goodwill by an acquirer if the company is sold.

Identifiable Intangibles

Under IFRS, identifiable intangible assets are recognized on the balance sheet if it is probable that future economic benefits will flow to the company and the cost of the asset can be measured reliably. Examples of identifiable intangible assets include patents, trademarks, copyrights, franchises, licenses, and other rights. Identifiable intangible assets may have been created internally or purchased by a company. Determining the cost of internally created intangible assets can be difficult and subjective. For these reasons, under IFRS and US GAAP, the general requirement is that internally created identifiable intangibles are expensed rather than reported on the balance sheet.

IFRS provides that for internally created intangible assets, the company must separately identify its research phase and development phase.[2] The research phase includes activities that seek new knowledge or products. The development phase occurs after the research phase and includes design or testing of prototypes and models. IFRS requires that costs to internally generate intangible assets during the research phase must be expensed on the income statement while costs incurred in the development stage can be capitalized as intangible assets if certain criteria are met, including technological feasibility, the ability to use or sell the resulting asset, and the ability to complete the project.

US GAAP prohibits the capitalization of most costs of internally developed intangibles and research and development. All such costs are expensed. Costs related to the following categories typically are expensed under IFRS and US GAAP. They include the following:

- internally generated brands, mastheads, publishing titles, and customer lists;
- start-up costs;
- training costs;
- administrative and other general overhead costs;
- advertising and promotion;
- relocation and reorganization expenses; and
- redundancy and other termination costs.

In contrast to internally created intangibles, *acquired* or *purchased* intangible assets are capitalized and reported as separately identifiable intangible, so long as they arise from contractual rights (such as a licensing agreement), other legal rights (such as patents), or have the ability to be separated and sold (such as a customer list).

MEASURING INTANGIBLE ASSETS

Alpha Inc., a motor vehicle manufacturer, has a research division that worked on the following projects during the year:

2 International Accounting Standard 38, *Intangible Assets*, paragraphs 51–67.

Project 1	Research aimed at finding a steering mechanism that does not operate like a conventional steering wheel but reacts to the impulses from a driver's fingers.
Project 2	The design of a prototype welding apparatus that is controlled electronically rather than mechanically. The apparatus has been determined to be technologically feasible, salable, and feasible to produce.

The following is a summary of the expenses of the research division (in thousands of euros):

Exhibit 1: Summary of Expenses

	General	Project 1	Project 2
Material and services	128	935	620
Labor			
▪ Direct labor	—	630	320
▪ Administrative personnel	720	—	—
Design, construction, and testing	270	450	470

1. Five percent of administrative personnel costs can be attributed to each project (Project 1 and 2). Explain the accounting treatment of Alpha's costs for Projects 1 and 2 under IFRS and US GAAP.

Solution:

Under IFRS, the capitalization of internal development costs for Projects 1 and 2 would be as follows:

		Amount Capitalized as an Asset (in thousands of euros)
Project 1:	Classified as in the research stage, so all costs are recognized as expenses	0
Project 2:	Classified as in the development stage, so costs may be capitalized. Note that administrative costs are not capitalized.	(620 + 320 + 470)= 1,410

Under US GAAP, there would no capitalization of these costs as US GAAP prohibits the capitalization of most costs of internally developed intangibles and research and development. All costs would be expensed.

Consider the balance sheet information presented in Exhibit 2 and 3 for SAP and Apple. SAP's 2017 balance sheet shows EUR2,967 million of intangible assets, and Apple's 2017 balance sheet shows acquired intangible assets, net of USD2,298 million. SAP's notes to financial statements disclose the types of intangible assets (software and database licenses, purchased software to be incorporated into its products, customer contracts, and acquired trademark licenses) and indicates that all of its purchased intangible assets other than goodwill have finite useful lives and are amortized either based on expected consumption of economic benefits or on a straight-line basis over their estimated useful lives, which range from 2 to 20 years. Apple's notes disclose that its acquired intangible assets consist primarily of patents and licenses, and almost the entire amount represents definite-lived and amortizable assets for which the remaining weighted-average amortization period is 3.4 years as of 2017.

Exhibit 2: SAP Group Consolidated Statements of Financial Position (Excerpt: Non-Current Assets Detail) (in millions of EUR)

	As of 31 December	
Assets	**2017**	**2016**
Total current assets	11,930	11,564
Goodwill	21,274	23,311
Intangible assets	2,967	3,786
Property, plant and equipment	2,967	2,580
Other financial assets	1,155	1,358
Trade and other receivables	118	126
Other non-financial assets	621	532
Tax assets	443	450
Deferred tax assets	1,022	571
Total non-current assets	30,567	32,713
Total assets	**42,497**	**44,277**
Total current liabilities	10,210	9,674
Total non-current liabilities	6,747	8,205
Total liabilities	**16,958**	**17,880**
Total equity	**25,540**	**26,397**
Total equity and liabilities	**€42,497**	**€44,277**

Source: SAP Group 2017 annual report.

Exhibit 3: Apple, Inc. Consolidated Balance Sheets (Excerpt: Non-Current Assets Detail) (in millions of US dollars)

Assets	**30 September 2017**	**24 September 2016**
Total current assets	128,645	106,869
Long-term marketable securities	194,714	170,430
Property, plant and equipment, net	33,783	27,010
Goodwill	5,717	5,414
Acquired intangible assets, net	2,298	3,206
Other non-current assets	10,162	8,757
[All other assets]	*246,674*	*214,817*
Total assets	375,319	321,686
Liabilities and shareholders' equity		
Total current liabilities	100,814	79,006
[Total non-current liabilities]	*140,458*	*114,431*

Assets	30 September 2017	24 September 2016
Total liabilities	241,272	193,437
Total shareholders' equity	134,047	128,249
Total liabilities and shareholders' equity	375,319	321,686

Note: The italicized subtotals presented in this excerpt are not explicitly shown on the face of the financial statement as prepared by the company.
Source: Apple Inc. 2017 annual report (Form 10K).

GOODWILL 3

☐ explain the financial reporting and disclosures related to goodwill

When one company acquires another, the purchase price is allocated to all of the identifiable assets (tangible and intangible) and liabilities acquired, based on fair value. If the purchase price is greater than the fair value of the identifiable assets and liabilities acquired, the excess amount is recognized as an asset, **goodwill**. To understand why an acquirer would pay more to purchase a company than the fair value of the target company's identifiable assets net of liabilities, consider the following three observations. First, certain items not recognized in the acquiree's financial statements (e.g., its reputation, established distribution system, trained employees) have value. Second, a target company's expenditures in research and development may not have resulted in a separately identifiable asset that meets the criteria for recognition but nonetheless may have created some value. Third, part of the value of an acquisition may arise from improved strategic positioning versus a competitor or from perceived synergies such as operating cost saving opportunities after the acquisition.

The subject of recognizing goodwill in financial statements has both proponents and opponents. The proponents of goodwill recognition assert that goodwill is the present value of excess returns that a company is expected to earn. This group claims that determining the present value of these excess returns is analogous to determining the present value of future cash flows associated with other assets and projects. Opponents of goodwill recognition claim that the prices paid for acquisitions often turn out to be based on unrealistic expectations, thereby leading to future write-offs of goodwill.

Analysts should distinguish between accounting goodwill and economic goodwill. Economic goodwill is based on the economic performance of the entity, whereas accounting goodwill is based on accounting standards and is reported only in the case of acquisitions. Economic goodwill is important to analysts and investors, and it is not necessarily reflected on the balance sheet. Instead, economic goodwill is reflected in the stock price (at least in theory). Some financial statement users believe that goodwill should not be listed on the balance sheet, because it cannot be sold separately from the entity. These financial statement users believe that only assets that can be separately identified and sold should be reflected on the balance sheet. Other financial statement users analyze goodwill and any subsequent impairment charges to assess management's performance on prior acquisitions.

Under both IFRS and US GAAP, accounting goodwill arising from acquisitions is capitalized. Goodwill is not amortized but is tested for impairment annually. If goodwill is deemed to be impaired, an impairment loss is charged against income in the current period, reducing earnings. An impairment loss also reduces total assets, so some performance measures, such as return on assets (net income divided by average total assets), may increase in future periods. An impairment loss is a non-cash item.

Accounting standards' requirements for recognizing goodwill can be summarized by the following steps:

Step 1 The total cost to purchase the target company (the acquiree) is determined.

Step 2 The acquiree's identifiable assets are measured at fair value. The acquiree's liabilities and contingent liabilities are measured at fair value. The difference between the fair value of identifiable assets and the fair value of the liabilities and contingent liabilities equals the net identifiable assets acquired.

Step 3 Goodwill arising from the purchase is the excess of (1) the cost to purchase the target company over (2) the net identifiable assets acquired. Occasionally, a transaction will involve the purchase of net identifiable assets with a value greater than the cost to purchase. Such a transaction is called a "bargain purchase." Any gain from a bargain purchase is recognized in profit and loss in the period in which it arises.[3]

Companies are also required to disclose information that enables users to evaluate the nature and financial effect of business combinations. The required disclosures include, for example, the acquisition date fair value of the total cost to purchase the target company, the acquisition date amount recognized for each major class of assets and liabilities, and a qualitative description of the factors that make up the goodwill recognized.

Despite the guidance incorporated in accounting standards, analysts should be aware that the estimations of fair value involve considerable management judgment. Values for intangible assets, such as computer software, might not be easily validated when analyzing acquisitions. Management judgment about valuation in turn affects current and future financial statements because identifiable intangible assets with definite lives are amortized over time. In contrast, neither goodwill nor identifiable intangible assets with indefinite lives are amortized; instead, as noted, both are tested annually for impairment.

The recognition and impairment of goodwill can significantly affect the comparability of financial statements between companies. Therefore, analysts often adjust the companies' financial statements by removing the impact of goodwill. Such adjustments include the following:

- excluding goodwill from balance sheet data used to compute financial ratios, and
- excluding goodwill impairment losses from income data used to examine operating trends.

In addition, analysts can develop expectations about a company's performance following an acquisition by taking into account the purchase price paid relative to the net assets and earnings prospects of the acquired company.

3 IFRS 3, *Business Combinations* and Financial Accounting Standards Board (FASB) Accounting Standards Codification (ASC) 805, *Business Combinations*.

GOODWILL IMPAIRMENT

Safeway, Inc., is a North American food and drug retailer. On 25 February 2010, Safeway issued a press release that included the following information:

- Safeway Inc. today reported a net loss of USD1,609.1 million (USD4.06 per diluted share) for the 16-week fourth quarter of 2009. Excluding a non-cash goodwill impairment charge of USD1,818.2 million, net of tax (USD4.59 per diluted share), net income would have been USD209.1 million (USD0.53 per diluted share). Net income was USD338.0 million (USD0.79 per diluted share) for the 17-week fourth quarter of 2008.
- In the fourth quarter of 2009, Safeway recorded a non-cash goodwill impairment charge of USD1,974.2 million (USD1,818.2 million, net of tax). The impairment was due primarily to Safeway's reduced market capitalization and a weak economy. . . . The goodwill originated from previous acquisitions.
- Safeway's balance sheet as of 2 January 2010 showed goodwill of USD426.6 million and total assets of USD14,963.6 million. The company's balance sheet as of 3 January 2009 showed goodwill of USD2,390.2 million and total assets of USD17,484.7 million.

1. How significant was this goodwill impairment charge?

   Solution:

   The goodwill impairment was more than 80 percent of the total value of goodwill and 11 percent of total assets, so it was clearly significant. (The charge of USD1,974.2 million equals 82.6 percent of the USD2,390.2 million of goodwill at the beginning of the year and 11.3 percent of the USD17,484.7 million total assets at the beginning of the year.)

2. With reference to acquisition prices, what might this goodwill impairment indicate?

   Solution:

   The goodwill had originated from previous acquisitions. The impairment charge implies that the acquired operations are now worth less than the price that was paid for their acquisition.

As presented in Exhibits 2 and 3, SAP's 2017 balance sheet shows EUR21,274 million of goodwill, and Apple's 2017 balance sheet shows goodwill of USD5,717 million. Goodwill represents 50.1 percent of SAP's total assets and only 1.5 percent of Apple's total assets. An analyst may be concerned that goodwill represents such a high proportion of SAP's total assets.

4 FINANCIAL INSTRUMENTS

☐ explain the financial reporting and disclosures related to financial instruments

IFRS defines a financial instrument as a contract that gives rise to a financial asset of one entity, and a financial liability or equity instrument of another entity.[4] This lesson focuses on financial assets, such as a company's investments in stocks issued by another company or its investments in the notes, bonds, or other fixed-income instruments issued by another company (or issued by a governmental entity). Financial liabilities, such as notes payable and bonds payable issued by the company, will be discussed later. Some financial instruments may be classified as either an asset or a liability depending on the contractual terms and current market conditions. One example of such a financial instrument is a derivative. **Derivatives** are financial instruments for which the value is derived based on some underlying factor (interest rate, exchange rate, commodity price, security price, or credit rating) and for which little or no initial investment is required.

Financial instruments are generally recognized when the entity becomes a party to the contractual provisions of the instrument. In general, the two basic alternative ways that financial instruments are measured subsequent to initial acquisition are fair value or amortized cost. Recall that fair value is the price that would be received to sell an asset or paid to transfer a liability in an orderly market transaction.[5] The amortized cost of a financial asset (or liability) is the amount at which it was initially recognized, minus any principal repayments, plus or minus any amortization of discount or premium, and minus any reduction for impairment.

Under IFRS, financial assets are subsequently measured at amortized cost if the asset's cash flows occur on specified dates and consist solely of principal and interest, and if the business model is to hold the asset to maturity. The concept is similar in US GAAP, where this category of asset is referred to as **held-to-maturity**. An example is an investment in a long-term bond issued by another company or by a government; the value of the bond will fluctuate, for example with interest rate movements, but if the bond is classified as a held-to-maturity investment, it will be measured at amortized cost on the balance sheet of the investing company. Other types of financial assets measured at amortized cost are loans to other companies.

For financial instruments measured at fair value, the two basic alternatives in how net changes in fair value are recognized are (1) as profit or loss on the income statement, or (2) as other comprehensive income (loss), which bypasses the income statement. Note that these alternatives refer to *unrealized* changes in fair value, that is, changes in the value of a financial asset that has not been sold and is still owned at the end of the period. Unrealized gains and losses also are referred to as holding period gains and losses. *Realized* gains or losses as a result of a sale are reported on the income statement.

Under IFRS, financial assets are subsequently measured at fair value through other comprehensive income (i.e., any unrealized holding gains or losses are recognized in other comprehensive income) if the business model's objective involves both collecting contractual cash flows and selling the financial assets. This IFRS category applies specifically to debt investments, namely assets with cash flows occurring on specified dates and consisting solely of principal and interest. However, IFRS also permits equity investments to be measured at fair value through other comprehensive income if,

4 IAS 32, *Financial Instruments: Presentation*, paragraph 11.
5 IFRS 13, *Fair Value Measurement*; and US GAAP ASC 820, *Fair Value Measurement*.

at the time a company buys an equity investment, the company decides to make an irrevocable election to measure the asset in this manner.[6] The concept is similar to the US GAAP investment category **available-for-sale** in which assets are measured at fair value, with any unrealized holding gains or losses recognized in other comprehensive income. Unlike IFRS, however, the US GAAP category available-for-sale applies only to debt securities and is not permitted for investments in equity securities.[7]

Under IFRS, financial assets are subsequently measured at fair value through profit or loss (i.e., any unrealized holding gains or losses are recognized in the income statement) if they are not assigned to either of the other two measurement categories described earlier. In addition, IFRS allows a company to make an irrevocable election at acquisition to measure a financial asset in this category. Under US GAAP, all investments in equity securities (other than investments giving rise to ownership positions that confer significant influence over the investee) are measured at fair value with unrealized holding gains or losses recognized in the income statement. Under US GAAP, debt securities designated as trading securities are also measured at fair value with unrealized holding gains or losses recognized in the income statement. The trading securities category pertains to a debt security that is acquired with the intent of selling it rather than holding it to collect the interest and principal payments.

Exhibit 4 summarizes how various financial assets are classified and measured subsequent to acquisition.

Exhibit 4: Measurement of Financial Assets

Measured at Cost or Amortized Cost	Measured at Fair Value through Other Comprehensive Income	Measured at Fair Value through Profit and Loss
▪ Debt securities that are to be held to maturity. ▪ Loans and notes receivable ▪ Unquoted equity instruments (in limited circumstances in which the fair value is not reliably measurable, cost may serve as a proxy [estimate] for fair value)	▪ "Available-for-sale" debt securities (US GAAP); debt securities for which the business model involves both collecting interest and principal and selling the security (IFRS) ▪ Equity investments for which the company irrevocably elects this measurement at acquisition (IFRS only)	▪ All equity securities unless the investment gives the investor significant influence (US GAAP only) ▪ "Trading" debt securities (US GAAP) ▪ Securities not assigned to either of the other two categories, or investments for which the company irrevocably elects this measurement at acquisition (IFRS only)

To illustrate the different accounting treatments of the gains and losses on financial assets, consider an entity that invests EUR100,000,000 on 1 January 202X in a fixed-income security investment, with a 5 percent coupon paid semi-annually. After six months, the company receives the first coupon payment of EUR2,500,000. Additionally, market interest rates have declined such that the value of the fixed-income investment has increased by EUR2,000,000 as of 30 June 202X. Exhibit 5 illustrates how this situation will be portrayed on the balance sheet and income statement (ignoring taxes) of the entity concerned, under each of the following three measurement categories of financial assets: assets held for trading purposes, assets available for sale, and held-to-maturity assets.

6 IFRS 7, *Financial Instruments: Disclosures*, paragraph 8(h); and IFRS 9 *Financial Instruments*, paragraph 5.7.5.

7 US GAAP, Accounting Standards Update (ASU) 2016-01, *Recognition and Measurement of Financial Assets and Financial Liabilities*; and US GAAP, ASC 32X, *Investments*.

Exhibit 5: Accounting for Gains and Losses on Marketable Securities

IFRS Categories	Measured at Cost or Amortized Cost	Measured at Fair Value through Other Comprehensive Income	Measured at Fair Value through Profit and Loss
US GAAP Comparable Categories	*Held to Maturity*	*Available-for-Sale Debt Securities*	*Trading Debt Securities*
Income Statement for period 1 January–30 June 202X			
Interest income	2,500,000	2,500,000	2,500,000
Unrealized gains	—	—	2,000,000
Impact on profit and loss	2,500,000	2,500,000	4,500,000
Balance Sheet as of 30 June 202X			
Assets			
Cash and cash equivalents	2,500,000	2,500,000	2,500,000
Cost of securities	100,000,000	100,000,000	100,000,000
Unrealized gains on securities	—	2,000,000	2,000,000
	102,500,000	104,500,000	104,500,000
Liabilities			
Equity			
Paid-in capital	100,000,000	100,000,000	100,000,000
Retained earnings	2,500,000	2,500,000	4,500,000
Accumulated other comprehensive income	—	2,000,000	—
	102,500,000	104,500,000	104,500,000

In the case of securities classified as Measured at Cost or Amortized Cost, or equivalently held-to-maturity (US GAAP), the income statement shows only the interest income (which is then reflected in retained earnings on the ending balance sheet). Because the securities are measured at cost rather than at fair value, no unrealized gain is recognized. On the balance sheet, the investment asset is shown at its amortized cost of EUR100,000,000.

In the case of securities classified as Measured at Fair Value through Other Comprehensive Income (IFRS), or equivalently as Available-for-Sale debt securities (US GAAP), the income statement shows only the interest income (which is then reflected in retained earnings on the ending balance sheet). The unrealized gain does not appear on the income statement; instead, it would appear on a Statement of Comprehensive Income as Other Comprehensive Income. On the balance sheet, the investment asset is shown at its fair value of EUR102,000,000. (Exhibit 5 shows the unrealized gain on a separate line solely to highlight the impact of the change in value. In practice, the investments would be shown at their fair value on a single line.) In the case of securities classified as Measured at Fair Value through Profit and Loss (IFRS), or equivalently as trading debt securities (US GAAP), both the interest income and the unrealized gain are included on the income statement and thus are reflected in retained earnings on the balance sheet.

From the information presented in Exhibits 2 and 6, SAP's 2017 balance sheet shows other financial assets of EUR990 million (current, Exhibit 6) and EUR1,155 million (non-current, Exhibit 2). The company's notes disclose that the largest component of the current financial assets are loans and other financial receivables (EUR793 million) and the largest component of the non-current financial assets is EUR827 million of available-for-sale equity investments.

Exhibit 6: SAP Group Consolidated Statements of Financial Position (Excerpt: Current Assets Detail) (in millions of euros)

	As of 31 December	
Assets	**2017**	**2016**
Cash and cash equivalents	€4,011	€3,702
Other financial assets	990	1,124
Trade and other receivables	5,899	5,924
Other non-financial assets	725	581
Tax assets	306	233
Total current assets	11,930	11,564
Total non-current assets	30,567	32,713
Total assets	**42,497**	**44,277**
Total current liabilities	10,210	9,674
Total non-current liabilities	6,747	8,205
Total liabilities	16,958	17,880
Total equity	25,540	26,397
Total equity and liabilities	**€42,497**	**€44,277**

Source: SAP Group 2017 annual report.

Exhibit 7: Apple, Inc. Consolidated Balance Sheets (Excerpt: Current Assets Detail) (in millions of US dollars)

Assets	**30 September, 2017**	**24 September, 2016**
Cash and cash equivalents	$20,289	$20,484
Short-term marketable securities	53,892	46,671
Accounts receivable, less allowances of $58 and $53, respectively	17,874	15,754
Inventories	4,855	2,132
Vendor non-trade receivables	17,799	13,545
Other current assets	13,936	8,283
Total current assets	128,645	106,869
[All other assets]	*246,674*	*214,817*
Total assets	**375,319**	**321,686**
Total current liabilities	100,814	79,006
[Total non-current liabilities]	*140,458*	*114,431*
Total liabilities	241,272	193,437

Assets	30 September, 2017	24 September, 2016
Total shareholders' equity	134,047	128,249
Total liabilities and shareholders' equity	**$375,319**	**$321,686**

Note: The italicized subtotals presented in this excerpt are not explicitly shown on the face of the financial statement as prepared by the company.
Source: Apple Inc. 2017 annual report (Form 10K).

In Exhibits 3 and 7, Apple's 2017 balance sheet shows USD53,892 million of short-term marketable securities (current, Exhibit 7) and USD194,714 million of long-term marketable securities (non-current, Exhibit 3). In total, marketable securities represent more than 66 percent of Apple's USD375.3 billion in total assets. Marketable securities plus cash and cash equivalents represent around 72 percent of the company's total assets. Apple's notes disclose that most of the company's marketable securities are fixed-income securities issued by the US government or its agencies (USD60,237 million) and by other companies, including commercial paper (USD153,451 million). In accordance with its investment policy, Apple invests in highly rated securities (which the company defines as investment grade) and limits its credit exposure to any one issuer. The company classifies its marketable securities as available for sale and reports them on the balance sheet at fair value. Unrealized gains and losses are reported in other comprehensive income.

5 NON-CURRENT LIABILITIES

☐ explain the financial reporting and disclosures related to non-current liabilities

All liabilities that are not classified as current are considered to be non-current or long-term. Exhibit 8 and Exhibit 9 present balance sheet excerpts for SAP Group and Apple Inc. showing the line items for the companies' non-current liabilities.

Both companies' balance sheets show non-current unearned revenue (deferred income for SAP Group and deferred revenue for Apple). These amounts represent unearned revenue relating to goods and services expected to be delivered in periods beyond 12 months following the reporting period. The sections that follow focus on two common types of non-current (long-term) liabilities: long-term financial liabilities and deferred tax liabilities.

Exhibit 8: SAP Group Consolidated Statements of Financial Position (Excerpt: Non-Current Liabilities Detail) (in millions of euros)

	As of 31 December	
	2017	2016
Assets		
Total current assets	11,930	11,564
Total non-current assets	30,567	32,713

	As of 31 December	
	2017	2016
Total assets	42,497	44,277
Financial liabilities (current)	1,561	1,813
Total current liabilities	10,210	9,674
Trade and other payables	119	127
Tax liabilities	470	365
Financial liabilities	5,034	6,481
Other non-financial liabilities	503	461
Provisions	303	217
Deferred tax liabilities	240	411
Deferred income	79	143
Total non-current liabilities	6,747	8,205
Total liabilities	16,958	17,880
Total equity	25,540	26,397
Total equity and liabilities	EUR42,497	EUR44,277

Source: SAP Group 2017 annual report.

Exhibit 9: Apple Inc. Consolidated Balance Sheet (Excerpt: Non-Current Liabilities Detail)* (in millions of US dollars)

Assets	30 September 2017	24 September 2016
Total current assets	128,645	106,869
[All other assets]	*246,674*	*214,817*
Total assets	375,319	321,686
Liabilities and shareholders' equity		
Total current liabilities	100,814	79,006
Deferred revenue, non-current	2,836	2,930
Long-term debt	97,207	75,427
Other non-current liabilities	40,415	36,074
[Total non-current liabilities]	*140,458*	*114,431*
Total liabilities	241,272	193,437
Total shareholders' equity	134,047	128,249
Total liabilities and shareholders' equity	375,319	321,686

Note: The italicized subtotals presented in this excerpt are not explicitly shown on the face of the financial statement as prepared by the company.
Source: Apple Inc. 2017 annual report (Form 10K).

Long-Term Financial Liabilities

Typical long-term financial liabilities include loans (i.e., borrowings from banks) and notes or bonds payable (i.e., fixed-income securities issued to investors). Liabilities such as loans payable and bonds payable are usually reported at amortized cost on the balance sheet. At maturity, the amortized cost of the bond (carrying amount) will be equal to the face value of the bond. For example, if a company issues USD10,000,000 of bonds at par value, the bonds are reported as a long-term liability of USD10 million. The carrying amount (amortized cost) from the date of issue to the date of maturity remains at USD10 million. As another example, if a company issues USD10,000,000 of bonds at a price of 97.50 percent of par value (a discount to par), the bonds are reported as a liability of USD9,750,000 at issue date. Over the bond's life, the discount of USD250,000 is amortized so that the bond will be reported as a liability of USD10,000,000 at maturity. Similarly, any bond premium would be amortized for bonds issued at a price in excess of par value.

In certain cases, liabilities such as bonds issued by a company are reported at fair value. Those cases include financial liabilities held for trading, derivatives that are a liability to the company, and some non-derivative instruments, such as those which are hedged by derivatives.

SAP's balance sheet in Exhibit 8 shows EUR5,034 million in financial liabilities, and the notes disclose that these liabilities are mostly for bonds payable. Apple's balance sheet in Exhibit 9 shows USD97,207 million in long-term debt, and the notes disclose that this debt includes floating- and fixed-rate notes with varying maturities.

Deferred Tax Liabilities

Deferred tax liabilities result from temporary timing differences between a company's income as reported for tax purposes (taxable income) and income as reported for financial statement purposes (reported income). Deferred tax liabilities result when taxable income, and the actual income tax payable in a period based on it, is less than the reported financial statement income before taxes and the income tax expense based on it. Deferred tax liabilities are defined as the amounts of income taxes payable in future periods in respect of taxable temporary differences.[8] In contrast, in the previous discussion of unearned revenue, inclusion of revenue in taxable income in an earlier period created a deferred tax asset (essentially prepaid tax).

Deferred tax liabilities typically arise when some expenses are included in taxable income in earlier periods than for financial statement net income. This results in taxable income being less than income before taxes in the earlier periods. As a result, taxes payable based on taxable income are less than income tax expense based on accounting income before taxes. The difference between taxes payable and income tax expense results in a deferred tax liability—for example, when companies use accelerated depreciation methods for tax purposes and straight-line depreciation methods for financial statement purposes. Deferred tax liabilities also arise when some income is included in taxable income in later periods—for example, when a company's subsidiary has profits that have not yet been distributed and thus have not yet been taxed.

SAP's balance sheet in Exhibit 8 shows EUR240 million of deferred tax liabilities. Apple's balance sheet in Exhibit 9 does not show a separate line item for deferred tax liabilities; however, note disclosures indicate that most of the USD40,415 million of other non-current liabilities reported on Apple's balance sheet represents deferred tax liabilities, which totaled USD31,504 million.

Non-current liabilities will be explored in greater detail in a later learning module.

8 IAS 12, *Income Taxes*, paragraph 5.

RATIOS AND COMMON-SIZE ANALYSIS

6

☐ calculate and interpret common-size balance sheets and related financial ratios

Analysis of a company's balance sheet can provide insight into the company's liquidity and solvency—as of the balance sheet date—as well as the economic resources the company controls. **Liquidity** refers to a company's ability to meet its short-term financial commitments. Assessments of liquidity focus on a company's ability to convert assets to cash to pay for operating needs. **Solvency** refers to a company's ability to meet its financial obligations over the longer term. Assessments of solvency focus on the company's financial structure and its ability to pay long-term financing obligations. This lesson describes two tools for analyzing the balance sheet: common-size analysis and balance sheet ratios.

Common-Size Analysis of the Balance Sheet

The first technique, vertical common-size analysis, involves stating each balance sheet item as a percentage of total assets.[9] Common-size balance sheets are useful in comparing a company's balance sheet composition over time (time-series analysis) and across companies in the same industry. To illustrate, Panel A of Exhibit 10 presents balance sheets for three hypothetical companies. Company C, with assets of USD9.75 million is much larger than Company A and Company B, each with only USD3.25 million in assets. The common-size balance sheet presented in Panel B facilitates a comparison of these different-size companies.

Exhibit 10: Balance Sheets for Companies A, B, and C

Panel A: Balance Sheets

(in thousands of US dollars)	A	B	C
ASSETS			
Current assets			
Cash and cash equivalents	1,000	200	3,000
Short-term marketable securities	900	—	300
Accounts receivable	500	1,050	1,500
Inventory	100	950	300
Total current assets	2,500	2,200	5,100
Property, plant, and equipment, net	750	750	4,650
Intangible assets	—	200	—
Goodwill	—	100	—
Total assets	3,250	3,250	9,750
LIABILITIES AND SHAREHOLDERS' EQUITY			
Current liabilities			

9 Another type of common-size analysis, known as "horizontal common-size analysis," states quantities in terms of a selected base-year value. Unless otherwise indicated, text references to "common-size analysis" refer to vertical analysis.

Panel A: Balance Sheets

(in thousands of US dollars)	A	B	C
Accounts payable	—	2,500	600
Total current liabilities	—	2,500	600
Long-term bonds payable	10	10	9,000
Total liabilities	10	2,510	9,600
Total shareholders' equity	3,240	740	150
Total liabilities and shareholders' equity	3,250	3,250	9,750

Panel B: Common-Size Balance Sheets

(Percent)	A	B	C
ASSETS			
Current assets			
Cash and cash equivalents	30.8	6.2	30.8
Short-term marketable securities	27.7	0.0	3.1
Accounts receivable	15.4	32.3	15.4
Inventory	3.1	29.2	3.1
Total current assets	76.9	67.7	52.3
Property, plant, and equipment, net	23.1	23.1	47.7
Intangible assets	0.0	6.2	0.0
Goodwill	0.0	3.1	0.0
Total assets	100.0	100.0	100.0
LIABILITIES AND SHAREHOLDERS' EQUITY			
Current liabilities			
Accounts payable	0.0	76.9	6.2
Total current liabilities	0.0	76.9	6.2
Long-term bonds payable	0.3	0.3	92.3
Total liabilities	0.3	77.2	98.5
Total shareholders' equity	99.7	22.8	1.5
Total liabilities and shareholders' equity	100.0	100.0	100.0

Most of the assets of Company A and B are current assets; however, Company A has nearly 60 percent of its total assets in cash and short-term marketable securities, whereas Company B has only 6 percent of its assets in cash. Company A is more liquid than Company B. Company A shows no current liabilities (its current liabilities round to less than USD10,000), and it has cash on hand of USD1.0 million to meet any near-term financial obligations it might have. In contrast, Company B has USD2.5 million of current liabilities, which exceed its available cash of only USD200,000. To pay those near-term obligations, Company B will need to collect some of its accounts receivables, sell more inventory, borrow from a bank, or raise more long-term capital (e.g., by issuing more bonds or more equity). Company C also appears more liquid than Company B. It holds more than 30 percent of its total assets in cash and short-term marketable securities, and its current liabilities are only 6.2 percent of the amount of total assets.

Company C's USD3.3 million in cash and short-term marketable securities is substantially more than its current liabilities of USD600,000. Turning to the question of solvency, however, note that 98.5 percent of Company C's assets are financed with liabilities. If Company C experiences significant fluctuations in cash flows, it may be unable to pay the interest and principal on its long-term bonds. Company A is far more solvent than Company C, with less than 1 percent of its assets financed with liabilities.

These examples are hypothetical only. Other than general comparisons, little more can be said without further detail. In practice, a wide range of factors affect a company's liquidity management and capital structure. The study **capital structure** is a fundamental issue addressed in Corporate Issuers modules.

Common-size balance sheets can also highlight differences in companies' strategies. Comparing the asset composition of the companies, Company C has made a greater proportional investment in property, plant, and equipment (PP&E)—possibly because it manufactures more of its products in-house. The presence of goodwill on Company B's balance sheet signifies that it has made one or more acquisitions in the past. In contrast, the lack of goodwill on the balance sheets of Company A and Company C suggests that these two companies may have pursued a strategy of internal growth rather than growth by acquisition. Company A may be in either a start-up or liquidation stage of operations as evidenced by the composition of its balance sheet. It has relatively little inventory and no accounts payable. It either has not yet established trade credit or it is in the process of paying off its obligations in the process of liquidating.

COMMON-SIZE ANALYSIS

1. Based on the information presented in Exhibits 2, 6, and 8, which of the following items increased as a percentage of total assets from 2016 to 2017? (Note: More than one answer may be correct.)

   A. Total current assets

   B. Total financial liabilities

   C. Cash and cash equivalents

   Solution:

   A and C are correct.

   Total current assets increased from 26.1 percent of total assets in 2016 (EUR11,564 ÷ EUR44,277) to 28.1 percent in 2017 (EUR11,930 ÷ EUR42,497).

   Cash and cash equivalents increased from 8.4 percent of total assets in 2016 (EUR3,702 EUR44,277) to 9.4 percent in 2017 (EUR4,011 ÷ EUR42,497).

   Total financial liabilities decreased in 2017 both in absolute euro amounts (EUR5,034) and as a percentage of total assets (EUR5,034 ÷ EUR42,497 = 11.8%) when compared with 2016 (EUR6,481 ÷ EUR44,277 = 14.6%).

   Overall, aspects of the company's liquidity position are somewhat stronger in 2017 than in 2016. The company's cash balances as a percentage of total assets increased. While current liabilities increased as a percentage of total assets and total liabilities remained approximately the same percentage, the mix of liabilities shifted. Financial liabilities, which represent future cash outlays, decreased as a percentage of total assets.

Common-size analysis of the balance sheet is particularly useful in cross-sectional analysis—comparing companies to each other for a particular time period or comparing a company with industry or sector data. The analyst could select individual peer companies for comparison, use industry data from published sources, or compile data from databases. When analyzing a company, many analysts prefer to select the peer companies for comparison or to compile their own industry statistics.

Exhibit 11 presents common-size balance sheet data compiled for the 10 sectors of the S&P 500 using 2017 data. The sector classification follows the S&P/MSCI Global Industrial Classification System (GICS). The exhibit presents mean and median common-size balance sheet data for those companies in the S&P 500 for which 2017 data was available in the Compustat database.[10]

Some interesting general observations can be made from these data:

- Energy and utility companies have the largest amounts of PP&E. Telecommunication services, followed by utilities, have the highest level of long-term debt. Utilities also use some preferred stock.
- Financial companies have the greatest percentage of total liabilities. Financial companies typically have relatively high financial leverage.
- Utility and real estate companies have the lowest level of receivables.
- Inventory levels are highest for consumer discretionary. Materials and consumer staples have the next highest inventories.
- Information technology companies use the least amount of leverage as evidenced by the lowest percentages for long-term debt and total liabilities and highest percentages for common and total equity.

Example 1 discusses an analyst using cross-sectional common-size balance sheet data.

EXAMPLE 1

Cross-Sectional Common-Size Analysis

Jason Lu is comparing two companies in the computer industry to evaluate their relative financial position as reflected on their balance sheets. He has compiled the following vertical common-size data for Apple and Microsoft, which is presented in Exhibit 12.

Exhibit 12: Cross-Sectional Analysis: Consolidated Balance Sheets (as percent of total assets)

	Apple	Microsoft
ASSETS:	**30 September 2017**	**30 June 2017**
Current assets:		
Cash and cash equivalents	5.4	3.2
Short-term marketable securities	14.4	52.0
Accounts receivable	4.8	8.2
Inventories	1.3	0.9
Vendor non-trade receivables	4.7	0.0
Other current assets	3.7	2.0
Total current assets	34.3	66.3
Long-term marketable securities	51.9	2.5

10 An entry of zero for an item (e.g., current assets) was excluded from the data, except in the case of preferred stock. Note that most financial institutions did not provide current asset or current liability data, so these are reported as not available in the database.

Exhibit 11: Common-Size Balance Sheet Statistics for the S&P 500 Grouped by S&P/MSCI GICS Sector, 2017 (in percent except for No. of Observations)

Panel A. Median Data											
	10	15	20	25	30	35	40	45	50	55	60
	Energy	Materials	Industrials	Consumer Discretionary	Consumer Staples	Health Care	Financials	Information Technology	Telecommunication Services	Utilities	Real Estate
Number of observation	34	27	68	81	33	59	64	64	4	29	30
Cash and short-term investments	6.8%	6.3%	8.1%	8.3%	4.1%	11.2%	6.2%	22.7%	1.2%	0.7%	1.4%
Receivables	5.8%	8.8%	12.9%	6.8%	6.5%	9.7%	20.4%	9.6%	3.7%	3.6%	2.0%
Inventories	1.6%	8.9%	6.9%	14.9%	9.6%	4.3%	0.0%	1.3%	0.3%	1.7%	0.0%
Total current assets	16.1%	26.0%	30.5%	41.5%	29.1%	31.4%	N.A.	48.7%	8.6%	7.3%	10.8%
PP&E	73.3%	36.3%	12.5%	19.8%	17.2%	8.1%	0.9%	6.2%	35.0%	72.0%	33.4%
Intangibles	1.6%	27.9%	33.3%	16.8%	41.9%	37.6%	2.8%	26.4%	49.6%	6.2%	1.0%
Goodwill	*0.7%*	*20.0%*	*28.3%*	*11.3%*	*26.2%*	*22.8%*	*2.2%*	*22.3%*	*26.0%*	*4.8%*	*0.0%*
Accounts payable	5.7%	7.3%	6.2%	8.0%	8.0%	3.1%	27.0%	2.7%	2.5%	3.0%	1.3%
Current liabilities	10.9%	16.5%	22.5%	25.8%	25.0%	16.5%	N.A.	21.2%	11.5%	11.5%	7.1%
Long-term debt	27.3%	31.4%	28.0%	28.7%	32.3%	24.3%	6.4%	22.9%	46.8%	32.5%	43.4%
Total liabilities	49.3%	64.2%	65.5%	64.9%	63.8%	59.2%	86.7%	59.9%	75.8%	71.8%	53.3%
Common equity	47.3%	33.8%	34.5%	34.7%	36.2%	39.4%	12.6%	39.3%	23.9%	27.7%	40.4%
Preferred stock	0.0%	0.0%	0.0%	0.0%	0.0%	0.0%	0.0%	0.0%	0.0%	0.0%	0.0%
Total equity	47.3%	33.8%	34.5%	34.7%	36.2%	39.4%	13.2%	39.3%	23.9%	28.0%	41.8%

(Continued from previous Exhibit)

Panel B. Mean Data (Continued from Previous Example)

	10	15	20	25	30	35	40	45	50	55	60
	Energy	Materials	Industrials	Consumer Discretionary	Consumer Staples	Health Care	Financials	Information Technology	Telecommunication Services	Utilities	Real Estate
Number of observations	34	27	68	81	33	59	64	64	4	29	30
Cash and short-term investments	6.9%	7.4%	9.2%	12.9%	7.3%	15.4%	11.2%	28.3%	3.6%	1.3%	2.9%
Receivables	6.6%	10.5%	15.2%	9.0%	7.7%	11.2%	31.5%	11.8%	5.0%	3.8%	3.8%
Inventories	3.4%	9.3%	7.8%	18.3%	10.6%	6.3%	3.8%	4.1%	0.3%	1.6%	0.1%
Total current assets	17.7%	28.8%	32.9%	40.6%	27.8%	36.4%	N.A.	49.4%	10.1%	8.6%	16.1%
PP&E	68.0%	36.9%	24.5%	25.1%	21.6%	11.2%	2.1%	10.3%	39.0%	69.9%	34.9%
Intangibles	7.8%	26.6%	35.6%	23.0%	43.6%	43.9%	11.4%	31.1%	48.2%	6.8%	10.3%
Goodwill	5.4%	18.4%	26.8%	14.6%	24.6%	27.3%	7.7%	24.5%	25.9%	5.7%	5.7%
Accounts payable	5.9%	8.1%	7.1%	11.8%	9.8%	8.1%	35.9%	5.1%	3.1%	2.9%	2.0%
Current liabilities	11.8%	17.0%	23.0%	26.8%	24.6%	21.2%	N.A.	26.1%	11.9%	11.8%	12.8%
Long-term debt	28.3%	31.2%	29.4%	31.3%	32.4%	28.5%	10.3%	24.8%	47.5%	35.0%	44.8%
Total liabilities	50.3%	63.4%	67.1%	67.5%	68.3%	60.1%	80.1%	61.8%	77.6%	73.9%	54.5%
Common equity	46.4%	34.2%	32.3%	32.3%	30.9%	38.9%	18.2%	37.5%	22.2%	24.7%	40.2%
Preferred stock	0.0%	0.0%	0.1%	0.0%	0.0%	0.1%	0.4%	0.3%	0.0%	0.3%	2.2%
Total equity	46.4%	34.2%	32.4%	32.3%	30.9%	39.0%	18.5%	37.8%	22.2%	25.0%	42.3%

PPE = Property, plant, and equipment, LT = Long term.
Source: Based on data from Compustat.

	Apple	Microsoft
ASSETS:	**30 September 2017**	**30 June 2017**
Property, plant, and equipment, net	9.0	9.8
Goodwill	1.5	14.6
Acquired intangible assets, net	0.6	4.2
Other assets	2.7	2.6
Total assets	100.0	100.0
LIABILITIES AND SHAREHOLDERS' EQUITY:		
Current liabilities:		
Accounts payable	13.1	3.1
Short-term debt	3.2	3.8
Current portion of long-term debt	1.7	0.4
Accrued expenses	6.9	2.7
Deferred revenue	2.0	14.1
Other current liabilities	0.0	2.6
Total current liabilities	26.9	26.8
Long-term debt	25.9	31.6
Deferred revenue non-current	0.8	4.3
Other non-current liabilities	10.8	7.3
Total liabilities	64.3	70.0
Commitments and contingencies		
Total shareholders' equity	35.7	30.0
Total liabilities and shareholders' equity	100.0	100.0

Source: Based on data from companies' annual reports.

From these data, Lu learns the following:

- Apple and Microsoft have high levels of cash and short-term marketable securities, consistent with the information technology sector as reported in Exhibit 11. Apple also has a high balance in long-term marketable securities. This may reflect the success of the company's business model, which has generated large operating cash flows in recent years.
- Apple's level of accounts receivable is lower than Microsoft's and lower than the industry average. Further research is necessary to learn the extent to which this is related to Apple's cash sales through its own retail stores. An alternative explanation would be that the company has been selling or factoring receivables to a greater degree than the other companies; however, that explanation is unlikely given Apple's cash position. Additionally, Apple shows vendor non-trade receivables, reflecting arrangements with its contract manufacturers.
- Apple and Microsoft both have low levels of inventory, similar to industry medians as reported in Exhibit 11. Apple uses contract manufacturers and can rely on suppliers to hold inventory until needed. Additionally, in the Management Discussion and Analysis section of their annual report, Apple discloses USD38 billion of noncancelable manufacturing purchase obligations, USD33 billion of which is due within 12 months. These amounts are not currently

recorded as inventory and reflect the use of contract manufacturers to assemble and test some finished products. The use of purchase commitments and contract manufacturers implies that inventory may be "understated." Microsoft's low level of inventory is consistent with its business mix, which is more heavily weighted to software than to hardware.

- Apple and Microsoft have a level of PP&E that is relatively close to the sector median, as reported in Exhibit 11.
- Apple has a very low amount of goodwill, reflecting its strategy to grow organically rather than through acquisition. Microsoft's level of goodwill, while higher than Apple's, is lower than the industry median and mean. Microsoft made a number of major acquisitions (e.g., Nokia in 2014), but subsequently (in 2015) it wrote off significant amounts of goodwill as an impairment charge.
- Apple's level of accounts payable is higher than the computer industry average, but given the company's high level of cash and investments, it is unlikely that this is a problem.
- Apple's and Microsoft's levels of long-term debt are slightly higher than industry averages. Again, given the companies' high level of cash and investments, it is unlikely that this is a problem.

Balance Sheet Ratios

Ratios facilitate time-series and cross-sectional analysis of a company's financial position. **Balance sheet ratios** are those involving balance sheet items only. Each of the line items on a vertical common-size balance sheet is a ratio in that it expresses a balance sheet amount in relation to total assets. Other balance sheet ratios compare one balance sheet item to another. For example, the current ratio expresses current assets in relation to current liabilities as an indicator of a company's liquidity. Balance sheet ratios include **liquidity ratios** (measuring the company's ability to meet its short-term obligations) and **solvency ratios** (measuring the company's ability to meet long-term and other obligations). These ratios and others are discussed in a later reading. Exhibit 13 summarizes the calculation and interpretation of selected balance sheet ratios.

Exhibit 13: Balance Sheet Ratios

Liquidity Ratios	Calculation	Indicates
Current	Current assets ÷ Current liabilities	Ability to meet current liabilities
Quick (acid test)	(Cash + Marketable securities + Receivables) ÷ Current liabilities	Ability to meet current liabilities
Cash	(Cash + Marketable securities) ÷ Current liabilities	Ability to meet current liabilities
Solvency Ratios		
Long-term debt-to-equity	Total long-term debt ÷ Total equity	Financial risk and financial leverage
Debt-to-equity	Total debt ÷ Total equity	Financial risk and financial leverage

Liquidity Ratios	Calculation	Indicates
Total debt	Total debt ÷ Total assets	Financial risk and financial leverage
Financial leverage	Total assets ÷ Total equity	Financial risk and financial leverage

RATIO ANALYSIS

1. Based on its balance sheet presented earlier, the current ratio for SAP Group at 31 December 2017 is *closest* to:

   A. 1.17.

   B. 1.20.

   C. 2.00.

   Solution:

   A is correct. SAP Group's current ratio (Current assets ÷ Current liabilities) at 31 December 2017 is 1.17 (EUR11,930 million ÷ EUR10,210 million).

2. Based on SAP's balance sheets presented earlier, which of the following liquidity ratios decreased in 2017 relative to 2016? (Note: More than one answer may be correct.)

   A. Cash

   B. Quick

   C. Current

   Solution:

   B and C are correct. The ratios are shown in the table below. The quick ratio and current ratio are lower in 2017 than in 2016. The cash ratio is slightly higher in 2017 than in 2016.

Liquidity Ratios	Calculation	2017 EUR in millions	2016 EUR in millions
Current	Current assets ÷ Current liabilities	EUR11,930 ÷ EUR10,210 = **1.17**	EUR11,564 ÷ EUR9,674 = **1.20**
Quick (acid test)*	(Cash + Marketable securities + Receivables) ÷ Current liabilities	(EUR4,011 + EUR990 + EUR5,899) ÷ EUR10,210 = **1.07**	(EUR3,702 + EUR1,124 + EUR5,924) ÷ EUR9,674 = **1.11**
Cash*	(Cash + Marketable securities) ÷ Current liabilities	(EUR4,011 + EUR990 ÷ EUR10,210 = **0.49**	(EUR3,702 + EUR1,124 ÷ EUR9,674 = **0.50**

* *Marketable securities is assumed to be equal to Other Financial Assets as shown in Exhibit 6.*

3. Based on SAP's balance sheets presented earlier, which of the following leverage ratios decreased in 2017 relative to 2016? (Note: more than one answer may be correct.)

   A. Debt-to-equity.

   B. Financial leverage.

C. Long-term debt-to-equity.

Solution:

A, B, and C are correct. All three leverage ratios decreased in 2017 relative to 2016.

Solvency Ratios

Long-term debt-to-equity	Total long-term debt ÷ Total equity	EUR5,034 ÷ EUR25,540 = **19.7%**	EUR6,481 ÷ EUR26,397 = **24.6%**
Debt-to-equity	Total debt ÷ Total equity	(EUR1,561 + EUR5,034) ÷ EUR25,540 = **25.8%**	(EUR 1,813 + EUR6,481) ÷ EUR26,397 = **31.4%**
Financial Leverage	Total assets ÷ Total equity	EUR42,497 ÷ EUR25,540 = **1.66**	EUR44,277 ÷ EUR26,397 = **1.68**

Cross-sectional financial ratio analysis can be limited by differences in accounting methods. In addition, lack of homogeneity of a company's operating activities can limit comparability. For diversified companies operating in different industries, using industry-specific ratios for different lines of business can provide better comparisons. Companies disclose information on operating segments. The financial position and performance of the operating segments can be compared to the relevant industry.

Ratio analysis requires a significant amount of judgment. One key area requiring judgment is understanding the limitations of any ratio. The current ratio, for example, is only a rough measure of liquidity at a specific point in time. The ratio captures only the amount of current assets, but the components of current assets differ significantly in their nearness to cash (e.g., marketable securities versus inventory). Another limitation of the current ratio is its sensitivity to end-of-period financing and operating decisions that potentially can affect current asset and current liability amounts. Another overall area requiring judgment is determining whether a ratio for a company is within a reasonable range for an industry. Yet another area requiring judgment is evaluating whether a ratio signifies a persistent condition or reflects only a temporary condition. Overall, evaluating specific ratios requires an examination of the entire operations of a company, its competitors, and the external economic and industry setting in which it is operating.

PRACTICE PROBLEMS

1. All of the following are current assets *except*:

   A. cash.

   B. goodwill.

   C. inventories.

2. The initial measurement of goodwill is *most likely* affected by:

   A. an acquisition's purchase price.

   B. the acquired company's book value.

   C. the fair value of the acquirer's assets and liabilities.

3. For financial assets classified as trading securities, how are unrealized gains and losses reflected in shareholders' equity?

   A. They are not recognized.

   B. They flow through income into retained earnings.

   C. They are a component of accumulated other comprehensive income.

4. For financial assets classified as available for sale, how are unrealized gains and losses reflected in shareholders' equity?

   A. They are not recognized.

   B. They flow through retained earnings.

   C. They are a component of accumulated other comprehensive income.

5. For financial assets classified as held to maturity, how are unrealized gains and losses reflected in shareholders' equity?

   A. They are not recognized.

   B. They flow through retained earnings.

   C. They are a component of accumulated other comprehensive income.

6. A company has total liabilities of GBP35 million and total stockholders' equity of GBP55 million. Total liabilities are represented on a vertical common-size balance sheet by a percentage *closest* to:

   A. 35 percent.

   B. 39 percent.

   C. 64 percent.

7. Which of the following would an analyst *most likely* be able to determine from a common-size analysis of a company's balance sheet over several periods?

   A. An increase or decrease in sales

B. An increase or decrease in financial leverage

C. A more efficient or less efficient use of assets

8. Defining total asset turnover as revenue divided by average total assets, all else equal, impairment write-downs of long-lived assets owned by a company will *most likely* result in an increase for that company in:

   A. the debt-to-equity ratio but not the total asset turnover.

   B. the total asset turnover but not the debt-to-equity ratio.

   C. both the debt-to-equity ratio and the total asset turnover.

9. An investor concerned about a company's ability to meet its near-term obligations is *most likely* to calculate the:

   A. current ratio.

   B. return on total capital.

   C. financial leverage ratio.

10. The most stringent test of a company's liquidity is its:

    A. cash ratio.

    B. quick ratio.

    C. current ratio.

11. An investor worried about a company's long-term solvency would *most likely* examine its:

    A. current ratio.

    B. return on equity.

    C. debt-to-equity ratio.

The following information relates to questions 12-15

Consider the common-size balance sheets in Exhibit 1 for Company A, Company B, as well as the industry average.

Exhibit 1: Balance Sheet and Industry Average

	Company A	Company B	Industry Average
ASSETS			
Current assets			
Cash and cash equivalents	5	5	7

	Company A	Company B	Industry Average
Marketable securities	5	0	2
Accounts receivable, net	5	15	12
Inventories	15	20	16
Prepaid expenses	5	15	11
Total current assets	35	55	48
Property, plant, and equipment, net	40	35	37
Goodwill	25	0	8
Other assets	0	10	7
Total assets	100	100	100
LIABILITIES AND SHAREHOLDERS' EQUITY			
Current liabilities			
Accounts payable	10	10	10
Short-term debt	25	10	15
Accrued expenses	0	5	3
Total current liabilities	35	25	28
Long-term debt	45	20	28
Other non-current liabilities	0	10	7
Total liabilities	80	55	63
Total shareholders' equity	20	45	37
Total liabilities and shareholders' equity	100	100	100

12. Which statement is correct?

    A. Company A has below-average liquidity risk.

    B. Company B has above-average solvency risk.

    C. Company A has made one or more acquisitions.

13. The quick ratio for Company A is *closest* to:

    A. 0.43.

    B. 0.57.

    C. 1.00.

14. The financial leverage ratio for Company B is *closest* to:

    A. 0.55.

    B. 1.22.

    C. 2.22.

15. Which ratio indicates lower liquidity risk for Company A compared with Company B?

    A. Cash ratio

B. Quick ratio

C. Current ratio

SOLUTIONS

1. B is correct. Goodwill is a long-term asset, and cash and inventories are current assets.

2. A is correct. Initially, goodwill is measured as the difference between the purchase price paid for an acquisition and the fair value of the acquired, not acquiring, company's net assets (identifiable assets less liabilities).

3. B is correct. For financial assets classified as trading securities, unrealized gains and losses are reported on the income statement and flow to shareholders' equity as part of retained earnings.

4. C is correct. For financial assets classified as available for sale, unrealized gains and losses are not recorded on the income statement and instead are part of *other* comprehensive income. Accumulated other comprehensive income is a component of shareholders' equity.

5. A is correct. Financial assets classified as held to maturity are measured at amortized cost. Gains and losses are recognized only when realized.

6. B is correct. Vertical common-size analysis involves stating each balance sheet item as a percentage of total assets. Total assets are the sum of total liabilities (GBP35 million) and total stockholders' equity (GBP55 million), or GBP90 million. Total liabilities are shown on a vertical common-size balance sheet as (GBP35 million ÷ GBP90 million) ≈ 39%.

7. B is correct. A common-size balance sheet analysis provides information about the composition of the balance sheet and it changes over time. As a result, it can provide information about an increase or decrease in a company's financial leverage.

8. C is correct. Impairment write-downs reduce equity in the denominator of the debt-to-equity ratio but do not affect debt, so the debt-to-equity ratio is expected to increase. Impairment write-downs reduce total assets but do not affect revenue. Thus, total asset turnover is expected to increase.

9. A is correct. The current ratio provides a comparison of assets that can be turned into cash relatively quickly and liabilities that must be paid within one year. The other ratios are more suited to evaluate longer-term concerns.

10. A is correct. The cash ratio determines how much of a company's near-term obligations can be settled with existing amounts of cash and marketable securities.

11. C is correct. The debt-to-equity ratio, a solvency ratio, is an indicator of financial risk.

12. C is correct. The presence of goodwill on Company A's balance sheet signifies that it has made one or more acquisitions in the past. The current, cash, and quick ratios are lower for Company A than for the sector average. These lower liquidity ratios imply above-average liquidity risk. The total debt, long-term debt-to-equity, debt-to-equity, and financial leverage ratios are lower for Company B than for the sector average. These lower solvency ratios imply below-average solvency risk.

    Current ratio is (35 ÷ 35) = 1.00 for Company A, versus (48 ÷ 28)

= 1.71 for the sector average.

Cash ratio is (5 + 5) ÷35 = 0.29 for Company A, versus (7 + 2) ÷28
= 0.32 for the sector average.

Quick ratio is (5 + 5 + 5) ÷35 = 0.43 for Company A, versus (7 + 2 + 12) ÷28
= 0.75 for the sector average.

Total debt ratio is (55 ÷ 100) = 0.55 for Company B, versus (63 ÷ 100)
= 0.63 for the sector average.

Long-term debt-to-equity ratio is (20 ÷ 45) = 0.44 for Company B, versus (28 ÷ 37)
= 0.76 for the sector average.

Debt-to-equity ratio is (55 ÷ 45) = 1.22 for Company B, versus (63 ÷ 37)
= 1.70 for the sector average.

Financial leverage ratio is (100 ÷ 45) = 2.22 for Company B, versus (100 ÷ 37)
= 2.70 for the sector average.

13. A is correct. The quick ratio is defined as (Cash and cash equivalents + Marketable securities + receivables) ÷ Current liabilities. For Company A, this calculation is (5 + 5 + 5) ÷ 35 = 0.43.

14. C is correct. The financial leverage ratio is defined as Total assets ÷ Total equity. For Company B, total assets are 100 and total equity is 45; hence, the financial leverage ratio is 100 ÷ 45 = 2.22.

15. A is correct. A higher cash ratio reflects lower liquidity risk. The cash ratio is defined as (Cash + Marketable securities) ÷ Current liabilities. Company A's cash ratio, (5 + 5) ÷ 35 = 0.29, is higher than (5 + 0) ÷ 25 = 0.20 for Company B.

LEARNING MODULE

4

Analyzing Statements of Cash Flows I

by Elaine Henry, PhD, CFA, Thomas R Robinson, PhD, CFA, CAIA, J. Hennie van Greuning, DCom, CFA, and Michael A Broihahn, CPA, CIA, CFA.

Elaine Henry, PhD, CFA, is at Stevens Institute of Technology (USA). Thomas R. Robinson, PhD, CFA, CAIA, Robinson Global Investment Management LLC, (USA). J. Hennie van Greuning, DCom, CFA, is at BIBD (Brunei). Michael A. Broihahn, CPA, CIA, CFA, is at Barry University (USA).

LEARNING OUTCOMES

Mastery	*The candidate should be able to:*
☐	describe how the cash flow statement is linked to the income statement and the balance sheet
☐	describe the steps in the preparation of direct and indirect cash flow statements, including how cash flows can be computed using income statement and balance sheet data
☐	demonstrate the conversion of cash flows from the indirect to direct method
☐	contrast cash flow statements prepared under International Financial Reporting Standards (IFRS) and US generally accepted accounting principles (US GAAP)

The two major accounting standard setters are as follows: 1) the International Accounting Standards Board (IASB) who establishes International Financial Reporting Standards (IFRS) and 2) the Financial Accounting Standards Board (FASB) who establishes US GAAP. Throughout this learning module both standards are referred to and many, but not all, of these two sets of accounting rules are identified. Note: changes in accounting standards as well as new rulings and/or pronouncements issued after the publication of this learning module may cause some of the information to become dated.

1 INTRODUCTION

The statement of cash flows provides important information about a company's cash receipts and cash payments during an accounting period, reconciling the cash accounts between balance sheet dates. Although the income statement provides similar measures on an accrual basis, cash flows and their timing are crucial to valuation as payments to investors are made in cash. Investors also use statement of cash flows to evaluate the company's liquidity, solvency, and financial flexibility. In this module, we discuss the components of the cash flow statement and its links to the other financial statements.

LEARNING MODULE OVERVIEW

- Understanding the interrelationships among the balance sheet, income statement, and cash flow statement is useful not only in evaluating the company's financial health but also in detecting accounting irregularities.
- The income statement and statement of cash flows provide key linkages between the current assets and current liabilities sections of the balance sheet.
- Companies can use either the direct or the indirect method for reporting their operating cash flow:
- The direct method discloses operating cash inflows by source (e.g., cash received from customers, cash received from investment income) and operating cash outflows by use (e.g., cash paid to suppliers, cash paid for interest) in the operating activities section of the cash flow statement.
- The indirect method reconciles net income to operating cash flow by adjusting net income for all non-cash items and the net changes in working capital accounts.
- Although the indirect method is most common, an analyst may desire to review direct-format operating cash flow to review trends in cash receipts and payments, such as cash received from customers or cash paid to suppliers.
- Cash flows from operating activities reported under the indirect method can generally be converted to an approximation of the direct format by following a simple three-step process.
- Cash flows from investing activities and from financing activities are both reported using a direct method, regardless of the method used for reporting operating cash flows.
- Compared with US GAAP, the International Financial Reporting Standards (IFRS) allow more flexibility in the classification of items as operating, investing, or financing activities, such as interest paid or received and dividends paid or received and in how income tax expense is classified.

LINKAGES BETWEEN THE FINANCIAL STATEMENTS 2

- [ ] describe how the cash flow statement is linked to the income statement and the balance sheet

Primary Financial Statements

Recall that the four primary financial statements are interrelated and each provides specific information to analysts about an entity. The primary financial statements are as follows:

1. Balance Sheet—shows the financial position of an entity *at a point in time*, reporting the balances of "permanent" or "stock" accounts showing the entity's assets and how those assets are financed.
2. Income Statement—provides information about a company's financial performance between balance sheet dates. The income statement is made up of revenue, expense, gain, and loss accounts. In contrast to the balance sheet, the income statement is a "flow" statement as it captures income activity between two balance sheet dates. Income statements prepared under IFRS or US GAAP are based on accrual accounting, so they do not necessarily reflect cash inflows and outflows.
3. Statement of Cash Flows—reports the change in an entity's cash, cash equivalents, and restricted cash between balance sheet dates. The statement classifies cash inflows and outflows during the period as operating, investing, or financing activities. Because the cash flow statement reports performance over a period of time, it is also a "flow" statement, like the income statement.
4. Statement of Shareholder's Equity—provides information about how a company's equity has changed between balance sheet dates. The statement identifies the significant components of shareholders equity that are reported on the balance sheet (e.g., common stock and retained earnings) and the activities that occurred during the period that impacted these accounts (e.g., share issuance, net income or loss). Like the income statement and statement of cash flows, the statement of shareholders equity is also a "flow" statement.

Relationship between Financial Statements

As illustrated in Exhibit 1, the income statement, cash flow statement and statement of shareholders' equity link the balance sheet from one period to the next.

Exhibit 1: Relationship between the Financial Statements

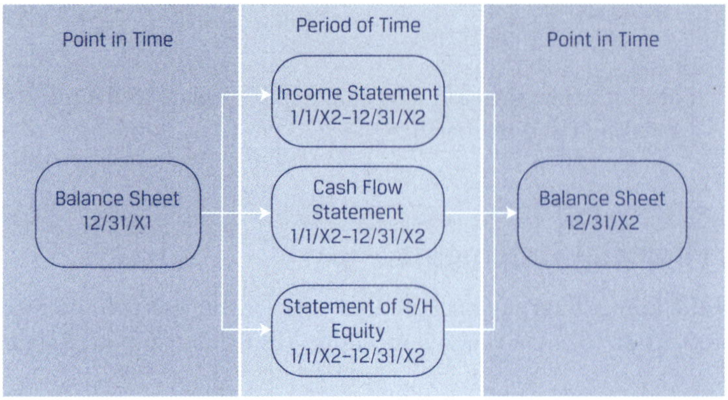

For example, the beginning and ending balances of cash are shown on the company's 20X1 and 20X2 balance sheets, and the bottom of the 20X2 cash flow statement reconciles 20X1 cash to 20X2 cash. The relationship, stated in general terms, is as shown in Exhibit 2.

Exhibit 2: Beginning and Ending Balances

Balance Sheet at 31 December 20X1	Statement of Cash Flows for Year Ended 31 December 20X2		Balance Sheet at 31 December 20X2
Beginning cash (as of Year-end 31 December 20x1)	Plus: Cash inflows (from operating, investing, and financing activities)	Less: Cash outflows (for operating, investing, and financing activities)	**Ending cash (as of Year-end 31 December 20x2)**

Exhibit 3 adds greater detail to Exhibit 1, tracing specific linkages through the four financial statements.

Exhibit 3: Interaction of Financial Statement Accounts

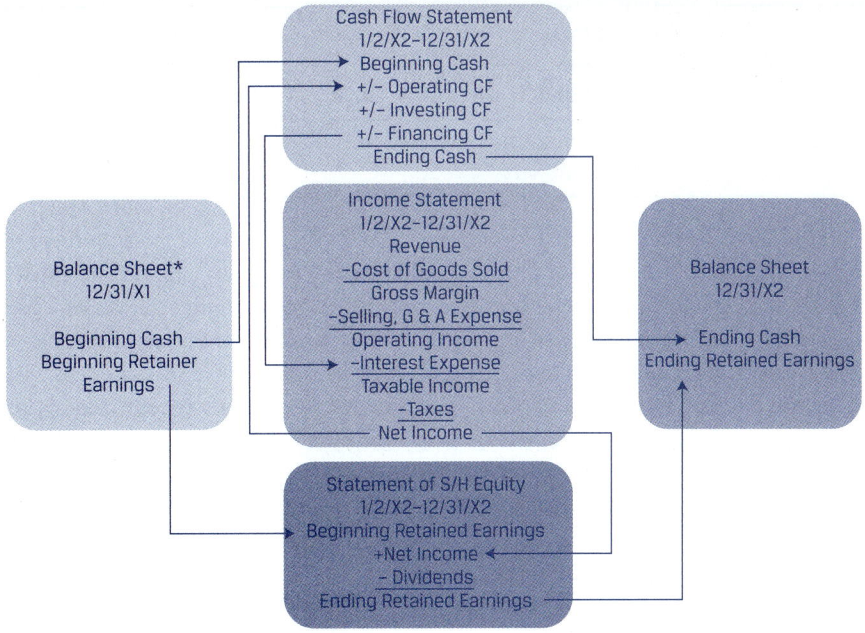

For example, the 20X2 statement of shareholders' equity reconciles the equity accounts reported on 20X1 balance sheet to the equity accounts reported on the 20X2 balance sheet, including additions (or subtractions) resulting from net income or loss reported on the income statement and dividends paid that are also reported on the statement of cash flows if made in cash.

Linkages Between Current Assets and Current Liabilities

The income statement and statement of cash flows also provide key linkages between the current assets and current liabilities sections of the balance sheet. Differences between the accrual and cash accounting recognition of operating activities result in an increase or decrease in a current asset or liability on the balance sheet. For example, accrual basis revenue in excess of cash collections will be accompanied by an increase in accounts receivable. If expenses reported using accrual accounting are lower than cash actually paid, the result will typically be a decrease in accounts payable or another accrued liability account. Finally, in situations in which a company is paid in advance for the delivery of a service or product in the future, it will recognize the cash received as an asset, but it also must recognize a liability for its obligation to deliver service or product in the future, typically referred to as deferred revenue. A deferred revenue liability account is derecognized upon the recognition of revenue when the entity satisfies its performance obligations.

If an analyst knows beginning accounts receivable, revenues, and cash collected from customers, they can compute ending accounts receivable, as the accounts are linked as shown in Exhibit 4.

Exhibit 4: Ending Accounts Receivable

Beginning Balance Sheet at 31 December 20X1	Income Statement for Year Ended 31 December 20X2	Statement of Cash Flows for Year Ended 31 December 20X2	Ending Balance Sheet at 31 December 20X2
Beginning accounts receivable	Plus: Revenues	Minus: Cash collected from customers	Equals: Ending accounts receivable

Understanding the interrelationships among the balance sheet, income statement, and cash flow statement is useful not only in evaluating the company's financial health but also in detecting accounting irregularities. Recall the extreme illustration of a hypothetical company that makes sales on account without regard to future collections and thus reports healthy sales and significant income on its income statement yet lacks cash inflow. Such a pattern would occur if a company improperly recognized revenue.

Example 1–Example 4 demonstrate how common business transactions affect a company's balance sheet, income statement, and statement of cash flows. Notice how all three financial statements are needed to fully account for the transactions.

EXAMPLE 1

Inventory Purchase and Sale Impact on Financial Statements

Assume fictional company ABC, a retailer, purchases USD100 of inventory on 1 January 1, 20X1 on credit with payment due to its supplier in 30 days. On 1 February, ABC sells the product to Customer X for USD150 with payment due by 16 February, 20X1. Customer X pays for the product on 15 February, 20X1.

This series of transaction would affect ABC's financial statements as follows shown in Exhibit 5.

Exhibit 5: ABC's Financial Statements

Date	Balance Sheet	Income Statement	Statement of Cash Flows
1 January	Inventory (asset) increases by USD100 Accounts Payable (liability) increases by USD100	N/A	N/A
30 January	Cash (asset) decreases by USD100 Accounts Payable (liability) decreases by USD100	N/A	Cash flows from operating activities decreases by USD100
1 February	Accounts Receivable (asset) increases by USD150 Inventory (asset) decreases by USD100	Revenue increases by USD150 Cost of sales increases by USD100	N/A
15 February	Cash (asset) increases by USD150 Accounts receivable (asset) decreases by USD150		Cash flows from operating activities increases by USD150

Note the statement of cash flows is affected only when the company pays or receives cash, which differs from recognition on the income statement.

EXAMPLE 2

Depreciation Impact on Financial Statements

On 1 January, fictional company Notion Ltd, a manufacturing company, owns USD100 of equipment used in the production of a product that is sold to wholesale customers. The equipment has a 10-year life and no salvage value. Notion uses straight-line depreciation, so the annual depreciation expense is USD10. On 1 July, Notion Ltd. makes a new capital investment for a different piece of equipment with a purchase price of USD200 and annual depreciation expense of USD50. Notion Ltd. pays for the equipment in cash upon receipt. Depreciation expense is recorded at the end of the fiscal year. The impact on Notion Ltd.'s financial statements is summarized in Exhibit 6.

Exhibit 6: Notion Ltd. Financial Statement

Date	Balance Sheet	Income Statement	Statement of Cash Flows
1 January	Equipment (asset) of USD100	N/A	N/A
1 July	Equipment (asset) increases by USD200 Cash (asset) decreases by USD200	N/A	Cash flows from investing activities decreases by USD200
31 December	Accumulated Depreciation (contra asset) increases by USD35	Depreciation expense increases by USD35	N/A

EXAMPLE 3

Borrowing Impact on Financial Statements

On 31 March, fictional Geneva Company borrows USD500 from Stockholm Bank (also fictional). The terms of the loan are interest accrues at 10 percent and payment is due along with principal upon maturity of the loan on 30 September. Accordingly, Geneva is to pay USD525 to Stockholm Bank on 30 September consisting of USD500 in loan principal and USD25 of interest (USD500 loan × 10% × ½ year.) The impact on Geneva's financial statements is summarized in Exhibit 7.

Exhibit 7: Geneva Financial Statement

Date	Balance Sheet	Income Statement	Statement of Cash Flows
31 March	Cash (asset) increases by USD500 Loans payable (liability) increases by USD500	N/A	Cash flows from financing activities increases by USD500
30 September	Cash (asset) decreases by USD525 Loans payable (liability) decreases by USD500	Interest expense increases by USD25	Cash flows from financing or operating activities decreases by USD25 Cash flows from financing activities decreases by USD500

EXAMPLE 4

Equipment Purchase Impact on Financial Statements

Assume Mountain Company, a fictional manufacturer, agrees to produce a custom-made piece of equipment for Cirrus Corp. (another fictional company) in two months for a sales price of USD1,000. On 1 October, Cirrus provides Mountain with a down payment of USD300 from Cirrus and agrees to pay the balance of USD700 when the equipment is delivered on 30 November. Mountain Company recognizes deferred revenue when it receives the USD300 on 1 October, which will be derecognized when Mountain fulfills its obligation and delivers the equipment. The impact on Mountain Company's financial statement is summarized in Exhibit 8.

Exhibit 8: Mountain Company Financial Statement

Date	Balance Sheet	Income Statement	Statement of Cash Flows
1 October	Cash (asset) increases by USD300 Deferred revenue (liability) increases by USD300	N/A	Cash flows from operating activities increases by USD300
30 September	Cash (asset) increases by USD700 Deferred revenue (liability) decreases by USD300	Revenue increases by USD1,000	Cash flows from operating activities increases by USD700

THE DIRECT METHOD FOR CASH FLOWS FROM OPERATING ACTIVITIES

3

☐ describe the steps in the preparation of direct and indirect cash flow statements, including how cash flows can be computed using income statement and balance sheet data

The first step in preparing the cash flow statement is to determine cash flows from operating activities, which can be presented using the direct or indirect method. The direct method uses the major categories of gross cash receipts and payments, and the indirect method reconciles net income to net cash flow. Cash flows from investing activities and from financing activities are identical regardless of whether the direct or indirect method is used to present operating cash flows.

- Companies often disclose only indirect operating cash flow information but understanding how cash flow information is put together will enable you to take an indirect statement apart and reconfigure it to approximate a direct cash flow statement, which—while not perfectly accurate—can be useful. This lesson demonstrates the approximate preparation of a direct cash flow statement using the income statement and the comparative balance sheets for Acme Corporation (a fictitious retail company) shown in Exhibit 9 and Exhibit 10.

Exhibit 9: Acme Corporation Income Statement Year Ended 31 December 2018

Revenue (net)		USD23,598
Cost of goods sold		11,456
Gross profit		12,142
Salary and wage expense	USD4,123	
Depreciation expense	1,052	
Other operating expenses	3,577	
Total operating expenses		8,752
Operating profit		3,390
Other revenues (expenses):		
Gain on sale of equipment	205	
Interest expense	(246)	(41)
Income before tax		3,349
Income tax expense		1,139
Net income		USD2,210

Exhibit 10: Acme Corporation Comparative Balance Sheets 31 December 2018 and 2017

	2018	2017	Net Change
Cash	USD1,011	USD1,163	USD(152)

Accounts receivable	1,012	957	55
Inventory	3,984	3,277	707
Prepaid expenses	155	178	(23)
Total current assets	6,162	5,575	587
Land	510	510	—
Buildings	3,680	3,680	—
Equipment*	8,798	8,555	243
Less: accumulated depreciation	(3,443)	(2,891)	(552)
Total long-term assets	9,545	9,854	(309)
Total assets	USD15,707	USD15,429	USD278
Accounts payable	USD3,588	USD3,325	USD263
Salary and wage payable	85	75	10
Interest payable	62	74	(12)
Income tax payable	55	50	5
Other accrued liabilities	1,126	1,104	22
Total current liabilities	4,916	4,628	288
Long-term debt	3,075	3,575	(500)
Common stock	3,750	4,350	(600)
Retained earnings	3,966	2,876	1,090
Total liabilities and equity	USD15,707	USD15,429	USD278

** During 2018, Acme purchased new equipment for a total cost of $1,300. No items impacted retained earnings other than net income and dividends.*

Operating Activities: Direct Method

We first determine how much cash Acme received from its customers (sometimes referred to as "cash collections"), followed by how much cash was paid to suppliers and to employees, as well as how much cash was paid for other operating expenses, interest, and income taxes.

Cash Received From Customers

The income statement for Acme reported revenue of USD23,598 for the year ended 31 December 2018. To determine the approximate cash receipts from its customers, it is necessary to adjust this revenue amount by the net change in accounts receivable for the year. If accounts receivable increase during the year, revenue on an accrual basis is higher than cash receipts from customers, and vice versa. For Acme Corporation, accounts receivable increased by USD55, so cash received from customers was USD23,543, as shown in Exhibit 11.

Exhibit 11: Cash Received from Customers

Revenue	USD23,598
Less: Increase in accounts receivable	(USD55)
Cash received from customers	**USD23,543**

Cash received from customers affects the accounts receivable account as shown in Exhibit 12.

Exhibit 12: Effect on Accounts Receivable, 1

Beginning accounts receivable	957
Plus revenue	23,598
Minus cash collected from customers	**(23,543)**
Ending accounts receivable	USD1,012

The accounts receivable account information can also be presented as shown in Exhibit 13.

Exhibit 13: Effect on Accounts Receivable, 2

Beginning accounts receivable	USD957
Plus revenue	23,598
Minus ending accounts receivable	(1,012)
Cash collected from customers	**USD23,543**

Acme did not have any deferred or unearned revenue. If it did, further adjustment would be required to arrive at cash collected from customers (a decrease in deferred revenue would be a negative adjustment and vice versa).

EXAMPLE 5

Computing Cash Received from Customers

1. Blue Bayou, a fictitious advertising company, reported revenues of USD50 million, total expenses of USD35 million, and net income of USD15 million in the most recent year. If accounts receivable decreased by USD12 million, how much cash did the company receive from customers?

   A. USD38 million

   B. USD50 million

   C. USD62 million

   Solution:

   C is correct. Revenues of USD50 million plus the decrease in accounts receivable of USD12 million equals USD62 million cash received from customers. The decrease in accounts receivable means that the company received more in cash than the amount of revenue it reported.

Cash Paid to Suppliers

For Acme, the cash paid to suppliers was USD11,900, determined as shown in Exhibit 14.

Exhibit 14: Cash Paid to Suppliers

Cost of goods sold	USD11,456
Plus: Increase in inventory	707
Equals purchases from suppliers	USD12,163
Less: Increase in accounts payable	(263)
Cash paid to suppliers	**USD11,900**

There are two pieces to this calculation: the amount of inventory purchased and the amount paid for it. To determine purchases from suppliers, cost of goods sold is adjusted for the change in inventory. If inventory increased during the year, then purchases during the year exceeded cost of goods sold, and vice versa. Acme reported cost of goods sold of USD11,456 for the year ended 31 December 2018. For Acme Corporation, inventory increased by USD707, so purchases from suppliers was USD12,163. Purchases from suppliers affect the inventory account, as shown in Exhibit 15.

Exhibit 15: Effect on Inventory

Beginning inventory	USD3,277
Plus purchases	12,163
Minus cost of goods sold	(11,456)
Ending inventory	USD3,984

Acme purchased USD12,163 of inventory from suppliers in 2018, but is this the amount of cash that Acme paid to its suppliers during the year? Not necessarily. Acme may not have yet paid for all of these purchases and may yet owe for some of the purchases made this year. In other words, Acme may have paid less cash to its suppliers than the amount of this year's purchases, in which case Acme's liability (accounts payable) will have increased by the difference. Alternatively, Acme may have paid even more to its suppliers than the amount of this year's purchases, in which case Acme's accounts payable will have decreased.

Therefore, once purchases have been determined, cash paid to suppliers can be calculated by adjusting purchases for the change in accounts payable. If the company made all purchases with cash, then accounts payable would not change and cash outflows would equal purchases. If accounts payable increased during the year, then purchases on an accrual basis would be higher than they would be on a cash basis, and vice versa. In this example, Acme made more purchases than it paid in cash, so the balance in accounts payable increased. For Acme, the cash paid to suppliers was USD11,900, determined as shown in Exhibit 16.

Exhibit 16: Cash Paid to Suppliers

Purchases from suppliers	USD12,163
Less: Increase in accounts payable	(263)
Cash paid to suppliers	**USD11,900**

The amount of cash paid to suppliers is reflected in the accounts payable account, as shown in Exhibit 17.

Exhibit 17: Cash Paid to Suppliers

Beginning accounts payable	USD3,325
Plus purchases	12,163
Minus cash paid to suppliers	**(11,900)**
Ending accounts payable	USD3,588

EXAMPLE 6

Computing Cash Paid to Suppliers

1. Orange Beverages Plc., a fictitious manufacturer of tropical drinks, reported cost of goods sold for the year of USD100 million. Total assets increased by USD55 million, but inventory declined by USD6 million. Total liabilities increased by USD45 million, but accounts payable decreased by USD2 million. How much cash did the company pay to its suppliers during the year?

   A. USD96 million

   B. USD104 million

   C. USD108 million

   Solution:

   A is correct. Cost of goods sold of USD100 million less the decrease in inventory of USD6 million equals purchases from suppliers of USD94 million. The decrease in accounts payable of USD2 million means that the company paid USD96 million in cash (USD94 million plus USD2 million).

Cash Paid to Employees

To determine the cash paid to employees, it is necessary to adjust salary and wage expenses by the net change in salary and wages payable for the year. If salary and wages payable increased during the year, then salary and wage expenses on an accrual basis would be higher than the amount of cash paid for this expense, and vice versa. For Acme, salary and wages payable increased by USD10, so cash paid for salary and wages was USD4,113, as shown in Exhibit 18.

Exhibit 18: Salary and Wages

Salary and wages expense	USD4,123
Less: Increase in salary and wages payable	(10)
Cash paid to employees	**USD4,113**

The amount of cash paid to employees is reflected in the salary and wages payable account, as shown in Exhibit 19.

Exhibit 19: Cash Paid to Employees

Beginning salary and wages payable	USD75
Plus salary and wages expense	4,123

Minus cash paid to employees	**(4,113)**
Ending salary and wages payable	USD85

Cash Paid for Other Operating Expenses

To determine the cash paid for other operating expenses, it is necessary to adjust the other operating expense amounts on the income statement by the net changes in prepaid expenses and accrued expense liabilities for the year. If prepaid expenses increased during the year, other operating expenses on a cash basis would be higher than on an accrual basis, and vice versa. Likewise, if accrued expense liabilities increased during the year, other operating expenses on a cash basis would be lower than on an accrual basis, and vice versa. For Acme Corporation, the amount of cash paid for operating expenses in 2018 was USD3,532, as shown in Exhibit 20.

Exhibit 20: Cash Paid for Operating Expenses

Other operating expenses	USD3,577
Less: Decrease in prepaid expenses	(23)
Less: Increase in other accrued liabilities	(22)
Cash paid for other operating expenses	**USD3,532**

EXAMPLE 7

Computing Cash Paid for Other Operating Expenses

1. Black Ice, a fictitious sportswear manufacturer, reported other operating expenses of USD30 million. Prepaid insurance expense increased by USD4 million, and accrued utilities payable decreased by USD7 million. Insurance and utilities are the only two components of other operating expenses. How much cash did the company pay in other operating expenses?

   A. USD19 million

   B. USD33 million

   C. USD41 million

   Solution:

   C is correct. Other operating expenses of USD30 million plus the increase in prepaid insurance expense of USD4 million plus the decrease in accrued utilities payable of USD7 million equals USD41 million.

Cash Paid for Interest

The cash paid for interest is included in operating cash flows under US GAAP and may be included in operating or financing cash flows under IFRS. To determine the cash paid for interest, it is necessary to adjust interest expense by the net change in interest payable for the year. If interest payable increases during the year, then interest expense on an accrual basis will be higher than the amount of cash paid for interest, and vice versa. For Acme Corporation, interest payable decreased by USD12, and cash paid for interest was USD258, as shown in Exhibit 21.

Exhibit 21: Cash Paid for Interest

Interest expense	USD246
Plus: Decrease in interest payable	12
Cash paid for interest	**USD258**

Alternatively, cash paid for interest may also be determined by an analysis of the interest payable account, as shown in Exhibit 22.

Exhibit 22: Interest Payable Account

Beginning interest payable	USD74
Plus interest expense	246
Minus cash paid for interest	**(258)**
Ending interest payable	USD62

Cash Paid for Income Taxes

To determine the cash paid for income taxes, it is necessary to adjust the income tax expense amount on the income statement by the net changes in taxes receivable, taxes payable, and deferred income taxes for the year. If taxes receivable or deferred tax assets increase during the year, income taxes on a cash basis will be higher than on an accrual basis, and vice versa. Likewise, if taxes payable or deferred tax liabilities increase during the year, income tax expense on a cash basis will be lower than on an accrual basis, and vice versa. For Acme Corporation, the amount of cash paid for income taxes in 2018 was USD1,134, as shown in Exhibit 23.

Exhibit 23: Cash Paid for Income Taxes

Income tax expense	USD1,139
Less: Increase in income tax payable	(5)
Cash paid for income taxes	**USD1,134**

THE INDIRECT METHOD FOR CASH FLOWS FROM OPERATING ACTIVITIES 4

☐ describe the steps in the preparation of direct and indirect cash flow statements, including how cash flows can be computed using income statement and balance sheet data

The alternative approach to reporting cash from operating activities is the indirect method. In this lesson, we reconcile Acme's net income to its operating cash flow using the indirect method.

Operating Activities: Indirect Method

To perform this reconciliation, net income is adjusted for the following: (1) any non-operating activities, (2) any non-cash expenses, and (3) changes in operating working capital items.

The only non-operating activity in Acme's income statement, the sale of equipment, resulted in a gain of USD205. This amount is removed from the operating cash flow section; the cash effects of the sale are shown in the investing section.

Acme's only non-cash expense was a depreciation expense of USD1,052. Under the indirect method, this depreciation expense must be added back to net income because it was a non-cash deduction in the calculation of net income.

Changes in working capital accounts include increases and decreases in the current operating asset and liability accounts. The changes in these accounts arise from applying accrual accounting—that is, recognizing revenues when they are earned and expenses when they are incurred instead of when the cash is received or paid. To make the working capital adjustments under the indirect method, any increase in a current operating asset account is subtracted from net income and a net decrease is added to net income. As described previously, the increase in accounts receivable, for example, resulted from Acme recording income statement revenue higher than the amount of cash received from customers. Therefore, to reconcile back to operating cash flow, that increase in accounts receivable must be deducted from net income. For current operating liabilities, a net increase is added to net income and a net decrease is subtracted from net income. As described previously, the increase in wages payable, for example, resulted from Acme recording income statement expenses higher than the amount of cash paid to employees.

Exhibit 24 presents a tabulation of the most common types of adjustments that are made to net income when using the indirect method to determine net cash flow from operating activities.

Exhibit 24: Adjustments to Net Income Using the Indirect Method

Additions	▪ Non-cash items • Depreciation expense of tangible assets • Amortization expense of intangible assets • Depletion expense of natural resources • Amortization of bond discount ▪ Non-operating losses • Loss on sale or write-down of assets • Loss on retirement of debt • Loss on investments accounted for under the equity method ▪ Increase in deferred income tax liability ▪ Changes in working capital resulting from accruing higher amounts for expenses than the amounts of cash payments or lower amounts for revenues than the amounts of cash receipts • Decrease in current operating assets (e.g., accounts receivable, inventory, and prepaid expenses) • Increase in current operating liabilities (e.g., accounts payable and accrued expense liabilities)
Subtractions	▪ Non-cash items (e.g., amortization of bond premium)

- Non-operating items
  - Gain on sale of assets
  - Gain on retirement of debt
  - Income on investments accounted for under the equity method
- Decrease in deferred income tax liability
- Changes in working capital resulting from accruing lower amounts for expenses than for cash payments or higher amounts for revenues than for cash receipts
  - Increase in current operating assets (e.g., accounts receivable, inventory, and prepaid expenses)
  - Decrease in current operating liabilities (e.g., accounts payable and accrued expense liabilities)

Accordingly, for Acme Corporation (using Exhibits 9 and 10), the USD55 increase in accounts receivable and the USD707 increase in inventory are subtracted from net income and the USD23 decrease in prepaid expenses is added to net income. For Acme's current liabilities, the increases in accounts payable, salary and wage payable, income tax payable, and other accrued liabilities (USD263, USD10, USD5, and USD22, respectively) are added to net income and the USD12 decrease in interest payable is subtracted from net income. Exhibit 25 presents the cash flow statement for Acme Corporation under the indirect method using the information that we have determined from our analysis of the income statement and the comparative balance sheets. Note that the investing and financing sections are identical to the statement of cash flows prepared using the direct method.

Exhibit 25: Acme Corporation Cash Flow Statement (Indirect Method) Year Ended 31 December 2018

Cash flow from operating activities:	
Net income	USD2,210
Depreciation expense	1,052
Gain on sale of equipment	(205)
Increase in accounts receivable	(55)
Increase in inventory	(707)
Decrease in prepaid expenses	23
Increase in accounts payable	263
Increase in salary and wage payable	10
Decrease in interest payable	(12)
Increase in income tax payable	5

Cash flow from operating activities:	
Increase in other accrued liabilities	22
Net cash provided by operating activities	2,606
Cash flow from investing activities:	
Cash received from sale of equipment	762
Cash paid for purchase of equipment	(1,300)
Net cash used for investing activities	(538)
Cash flow from financing activities:	
Cash paid to retire long-term debt	(500)
Cash paid to retire common stock	(600)
Cash paid for dividends	(1,120)
Net cash used for financing activities	(2,220)
Net decrease in cash	(152)
Cash balance, 31 December 2017	1,163
Cash balance, 31 December 2018	USD1,011

5 CONVERSION FROM THE INDIRECT TO DIRECT METHOD

☐ demonstrate the conversion of cash flows from the indirect to direct method

An analyst may desire to review direct-format operating cash flow to review trends in cash receipts and payments (such as cash received from customers or cash paid to suppliers). If a direct-format statement is not available, cash flows from operating activities reported under the indirect method can be converted to the direct method. Accuracy of conversion depends on adjustments using data available in published financial reports. The method described in this lesson is sufficiently accurate for most analytical purposes.

Method to Convert Cash Flow from Indirect to Direct

The three-step conversion process is demonstrated for Acme Corporation in Exhibit 26. Referring again to Exhibits 9 and 10 for Acme Corporation's income statement and balance sheet information, begin by disaggregating net income of USD2,210 into total revenues and total expenses (Step 1). Next, remove any non-operating and non-cash items (Step 2). For Acme, we therefore remove the non-operating gain on the sale of equipment of USD205 and the non-cash depreciation expense of USD1,052. Then, convert accrual amounts of revenues and expenses to cash flow amounts of receipts and payments by adjusting for changes in working capital accounts (Step 3). The results of these adjustments are the items of information for the direct format of operating cash flows. These line items are shown as the results of Step 3.

Exhibit 26: Conversion from the Indirect to the Direct Method

Step 1	Total revenues	USD23,803
Aggregate all revenue and all expenses	Total expenses	21,593
	Net income	USD2,210
Step 2	Total revenue less noncash item revenues:	
Remove all noncash items from aggregated revenues and expenses and break out remaining items into relevant cash flow items	(USD23,803 – USD205) =	USD23,598
	Revenue	USD23,598
	Total expenses less noncash item expenses:	
	(USD21,593 – USD1,052) =	USD20,541
	Cost of goods sold	USD11,456
	Salary and wage expenses	4,123
	Other operating expenses	3,577
	Interest expense	246
	Income tax expense	1,139
	Total	USD20,541
Step 3	Cash received from customers[a]	USD23,543
Convert accrual amounts to cash flow amounts by adjusting for working capital changes	Cash paid to suppliers[b]	(11,900)
	Cash paid to employees[c]	(4,113)
	Cash paid for other operating expenses[d]	(3,532)
	Cash paid for interest[e]	(258)
	Cash paid for income tax[f]	(1,134)
	Net cash provided by operating activities	USD2,606

Calculations for Step 3:

[a]Revenue of $23,598 less increase in accounts receivable of $55.

[b]Cost of goods sold of $11,456 plus increase in inventory of $707 less increase in accounts payable of $263.

[c]Salary and wage expense of $4,123 less increase in salary and wage payable of $10.

[d]Other operating expenses of $3,577 less decrease in prepaid expenses of $23 less increase in other accrued liabilities of $22.

[e]Interest expense of $246 plus decrease in interest payable of $12.

[f]Income tax expense of $1,139 less increase in income tax payable of $5.

CASH FLOWS FROM INVESTING ACTIVITIES 6

☐ describe the steps in the preparation of direct and indirect cash flow statements, including how cash flows can be computed using income statement and balance sheet data

The second and third steps in preparing the cash flow statement are to determine the total cash flows from investing activities and from financing activities. The presentation of this information is identical, regardless of whether the direct or indirect method is used for operating cash flows.

Cash Flows from Investing Activities

Purchases and sales of equipment were the only investing activities undertaken by Acme in 2018, as evidenced by the fact that the amounts reported for land and buildings were unchanged during the year. An informational note in Exhibit 10 tells us that Acme *purchased* new equipment in 2018 for a total cost of USD1,300. However, the amount of equipment shown on Acme's balance sheet increased by only USD243 (ending balance of USD8,798 minus beginning balance of USD8,555); therefore, Acme must have also *sold or otherwise disposed of* some equipment during the year. To determine the cash inflow from the sale of equipment, we analyze the equipment and accumulated depreciation accounts as well as the gain on the sale of equipment from Exhibits 9 and 10. Assuming that the entire accumulated depreciation is related to equipment, the cash received from sale of equipment is determined as follows.

The historical cost of the equipment sold was USD1,057. This amount is determined as shown in Exhibit 27:

Exhibit 27: Cost of Equipment Sold

Beginning balance equipment (from balance sheet)	USD8,555
Plus equipment purchased (from informational note)	1,300
Minus ending balance equipment (from balance sheet)	(8,798)
Equals historical cost of equipment sold	USD1,057

The accumulated depreciation on the equipment sold was USD500, determined as shown in Exhibit 28:

Exhibit 28: Accumulated Depreciation

Beginning balance accumulated depreciation (from balance sheet)	USD2,891
Plus depreciation expense (from income statement)	1,052
Minus ending balance accumulated depreciation (from balance sheet)	(3,443)
Equals accumulated depreciation on equipment sold	USD500

The historical cost information, accumulated depreciation information, and information from the income statement about the gain on the sale of equipment can be used to determine the cash received from the sale, as shown in Exhibit 29:

Exhibit 29: Cash Received from the Sale

Historical cost of equipment sold (calculated above)	USD1,057
Less accumulated depreciation on equipment sold (calculated above)	(500)
Equals book value of equipment sold	USD557

Plus gain on sale of equipment (from the income statement)	205
Equals cash received from sale of equipment	**USD762**

QUESTION SET

1. Copper, Inc., a fictitious brewery and restaurant chain, reported a gain on the sale of equipment of USD12 million. In addition, the company's income statement shows depreciation expense of USD8 million and the cash flow statement shows capital expenditure of USD15 million, all of which was for the purchase of new equipment.

Exhibit 30: Copper Inc.

Balance sheet item	31 December 2017	31 December 2018	Change
Equipment	USD100 million	USD109 million	USD9 million
Accumulated depreciation—equipment	USD30 million	USD36 million	USD6 million

Using the information in Exhibit 30 from the comparative balance sheets, how much cash did the company receive from the equipment sale?

A. USD12 million

B. USD16 million

C. USD18 million

Solution:

B is correct. Selling price (cash inflow) minus book value equals gain or loss on sale; therefore, gain or loss on sale plus book value equals selling price (cash inflow). The amount of gain is given, USD12 million. To calculate the book value of the equipment sold, find the historical cost of the equipment and the accumulated depreciation on the equipment.

- Beginning balance of equipment of USD100 million plus equipment purchased of USD15 million minus ending balance of equipment of USD109 million equals historical cost of equipment sold, or USD6 million.
- Beginning accumulated depreciation on equipment of USD30 million plus depreciation expense for the year of USD8 million minus ending balance of accumulated depreciation of USD36 million equals accumulated depreciation on the equipment sold, or USD2 million.
- Therefore, the book value of the equipment sold was USD6 million minus USD2 million, or USD4 million.
- Because the gain on the sale of equipment was USD12 million, the amount of cash received must have been USD16 million.

2. Silverago Incorporated, an international metals company, reported a loss on the sale of equipment of USD2 million in 2018. In addition, the company's income statement shows depreciation expense of USD8 million and the cash

flow statement shows capital expenditure of USD10 million, all of which was for the purchase of new equipment. Using the information in Exhibit 31 from the comparative balance sheets, how much cash did the company receive from the equipment sale?

Exhibit 31: Silverago Inc.

Balance Sheet Item	31 December 2017	31 December 2018	Change
Equipment	USD100 million	USD105 million	USD5 million
Accumulated depreciation—equipment	USD40 million	USD46 million	USD6 million

A. USD1 million

B. USD2 million

C. USD3 million

Solution:

A is correct. Selling price (cash inflow) minus book value equals gain or loss on sale; therefore, gain or loss on sale plus book value equals selling price (cash inflow). The amount of loss is given—USD2 million. To calculate the book value of the equipment sold, find the historical cost of the equipment and the accumulated depreciation on the equipment.

- Beginning balance of equipment of USD100 million plus equipment purchased of USD10 million minus ending balance of equipment of USD105 million equals the historical cost of equipment sold, or USD5 million.
- Beginning accumulated depreciation of USD40 million plus depreciation expense for the year of USD8 million minus ending balance of accumulated depreciation of USD46 million equals accumulated depreciation on the equipment sold, or USD2 million.
- Therefore, the book value of the equipment sold was USD5 million minus USD2 million, or USD3 million.
- Because the loss on the sale of equipment was USD2 million, the amount of cash received must have been USD1 million.

7 CASH FLOWS FROM FINANCING ACTIVITIES

☐ describe the steps in the preparation of direct and indirect cash flow statements, including how cash flows can be computed using income statement and balance sheet data

As with investing activities, the presentation of financing activities is identical, regardless of whether the direct or indirect method is used for operating cash flows.

Cash Flow from Financing activities: Long-Term Debt and Common Stock

The change in long-term debt, based on the beginning 2018 (ending 2017) and ending 2018 balances in Exhibit 10, was a decrease of USD500. Absent other information, this indicates that Acme retired USD500 of long-term debt. Retiring long-term debt is a cash outflow relating to financing activities.

Similarly, the change in common stock during 2018 was a decrease of USD600. Absent other information, this indicates that Acme repurchased USD600 of its common stock. Repurchase of common stock is also a cash outflow related to financing activity.

Computing Dividends Paid

Recall the following relationship:

Beginning retained earnings + Net income – Dividends = Ending retained earnings

Based on this relationship, the amount of cash dividends paid in 2018 can be determined from an analysis of retained earnings, as shown in Exhibit 32.

Exhibit 32: Analysis of Retained Earnings

Beginning balance of retained earnings (from the balance sheet)	USD2,876
Plus net income (from the income statement)	2,210
Minus ending balance of retained earnings (from the balance sheet)	(3,966)
Equals dividends paid	**USD1,120**

Note that dividends paid are presented in the statement of changes in equity.

EXAMPLE 8

Computing Cash Flow from Financing Activity

1. Jaderong Plinkett Stores reported net income of USD25 million. The company has no outstanding debt. Using the information in Exhibit 33 from the comparative balance sheets (in millions), what should the company report in the financing section of the statement of cash flows in 2018?

Exhibit 33: Jaderong Plinkett Stores

Balance Sheet Item	31 December 2017	31 December 2018	Change
Common stock	USD100	USD102	USD2
Additional paid-in capital common stock	USD100	USD140	USD40
Retained earnings	USD100	USD115	USD15
Total stockholders' equity	USD300	USD357	USD57

A. Issuance of common stock of USD42 million; dividends paid of USD10 million

B. Issuance of common stock of USD38 million; dividends paid of USD10 million

C. Issuance of common stock of USD42 million; dividends paid of USD40 million

Solution:

A is correct. The increase of USD42 million in common stock and additional paid-in capital indicates that the company issued stock during the year. The increase in retained earnings of USD15 million indicates that the company paid USD10 million in cash dividends during the year, determined as beginning retained earnings of USD100 million plus net income of USD25 million minus ending retained earnings of USD115 million, which equals USD10 million in cash dividends.

8 DIFFERENCES IN CASH FLOW STATEMENTS PREPARED UNDER US GAAP VERSUS IFRS

☐ contrast cash flow statements prepared under International Financial Reporting Standards (IFRS) and US generally accepted accounting principles (US GAAP)

The key differences between statements of cash flows prepared under IFRS and US GAAP are summarized in Exhibit 34. Most significantly, IFRS allow more flexibility in the reporting of such items as interest paid or received and dividends paid or received and in how income tax expense is classified.

US GAAP classify interest and dividends received from investments as operating activities, whereas IFRS allow companies to classify those items as either operating or investing cash flows. Likewise, US GAAP classify interest expense as an operating activity, even though the principal amount of the debt issued is classified as a financing activity. IFRS allow companies to classify interest expense as either an operating activity or a financing activity. US GAAP classify dividends paid to stockholders as a financing activity, whereas IFRS allow companies to classify dividends paid as either an operating activity or a financing activity.

US GAAP classify all income tax expenses as an operating activity. IFRS also classify income tax expense as an operating activity, unless the tax expense can be specifically identified with an investing or financing activity (e.g., the tax effect of the sale of a discontinued operation could be classified under investing activities).

Exhibit 34: Cash Flow Statements: Differences between IFRS and US GAAP

Topic	IFRS	US GAAP
Classification of cash flows:		
• Interest received	Operating or investing	Operating
• Interest paid	Operating or financing	Operating
• Dividends received	Operating or investing	Operating
• Dividends paid	Operating or financing	Financing
• Bank overdrafts	Considered part of cash equivalents	Not considered part of cash and cash equivalents and classified as financing

Topic	IFRS	US GAAP
• Taxes paid	Generally operating, but a portion can be allocated to investing or financing if it can be specifically identified with these categories	Operating
Format of statement:	Direct or indirect; direct is encouraged	Direct or indirect; direct is encouraged. A reconciliation of net income to cash flow from operating activities must be provided regardless of method used

Sources: IAS 7; FASB ASC Topic 230; and "IFRS and US GAAP: Similarities and Differences," PricewaterhouseCoopers (November 2017), available at www.pwc.com.

QUESTION SET

1. Which of the following is an example of a financing activity on the cash flow statement under US GAAP?

   A. Payment of interest

   B. Receipt of dividends

   C. Payment of dividends

   Solution:

   C is correct. Payment of dividends is a financing activity under US GAAP. Payment of interest and receipt of dividends are included in operating cash flows under US GAAP. Note that IFRS allow companies to include receipt of interest and dividends as either operating or investing cash flows and to include payment of interest and dividends as either operating or financing cash flows.

2. Interest paid is classified as an operating cash flow under:

   A. US GAAP but may be classified as either operating or investing cash flows under IFRS.

   B. IFRS but may be classified as either operating or investing cash flows under US GAAP.

   C. US GAAP but may be classified as either operating or financing cash flows under IFRS.

   Solution:

   C is correct. Interest expense is always classified as an operating cash flow under US GAAP but may be classified as either an operating or financing cash flow under IFRS.

3. Cash flows from taxes on income must be separately disclosed under:

   A. IFRS only.

   B. US GAAP only.

C. both IFRS and US GAAP.

Solution:

C is correct. Taxes on income are required to be separately disclosed under IFRS and US GAAP. The disclosure may be in the cash flow statement or elsewhere.

4. Mabel Corporation (MC) reported accounts receivable of USD66 million at the end of its second fiscal quarter. MC had revenues of USD72 million for its third fiscal quarter and reported accounts receivable of USD55 million at the end of its third fiscal quarter. Based on this information, the amount of cash MC collected from customers during the third fiscal quarter is:

   A. USD61 million.

   B. USD72 million.

   C. USD83 million.

   Solution:

   C is correct. The amount of cash collected from customers during the quarter is equal to beginning accounts receivable plus revenues minus ending accounts receivable: USD66 million + USD72 million – USD55 million = USD83 million. A reduction in accounts receivable indicates that cash collected during the quarter was greater than revenue on an accrual basis.

5. Red Road Company, a consulting company, reported total revenues of USD100 million, total expenses of USD80 million, and net income of USD20 million in the most recent year. If accounts receivable increased by USD10 million, how much cash did the company receive from customers?

   A. USD90 million.

   B. USD100 million.

   C. USD110 million.

   Solution:

   A is correct. Revenues of USD100 million minus the increase in accounts receivable of USD10 million equal USD90 million cash received from customers. The increase in accounts receivable means that the company received less in cash than it reported as revenue.

PRACTICE PROBLEMS

1. Based on the information in Exhibit 1 for Pinkerly Inc., a fictitious company, what are the total adjustments that the company would make to net income in order to derive operating cash flow?

Exhibit 1: Pinkerly Inc.

		Year Ended	
Income statement item		12/31/2018	
Net income		USD30 million	
Depreciation		USD7 million	
Balance sheet item	12/31/2017	12/31/2018	Change
Accounts receivable	USD15 million	USD30 million	USD15 million
Inventory	USD16 million	USD13 million	(USD3 million)
Accounts payable	USD10 million	USD20 million	USD10 million

A. Add USD5 million

B. Add USD21 million

C. Subtract USD9 million

2. When computing net cash flow from operating activities using the indirect method, an addition to net income is *most likely* to occur when there is a:

A. gain on the sale of an asset.

B. loss on the retirement of debt.

C. decrease in a deferred tax liability.

3. An analyst gathered the information in Exhibit 1 from a company's 2018 financial statements:

Exhibit 1: 2018 Financial Statement (US dollars, millions)

Balances as of Year Ended 31 December	2017	2018
Retained earnings	120	145
Accounts receivable	38	43
Inventory	45	48
Accounts payable	36	29

In 2018, the company declared and paid cash dividends of USD10 million and recorded depreciation expense in the amount of USD25 million. The company considers dividends paid a financing activity. The company's 2018 cash flow from operations (in USD millions) was *closest* to:

A. 25.

B. 45.

C. 75.

4. Based on the information in Exhibit 1 for Star Inc., what are the total net adjustments that the company would make to net income to derive operating cash flow?

Exhibit 1: Star Inc.

	Year Ended		
Income Statement Item		**12/31/2018**	
Net income		USD20 million	
Depreciation		USD2 million	
Balance Sheet Item	**12/31/2017**	**12/31/2018**	**Change**
Accounts receivable	USD25 million	USD22 million	(USD3 million)
Inventory	USD10 million	USD14 million	USD4 million
Accounts payable	USD8 million	USD13 million	USD5 million

A. Add USD2 million

B. Add USD6 million

C. Subtract USD6 million.

5. In 2018, a company using US GAAP made cash payments of USD6 million for salaries, USD2 million for interest expense, and USD4 million for income taxes. Additional information for the company is provided in the Exhibit 1:

Exhibit 1: Cash Payments

(US dollars, millions)	2017	2018
Revenue	42	37
Cost of goods sold	18	16
Inventory	36	40
Accounts receivable	22	19
Accounts payable	14	12

Based only on the information in Exhibit 1, the company's operating cash flow for 2018 is *closest to*:

A. USD6 million.

B. USD10 million.

C. USD14 million.

6. Green Glory Corp., a garden supply wholesaler, reported cost of goods sold for

the year of USD80 million. Total assets increased by USD55 million, including an increase of USD5 million in inventory. Total liabilities increased by USD45 million, including an increase of USD2 million in accounts payable. The cash paid by the company to its suppliers is most likely *closest* to:

A. USD73 million.

B. USD77 million.

C. USD83 million.

7. Purple Fleur S.A., a retailer of floral products, reported cost of goods sold for the year of USD75 million. Total assets increased by USD55 million, but inventory declined by USD6 million. Total liabilities increased by USD45 million, and accounts payable increased by USD2 million. The cash paid by the company to its suppliers is most likely *closest* to:

A. USD67 million.

B. USD79 million.

C. USD83 million.

8. White Flag, a women's clothing manufacturer, reported salaries expense of USD20 million. The beginning balance of salaries payable was USD3 million, and the ending balance of salaries payable was USD1 million. How much cash did the company pay in salaries?

A. USD18 million

B. USD21 million

C. USD22 million

9. An analyst gathered the information in Exhibit 1 from a company's 2018 financial statements:

Exhibit 1: 2018 Financial Statements (US dollars, millions)

Year ended 31 December	2017	2018
Net sales	245.8	254.6
Cost of goods sold	168.3	175.9
Accounts receivable	73.2	68.3
Inventory	39.0	47.8
Accounts payable	20.3	22.9

Based only on the information in Exhibit 1, the company's 2018 statement of cash flows in the direct format would include amounts (in US dollars millions) for cash received from customers and cash paid to suppliers, respectively, that are *closest* to:

	Cash received from customers	Cash paid to suppliers
A.	249.7	169.7
B.	259.5	174.5
C.	259.5	182.1

10. Golden Cumulus Corp., a commodities trading company, reported interest expense of USD19 million and taxes of USD6 million. Interest payable increased by USD3 million, and taxes payable decreased by USD4 million over the period. How much cash did the company pay for interest and taxes?

    A. USD22 million for interest and USD10 million for taxes

    B. USD16 million for interest and USD2 million for taxes

    C. USD16 million for interest and USD10 million for taxes

11. The information in Exhibit 1 is extracted from Sweetfall Incorporated's financial statements.

Exhibit 1: Sweetfall Inc.

Income Statement		Balance Sheet Changes	
Revenue	USD56,800	Decrease in accounts receivable	USD1,324
Cost of goods sold	27,264	Decrease in inventory	501
Other operating expense	562	Increase in prepaid expense	6
Depreciation expense	2,500	Increase in accounts payable	1,063

The amount of cash Sweetfall Inc. paid to suppliers is:

A. USD25,700.

B. USD26,702.

C. USD27,826.

SOLUTIONS

1. A is correct. To derive operating cash flow, the company would make the following adjustments to net income: add depreciation (a non-cash expense) of USD7 million; add the decrease in inventory of USD3 million; add the increase in accounts payable of USD10 million; and subtract the increase in accounts receivable of USD15 million. Total additions of USD20 million and total subtractions of USD15 million result in net total additions of USD5 million.

2. B is correct. An addition to net income is made when there is a loss on the retirement of debt, which is a non-operating loss. A gain on the sale of an asset and a decrease in deferred tax liability are both subtracted from net-income.

3. B is correct. All dollar amounts are in millions. Net income (NI) for 2018 is USD35. This amount is the increase in retained earnings, USD25, plus the dividends paid, USD10. Depreciation of USD25 is added back to net income, and the increases in accounts receivable, USD5, and in inventory, USD3, are subtracted from net income because they are uses of cash. The decrease in accounts payable is also a use of cash and, therefore, a subtraction from net income. Thus, cash flow from operations is USD25 + USD10 + USD25 – USD5 – USD3 – USD7 = USD45.

4. B is correct. To derive operating cash flow, the company would make the following adjustments to net income: Add depreciation (a non-cash expense) of USD2 million; add the decrease in accounts receivable of USD3 million; add the increase in accounts payable of USD5 million; and subtract the increase in inventory of USD4 million. Total additions would be USD10 million, and total subtractions would be USD4 million, which gives net additions of USD6 million.

5. A is correct.

   Operating cash flows

   = Cash received from customers – (Cash paid to suppliers + Cash paid to employees + Cash paid for other operating expenses + Cash paid for interest + Cash paid for income taxes)

   Cash received from customers = Revenue + Decrease in accounts receivable

   = USD37 + USD3 = USD40 million

   Cash paid to suppliers

   = Cost of goods sold + Increase in inventory + Decrease in accounts payable

   = USD16 + USD4 + USD2 = USD22 million

   Therefore, the company's operating cash flow = USD40 – USD22 – Cash paid for salaries – Cash paid for interest – Cash paid for taxes = USD40 – USD22 – USD6 – USD2 – USD4 = USD6 million.

6. C is correct. Cost of goods sold of USD80 million plus the increase in inventory of USD5 million equals purchases from suppliers of USD85 million. The increase in accounts payable of USD2 million means that the company paid USD83 million in cash (USD85 million minus USD2 million) to its suppliers.

7. A is correct. Cost of goods sold of USD75 million less the decrease in inventory of USD6 million equals purchases from suppliers of USD69 million. The increase

in accounts payable of USD2 million means that the company paid USD67 million in cash (USD69 million minus USD2 million).

8. C is correct. Beginning salaries payable of USD3 million plus salaries expense of USD20 million minus ending salaries payable of USD1 million equals USD22 million. Alternatively, the expense of USD20 million plus the USD2 million decrease in salaries payable equals USD22 million.

9. C is correct. Cash received from customers = Sales + Decrease in accounts receivable = 254.6 + 4.9 = 259.5. Cash paid to suppliers = Cost of goods sold + Increase in inventory – Increase in accounts payable = 175.9 + 8.8 – 2.6 = 182.1.

10. C is correct. Interest expense of USD19 million less the increase in interest payable of USD3 million equals interest paid of USD16 million. Tax expense of USD6 million plus the decrease in taxes payable of USD4 million equals taxes paid of USD10 million.

11. A is correct. The amount of cash paid to suppliers is calculated as follows:

    = Cost of goods sold – Decrease in inventory – Increase in accounts payable

    = USD27,264 – USD501 – USD1,063

    = USD25,700.

LEARNING MODULE

5

Analyzing Statements of Cash Flows II

LEARNING OUTCOMES

Mastery	The candidate should be able to:
☐	analyze and interpret both reported and common-size cash flow statements
☐	calculate and interpret free cash flow to the firm, free cash flow to equity, and performance and coverage cash flow ratios

INTRODUCTION

1

An analysis of a company's statement of cash flows provides crucial information for evaluating a company's financial position and for forecasting its future cash flows, which is foundational to the valuation of the company's debt and equity securities. This module discusses tools and techniques for analyzing the statement of cash flows, including the analysis of sources and uses of cash and cash flow, common-size analysis, and the calculation of free cash flow measures and cash flow ratios.

LEARNING MODULE OVERVIEW

- An evaluation of a cash flow statement involves an assessment of the sources and uses of cash and the main drivers of cash flow within operating, investing, and financing activities.
- Analyst can use common-size statement analysis for the cash flow statement by expressing cash flow items as a percentage of total cash inflows/total cash outflows or as a percentage of net revenues.
- The cash flow statement can be used to calculate free cash flow to the firm (FCFF) and free cash flow to equity (FCFE), which are important profit measures for investors.
- The cash flow statement may also be used to calculate financial ratios that measure a company's profitability, performance, and financial position. Analysts use these ratios to evaluate the company over time and to compare multiple companies.

The two major accounting standard setters are as follows: 1) the International Accounting Standards Board (IASB) who establishes International Financial Reporting Standards (IFRS) and 2) the Financial Accounting Standards Board (FASB) who establishes US GAAP. Throughout this learning module both standards are referred to and many, but not all, of these two sets of accounting rules are identified. Note: changes in accounting standards as well as new rulings and/or pronouncements issued after the publication of this learning module may cause some of the information to become dated.

2 EVALUATING SOURCES AND USES OF CASH

☐ analyze and interpret both reported and common-size cash flow statements

Evaluation of the cash flow statement should involve an overall assessment of the sources and uses of cash between the three main categories as well as an assessment of the main drivers of cash flow within each category, as follows:

Step 1 Evaluate the major sources and uses of cash flow, including operating, investing, and financing activities.

Step 2 Evaluate the primary determinants of operating cash flow.

Step 3 Evaluate the primary determinants of investing cash flow.

Step 4 Evaluate the primary determinants of financing cash flow.

Step 1. Evaluate the major sources and uses of cash flow

The major sources of cash for a company can vary with its stage of growth. For a mature company, it is expected and desirable that operating activities are the primary source of cash flows. Over the long term, a company must generate cash from its operating activities. If operating cash flow were consistently negative, a company would need to borrow money or issue stock (financing activities) to fund the shortfall. Eventually, these providers of capital need to be repaid from operations or they will no longer be willing to provide capital. Cash generated from operating activities can be used in either investing or financing activities. If the company has value-creative investment opportunities, it is desirable to use the cash in investing activities. If the company does not have profitable investment opportunities, the cash should be returned to capital providers, a financing activity.

For a new or growth stage company, operating cash flow may be negative for some period of time as it invests in such assets as inventory and receivables (extending credit to new customers) to grow the business. This situation is not sustainable over the long term, so eventually the cash must start to come primarily from operating activities so that capital can be returned to the providers of capital. Lastly, it is desirable that operating cash flows are sufficient to cover capital expenditures (in other words, the company has free cash flow as discussed further in Lesson 3). In summary, major points to consider at this step are:

- What are the major sources and uses of cash flow?
- Is operating cash flow positive and sufficient to cover capital expenditures?

Step 2. Evaluate the primary determinants of operating cash flow

Turning to the operating section, analysts should examine the most significant determinants of operating cash flow. Companies need cash for use in operations (e.g., to hold receivables and inventory and to pay employees and suppliers) and receive cash from operating activities (e.g., payments from customers). Increases and decreases in receivables, inventory, payables, and so on can be examined to determine whether the company is using or generating cash in operations and why.

It is also useful to compare operating cash flow with net income. For a mature company, because net income includes non-cash expenses (depreciation and amortization), it is expected and desirable that operating cash flow exceeds net income. The relationship between net income and operating cash flow is also an indicator of earnings quality. If a company has large net income but poor operating cash flow, it may be a sign of poor earnings quality. The company may be making aggressive accounting choices to increase net income but may not be generating cash for its business. Analysts also should examine the variability of both earnings and cash flow and consider the impact of this variability on the company's risk as well as the ability to forecast future cash flows for valuation purposes. In summary:

- What are the major determinants of operating cash flow?
- Is operating cash flow higher or lower than net income? Why?
- How consistent are operating cash flows?

Step 3. Evaluate the primary determinants of investing cash flow

Within the investing section, analysts should evaluate each line item. Each line item represents either a source or use of cash. This enables analysts to understand where the cash is being spent (or received). This section will reveal how much cash is being invested for the future in property, plant, and equipment; how much is used to acquire entire companies; and how much is put aside in liquid investments, such as stocks and bonds. It will also tell show how much cash is being raised by selling these types of assets. If the company is making major capital investments, analysts should consider where the cash is coming from to cover these investments (e.g., is the cash coming from excess operating cash flow or from the financing activities described in Step 4). If assets are being sold, it is important to determine why and to assess the effects on the company.

Step 4. Evaluate the primary determinants of financing cash flow

Within the financing section, analysts should examine each line item to understand whether the company is raising capital or repaying capital and what the nature of its capital sources are. If the company is borrowing each year, analysts should consider when repayment may be required. The financing section will also present dividend payments and repurchases of stock that are alternative means of returning capital to owners. It is important to assess why capital is being raised or repaid.

EXAMPLE 1

Analysis of the Cash Flow Statement

Derek Yee, CFA, is preparing to forecast cash flow for Groupe Danone as an input into his valuation model. He reviews the historical cash flow statement of Groupe Danon for 2016 and 2017, which is presented in Exhibit 1, and excerpts from Danone's 2017 Registration Document, which is presented in Exhibit 2. Yee notes that Groupe Danone prepares its financial statements in conformity with International Financial Reporting Standards (IFRS).

Exhibit 1: Groupe Danone Consolidated Financial Statements Consolidated Statements of Cash Flows (in EUR millions)

Years Ended 31 December	2016	2017
Net income	1,827	2,563
Share of profits of associates net of dividends received	52	(54)
Depreciation, amortization, and impairment of tangible and intangible assets	786	974
Increases in (reversals of) provisions	51	153
Change in deferred taxes	(65)	(353)
(Gains) losses on disposal of property, plant and equipment and financial investments	(74)	(284)
Expense related to group performance shares	24	22
Cost of net financial debt	149	265
Net interest paid	(148)	(186)
Net change in interest income (expense)	—	80
Other components with no cash impact	13	(15)
Cash flows provided by operating activities, before changes in net working capital	**2,615**	**3,085**
(Increase) decrease in inventories	(24)	(122)
(Increase) decrease in trade receivables	(110)	(190)
Increase (decrease) in trade payables	298	145
Changes in other receivables and payables	(127)	40
Change in other working capital requirements	37	(127)
Cash flows provided by (used in) operating activities	**2,652**	**2,958**
Capital expenditure	(925)	(969)
Proceeds from the disposal of property, plant, and equipment	27	45
Net cash outflows on purchases of subsidiaries and financial investments	(66)	(10,949)
Net cash inflows on disposal of subsidiaries and financial investments	110	441
(Increase) decrease in long-term loans and other long-term financial assets	6	(4)
Cash flows provided by (used in) investing activities	**(848)**	**(11,437)**
Increase in capital and additional paid-in capital	46	47
Purchases of treasury stock (net of disposals) and Danone call options	32	13
Issue of perpetual subordinated debt securities	—	1,245
Interest on perpetual subordinated debt securities	—	—
Dividends paid to Danone shareholders	(985)	(279)
Buyout of non-controlling interests	(295)	(107)
Dividends paid	(94)	(86)
Contribution from non-controlling interests to capital increases	6	1
Transactions with non-controlling interests	(383)	(193)
Net cash flows on hedging derivatives	50	(52)
Bonds issued during the period	11,237	—

Years Ended 31 December	2016	2017
Bonds repaid during the period	(638)	(1,487)
Net cash flows from other current and non-current financial debt	(442)	(564)
Net cash flows from short-term investments	(10,531)	9,559
Cash flows provided by (used in) financing activities	**(1,616)**	**8,289**
Effect of exchange rate and other changes	(151)	272
Increase (decrease) in cash and cash equivalents	**38**	**81**
Cash and cash equivalents at beginning of period	519	557
Cash and cash equivalents at end of period	557	638
Supplemental disclosures		
Income tax payments during the year	(891)	(1,116)

Note: the numbers in the consolidated statement of cash flows were derived straight from company filings; some sub-totals may not sum exactly due to rounding by the company.

Exhibit 2: Excerpt from Groupe Danone 2017 Registration Statement

Footnote 2 to the financial statements:

"On July 7, 2016, Danone announced the signing of an agreement to acquire The WhiteWave Foods Company ("WhiteWave"), the global leader in plant-based foods and beverages and organic produce. The acquisition in cash, for USD 56.25 per share, represented, as of the date of the agreement, a total enterprise value of approximately USD 12.5 billion, including debt and certain other WhiteWave liabilities. ...

"Acquisition expenses recognized in Danone's consolidated financial statements totaled €51 million before tax, of which €48 million was recognized in 2016 in Other operating income (expense), with the balance recognized in 2017.

"WhiteWave's contribution to 2017 consolidated sales totaled €2.7 billion. Had the transaction been completed on January 1, 2017, the Group's 2017 consolidated sales would have been €25.7 billion, with recurring operating income of €3.6 billion.

"Meanwhile, integration expenses for the period totaled €91 million, recognized under Other operating income (expense)."

Overview of Activities:

"As part of its transformation plan aimed at ensuring a safe journey to deliver strong, profitable and sustainable growth, Danone set objectives for 2020 that include like-for-like sales growth between 4% and 5% .... a recurring operating margin of over 16% in 2020 ... Finally, Danone will continue to focus on growing its free cash flow, which will contribute to financial deleverage with an objective of a ratio of Net debt/EBITDA below 3x in 2020. Danone is committed to reaching a ROIC level around 12% in 2020."

1. What are the major sources and uses of cash for Groupe Danone?

   Solution:

   The major categories of cash flows can be summarized as follows (in EUR millions):

	2016	2017
Cash flows provided by operating activities	2,652	2,958
Cash flows provided by (used in) investing activities	(848)	(11,437)
Cash flows provided by (used in) financing activities	(1,616)	8,289
Exchange rate effects on cash	(151)	272
Increase in cash	38	81

   The primary source of cash for Groupe Danone in 2016 was operating activities of 2,652. During that year, the company spent 925 on capital expenditures, representing most of the outflow of 848 from investing activities. In 2017, however, the primary source of cash for Groupe Danone was from financing activities. The investing section shows significant use of cash in 2017 for purchase of subsidiaries within investing activities.

2. Is cash flow from operating activities sufficient to cover capital expenditures?

   Solution:

   Yes, in both 2016 and 2017, there was sufficient operating cash flow to cover usual capital expenditures.

3. What is the relationship between net income and cash flow from operating activities?

   Solution:

   In both years, operating cash flow exceeded net income. The fact that operating cash flow exceeds net income in both years is a positive sign.

4. What types of financing cash flows does Groupe Danone have?

   Solution:

   Footnotes disclose a major acquisition with an aggregate value of USD12.5 billion, some of which was funded through proceeds from an earlier bond issuance, which appears as a financing cash flow in the financing section for 2016.

3 RATIOS AND COMMON-SIZE ANALYSIS

☐ calculate and interpret free cash flow to the firm, free cash flow to equity, and performance and coverage cash flow ratios

In common-size analysis of a company's income statement, each income and expense line item is expressed as a percentage of net revenues (net sales). For the common-size balance sheet, each asset, liability, and equity line item is expressed as a percentage of total assets. The common-size cash flow statement has two alternative approaches. The first approach is to express each line item of cash inflow (outflow) as a percentage of total inflows (outflows) of cash, and the second approach is to express each line item as a percentage of net revenue. The common-size format makes it easier to see trends in cash flow rather than just looking at the total amount.

Consider the statement of cash flows for Acme Corporation in Exhibit 3. Exhibit 4 demonstrates the total cash inflows/total cash outflows common-size method for Acme Corporation. Under this approach, each of the cash inflows is expressed as a percentage of the total cash inflows, whereas each of the cash outflows is expressed as a percentage of the total cash outflows. In Panel A, Acme's common-size statement is based on a cash flow statement using the direct method of presenting operating cash flows. Operating cash inflows and outflows are separately presented on the cash flow statement, and therefore, the common-size cash flow statement shows each of these operating inflows (outflows) as a percentage of total inflows (outflows).

In Panel B of Exhibit 4, Acme's common-size statement is based on a cash flow statement using the indirect method of presenting operating cash flows. When a cash flow statement has been presented using the indirect method, operating cash inflows and outflows are not separately presented; therefore, the common-size cash flow statement shows only the net operating cash flow (net cash provided by or used in operating activities) as a percentage of total inflows or outflows, depending on whether the net amount was a cash inflow or outflow. Because Acme's net operating cash flow is positive, it is shown as a percentage of total inflows.

Exhibit 3: Acme Corporation Cash Flow Statement (Direct Method) for Year Ended 31 December 2018

Cash flow from operating activities:	
Cash received from customers	$23,543
Cash paid to suppliers	(11,900)
Cash paid to employees	(4,113)
Cash paid for other operating expenses	(3,532)
Cash paid for interest	(258)
Cash paid for income tax	(1,134)
Net cash provided by operating activities	2,606
Cash flow from investing activities:	
Cash received from sale of equipment	762
Cash paid for purchase of equipment	(1,300)
Net cash used for investing activities	(538)
Cash flow from financing activities:	
Cash paid to retire long-term debt	(500)
Cash paid to retire common stock	(600)
Cash paid for dividends	(1,120)
Net cash used for financing activities	(2,120)
Net increase (decrease) in cash	(152)
Cash balance, 31 December 2017	1,163
Cash balance, 31 December 2018	1,011

Exhibit 4: Acme Corporation Common-Size Cash Flow Statement: Percentage of Inflows/Outflows Approach

Panel A. Direct Format for Cash Flow

Inflows		Percentage of Total Inflows
Receipts from customers	USD23,543	96.86%
Sale of equipment	762	3.14
Total	USD24,305	100.00%

Outflows		Percentage of Total Outflows
Payments to suppliers	USD11,900	48.66%
Payments to employees	4,113	16.82
Payments for other operating expenses	3,532	14.44
Payments for interest	258	1.05
Payments for income tax	1,134	4.64
Purchase of equipment	1,300	5.32
Retirement of long-term debt	500	2.04
Retirement of common stock	600	2.45
Dividend payments	1,120	4.58
Total	USD24,457	100.00%
Net increase (decrease) in cash	(USD152)	

Panel B. Indirect Format for Cash Flow

Inflows		Percentage of Total Inflows
Net cash provided by operating activities	USD2,606	77.38%
Sale of equipment	762	22.62
Total	USD3,368	100.00%

Outflows		Percentage of Total Outflows
Purchase of equipment	USD1,300	36.93%
Retirement of long-term debt	500	14.20
Retirement of common stock	600	17.05
Dividend payments	1,120	31.82
Total	USD3,520	100.00%
Net increase (decrease) in cash	(USD152)	

Exhibit 5 demonstrates the second method of common-sizing the statement of cash flows: the net revenue approach. Under the net revenue approach, each line item in the cash flow statement is shown as a percentage of net revenue. The common-size statement in Exhibit 5 has been developed based on Acme's cash flow statement using the indirect method for operating cash flows and using net revenue (cash received from customers) for the company in 2018 of USD23,543 from Exhibit 3.

This method is also useful to the analyst in forecasting future cash flows because individual items in the common-size statement (e.g., depreciation, fixed capital expenditures, debt borrowing, and repayment) are expressed as a percentage of net revenue. Thus, once the analyst has forecasted revenue, the common-size statement provides a basis for forecasting cash flows for those items with an expected relation to net revenue.

Exhibit 5: Acme Corporation Common-Size Cash Flow Statement: Net Revenue Approach

		Percentage of Net Revenue
Cash flow from operating activities:		
Net income	USD2,210	9.37%
Depreciation expense	1,052	4.46
Gain on sale of equipment	(205)	(0.87)
Increase in accounts receivable	(55)	(0.23)
Increase in inventory	(707)	(3.00)
Decrease in prepaid expenses	23	0.10
Increase in accounts payable	263	1.11
Increase in salary and wage payable	10	0.04
Decrease in interest payable	(12)	(0.05)
Increase in income tax payable	5	0.02
Increase in other accrued liabilities	22	0.09
Net cash provided by operating activities	USD2,606	11.04%
Cash flow from investing activities:		
Cash received from sale of equipment	USD762	3.23%
Cash paid for purchase of equipment	(1,300)	(5.51)
Net cash used for investing activities	USD(538)	(2.28)%
Cash flow from financing activities:		
Cash paid to retire long-term debt	USD(500)	(2.12)%
Cash paid to retire common stock	(600)	(2.54)
Cash paid for dividends	(1,120)	(4.75)
Net cash used for financing activities	USD(2,220)	(9.41)%
Net decrease in cash	USD(152)	(0.64)%

EXAMPLE 2

Analysis of a Common-Size Cash Flow Statement

1. Andrew Potter is examining an abbreviated common-size cash flow statement for Apple Inc., a multinational technology company. The common-size cash flow statement, presented in Exhibit 6, was prepared by dividing each line item by total net sales for the same year.

Exhibit 6: Apple Inc. Common-Size Statements of Cash Flows as Percentage of Total Net Sales

	12 Months Ended		
	30 September 2017	24 September 2016	26 September 2015
Statement of Cash Flows [Abstract]			
Operating activities:			
Net income	21.1%	21.2%	22.8%
Adjustments to reconcile net income to cash generated by operating activities:			
Depreciation and amortization	4.4%	4.9%	4.8%
Share-based compensation expense	2.1%	2.0%	1.5%
Deferred income tax expense	2.6%	2.3%	0.6%
Other	−0.1%	0.2%	0.2%
Changes in operating assets and liabilities:			
Accounts receivable, net	−0.9%	0.2%	0.2%
Inventories	−1.2%	0.1%	−0.1%
Vendor non-trade receivables	−1.9%	0.0%	−1.6%
Other current and non-current assets	−2.3%	0.5%	−0.1%
Accounts payable	4.2%	0.9%	2.1%
Deferred revenue	−0.3%	−0.7%	0.4%
Other current and non-current liabilities	−0.1%	−0.9%	3.9%
Cash generated by operating activities	27.7%	30.5%	34.8%
Investing activities:			
Purchases of marketable securities	−69.6%	−66.0%	−71.2%
Proceeds from maturities of marketable securities	13.9%	9.9%	6.2%
Proceeds from sales of marketable securities	41.3%	42.0%	46.0%
Payments made in connection with business acquisitions, net	−0.1%	−0.1%	−0.1%

	12 Months Ended		
	30 September 2017	24 September 2016	26 September 2015
Payments for acquisition of property, plant and equipment	−5.4%	−5.9%	−4.8%
Payments for acquisition of intangible assets	−0.2%	−0.4%	−0.1%
Payments for strategic investments, net	−0.2%	−0.6%	0.0%
Other	0.1%	−0.1%	0.0%
Cash used in investing activities	−20.3%	−21.3%	−24.1%
Financing activities:			
Proceeds from issuance of common stock	0.2%	0.2%	0.2%
Excess tax benefits from equity awards	0.3%	0.2%	0.3%
Payments for taxes related to net share settlement of equity awards	−0.8%	−0.7%	−0.6%
Payments for dividends and dividend equivalents	−5.6%	−5.6%	−4.9%
Repurchases of common stock	−14.4%	−13.8%	−15.1%
Proceeds from issuance of term debt, net	12.5%	11.6%	—
Repayments of term debt	−1.5%	−1.2%	0.0%
Change in commercial paper, net	1.7%	−0.2%	0.9%
Cash used in financing activities	−7.6%	−9.5%	−7.6%
Increase/(Decrease) in cash and cash equivalents	−0.1%	−0.3%	3.1%

2. Based on the information in Exhibit 6, discuss the trends in Apple's:

   A. depreciation and amortization expense.

   B. capital expenditures.

Solution:

A. Apple's depreciation and amortization expense was consistently just less than 5 percent of total net revenue in 2015 and 2016, declining to 4.4 percent in 2017.

B. Apple's level of capital expenditures is greater than its depreciation and amortization in 2016 and 2017, whereas it was at about the same level as depreciation and amortization in 2015. In 2017, capital expenditures approached 6 percent. This is an indication that Apple is doing more than replacing property, plant, and equipment, and is expanding those investments. With cash generated from operating activities exceeding 27 percent of sales in every year, however, Apple has more than enough cash flow from operations to fund these expenditures.

3. Compare Apple's operating cash flow as a percentage of revenue with Apple's net profit margin.

Solution:

Apple's operating cash flow as a percentage of sales is much higher than net profit margin in every year. This gap appears to be declining however over the three-year period. In 2015 net profit margin was 22.8 percent, while operating cash flow as a percentage of sales was 34.8 percent. By 2017, the net profit margin declined slightly to 21.1 percent, while the operating cash flow as a percentage of sales declined more to 27.7 percent. The primary difference appears to have been an increase in the level of receivables and inventory purchases, somewhat offset by an increase in accounts payable.

4. Discuss Apple's use of its positive operating cash flow.

Solution:

Apple generated a large amount of operating cash flow each year, exceeding net income. This cash flow is used for relatively modest purchases of property, plant, and equipment, substantial purchases of marketable securities (investments), dividend payments and repurchases of its own stock.

4 FREE CASH FLOW MEASURES

☐ calculate and interpret free cash flow to the firm, free cash flow to equity, and performance and coverage cash flow ratios

As noted earlier, it is desirable that operating cash flows are sufficient to cover capital expenditures. The excess of operating cash flow over capital expenditures is known generically as **free cash flow**. For purposes of valuing a company or its equity securities, an analyst may want to determine and use other cash flow measures, such as free cash flow to the firm (FCFF) or free cash flow to equity (FCFE).

FCFF is the cash flow available to both debt and equity investors after all operating expenses (including income taxes) have been paid and necessary investments in working capital and fixed capital have been made. FCFF can be computed starting with net income as follows:

$$\text{FCFF} = \text{NI} + \text{NCC} + \text{Int}(1 - \text{Tax rate}) - \text{FCInv} - \text{WCInv}$$

where:

NI = Net income,

NCC = Non-cash charges (such as depreciation and amortization),

Int = Interest expense,

FCInv = Capital expenditures (fixed capital, such as equipment), and

WCInv = Working capital expenditures.

The reason for adding back interest is that FCFF is the cash flow available to the suppliers of debt capital as well as equity capital. Conveniently, FCFF can also be computed from cash flow from operating activities as follows

FCFF = CFO + Int(1 – Tax rate) – FCInv.

CFO represents cash flow from operating activities under US GAAP or under IFRS, where the company has included interest paid in operating activities. If interest paid was included in financing activities, then CFO does not have to be adjusted for Int(1 – Tax rate). Under IFRS, if the company has placed interest and dividends received in investing activities, these should be added back to CFO to determine FCFF. Additionally, if dividends paid were subtracted in the operating section, these should be added back in to compute FCFF.

Assuming a marginal tax rate of 34 percent for Acme in 2018, the computation of FCFF for Acme Corporation (based on the data from Exhibit 3) is shown in Exhibit 7.

Exhibit 7: FCFF for Acme Corporation

CFO	USD2,606
Plus: Interest paid times (1 – income tax rate)	
{USD258 [1 – 0.34][a]}	170
Less: Net investments in fixed capital (USD1,300 – USD762)	(538)
FCFF	USD2,238

[a]*Income tax rate of 0.34 = (Tax expense ÷ Pretax income) = ($1,139 ÷ $3,349).*

FCFE is the cash flow available to the company's common stockholders after all operating expenses and borrowing costs (principal and interest) have been paid and necessary investments in working capital and fixed capital have been made. FCFE can be computed as follows:

FCFE = CFO – FCInv + Net borrowing.

When net borrowing is negative, debt repayments exceed receipts of borrowed funds. In this case, FCFE can be expressed as follows:

FCFE = CFO – FCInv – Net debt repayment.

The computation of FCFE for Acme Corporation (again, based on the data from Exhibit 3) is shown in Exhibit 8.

Exhibit 8: FCFE for Acme Corporation

CFO	USD2,606
Less: Net investments in fixed capital (USD1,300 – USD762)	(538)
Less: Debt repayment	(500)
FCFE	USD1,568

Positive FCFE means that the company has an excess of operating cash flow over amounts needed for capital expenditures and repayment of debt. This cash would be available for distribution to owners.

5 CASH FLOW STATEMENT ANALYSIS: CASH FLOW RATIOS

☐ calculate and interpret free cash flow to the firm, free cash flow to equity, and performance and coverage cash flow ratios

Ratios based on information in statements of cash flows can be used to compare the performance and prospects of different companies in an industry and of different industries. These ratios generally fall into cash flow performance (profitability) ratios and cash flow coverage (solvency) ratios. Exhibit 9 summarizes the calculation and interpretation of some of these ratios.

Exhibit 9: Cash Flow Ratios

Performance Ratios	Calculation	What It Measures
Cash flow to revenue	CFO ÷ Net revenue	Operating cash generated per dollar of revenue
Cash return on assets	CFO ÷ Average total assets	Operating cash generated per dollar of asset investment
Cash return on equity	CFO ÷ Average shareholders' equity	Operating cash generated per dollar of owner investment
Cash to income	CFO ÷ Operating income	Cash generating ability of operations
Cash flow per share[a]	(CFO – Preferred dividends) ÷ Number of common shares outstanding	Operating cash flow on a per-share basis

Coverage Ratios	Calculation	What It Measures
Debt coverage	CFO ÷ Total debt	Financial risk and financial leverage
Interest coverage[b]	(CFO + Interest paid + Taxes paid) ÷ Interest paid	Ability to meet interest obligations
Reinvestment	CFO ÷ Cash paid for long-term assets	Ability to acquire assets with operating cash flows
Debt payment	CFO ÷ Cash paid for long-term debt repayment	Ability to pay debts with operating cash flows

Coverage Ratios	Calculation	What It Measures
Dividend payment	CFO ÷ Dividends paid	Ability to pay dividends with operating cash flows
Investing and financing	CFO ÷ Cash outflows for investing and financing activities	Ability to acquire assets, pay debts, and make distributions to owners

Notes:

[a] If the company reports under IFRS and includes total dividends paid as a use of cash in the operating section, total dividends should be added back to CFO as reported and then preferred dividends should be subtracted. Recall that CFO reported under US GAAP and IFRS may differ depending on the treatment of interest and dividends, received and paid.

[b] If the company reports under IFRS and included interest paid as a use of cash in the financing section, then interest paid should not be added back to the numerator.

EXAMPLE 3

A Cash Flow Analysis of Comparables

1. Andrew Potter is analyzing operating cash flow trends for Microsoft and Apple, which are presented in Exhibits 10 and 11.

Exhibit 10: Cash Flow from Operating Activities as a Percentage of Total Net Revenue

	2017	2016	2015
Microsoft	43.9%	39.1%	31.7%
Apple Inc.	27.7%	30.5%	34.8%

Exhibit 11: Cash Flow from Operating Activities as a Percentage of Average Total Assets

	2017	2016	2015
Microsoft	18.2%	18.1%	17.1%
Apple Inc.	18.2%	21.5%	31.1%

What is Potter *most likely* to conclude about the relative operating cash-flow-generating ability of these two companies?

Solution:

On both measures—operating cash flow divided by revenue and operating cash flow divided by assets—both companies have overall strong results. However, Microsoft has higher cash flow from operating activities as a percentage of revenues in both 2016 and 2017. Further, Microsoft has an increasing trend. While Apple had a higher operating cash flow as a percent of revenue in 2015 compared to Microsoft, it has had a declining trend and was below Microsoft in the two more recent years. Microsoft's operating cash flow relative to assets is the same as Apple's in 2017 and relatively stable with a slight increase since 2015. Apple started the three years with a much stronger ratio but saw a declining trend such that its ratio is now at the same level as Microsoft. We should note that this ratio is heavily influenced by substantial investments in financial instruments that Apple has made over the years due to its strong historic cash flow.

PRACTICE PROBLEMS

1. One appropriate method of preparing a common-size cash flow statement is to show each line item:

   A. of revenue and expense as a percentage of net revenue.

   B. on the cash flow statement as a percentage of net revenue.

   C. on the cash flow statement as a percentage of total cash outflows.

2. Which of the following is an appropriate method of computing free cash flow to the firm?

   A. Add operating cash flows to capital expenditures and deduct after-tax interest payments.

   B. Add operating cash flows to after-tax interest payments and deduct capital expenditures.

   C. Deduct both after-tax interest payments and capital expenditures from operating cash flows.

3. The first step in cash flow statement analysis should be to:

   A. evaluate consistency of cash flows.

   B. determine operating cash flow drivers.

   C. identify the major sources and uses of cash.

4. An analyst has calculated a ratio using as the numerator the sum of operating cash flow, interest, and taxes and as the denominator the amount of interest. What is this ratio, what does it measure, and what does it indicate?

   A. This ratio is an interest coverage ratio, measuring a company's ability to meet its interest obligations and indicating a company's solvency.

   B. This ratio is an effective tax ratio, measuring the amount of a company's operating cash flow used for taxes and indicating a company's efficiency in tax management.

   C. This ratio is an operating profitability ratio, measuring the operating cash flow generated accounting for taxes and interest and indicating a company's liquidity.

SOLUTIONS

1. B is correct. An appropriate method to prepare a common-size cash flow statement is to show each line item on the cash flow statement as a percentage of net revenue. An alternative way to prepare a statement of cash flows is to show each item of cash inflow as a percentage of total inflows and each item of cash outflows as a percentage of total outflows.

2. B is correct. Free cash flow to the firm can be computed as operating cash flows plus after-tax interest expense less capital expenditures.

3. C is correct. An overall assessment of the major sources and uses of cash should be the first step in evaluating a cash flow statement.

4. A is correct. This ratio is an interest coverage ratio, measuring a company's ability to meet its interest obligations and indicating a company's solvency. This coverage ratio is based on cash flow information; another common formulation of the interest coverage ratio uses EBITDA based on the income statement as the numerator.

LEARNING MODULE

6

Analysis of Inventories

LEARNING OUTCOMES

Mastery	The candidate should be able to:
☐	describe the measurement of inventory at the lower of cost and net realisable value and its implications for financial statements and ratios
☐	calculate and explain how inflation and deflation of inventory costs affect the financial statements and ratios of companies that use different inventory valuation methods
☐	describe the presentation and disclosures relating to inventories and explain issues that analysts should consider when examining a company's inventory disclosures and other sources of information

The two major accounting standard setters are as follows: 1) the International Accounting Standards Board (IASB) who establishes International Financial Reporting Standards (IFRS) and 2) the Financial Accounting Standards Board (FASB) who establishes US GAAP. Throughout this learning module both standards are referred to and many, but not all, of these two sets of accounting rules are identified. Note: changes in accounting standards as well as new rulings and/or pronouncements issued after the publication of this learning module may cause some of the information to become dated.

1 INTRODUCTION

The choice of inventory valuation method (also known as the cost formula or cost flow assumption) can have a significant impact on inventory carrying amounts and cost of sales. These items in turn affect other financial statement items, such as current assets, total assets, gross profit, and net income. A company's financial statements and accompanying notes provide important information about its inventory accounting policies that the analyst needs to correctly assess financial performance and compare it with that of other companies.

LEARNING MODULE OVERVIEW

- Inventories are a major factor in the analysis of merchandising and manufacturing companies. Such companies generate their sales and profits through inventory transactions on a regular basis. An important consideration in determining profits for these companies is measuring the cost of sales when inventories are sold.
- The choice of inventory method affects the financial statements and any financial ratios that are based on them. As a consequence, the analyst must carefully consider inventory valuation method differences when evaluating a company's performance over time or in comparison to industry data or industry competitors.
- Under International Financial Reporting Standards (IFRS), inventories are measured at the lower of cost and net realizable value. Net realizable value is the estimated selling price in the ordinary course of business less the estimated costs necessary to make the sale. Under US GAAP, inventories are measured at the lower of cost, market value, or net realizable value depending upon the inventory method used. Market value is defined as the current replacement cost subject to an upper limit of net realizable value and a lower limit of net realizable value less a normal profit margin. Reversals of previous write-downs are permissible under IFRS but not under US GAAP.
- Reversals of inventory write-downs may occur under IFRS but are not allowed under US GAAP.
- Changes in the carrying amounts within inventory classifications (such as raw materials, work-in-process, and finished goods) may provide signals about a company's future sales and profits. Relevant information with respect to inventory management and future sales may be found in the management discussion and analysis or similar section within the annual or quarterly reports, industry news and publications, and industry economic data.
- The inventory turnover ratio, number of days of inventory ratio, and gross profit margin ratio are useful in evaluating the management of a company's inventory.
- Financial statement disclosures provide information regarding the accounting policies adopted in measuring inventories, the principal uncertainties regarding the use of estimates related to inventories, and details of the inventory carrying amounts and costs. This information can greatly assist analysts in their evaluation of a company's inventory management.

INVENTORY VALUATION

2

☐ describe the measurement of inventory at the lower of cost and net realisable value and its implications for financial statements and ratios

Significant financial risk can result from the holding of inventory. The cost of inventory may not be recoverable due to spoilage, obsolescence, or declines in selling prices. IFRS states that inventories shall be measured (and carried on the balance sheet) at the lower of cost and net realizable value.[1]Net realizable value is the estimated selling price in the ordinary course of business, less the estimated costs necessary to make the sale and estimated costs to get the inventory in condition for sale. The assessment of net realizable value is typically done item by item or by groups of similar or related items. In the event that the value of inventory declines below the carrying amount on the balance sheet, the inventory carrying amount must be written down to its net realizable value[2] and the loss (reduction in value) recognized as an expense on the income statement. This expense may be included as part of cost of sales or reported separately.

In each subsequent period, a new assessment of net realizable value is made. Reversal (limited to the amount of the original write-down) is required for a subsequent increase in value of inventory previously written down. The reversal of any write-down of inventories is recognized as a reduction in cost of sales (reduction in the amount of inventories recognized as an expense).

US GAAP used to specify the lower of cost or market to value inventories.[3] For fiscal years beginning after 15 December 2016, inventories measured using other than last-in, first-out (LIFO) and retail inventory methods are measured at the lower of cost or net realizable value. This is broadly consistent with IFRS with one major difference: US GAAP prohibits the reversal of write-downs. For inventories measured using LIFO and retail inventory methods, market value is defined as current replacement cost subject to upper and lower limits. Market value cannot exceed net realizable value (i.e., the selling price less reasonably estimated costs of completion and disposal). The lower limit of market value is net realizable value less a normal profit margin. Any write-down to market value or net realizable value reduces the value of the inventory, and the loss in value (expense) generally is reflected in the income statement in the cost of goods sold.

An inventory write-down reduces both profit and the carrying amount of inventory on the balance sheet and thus has a negative effect on profitability, liquidity, and solvency ratios. However, activity ratios (e.g., inventory turnover and total asset turnover) will be positively affected by a write-down because the asset base (denominator) is reduced. The negative impact on some key ratios, due to the decrease in profit, may result in the reluctance by some companies to record inventory write-downs unless evidence is strong that the decline in the value of inventory is permanent. This is especially true under US GAAP, in which case reversal of a write-down is prohibited.

International Accounting Standards 2 (IAS 2), *Inventories*, does not apply to the inventories of producers of agricultural and forest products and minerals and mineral products, nor to commodity broker–traders. These inventories may be measured at net

1 IAS 2, paragraphs 28–33, *Inventories– Net realizable value.*

2 Frequently, rather than writing down inventory directly, an inventory valuation allowance account is used. The allowance account is netted with the inventory accounts to arrive at the carrying amount that appears on the balance sheet.

3 Financial Accounting Standards Board (FASB), Accounting Standards Codification (ASC), Section 330-10-35, *Inventory–Overall–Subsequent Measurement.*

realizable value (fair value less costs to sell and complete) according to well-established industry practices. If an active market exists for these products, the quoted market price in that market is the appropriate basis for determining the fair value of that asset. If an active market does not exist, a company may use market determined prices or values (such as the most recent market transaction price) when available for determining fair value. Changes in the value of inventory (increase or decrease) are recognized in profit or loss in the period of the change. US GAAP is similar to IFRS in its treatment of inventories of agricultural and forest products and mineral ores. Mark-to-market inventory accounting is allowed for bullion.

EXAMPLE 1

Accounting for Declines and Recoveries of Inventory Value

Hatsumei Enterprises, a hypothetical company, manufactures computers and prepares its financial statements in accordance with IFRS. In 2017, the cost of ending inventory was EUR5.2 million, but its net realizable value was EUR4.9 million. The current replacement cost of the inventory is EUR4.7 million. This figure exceeds the net realizable value less a normal profit margin. In 2018, the net realizable value of Hatsumei's inventory was EUR0.5 million greater than the carrying amount.

1. What was the effect of the write-down on Hatsumei's 2017 financial statements? What was the effect of the recovery on Hatsumei's 2018 financial statements?

   Solution:

   For 2017, Hatsumei would write down its inventory to EUR4.9 million and record the change in value of EUR0.3 million as an expense on the income statement. For 2018, Hatsumei would increase the carrying amount of its inventory and reduce the cost of sales by EUR0.3 million (the recovery is limited to the amount of the original write-down).

2. Under US GAAP, if Hatsumei used the LIFO method, what would be the effects of the write-down on Hatsumei's 2017 financial statements and of the recovery on Hatsumei's 2018 financial statements?

   Solution:

   Under US GAAP, for 2017, Hatsumei would write down its inventory to EUR4.7 million and typically include the change in value of EUR0.5 million in cost of goods sold on the income statement. For 2018, Hatsumei would not reverse the write-down.

3. What would be the effect of the recovery on Hatsumei's 2018 financial statements if Hatsumei's inventory were agricultural products instead of computers?

   Solution:

   If Hatsumei's inventory were agricultural products instead of computers, inventory would be measured at net realizable value and Hatsumei, therefore, would increase inventory and record a gain of EUR0.5 million for 2018.

Analysts should consider the possibility of an inventory write-down because the impact on a company's financial ratios may be substantial. The potential for inventory write-downs can be high for companies in industries in which technological obsolescence of inventories is a significant risk. Analysts should carefully evaluate prospective inventory impairments (as well as other potential asset impairments) and their potential effects on the financial ratios when debt covenants include financial ratio requirements. The breaching of debt covenants can have a significant impact on a company.

Companies that use specific identification, weighted average cost, or FIFO methods are more likely to incur inventory write-downs than companies that use the LIFO method. Under the LIFO method, the *oldest* costs are reflected in the inventory carrying amount on the balance sheet. Given increasing inventory costs, the inventory carrying amounts under the LIFO method are already conservatively presented at the oldest and lowest costs. Thus, it is far less likely that inventory write-downs will occur under LIFO—and if a write-down does occur, it is likely to be of a lesser magnitude.

EXAMPLE 2

Effect of Inventory Write-Downs on Financial Ratios

The Volvo Group, based in Göteborg, Sweden, is a leading supplier of commercial transport products, such as construction equipment, trucks, busses, and drive systems for marine and industrial applications as well as aircraft engine components.[4] Excerpts from Volvo's consolidated financial statements are shown in Exhibits 1 and 2. Notes pertaining to Volvo's inventories are presented in Exhibit 3.

Exhibit 1: Volvo Group Consolidated Income Statements (Swedish krona in millions, except per share data)

For the years ended 31 December	2017	2016	2015
Net sales	334,748	301,914	312,515
Cost of sales	(254,581)	(231,602)	(240,653)
Gross income	80,167	70,312	71,862
⋮	⋮	⋮	⋮
Operating income	30,327	20,826	23,318
Interest income and similar credits	164	240	257
Income expenses and similar charges	(1,852)	(1,847)	(2,366)
Other financial income and expenses	(386)	11	(792)
Income after financial items	28,254	19,230	20,418
Income taxes	(6,971)	(6,008)	(5,320)
Income for the period	21,283	13,223	15,099
Attributable to:			
Equity holders of the parent company	20,981	13,147	15,058
Minority interests	302	76	41
Profit	21,283	13,223	15,099

4 The Volvo line of automobiles has not been under the control and management of the Volvo Group since 1999.

Exhibit 2: Volvo Group Consolidated Balance Sheets (Swedish krona in millions)

31 December	2017	2016	2015
Assets			
Total non-current assets	213,455	218,465	203,478
Current assets:			
Inventories	52,701	48,287	44,390
⋮	⋮	⋮	⋮
Cash and cash equivalents	36,092	23,949	21,048
Total current assets	199,039	180,301	170,687
Total assets	412,494	398,916	374,165
Shareholders' equity and liabilities			
Equity attributable to equity holders of the parent company	107,069	96,061	83,810
Minority interests	1,941	1,703	1,801
Total shareholders' equity	109,011	97,764	85,610
Total non-current provisions	29,147	29,744	26,704
Total non-current liabilities	96,213	104,873	91,814
Total current provisions	10,806	11,333	14,176
Total current liabilities	167,317	155,202	155,860
Total shareholders' equity and liabilities	412,404	398,916	374,165

Exhibit 3: Volvo Group Selected Notes to Consolidated Financial Statements

Note 17. Inventories

Accounting Policy

Inventories are reported at the lower of cost and net realizable value. The cost is established using the first-in, first-out principle (FIFO) and is based on the standard cost method, including costs for all direct manufacturing expenses and the attributable share of capacity and other related manufacturing-related costs. The standard costs are tested regularly and adjustments are made based on current conditions. Costs for research and development, selling, administration and financial expenses are not included. Net realizable value is calculated as the selling price less costs attributable to the sale.

Sources of Estimation Uncertainty

Inventory obsolescence

If the net realizable value is lower than cost, a valuation allowance is established for inventory obsolescence. The total inventory value, net of inventory obsolescence allowance, was SEK52,701 (in millions) as of December 2017, and SEK48,287 as of 31 December 2016.

Panel A: Inventory

31 December (millions of krona)	2017	2016	2015
Finished products	32,304	31,012	27,496
Production materials, etc.	20,397	17,275	16,894
Total	**52,701**	**48,287**	**44,390**

Panel B: Increase (decrease) in allowance for inventory obsolescence

31 December (millions of krona)	2017	2016	2015
Opening balance	3,683	3,624	3,394
Change in allowance for inventory obsolescence charged to income	304	480	675
Scrapping	(391)	(576)	(435)
Translation differences	(116)	177	(29)
Reclassifications, etc.	8	(23)	20
Allowance for inventory obsolescence as of 31 December	3,489	3,683	3,624

1. What inventory values would Volvo have reported for 2017, 2016, and 2015 if it had no allowance for inventory obsolescence?

   Solution:

31 December (Swedish krona in millions)	2017	2016	2015
Total inventories, net	52,701	48,287	44,390
From Note 17. (Allowance for obsolescence)	3,489	3,683	3,624
Total inventories (without allowance)	56,190	51,970	48,014

2. Assuming that any changes to the allowance for inventory obsolescence are reflected in the cost of sales, what amount would Volvo's cost of sales be for 2017 and 2016 if it had not recorded inventory write-downs in 2017 and 2016?

   Solution:

31 December (Swedish krona in millions)	2017	2016
Cost of sales	254,581	231,602
(Increase) decrease in allowance for obsolescence*	194	(59)
Cost of sales without allowance	254,775	231,543

** From Note 17, the decrease in the allowance for obsolescence for 2017 is 194 (3,489 – 3,683) and the increase for 2016 is 59 (3,683 – 3,624).*

3. What amount would Volvo's profit (net income) be for 2017 and 2016 if it had not recorded inventory write-downs in 2017 and 2016? Volvo's effec-

tive income tax rate was reported as 25 percent for 2017 and 31 percent for 2016.

Solution:

31 December (Swedish krona in millions)	2017	2016
Profit (Net income)	21,283	13,223
Increase (reduction) in cost of sales	(194)	59
Taxes (tax reduction) on operating profit*	49	(18)
Profit (without allowance)	21,138	13,264

* *Taxes (tax deductions) on the operating profit are assumed to be 49 (194 x 25%) for 2017 and −18 (−59 x 31%) for 2016.*

4. What would Volvo's 2017 profit (net income) have been if it had reversed all past inventory write-downs in 2017? This question is independent of 1, 2, and 3. The effective income tax rate was 25 percent for 2017.

Solution:

31 December (Swedish krona in millions)	2017
Profit (Net income)	21,283
Reduction in cost of sales (increase in operating profit)	3,489
Taxes on increased operating profit*	-872
Profit (after recovery of previous write-downs)	23,900

* *Taxes on the increased operating profit are assumed to be 872 (3,489 × 25%) for 2017.*

5. Compare the following for 2017 based on the numbers as reported and those assuming no allowance for inventory obsolescence as in questions 1, 2, and 3: inventory turnover ratio, days of inventory on hand, gross profit margin, and net profit margin.

Solution:

The Volvo Group's financial ratios for 2017 with the allowance for inventory obsolescence and without the allowance for inventory obsolescence are as follows:

	With Allowance (As Reported)	Without Allowance (Adjusted)
Inventory turnover ratio	5.04	4.71
Days of inventory on hand	72.4	77.5
Gross profit margin	23.95%	23.89%
Net profit margin	6.36%	6.31%

Inventory turnover ratio = Cost of sales ÷ Average inventory

With allowance (as reported) = 5.04 = 254,581 ÷ [(52,701 + 48,287) ÷ 2]

Without allowance (adjusted) = 4.71 = 254,775 ÷ [(56,190 + 51,970) ÷ 2]

Inventory turnover is higher based on the numbers as reported because inventory carrying amounts will be lower with an allowance for inventory obsolescence. The company might appear to manage its inventory more efficiently when it has inventory write-downs.

Days of inventory on hand

= Number of days in period ÷ Inventory turnover ratio

With allowance (as reported) = 72.4 days = (365 days ÷ 5.04)

Without allowance (adjusted) = 77.5 days = (365 days ÷ 4.71)

Days of inventory on hand are lower based on the numbers as reported because the inventory turnover is higher. A company with inventory write-downs might appear to manage its inventory more effectively. This is primarily the result of the lower inventory carrying amounts.

Gross profit margin = Gross profit ÷ Net sales

With allowance (as reported) = 23.95% = (80,167 ÷ 334,748)

Without allowance (adjusted) = 23.89% = [(80,167 − 194) ÷ 334,748]

In this instance, the gross profit margin is slightly higher with inventory write-downs because the cost of sales is lower (due to the reduction in the allowance for inventory obsolescence). This assumes that inventory write-downs (and inventory write-down recoveries) are reported as part of cost of sales.

Net profit margin = Profit ÷ Net sales

With allowance (as reported) = 6.36% = (21,283 ÷ 334,748)

Without allowance (adjusted) = 6.31% = (21,138 ÷ 334,748)

In this instance, the net profit margin is higher with inventory write-downs because the cost of sales is lower (due to the reduction in the allowance for inventory obsolescence). The absolute percentage difference is less than that of the gross profit margin because of the income tax reduction on the decreased income without write-downs.

The profitability ratios (gross profit margin and net profit margin) for Volvo Group would have been slightly lower for 2017 if the company had not recorded inventory write-downs. The activity ratio (inventory turnover ratio) would appear less attractive without the write-downs. The inventory turnover ratio is slightly better (higher) with inventory write-downs because inventory write-downs decrease the average inventory (denominator), making inventory management appear more efficient with write-downs.

3 THE EFFECTS OF INFLATION AND DEFLATION ON INVENTORIES, COSTS OF SALES, AND GROSS MARGIN

☐ calculate and explain how inflation and deflation of inventory costs affect the financial statements and ratios of companies that use different inventory valuation methods

The allocation of the total cost of goods available for sale to cost of sales on the income statement and to ending inventory on the balance sheet varies under the different inventory valuation methods. In an environment of declining inventory unit costs and constant or increasing inventory quantities, first-in, first-out (FIFO) (in comparison with weighted average cost or LIFO) will allocate a higher amount of the total cost of goods available for sale to cost of sales on the income statement and a lower amount to ending inventory on the balance sheet. Accordingly, because cost of sales will be higher under FIFO, a company's gross profit, operating profit, and income before taxes will be lower.

Conversely, in an environment of rising inventory unit costs and constant or increasing inventory quantities, FIFO (in comparison with weighted average cost or LIFO) will allocate a lower amount of the total cost of goods available for sale to cost of sales on the income statement and a higher amount to ending inventory on the balance sheet. Accordingly, because cost of sales will be lower under FIFO, a company's gross profit, operating profit, and income before taxes will be higher.

The carrying amount of inventories under FIFO will more closely reflect current replacement values because inventories are assumed to consist of the most recently purchased items. The cost of sales under LIFO will more closely reflect current replacement value. LIFO ending inventory amounts typically are not reflective of current replacement value because the ending inventory is assumed to be the oldest inventory and costs are allocated accordingly. Example 3 illustrates the different results obtained by using either the FIFO or LIFO methods to account for inventory.

EXAMPLE 3

Impact of Inflation Using LIFO Compared to FIFO

Company L and Company F are identical in all respects except that Company L uses the LIFO method and Company F uses the FIFO method. Each company has been in business for five years and maintains a base inventory of 2,000 units each year. Each year, except the first year, the number of units purchased equaled the number of units sold. Over the five year period, unit sales increased 10 percent each year and the unit purchase and selling prices increased at the beginning of each year to reflect inflation of 4 percent per year. In the first year, 20,000 units were sold at a price of USD15.00 per unit and the unit purchase price was USD8.00.

1. What was the end-of-year inventory, sales, cost of sales, and gross profit for each company for each of the five years?

   Solution:

Company L using LIFO (in USD)	**Year 1**	**Year 2**	**Year 3**	**Year 4**	**Year 5**
Ending inventory[a]	16,000	16,000	16,000	16,000	16,000
Sales[b]	300,000	343,200	392,621	449,158	513,837
Cost of sales[c]	160,000	183,040	209,398	239,551	274,046
Gross profit	140,000	160,160	183,223	209,607	239,791

[a] *Inventory is unchanged at USD16,000 each year (2,000 units × USD8). 2,000 of the units acquired in the first year are assumed to remain in inventory.*
[b] *Sales Year X = (20,000 × USD15)$(1.10)^{X-1}(1.04)^{X-1}$. The quantity sold increases by 10 percent each year and the selling price increases by 4 percent each year.*
[c] *Cost of sales Year X = (20,000 × USD8)$(1.10)^{X-1}(1.04)^{X-1}$. In Year 1, 20,000 units are sold with a cost of USD8. In subsequent years, the number of units purchased equals the number of units sold and the units sold are assumed to be those purchased in the year. The quantity purchased increases by 10 percent each year and the purchase price increases by 4 percent each year.*

If the company sold more units than it purchased in a year, inventory would decrease. This is referred to as LIFO liquidation. The cost of sales of the units sold in excess of those purchased would reflect the inventory carrying amount. In this example, each unit sold in excess of those purchased would have a cost of sales of USD8 and a higher gross profit.

Company F using FIFO (in US dollars)	**Year 1**	**Year 2**	**Year 3**	**Year 4**	**Year 5**
Ending inventory[a]	16,000	16,640	17,306	17,998	18,718
Sales[b]	300,000	343,200	392,621	449,158	513,837
Cost of sales[c]	160,000	182,400	208,732	238,859	273,326
Gross profit	140,000	160,800	183,889	210,299	240,511

[a] *Ending Inventory Year X = 2,000 units × Cost in Year X = 2,000 units [USD8 × $(1.04)^{X-1}$]; 2,000 units of the units acquired in Year X are assumed to remain in inventory.*
[b] *Sales Year X = (20,000 x USD15)$(1.10)^{X-1}(1.04)^{X-1}$.*
[c] *Cost of sales Year 1 = USD160,000 (= 20,000 units × USD8). There was no beginning inventory.*

Cost of sales Year X (where $X \neq 1$)

= Beginning inventory plus purchases less ending inventory

= (Inventory at Year X–1) + [(20,000 × USD8)$(1.10)^{X-1}(1.04)^{X-1}$]
– (Inventory at Year X)

= 2,000(USD8)$(1.04)^{X-2}$ + [(20,000 × USD8)$(1.10)^{X-1}(1.04)^{X-1}$] – [2,000 (USD8)$(1.04)^{X-1}$].

For example, cost of sales Year 2

= 2,000(USD8) + [(20,000 x USD8)(1.10)(1.04)] – [2,000(USD8)(1.04)]

= USD16,000 + USD183,040 – USD16,640 = USD182,400.

2. Compare the inventory turnover ratios (based on ending inventory carrying amounts) and gross profit margins over the five-year period and between companies.

Solution:

	Company L					Company F				
Year	**1**	**2**	**3**	**4**	**5**	**1**	**2**	**3**	**4**	**5**
Inventory turnover	10.0	11.4	13.1	15.0	17.1	10.0	11.0	12.1	13.3	14.6
Gross profit margin (%)	46.7	46.7	46.7	46.7	46.7	46.7	46.9	46.8	46.8	46.8

Inventory turnover ratio = Cost of sales ÷ Ending inventory.

The inventory turnover ratio increased each year for both companies because the units sold increased, whereas the units in ending inventory remained unchanged. The increase in the inventory turnover ratio is higher for Company L because Company L's cost of sales is increasing for inflation, but the inventory carrying amount is unaffected by inflation. It might appear that a company using the LIFO method manages its inventory more effectively, but this is deceptive. Both companies have identical quantities and prices of purchases and sales and only differ in the inventory valuation method used.

Gross profit margin = Gross profit ÷ Sales.

The gross profit margin is stable under LIFO because both sales and cost of sales increase at the same rate of inflation. The gross profit margin is slightly higher under the FIFO method after the first year because a proportion of the cost of sales reflects an older purchase price.

4 PRESENTATION AND DISCLOSURE

☐ describe the presentation and disclosures relating to inventories and explain issues that analysts should consider when examining a company's inventory disclosures and other sources of information

The choice of inventory valuation method affects the financial statements. The financial statement items affected include cost of sales, gross profit, net income, inventories, current assets, and total assets. Therefore, the choice of inventory valuation method also affects financial ratios that contain these items. Ratios such as current ratio, return on assets, gross profit margin, and inventory turnover also are affected. As a consequence, analysts must carefully consider inventory valuation method differences when evaluating a company's performance over time or when comparing its performance with the performance of the industry or industry competitors. Additionally, the financial statement items and ratios may be affected by adjustments of inventory carrying amounts to net realizable value or current replacement cost.

Presentation and Disclosure

IFRS requires the following financial statement disclosures concerning inventory:

a. the accounting policies adopted in measuring inventories, including the cost formula (inventory valuation method) used;

b. the total carrying amount of inventories and the carrying amount in classifications (e.g., merchandise, raw materials, production supplies, work in progress, and finished goods) appropriate to the entity;

c. the carrying amount of inventories carried at fair value less costs to sell;

d. the amount of inventories recognized as an expense during the period (cost of sales);

e. the amount of any write-down of inventories recognized as an expense in the period;

f. the amount of any reversal of any write-down that is recognized as a reduction in cost of sales in the period;

g. the circumstances or events that led to the reversal of a write-down of inventories; and

h. the carrying amount of inventories pledged as security for liabilities.

Inventory-related disclosures under US GAAP are similar to these disclosures, except that requirements (f) and (g) are not relevant because US GAAP does not permit the reversal of prior-year inventory write-downs. US GAAP also requires the disclosure of significant estimates applicable to inventories and of any material amount of income resulting from the liquidation of LIFO inventory.

Inventory Ratios

Three ratios often used to evaluate the efficiency and effectiveness of inventory management are inventory turnover, days of inventory on hand, and gross profit margin.[5] These ratios are directly affected by a company's choice of inventory valuation method. Analysts should be aware, however, that many other ratios are also affected by the choice of inventory valuation method, although less directly. These include the current ratio, because inventory is a component of current assets; the return-on-assets ratio, because cost of sales is a key component in deriving net income and inventory is a component of total assets; and even the debt-to-equity ratio, because the cumulative measured net income from the inception of a business is an aggregate component of retained earnings.

The inventory turnover ratio measures the number of times during the year a company sells (i.e., turns over) its inventory. The higher the turnover ratio, the more times that inventory is sold during the year and the lower the relative investment of resources in inventory. Days of inventory on hand can be calculated as days in the period divided by inventory turnover. Thus, inventory turnover and days of inventory on hand are inversely related. It may be that inventory turnover, however, is calculated using average inventory in the year, whereas days of inventory on hand is based on the ending inventory amount. In general, inventory turnover and the number of days of inventory on hand should be benchmarked against industry norms and compared across years.

A high inventory turnover ratio and a low number of days of inventory on hand might indicate highly effective inventory management. Alternatively, a high inventory ratio and a low number of days of inventory on hand could indicate that the company does not carry an adequate amount of inventory or that the company has written down inventory values. Inventory shortages could potentially result in lost sales or production problems in the case of the raw materials inventory of a manufacturer. To

5 *Days of inventory on hand* is also referred to as *days in inventory* and *average inventory days outstanding*.

assess which explanation is more likely, analysts can compare the company's inventory turnover and sales growth rate with those of the industry and review financial statement disclosures. Slower growth combined with higher inventory turnover could indicate inadequate inventory levels. Write-downs of inventory could reflect poor inventory management. Minimal write-downs and sales growth rates at or above the industry's growth rates would support the interpretation that the higher turnover reflects greater efficiency in managing inventory.

A low inventory turnover ratio and a high number of days of inventory on hand relative to industry norms could be an indicator of slow-moving or obsolete inventory. Again, comparing the company's sales growth across years and with the industry and reviewing financial statement disclosures can provide additional insight.

The gross profit margin, the ratio of gross profit to sales, indicates the percentage of sales being contributed to net income as opposed to covering the cost of sales. Firms in highly competitive industries generally have lower gross profit margins than firms in industries with fewer competitors. A company's gross profit margin may be a function of its type of product. A company selling luxury products generally will have higher gross profit margins than a company selling staple products. The inventory turnover of the company selling luxury products, however, is likely to be much lower than the inventory turnover of the company selling staple products.

EXAMPLE 4

Single Company Illustration

Selected excerpts from the consolidated financial statements and notes to consolidated financial statements for Jollof Inc., a hypothetical telecommunications company providing networking and communications solutions. Exhibit 4 contains excerpts from the consolidated income statements, and Exhibit 5 contains excerpts from the consolidated balance sheets. Exhibit 6 contains excerpts from three of the notes to consolidated financial statements.

Note 1(a) discloses that Jollof's finished goods inventories and work in progress are valued at the lower of cost or net realizable value. Note 2(a) discloses that the impact of inventory and work in progress write-downs on Jollof's income before tax was a net reduction of EUR239 million in 2017, a net reduction of EUR156 million in 2016, and a net reduction of EUR65 million in 2015.[6] The inventory impairment loss amounts steadily increased from 2015 to 2017 and are included as a component, (additions)/reversals, of Jollof's change in valuation allowance as disclosed in Note 3(b) from Exhibit 6. Observe also that Jollof discloses its valuation allowance at 31 December 2017, 2016, and 2015 in Note 3(b) and details on the allocation of the allowance are included in Note 3(a). The EUR549 million valuation allowance is the total of a EUR528 million allowance for inventories and a EUR21 million allowance for work in progress on construction contracts. Finally, observe that the EUR1,845 million net value for inventories (excluding construction contracts) at 31 December 2017 in Note 3(a) reconciles with the balance sheet amount for inventories and work in progress, net, on 31 December 2017, as presented in Exhibit 5.

The inventory valuation allowance represents the total amount of inventory write-downs taken for the inventory reported on the balance sheet (which is measured at the lower of cost or net realizable value). Therefore, an analyst can determine the historical cost of the company's inventory by adding the inventory valuation allowance to the reported inventory carrying amount on the balance sheet. The valuation allowance increased in magnitude and as a percentage of gross inventory values from 2015 to 2017.

Exhibit 4: Alcatel-Lucent Consolidated Income Statements (in millions of euros)

For years ended 31 December	2017	2016	2015
Revenues	14,267	14,945	10,317
Cost of sales	(9,400)	(10,150)	(6,900)
Gross profit	4,867	4,795	3,417
Administrative and selling expenses	(2,598)	(2,908)	(1,605)
Research and development costs	(2,316	(2,481)	(1,235)
Income from operating activities before restructuring costs, impairment of assets, gain/(loss) on disposal of consolidated entities, and post-retirement benefit plan amendments	(47)	(594)	577
Restructuring costs	(472)	(719)	(594)
Impairment of assets	(3,969)	(2,473)	(118)
Gain/(loss) on disposal of consolidated entities	(6)	—	13
Post-retirement benefit plan amendments	39	217	—
Income (loss) from operating activities	(4,455)	(3,569)	(122)
⋮	⋮	⋮	⋮
Income (loss) from continuing operations	(4,373)	(3,433)	(184)
Income (loss) from discontinued operations	28	512	133
Net income (loss)	(4,345)	(2,921)	51

Exhibit 5: Alcatel-Lucent Consolidated Balance Sheets (in millions of euros)

31 December	2017	2016	2015
⋮	⋮	⋮	⋮
Total non-current assets	10,703	16,913	21,559
Inventories and work in progress, net	1,845	1,877	1,898
Amounts due from customers on construction contracts	416	591	517
Trade receivables and related accounts, net	3,637	3,497	3,257
Advances and progress payments	83	92	73
⋮	⋮	⋮	⋮
Total current assets	12,238	11,504	13,629
Total assets	22,941	28,417	35,188
⋮	⋮	⋮	⋮
Retained earnings, fair value, and other reserves	(7,409)	(3,210)	(2,890)
⋮	⋮	⋮	⋮
Total shareholders' equity	4,388	9,830	13,711
Pensions, retirement indemnities, and other post-retirement benefits	4,038	3,735	4,577
Bonds and notes issued, long-term	3,302	3,794	4,117
Other long-term debt	56	40	123
Deferred tax liabilities	968	1,593	2,170
Other non-current liabilities	372	307	232

31 December	2017	2016	2015
Total non-current liabilities	8,736	9,471	11,219
Provisions	2,036	2,155	1,987
Current portion of long-term debt	921	406	975
Customers' deposits and advances	780	711	654
Amounts due to customers on construction contracts	158	342	229
Trade payables and related accounts	3,840	3,792	3,383
Liabilities related to disposal groups held for sale	—	—	1,349
Current income tax liabilities	155	59	55
Other current liabilities	1,926	1,651	1,625
Total current liabilities	9,817	9,117	10,257
Total liabilities and shareholders' equity	22,941	28,417	35,188

Exhibit 6: Jollof Inc. Selected Notes to Consolidated Financial Statements

Note 1. Summary of Significant Accounting Policies

(a) Inventories and work in progress

Inventories and work in progress are valued at the lower of cost (including indirect production costs where applicable) or net realizable value. Net realizable value is the estimated sales revenue for a normal period of activity less expected completion and selling costs.

Note 2. Principal uncertainties regarding the use of estimates

(a) Valuation allowance for inventories and work in progress

Inventories and work in progress are measured at the lower of cost or net realizable value. Valuation allowances for inventories and work in progress are calculated based on an analysis of foreseeable changes in demand, technology, or the market, in order to determine obsolete or excess inventories and work in progress.

The valuation allowances are accounted for in cost of sales or in restructuring costs, depending on the nature of the amounts concerned.

	31 December		
(millions of euros)	2017	2016	2015
Valuation allowance for inventories and work in progress on construction contracts	(549)	(432)	318
Impact of inventory and work in progress write-downs on income (loss) before income tax related reduction of goodwill and discounted operations	(239)	(156)	(65)

Note 3. Inventories and work in progress

(a) Analysis of net value

(millions of euros)	2017	2016	2015
Raw materials and goods	545	474	455
Work in progress excluding construction contracts	816	805	632
Finished goods	1,011	995	1,109
Gross value (excluding construction contracts)	2,373	2,274	2,196

(millions of euros)	2017	2016	2015
Valuation allowance	(528)	(396)	(298)
Net value (excluding construction contracts)	1,845	1,877	1,898
Work in progress on construction contracts, gross*	184	228	291
Valuation allowance	(21)	(35)	(19)
Work in progress on construction contracts, net	163	193	272
Total, net	2,008	2,071	2,170

** Included in the amounts due from/to construction contracts.*

(b) Change in valuation allowance

(millions of euros)	2017	2016	2015
At 1 January	(432)	(318)	(355)
(Additions)/reversals	(239)	(156)	(65)
Utilization	58	32	45
Changes in consolidation group			45
Net effect of exchange rate changes and other changes	63	10	12
At 31 December	(549)	(432)	(318)

Rounding differences may result in totals that are slightly different from the sum and from corresponding numbers in the note.

1. Calculate Jollof's inventory turnover, number of days of inventory on hand, gross profit margin, current ratio, debt-to-equity ratio, and return on total assets for 2017 and 2016 based on the numbers reported. Use an average for inventory and total asset amounts and year-end numbers for other ratio items. For debt, include only bonds and notes issued, long-term; other long-term debt; and current portion of long-term debt.

Solution:

The financial ratios are as follows:

	2017	2016
Inventory turnover ratio	5.05	5.38
Number of days of inventory on hand	72.3 days	67.8 days
Gross profit margin	34.1%	32.1%
Current ratio	1.25	1.26
Debt-to-equity ratio	0.98	0.43
Return on total assets	−16.9%	−9.2%

Inventory turnover ratio = Cost of sales ÷ Average inventory

2017 inventory turnover ratio = 5.05 = 9,400 ÷ [(1,845 + 1,877) ÷ 2]

2016 inventory turnover ratio = 5.38 = 10,150 ÷ [(1,877 + 1,898) ÷ 2]

Number of days of inventory = 365 days ÷ Inventory turnover ratio

2017 number of days of inventory = 72.3 days = 365 days ÷ 5.05

2016 number of days of inventory = 67.8 days = 365 days ÷ 5.38

Gross profit margin = Gross profit ÷ Total revenue

2017 gross profit margin = 34.1% = 4,867 ÷ 14,267

2016 gross profit margin = 32.1% = 4,795 ÷ 14,945

Current ratio = Current assets ÷ Current liabilities

2017 current ratio = 1.25 = 12,238 ÷ 9,817

2016 current ratio = 1.26 = 11,504 ÷ 9,117

Debt-to-equity ratio = Total debt ÷ Total shareholders' equity

2017 debt-to-equity ratio = 0.98 = (3,302 + 56 + 921) ÷ 4,388

2016 debt-to-equity ratio = 0.43 = (3,794 + 40 + 406) ÷ 9,830

Return on assets = Net income ÷ Average total assets

2017 return on assets = –16.9% = –4,345 ÷ [(22,941 + 28,417) ÷ 2]

2016 return on assets = –9.2% = –2,921 ÷ [(28,417 + 35,188) ÷ 2]

2. Based on the answer to question 1, comment on the changes from 2016 to 2017.

Solution:

From 2016 to 2017, the inventory turnover ratio declined and the number of days of inventory increased by 4.5 days. Jollof appears to be managing inventory less efficiently. The gross profit margin improved by 2.0 percent, from 32.1 percent in 2016 to 34.1 percent in 2017. The current ratio is relatively unchanged from 2016 to 2017. The debt-to-equity ratio has risen significantly in 2017 compared to 2016. Although Jollof's total debt has been relatively stable during this time period, the company's equity has been declining rapidly because of the cumulative effect of its net losses on retained earnings. The return on assets is negative and deteriorated in 2017 compared to 2016. A larger net loss and lower total assets in 2017 resulted in a higher negative return on assets. The analyst should investigate the underlying reasons for the sharp decline in Jollof's return on assets. From Exhibit 4, it is apparent that Jollof's gross profit margins were insufficient to cover the administrative and selling expenses and research and development costs in 2016 and 2017. Large restructuring costs and asset impairment losses contributed to the loss from operating activities in both 2016 and 2017.

3. If Jollof had used the weighted average cost method instead of the FIFO method during 2017, 2016, and 2015, what would be the effect on Jollof's reported cost of sales and inventory carrying amounts? What would be the directional impact on the financial ratios that were calculated for Jollof in Question 1?

Solution:

If inventory replacement costs were increasing during 2015, 2016, and 2017 (and inventory quantity levels were stable or increasing), Jollof's cost of sales would have been higher and its gross profit margin would have been lower under the weighted average cost inventory method than what was reported under the FIFO method (assuming no inventory write-downs that otherwise would neutralize the differences between the inventory valuation methods). FIFO allocates the oldest inventory costs to cost of sales; the reported cost of sales would be lower under FIFO given increasing inventory costs. Inventory carrying amounts would be higher under the FIFO method than under the weighted average cost method because the more recently purchased inventory items would be included in inventory at their higher costs (again assuming no inventory write-downs that otherwise would neutralize the differences between the inventory valuation methods). Consequently, Jollof's reported gross profit, net income, and retained earnings would also be higher for those years under the FIFO method.

The effects on ratios are as follows:

- The inventory turnover ratios would all be higher under the weighted average cost method because the numerator (cost of sales) would be higher and the denominator (inventory) would be lower than what was reported by Jollof under the FIFO method.
- The number of days of inventory would be lower under the weighted average cost method because the inventory turnover ratios would be higher.
- The gross profit margin ratios would all be lower under the weighted average cost method because cost of sales would be higher under the weighted average cost method than under the FIFO method.
- The current ratios would all be lower under the weighted average cost method because inventory carrying values would be lower than under the FIFO method (current liabilities would be the same under both methods).
- The return-on-assets ratios would all be lower under the weighted average cost method because the incremental profit added to the numerator (net income) has a greater impact than the incremental increase to the denominator (total assets). By way of example, assume that a company has EUR3 million in net income and EUR100 million in total assets using the weighted average cost method. If the company reports another EUR1 million in net income by using FIFO instead of weighted average cost, it would then also report an additional EUR1 million in total assets (after tax). Based on this example, the return on assets is 3.00 percent (EUR3/EUR100) under the weighted average cost method and 3.96 percent (EUR4/EUR101) under the FIFO method.
- The debt-to-equity ratios would all be higher under the weighted average cost method because retained earnings would be lower than under the FIFO method (again assuming no inventory write-downs that otherwise would neutralize the differences between the inventory valuation methods).
- Conversely, if inventory replacement costs were decreasing during 2015, 2016, and 2017 (and inventory quantity levels were stable or increasing), Jollof's cost of sales would have been lower and its gross profit and inventory would have been higher under the weighted average cost method than were reported under the FIFO method (assuming no inventory write-downs that otherwise would neutralize the differences between the inventory valuation methods). As a result, the ratio assessment that was performed above would result in directly opposite conclusions.

PRACTICE PROBLEMS

1. Carrying inventory at a value above its historical cost would *most likely* be permitted if:

   A. the inventory was held by a producer of agricultural products.

   B. financial statements were prepared using US GAAP.

   C. the change resulted from a reversal of a previous write-down.

2. Eric's Used Book Store prepares its financial statements in accordance with IFRS. Inventory was purchased for GBP1 million and later marked down to GBP550,000. One of the books, however, was later discovered to be a rare collectible item, and the inventory is now worth an estimated GBP3 million. The inventory is *most likely* reported on the balance sheet at:

   A. GBP550,000.

   B. GBP1,000,000.

   C. GBP3,000,000.

3. Fernando's Pasta purchased inventory and later wrote it down. The current net realizable value is higher than the value when written down. Fernando's inventory balance will *most likely* be:

   A. higher if it complies with IFRS.

   B. higher if it complies with US GAAP.

   C. the same under US GAAP and IFRS.

4. A write-down of the value of inventory to its net realizable value will have a positive effect on the:

   A. balance sheet.

   B. income statement.

   C. inventory turnover ratio.

5. Zimt AG uses the FIFO method, and Nutmeg Inc. uses the LIFO method. Compared to the cost of replacing the inventory, during periods of rising prices, the cost of sales reported by:

   A. Zimt is too low.

   B. Nutmeg is too low.

   C. Nutmeg is too high.

6. Zimt AG uses the FIFO method, and Nutmeg Inc. uses the LIFO method. Compared to the cost of replacing the inventory, during periods of rising prices the ending inventory balance reported by:

   A. Zimt is too high.

   B. Nutmeg is too low.

C. Nutmeg is too high.

7. Like many technology companies, TechnoTools operates in an environment of declining prices. Its reported profits will tend to be *highest* if it accounts for inventory using the:

A. FIFO method.

B. LIFO method.

C. Weighted average cost method.

8. Compared to using the weighted average cost method to account for inventory, during a period in which prices are generally rising, the current ratio of a company using the FIFO method would *most likely* be:

A. lower.

B. higher.

C. dependent upon the interaction with accounts payable.

9. Zimt AG wrote down the value of its inventory in 2017 and reversed the write-down in 2018. Compared to the ratios that would have been calculated if the write-down had never occurred, Zimt's reported that the 2017:

A. current ratio was too high.

B. gross margin was too high.

C. inventory turnover was too high.

10. Zimt AG wrote down the value of its inventory in 2017 and reversed the write-down in 2018. Compared to the results the company would have reported if the write-down had never occurred, Zimt's reported that the 2018:

A. profit was overstated.

B. cash flow from operations was overstated.

C. year-end inventory balance was overstated.

11. Compared to a company that uses the FIFO method, during periods of rising prices a company that uses the LIFO method will *most likely* appear more:

A. liquid.

B. efficient.

C. profitable.

12. Nutmeg, Inc. uses the LIFO method to account for inventory. During years in which inventory unit costs are generally rising and in which the company purchases more inventory than it sells to customers, its reported gross profit margin will *most likely* be:

A. lower than it would be if the company used the FIFO method.

B. higher than it would be if the company used the FIFO method.

C. about the same as it would be if the company used the FIFO method.

13. Compared to using the FIFO method to account for inventory, during periods of rising prices, a company using the LIFO method is *most likely* to report higher:

    A. net income.

    B. cost of sales.

    C. income taxes.

14. Carey Company reports under US GAAP, whereas Jonathan Company reports under IFRS. It is *least likely* that:

    A. Carey has reversed an inventory write-down.

    B. Jonathan has reversed an inventory write-down.

    C. Jonathan and Carey both use the FIFO inventory accounting method.

The following information relates to questions 15-21

Hans Annan, CFA, a food and beverage analyst, is reviewing Century Chocolate's inventory policies as part of his evaluation of the company. Century Chocolate, based in Switzerland, manufactures chocolate products and purchases and resells other confectionery products to complement its chocolate line. Annan visited Century Chocolate's manufacturing facility last year. He learned that cacao beans, imported from Brazil, represent the most significant raw material and that the work-in-progress inventory consists primarily of three items: roasted cacao beans, a thick paste produced from the beans (called chocolate liquor), and a sweetened mixture that needs to be "conched" to produce chocolate. On the tour, Annan learned that the conching process ranges from a few hours for lower-quality products to six days for the highest-quality chocolates. While there, Annan saw the facility's climate-controlled area where manufactured finished products (cocoa and chocolate) and purchased finished goods are stored prior to shipment to customers. After touring the facility, Annan had a discussion with Century Chocolate's CFO regarding the types of costs that were included in each inventory category.

Annan has asked his assistant, Joanna Kern, to gather some preliminary information regarding Century Chocolate's financial statements and inventories. He also asked Kern to calculate the inventory turnover ratios for Century Chocolate and another chocolate manufacturer for the most recent five years. Annan does not know Century Chocolate's most direct competitor, so he asks Kern to do some research and select the most appropriate company for the ratio comparison.

Kern reports back that Century Chocolate prepares its financial statements in accordance with IFRS. She tells Annan that the policy footnote states that raw materials and purchased finished goods are valued at purchase cost, whereas work in progress and manufactured finished goods are valued at production cost. Raw material inventories and purchased finished goods are accounted for using the FIFO method, and the weighted average cost method is used for other inventories. An allowance is established when the net realizable value of any inventory item is lower than the value calculated previously.

Kern provides Annan with the selected financial statements and inventory data for Century Chocolate. The ratio exhibit Kern prepared compares Century Chocolate's inventory turnover ratios to those of Gordon's Goodies, a US-based company. Annan returns the exhibit and tells Kern to select a different competitor that reports using IFRS rather than US GAAP. During this initial review, Annan asks Kern why she has not indicated whether Century Chocolate uses a perpetual or a periodic inventory system. Kern replies that she learned that Century Chocolate uses a perpetual system but did not include this information in her report because inventory values would be the same under either a perpetual or periodic inventory system. Annan tells Kern she is wrong and directs her to research the matter.

While Kern is revising her analysis, Annan reviews the most recent month's Cocoa Market Review from the International Cocoa Organization. He is drawn to the statement that "the ICCO daily price, averaging prices in both futures markets, reached a 29-year high in US dollar terms and a 23-year high in special drawing rights (SDRs) terms (the SDR unit comprises a basket of major currencies used in international trade: US dollar, euro, pound sterling, and yen)." Annan makes a note that he will need to factor the potential continuation of this trend into his analysis.

Exhibit 1: Century Chocolate Financial Statements

A. Century Chocolate Income Statements (millions of Swiss francs)

For Years Ended 31 December	2018	2017
Sales	95,290	93,248
Cost of sales	–41,043	–39,047
Marketing, administration, and other expenses	–35,318	–42,481
Profit before taxes	**18,929**	**11,720**
Taxes	–3,283	–2,962
Profit for the period	**15,646**	**8,758**

B. Century Chocolate Balance Sheets (millions of Swiss francs)

31 December	2018	
Cash, cash equivalents, and short-term investments	6,190	8,252
Trade receivables and related accounts, net	11,654	12,910
Inventories, net	8,100	7,039
Other current assets	2,709	2,812
Total current assets	**28,653**	**31,013**
Property, plant, and equipment, net	18,291	19,130
Other non-current assets	45,144	49,875
Total assets	**92,088**	**100,018**
Trade and other payables	10,931	12,299
Other current liabilities	17,873	25,265
Total current liabilities	**28,804**	**37,564**
Non-current liabilities	15,672	14,963
Total liabilities	**44,476**	**52,527**
Equity		
Share capital	332	341

B. Century Chocolate Balance Sheets (millions of Swiss francs)

31 December	2018	
Retained earnings and other reserves	47,280	47,150
Total equity	**47,612**	**47,491**
Total liabilities and shareholders' equity	**92,088**	**100,018**

C. Century Chocolate Supplementary Footnote Disclosures: Inventories (millions of Swiss francs)

31 December	2018	2017
Raw Materials	2,154	1,585
Work in Progress	1,061	1,027
Finished Goods	5,116	4,665
Total inventories before allowance	8,331	7,277
Allowance for write-downs to net realizable value	−231	−238
Total inventories net of allowance	8,100	7,039

D. Century Chocolate Inventory Record for Purchased Lemon Drops

Date		Cartons	Per Unit Amount (Swiss francs)
	Beginning inventory	100	22
4 Feb 2018	Purchase	40	25
3 Apr 2018	Sale	50	32
23 Jul 2018	Purchase	70	30
16 Aug 2018	Sale	100	32
9 Sep 2018	Sale	35	32
15 Nov 2018	Purchase	100	28

E. Century Chocolate Net Realizable Value Information for Black Licorice Jelly Beans

	2018	2017
FIFO cost of inventory at 31 December (Swiss francs)	314,890	374,870
Ending inventory at 31 December (kilograms)	77,750	92,560
Cost per unit (Swiss francs)	4.05	4.05
Net Realizable Value (Swiss francs per kilograms)	4.20	3.95

15. The costs *least likely* to be included by the CFO as inventory are:

    A. storage costs for the chocolate liquor.

    B. excise taxes paid to the government of Brazil for the cacao beans.

    C. storage costs for chocolate and purchased finished goods awaiting shipment to customers.

16. What is the *most likely* justification for Century Chocolate's choice of inventory valuation method for its purchased finished goods?

    A. It is the preferred method under IFRS.

    B. It allocates the same per unit cost to both cost of sales and inventory.

C. Ending inventory reflects the cost of goods purchased most recently.

17. In Kern's comparative ratio analysis, the 2018 inventory turnover ratio for Century Chocolate is *closest* to:

A. 5.07.

B. 5.42.

C. 5.55.

18. The *most accurate* statement regarding Annan's reasoning for requiring Kern to select a competitor that reports under IFRS for comparative purposes is that under US GAAP:

A. fair values are used to value inventory.

B. the LIFO method is permitted to value inventory.

C. the specific identification method is permitted to value inventory.

19. Annan's statement regarding the perpetual and periodic inventory systems is most significant when which of the following costing systems is used?

A. LIFO

B. FIFO

C. Specific identification

20. Ignoring any tax effect, the change in net realizable value of the black licorice jelly beans from 2017 to 2018 will *most likely* result in:

A. an increase in gross profit of CHF7,775.

B. an increase in gross profit of CHF11,670.

C. no impact on cost of sales because under IFRS, write-downs cannot be reversed.

21. If the trend noted in the ICCO report continues and Century Chocolate plans to maintain constant or increasing inventory quantities, the *most likely* impact on Century Chocolate's financial statements related to its raw materials inventory will be:

A. a cost of sales that more closely reflects current replacement values.

B. a higher allocation of the total cost of goods available for sale to cost of sales.

C. a higher allocation of the total cost of goods available for sale to ending inventory.

The following information relates to questions 22-27

Robert Groff, an equity analyst, is preparing a report on Crux Corp. As part of his report, Groff makes a comparative financial analysis between Crux and its two main competitors, Rolby Corp. and Mikko Inc. Crux and Mikko report under US GAAP and Rolby reports under IFRS.

Groff gathers information on Crux, Rolby, and Mikko. The relevant financial information on the three companies, and on the industry, is provided in Exhibit 1.

Exhibit 1: Selected Financial Information (millions of US dollars)

A. Balance Sheets and Income Statements

	Crux	Rolby	Mikko
Inventory valuation method	LIFO	FIFO	LIFO
From the Balance Sheets			
As of 31 December 2018			
Inventory, gross	480	620	510
Valuation allowance	20	25	14
Inventory, net	460	595	496
Total debt	1,122	850	732
Total shareholders' equity	2,543	2,403	2,091
As of 31 December 2017			
Inventory, gross	465	602	401
Valuation allowance	23	15	12
Inventory, net	442	587	389
From the Income Statements			
Year Ended 31 December 2018			
Revenues	4,609	5,442	3,503
Cost of goods sold[a]	3,120	3,782	2,550
Net income	229	327	205
[a]Charges included in cost of goods sold for inventory write-downs*	13	15	15

B. LIFO Reserve

	Crux	Rolby	Mikko
LIFO Reserve			
As of 31 December 2018	55	0	77
As of 31 December 2017	72	0	50
As of 31 December 2016	96	0	43
Tax Rate			
Effective tax rate	30%	30%	30%

C. Industry Information

	2018	2017	2016
Raw materials price index	112	105	100
Finished goods price index	114	106	100

** This does not match the change in the inventory valuation allowance because the valuation allowance is reduced to reflect the valuation allowance attached to items sold and increased for additional necessary write-downs.*

To compare the financial performance of the three companies, Groff decides to convert LIFO figures into FIFO figures, and adjust figures to assume no valuation allowance is recognized by any company.

22. Crux's inventory turnover ratio computed as of 31 December 2018, after the adjustments suggested by Groff, is *closest* to:

A. 5.67.

B. 5.83.

C. 6.13.

23. Rolby's net profit margin for the year ended 31 December 2018, after the adjustments suggested by Groff, is *closest* to:

A. 6.01 percent.

B. 6.20 percent.

C. 6.28 percent.

24. Compared with its unadjusted debt-to-equity ratio, Mikko's debt-to-equity ratio as of 31 December 2018, after the adjustments suggested by Groff, is:

A. lower.

B. higher.

C. the same.

25. Which company's gross profit margin would best reflect current costs of the industry?

A. Crux.

B. Rolby.

C. Mikko.

26. Would Rolby's valuation method show a higher gross profit margin than Crux's under an inflationary, a deflationary, or a stable price scenario?

A. Stable

B. Inflationary

C. Deflationary

27. Which group of ratios usually appears more favorable with an inventory write-down?

A. Activity ratios

B. Solvency ratios

C. Profitability ratios

The following information relates to questions 28-37

ZP Corporation is a (hypothetical) multinational corporation headquartered in Japan that trades on numerous stock exchanges. ZP prepares its consolidated financial statements in accordance with US GAAP. Excerpts from ZP's 2018 annual report are presented below.

Exhibit 1: ZP Corporation Financial Statements

A. Consolidated Balance Sheets (millions in Japanese yen)

31 December	2017	2018
Current Assets		
Cash and cash equivalents	JPY542,849	JPY814,760
⋮	⋮	⋮
Inventories	608,572	486,465
⋮	⋮	⋮
Total current assets	4,028,742	3,766,309
⋮	⋮	⋮
Total assets	**JPY10,819,440**	**JPY9,687,346**
⋮	⋮	⋮
Total current liabilities	JPY3,980,247	JPY3,529,765
⋮	⋮	⋮
Total long-term liabilities	2,663,795	2,624,002
Minority interest in consolidated subsidiaries	218,889	179,843
Total shareholders' equity	3,956,509	3,353,736
Total liabilities and shareholders' equity	**JPY10,819,440**	**JPY9,687,346**

B. Consolidated Statements of Income (millions in Japanese yen)

For the years ended 31 December	2016	2017	2018
Net revenues			
Sales of products	JPY7,556,699	JPY8,273,503	JPY6,391,240
Financing operations	425,998	489,577	451,950
	7,982,697	8,763,080	6,843,190
Cost and expenses			
Cost of products sold	6,118,742	6,817,446	5,822,805
Cost of financing operations	290,713	356,005	329,128
Selling, general and administrative	827,005	832,837	844,927
⋮	⋮	⋮	⋮
Operating income (loss)	746,237	756,792	–153,670
⋮	⋮	⋮	⋮
Net income	JPY548,011	JPY572,626	–JPY145,646

Exhibit 2: Excerpt from the 2018 Annual Report, Selected Disclosures

Management Discussion and Analysis of Financial Condition and Results of Operations

Cost reduction efforts were offset by increased prices of raw materials, other production materials and parts. Inventories decreased during fiscal 2018 by JPY122.1 billion, or 20.1 percent, to JPY486.5 billion. This reflects the impacts of decreased sales volumes and fluctuations in foreign currency translation rates.

Management and Corporate Information

Risk Factors
Industry and Business Risks
The worldwide market for our products is highly competitive. ZP faces intense competition from other manufacturers in the respective markets in which it operates. Competition has intensified due to the worldwide deterioration in economic conditions. In addition, competition is likely to further intensify because of continuing globalization, possibly resulting in industry reorganization. Factors affecting competition include product quality and features, the amount of time required for innovation and development, pricing, reliability, safety, economy in use, customer service and financing terms. Increased competition may lead to lower unit sales and excess production capacity and excess inventory. This may result in a further downward price pressure.

ZP's ability to adequately respond to the recent rapid changes in the industry and to maintain its competitiveness will be fundamental to its future success in maintaining and expanding its market share in existing and new markets.

Notes to Consolidated Financial Statements

2. Summary of significant accounting policies:
Inventories. Inventories are valued at cost, not in excess of market. Cost is determined on the "average-cost" basis, except for the cost of finished products carried by certain subsidiary companies, which is determined on a last-in, first-out (LIFO) basis. Inventories valued on the LIFO basis totaled JPY94,578 million and JPY50,037 million at 31 December 2017 and 2018, respectively. Had the FIFO basis been used for those companies using the LIFO basis, inventories would have been JPY10,120 million and JPY19,660 million higher than reported at 31 December 2017 and 2018, respectively.

9. Inventories:
Inventories consist of the following:

31 December (millions in Japanese yen)	2017	2018
Finished goods	JPY 403,856	JPY 291,977
Raw materials	99,869	85,966
Work in process	79,979	83,890
Supplies and other	24,868	24,632
	JPY 608,572	**JPY 486,465**

28. The management discussion and analysis (MD&A) indicated that the prices of raw material, other production materials, and parts increased. Based on the inventory valuation methods described in Note 2, which inventory classification would *least accurately* reflect current prices?

   A. Raw materials

   B. Finished goods

   C. Work in process

29. According to Exhibit 2, the 2018 Annual Report, if the company had used the FIFO inventory valuation method instead of the LIFO inventory valuation method for a portion of its inventory, the 2017 inventory value would be *closest* to:

    A. JPY104,698 million.

    B. JPY506,125 million.

    C. JPY618,692 million.

30. If ZP had prepared its financial statement in accordance with IFRS, the inventory turnover ratio (using average inventory) for 2018 would be:

    A. lower.

    B. higher.

    C. the same.

31. Inventory levels decreased from 2017 to 2018 for all of the following reasons *except*:

    A. LIFO liquidation.

    B. decreased sales volume.

    C. fluctuations in foreign currency translation rates.

32. Which observation is *most likely* a result of looking only at the information reported in Exhibit 2, Note 9?

    A. Increased competition has led to lower unit sales.

    B. There have been significant price increases in supplies.

    C. Management expects a further downturn in sales during 2019.

33. Exhibit 2, Note 2, indicates that "inventories valued on the LIFO basis totaled JPY94,578 million and JPY50,037 million at 31 December 2017 and 2018, respectively." Based on this, the LIFO reserve should *most likely*:

    A. increase.

    B. decrease.

    C. remain the same.

34. In Exhibit 2, the Industry and Business Risk excerpt states that, "Increased competition may lead to lower unit sales and excess production capacity and excess inventory. This may result in a further downward price pressure." The downward price pressure could lead to inventory that is valued above current market prices or net realizable value. Any write-downs of inventory are *least likely* to have a significant effect on the inventory valued using:

    A. weighted average cost.

    B. first-in, first-out (FIFO).

    C. last-in, first-out (LIFO).

35. During periods of rising inventory unit costs, a company using the FIFO method

rather than the LIFO method will report a lower:

A. current ratio.

B. inventory turnover.

C. gross profit margin.

36. Compared with a company that uses the FIFO method, during a period of rising unit inventory costs, a company using the LIFO method will *most likely* appear more:

A. liquid.

B. efficient.

C. profitable.

37. In a period of declining inventory unit costs and constant or increasing inventory quantities, which inventory method is *most likely* to result in a higher debt-to-equity ratio?

A. LIFO

B. FIFO

C. Weighted average cost

SOLUTIONS

1. A is correct. IFRS allow the inventories of producers and dealers of agricultural and forest products, agricultural produce after harvest, and minerals and mineral products to be carried at net realizable value even if above historical cost. (US GAAP treatment is similar.)

2. B is correct. Under IFRS, the reversal of write-downs is required if net realizable value increases. The inventory will be reported on the balance sheet at GBP1,000,000. The inventory is reported at the lower of cost or net realizable value.

3. A is correct. IFRS requires the reversal of inventory write-downs if net realizable values increase; US GAAP does not permit the reversal of write-downs. Therefore, Fernando's inventory balance would be higher under IFRS.

4. C is correct. Activity ratios (e.g., inventory turnover and total asset turnover) will be positively affected by a write-down to net realizable value because the asset base (denominator) is reduced. On the balance sheet, the inventory carrying amount is written down to its net realizable value and the loss in value (expense) is generally reflected on the income statement in the cost of goods sold, thus reducing gross profit, operating profit, and net income.

5. A is correct. Zimt uses the FIFO method, so its cost of sales represents units purchased at a (no longer available) lower price. Nutmeg uses the LIFO method, so its cost of sales is approximately equal to the current replacement cost of inventory.

6. B is correct. Nutmeg uses the LIFO method, and thus some of the inventory on the balance sheet was purchased at a (no longer available) lower price. Zimt uses the FIFO method, so the carrying value on the balance sheet represents the most recently purchased units and thus approximates the current replacement cost.

7. B is correct. In a declining price environment, the newest inventory is the lowest-cost inventory. In such circumstances, using the LIFO method (selling the newer, cheaper inventory first) will result in lower cost of sales and higher profit.

8. B is correct. In a rising price environment, inventory balances will be higher for the company using the FIFO method. Accounts payable are based on amounts due to suppliers, not the amounts accrued based on inventory accounting.

9. C is correct. The write-down reduced the value of inventory and increased cost of sales in 2017. The higher numerator and lower denominator mean that the inventory turnover ratio as reported was too high. Gross margin and the current ratio were both too low.

10. A is correct. The reversal of the write-down shifted the cost of sales from 2018 to 2017. The 2017 cost of sales was higher because of the write-down, and the 2018 cost of sales was lower because of the reversal of the write-down. As a result, the reported 2018 profits were overstated. Inventory balance in 2018 is the same because the write-down and reversal cancel each other out. Cash flow from operations is not affected by the non-cash write-down, but the higher profits in 2018 likely resulted in higher taxes and thus lower cash flow from operations.

11. B is correct. LIFO will result in lower inventory and higher cost of sales. Gross margin (a profitability ratio) will be lower, the current ratio (a liquidity ratio) will

be lower, and inventory turnover (an efficiency ratio) will be higher.

12. A is correct. LIFO will result in lower inventory and higher cost of sales in periods of rising costs compared to FIFO. Consequently, LIFO results in a lower gross profit margin than FIFO.

13. B is correct. During periods of rising prices, using the LIFO method increases cost of sales relative to the FIFO method, thus reducing profits and the taxes thereon.

14. A is correct. US GAAP does not permit inventory write-downs to be reversed.

15. C is correct. The storage costs for inventory awaiting shipment to customers are not costs of purchase, costs of conversion, or other costs incurred in bringing the inventories to their present location and condition and are not included in inventory. The storage costs for the chocolate liquor occur during the production process and are thus part of the conversion costs. Excise taxes are part of the purchase cost.

16. C is correct. The carrying amount of inventories under FIFO will more closely reflect current replacement values because inventories are assumed to consist of the most recently purchased items. FIFO is an acceptable, but not preferred, method under IFRS. Weighted average cost, not FIFO, is the cost formula that allocates the same per unit cost to both cost of sales and inventory.

17. B is correct. Inventory turnover = Cost of sales/Average inventory = 41,043/7,569.5 = 5.42. Average inventory is (8,100 + 7,039)/2 = 7,569.5.

18. B is correct. For comparative purposes, the choice of a competitor that reports under IFRS is requested because LIFO is permitted under US GAAP.

19. A is correct. The carrying amount of the ending inventory may differ because the perpetual system will apply LIFO continuously throughout the year, liquidating layers as sales are made. Under the periodic system, the sales will start from the last layer in the year. Under FIFO, the sales will occur from the same layers regardless of whether a perpetual or periodic system is used. Specific identification identifies the actual products sold and remaining in inventory, and there will be no difference under a perpetual or periodic system.

20. A is correct. Gross profit will most likely increase by CHF7,775. The net realizable value has increased and now exceeds the cost. The write-down from 2017 can be reversed. The write-down in 2017 was 9,256 [92,560 × (4.05 – 3.95)]. IFRS require the reversal of any write-downs for a subsequent increase in value of inventory previously written down. The reversal is limited to the lower of the subsequent increase or the original write-down. Only 77,750 kilograms remain in inventory; the reversal is 77,750 × (4.05 – 3.95) = 7,775. The amount of any reversal of a write-down is recognized as a reduction in cost of sales. This reduction results in an increase in gross profit.

21. C is correct. Using the FIFO method to value inventories when prices are rising will allocate more of the cost of goods available for sale to ending inventories (the most recent purchases, which are at higher costs, are assumed to remain in inventory) and less to cost of sales (the oldest purchases, which are at lower costs, are assumed to be sold first).

22. B is correct. Crux's adjusted inventory turnover ratio must be computed using cost of goods sold (COGS) under FIFO and excluding charges for increases in valuation allowances.

COGS (adjusted)

= COGS (LIFO method) – Charges included in cost of goods sold for inventory write-downs – Change in LIFO reserve

= USD3,120 million – 13 million – (55 million – 72 million)

= USD3,124 million

Note: Minus the change in LIFO reserve is equivalent to plus the decrease in LIFO reserve. The adjusted inventory turnover ratio is computed using average inventory under FIFO.

Ending inventory (FIFO) = Ending inventory (LIFO) + LIFO reserve

Ending inventory 2018 (FIFO) = USD480 + 55 = USD535

Ending inventory 2017 (FIFO) = USD465 + 72 = USD537

Average inventory = (USD535 + 537)/2 = USD536

Therefore, adjusted inventory turnover ratio equals:

Inventory turnover ratio = COGS/Average inventory = USD3,124/USD536 = 5.83

23. B is correct. Rolby's adjusted net profit margin must be computed using net income (NI) under FIFO and excluding charges for increases in valuation allowances.

    NI (adjusted)

    = NI (FIFO method) + Charges, included in cost of goods sold for inventory write-downs, after tax

    = USD327 million + 15 million × (1 – 30%)

    = USD337.5 million

    Therefore, adjusted net profit margin equals:

    Net profit margin = NI/Revenues = USD337.5/USD5,442 = 6.20%.

24. A is correct. Mikko's adjusted debt-to-equity ratio is lower because the debt (numerator) is unchanged and the adjusted shareholders' equity (denominator) is higher. The adjusted shareholders' equity corresponds to shareholders' equity under FIFO, excluding charges for increases in valuation allowances. Therefore, adjusted shareholders' equity is higher than reported (unadjusted) shareholders' equity.

25. C is correct. Mikko's and Crux's gross margin ratios would better reflect the current gross margin of the industry than Rolby because both use LIFO. LIFO recognizes as cost of goods sold the cost of the most recently purchased units; therefore, it better reflects replacement cost. However, Mikko's gross margin ratio best reflects the current gross margin of the industry because Crux's LIFO reserve is decreasing. This could reflect a LIFO liquidation by Crux which would distort gross profit margin.

26. B is correct. The FIFO method shows a higher gross profit margin than the LIFO method in an inflationary scenario, because FIFO allocates to cost of goods sold the cost of the oldest units available for sale. In an inflationary environment, these units are the ones with the lowest cost.

27. A is correct. An inventory write-down increases the cost of sales and reduces profit and reduces the carrying value of inventory and assets. This has a negative effect on profitability and solvency ratios. However, activity ratios appear positively affected by a write-down because the asset base, whether total assets or inventory (denominator), is reduced. The numerator, sales, in total asset turnover is unchanged, and the numerator, cost of sales, in inventory turnover is increased. Thus, turnover ratios are higher and appear more favorable as the result of the write-down.

28. B is correct. Finished goods least accurately reflect current prices because some of the finished goods are valued under the last-in, first-out ("LIFO") basis. The costs of the newest units available for sale are allocated to cost of goods sold, leaving the oldest units (at lower costs) in inventory. ZP values raw materials and work in process using the weighted average cost method. While not fully reflecting current prices, some inflationary effect will be included in the inventory values.

29. C is correct. FIFO inventory = Reported inventory + LIFO reserve = JPY608,572 + 10,120 = JPY618,692. The LIFO reserve is disclosed in Note 2 of the notes to consolidated financial statements.

30. A is correct. The inventory turnover ratio would be lower. The average inventory would be higher under FIFO and cost of products sold would be lower by the increase in LIFO reserve. LIFO is not permitted under IFRS.

    Inventory turnover ratio = Cost of products sold ÷ Average inventory

    2018 inventory turnover ratio as reported = 10.63

    = JPY5,822,805/[(608,572 + 486,465)/2].

    2018 inventory turnover ratio adjusted to FIFO as necessary = 10.34

    = [JPY5,822,805 – (19,660 – 10,120)]/[(608,572 + 10,120 + 486,465 + 19,660)/2].

31. A is correct. No LIFO liquidation occurred during 2018; the LIFO reserve increased from JPY10,120 million in 2017 to JPY19,660 million in 2018. Management stated in the MD&A that the decrease in inventories reflected the impact of decreased sales volumes and fluctuations in foreign currency translation rates.

32. C is correct. Finished goods and raw materials inventories are lower in 2018 when compared to 2017. Reduced levels of inventory typically indicate an anticipated business contraction.

33. B is correct. The decrease in LIFO inventory in 2018 would typically indicate that more inventory units were sold than produced or purchased. Accordingly, one would expect a liquidation of some of the older LIFO layers and the LIFO reserve to decrease. In actuality, the LIFO reserve *increased* from JPY10,120 million in 2017 to JPY19,660 million in 2018. This is not to be expected and is likely caused by the increase in prices of raw materials, other production materials, and parts of foreign currencies as noted in the MD&A. An analyst should seek to confirm this explanation.

34. C is correct. In a period of rising inventory costs, inventory valued using FIFO would have relatively higher values compared to inventory valued using LIFO. Thus, any mark downs of inventory values to NRV would have the least impact on inventories valued using the LIFO method as they are already conservatively valued.

35. B is correct. During a period of rising inventory costs, a company using the FIFO method will allocate a lower amount to cost of goods sold and a higher amount to ending inventory as compared with the LIFO method. The inventory turnover ratio is the ratio of cost of sales to ending inventory. A company using the FIFO method will produce a lower inventory turnover ratio as compared with the LIFO method. The current ratio (current assets/current liabilities) and the gross profit margin [gross profit/sales = (sales less cost of goods sold)/sales] will be higher under the FIFO method than under the LIFO method in periods of rising inventory unit costs.

36. B is correct. During a period of rising inventory prices, a company using the LIFO method will have higher cost of goods sold and a lower inventory compared with a company using the FIFO method. The inventory turnover ratio will be higher for the company using the LIFO method, thus making it appear more efficient. Current assets and gross profit margin will be lower for the company using the LIFO method, thus making it appear to be less liquid and less profitable.

37. B is correct. In an environment of declining inventory unit costs and constant or increasing inventory quantities, FIFO (in comparison with weighted average cost or LIFO) will have higher cost of goods sold and lower net income and inventory. Because both inventory and net income are lower, total equity is lower, resulting in a higher debt-to-equity ratio.

LEARNING MODULE

7

Analysis of Long-Term Assets

LEARNING OUTCOMES	
Mastery	***The candidate should be able to:***
☐	compare the financial reporting of the following types of intangible assets: purchased, internally developed, and acquired in a business combination
☐	explain and evaluate how impairment and derecognition of property, plant, and equipment and intangible assets affect the financial statements and ratios
☐	analyze and interpret financial statement disclosures regarding property, plant, and equipment and intangible assets

INTRODUCTION

1

Long-term assets such as property, plant, and equipment and intangibles typically account for most issuers' assets and are employed to generate economic benefits for many years. While an "economic" balance sheet would include a wide range of assets such as a company's reputation and its trained, experienced workforce, "accounting" balance sheets prepared under IFRS and US GAAP permit the recognition of a narrow range of assets. Once a long-lived asset is recognized, either the cost or revaluation models are used for measurement, while US GAAP requires the cost model. The choice of different methods and varying accounting policies for long-lived assets can create challenges for analysts comparing companies.

The two major accounting standard setters are as follows: 1) the International Accounting Standards Board (IASB) who establishes International Financial Reporting Standards (IFRS) and 2) the Financial Accounting Standards Board (FASB) who establishes US GAAP. Throughout this learning module both standards are referred to and many, but not all, of these two sets of accounting rules are identified. Note: changes in accounting standards as well as new rulings and/or pronouncements issued after the publication of this learning module may cause some of the information to become dated.

LEARNING MODULE OVERVIEW

- IFRS requires expensing research costs but allows development costs (not only software development costs) to be capitalized under certain conditions. Generally, US GAAP requires that both research and development costs be expensed; however, certain development costs related to software must be capitalized.
- When one company acquires another company, the transaction is accounted for using the acquisition method of accounting in which the company identified as the acquirer allocates the purchase price

to each asset acquired (and each liability assumed) on the basis of its fair value. Any excess of the purchase price over the fair value of net identifiable assets acquired is recorded as goodwill.

- The capitalized costs of long-lived tangible assets and of intangible assets with finite useful lives are allocated to expense in subsequent periods over their useful lives. For tangible assets, this process is referred to as depreciation, and for intangible assets, it is referred to as amortization.
- Long-lived tangible assets and intangible assets with finite useful lives are reviewed for impairment whenever changes in events or circumstances indicate that the carrying amount of an asset may not be recoverable.
- Intangible assets with an indefinite useful life are not amortized. Instead, they are reviewed for impairment annually.
- In contrast with depreciation and amortization charges, which serve to allocate the cost of a long-lived asset over its useful life, impairment charges reflect an unexpected decline in the fair value of an asset to an amount lower than its carrying amount.
- IFRS permit impairment losses to be reversed, with the reversal reported in profit. US GAAP do not permit the reversal of impairment losses.
- The gain or loss on the sale of long-lived assets is computed as the sale proceeds minus the carrying amount of the asset at the time of sale.

2 ACQUISITION OF INTANGIBLE ASSETS

☐ compare the financial reporting of the following types of intangible assets: purchased, internally developed, and acquired in a business combination

Intangible assets are non-monetary assets lacking physical substance. Intangible assets include items that involve exclusive rights, such as patents, copyrights, trademarks, and franchises. Under IFRS, identifiable intangible assets must meet three definitional criteria. They must be (1) identifiable (either capable of being separated from the entity or arising from contractual or legal rights), (2) under the control of the company, and (3) expected to generate future economic benefits. In addition, two recognition criteria must be met: (1) It is probable that the expected future economic benefits of the asset will flow to the company, and (2) the cost of the asset can be reliably measured. Goodwill, which is not considered an identifiable intangible asset,[1] arises when one company purchases another and the acquisition price exceeds the fair value of the net identifiable assets (both the tangible assets and the identifiable intangible assets, minus liabilities) acquired.

1 The IFRS definition of an intangible asset as an "identifiable non-monetary asset without physical substance" applies to intangible assets not specifically dealt with in standards other than International Accounting Standards (IAS) 38. The definition of intangible assets under US GAAP—"assets (other than financial assets) that lack physical substance"—includes goodwill in the definition of an intangible asset.

Accounting for an intangible asset depends on how it is acquired. The following sections describe accounting for intangible assets obtained in three ways: purchased in situations other than business combinations, developed internally, and acquired in business combinations.

Intangible Assets Purchased in Situations Other Than Business Combinations

Intangible assets purchased in situations other than business combinations, such as buying a patent, are treated at acquisition the same as long-lived tangible assets; they are recorded at their fair value when acquired, which is assumed to be equivalent to the purchase price. If several intangible assets are acquired as part of a group, the purchase price is allocated to each asset on the basis of its fair value.

In deciding how to treat individual intangible assets for analytical purposes, analysts are particularly aware that companies must use a substantial amount of judgment and numerous assumptions to determine the fair value of individual intangible assets. For analysis, therefore, understanding the types of intangible assets acquired can often be more useful than focusing on the values assigned to the individual assets. In other words, an analyst would typically be more interested in understanding what assets a company acquired (e.g., franchise rights) than in the precise portion of the purchase price a company allocated to each asset. Understanding the types of assets a company acquires can offer insights into the company's strategic direction and future operating potential.

Intangible Assets Developed Internally

In contrast with the treatment of construction costs of tangible assets, the costs to internally develop intangible assets are generally expensed when incurred. In some situations, however, the costs incurred to internally develop an intangible asset are capitalized. The general analytical issues related to the capitalizing-versus-expensing decision apply here—namely, comparability across companies and the effect on an individual company's trend analysis.

The general requirement that costs to internally develop intangible assets be expensed should be compared with capitalizing the cost of acquiring intangible assets in situations other than business combinations. Because costs associated with internally developing intangible assets are usually expensed, a company that has internally developed intangible assets, such as patents, copyrights, or brands through expenditures on R&D or advertising, will recognize a lower amount of assets than a company that has obtained intangible assets through external purchase. In addition, on the statement of cash flows, costs of internally developing intangible assets are classified as operating cash outflows whereas costs of acquiring intangible assets are classified as investing cash outflows. Differences in strategy (developing versus acquiring intangible assets) can thus impact financial ratios.

IFRS requires that expenditures on research (or during the research phase of an internal project) be expensed rather than capitalized as an intangible asset.[2] Research is defined as "original and planned investigation undertaken with the prospect of gaining new scientific or technical knowledge and understanding."[3] The "research phase of an internal project" refers to the period during which a company cannot demonstrate that an intangible asset is being created—for example, the search for alternative materials or systems to use in a production process. In contrast with the

2 IAS 38, *Intangible Assets.*

3 IAS 38, *Intangible Assets*, paragraph 8, *Definitions.*

treatment of research-phase expenditures, IFRS allow companies to recognize an intangible asset arising from development expenditures (or the development phase of an internal project) if certain criteria are met, including a demonstration of the technical feasibility of completing the intangible asset and the intent to use or sell the asset. Development is defined as "the application of research findings or other knowledge to a plan or design for the production of new or substantially improved materials, devices, products, processes, systems or services before the start of commercial production or use."[4]

Generally, US GAAP requires that both research and development costs be expensed as incurred but require capitalization of certain costs related to software development.[5] Costs incurred to develop a software product for sale are expensed until the product's technological feasibility is established and are capitalized thereafter. Similarly, companies expense costs related to the development of software for internal use until it is probable that the project will be completed and that the software will be used as intended. Thereafter, development costs are capitalized. The probability that the project will be completed is easier to demonstrate than is technological feasibility. The capitalized costs, related directly to developing software for sale or internal use, include the costs of employees who help build and test the software. The treatment of software development costs under US GAAP is similar to the treatment of all costs of internally developed intangible assets under IFRS.

EXAMPLE 1

Software Development Costs

REH AG, a fictional company that reports under IFRS, incurs expenditures of EUR1,000 per month during the fiscal year ended 31 December 2019 to develop software for internal use.

1. What is the accounting impact of the company being able to demonstrate that the software met the criteria for recognition as an intangible asset on 1 February versus 1 December?

   Solution:

   If the company is able to demonstrate that the software met the criteria for recognition as an intangible asset on 1 February, the company would recognize the EUR1,000 expended in January as an expense on the income statement for the fiscal year ended 31 December 2019. The other EUR11,000 of expenditures would be recognized as an intangible asset (on the balance sheet). Alternatively, if the company is not able to demonstrate that the software met the criteria for recognition as an intangible asset until 1 December, the company would recognize the EUR11,000 expensed in January through November as an expense on the income statement for the fiscal year ended 31 December 2019, with the other EUR1,000 of expenditures recognized as an intangible asset.

4 IAS 38, *Intangible Assets*, paragraph 8, *Definitions*.

5 Financial Accounting Standards Board (FASB) Accounting Standards Codification (ASC), Section 350-40-25, *Intangibles—Goodwill and Other – Internal-Use Software – Recognition*; and FASB ASC, Section 985-20-25, *Software – Costs of Software to be Sold, Leased, or Marketed – Recognition*, specify US GAAP accounting for software development costs for software for internal use and for software to be sold, respectively.

2. How would the treatment of expenditures differ if the company reported under US GAAP and it had established in 2018 that the project was likely to be completed and the software used to perform the function intended?

Solution:

Under US GAAP, the company would capitalize the entire EUR12,000 spent to develop software for internal use.

Intangible Assets Acquired in a Business Combination

When one company acquires another company, the transaction is accounted for using the acquisition method of accounting.[6] Under the acquisition method, the company identified as the acquirer allocates the purchase price to each asset acquired (and each liability assumed) on the basis of its fair value. If the purchase price exceeds the sum of the amounts that can be allocated to individual identifiable assets and liabilities, the excess is recorded as goodwill. Goodwill cannot be identified separately from the business as a whole.

Under IFRS, the acquired individual assets include identifiable intangible assets that meet the definitional and recognition criteria.[7] Otherwise, if the item is acquired in a business combination and cannot be recognized as a tangible or identifiable intangible asset, it is recognized as goodwill. Under US GAAP, there are two criteria to judge whether an intangible asset acquired in a business combination should be recognized separately from goodwill: The asset must be either an item arising from contractual or legal rights or an item that can be separated from the acquired company. Examples of intangible assets treated separately from goodwill include the intangible assets previously mentioned that involve exclusive rights (patents, copyrights, franchises, licenses), as well as such items as internet domain names and video and audiovisual materials.

Exhibit 1 describes how AB InBev allocated the USD103 billion purchase consideration in its 2016 acquisition of SABMiller Group. The combined company was renamed Anheuser-Busch InBev SA/NV. The majority of the intangible asset valuation relates to brands with indefinite life (USD19.9 billion of the USD20.0 billion total). Of USD63.0 billion total assets acquired, assets to be divested were valued at USD24.8 billion and assets to be held for were valued at USD38.2 billion. In total, intangible assets represent 52 percent of the total assets to be held for use. In addition, USD74.1 billion of goodwill was recognized in the transaction.

Exhibit 1: Acquisition of Intangible Assets through a Business Combination

Excerpt from the 2016 Annual Report of AB InBev:

> "On 10 October 2016, AB InBev announced the … successful completion of the business combination with the former SABMiller Group ("SAB").
>
> "The transaction resulted in 74.1 billion US dollar of goodwill provisionally allocated primarily to the businesses in Colombia, Ecuador, Peru, Australia, South Africa and other African, Asia Pacific and Latin American countries. The factors that contributed to the recognition of goodwill include the acquisition of an assembled workforce and the premiums paid for cost synergies expected to be achieved in SABMiller. Management's

6 Both IFRS and US GAAP require the use of the acquisition method in accounting for business combinations (IFRS 3 and FASB ASC, Section 805).

7 As previously described, the definitional criteria are identifiability, control by the company, and expected future benefits. The recognition criteria are probable flows of the expected economic benefits to the company and measurability.

assessment of the future economic benefits supporting recognition of this goodwill is in part based on expected savings through the implementation of AB InBev best practices such as, among others, a zero based budgeting program and initiatives that are expected to bring greater efficiency and standardization, generate cost savings and maximize purchasing power. Goodwill also arises due to the recognition of deferred tax liabilities in relation to the preliminary fair value adjustments on acquired intangible assets for which the amortization does not qualify as a tax deductible expense. None of the goodwill recognized is deductible for tax purposes.

"The majority of the intangible asset valuation relates to brands with indefinite life, valued for a total amount of 19.9 billion US dollar. The valuation of the brands with indefinite life is based on a series of factors, including the brand history, the operating plan and the countries in which the brands are sold. The fair value of brands was estimated by applying a combination of known valuation methodologies, such as the royalty relief and excess earnings valuation approaches.

"The intangibles with an indefinite life mainly include the Castle and Carling brand families in Africa, the Aguila and Poker brand families in Colombia, the Cristal and Pilsner brand families in Ecuador, and the Carlton brand family in Australia.

"Assets held for sale were recognized in relation to the divestiture of SABMiller's interests in the MillerCoors LLC joint venture and certain of SABMiller's portfolio of Miller brands outside of the US to Molson Coors Brewing company; the divestiture of SABMiller's European premium brands to Asahi Group Holdings, Ltd and the divestiture of SABMiller's interest in China Resources Snow Breweries Ltd. to China Resources Beer (Holdings) Co. Ltd."

The following is a summary of the provisional allocation of AB InBev's purchase price of SABMiller:

Assets	USD million
Property, plant and equipment	9,060
Intangible assets	20,040
Investment in associates	4,386
Inventories	977
Trade and other receivables	1,257
Cash and cash equivalents	1,410
Assets held for sale	24,805
All other assets	*1,087*
Total assets	*63,022*
Total liabilities	*–27,769*
Net identified assets and liabilities	**35,253**
Non-controlling interests	–6,200
Goodwill on acquisition	**74,083**
Purchase consideration	**103,136**

Table is excerpted from the company's 2016 Annual Report. Portions of detail are omitted, and subtotals are shown in italics.

Source: AB InBev 2016 Annual Report, 82–85.

IMPAIRMENT AND DERECOGNITION OF ASSETS

3

- [ ] explain and evaluate how impairment and derecognition of property, plant, and equipment and intangible assets affect the financial statements and ratios

In contrast with depreciation and amortization charges, which serve to allocate the depreciable cost of a long-lived asset over its useful life, impairment charges reflect an unanticipated decline in the value of an asset. Both IFRS and US GAAP require companies to write down the carrying amount of impaired assets. Impairment reversals for identifiable, long-lived assets are permitted under IFRS but typically not under US GAAP.

An asset is considered to be impaired when its carrying amount exceeds its recoverable amount. Although IFRS and US GAAP define recoverability differently (as described below), in general, impairment losses are recognized when the asset's carrying amount is not recoverable. The following paragraphs describe accounting for impairment for different categories of assets.

Impairment of Property, Plant, and Equipment

Accounting standards do not require that property, plant, and equipment be tested annually for impairment. Rather, at the end of each reporting period (generally, a fiscal year), a company assesses whether there are indications of asset impairment. If there is no indication of impairment, the asset is not tested for impairment. If there is an indication of impairment, such as evidence of obsolescence, decline in demand for products, or technological advancements, the recoverable amount of the asset should be measured in order to test for impairment. For property, plant, and equipment, impairment losses are recognized when the asset's carrying amount is not recoverable (i.e. the carrying amount is more than the recoverable amount). The amount of the impairment loss will reduce the carrying amount of the asset on the balance sheet and will reduce net income on the income statement. The impairment loss is a non-cash item and will not affect cash from operations.

IFRS and US GAAP differ somewhat both in the guidelines for determining that impairment has occurred and in the measurement of an impairment loss. Under IAS 36, an impairment loss is measured as the excess of carrying amount over the recoverable amount of the asset. The recoverable amount of an asset is defined as "the higher of its fair value less costs to sell and its value in use." Value in use is based on the present value of expected future cash flows. Under US GAAP, assessing recoverability is separate from measuring the impairment loss. The carrying amount of an asset "group" is considered not recoverable when it exceeds the undiscounted expected future cash flows of the group. If the asset's carrying amount is considered not recoverable, the impairment loss is measured as the difference between the asset's fair value and carrying amount.

EXAMPLE 2

Impairment of Property, Plant, and Equipment

Sussex, a fictional manufacturing company in the United Kingdom, owns a machine it uses to produce a single product. The demand for the product has declined substantially since the introduction of a competing product. The company has assembled the following information with respect to the machine:

Carrying amount	GBP18,000
Undiscounted expected future cash flows	GBP19,000
Present value of expected future cash flows	GBP16,000
Fair value if sold	GBP17,000
Costs to sell	GBP2,000

1. Under IFRS, what would the company report for the machine?

   Solution:

   Under IFRS, the company would compare the carrying amount (GBP18,000) with the higher of its fair value less costs to sell (GBP15,000) and its value in use (GBP16,000). The carrying amount exceeds the value in use, the higher of the two amounts, by GBP2,000. The machine would be written down to the recoverable amount of £16,000, and a loss of £2,000 would be reported in the income statement. The carrying amount of the machine is now GBP16,000. A new depreciation schedule based on the carrying amount of GBP16,000 would be developed.

2. Under US GAAP, what would the company report for the machine?

   Solution:

   Under US GAAP, the carrying amount (GBP18,000) is compared with the undiscounted expected future cash flows (GBP19,000). The carrying amount is less than the undiscounted expected future cash flows, so the carrying amount is considered recoverable. The machine would continue to be carried at GBP18,000, and no loss would be reported.

In Example 2, a write down in the value of a piece of property, plant, and equipment occurred under IFRS but not under US GAAP. In Example 3, a write down occurs under both IFRS and US GAAP.

EXAMPLE 3

Impairment of Property, Plant, and Equipment

Essex, a fictional manufacturing company in the United Kingdom, owns a machine it uses to produce a single product. The demand for the product has declined substantially since the introduction of a competing product. The company has assembled the following information with respect to the machine:

Carrying amount	GBP18,000
Undiscounted expected future cash flows	GBP16,000
Present value of expected future cash flows	GBP14,000
Fair value if sold	GBP10,000
Costs to sell	GBP2,000

1. Under IFRS, what would the company report for the machine?

   Solution:

   Under IFRS, the company would compare the carrying amount (GBP18,000) with the higher of its fair value less costs to sell (GBP8,000) and its value in use (GBP14,000). The carrying amount exceeds the value in use, the higher of the two amounts, by GBP4,000. The machine would be written down to the recoverable amount of GBP14,000, and a loss of GBP4,000 would be reported in the income statement. The carrying amount of the machine is now GBP14,000. A new depreciation schedule based on the carrying amount of GBP14,000 would be developed.

2. Under US GAAP, what would the company report for the machine?

Solution:

Under US GAAP, the carrying amount (GBP18,000) is compared with the undiscounted expected future cash flows (GBP16,000). The carrying amount exceeds the undiscounted expected future cash flows, so the carrying amount is considered not recoverable. The machine would be written down to fair value of GBP10,000, and a loss of GBP8,000 would be reported in the income statement. The carrying amount of the machine is now GBP10,000. A new depreciation schedule based on the carrying amount of GBP10,000 would be developed.

Example 3 shows that the write down to value in use under IFRS can be less than the write down to fair value under US GAAP. The difference in recognition of impairment losses is ultimately reflected in differences in book value of equity.

Impairment of Intangible Assets with a Finite Life

Intangible assets with a finite life are amortized (carrying amount decreases over time) and may become impaired. As is the case with property, plant, and equipment, the assets are not tested annually for impairment. Instead, they are tested only when significant events suggest the need to test. The company assesses at the end of each reporting period whether a significant event suggesting the need to test for impairment has occurred. Examples of such events include a significant decrease in the market price or a significant adverse change in legal or economic factors. Impairment accounting for intangible assets with a finite life is essentially the same as for tangible assets; the amount of the impairment loss will reduce the carrying amount of the asset on the balance sheet and will reduce net income on the income statement.

Impairment of Intangibles with Indefinite Lives

Intangible assets with indefinite lives are not amortized. Instead, they are carried on the balance sheet at historical cost but are tested at least annually for impairment. Impairment exists when the carrying amount exceeds its fair value.

Impairment of Long-Lived Assets Held for Sale

A long-lived (non-current) asset is reclassified as held for sale rather than held for use when management's intent is to sell it and its sale is highly probable. (Additionally, accounting standards require that the asset must be available for immediate sale in its present condition.)[8] For instance, assume a building is no longer needed by a company and management's intent is to sell it. If the transaction meets the accounting criteria, the building is reclassified from property, plant, and equipment to non-current assets held for sale. At the time of reclassification, assets previously held for use are tested for impairment. If the carrying amount at the time of reclassification exceeds the fair

8 IFRS 5, *Non-current Assets Held for Sale and Discontinued Operations.*

value less costs to sell, an impairment loss is recognized and the asset is written down to fair value less costs to sell. Long-lived assets held for sale cease to be depreciated or amortized.

Reversals of Impairments of Long-Lived Assets

After an asset has been deemed impaired and an impairment loss has been reported, the asset's recoverable amount could potentially increase. For instance, a lawsuit appeal may successfully challenge a patent infringement by another company, with the result that a patent previously written down has a higher recoverable amount. IFRS permit impairment losses to be reversed if the recoverable amount of an asset increases regardless of whether the asset is classified as held for use or held for sale. Note that IFRS permit the reversal of impairment losses only. IFRS do not permit the revaluation to the recoverable amount if the recoverable amount exceeds the previous carrying amount. Under US GAAP, the accounting for reversals of impairments depends on whether the asset is classified as held for use or held for sale.[9] Under US GAAP, once an impairment loss has been recognized for assets held for use, it cannot be reversed. In other words, once the value of an asset held for use has been decreased by an impairment charge, it cannot be increased. For assets held for sale, if the fair value increases after an impairment loss, the loss can be reversed.

Derecognition

A company derecognizes an asset (i.e., removes it from the financial statements) when the asset is disposed of or is expected to provide no future benefits from either use or disposal. A company may dispose of a long-lived operating asset by selling it, exchanging it, abandoning it, or distributing it to existing shareholders. As previously described, non-current assets that management intends to sell or to distribute to existing shareholders and which meet the accounting criteria (immediately available for sale in current condition and the sale is highly probable) are reclassified as non-current assets held for sale.

Sale of Long-Lived Assets

The gain or loss on the sale of long-lived assets is computed as the sales proceeds minus the carrying amount of the asset at the time of sale. An asset's carrying amount is typically the net book value (i.e., the historical cost minus accumulated depreciation), unless the asset's carrying amount has been changed to reflect impairment and/or revaluation, as previously discussed.

EXAMPLE 4

Calculation of Gain or Loss on the Sale of Long-Lived Assets

1. Moussilauke Diners Inc., a fictional company, is revamping its menus to focus on healthier food items. The company sells 450 used pizza ovens for $3.1 million. At the time of sale, the oven had a carrying amount that reflected an original cost of $5.1 million and $3.2 million in accumulated depreciation. What would be the reported gain or loss from selling the ovens?

   A. $0.1 million loss

9 FASB ASC, Section 360-10-35, *Property, Plant, and Equipment–Overall–Subsequent Measurement.*

B. $1.2 million gain

C. $3.1 million gain

Solution:

B is correct. The ovens had a carrying amount of $5.1 – $3.2 = $1.9 million, and Moussilauke sold the ovens at a price of $3.1 million, resulting in a gain on the sale of $1.2 million. Ignoring taxes, the cash flow from the sale is $3.1 million, which would be reported as a cash inflow from investing.

A gain or loss on the sale of an asset is disclosed on the income statement, either as a component of other gains and losses or in a separate line item when the amount is material. A company typically discloses further detail about the sale in the management discussion and analysis and/or financial statement footnotes. In addition, a statement of cash flows prepared using the indirect method adjusts net income to remove any gain or loss on the sale from operating cash flow and to include the amount of proceeds from the sale in cash from investing activities. Recall that the indirect method of the statement of cash flows begins with net income and makes all adjustments to arrive at cash from operations, including removal of gains or losses from non-operating activities.

Long-Lived Assets Disposed of Other Than by a Sale

Long-lived assets to be disposed of other than by a sale (e.g., abandoned, exchanged for another asset, or distributed to owners in a spin-off) are classified as held for use until disposal or until they meet the criteria to be classified as held for sale or held for distribution.[10] Thus, the long-lived assets continue to be depreciated and tested for impairment, unless their carrying amount is zero, as required for other long-lived assets owned by the company.

When an asset is retired or abandoned, the accounting is similar to a sale, except that the company does not record cash proceeds. Assets are reduced by the carrying amount of the asset at the time of retirement or abandonment, and a loss equal to the asset's carrying amount is recorded.

When an asset is exchanged, accounting for the exchange typically involves removing the carrying amount of the asset given up, adding a fair value for the asset acquired, and reporting any difference between the carrying amount and the fair value as a gain or loss. The fair value used is the fair value of the asset given up unless the fair value of the asset acquired is more clearly evident. If no reliable measure of fair value exists, the acquired asset is measured at the carrying amount of the asset given up. A gain is reported when the fair value used for the newly acquired asset exceeds the carrying amount of the asset given up. A loss is reported when the fair value used for the newly acquired asset is less than the carrying amount of the asset given up. If the acquired asset is valued at the carrying amount of the asset given up because no reliable measure of fair value exists, no gain or loss is reported.

When a spin-off occurs, typically, an entire cash generating unit of a company with all its assets is spun off. As an illustration of a spin-off, Fiat Chrysler Automobiles (FCA) spun off its ownership of Ferrari in 2016. Prior to the spin-off, FCA had sold 10 percent of its ownership of Ferrari in an IPO and recognized an increase in Shareholders' equity of EUR873 million (the difference between the consideration it received in the IPO of EUR866 million and the carrying amount of the equity interest sold of EUR7 million.) In contrast, the spin-off, in which FCA distributed its ownership in Ferrari to the existing FCA shareholders, did not result in any gain or loss.

10 In a spin-off, shareholders of the parent company receive a proportional number of shares in a new, separate entity.

FCA's spin-off was completed on 3 January 2016, with each FCA shareholder receiving one common share of Ferrari N.V. for every ten common shares of FCA. In its financial statements for the prior fiscal year, FCA shows the assets and liabilities of Ferrari as held for distribution. Specifically, its balance sheet includes € 3,650 million in Assets Held for Distribution as a component of current assets and € 3,584 million Liabilities Held for Distribution. Exhibit 2 includes excerpts from the company's 31 December 2015 annual report.

Exhibit 2: Excerpt from Fiat Chrysler Automobiles (FCA) Notes to the Consolidated Financial Statements, 2015 Annual Report

Ferrari Spin-off and Discontinued Operations

"As the spin-off of Ferrari N.V. became highly probable with the aforementioned shareholders' approval and since it was available for immediate distribution at that date, the Ferrari segment met the criteria to be classified as a disposal group held for distribution to owners and a discontinued operation pursuant to IFRS 5 - *Non-current Assets Held for Sale and Discontinued Operations*."

The following assets and liabilities of the Ferrari segment were classified as held for distribution on 31 December 2015:

	At 31 December 2015
Assets classified as held for distribution	(euro millions)
Goodwill	786
Other intangible assets	297
Property, plant, and equipment	627
Other non-current assets	134
Receivables from financing activities	1,176
Cash and cash equivalents	182
Other current assets	448
Total Assets held for distribution	**3,650**
Liabilities classified as held for distribution	
Provisions	224
Debt	2,256
Other current liabilities	624
Trade payables	480
Total Liabilities held for distribution	**3,584**

4 PRESENTATION AND DISCLOSURE

☐ analyze and interpret financial statement disclosures regarding property, plant, and equipment and intangible assets

Under IFRS, for each class of property, plant, and equipment, a company must disclose the measurement basis, the depreciation method, the useful life (or, equivalently, the depreciation rate) used, the gross carrying amount, and the accumulated depreciation at the beginning and end of the period, and a reconciliation of the carrying amount at the beginning and end of the period.[11] In addition, disclosures of restrictions on title and pledges as security of property, plant, and equipment and contractual agreements to acquire property, plant, and equipment are required. If the revaluation model is used, the date of revaluation, details of how the fair value was obtained, the carrying amount under the cost model, and the revaluation surplus must be disclosed. A company must also disclose the depreciation expense for the period, the balances of major classes of depreciable assets, accumulated depreciation by major classes or in total, and a general description of the depreciation method(s) used in computing depreciation expense with respect to the major classes of depreciable assets.

Under IFRS, for each class of intangible assets, a company must disclose whether the useful lives are indefinite or finite. If finite, for each class of intangible asset, a company must disclose the useful lives (or, equivalently, the amortization rate) used, the amortization methods used, the gross carrying amount and the accumulated amortization at the beginning and end of the period, where amortization is included on the income statement, and a reconciliation of the carrying amount at the beginning and end of the period.[12] If an asset has an indefinite life, the company must disclose the carrying amount of the asset and why it is considered to have an indefinite life. Similar to property, plant, and equipment, disclosures of restrictions on title and pledges as security of intangible assets and contractual agreements to acquire intangible assets are required. If the revaluation model is used, the date of revaluation, details of how the fair value was obtained, the carrying amount under the cost model, and the revaluation surplus must be disclosed.

Under US GAAP, companies are required to disclose the gross carrying amounts and accumulated amortization in total and by major class of intangible assets, the aggregate amortization expense for the period, and the estimated amortization expense for the next five fiscal years.[13]

The disclosures related to impairment losses also differ under IFRS and US GAAP. Under IFRS, a company must disclose for each class of assets the amounts of impairment losses and reversals of impairment losses recognized in the period and where those are recognized on the financial statements.[14] The company must also disclose in aggregate the main classes of assets affected by impairment losses and reversals of impairment losses and the main events and circumstances leading to recognition of these impairment losses and reversals of impairment losses. Under US GAAP, there is no reversal of impairment losses for assets held for use. The company must disclose a description of the impaired asset, what led to the impairment, the method of determining fair value, the amount of the impairment loss, and where the loss is recognized on the financial statements.[15]

Disclosures about long-lived assets appear throughout the financial statements: in the balance sheet, the income statement, the statement of cash flows, and the notes. The balance sheet reports the carrying value of the asset. For the income statement, depreciation expense may or may not appear as a separate line item. Under IFRS, whether the income statement discloses depreciation expense separately depends on whether the company is using a 'nature of expense' method or a 'function of expense' method. Under the nature of expense method, a company aggregates expenses "according to their nature (e.g., depreciation, purchases of materials, transport costs, employee benefits and advertising costs), and does not reallocate them among functions within the entity."[16] Under the function of expense method, a company classifies expenses

11 IAS 16, *Property, Plant and Equipment*, paragraphs 73–79, *Disclosure*.
12 IAS 38, *Intangible Assets*, paragraphs 118–128, *Disclosure*.
13 FASB ASC, Section 350-30-50, *Intangibles–General–Disclosure*.
14 IAS 36, *Impairment of Assets*, paragraphs 126–137, *Disclosure*.
15 IAS 36, *Impairment of Assets*, paragraphs 126–137, *Disclosure*.
16 IAS 1, paragraph 102.

according to the function, for example as part of cost of sales or of SG&A (selling, general, and administrative) expenses. At a minimum, a company using the function of expense method must disclose cost of sales, but the other line items vary.

The statement of cash flows reflects acquisitions and disposals of fixed assets in the investing section. In addition, when prepared using the indirect method, the statement of cash flows typically shows depreciation expense (or depreciation plus amortization) as a line item in the adjustments of net income to cash flow from operations. The notes to the financial statements describe the company's accounting method(s), the range of estimated useful lives, historical cost by main category of fixed asset, accumulated depreciation, and annual depreciation expense.

The following example provides excerpts relating to intangible assets and property, plant, and equipment from the annual report of Orange SA for the year ended 31 December 2017.

EXAMPLE 5

Financial Statement Presentation and Disclosures for Long-Lived Assets

The following exhibits include excerpts from the annual report for the year ended 31 December 2017 of Orange SA, an international telecommunications company based in France.

Exhibit 3: Orange SA, 2017 Consolidated Financial Statement

Excerpt from Consolidated Income Statement (euro millions)

(Note that only selected line items/data are shown for illustrative purposes)

	12 Months Ended		
	31 Dec. 2017	**31 Dec. 2016**	**31 Dec. 2015**
Revenues	€41,096	€40,918	€40,236
...	...	...	...
Depreciation and amortization	(6,846)	(6,728)	(6,465)
...	...	...	...
Impairment of goodwill	(20)	(772)	
Impairment of fixed assets	(190)	(207)	(38)
...	...	...	...
Operating income	4,917	4,077	4,742
...	...	...	...
Consolidated net income of continuing operations	2,114	1,010	2,510
Consolidated net income of discontinued operations (EE)	29	2,253	448
Consolidated net income	**2,143**	**3,263**	**2,958**
Net income attributable to owners of the parent company	1,906	2,935	2,652
Non-controlling interests	€237	€328	€306

Excerpt from the Consolidated Statement of Financial Position (euro millions)

Assets	31 Dec. 2017	31 Dec. 2016	31 Dec. 2015
Goodwill	€27,095	€27,156	€27,071
Other intangible assets	14,339	14,602	14,327
Property, plant, and equipment	26,665	25,912	25,123
...	...	...	...
Total non-current assets	74,035	74,819	71,330
...	...	...	...
Total current assets	20,679	19,849	14,312
Assets held for sale			5,788
Total assets	**94,714**	**94,668**	**91,430**
Equity and liabilities			
...	...	...	...
Total equity	32,942	33,174	33,267
...	...	...	...
Total non-current liabilities	32,736	35,590	36,537
...	...	...	...
Total current liabilities	29,036	25,904	21,626
Total equity and liabilities	**94,714**	**94,668**	**91,430**

Exhibit 4: Orange SA, 2017 Notes to the Consolidated Financial Statement

Excerpt from Note 7.2 Goodwill

Excerpt from Reconciliation of Changes in Goodwill (euro millions)

	12 Months Ended		
	31 Dec. 2017	**31 Dec. 2016**	**31 Dec. 2015**
Gross value in the opening balance	€32,689	€32,606	€30,271
Acquisitions	38	904	2,333
Disposals	0	(6)	(69)
Translation adjustment	(40)	(815)	73
Reclassifications and other items	0	0	(2)
Reclassification to assets held for sale	0	0	0
Gross value in closing balance	32,687	32,689	32,606
Accumulated impairment losses in the opening balance	(5,533)	(5,535)	(5,487)
Impairment	(20)	(772)	0
Disposals	0	0	0
Translation adjustment	(39)	774	(48)
Reclassifications and other items	0	0	0
Reclassification to assets held for sale	0	0	0

Excerpt from Reconciliation of Changes in Goodwill (euro millions)

	12 Months Ended		
	31 Dec. 2017	31 Dec. 2016	31 Dec. 2015
Accumulated impairment losses in the closing balance	€(5,592)	€(5,533)	€(5,535)
Net book value of goodwill	27,095	27,156	27,071

Excerpt* from Note 7.3 Key assumptions used to determine recoverable amounts as of 31 December 2017*

The parameters used for the determination of recoverable amount of the main consolidated operations are set forth below:

	France	Spain	Poland	Belgium	Romania
Perpetuity growth rate	0.8%	1.5%	1.0%	0.5%	2.3%
Post-tax discount rate	5.5%	8.6%	8.3%	6.8%	8.8%

Excerpt from Note 7.4 Sensitivity of recoverable amounts as of 31 December 2017*

The level of sensitivity presented allows readers of the financial statements to estimate the impact in their own assessment.

(in billions of euros)	France	Spain	Poland	Belgium	Romania
Decrease by 1% in perpetuity growth rate	10.4	1.6	0.6	0.3	0.3
An increase by 1% in post-tax discount rate	11.4	2.0	0.6	0.3	0.3

** Table extracted presents only selected assumptions and selected countries.*

The company's annual report provides more detail.

"Goodwill is not amortized. It is tested for impairment at least annually and more frequently when there is an indication that it may be impaired .... These tests are performed at the level of each Cash Generating Unit (CGU) (or group of CGUs)... To determine whether an impairment loss should be recognized, the carrying value of the assets and liabilities of the CGUs or groups of CGUs is compared to recoverable amount, for which Orange uses mostly the value in use.... Value in use is the present value of the future expected cash flows. Cash flow projections are based on economic and regulatory assumptions, license renewal assumptions and forecast trading and investment activity drawn up by the Group's management..."

Excerpt from Note 8.3 Other intangible assets—Net book value

	31 December		
(in millions of euros)	2017	2016	2015
Telecommunications licenses	6,233	6,440	5,842
Orange brand	3,133	3,133	3,133
Other brands	88	102	137
Customer bases	555	703	729

	31 December		
(in millions of euros)	**2017**	**2016**	**2015**
Software	3,946	3,781	3,815
Other intangible assets	384	443	671
Total	€14,339	€14,602	€14,327

Excerpt from Note 8.4 Property, plant and equipment—Net book value

	31 December		
(in millions of euros)	**2017**	**2016**	**2015**
Land and buildings	2,535	2,661	2,733
Network and terminals	22,880	21,984	21,194
IT equipment	802	784	787
Other property, plant, and equipment	448	483	409
Total	€26,665	€25,912	€25,123

Exhibit 5: Orange SA, 2017 Analysis of the Group's Financial Position and Earnings

"Orange group operating income stood at 4,077 million euros in 2016, compared with 4,742 million euros in 2015 on a historical basis, a drop of 14.0% or 665 million euros. This drop on a historical basis was largely attributable to:

- the recognition, in 2016, of 772 million euros in impairment loss of goodwill ... and 207 million euros in impairment loss of fixed assets ... primarily relating to:
  - Poland for 507 million euros. This impairment loss mainly reflects a decline in competitiveness in the ADSL market, a deterioration in revenue assumptions in the mobile market and an increase in the post-tax discount rate due to the downgrading of the country's sovereign rating by the rating agencies,
  - Egypt for 232 million euros. This impairment loss reflects the financial terms of the 4G license awarded in 2016, the sharp depreciation of the Egyptian pound and increased political and economic uncertainty,
  - in the Congo (DRC), for 109 million euros. This impairment loss reflects political and economic uncertainty, a decline in purchasing power with a knock-on effect on the consumption of telecommunications products and services and an increased regulatory burden (particularly connected with the implementation of customer identification),
  - Cameroon for 90 million euros. This impairment loss reflects a decline in voice revenues following the surge in messaging services and in VoIP of Over-The-Top (OTT) providers and heightened competition in the mobile market,

- and Niger for 26 million euros;

- and the 263 million euro increase in depreciation and amortization."

1. What proportion of Orange's total assets as of 31 December 2017 is represented by goodwill and other intangible assets?

Solution:

As of 31 December 2017, goodwill represents 28.6 percent (= 27,095 ÷ 94,714) of Orange's total assets. Other intangible assets represent 15.1 percent (= 14,339 ÷ 94,714). Data are from the company's balance sheet in Exhibit 3.

2. What is the largest component of the company's impairment losses during the year ending December 2016?

Solution:

The largest component of the EUR772 impairment loss on goodwill and the EUR207 million impairment loss of fixed assets related to a EUR507 million loss in Poland. The company attributed the loss to a decline in the competitiveness of the market for its ADSL technology, a reduction in revenue assumptions, and an increase in the discount rate resulting from the downgrading of the country's debt rating. From Exhibit 4:
[The company's financial statements define ADSL (Asymmetrical Digital Subscriber Line) as a "broadband data transmission technology on the traditional telephone network. It enables broadband data transmission (first and foremost Internet access) via twisted paired copper cable (the most common type of telephone line found in buildings)."]

3. The company discloses that it determines whether an impairment loss should be recognized by comparing the carrying value of a unit's assets and liabilities to the "recoverable amount," equal to the company's estimate of its value in use. How does the company determine value in use?

Solution:

The company determines value in use – which it uses as a unit's assets and liabilities "recoverable amount" in impairment testing – as the present value of the future expected cash flows. The cash flow projections are based on management's assumptions. From Note 7.4 in Exhibit 4.

4. By what amount would the estimated recoverable value of the company's operations in France, Spain, Poland, Belgium, and Romania change if the company decreased its estimate of the perpetuity growth rate by 1 percent? By what amount would the estimated recoverable value of these operations change if the company increased its estimate of the post-tax discount rate by 1 percent?

Solution:

If the company decreased its estimate of the perpetuity growth rate by 1 percent, the estimated recoverable value of the company's operations in France, Spain, Poland, Belgium and Romania would be reduced by EUR13.2 billion (=10.4 + 1.6 + 0.6 + 0.3 + 0.3). A decrease in estimated growth decreases the present value of the cash flows. If the company increased its estimate of the post-tax discount rate by 1 percent, the estimated recoverable value of these operations would be reduced by EUR14.6 billion (=11.4 +

2.0 + 0.6 + 0.3 + 0.3). An increase in the discount rate decreases the present value of cash flows. Data are from Note 7.4 in Exhibit 4.

5. What are the largest components of other intangible assets as of 31 December 2017? What is the largest component of property, plant and equipment as of 31 December 2017?

Solution:

The largest components of other intangible assets as of 31 December 2017 are telecommunications licenses, software, and the Orange brand, reported at EUR6,233 million, EUR3,946 million, and EUR3,133 million, respectively. The largest component of property, plant, and equipment as of 31 December 2017 is network and terminals (EUR22,880 million). Data are from Notes 8.3 and 8.4 in Exhibit 4.

Note that the exhibits in the previous example contain relatively brief excerpts from the company's disclosures. The complete text of the disclosures concerning the company's non-current assets spans numerous different footnotes, some of which are several pages long. Overall, an analyst can use the disclosures to understand a company's investments in tangible and intangible assets, how those investments changed during a reporting period, how those changes affected current performance, and what those changes might indicate about future performance.

USING DISCLOSURES IN ANALYSIS 5

☐ analyze and interpret financial statement disclosures regarding property, plant, and equipment and intangible assets

Ratios used in analyzing fixed assets include the fixed asset turnover ratio and several asset age ratios. The fixed asset turnover ratio (total revenue divided by average net fixed assets) reflects the relationship between total revenues and investment in PPE (property, plant, & equipment). The higher this ratio, the higher the amount of sales a company is able to generate with a given amount of investment in fixed assets. A higher asset turnover ratio is often interpreted as an indicator of greater efficiency.

Asset age ratios generally rely on the relationship between historical cost and depreciation. Under the revaluation model (permitted under IFRS but not US GAAP), the relationship between carrying amount, accumulated depreciation, and depreciation expense will differ when the carrying amount differs significantly from the depreciated historical cost. Therefore, the following discussion of asset age ratios applies primarily to PPE reported under the cost model.

Asset age and remaining useful life, two asset age ratios, are important indicators of a company's need to reinvest in productive capacity. The older the assets and the shorter the remaining life, the more a company may need to reinvest to maintain productive capacity. The average age of a company's asset base can be estimated as accumulated depreciation divided by depreciation expense. The average remaining life of a company's asset base can be estimated as net PPE divided by depreciation expense. These estimates simply reflect the following relationships for assets accounted for on a historical cost basis: total historical cost minus accumulated depreciation equals net PPE; and, under straight-line depreciation, total historical cost less salvage value divided by estimated useful life equals annual depreciation expense. Equivalently, total historical cost less salvage value divided by annual depreciation expense equals estimated useful life. Assuming straight-line depreciation and no salvage value (for simplicity), we have the following:

Estimated total useful life	=	Time elapsed since purchase (Age)	+	Estimated remaining life
Historical cost ÷ annual depreciation expense	=	Estimated total useful life		
Historical cost	=	Accumulated depreciation	+	Net PPE

Equivalently,

Estimated total useful life	=	Estimated age of equipment	+	Estimated remaining life
Historical cost ÷ annual depreciation expense	=	Accumulated depreciation ÷ annual depreciation expense	+	Net PPE ÷ annual depreciation expense

The application of these estimates can be illustrated by a hypothetical example of a company with a single depreciable asset. Assume the asset initially cost USD100, had an estimated useful life of 10 years, and an estimated salvage value of USD0. Each year, the company records a depreciation expense of USD10, so accumulated depreciation will equal USD10 times the number of years since the asset was acquired (when the asset is 7 years old, accumulated depreciation will be USD70). Equivalently, the age of the asset will equal accumulated depreciation divided by the annual depreciation expense.

In practice, such estimates are difficult to make with great precision. Companies use depreciation methods other than the straight-line method and have numerous assets with varying useful lives and salvage values, including some assets that are fully depreciated, so this approach produces an estimate only. Moreover, fixed asset disclosures are often quite general. Consequently, these estimates may be primarily useful to identify areas for further investigation.

One further measure compares a company's current reinvestment in productive capacity. Comparing annual capital expenditures to annual depreciation expense provides an indication of whether productive capacity is being maintained. It is a very general indicator of the rate at which a company is replacing its PPE relative to the rate at which PPE is being depreciated.

EXAMPLE 6

Using Fixed Asset Disclosure to Compare Companies' Fixed Asset Turnover and Average Age of Depreciable Assets

Consider the property, plant, and equipment for the following three international telecommunications companies:

- Orange SA, which we discussed previously, has been listed on Euronext Paris (symbol ORA) and on the New York Stock Exchange (symbol ORAN) since 1997. At 31 December 2017, the French government retained 22.95 percent of the share capital.
- BCE Inc., Canada's largest communications company, provides wireless, wireline, Internet, TV, and business communications across Canada. BCE's shares are publicly traded on the Toronto Stock Exchange and on the New York Stock Exchange (TSX, NYSE: BCE).

- Verizon Communications Inc. is a US-based global provider of communications, information, and entertainment products and services to consumers, businesses, and governmental agencies. Verizon's shares are listed on the New York Stock Exchange and the NASDAQ Global Select Market (symbol VZ).

Exhibit 6: Selected Information from the Companies' Financial Statements

	Orange	BCE Inc	Verizon
Currency, Millions of:	**Euro**	**Canadian dollars**	**US dollars**
Historical cost total PPE, end of year	97,092	69,230	246,498
Accumulated depreciation, end of year	70,427	45,197	157,930
Net PPE, end of year	26,665	24,033	88,568
Net PPE, beginning of year	25,912	22,346	84,751
Revenues	41,096	22,719	126,034
Annual depreciation expense	4,708	3,037	14,741
Capital expenditure	5,677	4,149	17,247
Land included in PPE	Not separated	Not separated	806
Accounting standards	IFRS	IFRS	US GAAP
PPE measurement	Historical cost	Historical cost	Historical cost
Depreciation method	Straight-line	Straight-line	Straight-line

Sources: Companies' 2017 Annual Financial Reports."

1. Based on the data for each company in Exhibit 5, estimate the total useful life, age, and remaining useful life of PPE.

   Solution:

   The following table presents the estimated total useful life, estimated age, and estimated remaining useful life of PPE for each of the companies.

Estimates	Orange	BCE Inc	Verizon
Estimated total useful life (years)	20.6	22.8	16.7
Estimated age (years)	15.0	14.9	10.7
Estimated remaining life (years)	5.7	7.9	6.0

The computations are demonstrated using Verizon's data ($ in millions). The estimated total useful life of PPE is total historical cost of PPE of USD246,498 divided by annual depreciation expense of USD14,741, giving 16.7 years. Estimated age and estimated remaining life are obtained by dividing accumulated depreciation of USD157,930 and net PPE of USD88,568 by the annual depreciation expense of USD14,741, giving 10.7 years and 6.0 years, respectively.

Ideally, the estimates of asset lives illustrated in this example should exclude land, which is not depreciable, when the information is available; however, both Orange and BCE report Land and Buildings as a combined amount. We will use Verizon, for which land appeared to be disclosed separately in the above table, to illustrate the estimates with adjusting for land. As an illustration of the calculations to exclude land, excluding Verizon's land would give an estimated total useful life for the non-land PPE of 16.7 years [(total cost EUR246,498 minus land cost of USD806) divided by annual depreciation expense of EUR14,741 million]. The estimate is essentially unchanged from the estimate including land because land represents such a small component of Verizon's PPE.

2. Interpret the estimates of estimated total useful life, age, and remaining life. What items might affect comparisons across the three companies?

Solution:

The estimated total useful life suggests that Orange and BCE depreciate PPE over a much longer period than Verizon: 20.6 and 22.8 years for Orange and BCE, respectively, versus 16.7 years for Verizon.

The estimated age of the equipment suggests that Verizon has the newest PPE with an estimated age of 10.7 years. Additionally, the estimates suggest that around 73 percent of Orange's assets' useful lives have passed (15.0 years ÷ 20.6 years, or equivalently, EUR70,427 million ÷ EUR97,092 million). In comparison, around 65 and 64 percent of the useful lives of the PPE of BCE and Verizon, respectively, have passed.

Items that can affect comparisons across the companies include business differences, such as differences in composition of the companies' operations and differences in acquisition and divestiture activity. This result can be compared, to an extent, to the useful lives and asset mix disclosed in the companies' footnotes; however, differences in disclosures (e.g., in the categories of assets disclosed) can affect comparisons.

3. How does each company's 2017 depreciation expense compare to its capital expenditures for the year?

Solution:

All three companies' capital expenditure exceeds its depreciation expense. Rounding to the nearest 10 percent, capital expenditure as a percentage of depreciation is 120 percent for Orange, 140 percent for BCE, and 120 percent for Verizon. All three companies are replacing PPE at a faster rate than the PPE is being depreciated, consistent with the companies' somewhat older asset base.

4. Calculate and compare fixed asset turnover for each company.

Solution:

Fixed asset turnover is calculated as total revenues divided by average net PPE. Orange's fixed asset turnover is 1.6 (= 41,096/((26,665 + 25,912)/2)). BCE's fixed asset turnover is 1.0, and Verizon's fixed asset turnover is 1.5. Orange's and Verizon's higher levels of fixed asset turnover indicate these companies, compared to BCE, are able to generate more sales per unit of investment in fixed assets.

PRACTICE PROBLEMS

The following information relates to questions 1-3

An analyst is studying the impairment of the manufacturing equipment of WLP Corp., a UK-based corporation that reports under IFRS. He gathers the following information about the equipment:

Fair value	GBP16,800,000
Costs to sell	GBP800,000
Value in use	GBP14,500,000
Net carrying amount	GBP19,100,000

1. Based on this information, the amount of impairment loss that WLP will need to report on its income statement related to the manufacturing equipment is *closest* to:

   A. GBP2,300,000.

   B. GBP3,100,000.

   C. GBP4,600,000.

2. Under IFRS, an impairment loss on a property, plant, and equipment asset is measured as the excess of the carrying amount over the asset's:

   A. fair value.

   B. recoverable amount.

   C. undiscounted expected future cash flows.

3. The impairment of intangible assets with finite lives affects:

   A. only the balance sheet.

   B. only the income statement.

   C. both the balance sheet and the income statement.

The following information relates to questions 4-7

Melanie Hart, CFA, is a transportation analyst. Hart has been asked to write a research report on Altai Mountain Rail Company (AMRC). Like other companies in the railroad industry, AMRC's operations are capital intensive, with significant investments in long-lived tangible assets as property, plant, and equipment. In November of 2021, AMRC's board of directors hired a new team to manage the company. In reviewing the company's 2022 annual report, Hart is concerned about some of the accounting choices that the new management has made. These choices differ from those of the previous management and from common industry practice. Hart has highlighted the following statements from the company's annual report:

Statement 1 "In 2022, AMRC spent significant amounts on track replacement and similar improvements. AMRC expensed rather than capitalized a significant proportion of these expenditures."

Statement 2 "AMRC uses the straight-line method of depreciation for both financial and tax reporting purposes to account for plant and equipment."

Statement 3 "In 2022, AMRC recognized an impairment loss of €50 million on a fleet of locomotives. The impairment loss was reported as 'other income' in the income statement and reduced the carrying amount of the assets on the balance sheet."

Exhibit 1 and Exhibit 2 contain AMRC's 2022 consolidated income statement and balance sheet. AMRC prepares its financial statements in accordance with International Financial Reporting Standards.

Exhibit 1: Consolidated Statement of Income

	2022		2021	
For the Years Ended 31 December	**Euros millions**	**Revenues (%)**	**Euros millions**	**Revenues (%)**
Operating revenues	2,600	100.0	2,300	100.0
Operating expenses				
Depreciation	(200)	(7.7)	(190)	(8.3)
Other operating expense	(1,590)	(61.1)	(1,515)	(65.9)
Total operating expenses	(1,790)	(68.8)	(1,705)	(74.2)
Operating income	810	31.2	595	25.8
Other income	(50)	(1.9)		0.0
Interest expense	(73)	(2.8)	(69)	(3.0)
Income before taxes	687	26.5	526	22.8
Income taxes	(272)	(10.5)	(198)	(8.6)
Net income	415	16	328	14.2

Exhibit 2: Consolidated Balance Sheet

As of 31 December	2022		2021	
Assets	**Euros millions**	**Assets (%)**	**Euros millions**	**Assets (%)**
Current assets	500	9.4	450	8.5
Property & equipment:				
Land	700	13.1	700	13.2
Plant & equipment	6,000	112.1	5,800	109.4

Total property & equipment	6,700	125.2	6,500	122.6
Accumulated depreciation	(1,850)	(34.6)	(1,650)	(31.1)
Net property & equipment	4,850	90.6	4,850	91.5
Total assets	5,350	100.0	5,300	100.0
Liabilities and Shareholders' Equity				
Current liabilities	480	9.0	430	8.1
Long-term debt	1,030	19.3	1,080	20.4
Other long-term provisions and liabilities	1,240	23.1	1,440	27.2
Total liabilities	2,750	51.4	2,950	55.7
Shareholders' equity				
Common stock and paid-in-surplus	760	14.2	760	14.3
Retained earnings	1,888	35.5	1,600	30.2
Other comprehensive losses	(48)	(0.9)	(10)	(0.2)
Total shareholders' equity	2,600	48.6	2,350	44.3
Total liabilities & shareholders' equity	5,350	100.0	5,300	100.0

4. With respect to Statement 1, which of the following is the *most likely* effect of management's decision to expense rather than capitalize these expenditures?

   A. 2022 net profit margin is higher than if the expenditures had been capitalized.

   B. 2022 total asset turnover is lower than if the expenditures had been capitalized.

   C. Future profit growth will be higher than if the expenditures had been capitalized.

5. With respect to Statement 2, what would be the *most likely* effect in 2023 if AMRC were to switch to an accelerated depreciation method for both financial and tax reporting?

   A. Net profit margin would increase.

   B. Total asset turnover would decrease.

   C. Cash flow from operating activities would increase.

6. With respect to Statement 3, what is the *most likely* effect of the impairment loss?

   A. Net income in years prior to 2022 was likely understated.

   B. Net profit margins in years after 2022 will likely exceed the 2022 net profit margin.

   C. Cash flow from operating activities in 2022 was likely lower due to the impairment loss.

7. Based on Exhibit 1, the *best estimate* of the average remaining useful life of the

company's plant and equipment at the end of 2022 is:

A. 20.75 years.

B. 24.25 years.

C. 30.00 years.

The following information relates to questions 8-13

Brian Jordan is interviewing for a junior equity analyst position at Orion Investment Advisors. As part of the interview process, Mary Benn, Orion's Director of Research, provides Jordan with information about two hypothetical companies, Alpha and Beta, and asks him to comment on the companies' financial statements and ratios. Both companies prepare their financial statements in accordance with International Financial Reporting Standards (IFRS) and are identical in all respects except for their accounting choices.

Jordan is told that, at the beginning of the current fiscal year, both companies purchased a major new computer system and began building new manufacturing plants for their own use. Alpha capitalized and Beta expensed the cost of the computer system; Alpha capitalized and Beta expensed the interest costs associated with the construction of the manufacturing plants.

Benn asks Jordan, "What was the impact of these decisions on each company's current fiscal year financial statements and ratios?"

Jordan responds, "Alpha's decision to capitalize the cost of its new computer system instead of expensing it results in lower net income, lower total assets, and higher cash flow from operating activities in the current fiscal year. Alpha's decision to capitalize its interest costs instead of expensing them results in a lower fixed asset turnover ratio and a higher interest coverage ratio."

Jordan is told that Alpha uses the straight-line depreciation method and Beta uses an accelerated depreciation method; both companies estimate the same useful lives for long-lived assets. Many companies in their industry use the units-of-production method.

Benn asks Jordan, "What are the financial statement implications of each depreciation method, and how do you determine a company's need to reinvest in its productive capacity?"

Jordan replies, "All other things being equal, the straight-line depreciation method results in the least variability of net profit margin over time, while an accelerated depreciation method results in a declining trend in net profit margin over time. The units-of-production can result in a net profit margin trend that is quite variable. I use a three-step approach to estimate a company's need to reinvest in its productive capacity. First, I estimate the average age of the assets by dividing net property, plant, and equipment by annual depreciation expense. Second, I estimate the average remaining useful life of the assets by dividing accumulated depreciation by depreciation expense. Third, I add the estimates of the average remaining useful life and the average age of the assets in order to determine the total useful life."

Jordan is told that at the end of the current fiscal year, Alpha revalued a manufacturing plant; this increased its reported carrying amount by 15 percent. There was no previous downward revaluation of the plant. Beta recorded an impairment loss on a manufacturing plant; this reduced its carrying value by 10 percent.

Benn asks Jordan "What was the impact of these decisions on each company's current fiscal year financial ratios?"

Jordan responds, "Beta's impairment loss increases its debt to total assets and fixed asset turnover ratios, and lowers its cash flow from operating activities. Alpha's revaluation increases its debt to capital and return on assets ratios, and reduces its return on equity."

8. Jordan's response about the financial statement impact of Alpha's decision to capitalize the cost of its new computer system is correct with respect to:

   A. lower net income.

   B. lower total assets.

   C. higher cash flow from operating activities.

9. Jordan's response about the ratio impact of Alpha's decision to capitalize interest costs is most likely *correct* with respect to the:

   A. interest coverage ratio.

   B. fixed asset turnover ratio.

   C. interest coverage and fixed asset turnover ratios.

10. Jordan's response about the impact of the different depreciation methods on net profit margin is most likely *incorrect* with respect to:

    A. accelerated depreciation.

    B. straight-line depreciation.

    C. units-of-production depreciation.

11. Jordan's response about his approach to estimating a company's need to reinvest in its productive capacity is most likely *correct* regarding estimating the:

    A. average age of the asset base.

    B. total useful life of the asset base.

    C. average remaining useful life of the asset base.

12. Jordan's response about the effect of Beta's impairment loss is *incorrect* with respect to the impact on its:

    A. debt to total assets.

    B. fixed asset turnover.

    C. cash flow from operating activities.

13. Jordan's response about the effect of Alpha's revaluation is most likely *correct* with respect to the impact on its:

    A. return on equity.

    B. return on assets.

    C. debt to capital ratio.

The following information relates to questions 14-19

A financial analyst at BETTO S.A. is analyzing the result of the sale of a vehicle for 85,000 Argentine pesos (ARP) on 31 December 2021. The analyst compiles the following information about the vehicle:

Acquisition cost of the vehicle	ARP100,000
Acquisition date	1 January 2019
Estimated residual value at acquisition date	ARP10,000
Expected useful life	9 years
Depreciation method	Straight-line

14. The result of the sale of the vehicle is *most likely*:

    A. a loss of ARP 15,000.

    B. a gain of ARP 15,000.

    C. a gain of ARP 18,333.

15. CROCO S.p.A sells an intangible asset with a historical acquisition cost of EUR12 million and an accumulated amortization of EUR2 million and reports a loss on the sale of EUR3.2 million. Which of the following amounts is *most likely* the sale price of the asset?

    A. EUR6.8 million

    B. EUR8.8 million

    C. EUR13.2 million

16. The gain or loss on a sale of a long-lived asset to which the revaluation model has been applied is *most likely* calculated using sales proceeds less:

    A. carrying amount.

    B. carrying amount adjusted for impairment.

    C. historical cost net of accumulated depreciation.

17. According to IFRS, all of the following pieces of information about property, plant, and equipment must be disclosed in a company's financial statements and footnotes *except for*:

    A. useful lives.

    B. acquisition dates.

    C. amount of disposals.

18. According to IFRS, all of the following pieces of information about intangible assets must be disclosed in a company's financial statements and footnotes *except for*:

    A. fair value.

    B. impairment loss.

C. amortization rate.

19. Which of the following is a required financial statement disclosure for long-lived intangible assets under US GAAP?

    A. The useful lives of assets

    B. The reversal of impairment losses

    C. Estimated amortization expense for the next five fiscal years

The following information relates to questions 20-23

After reading the financial statements and footnotes of a company that reports under IFRS, an analyst identified the following three intangible assets:

- product patent expiring in 40 years;
- copyright with no expiration date; and
- goodwill acquired 2 years ago in a business combination.

20. Which of the three assets is an intangible asset with a finite useful life?

    A. Patent

    B. Goodwill

    C. Copyright

21. Intangible assets with finite useful lives *mostly* differ from intangible assets with infinite useful lives with respect to accounting treatment of:

    A. revaluation.

    B. impairment.

    C. amortization.

22. Costs incurred for intangible assets are generally expensed when they are:

    A. internally developed.

    B. individually acquired.

    C. acquired in a business combination.

23. Under US GAAP, when assets are acquired in a business combination, goodwill *most likely* arises from:

    A. contractual or legal rights.

    B. assets that can be separated from the acquired company.

    C. assets that are neither tangible nor identifiable intangible assets.

SOLUTIONS

1. B is correct. The impairment loss equals GBP3,100,000, calculated as:

   Impairment = max(Fair value less costs to sell; Value in use) – Net carrying amount

   = max(16,800,000 – 800,000; 14,500,000) – 19,100,000

   = –3,100,000.

2. B is correct. Under IFRS, an impairment loss is measured as the excess of the carrying amount over the asset's recoverable amount. The recoverable amount is the higher of the asset's fair value less costs to sell and its value in use. Value in use is a discounted measure of expected future cash flows. Under US GAAP, assessing recoverability is separate from measuring the impairment loss. If the asset's carrying amount exceeds its undiscounted expected future cash flows, the asset's carrying amount is considered unrecoverable and the impairment loss is measured as the excess of the carrying amount over the asset's fair value.

3. C is correct. The carrying amount of the asset on the balance sheet is reduced by the amount of the impairment loss, and the impairment loss is reported on the income statement.

4. C is correct. Expensing, rather than capitalizing, an investment in long-term assets will result in higher expenses and lower net income and net profit margin in the current year. Future years' incomes will not include depreciation expense related to these expenditures. Consequently, year-to-year growth in profitability will be higher. If the expenses had been capitalized, the carrying amount of the assets would have been higher and the 2022 total asset turnover would have been lower.

5. C is correct. Switching to an accelerated depreciation method would increase depreciation expense and decrease income before taxes, taxes payable, and net income. Cash flow from operating activities would increase because of the resulting tax savings.

6. B is correct. 2022 net income and net profit margin are lower because of the impairment loss. Consequently, net profit margins in subsequent years are likely to be higher. An impairment loss suggests that insufficient depreciation expense was recognized in prior years, and net income was overstated in prior years. The impairment loss is a non-cash item and will not affect operating cash flows.

7. A is correct. The estimated average remaining useful life is 20.75 years, calculated as:

   Estimate of remaining useful life = Net plant and equipment ÷ Annual depreciation expense

   Net plant and equipment = Plant & equipment – Accumulated depreciation

   = EUR6,000 – EUR1,850 = EUR4,150

   Estimate of remaining useful life = Net P & E ÷ Depreciation expense

   = EUR4,150 ÷ EUR200 = 20.75

8. C is correct. The decision to capitalize the costs of the new computer system results in higher cash flow from operating activities; the expenditure is reported as an outflow of investing activities. The company allocates the capitalized amount over the asset's useful life as depreciation or amortization expense rather than expensing it in the year of expenditure. Net income and total assets are higher in

the current fiscal year.

9. B is correct. Alpha's fixed asset turnover will be lower because the capitalized interest will appear on the balance sheet as part of the asset being constructed. Therefore, fixed assets will be higher and the fixed asset turnover ratio (total revenue/average net fixed assets) will be lower than if it had expensed these costs. Capitalized interest appears on the balance sheet as part of the asset being constructed instead of being reported as interest expense in the period incurred. However, the interest coverage ratio should be based on interest payments, not interest expense (earnings before interest and taxes/interest payments) and should be unchanged. To provide a true picture of a company's interest coverage, the entire amount of interest expenditure, both the capitalized portion and the expensed portion, should be used in calculating interest coverage ratios.

10. A is correct. Accelerated depreciation will result in an improving, not declining, net profit margin over time, because the amount of depreciation expense declines each year. Under straight-line depreciation, the amount of depreciation expense will remain the same each year. Under the units-of-production method, the amount of depreciation expense reported each year varies with the number of units produced.

11. B is correct. The estimated average total useful life of a company's assets is calculated by adding the estimates of the average remaining useful life and the average age of the assets. The average age of the assets is estimated by dividing accumulated depreciation by depreciation expense. The average remaining useful life of the asset base is estimated by dividing net property, plant, and equipment by annual depreciation expense.

12. C is correct. The impairment loss is a non-cash charge and will not affect cash flow from operating activities. The debt to total assets and fixed asset turnover ratios will increase, because the impairment loss will reduce the carrying amount of fixed assets and therefore total assets.

13. A is correct. In an asset revaluation, the carrying amount of the assets increases. The increase in the asset's carrying amount bypasses the income statement and is reported as other comprehensive income and appears in equity under the heading of revaluation surplus. Therefore, shareholders' equity will increase but net income will not be affected, so return on equity will decline. Return on assets and debt to capital ratios will also decrease.

14. B is correct. The result on the sale of the vehicle is a gain of 15,000, calculated as:

    Gain or loss on the sale = Sale proceeds – Carrying amount

    = Sale proceeds – (Acquisition cost – Accumulated depreciation)

    = 85,000 – {100,000 – [((100,000 – 10,000)/9 years) × 3 years]}

    = 15,000.

15. A is correct. Gain or loss on the sale = Sale proceeds – Carrying amount. Rearranging this equation, Sale proceeds = Carrying amount + Gain or loss on sale. Thus, Sale price = (12 million – 2 million) + (–3.2 million) = 6.8 million.

16. A is correct. The gain or loss on the sale of long-lived assets is computed as the sales proceeds minus the carrying amount of the asset at the time of sale. This is true under the cost and revaluation models of reporting long-lived assets. In the absence of impairment losses, under the cost model, the carrying amount will equal historical cost net of accumulated depreciation.

17. B is correct. IFRS do not require acquisition dates to be disclosed.

18. A is correct. IFRS do not require fair value of intangible assets to be disclosed.

19. C is correct. Under US GAAP, companies are required to disclose the estimated amortization expense for the next five fiscal years. Under US GAAP, there is no reversal of impairment losses. Disclosure of the useful lives—finite or indefinite and additional related details—is required under IFRS.

20. A is correct. A product patent with a defined expiration date is an intangible asset with a finite useful life. A copyright with no expiration date is an intangible asset with an indefinite useful life. Goodwill is no longer considered an intangible asset under IFRS and is considered to have an indefinite useful life.

21. C is correct. An intangible asset with a finite useful life is amortized, whereas an intangible asset with an indefinite useful life is not amortized. Rather, they are carried on the balance sheet at historical cost and are tested at least annually for impairment.

22. A is correct. The costs to internally develop intangible assets are generally expensed when incurred.

23. C is correct. Under both IFRS and US GAAP, if an item is acquired in a business combination and cannot be recognized as a tangible asset or identifiable intangible asset, it is recognized as goodwill. Under US GAAP, assets arising from contractual or legal rights and assets that can be separated from the acquired company are recognized separately from goodwill.

LEARNING MODULE

8

Topics in Long-Term Liabilities and Equity

by Elizabeth A. Gordon, PhD, MBA, and Elaine Henrik, Phd, CFA.

Elizabeth A. Gordon, PhD, MBA, CPA, is at Temple University (USA), and Elaine Henrik, Phd, CFA, is at Stevens Institute of Technology (USA).

LEARNING OUTCOMES

Mastery	The candidate should be able to:
☐	explain the financial reporting of leases from the perspectives of lessors and lessees
☐	explain the financial reporting of defined contribution, defined benefit, and stock-based compensation plans
☐	describe the financial statement presentation of and disclosures relating to long-term liabilities and share-based compensation

The two major accounting standard setters are as follows: 1) the International Accounting Standards Board (IASB) who establishes International Financial Reporting Standards (IFRS) and 2) the Financial Accounting Standards Board (FASB) who establishes US GAAP. Throughout this learning module both standards are referred to and many, but not all, of these two sets of accounting rules are identified. Note: changes in accounting standards as well as new rulings and/or pronouncements issued after the publication of this learning module may cause some of the information to become dated.

1 INTRODUCTION

Non-current liabilities arise from different sources of financing and different types of creditors. While the financial reporting of bonds and loans is straightforward and is covered in the prerequisite materials, the reporting of leases and postemployment liabilities is more complex. Leases are an alternative to asset ownership and have become a common means of financing real estate and capital equipment. Postretirement and stock-based compensation are a large and growing share of employee compensation and operating expenses. Given their importance, this learning module introduces the reporting of leases, pension plans, and stock-based compensation under International Financial Reporting Standards (IFRS) and US GAAP. It concludes by reviewing the presentation and disclosure requirements for these items.

LEARNING MODULE OVERVIEW

- Leasing has several advantages over purchasing an asset outright: less upfront cash commitment, typically low financing costs, and lower risks associated with ownership, such as obsolescence.
- Under IFRS and US GAAP, leases are classified as operating or finance leases. Finance leases resemble an asset purchase or sale while operating leases resemble a rental agreement.
- The financial reporting of a lease depends on whether the party is the lessee or lessor, whether the party reports with IFRS or US GAAP, and the classification of the lease as finance or operating.
- US GAAP and IFRS share the same accounting treatment for lessors but differ slightly for lessees. IFRS has a single accounting model for both operating leases and finance lease lessees, while US GAAP has an accounting model for each.
- Two types of pension plans are defined contribution plans and defined benefits plans. In a defined contribution plan, the amount of employer contribution into the plan is specified (i.e., defined) and the amount of pension that is ultimately paid by the plan (received by the retiree) depends on the performance of the plan's assets. In a defined benefit plan, the amount of pension that is ultimately paid by the plan (received by the retiree) is defined, usually according to a benefit formula.
- In a defined contribution plan, employees bear investment risks (i.e., the potential for investment returns on plan assets to differ from expectations) and actuarial risks (i.e. the potential for retirement and death timing to differ from expectations). In a defined benefit plan, employers bear both investment and actuarial risks.
- Under a defined contribution pension plan, the cash payment made into the plan is recognized as pension expense.
- For defined benefit pension plans, companies must report the difference between the defined benefit pension obligation and the fair value of pension assets as an asset or liability on the balance sheet. An underfunded defined benefit pension plan is shown as a non-current liability. The change in the net asset or liability between balance sheet dates is recognized as a cost of the period, with service cost and net interest expense or income recognized in profit and loss and

remeasurement changes recognized in other comprehensive income. There are modest differences in accounting treatment under US GAAP.

- Employee compensation packages are structured to fulfill various objectives, including satisfying employees' needs for liquidity, retaining employees, and providing incentives to employees.
- Share-based compensation serves to align employees' interests with those of the shareholders. It typically includes stock grants and stock options, which have the advantage of requiring no current-period cash outlays. Stock-based compensation is measured using fair value at the grant date and recognized as compensation expense over the vesting period.
- The valuation technique, or option pricing model, that a company uses is an important choice in determining fair value of options used in a compensation agreement and is disclosed in the notes to financial statements. Key inputs into option pricing models include such items as exercise price, stock price volatility, estimated life of each award, estimated number of options that will be forfeited, dividend yield, and the risk-free rate of interest.

LEASES

2

☐ explain the financial reporting of leases from the perspectives of lessors and lessees

Firms typically acquire the rights to use assets by outright purchase. As an alternative, a lease is a contract that conveys the right to use an asset for a period of time in exchange for consideration. The party who uses the asset and pays the consideration is the **lessee**, and the party who owns the asset, grants the right to use the asset, and receives consideration is the **lessor**.

Leasing is a way to obtain the benefits of the asset without purchasing it outright. From the perspective of a lessee, it is a form of financing that resembles acquiring an asset with a note payable. From the perspective of a lessor, a lease is a form of investment and can also be an effective selling strategy, because customers generally prefer to pay in installments.

After reviewing the contractual requirements for a lease, this lesson examines the advantages and classification of leases and their financial reporting.

Requirements for Lease Accounting

For a contract to be a lease or contain a lease, it must

- identify a specific underlying asset;
- give the customer the right to obtain largely all of the economic benefits from the asset over the contract term; and
- give the customer, not the supplier, the ability to direct how and for what objective the underlying asset is used.

For example, a contract between a customer and a trucking company is a lease if the contract identifies a specific truck, allows the customer exclusive use of it during the contract term, and lets the customer direct its use. If, however, the customer contracts with a trucking company to ship goods for a fee, the contract would not be a lease, because a specific truck is not identified nor does the customer obtain largely all of the economic benefits from the truck over the contract term.

Examples of Leases

Leasing is among the most prevalent forms of financing. Most companies are lessees of real estate and information technology assets. In 2014, the International Accounting Standards Board found that more than 14,000 publicly listed companies were lessees and that they owed more than USD3.3 trillion in future lease payments in aggregate.[1] Exhibit 1 illustrates several examples of these arrangements.

Exhibit 1: Examples of Leases

Lessee	Lease Disclosure Excerpt
Alibaba	"The Company entered into operating lease agreements primarily for shops and malls, offices, warehouses, and land."
Copa Airlines	"The Company leases some aircraft under long-term lease agreements with an average duration of 10 years. Other leased assets include real estate, airport and terminal facilities, sales offices, maintenance facilities, and general offices."
Meta (formerly Facebook)	"We have entered into various non-cancelable operating lease agreements for certain of our offices, data center, land, colocations, and equipment."
Standard Bank	"The group leases various offices, branch space, and ATM space."

Sources: Companies' 2020 and 2019 annual reports.

Lessors are often real estate investment companies or banks, although there are independent specialist leasing companies, such as AerCap Holdings N.V., which describes itself as "the global leader in aircraft leasing." As of 30 June 2022, the company owned 1,557 passenger aircraft that are leased to airlines.[2]

Advantages of Leasing

There are several advantages to leasing an asset compared with purchasing it:

- Less cash is needed up front. Leases typically require little, if any, down payment.
- Cost effectiveness: Leases are a form of secured borrowing; in the event of non-payment, the lessor simply repossesses the leased asset. As a result, the effective interest rate for a lease is typically lower than what the lessee would pay on an unsecured loan or bond.

1 IFRS, "IASB Shines Light on Leases by Bringing Them onto the Balance Sheet," 13 January 2016, www.ifrs.org/news-and-events/2016/01/iasb-shines-light-on-leases-by-bringing-them-onto-the-balance-sheet.
2 AerCap Holdings N.V. annual report for the fiscal year ended 31 December 31 2019 on Form 20-F.

- Convenience and lower risks associated with asset ownership, such as obsolescence.[3]

From the perspective of a lessor, leasing has advantages over selling outright, which include earning interest income over the lease term and increasing the addressable market for its product by offering customers the ability to use or control an asset while paying smaller amounts over time.

Lease Classification as Finance or Operating

Leases can resemble either the purchase of an asset or a rental contract. For example, a ten-year lease of an automobile with a ten-year useful life for monthly payments that, in aggregate, are equal to or greater than the fair value of the automobile is effectively a debt-financed purchase of that automobile. In contrast, a one-year lease of a machine with a twenty-year useful life resembles a rental contract. A lease that resembles a purchase is classified as a **finance lease**. All other leases are **operating leases**.

More specifically, a lease is a finance lease if *any* of the following five criteria are met. These criteria are the same for IFRS and US GAAP. If *none* of the criteria are met, the lease is an operating lease. The same criteria are used by lessees and lessors in classifying a lease.

1. The lease transfers ownership of the underlying asset to the lessee.
2. The lessee has an option to purchase the underlying asset and is reasonably certain it will do so.
3. The lease term is for a major part of the asset's useful life.
4. The present value of the sum of the lease payments equals or exceeds substantially all of the fair value of the asset.
5. The underlying asset has no alternative use to the lessor.

EXAMPLE 1

Lease Identification and Classification

Company C enters a contract with Company D that requires Company C to pay JPY100 million at the end of each of the next two years to Company D for exclusive use of a specific machine over that time period. The present value of the payments is JPY186 million. At the end of the contract, Company C will return the machine to Company D. The contract does not contain a purchase option. The machine can be used in many applications by many types of customers. The remaining useful life of the machine is four years, and its fair value is JPY190 million.

1. This contract is:

   A. not a lease.

   B. an operating lease.

   C. a finance lease.

   Solution:

   C is correct. This contract is a lease because a specific asset is identified, Company C will exclusively use it, and Company C *will* have the ability to direct its use. The contract is a finance lease because one of the five criteria

3 Lessors are aware of asset obsolescence, however, and impound its costs and risks in lease payments.

is met: The present value of the lease payments equals substantially all of the fair value (186/190 = 98%).

2. If the fair value of the machine in question 1 was JPY300 million, would the classification of the contract change?

   A. No

   B. Yes, from an operating lease to a finance lease

   C. Yes, from a finance lease to an operating lease

Solution:

C is correct. This change would result in the lease not meeting any of the five criteria for a finance lease. If a lease does not meet any of the five criteria, it is an operating lease.

Financial Reporting of Leases

The financial reporting of a lease depends on whether the party is the lessee or lessor, whether the party reports with IFRS or US GAAP, and the classification of the lease as finance or operating. Additionally, for lessees, there are lease accounting exemptions for certain lease contracts: If its term is 12 months or less (IFRS and US GAAP) or it is for a "low-value asset," up to USD5,000 in sales price (IFRS only), then the lessee can elect to simply expense the lease payments on a straight-line basis. These exemptions are not available to lessors. Exhibit 2 illustrates the different permutations for lease accounting.

Exhibit 2: Lease Classifications for Lessee and Lessor

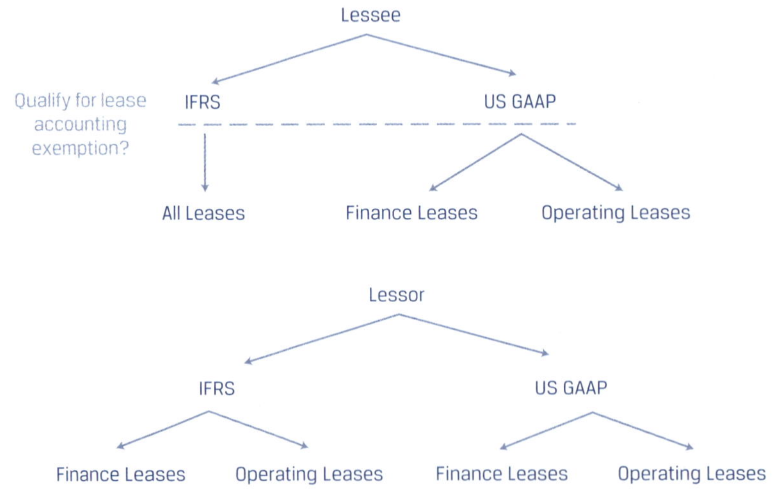

Fortunately, lessor accounting under both IFRS and US GAAP is substantially identical, and the differences in treatment for lessees are modest.

Lessee Accounting—IFRS

Under IFRS, there is a single accounting model for both finance and operating leases for lessees. At lease inception, the lessee records a lease payable liability and a right-of-use (ROU) asset on its balance sheet, both equal to the present value of future lease payments. The discount rate used in the present value calculation is either the rate implicit in the lease or an estimated secured borrowing rate.

The lease liability is subsequently reduced by each lease payment using the effective interest method. Each lease payment is composed of interest expense, which is the product of the lease liability and the discount rate, and principal repayment, which is the difference between the interest expense and lease payment.

The ROU asset is subsequently amortized, often on a straight-line basis, over the lease term. So, although the lease liability and ROU asset begin with the same carrying value on the balance sheet, they typically diverge in subsequent periods because the principal repayment that reduces the lease liability and the amortization expense that reduces the ROU asset are calculated differently.

The following list shows how the transaction affects the financial statements:

- The lease liability net of principal repayments and the ROU asset net of accumulated amortization are reported on the balance sheet.
- Interest expense on the lease liability and the amortization expense related to the ROU asset are reported separately on the income statement.
- The principal repayment component of the lease payment is reported as a cash outflow under financing activities on the statement of cash flows, and depending on the lessee's reporting policies, interest expense is reported under either operating or financing activities on the statement of cash flows.

EXAMPLE 2

Lease Impact on Balance Sheet and Income Statement

Proton Enterprises, a hypothetical manufacturer based in Germany, is offered the following terms to lease a machine: five-year lease with an implied interest rate of 10 percent and an annual lease payment of EUR100,000 per year payable at the end of each year. The present value of the machinery is therefore EUR379,079 (in Microsoft Excel, the formula is =PV(10%,5,-100,000). The asset will be amortized over the five-year lease term on a straight-line basis. Proton reports under IFRS.

1. What would be the impact of this lease on Proton's balance sheet at the beginning of the year?

   Solution:

   Proton would report a EUR379,079 lease liability and ROU asset.

2. What would be the impact of this lease on Proton's income statement during the following year?

   Solution:

   Interest expense and amortization expense are reported on the income statement. In Year 2, interest expense is EUR31,699 and amortization expense is EUR 75,816, as illustrated in the following tables:

	Lease Payment	Interest Expense (10% × Lease Liability)	Principal Repayment (Payment – Interest)	Lease Liability
	FO.1	FO.2	FO.3	FO.4
Year 0				379,079
Year 1	100,000	37,908	62,092	316,987
Year 2	100,000	31,699	68,301	248,685
Year 3	100,000	24,869	75,131	173,554
Year 4	100,000	17,355	82,645	90,909
Year 5	100,000	9,091	90,909	0
Total	500,000	120,921	379,079	

	Amortization Expense	ROU Asset
	Straight-Line F.1	F.2
Year 0		379,079
Year 1	75,816	303,263
Year 2	75,816	227,447
Year 3	75,816	151,631
Year 4	75,816	75,816
Year 5	75,816	0
Total	379,079	

Note: Totals may not sum due to rounding.

3. What would be the impact of this lease on Proton's statement of cash flows during the following year?

   Solution:

   Principal repayments are reported as a cash outflow under financing activities on the statement of cash flows, and depending on Proton's reporting policies, interest expense is reported under operating or financing activities on the statement of cash flows. From the previous tables, Year 2 principal repayment is EUR68,301 and interest expense is EUR31,699, for a total of EUR100,000.

Lessee Accounting—US GAAP

Under US GAAP, there are two accounting models for lessees: one for finance leases and another for operating leases. The finance lease accounting model is identical to the lessee accounting model for IFRS. The operating lease accounting model is different.

At operating lease inception, the lessee records a lease payable liability and a corresponding right-of-use asset on its balance sheet that are subsequently reduced by the principal repayment component of the lease payment and amortization, respectively, in the same manner that an IFRS lessee would.

The key difference between an operating lease and a finance lease is how the amortization of the ROU asset is calculated. For an operating lease, the lessee's ROU asset amortization expense is the lease payment minus the interest expense. The implication is that the total expense reported on the income statement (interest plus amortization) will equal the lease payment and that the lease liability and the ROU asset will always equal each other because the principal repayment and amortization are calculated in an identical manner.

The following list shows how the transaction appears on the financial statements:

- The lease liability net of principal repayments and the ROU asset net of accumulated amortization are reported on the balance sheet.
- Interest expense on the lease liability and the amortization expense related to the ROU asset are reported as a single line titled "lease expense" as an operating expense on the income statement. The interest and amortization components are *not* reported separately, nor are they grouped with other types of interest and amortization expense (e.g., interest on a bond, amortization of an intangible asset).
- The entire lease payment is reported as a cash outflow under operating activities on the statement of cash flows. The interest and principal repayment components are *not* reported separately.

EXAMPLE 3

Lessee Accounting—Operating Lease under US GAAP

Consider the differences in accounting if Proton Enterprises classified the lease of the machinery from Example 2 as an operating lease.

1. How would its financial statements differ, if at all?

Solution:

The first step is to construct the lease liability and ROU asset amortization tables under an operating lease scenario. The lease liability amortization is the same as the finance lease columns FO.1–FO.4 in Example 2.

	Amortization Expense (Lease Payment – Interest)	ROU Asset	Lease Expense (Amortization + Interest)
	O.1	O.2	O.3
Year 0		379,079	
Year 1	62,092	316,987	100,000
Year 2	68,301	248,685	100,000
Year 3	75,131	173,554	100,000
Year 4	82,645	90,909	100,000
Year 5	90,909	0	100,000
Total	379,078		500,000

Now we can compare the financial statement impacts under both finance and operating lease scenarios.

Balance Sheet	Year 1	Year 2	Year 3	Year 4	Year 5
Finance lease:					
ROU asset, net: F.2	303,263	227,447	151,631	75,816	0
Lease liability, net: FO.4	316,987	248,685	173,554	90,909	0
Operating lease:					

Balance Sheet	Year 1	Year 2	Year 3	Year 4	Year 5
ROU asset, net: O.2	316,987	248,685	173,554	90,909	0
Lease liability, net: FO.4	316,987	248,685	173,554	90,909	0

The ROU asset is lower in each period under a finance lease because the amortization expense is higher.

Income Statement	Year 1	Year 2	Year 3	Year 4	Year 5
Finance lease:					
Amortization: F.1	75,816	75,816	75,816	75,816	75,816
Interest: FO.2	37,908	31,699	24,869	17,355	9,091
Total	113,724	107,515	100,685	93,171	84,907
Operating lease:					
Lease expense: O.3	100,000	100,000	100,000	100,000	100,000

Total expense is higher for a finance lease in Years 1–3 but lower in Years 4 and 5. The largest difference is classification; amortization and interest are presented separately for a finance lease, whereas operating lease expense is an operating expense.

Statement of Cash Flows	Year 1	Year 2	Year 3	Year 4	Year 5
Finance lease:					
Cash flow from operating activities	(37,908)	(31,699)	(24,869)	(17,355)	(9,091)
Cash flow from financing activities	(62,902)	(68,301)	(75,131)	(82,645)	(90,909)
Total	(100,000)	(100,000)	(100,000)	(100,000)	(100,000)
Operating lease:					
Cash flows from operating activities	(100,000)	(100,000)	(100,000)	(100,000)	(100,000)

The difference on the statement of cash flows is only in classification, because in both cases the total cash outflow is equal to the lease payment.

2. How would the classification, all else equal, affect EBITDA margin, total asset turnover, and cash flow per share?

Solution:

The following table shows how the classification affects the indicated financial ratios.

Ratio	Formula	Impact of Using an Operating Lease Instead of a Finance Lease
EBITDA margin	$\frac{\text{EBITDA}}{\text{Total revenues}}$	Lower: Lease expense is classified as an operating expense rather than interest and amortization.
Asset turnover	$\frac{\text{Total revenues}}{\text{Total assets}}$	Lower: Total assets are higher under an operating lease because the ROU asset is amortized at a slower pace in Years 1–3.
Cash flow per share	$\frac{\text{Cash flow from operations}}{\text{Shares outstanding}}$	Lower: Cash flow from operations is lower because the entire lease payment is included in operating activities versus solely interest expense for a finance lease.

Lessor Accounting

The accounting for lessors is substantially identical under IFRS and US GAAP. Under both accounting standards, lessors classify leases as finance or operating leases, which determines the financial reporting. Although lessors under US GAAP recognize finance leases as either "sales-type" or "direct financing," the distinction is immaterial from an analyst's perspective.

At finance lease inception, the lessor recognizes a lease receivable asset equal to the present value of future lease payments and de-recognizes the leased asset, simultaneously recognizing any difference as a gain or loss. The discount rate used in the present value calculation is the rate implicit in the lease.

The lease receivable is subsequently reduced by each lease payment using the effective interest method. Each lease payment is composed of interest income, which is the product of the lease receivable and the discount rate, and principal proceeds, which equals the difference between the interest income and cash receipt.

The transaction affects the financial statements in the following ways:

- Lease receivable net of principal proceeds is reported on the balance sheet.
- Interest income is reported on the income statement. If leasing is a primary business activity for the entity, as it commonly is for financial institutions and independent leasing companies, it is reported as revenue.
- The entire cash receipt is reported under operating activities on the statement of cash flows.

The accounting treatment for an operating lease is different: because the contract is essentially a rental agreement, the lessor keeps the leased asset on its books and recognizes lease revenue on a straight-line basis. Interest revenue is not recognized because the transaction is not considered a financing.

The transaction affects the financial statements in the following ways:

- The balance sheet is not affected. The lessor continues to recognize the leased asset at cost net of accumulated depreciation.
- Lease revenue is recognized on a straight-line basis on the income statement. Depreciation expense continues to be recognized.

- The entire cash receipt is reported under operating activities on the statement of cash flows. This is the same as a finance lease.

EXAMPLE 4

Lessor Accounting

Let's examine Proton's machine lease from Example 2 and Example 3 from the perspective of the lessor. Assume that the carrying value of the asset immediately prior to the lease is EUR350,000, accumulated depreciation is zero, and the lessor elects to depreciate it on a straight-line basis over five years.

1. How are the lessor's financial statements affected by the classification of the lease as a finance or operating lease?

   Solution:

   The difference on the balance sheet is material, because a finance lease requires the lessor to de-recognize the asset and recognize a lease receivable, whereas an operating lease lessor continues to recognize the asset and depreciate it over its useful life. In this case, where the present value of the lease payments is well above the carrying value of the asset, the finance lease classification results in a significant increase in assets.

Balance Sheet	Year 1	Year 2	Year 3	Year 4	Year 5
Finance lease:					
Lease receivable, net	316,987	248,685	173,554	90,909	0
Operating lease:					
Property, plant, and equipment, net	280,000	210,000	140,000	70,000	0

   The difference on the income statement is also material, because a finance lease lessor recognizes interest revenue under the effective interest method whereas the operating lease lessor recognizes straight-line lease revenue.

Income Statement	Year 1	Year 2	Year 3	Year 4	Year 5
Finance lease:					
Interest revenue	37,908	31,699	24,869	17,355	9,091
Operating lease:					
Lease revenue	100,000	100,000	100,000	100,000	100,000

   The statement of cash flows, however, is no different for the lessor under a finance or operating lease: The entire cash inflow from the lease payment is recognized under operating activities.

Statement of Cash Flows	Year 1	Year 2	Year 3	Year 4	Year 5
Finance lease:					
Cash flows from operating activities	100,000	100,000	100,000	100,000	100,000

Statement of Cash Flows	Year 1	Year 2	Year 3	Year 4	Year 5
Operating lease:					
Cash flows from operating activities	100,000	100,000	100,000	100,000	100,000

FINANCIAL REPORTING FOR POSTEMPLOYMENT AND SHARE-BASED COMPENSATION PLANS

3

☐ explain the financial reporting of defined contribution, defined benefit, and stock-based compensation plans

Employee Compensation

Employee compensation packages are structured to achieve various objectives, including satisfying employees' needs for liquidity, retaining employees, and motivating employees. Common components of employee compensation are salary, bonuses, health and life insurance premiums, defined contribution and benefit pension plans, and share-based compensation. The amount of compensation and its composition are determined in labor markets, which vary significantly by the types of skills needed, geography, the stage of the business cycle, and labor laws and customs.

The salary component of compensation provides for the liquidity needs of an employee. Bonuses, generally in the form of cash, motivate and reward employees for short- or long-term performance or goal achievement by linking pay to performance. Non-monetary benefits, such as health and life insurance premiums, housing, and vehicles, may be provided to facilitate employees performing their jobs. Salary, bonuses, and non-monetary benefits tend to **vest** (i.e., employee earns the right to the consideration) immediately or shortly after their grant date. In terms of financial reporting, a company reports compensation expense on the income statement in the period in which compensation vests. Immediate or short-term vesting makes the accounting for salary, most non-monetary benefits, and bonuses straightforward: when the employee has earned the salary or bonus, an expense is recorded for the fair value of the compensation, and a cash outflow or accrued compensation liability (a current liability) is recognized. Expenses and cash outflows for short-term compensation tend to be well matched.

Deferred Compensation

Deferred compensation vests over time and can provide valuable retirement savings and financial upside to employees and often serve as an effective retention and stakeholder alignment tool for employers. The financial reporting for deferred compensation plans is generally more complex than that for compensation that vests immediately because of the difficulty in measurement and potential lags between employee service and cash outflows. Employees may earn compensation in the current period but receive consideration in future periods, and the amount of consideration can be based on factors such as their future salary or the employer's stock price. Management judgment and assumptions are required.

Pensions and other postemployment benefit plans are a common type of deferred compensation. Two common types of pension plans are **defined contribution pension plans** and **defined benefit pension plans**. Under a defined-contribution plan, a company contributes an agreed-upon amount into the plan, which may be structured as a match to employees' contributions into the plan (e.g., 50 percent of 5 percent of employees' contribution up to a certain limit). The company contribution is the pension expense and is reported as an operating cash outflow. The only impact on assets and liabilities is a decrease in cash, although if some portion of the agreed-upon amount has not been paid by fiscal year-end, an accrued compensation liability would be recognized on the balance sheet. Because the amount of the contribution is defined and the company has no further obligation once the contribution has been made, accounting for a defined-contribution plan is straightforward.

Companies may also offer other types of postemployment benefit plans, such as retiree healthcare plans. These plans also incur non-current liabilities for employers but tend to be far smaller than pension plans and are typically *not* funded in advance; thus, benefit payments are often expensed as incurred.

Defined-Benefit Pension Plans

Under a defined-benefit pension plan, a company makes promises of future benefits to be paid to the employee during retirement. For example, a company could promise an employee annual pension payments equal to 70 percent of her final salary at retirement until death. Measuring the obligation arising from that promise requires the company to make many assumptions, such as the employee's expected salary at retirement and the number of years the employee is expected to live beyond retirement. The company estimates the future amounts to be paid and discounts the future estimated amounts to a present value (using a discount rate equal to the yield on a high-quality corporate bond) to determine the pension obligation today. The discount rate and other assumptions used to determine the pension obligation significantly affects the size of the pension obligation.

Most defined-benefit pension plans are funded through assets held in a separate legal entity, typically a pension trust fund. A company makes payments into the pension fund and retirees are paid from the fund. The payments that a company makes into the fund are invested until they are needed to pay the retirees. If the fair value of the plan's assets is higher than the present value of the estimated pension obligation, the plan has a surplus and the company will report a net pension asset on its balance sheet. Conversely, if the present value of the estimated pension obligation exceeds the fair value of the fund's assets, the plan has a deficit and the company will report a net pension liability on its balance sheet.

Accounting for Defined-Benefit Plans under IFRS

Under IFRS, the change in the net pension asset or liability each period is viewed as having three general components. Two of the components of this change are recognized as pension expense on the income statement: (1) employees' service costs, and (2) the net interest expense or income accrued on the beginning net pension asset or liability.

The service cost during the period for an employee is the present value of the increase in the pension benefit earned by the employee as a result of providing one more year of service. The service cost also includes any effects from changes in the plan, known as past service costs.

The net interest expense or income represents the change in the present value of the net defined benefit pension asset or liability from the passage of time (i.e., a liability would increase over time as payout dates near) and is calculated as the net pension asset or liability multiplied by the discount rate.

The third component of the change in the net pension asset or liability during a period (i.e., "remeasurements") is recognized in other comprehensive income. Remeasurements are not amortized into profit or loss over time. Remeasurements include (1) actuarial gains and losses and (2) the actual return on plan assets less any return included in the net interest expense or income. Actuarial gains and losses can occur when changes are made to the assumptions on which a company bases its estimated pension obligation (e.g., employee turnover, mortality rates, retirement ages, compensation increases). The actual return on plan assets includes interest, dividends, and other income derived from the plan assets, including realized and unrealized gains or losses. The actual return typically differs from the amount included in the net interest expense or income, which is calculated using a rate reflective of a high-quality corporate bond yield; plan assets are typically allocated across various asset classes, including equity as well as bonds.

Accounting for Defined-Benefit Plan under US GAAP

Under US GAAP, the change in net pension asset or liability each period is viewed as having five components, some of which are recognized in profit and loss in the period incurred and some of which are recognized in other comprehensive income and amortized into profit and loss over time.

The three components recognized on the income statement in the period incurred are as follows:

1. employees' service costs for the period;
2. interest expense accrued on the beginning pension obligation; and
3. expected return on plan assets, which is a reduction in the amount of expense recognized.

The other two components are past service costs and actuarial gains and losses. Past service costs are recognized in other comprehensive income in the period in which they arise and then subsequently amortized into pension expense over the future service period of the employees covered by the plan. Actuarial gains and losses are typically also recognized in other comprehensive income in the period in which they occur and then amortized into pension expense over time. In effect, this treatment allows companies to "smooth" the effects on pension expense over time for these latter two components. US GAAP does permit companies to immediately recognize actuarial gains and losses in profit and loss.

Pension expense on the income statement is classified on a functional basis like other employee compensation expenses. For a manufacturing company, pension expense related to production employees is added to inventory and expensed through cost of sales (cost of goods sold). For other employees, the pension expense is included in selling, general, and administrative expenses. Therefore, pension expense is typically not directly reported on the income statement. Rather, extensive disclosures are included in the notes to the financial statements.

Exhibit 3 presents excerpts from the balance sheet and pension-related disclosures in BT Group plc's Annual Report for the year ended 31 March 2018. BT reports under IFRS.

Exhibit 3: BT Group plc: Excerpts from Balance Sheet and Pension-Related Disclosures

Non-current liabilities, GBP millions	Mar. 31, 2018	Mar. 31, 2017	Mar. 31, 2016
Loans and other borrowings	11,994	10,081	11,025
Derivative financial instruments	787	869	863
Retirement benefit obligations	6,371	9,088	6,382
Other payables	1,326	1,298	1,106
Deferred tax liabilities	1,340	1,240	1,262
Provisions	452	536	565
Non-current liabilities	22,270	23,112	21,203

Pension-Related Disclosures

The following are excerpts of pension-related disclosures from BT Group plc's 2018 Annual Report.

Extract from Note 3 "Summary of Significant Accounting Policies"

Retirement benefits

The group's net obligation in respect of defined benefit pension plans is the present value of the defined benefit obligation less the fair value of the plan assets.

The calculation of the obligation is performed by a qualified actuary using the projected unit credit method and key actuarial assumptions at the balance sheet date.

The income statement expense is allocated between an operating charge and net finance income or expense. The operating charge reflects the increase in the defined benefit obligation resulting from the pension benefit earned by active employees in the current period, the costs of administering the plans and any past service costs/credits such as those arising from curtailments or settlements. The net finance income or expense reflects the interest on the net retirement benefit obligations recognised in the group balance sheet, based on the discount rate at the start of the year. Actuarial gains and losses are recognised in full in the period in which they occur and are presented in the group statement of comprehensive income.

The group also operates defined contribution pension plans and the income statement expense represents the contributions payable for the year.

Extract from Note 20 "Retirement Benefit Plans Information on Defined Benefit Pension Plans"

GBP millions	2018	2017	2016
Present value of liabilities	**57,327**	60,200	50,350
Fair value of plan assets	**50,956**	51,112	43,968

EXAMPLE 5

BT Group's Pension Plan

Use information in the excerpts in Exhibit 3 to answer the following questions:

1. What type(s) of pension plans does BT have?

   Solution:

   Note 3 "Summary of Significant Accounting Policies" indicates that the company has both defined contribution and defined benefit pension plans.

2. What proportion of BT's total non-current liabilities are related to its retirement benefit obligations?

   Solution:

   Retirement benefit obligations represent 29 percent, 39 percent, and 30 percent of BT's total non-current liabilities for the years 2018, 2017, and 2016. Using 2018 to illustrate, GBP6,371/GBP22,270 = 29%. (GBP million)

3. Describe how BT's retirement benefit obligation is calculated.

   Solution:

   Note 3 "Summary of Significant Accounting Policies" indicates that BT's Retirement benefit obligation is calculated as the present value of the defined benefit obligation minus the fair value of the plan assets.
   Using data from Note 20 "Retirement Benefit Plans" the retirement benefit obligation for each year can be calculated. Using 2018 to illustrate, GBP57,327 – GBP50,956 = GBP6,371 (GBP million).

Share-Based Compensation

Share-based compensation is intended to align employees' interests with those of the shareholders and is another common type of deferred compensation. Unlike pension plans, share-based compensation tends to be highly concentrated among more senior-level employees such as executives as well as directors. Both IFRS and US GAAP require a company to disclose in their annual report key elements of management compensation. Regulators may require additional disclosure. The disclosures enable analysts to understand the nature and extent of compensation, including the share-based payment arrangements that existed during the reporting period. In the United States, these disclosures are typically provided in a company's proxy statement that is filed with the SEC. Exhibit 4 shows the disclosure of Apple Inc.'s 2021 Named Executive Officer Compensation:

Exhibit 4: Apple Inc.'s 2021 Named Executive Officer Compensation

Our executive compensation program is designed to motivate and reward outstanding performance in a straightforward, consistent, and effective way, commensurate with Apple's size, performance, and profitability. The compensation of our named executive officers has three basic components: annual base salary, annual cash incentive, and long-term equity awards.

Annual Base Salary

Base salary is a customary, fixed element of compensation intended to attract and retain executives. When setting the annual base salaries of our named executive officers, the Compensation Committee considers market data provided by its independent compensation consultant, internal pay equity, and Apple's financial performance and size relative to peer companies. The annual base salaries for our named executive officers did not change for 2021.

Annual Cash Incentive

Our annual cash incentive program is a performance-based, at-risk component of our named executive officers' compensation. Variable payouts are designed to motivate our named executive officers to deliver strong annual financial results, while advancing Apple values and key community initiatives. The financial performance measures and payout opportunities under the annual incentive program did not change for 2021, although the design of the program was enhanced to include a modifier based on Apple values and key community initiatives ("ESG Modifier"), as described below.

Long-Term Equity Awards

We pay for performance and manage Apple for the long-term. Consistent with this approach and our guiding compensation principles, the majority of our named executive officers' annual compensation is provided in the form of long-term equity incentives that emphasize long-term shareholder value creation and the retention of a strong executive leadership team through a balanced mix of performance-based and time-based RSU awards.

Performance-Based RSUs

RSU awards with performance-based vesting are a substantial, at-risk component of our named executive officers' compensation tied to Apple's long-term performance. The number of performance-based RSUs that vest depends entirely on Apple's total shareholder return relative to the other companies in the S&P 500 ("Relative TSR") for the applicable performance period. To earn a target award, Apple must achieve performance at the 55th percentile of the S&P 500. The Compensation Committee chose Relative TSR as it continues to be an objective and meaningful metric to evaluate our performance against the performance of other large companies and to align the interests of our named executive officers with the interests of our shareholders in creating long-term value.

We measure Relative TSR for the applicable performance period based on the change in each company's stock price during that period, taking into account any dividends paid during that period, which are assumed to be reinvested in the stock. A 20-trading-day averaging period is used to determine the beginning and ending stock price values used to calculate the total shareholder return of Apple and the other companies in the S&P 500. This averaging period mitigates the impact on the long-term Relative TSR results of one-day or short-term stock price fluctuations at the beginning or end of the performance period. The change in stock price value from the beginning to the end of the period is divided by the beginning stock price value to determine TSR.

Time-Based RSUs

RSU awards with time-based vesting align the interests of our named executive officers with the interests of our shareholders by promoting the stability and retention of a high-performing executive team over the longer term. Vesting schedules for time-based awards are generally longer than typical peer company practices, as described below.

Dividend Equivalents

All RSUs granted to our employees in 2021, including our named executive officers, have dividend equivalent rights. The dividend equivalents will only pay out if the time-based vesting and performance conditions have been met for the RSUs to which the dividend equivalents relate.

Source: Apple Inc's 2022 Proxy Statement Form DEF14A, filed 6 January 2022, p. 43.

Share-based compensation, in addition to theoretically aligning the interests of employees with shareholders, has the advantage of potentially requiring no cash outlay. However, share-based compensation is treated as an expense and thus as a reduction of earnings even when no cash changes hands. In addition to decreasing earnings through compensation expense, share-based compensation has the potential to dilute earnings per share. Share-based compensation arrangements can also be cash-settled, which can result in the accrual of a liability.

Although share-based compensation is generally viewed positively as it aligns managers' interests with those of the shareholders, there are several disadvantages. First is that issuing shares to employees dilutes existing shareholders. Second, the recipient may have limited influence over the company's market value (especially with respect to the performance of the broad stock market), so share-based compensation does not necessarily provide the desired incentives and may improperly reward or punish employee performance. Another disadvantage is that the increased ownership may lead managers to be risk averse. Fearing a large market value decline (and loss in individual wealth), shareholder managers may seek less risky (and less profitable) projects. An opposite effect, excessive risk taking, can also occur with the awarding of stock options. Options have skewed payouts that reward the upside while the downside is limited to zero; as a result, managers may seek high-risk, high-reward investments.

For financial reporting of share-based compensation plans, under both IFRS and US GAAP, companies generally estimate the fair value of the share-based compensation at the grant date and recognize it as compensation expense ratably over the plan's vesting schedule. Any changes in the employee's stock price after the grant date does not affect the financial reporting. Specifically, the financial reporting depends on the type of plan. Two common forms of equity-settled share-based compensation are stock grants and stock options.

Stock Grants

A company can grant stock to employees outright, with restrictions, or contingent on performance. For an outright stock grant, compensation expense is reported on the basis of the fair value of the stock on the grant date—generally the market value at grant date. Compensation expense is allocated over the period benefited by the employee's service, referred to as the service period. The employee service period is presumed to be the current period unless there are some specific requirements, such as three years of future service, before the employee is vested (has the right to receive the compensation).

Another type of stock award is a restricted stock grant, which requires the employee to return ownership of those shares to the company if certain conditions are not met. Common restrictions include the requirements that employees remain with the company for a specified period or that certain performance goals are met. Compensation expense for restricted stock grants is measured as the fair value (usually market value) of the shares issued at the grant date. This compensation expense is allocated over the employee's service period.

Shares granted contingent on meeting performance goals are called performance shares. The amount of the grant is usually determined by performance measures other than the change in stock price, such as accounting earnings or return on assets. Basing the grant on accounting performance addresses employees' potential concerns that the stock price is beyond their control and thus should not form the basis for compensation. However, performance shares can potentially have the unintended impact of providing incentives to manipulate accounting numbers. Compensation expense is equal to the fair value (usually market value) of the shares issued at the grant date. This compensation expense is allocated over the employee service period.

Generally, companies have increased their use of stock grants, particularly restricted stock grants in the form of restricted stock units (RSUs), and have decreased their use of stock options to compensate employees over time. Stock grants benefit employees as they are valuable so long as the employer's stock price is greater than zero, while stock options can expire worthless if the employer's stock price does not exceed the exercise price.

Stock Options

Like stock grants, compensation expense related to option grants is reported at fair value under both IFRS and US GAAP. Both require that fair value be estimated using an appropriate valuation model.

Whereas the fair value of stock grants is usually the market value at the date of the grant (adjusted for dividends prior to vesting), the fair value of option grants must be estimated. Companies cannot rely on market prices of options to measure the fair value of employee stock options because features of employee stock options typically differ from traded options. The choice of valuation or option pricing model is one of the critical elements in estimating fair value. Several models are commonly used, such as the Black–Scholes option pricing model or a binomial model. Accounting standards do not prescribe a particular model. Generally, though, the valuation method should (1) be consistent with fair value measurement, (2) be based on established principles of financial economic theory, and (3) reflect all substantive characteristics of the award.

Once a valuation model is selected, a company must determine the inputs to the model, typically including exercise price, stock price volatility, estimated life of each award, estimated number of options that will be forfeited, dividend yield, and the risk-free rate of interest. Some inputs, such as the exercise price, are known at the time of the grant. Other critical inputs are highly subjective—such as stock price volatility or the estimated life of stock options—and can greatly change the estimated fair value and thus compensation expense. Higher volatility, a longer estimated life, and a higher risk-free interest rate increase the estimated fair value, whereas a higher assumed dividend yield decreases the estimated fair value. Combining different assumptions with alternative valuation models can significantly affect the fair value of employee stock options.

In Exhibit 5, an excerpt from GlaxoSmithKline, plc's 2021 Annual Report explains the assumptions and model used in valuing its stock options.

Exhibit 5: GlaxoSmithKline, plc's Assumptions and Model Used in Valuing Its Stock Option

Share options and savings-related options

For the purposes of valuing savings-related options to arrive at the share-based payment charge, a Black-Scholes option pricing model has been used. The assumptions used in the model are as follows:

	2021 Grant	2020 Grant	2019 Grant
Risk-free interest rate	0.74%	(0.07%)	0.44%
Dividend yield	3.8%	6.2%	4.5%
Volatility	27%	27%	22%
Expected life	3 years	3 years	3 years
Savings-related options grant price (including 20% discount)	£12.07	£10.34	£14.15

Options outstanding

	Savings-related share options scheme	
	Number	Weighted exercise price
At 31 December 2021	7,165	£11.58
Range of exercise prices on options outstanding at year end	£10.34–14.15	
Weighted average market price on exercise during year		£13.30
Weighted average remaining contractual life		2.1 years

Options over 1.9 million shares were granted during the year under the savings-related share option scheme at a weighted average fair value of £3.22. At 31 December 2021, 5.3 million of the savings-related share options were not exercisable.

There has been no change in the effective exercise price of any outstanding options during the year.

Source: GSK, *2021 Annual Report*, p. 246.

Accounting for Stock Options

In accounting for stock options, the basic requirement is that the value of options granted to employees as compensation must be expensed ratably over the period that services are provided. Several important dates affect the accounting, including the grant date, the vesting date, the exercise date, and the expiration date. The **grant date** is the day that options are granted to employees. The **service period** is usually the period between the grant date and the vesting date.

The **vesting date** is the date that employees can first exercise the stock options. The vesting can be immediate or over a future period. If the share-based payments vest immediately (i.e., no further period of service is required), then expense is recognized on the grant date. If the share-based awards do not vest until a specified service period is completed, compensation expense is recognized and allocated over the service period. If the share-based awards are conditional upon the achievement of a performance condition or a market condition (i.e., a target share price), then compensation expense is recognized over the estimated service period. The **exercise date** is the date when employees exercise the options and convert them to stock. If the options go unexercised, they may expire at some predetermined future date, commonly 5 or 10 years from the grant date.

The grant date is also the date that compensation expense is measured if both the number of shares and the option price are known. If facts affecting the value of options granted depend on events after the grant date, then compensation expense is measured when those facts are known.

EXAMPLE 6

Disclosure of Stock Options' Current Compensation Expense, Vesting, and Future Compensation Expense

Exhibit 6: Excerpts from Note 12—Stock Compensation Plans in the Notes to Financial Statements of Coca Cola, Inc.

Our Company grants long-term equity awards under its stock-based compensation plans to certain employees of the Company.

Total stock-based compensation expense was $337 million, $141 million and $201 million in 2021, 2020 and 2019, respectively. In 2020, for certain employees who accepted voluntary separation from the Company as a result of our strategic realignment initiatives, the Company modified their outstanding equity awards granted prior to 2020 so that the employees

As of December 31, 2021, we had $335 million of total unrecognized compensation cost related to nonvested stock-based compensation awards granted under our plans, which we expect to recognize over a weighted-average period of 1.9 years as stock-based compensation expense. This expected cost does not include the impact of any future stockbased compensation awards.

Source: Coca Cola, Inc. Form 10-K, filed 22 February 2022.

Using the information in Exhibit 6, from Coca Cola, Inc.'s Notes to Financial Statements, determine the following:

1. Total compensation expense relating to options already granted that will be recognized in future years as options vest.

Solution:

Coca Cola, Inc. discloses that unrecognized compensation expense relating to stock options already granted, but not yet vested, totals USD335 million.

2. Approximate compensation expense in 2022 and 2023 relating to options already granted.

Solution:

The options already granted will vest over the next 1.9 years. Compensation expense related to stock options already granted will be USD176 million (USD335/1.9 years) in 2022 and USD159 million in 2023 (USD335 total less USD176 expensed in 2022). New options granted in the future will likely raise the total reported compensation expense.

When an option is exercised, the market price of the option at the time of exercise is not relevant. The amount of expense is determined based on the fair value of the option at the grant date. The fair value amount is recognized as compensation expense over the vesting period.

The exercise of an option is accounted for in a similar way to the issuance of stock. Upon exercise, the company increases its cash for the exercise price of the option (paid by the option holder) and credits common stock for the par value of the stock issued. Additional paid-in capital is increased by the difference between the par value of the stock and the sum of the fair value of the option at the grant date and the cash received.

In sum, the key accounting requirements are as follows:

1. Recognize compensation expense based on the fair value of the award. Since no cash is exchanged upon the grant, the offsetting account for the compensation expense is additional paid in capital.
2. The grant date fair value is recognized as compensation expense over the vesting period.
3. Upon exercise, the company increases equity by the fair value of the options on the grant date plus the cash provided by the employee upon exercise.

As the option expense is recognized over the relevant vesting period, the impact on the financial statements is to ultimately reduce retained earnings (as with any other expense). The offsetting entry is an increase in paid-in capital. Thus, the recognition of option expense has no net impact on total equity.

Other Types of Share-Based Compensation

Both stock grants and stock options allow the employee to obtain ownership in the company. Other types of share-based compensation, such as stock appreciation rights (SARs) or phantom stock, compensate an employee on the basis of changes in the value of shares without requiring the employee to hold the shares. These are referred to as cash-settled share-based compensation. With SARs, an employee's compensation is based on increases in a company's share price. Like other forms of share-based compensation, SARs serve to motivate employees and align their interests with shareholders. The following are two additional advantages of SARs:

- The potential for risk aversion is limited because employees have limited downside risk and unlimited upside potential similar to employee stock options.
- Shareholder ownership is not diluted.

Similar to other share-based compensation, SARs are valued at fair value and compensation expense is allocated over the service period of the employee. While phantom share plans are similar to other types of share-based compensation, they differ somewhat because compensation is based on the performance of hypothetical stock rather than the company's actual stock. Unlike SARs, phantom shares can be used by private companies or business units within a company that are not publicly traded or by highly illiquid companies.

4 PRESENTATION AND DISCLOSURE

☐ describe the financial statement presentation of and disclosures relating to long-term liabilities and share-based compensation

This lesson examines the presentation and disclosure requirements for leases, post-retirement benefits, and share-based compensation. These disclosures are typically included as notes to the financial statements.

Presentation and Disclosure of Leases

Both IFRS and US GAAP indicate that the objective of lease disclosure is to provide the user of the financial statement with information to assess the amount, timing and uncertainty of cash flows associated with leases.

The non-current portion of the balance sheet will typically contain a "right of use" asset and the non-current (long-term) liabilities section will typically show the lease liability. However, depending on the size of leased assets and lease obligations, some companies may not have discrete lease line items on the balance sheet and instead will report leases in "Other assets" or "Other liabilities." In addition to amounts reported on the balance sheet, both lessees and lessors must disclose quantitative and qualitative information about its leases, significant judgments made to comply with lease accounting requirements and the amounts recognized in the financial statements relating to those leases and their location on the statements.

Lessee Disclosure

Specifically, as indicated in IFRS 16, lessee disclosures must include the following amounts for the current reporting period:

- the carrying amount of right of use assets and the end of the reporting period by class of underlying asset;
- total cash outflow for leases;
- interest expense on lease liabilities;
- depreciation charges for right-of-use assets by class of underlying asset; and
- additions to right of use assets.

In addition, lessees should disclose a maturity analysis of lease liabilities (separately from the maturity analysis of other financial liabilities like bonds and loans) and additional quantitative and qualitative information about leasing activity to enable users of financial statements to assess the nature of the lessee's leasing activities and future cash outflows. This analysis should include the following:

- the nature of the lessee's leasing activities;
- future cash outflows to which the lessee is potentially exposed that are not reflected in the measurement of lease liabilities;
- restrictions or covenants imposed by leases; and
- sale and leaseback transactions.

Exhibit 7 is a reproduction of Apple's Corp's lease disclosure in its notes to financial statements.

Exhibit 7: Apple Corp's 2021 Lease Note

Note 6 - Leases

The Company has lease arrangements for certain equipment and facilities, including retail, corporate, manufacturing and data center space. These leases typically have original terms not exceeding 10 years and generally contain multiyear renewal options, some of which are reasonably certain of exercise. The Company's lease arrangements may contain both lease and nonlease components. The Company has elected to combine and account for lease and nonlease components as a single lease component for leases of retail, corporate, and data center facilities.

Payments under the Company's lease arrangements may be fixed or variable, and variable lease payments are primarily based on purchases of output of the underlying leased assets. Lease costs associated with fixed payments on the Company's operating leases were \$1.7 billion and \$1.5 billion for 2021 and 2020, respectively. Lease costs associated with variable payments on the Company's leases were \$12.9 billion and \$9.3 billion for 2021 and 2020, respectively. Rent expense for operating leases, as previously reported under former lease accounting standards, was \$1.3 billion in 2019.

The Company made \$1.4 billion and \$1.5 billion of fixed cash payments related to operating leases in 2021 and 2020, respectively. Noncash activities involving right-of-use ("ROU") assets obtained in exchange for lease liabilities were \$3.3 billion for 2021 and \$10.5 billion for 2020, including the impact of adopting FASB ASU No. 2016-02, Leases (Topic 842) in the first quarter of 2020.

The following table shows ROU assets and lease liabilities, and the associated financial statement line items, as of September 25, 2021 and September 26, 2020 (in millions of USD):

Lease-Related Assets and Liabilities	Financial Statement Line Items	2021	2020
Right-of-use assets:			
Operating leases	Other non-current assets	10,087	8,570
Finance leases	Property, plant and equipment, net	861	629
Total right-of-use assets		10,948	9,199
Lease liabilities:			
Operating leases	Other current liabilities	1,449	1,436
	Other non-current liabilities	9,506	7,745
Finance leases	Other current liabilities	79	24
	Other non-current liabilities	769	637
Total lease liabilities		11,803	9,482

Lease liability maturities as of 25 September 2021 are as follows (in millions of USD):

	Operating Leases	Finance Leases	Total
2022	1,629	104	1,733
2023	1,560	123	1,683
2024	1,499	99	1,598

	Operating Leases	Finance Leases	Total
2025	1,251	46	1,297
2026	1,061	26	1,087
Thereafter	5,187	868	6,055
Total undiscounted liabilities	12,187	1,266	13,453
Less: imputed interest	(1,232)	(418)	(1,650)
Total lease liabilities	10,955	848	11,803

The weighted-average remaining lease term related to the Company's lease liabilities as of September 25, 2021 and September 26, 2020 was 10.8 years and 10.3 years, respectively.

The discount rate related to the Company's lease liabilities as of both September 25, 2021 and September 26, 2020 was 2.0%. The discount rates are generally based on estimates of the Company's incremental borrowing rate, as the discount rates implicit in the Company's leases cannot be readily determined.

As of September 25, 2021, the Company had $1.1 billion of future payments under additional leases, primarily for corporate facilities and retail space, that had not yet commenced. These leases will commence between 2022 and 2023, with lease terms ranging from 3 years to 20 years.

Source: Apple Corp. 2021 Annual Report on Form 10-K.

Lessor Disclosure

IFRS 16 specifies different disclosure requirements for lessors. Similar to lessees, lessors must disclose information (either in the notes or the financial statements) that enables users of financial statements to assess the effect that leases have on the financial position, performance, and cash flows of the lessor. At a minimum, lessors should disclose:

- for finance leases,
- the amount of selling profit or loss; and
- finance income on the net investment in the lease; and income relating to variable lease payments not included in the measurement of the lease;
- for operating leases, lease income with separate disclosure for income relating to variable lease payments no based on an index or rate.

In addition, a lessor must provide additional qualitative and quantitative information about its leasing activities, including information to help users assess the nature of the lessor's leasing activities and how the lessor manages risk associated with any rights it retains in the underlying leased assets.

For finance leases, lessors should provide a qualitative and quantitative explanation of significant changes in the carrying amount of the net investment, along with a maturity analysis of the lease payments receivable showing undiscounted lease payments to be received on an annual basis for a minimum of each of the first five years and a total amount for any remaining years

For operating leases, a lessor should disclose disaggregated information about each class of property, plant, and equipment subject to operating leases and disclose a maturity analysis of lease payments showing the undiscounted lease payments to be received on an annual basis for a minimum of each of the first five years and a total of the amounts for the remaining years.

Presentation and Disclosure of Postemployment Plans

Disclosures for defined benefit and defined contribution pension plans are typically included as a note to the financial statements, with disclosures for defined benefit plans being far more extensive. For defined contribution plans, International Accounting Standard 19 (IAS 19) requires issuers to simply disclose the amount recognized on the income statement during the period. Regulators can require more extensive disclosures. For example, the US SEC requires issuers to file a separate annual report on Form 11-K for employee benefit plans that includes audited plan financial statements and descriptions of the plan's structure and holdings.

IAS 19 defines the following objectives for issuers' disclosures of their defined benefit pension plans:

- explain the characteristics of its defined benefit plans and risks associated with them;
- identify and explain the amounts in its financial statements arising from its defined benefit plans (i.e., the net pension asset or liability); and
- describe how its defined benefit plans may affect the amount, timing and uncertainty of the entity's future cash flows.

While IAS 19 is principles-based, giving issuers discretion in how best to achieve the disclosure objectives, it does give several specific prescriptions, requiring issuers to make disclosures, such as the following:

- the nature of benefits provided, the regulatory framework in which the plan operates, governance of the plan, and risks to which the plan exposes the entity;
- a reconciliation from the opening balance to the closing balance of the net pension asset or liability, with separate reconciliations for plan assets and the present value of the defined benefit obligation, showing service costs, interest income or expense, remeasurements, past service costs, contributions to the plan, and other components of the change;
- a sensitivity analysis showing how changes in significant assumptions (such as the discount rate used to measure the defined benefit pension obligation) would affect the amounts reported on the financial statements;
- the composition of plan assets by category, such as equity securities, fixed-income securities, and real estate; and
- indications of the effect of the defined benefit pension plans on the entity's future cash flows.

The disclosures in Exhibit 8 are included in the 2021 Annual Report of Roche AG, a Swiss biopharmaceutical and diagnostics company. Roche provides extensive detail on its postemployment plans in a note to its financial statements titled "Pensions and other postemployment benefits."

Exhibit 8: Roche AG's Pensions and Other Postemployment Benefits

Note 26. Pensions and other post-employment benefits

[Roche AG's] ("Group") objective is to provide attractive and competitive post-employment benefits to employees, while at the same time ensuring that the various plans are appropriately financed and managing any potential impacts on the Group's long-term financial position. Most employees are covered by pension plans sponsored by Group companies. The nature of such plans varies according to legal regulations, fiscal requirements and market practice in the countries in which the employees are employed. Post-employment benefit plans are classified for IFRS as 'defined contribution plans' if the Group pays fixed contributions into a separate fund or to a third-party financial institution and will have no further legal or constructive obligation to pay further contributions. All other plans are classified as 'defined benefit plans'

Defined contribution plans

Defined contribution plans are funded through payments by employees and by the Group to funds administered by third parties. The Group's expenses for these plans were CHF 419 million (2020: CHF 409 million). No assets or liabilities are recognised in the Group's balance sheet in respect of such plans, apart from regular prepayments and accruals of the contributions withheld from employees' wages and salaries and of the Group's contributions. The Group's major defined contribution plan is the US Roche 401(k) Savings Plan.

Defined benefit plans

Plans are usually established as trusts independent of the Group and are funded by payments from Group companies and by employees. In some cases, notably for the major defined benefit plans in Germany, the plans are unfunded and the Group pays pensions to retired employees directly from its own financial resources. Plans are usually governed by a senior governing body, such as a Board of Trustees, which is typically composed of both employee and employer representatives. Funding of these plans is determined by local regulations using independent actuarial valuations. Separate independent actuarial valuations are prepared in accordance with the requirements of IAS 19 for use in the Group's financial statements. The Group's major pension plans are located in Switzerland, the US and Germany, which in total account for 85% of the Group's defined benefit obligation (2020: 85%).

Defined Benefit Plans: Income Statement (in millions of CHF)

	2021			2020		
	Pension plans	Other post-employment benefit plans	Total expense	Pension plans	Other post-employment benefit plans	Total expense
Current service cost	695	13	708	644	13	657
Past service cost (income)	(30)	0	(30)	1	0	1
Settlement (gain) loss	0	0	0	(2)	0	(2)
Total operating expenses	665	13	678	643	13	656
Net interest cost of defined benefit plans	53	18	71	78	23	101
Total expense recognized on the income statement	718	31	749	721	36	757

Defined Benefit Plans: Funding Status (in millions of CHF)

	2021			2020		
	Pension plans	**Other post-employment benefit plans**	**Total expense**	**Pension plans**	**Other post-employment benefit plans**	**Total expense**
Funded plans:						
Fair value of plan assets	18,817	347	19,164	17,639	328	17,967
Defined benefit obligation	(17,609)	(683)	(18,292)	(18,290)	(757)	(19,047)
Over (under) funding	1,208	(336)	872	(651)	(429)	(1,080)
Unfunded plans:						
Defined benefit obligation	(5,211)	(371)	(5,582)	(5,506)	(396)	(5,902)
Total funding status	(4,003)	(707)	(4,710)	(6,157)	(825)	(6,982)
Limit on asset recognition	(3)	0	(3)	0	0	0
Reimbursement rights	0	108	108	0	118	118
Net recognized asset (liability)	(4,006)	(599)	(4,605)	(6,157)	(707)	(6,864)

Defined Benefit Plans: Cash Flows (in millions of CHF)

	2021	2020
Employer contributions, net of reimbursements – funded plans	(413)	(410)
Benefits paid – unfunded plans	(206)	(191)
Total cash inflow (outflow)	(619)	(601)

Based on the most recent actuarial valuations, the Group expects that employer contributions for funded plans in 2022 will be approximately CHF 411 million, which includes an estimated CHF 10 million of additional voluntary contributions related to the Chugai benefit plans. Benefits paid for unfunded plans in 2022 are estimated to be approximately CHF 204 million, which mostly relate to the German defined benefit plans.

Source: Roche AG 2021 Finance Report.

Presentation and Disclosure of Share-Based Compensation

Companies are required to provide disclosures about their share-based compensation programs that enable users of the financial statements to understand the nature and extent of share-based payment arrangements, including the current expected future cash flows and expenses relating to those plans. Issuers typically include these disclosures in a note to the financial statements. As specified in IFRS 2, required disclosures include the following:

- A description of each type of share-based payment arrangement, including its general terms and conditions, such as vesting requirements, the maximum term of options granted and the method of settlement (i.e., cash or equity)

- Details about the number and weighted average exercises price of options, including:
    - the number outstanding at the beginning of the period,
    - granted during the period,
    - forfeited during the period,
    - exercised during the period,
    - expired during the period,
    - outstanding at the end of the period, and
    - exercisable at the end of the period.
- For other equity instruments granted during the period (i.e., other than share options), the number and weighted average fair value of those equity instruments at the measurement date, and information on how that fair value was measured.

Exhibit 9 is an excerpt of Apple Inc.'s note disclosure for its share-based compensation, which is composed of grants of RSUs and an employee stock purchase plan. Note that Apple Inc.'s share price at the last balance sheet date (25 September 2021) was USD146.10, up significantly over the prior three years, which is evident in the increase in the fair value of RSU grants. Second, Apple Inc.'s primary share-based compensation plan is named the "2014 Employee Stock Plan." The name of these plans usually refers to the date it was approved by shareholders. A new plan, with a new date name, can be created at the discretion of the board and submitted to a shareholder vote; the company does not necessarily have to wait until all stock grants under the prior plan have been made, however. Some issuers will have several active stock compensation plans outstanding.

Exhibit 9: Apple Inc. 2021 Note Disclosure on Share-Based Compensation

2014 Employee Stock Plan

The 2014 Employee Stock Plan (the "2014 Plan") is a shareholder-approved plan that provides for broad-based equity grants to employees, including executive officers, and permits the granting of restricted stock units ("RSUs"), stock grants, performance-based awards, stock options and stock appreciation rights, as well as cash bonus awards. RSUs granted under the 2014 Plan generally vest over four years, based on continued employment, and are settled upon vesting in shares of the Company's common stock on a one-for-one basis. RSUs granted under the 2014 Plan reduce the number of shares available for grant under the plan by a factor of two times the number of RSUs granted. RSUs canceled and shares withheld to satisfy tax withholding obligations increase the number of shares available for grant under the 2014 Plan utilizing a factor of two times the number of RSUs canceled or shares withheld. All RSUs granted under the 2014 Plan have dividend equivalent rights ("DERs"), which entitle holders of RSUs to the same dividend value per share as holders of common stock. DERs are subject to the same vesting and other terms and conditions as the underlying RSUs. As of September 25, 2021, approximately 760 million shares were reserved for future issuance under the 2014 Plan. Shares subject to outstanding awards under the 2003 Employee Stock Plan that expire, are canceled or otherwise terminate, or are withheld to satisfy tax withholding obligations for RSUs, will also be available for awards under the 2014 Plan.

Employee Stock Purchase Plan

The Employee Stock Purchase Plan (the "Purchase Plan") is a shareholder-approved plan under which substantially all employees may voluntarily enroll to purchase the Company's common stock through payroll deductions at a price equal to 85% of the lower of the fair market values of the stock as of the beginning or the end of six-month offering periods. An employee's payroll deductions under the Purchase Plan are limited to 10% of the employee's compensation and employees may not purchase more than $25,000 of stock during any calendar year. As of September 25, 2021, approximately 96 million shares were reserved for future issuance under the Purchase Plan.

Restricted Stock Units

A summary of the Company's RSU activity and related information for 2021, 2020 and 2019, is as follows:

	Number of RSUs (thousands)	Weighted-Average Grant Date Fair Value per RSU	Aggregate Fair Value (millions)
Balance as of 29 September, 2018	368,618	33.65	
RSUs granted	147,409	53.99	
RSUs vested	(168,350)	33.80	
RSUs canceled	(21,609)	40.71	
Balance as of 28 September, 2019	326,068	42.30	
RSUs granted	156,800	59.20	
RSUs vested	(157,743)	40.29	
RSUs canceled	(14,347)	48.07	
Balance as of 26 September, 2020	310,778	51.58	
RSUs granted	89,363	116.33	
RSUs vested	(145,766)	50.71	
RSUs canceled	(13,948)	68.95	
Balance as of 25 September, 2021	240,427	75.16	35,324

The fair value as of the respective vesting dates of RSUs was $19.0 billion, $10.8 billion and $8.6 billion for 2021, 2020 and 2019, respectively. The majority of RSUs that vested in 2021, 2020 and 2019 were net share settled such that the Company withheld shares with a value equivalent to the employees' obligation for the applicable income and other employment taxes, and remitted the cash to the appropriate taxing authorities. The total shares withheld were approximately 53 million, 56 million and 59 million for 2021, 2020 and 2019, respectively, and were based on the value of the RSUs on their respective vesting dates as determined by the Company's closing stock price. Total payments for the employees' tax obligations to taxing authorities were $6.8 billion, $3.9 billion and $3.0 billion in 2021, 2020 and 2019, respectively.

As of September 25, 2021, the total unrecognized compensation cost related to outstanding RSUs and stock options was $13.6 billion, which the Company expects to recognize over a weighted-average period of 2.5 years.

Source: Apple Inc., *2021 Annual Report* on Form 10-K, p. 47.

PRACTICE PROBLEMS

1. Which of the following is a potential drawback of compensating employees with stock options?
   - **A.** The grant may make employees adverse to risk.
   - **B.** The grant may make employees seek more risk.
   - **C.** Both of the above are potential drawbacks.:

2. Which of the following is typically an objective of a share-based compensation plan?
   - **A.** Attracting new employees
   - **B.** Maximizing executive compensation
   - **C.** Alignment of employees' interest with those of management

3. Which of the following statements is true?
   - **A.** Share-based compensation does not have to be treated as an expense, when no cash is exchanged.
   - **B.** Share-based compensation programs can take a variety of forms, including those that are equity-settled and those that are cash settled.
   - **C.** Employees will receive a benefit of the stock option as long as they work long enough for the option to vest.

4. Which of the following is a difference between a stock grant and a stock option grant?
   - **A.** Whereas the fair value of stock grants is usually based on the market value at the date of the grant, the fair value of option grants must be estimated.
   - **B.** Companies account for stock grants by allocating compensation expense over the employee service period, whereas compensation expense for stock options is expensed immediately.
   - **C.** Compensation expense is determined based on the market value of a share of stock on the grant date, whereas the measurement date for the value of an option is when the employee exercises the option.

5. Assume ABC Company, a fictional company provides the following disclosure about its stock compensation plans:
   "The average fair value of shares granted was USD20.86, USD16.42, and USD17.80 in 2021, 2020, and 2019 respectively." If the company granted 18,000 shares, with a three-year vesting period in 2021, what is the annual compensation expense for the 2021 shares granted?
   - **A.** USD125,160
   - **B.** USD339,480
   - **C.** USD375,480

6. Assume XYZ Company discloses the following information in its Stock Compensation note: As of 31 December 2021, we had USD630 million of unrecognized compensation cost related to nonvested stock-based compensation awards granted under our plan. We expect to recognize this cost over a weighted average period of 3.2 years as stock-based compensation expense. What is the expected compensation expense in 2025?

   A. USD39 million

   B. USD197 million

   C. USD630 million

7. Beginning with fiscal year 2019, for leases with a term longer than one year, lessees report a right-to-use asset and a lease liability on the balance sheet:

   A. only for finance leases.

   B. only for operating leases.

   C. for both finance and operating leases.

8. For a lessor, the leased asset appears on the balance sheet and continues to be depreciated when the lease is classified as:

   A. a finance lease.

   B. a sales-type lease.

   C. an operating lease.

9. Under US GAAP, a lessor's reported revenues at lease inception will be *highest* if the lease is classified as:

   A. a sales-type lease.

   B. an operating lease.

   C. a direct financing lease.

10. Under both IFRS and US GAAP, a lessor in an operating lease recognizes:

    A. selling profit at lease inception.

    B. a lease asset comprising the lease receivable and relevant residual value at lease inception.

    C. lease receipts as income and related costs, including depreciation, as expenses over the lease term.

11. Compared with a finance lease, an operating lease:

    A. is similar to renting an asset.

    B. is equivalent to the purchase of an asset.

    C. has a term for the majority of the economic life of the leased asset.

12. Under US GAAP, a lessee's accounting for a long-term finance lease after incep-

tion will include:

A. recognizing a single lease expense.

B. recording depreciation expense on the right-of-use asset.

C. increasing the balance of the lease liability by a portion of the lease payment.

13. A company enters into a finance lease agreement to acquire the use of an asset for three years with lease payments of EUR19,000,000 starting next year. The leased asset has a fair market value of EUR49,000,000 and the present value of the lease payments is EUR47,250,188. Based on this information, the value of the lease liability reported on the company's balance sheet at lease inception is *closest* to:

A. EUR47,250,188.

B. EUR49,000,000.

C. EUR57,000,000.

14. Penben Corporation has a defined benefit pension plan. At 31 December, its pension obligation is EUR10 million and pension assets are EUR9 million. Under either IFRS or US GAAP, the reporting on the balance sheet would be *closest* to which of the following?

A. EUR10 million is shown as a liability, and EUR9 million appears as an asset.

B. EUR1 million is shown as a net pension obligation.

C. Pension assets and obligations are not required to be shown on the balance sheet but only disclosed in footnotes.

15. The information below is associated with a company that offers its employees a defined benefit plan:

Fair value of fund's assets	USD1,500,000,000
Estimated pension obligations	USD2,600,000,000
Present value of estimated pension obligations	USD1,200,000,000

Based on this information, the company's balance sheet will present a net pension:

A. asset of USD300,000,000.

B. asset of USD1,400,000,000.

C. liability of USD1,100,000,000.

SOLUTIONS

1. C is correct. Stock option grants may lead managers to be either risk adverse or have the opposite effect (i.e., encourage excessive risk taking). Therefore, B and C are both potential drawbacks.

2. The correct answer is A. The objectives of employee compensation plans include attracting new employees, retaining and motivating existing employees and aligning employee interests with those of shareholders. Answer B, maximizing executive compensation is not typically an objective of a share-based compensation programs. Answer C is not correct because an objective is to align employee interests with shareholders, not necessarily management.

3. The correct answer is B. There are numerous types of share-based compensation programs; some result in the issuance of shares to employees, and others result in a cash payment based on the value of company shares. Answer A is not correct because even if no cash is exchanged at the time of grant, the compensation expense is recognized based on the fair value of the grant. Answer C is not correct because, in some cases, employees may not receive the benefit of a stock option. For example, if the stock option expires when the exercise price exceeds the market value of the company's stock, the recipient may not benefit from the grant.

4. A is correct. The compensation for a stock grant is based on the market value at the date of the stock grant. For a stock option, the value is not definitively known and must be estimated. Answer B is not correct because companies account for both stock grants and option grants by allocating the value of the grant over the service period (often the vesting period). Answer C is not correct because for both a share grant and an option grant, the value of the grant is determined based on the date of the grant.

5. The correct answer is A, calculated as follows: 18,000 shares × by average fair value at grant date of USD20.86 = USD375,480 total compensation. Divide this amount by the three-year vesting period, and the result is USD125,160 annual compensation expense.

6. The correct answer is A. USD39 million calculated as follows: USD630 million/3.2 years = USD197 million per year for years 2022, 2023, and 2024. The amount remaining in 2025 would be USD39 million: USD630 – USD197 – USD197 – USD197 = USD39 million.

7. C is correct. Beginning with fiscal year 2019, lessees report a right-of-use asset and a lease liability for all leases longer than one year. An exception under IFRS exists for leases when the underlying asset is of low value.

8. C is correct. When a lease is classified as an operating lease, the underlying asset remains on the lessor's balance sheet. The lessor will record a depreciation expense that reduces the asset's value over time.

9. A is correct. A sales-type lease treats the lease as a sale of the asset, and revenue is recorded at the time of sale equal to the value of the leased asset. Under a direct financing lease, only interest income is reported as earned. Under an operating lease, revenue from lease receipts is reported when collected.

10. C is correct. Lessor accounting for an operating lease under US GAAP is similar to that under IFRS: Over the lease term, the lessor recognizes lease receipts

as income and recognizes related costs, including depreciation of the leased asset, as expenses. Under IFRS, at inception of a finance lease—not an operating lease—the lessor derecognizes the underlying leased asset and recognizes a lease asset comprising the lease receivable and relevant residual value. Further, an IFRS-reporting lessor will recognize selling profit at the beginning of all leases that are not classified as operating leases. In contrast, a US GAAP–reporting lessor will recognize selling profit only on sales-type leases at the beginning of the lease term.

11. A is correct. An operating lease is an agreement that allows the lessee to use an asset for a period of time. Thus, an operating lease is similar to renting an asset, whereas a finance lease is equivalent to the purchase of an asset by the lessee that is directly financed by the lessor.

12. B is correct. A lessee's accounting for a long-term finance lease under US GAAP and after lease inception includes recording depreciation expense on the right-of-use asset, recognizing interest expense on the lease liability, and reducing the balance of the lease liability for the portion of the lease payments that represents repayment of the lease liability. A lessee's accounting for an operating lease under US GAAP and after lease inception will recognize a single lease expense, which is a straight-line allocation of the cost of the lease over its term.

13. A is correct. Under the revised reporting standards under IFRS and US GAAP, a lessee must recognize an asset and a lease liability at inception of each of its leases (with an exception for short-term leases). The lessee reports a right-of-use (ROU) asset and a lease liability, calculated essentially as the present value of fixed lease payments, on its balance sheet. Thus, at lease inception, the company will record a lease liability on the balance sheet of EUR47,250,188.

14. B is correct. The company will report a net pension obligation of EUR1 million equal to the pension obligation (EUR10 million) less the plan assets (EUR9 million).

15. A is correct. A company that offers a defined benefit plan makes payments into a pension fund and the retirees are paid from the fund. The payments that a company makes into the fund are invested until they are needed to pay retirees. If the fair value of the fund's assets is higher than the present value of the estimated pension obligation, the plan has a surplus and the company's balance sheet will reflect a net pension asset. Because the fair value of the fund's assets is USD1,500,000,000 and the present value of estimated pension obligations is USD1,200,000,000, the company will present a net pension asset of USD300,000,000 on its balance sheet.

LEARNING MODULE

9

Analysis of Income Taxes

by Elbie Louw, PhD, CFA, CIPM, and Michael A. Broihahn, CPA, CIA, CFA.

Elbie Louw, PhD, CFA, CIPM (South Africa). Michael A. Broihahn, CPA, CIA, CFA, is at Barry University (USA).

LEARNING OUTCOMES

Mastery	The candidate should be able to:
☐	contrast accounting profit, taxable income, taxes payable, and income tax expense and temporary versus permanent differences between accounting profit and taxable income
☐	explain how deferred tax liabilities and assets are created and the factors that determine how a company's deferred tax liabilities and assets should be treated for the purposes of financial analysis
☐	calculate, interpret, and contrast an issuer's effective tax rate, statutory tax rate, and cash tax rate
☐	analyze disclosures relating to deferred tax items and the effective tax rate reconciliation and explain how information included in these disclosures affects a company's financial statements and financial ratios

The two major accounting standard setters are as follows: 1) the International Accounting Standards Board (IASB) who establishes International Financial Reporting Standards (IFRS) and 2) the Financial Accounting Standards Board (FASB) who establishes US GAAP. Throughout this learning module both standards are referred to and many, but not all, of these two sets of accounting rules are identified. Note: changes in accounting standards as well as new rulings and/or pronouncements issued after the publication of this learning module may cause some of the information to become dated.

1 INTRODUCTION

Differences between tax laws and financial accounting standards result in differences between accounting profit (i.e., income before taxes on the income statement) and taxable income, or income computed under the prevailing tax laws in a given jurisdiction. These differences can be temporary or permanent. Temporary differences result in deferred tax assets and liabilities on the balance sheet and are important for capturing the income tax effects of all current period activities, even if tax consequences occur in the future. Current and deferred income tax expenses are used to calculate the effective tax rate, which is commonly used by analysts in estimating after-tax profitability measures like free cash flow. Given temporary and permanent differences, the effective tax rate typically differs from the statutory and cash tax rates for an issuer. Company disclosures of income tax related information in the notes to financial statements is typically one of the most extensive note disclosures.

LEARNING MODULE OVERVIEW

- Accounting profit is reported on a company's income statement in accordance with prevailing accounting standards and does not include a provision for income tax expense.
- A company's taxable income is its income subject to income taxes under the tax laws of the relevant jurisdiction and is the basis for its income tax payable (a liability), which appears on its balance sheet.
- Taxable and deductible temporary differences reverse in future periods while permanent differences do not.
- Deferred tax assets and liabilities arise from temporary differences in accounting profit and taxable income.
- Deferred tax assets represent taxes that have been paid but have not yet been recognized on the income statement, and deferred tax liabilities occur when financial accounting income tax expense is greater than regulatory income tax expense.
- The changes in deferred tax assets and liabilities are added to income tax payable to determine the company's income tax expense as it is reported on the income statement.
- Income taxes payable are primarily determined by the geographic composition of taxable income and the tax rates in each jurisdiction.
- Three types of tax rates are relevant to analysts: the statutory tax rate, the effective tax rate, and the cash tax rate.
- The notes in the financial statements disclose a reconciliation of the statutory tax rate to the effective rate and identify the items that significantly contribute to a temporarily high or low effective tax rate.
- Companies present and disclose income tax–related information through income statements, balance sheets, and income tax note disclosures.
- Companies will disclose how the income tax provision was derived from the US federal statutory rate.
- In the income tax note disclosure, companies will provide detailed information about the derivation of the deferred tax assets and deferred tax liabilities.

2 DIFFERENCES BETWEEN ACCOUNTING PROFIT AND TAXABLE INCOME

☐ contrast accounting profit, taxable income, taxes payable, and income tax expense and temporary versus permanent differences between accounting profit and taxable income

A company's **accounting profit** is reported on its income statement in accordance with prevailing accounting standards. Accounting profit (also referred to as income before taxes or pretax income) does not include a provision for income tax expense.[1] A company's **taxable income** is its income subject to income taxes under the tax laws of the relevant jurisdiction. A company's taxable income is the basis for its **income tax payable** (a liability) or recoverable (an asset), which appears on its balance sheet. **Income tax paid** in a period is the cash amount paid for income and reduces the income tax payable.

The **tax base** of an asset or liability is the amount at which the asset or liability is valued for tax purposes, whereas the **carrying amount** is the amount at which the asset or liability is recorded in the financial statements.[2] The tax bases and carrying amounts of assets and liabilities can differ based on differences in accounting standards and the relevant tax laws. Common differences are as follows:

- Revenues and expenses may be recognized in one period for accounting purposes and a different period for tax purposes.
- Specific revenues and expenses may be either recognized for accounting purposes and not at all for tax purposes, or vice versa.
- The deductibility of gains and losses of assets and liabilities may vary for accounting and income tax purposes.
- Subject to tax rules, tax losses in prior years might be used to reduce taxable income in later years, resulting in differences in accounting and taxable income (tax loss carryforward).
- Adjustments of reported financial data from prior years might not be recognized equally for accounting and tax purposes or might be recognized in different periods.

A common example is accelerated depreciation of an asset for tax reporting (to increase expense and lower tax payments in the early years) while using the straight-line depreciation method on the financial statements. Although different on a year-to-year basis (e.g., depreciation of 10 percent on a straight-line basis may be used for accounting purposes, whereas 50 percent might be allowed for tax purposes in the first year) both approaches allow for the total cost of the asset to be depreciated over its useful life.

Differences between the tax base and carrying amount of liabilities (and, by extension, between taxable income and accounting profit) can either be temporary or permanent. Temporary differences, like the aforementioned accelerated versus straight-line depreciation example, reverse in future periods, whereas permanent differences do not.

1 As defined under International Accounting Standard 12 (IAS 12), paragraph 5.

2 The terms "tax base" and "tax basis" are interchangeable. "Tax basis" is more commonly used in the United States. Similarly, "carrying amount" and "book value" refer to the same concept.

Taxable Temporary Differences

Temporary differences are further divided into two categories, namely taxable temporary differences and deductible temporary differences. **Taxable temporary differences** result from the carrying amount of an asset exceeding its tax base (like the aforementioned accelerated depreciation example at the end of Year 1) or when the tax base of a liability exceeds its carrying amount. Taxable temporary differences result in the recognition of **deferred tax liabilities**.

Deductible Temporary Differences

Deductible temporary differences are temporary differences that result in a reduction or deduction of taxable income in a future period when the balance sheet item is recovered or settled. Deductible temporary differences result in a **deferred tax asset** when the tax base of an asset exceeds its carrying amount and, in the case of a liability, when the carrying amount of the liability exceeds its tax base. The recognition of a deferred tax asset is allowed only to the extent there is a reasonable expectation of future profits against which the asset or liability (that gave rise to the deferred tax asset) can be recovered or settled.

To determine the probability of sufficient future profits for utilization, one must consider the following: (1) sufficient taxable temporary differences must exist that are related to the same tax authority and the same taxable entity; and (2) the taxable temporary differences that are expected to reverse in the same periods as expected for the reversal of the deductible temporary differences.

Taxable and Deductible Temporary Differences

Exhibit 1 summarizes how differences between the tax bases and carrying amounts of assets and liabilities give rise to deferred tax assets or deferred tax liabilities.

Exhibit 1: Treatment of Temporary Differences

Balance Sheet Item	Carrying Amount vs. Tax Base	Results in Deferred Tax Asset/Liability
Asset	Carrying amount > tax base	Deferred tax liability
Asset	Carrying amount < tax base	Deferred tax asset
Liability	Carrying amount > tax base	Deferred tax asset
Liability	Carrying amount < tax base	Deferred tax liability

Example 1 and 2 illustrate the difference in the tax base and carrying amount of the assets and liabilities, whether they are temporary or permanent differences, and whether a deferred tax asset or liability will be recognized.

EXAMPLE 1

Differences in Tax Base and Carrying Amount of Assets and Liabilities

Exhibit 2: Tax Base and Carrying Amounts

	Carrying Amount (euros)	Tax Base (euros)	Temporary Difference (euros)	*Will Result in Deferred Tax Asset/Liability*
1. Dividends receivable	1,000,000	1,000,000	0	*N/A*
2. Development costs	2,500,000	2,250,000	250,000	*Deferred tax liability*
3. Research costs	0	375,000	(375,000)	*Deferred tax asset*
4. Accounts receivable	1,500,000	1,218,750	281,250	*Deferred tax liability*

1. *Dividends receivable*: As a result of non-taxability, the carrying amount equals the tax base of dividends receivable. This constitutes a permanent difference and will not result in the recognition of any deferred tax asset or liability. A temporary difference constitutes a difference that will, at some future date, be reversed. Although the timing of recognition is different for tax and accounting purposes, in the end the full carrying amount will be expensed/recognized as income. A permanent difference will never be reversed. Based on tax legislation, dividends from a subsidiary are not recognized as income. Therefore, no amount will be reflected as dividend income when calculating the taxable income, and the tax base of dividends receivable must be the total amount received, namely EUR1,000,000. The taxable income and accounting profit will permanently differ with the amount of dividends receivable, even on future financial statements as an effect on the retained earnings reflected on the balance sheet.
2. *Development costs*: The difference between the carrying amount and tax base is a temporary difference that, in the future, will reverse. In this fiscal year, it will result in a deferred tax liability.
3. *Research costs*: The difference between the carrying amount and tax base is a temporary difference that results in a deferred tax asset. Remember that a deferred tax asset arises because of an excess amount paid for taxes (when taxable income is greater than accounting profit), which is expected to be recovered from future operations. Based on accounting principles, the full amount was deducted resulting in a lower accounting profit, while the taxable income by implication, should be greater because of the lower amount expensed.
4. *Accounts receivable*: The difference between the carrying amount and tax base of the asset is a temporary difference that will result in a deferred tax liability.

EXAMPLE 2

Differences in Tax Base and Carrying Amount of Assets and Liabilities

Exhibit 3: Tax Base and Carrying Amounts

	Carrying Amount (euros)	Tax Base (euros)	Temporary Difference (euros)	*Will Result in Deferred Tax Asset/ Liability*
1. Donations	0	0	0	*N/A*
2. Interest received in advance	300,000	0	(300,000)	*Deferred tax asset*
3. Rent received in advance	10,000,000	0	(10,000,000)	*Deferred tax asset*
4. Loan (capital)	550,000	550,000	0	*N/A*
4. Interest paid	0	0	0	*N/A*

1. *Donations*: It was assumed that tax legislation does not allow donations to be deducted for tax purposes. No temporary difference results from donations, and thus a deferred tax asset or liability will not be recognized. This constitutes a permanent difference.
2. *Interest received in advance*: Interest received in advance results in a temporary difference that gives rise to a deferred tax asset. A deferred tax asset arises because of an excess amount paid for taxes (when taxable income is greater than accounting profit), which is expected to be recovered from future operations.
3. *Rent received in advance*: The difference between the carrying amount and tax base is a temporary difference that leads to the recognition of a deferred tax asset.
4. *Loan*: There are no temporary differences, as a result of the loan or interest paid, and thus no deferred tax item is recognized.

Permanent Differences

Permanent differences are differences between tax laws and accounting standards that *will not* be reversed at some future date. Because they will not be reversed at a future date, these differences do not give rise to deferred tax. These items typically include the following:

- income or expense items not allowed by tax legislation, such as penalties and fines that are considered expenses for financial reporting purposes, but are not deductible for tax purposes; and
- tax credits for some expenditures that directly reduce taxes. An example is tax credits provided by tax authorities to encourage the purchase of solar power or an electric vehicle.

Because no deferred tax item is created for permanent differences, all permanent differences result in a difference between the company's tax rate and its statutory corporate income tax rate.

Tax Expense

A company's **tax expense** or its provision for income taxes, appears on its income statement and is an aggregate of its income tax payable (or recoverable in the case of a tax benefit) and any changes in deferred tax assets and liabilities. This approach, rather than simply reporting income taxes paid, follows the matching principle by reporting the tax consequences of all current period activities.

QUESTION SET

1. When accounting standards require recognition of an expense that is not permitted under tax laws, the result is a:

   A. deferred tax liability.

   B. temporary difference.

   C. permanent difference.

   Solution:

   C is correct. Accounting items that are not deductible for tax purposes will not be reversed and thus result in permanent differences.

2. When certain expenditures result in tax credits that directly reduce taxes, the company will *most likely* record:

   A. a deferred tax asset.

   B. a deferred tax liability.

   C. no deferred tax asset or liability.

   Solution:

   C is correct. Tax credits that directly reduce taxes are a permanent difference, and permanent differences do not give rise to deferred tax.

3. In early 2018, Sanborn Company must pay the tax authority EUR37,000 on the income it earned in 2017. This amount was *most likely* recorded on the company's 31 December 2017 financial statements as:

   A. taxes payable.

   B. income tax expense.

   C. a deferred tax liability.

   Solution:

   A is correct. The taxes a company must pay in the immediate future are taxes payable.

DEFERRED TAX ASSETS AND LIABILITIES 3

☐ explain how deferred tax liabilities and assets are created and the factors that determine how a company's deferred tax liabilities and assets should be treated for the purposes of financial analysis

Deferred tax assets and liabilities arise from temporary differences in accounting profit and taxable income. Deferred tax assets represent taxes that have been paid (or often the carrying forward of losses from previous periods) but have not yet been recognized on the income statement. Deferred tax liabilities occur when financial accounting income tax expense is greater than regulatory income tax expense. At the end of each reporting period, deferred tax assets and liabilities are recalculated by comparing the tax bases and carrying amounts of the balance sheet items. The changes in deferred tax assets and liabilities are added to income tax payable to determine the company's income tax expense (or credit) as it is reported on the income statement.

If statutory tax rates change, the recorded value of a deferred tax asset or deferred tax liability would also change. For example, assume a tax authority reduces the statutory corporate tax rate from 35 percent to 21 percent. Because the future tax benefit would be reduced, the recorded value of a deferred tax asset would decrease. Similarly, because the amount of a future tax obligation decreases, the value of a corresponding deferred tax liability would also decrease.

Realizability of Deferred Tax Assets

Pinto Construction receives advance payments from customers that are immediately taxable but these payments are not recognized as accounting income until Pinto Construction fulfills its obligations in later reporting periods. A deferred tax liability may be created only if the company expects to be able to realize the economic benefit of the deferred tax liability in the future. In this example, the equipment is used in the core business of Pinto Construction. If the company is a going concern and has stable earnings, there should be no doubt that future economic benefits will result from the equipment, and it would be appropriate to create the deferred tax item.

If, however, it were doubtful that future economic benefits will be realized from a temporary difference (i.e., if Pinto Construction was being liquidated), the temporary difference will not lead to recognition of a deferred tax asset. If a deferred tax asset was recognized previously, but there was sufficient doubt about the economic benefits being realized, then, under IFRS, an existing deferred tax asset would be reversed. Under US GAAP, a valuation allowance would be established to reduce the amount of the deferred tax asset to the amount that is more likely than not to be realized. In assessing future economic benefits, much is left to the discretion of management in assessing the temporary differences and the issue of future economic benefits.

EXAMPLE 3

Reston Partners

The information in Exhibit 4 pertains to a hypothetical company, Reston Partners.

Exhibit 4: Reston Partners Consolidated Income Statement

Period Ending 31 March	Year 3	Year 2	Year 1
Revenue	GBP40,000	GBP30,000	GBP25,000
Other net gains	2,000	0	0
Changes in inventories of finished goods and work in progress	400	180	200
Raw materials and consumables used	(5,700)	(4,000)	(8,000)
Depreciation expense	(2,000)	(2,000)	(2,000)
Other expenses	(6,000)	(5,900)	(4,500)

Period Ending 31 March	Year 3	Year 2	Year 1
Interest expense	(2,000)	(3,000)	(6,000)
Profit before tax	GBP26,700	GBP15,280	GBP4,700

The financial performance and accounting profit of Reston Partners on this income statement is based on accounting principles appropriate for the jurisdiction in which Reston Partners operates. The principles used to calculate accounting profit (profit before tax) may differ from the principles applied for tax purposes (the calculation of taxable income). For illustrative purposes, however, assume that all income and expenses on the income statement are treated identically for tax and accounting purposes *except* depreciation.

The depreciation is related to equipment owned by Reston Partners. For simplicity, assume that the equipment was purchased at the beginning of Year 1. Depreciation should thus be calculated and expensed for the full year. Assume that accounting standards permit equipment to be depreciated on a straight-line basis over a 10-year period, whereas the tax standards in the jurisdiction specify that equipment should be depreciated on a straight-line basis over a seven-year period. For simplicity, assume a salvage value of GBP0 at the end of the equipment's useful life. Both methods will result in the full depreciation of the asset over the respective tax or accounting life.

The equipment was originally purchased for GBP20,000. In accordance with accounting standards, over the next 10 years the company will recognize annual depreciation of GBP2,000 (GBP20,000 ÷ 10) as an expense on its income statement and for the determination of accounting profit. For tax purposes, however, the company will recognize GBP2,857 (GBP20,000 ÷ 7) in depreciation each year. Each fiscal year the depreciation expense related to the use of the equipment will, therefore, differ for tax and accounting purposes (tax base vs. carrying amount), resulting in a difference between accounting profit and taxable income.

The previous income statement reflects accounting profit (depreciation at GBP2,000 per year). Exhibit 5 shows the taxable income for each fiscal year.

Exhibit 5: Taxable Income (British pound millions)

Taxable Income	Year 3	Year 2	Year 1
Revenue	GBP40,000	GBP30,000	GBP25,000
Other net gains	2,000	0	0
Changes in inventories of finished goods and work in progress	400	180	200
Raw materials and consumables used	(5,700)	(4,000)	(8,000)
Depreciation expense	(2,857)	(2,857)	(2,857)
Other expenses	(6,000)	(5,900)	(4,500)
Interest expense	(2,000)	(3,000)	(6,000)
Taxable income	GBP25,843	GBP14,423	GBP3,843

The carrying amount and tax base for the equipment is shown in Exhibit 6:

Exhibit 6: Tax Base for Equipment (British pound millions)

	Year 3	Year 2	Year 1
Equipment value for accounting purposes (*carrying amount*) (depreciation of GBP2,000/year)	GBP14,000	GBP16,000	GBP18,000
Equipment value for tax purposes (*tax base*) (depreciation of GBP2,857/year)	GBP11,429	GBP14,286	GBP17,143
Difference	GBP2,571	GBP1,714	GBP857

At each balance sheet date, the tax base and carrying amount of all assets and liabilities must be determined. The income tax payable by Reston Partners will be based on the taxable income of each fiscal year. If a tax rate of 30 percent is assumed, then the income taxes payable for years 1, 2, and 3 are GBP1,153 (30% × 3,843), GBP4,327 (30% × 14,423), and GBP7,753 (30% × 25,843), respectively.

Remember, though, that if the tax obligation is calculated based on accounting profits, it will differ because of the differences between the tax base and the carrying amount of equipment. The difference in each fiscal year is reflected in the table above. In each fiscal year the carrying amount of the equipment exceeds its tax base. For tax purposes, therefore, the asset tax base is less than its carrying value under financial accounting principles. The difference results in a deferred tax liability as shown in Exhibit 7.

Exhibit 7: Deferred Tax Liability (British pound millions)

	Year 3	Year 2	Year 1
Deferred tax liability	**GBP771**	**GBP514**	**GBP257**
(Difference between tax base and carrying amount) × tax rate			
Year 1: GBP(18,000 – 17,143) × 30 percent = 257			
Year 2: GBP(16,000 – 14,286) × 30 percent = 514			
Year 3: GBP(14,000 – 11,429) × 30 percent = 771			

The comparison of the tax base and carrying amount of equipment shows what the deferred tax liability should be on a particular balance sheet date. In each fiscal year, only the change in the deferred tax liability should be included in the calculation of the income tax expense reported on the income statement prepared for accounting purposes.

On the income statement, the company's income tax expense will be the sum of change in the deferred tax liability and the income tax payable.

Exhibit 8: Deferred Tax Liability (British pound millions)

	Year 3	Year 2	Year 1
Income tax payable (based on tax accounting)	GBP7,753	GBP4,327	GBP1,153
Change in deferred tax liability	257	257	257
Income tax (based on financial accounting)	GBP8,010	GBP4,584	GBP1,410

Note that because the different treatment of depreciation is a temporary difference, the income tax on the income statement is 30 percent of the accounting profit, although only a part is income tax payable and the rest is a deferred tax liability.

The consolidated income statement of Reston Partners including income tax is presented in Exhibit 9:

Exhibit 9: Reston Partners Consolidated Income Statement (British pound millions)

Period Ending 31 March	Year 3	Year 2	Year 1
Revenue	GBP40,000	GBP30,000	GBP25,000
Other net gains	2,000	0	0
Changes in inventories of finished goods and work in progress	400	180	200
Raw materials and consumables used	(5,700)	(4,000)	(8,000)
Depreciation expense	(2,000)	(2,000)	(2,000)
Other expenses	(6,000)	(5,900)	(4,500)
Interest expense	(2,000)	(3,000)	(6,000)
Profit before tax	GBP26,700	GBP15,280	GBP4,700
Income tax	(8,010)	(4,584)	(1,410)
Profit after tax	GBP18,690	GBP10,696	GBP3,290

Any amount paid to the tax authorities will reduce the liability for income tax payable and be reflected on the statement of cash flows of the company.

QUESTION SET

1. Using the straight-line method of depreciation for reporting purposes and accelerated depreciation for tax purposes would *most likely* result in a:

   A. deferred tax asset.

   B. valuation allowance.

   C. temporary difference.

   Solution:

   C is correct. Because the differences between tax and financial accounting will correct over time, the resulting deferred tax liability, for which the expense was charged to the income statement but the tax authority has not yet been paid, will be a temporary difference. A valuation allowance would only arise if there was doubt over the company's ability to earn sufficient income in the future to require paying the tax.

2. Income tax expense reported on a company's income statement equals taxes payable, plus the net increase in:

   A. deferred tax assets and deferred tax liabilities.

   B. deferred tax assets, less the net increase in deferred tax liabilities.

   C. deferred tax liabilities, less the net increase in deferred tax assets.

   Solution:

   C is correct. Higher reported tax expense relative to taxes paid will increase the deferred tax liability, whereas lower reported tax expense relative to taxes paid increases the deferred tax asset.

3. Analysts should treat deferred tax liabilities that are expected to reverse as:

   A. equity.

   B. liabilities.

   C. neither liabilities nor equity.

   Solution:

   B is correct. If the liability is expected to reverse (and thus require a cash tax payment) the deferred tax represents a future liability.

4. When accounting standards require an asset to be expensed immediately but tax rules require the item to be capitalized and amortized, the company will *most likely* record:

   A. a deferred tax asset.

   B. a deferred tax liability.

   C. no deferred tax asset or liability.

   Solution:

   A is correct. The capitalization will result in an asset with a positive tax base and zero carrying value. The amortization means the difference is temporary. Because there is a temporary difference on an asset resulting in a higher tax base than carrying value, a deferred tax asset is created.

5. A company incurs a capital expenditure that may be amortized over five years for accounting purposes, but over four years for tax purposes. The company will *most likely* record:

   A. a deferred tax asset.

   B. a deferred tax liability.

   C. no deferred tax asset or liability.

   Solution:

   B is correct. The difference is temporary, and the tax base will be lower (because of more rapid amortization) than the carrying value of the asset. The result will be a deferred tax liability.

6. A company receives advance payments from customers that are immediately taxable but will not be recognized for accounting purposes until the company fulfills its obligation. The company will *most likely* record:

   A. a deferred tax asset.

   B. a deferred tax liability.

   C. no deferred tax asset or liability.

   Solution:

   A is correct. The advances represent a liability for the company. The carrying value of the liability exceeds the tax base (which is now zero). A deferred tax asset arises when the carrying value of a liability exceeds its tax base.

The information in Exhibit 10 pertains to questions 7–9.

The tax effects of temporary differences that give rise to deferred tax assets and liabilities are as follows (US dollar thousands):

Exhibit 10: Tax Assets and Liabilities

	Year 3	Year 2
Deferred tax assets:		
Accrued expenses	USD8,613	USD7,927
Tax credit and net operating loss carryforwards	2,288	2,554
LIFO and inventory reserves	5,286	4,327
Other	2,664	2,109
Deferred tax assets	18,851	16,917
Valuation allowance	(1,245)	(1,360)
Net deferred tax assets	USD17,606	USD15,557
Deferred tax liabilities:		
Depreciation and amortization	(USD27,338)	(USD29,313)
Compensation and retirement plans	(3,831)	(8,963)
Other	(1,470)	(764)
Deferred tax liabilities	(32,639)	(39,040)
Net deferred tax liability	(USD15,033)	(USD23,483)

7. A reduction in the statutory tax rate would *most likely* benefit the company's:

   A. income statement and balance sheet.

   B. income statement but not the balance sheet.

   C. balance sheet but not the income statement.

   Solution:

   A is correct. A lower tax rate would increase net income on the income statement, and because the company has a net deferred tax liability, the net liability position on the balance sheet would also improve (be smaller).

8. If the valuation allowance had been the same in Year 3 as it was in Year 2, the company would have reported USD115 *higher*:

   A. net income.

B. deferred tax assets.

C. income tax expense.

Solution:

C is correct. The reduction in the valuation allowance resulted in a corresponding reduction in the income tax provision.

9. Relative to the provision for income taxes in Year 3, the company's cash tax payments were:

A. lower.

B. higher.

C. the same.

Solution:

B is correct. The net deferred tax liability was smaller in Year 3 than it was in Year 2, indicating that in addition to meeting the tax payments provided for in Year 3 the company also paid taxes that had been deferred in prior periods.

4 CORPORATE INCOME TAX RATES

☐ calculate, interpret, and contrast an issuer's effective tax rate, statutory tax rate, and cash tax rate

Income taxes payable are primarily determined by the geographic composition of taxable income and the tax rates in each jurisdiction but can also be influenced by the nature of a business. Some companies benefit from special tax treatment—for example, from R&D tax credits or accelerated depreciation of fixed assets. Analysts should also be aware of any governmental or business changes that can alter tax rates.

Differences in tax rates can be an important driver of value. Generally, three types of tax rates are relevant to analysts:

- The **statutory tax rate**, which is the corporate income tax rate in the country in which the company is domiciled.
- The **effective tax rate**, which is calculated as the reported income tax expense amount on the income statement divided by the pre-tax income.
- The **cash tax rate**, which is the tax paid in cash that period (cash tax) divided by pre-tax income.

As discussed previously, differences between cash taxes and reported taxes typically result from differences between financial accounting standards and tax laws and result from changes in deferred tax assets or deferred tax liabilities.

In forecasting tax expense and cash taxes, respectively, the effective tax rate and cash tax rate are key. A good understanding of their operational drivers and the financial structure of a company is useful in forecasting these tax rates.

Differences between the statutory tax rate and the effective tax rate can arise for many reasons. Tax credits, withholding tax on dividends, adjustments to previous years, and expenses not deductible for tax purposes are among the reasons for differences. Effective tax rates can also differ when companies are active outside the country in which they are domiciled. The effective tax rate becomes a blend of the different tax rates of the countries in which the activities take place in relation to the profit generated in each country. If a company reports a high profit in a country with a high tax rate and a low profit in a country with a low tax rate, the effective tax rate will be the weighted average of the rates and higher than the simple average tax rate of both countries.

In general, an effective tax rate that is consistently lower than statutory rates or the effective tax rates reported by competitors is not necessarily unusual but might warrant additional attention when forecasting future tax expenses. The notes in the financial statements should disclose a reconciliation of the statutory tax rate to the effective rate and identify the items that significantly contribute to a temporarily high or low effective tax rate. The cash tax rate is used for forecasting cash flows, and the effective tax rate is relevant for projecting earnings on the income statement.

In developing an estimated tax rate for forecasts, analysts should adjust for one-time events. If the income from equity-method investees is a substantial part of pre-tax income and, also a volatile component of it, the effective tax rate excluding this amount is likely to be a better estimate for the future tax costs for a company. The tax impact from income from participations is disclosed in the notes on the financial statements.

Often, a good starting point for estimating future tax expense is a tax rate based on normalized operating income, before the results from associates and special items. This normalized tax rate should be a good indication of the future tax expense, adjusted for special items, in an analyst's earnings model.

Building a model allows the effective tax amount to be found in the profit and loss projections and the cash tax amount on the cash flow statement (or given as supplemental information). The reconciliation between the profit and loss tax amount and the cash flow tax figures should be the change in the deferred tax asset or liability.

EXAMPLE 4

Tax Rate Estimates

ABC, a hypothetical company, operates in Countries A and B. The tax rate in Country A is 40 percent, and the tax rate in Country B is 10 percent. In the first year, the company generates an equal amount of profit before tax in each country, as shown in Exhibit 11.

Exhibit 11: Tax Rates That Differ by Jurisdiction

	A	B	Total
Profit before tax	100	100	200
Effective tax rate	40%	10%	25%
Tax	40	10	50
Net profit	60	90	150

1. What will happen to the effective tax rate for the next three years if the profit before tax in Country A is stable but the profit before tax in Country B grows 15 percent annually?

   Solution:

   The effective tax rate will gradually decline because a higher proportion of profit will be generated in the country with the lower tax rate each year. In Exhibit 12, the effective tax rate declines from 25 percent in the beginning to 22 percent in the third year.

Exhibit 12: Worksheet for Tax Rate Estimates Problem

	Year			
	0	1	2	3
Profit before tax, Country A	100	100	100	100
Growth rate		0%	0%	0%
Profit before tax, Country B	100	115	132	152
Growth rate		15%	15%	15%
Total profit before tax	200	215	232	252
Effective tax rate, Country A	40%	40%	40%	40%
Effective tax rate, Country B	10%	10%	10%	10%
Total tax	50	52	53	55
Total effective tax rate	25%	24%	23%	22%

2. Evaluate the cash tax and effective tax rates for the next three years if the tax authorities in Country A allow some costs (e.g., accelerated depreciation) to be taken sooner for tax purposes. Specifically, assume for Country A, the result is a 50 percent reduction in taxes paid in the current year (Year 0) but an increase in taxes paid by the same amount in the following year (Year 1) and in subsequent years. Assume stable profit before tax in Country A and 15 percent annual before-tax-profit growth in Country B.

Solution:

The combined cash tax rate (last line in Exhibit 13) will be 15 percent in the first year and then rebound in subsequent years. Only the rate for the first year will benefit from a tax deferral; in subsequent years, the deferral for a given year will be offset by the addition of the amount postponed from the previous year. The combined effective tax rate will be unaffected by the deferral. As shown in Exhibit 13, beginning with the second year (Year 1), the combined cash tax and effective tax rates decline over time because the growth in taxable income occurs in Country B, which has the lower tax rate.

Exhibit 13: Worksheet for Tax Rate Estimates Problem

	Year			
	0	1	2	3
Profit before tax, Country A	100	100	100	100
Growth rate		0%	0%	0%
Profit before tax, Country B	100	115	132	152
Growth rate		15%	15%	15%
Total profit before tax	200	215	232	252
Effective tax rate, Country A	40%	40%	40%	40%
Effective tax rate, Country B	10%	10%	10%	10%

	Year			
	0	1	2	3
Total tax per income statement	50	52	53	55
Total effective tax rate	25%	24%	23%	22%
Cash taxes, Country A	20	40	40	40
Cash taxes, Country B	10	12	13	15
Total cash tax	30	52	53	55
Cash tax rate	15%	24%	23%	22%

3. Repeat the exercise of the Tax Rate Estimates Problem, but now assume that Country B, rather than Country A, allows some costs to be taken sooner for tax purposes and that the tax effect described applies to Country B. Continue to assume stable profit before tax in Country A and 15 percent annual profit growth in Country B.

Solution:

The combined effective tax rate is unchanged from Exhibit 12 and Exhibit 13. Because of the growth assumed for Country B, however, the annual tax postponement will result in a lower cash tax rate in Country B than the effective tax rate in Country B. Consequently, as shown in Exhibit 14, the combined cash tax rate will be less than the effective tax rate in Year 0.

Exhibit 14: Worksheet for Tax Rate Estimates Problem

	Year			
	0	1	2	3
Profit before tax, Country A	100	100	100	100
Growth rate		0%	0%	0%
Profit before tax, Country B	100	115	132	152
Growth rate		15%	15%	15%
Total profit before tax	200	215	232	252
Effective tax rate, Country A	40%	40%	40%	40%
Effective tax rate, Country B	10%	10%	10%	10%
Total tax per income statement	50	52	53	55
Total effective tax rate	25%	24%	23%	22%
Cash taxes, Country A	40	40	40	40
Cash taxes, Country B	5	11	12	14
Total cash tax	45	51	52	54
Cash tax rate	23%	24%	23%	22%

EXAMPLE 5

Johnson & Johnson

The difference between the effective tax rate and the cash tax rate for Johnson & Johnson (JNJ) is shown in Exhibit 15.

Exhibit 15: Johnson & Johnson Consolidated Statement of Earnings (US dollar millions)

	2021	2020	2019
Sales to customers	93,775	82,584	82,059
Cost of products sold	29,855	28,427	27,556
Gross profit	63,920	54,157	54,503
Selling, marketing, and administrative expense	24,659	22,084	22,178
Research and development expense	14,714	12,159	11,355
In-process research and development	900	181	890
Interest income	(53)	(111)	(357)
Interest expense	183	201	318
Other (income) expense, net	489	2,899	2,525
Restructuring	252	247	266
Income before income taxes	22,776	16,497	17,328
Provision for income taxes	1,898	1,783	2,209
Net income	20,878	14,714	15,119

JNJ's income tax expense for 2021 was USD1,898 million. Accordingly, JNJ's effective tax rate was 8.3 percent (USD1,898/USD22,776). This is substantially lower than JNJ's statutory tax rate of 21 percent as a US corporation. JNJ's reconciliation of its statutory tax rate to its effective tax rate reported in its notes to financial statements shows that the primary driver of this differences is a lower tax rate on its business outside the United States.

Tax rates:	2021	2020	2019
US statutory rate	21.0%	21.0%	21.0%
International operations	(16.4)	(9.9)	(5.9)
US taxes on international income	6.7	2.7	1.8
Tax benefits from loss on capital assets	(1.3)	(1.2)	(0.3)
Tax benefits on share-based compensation	(1.0)	(1.5)	(0.5)
Tax Cuts And Jobs Act related impacts	(0.5)	0.7	(3.9)
All Other	(0.2)	(1.0)	0.5
Effective tax rate	8.3%	10.8%	12.7%

QUESTION SET

1. Which of the following *best* describes a statutory tax rate?

   A. Tax paid in cash that period divided by pre-tax income

B. Corporate income tax rate in the country in which the company is domiciled

C. Reported income tax expense amount on the income statement divided by the pre-tax income

Solution:

B is correct. The statutory tax rate is the corporate income tax rate in the country in which the company is domiciled. A is incorrect because it describes the cash tax rate. C is incorrect because it describes the effective tax rate.

Please use the following information and Exhibit 16 and Exhibit 17 from Walmart's 2021 Form 10-K to answer questions 2 and 3:

Walmart reported total revenues of USD572,762 million, income before taxes of USD18,696 million and consolidated net income of USD13,940 million. In addition, it disclosed the following information in its tax footnote:

Exhibit 16: Walmart's 2021 Form 10-K

Note 9: Taxes

The components of income before income taxes are as follows:

	Fiscal Years Ended 31 January		
(in millions USD)	**2022**	**2021**	**2020**
US	15,536	18,068	15,019
Non-US	3,160	2,496	5,097
Total income before income taxes	18,696	20,564	20,116

A summary of the provision for income taxes is as follows:

Exhibit 17: Walmart's 2021 Form 10-K

	Fiscal Years Ended 31 January		
(in millions USD)	**2022**	**2021**	**2020**
Current:			
US Federal	3,313	2,991	2,794
US State and Local	649	742	587
International	1,553	1,127	1,205
Total current tax provision	5,515	4,860	4,586
Deferred:			
US Federal	(671)	2,316	663
US State and Local	41	23	35
International	(129)	(341)	(369)
Total deferred tax expense (benefit)	(759)	1,998	329
Total provision for income taxes	4,756	6,858	4,915

2. Based on the information in Exhibit 16 and Exhibit 17, Walmart's effective tax rate is *closest* to:

   A. 25.4 percent.

   B. 29.5 percent.

   C. 34.1 percent.

   Solution:

   A is correct. The effective tax rate is calculated as the total provision for income taxes (USD4,756 million) divided by Total income before taxes (USD18,696 million).

3. Based on the information in Exhibit 16 and Exhibit 17, Walmart's cash tax rate is *closest* to:

   A. 25.4 percent.

   B. 29.5 percent.

   C. 34.1 percent.

   Solution:

   B is correct. The cash tax rate is calculated as the current tax expense (USD5,515 million) divided by Total income before taxes (USD18,696 million).

Please use the following information to answer questions 4 and 5 below:

Neutrino is a hypothetical company that is domiciled in the United States and that has significant operations in Ireland. The Statutory Tax rate in the United States is 21 percent, and the statutory tax rate in Ireland is 12 percent. Assume that Neutrino earns USD1,000 in profit before taxes in each country during year 20X1.

4. Assuming that there are no other differences between Neutrino's effective and statutory tax rates, Neutrino's combined effective tax rate is *closest* to:

   A. 12.0 percent.

   B. 16.5 percent.

   C. 21.0 percent.

   Solution:

   B is correct. Taxes are calculated as: (USD1,000 × 21%) + (USD1,000 × 12%) = USD330; Effective tax rate = USD330/USD2,000 = 16.5%.

5. Assume on January 1 the following year, 20X2, Neutrino acquires company EFG, which is domiciled in South Korea. The statutory tax rate in South Korea is 25 percent. EFG earns USD500 in profits in 20X2. Assuming US and Ireland operations each increase pre-tax profits by 25 percent, the effective tax rate in 20X2 for the consolidated entity is *closest* to:

   A. 6.5 percent.

   B. 17.9 percent.

   C. 22.0 percent.

   Solution:

   B is correct. The effective tax rate in 20X2 for the consolidated entity is calculated as follows:

Country	Taxable Income	Statutory Rate	Taxes
United States	USD1,250	21%	USD262.50
Ireland	1,250	12	150.00
South Korea	500	25	125.00
Total	USD3,000		537.50
Effective tax rate:		537.50/3,000	**17.9%**

PRESENTATION AND DISCLOSURE

5

☐ analyze disclosures relating to deferred tax items and the effective tax rate reconciliation and explain how information included in these disclosures affects a company's financial statements and financial ratios

The Consolidated Statements of Operations (Income Statements) and Consolidated Balance Sheets for Micron Technology (MU), a global technology company based in the US, are provided in Exhibit 18 and Exhibit 19, respectively. Exhibit 18 provides the income tax note disclosures for MU for the 2015, 2016, and 2017 fiscal years.

MU's income tax provision (i.e., income tax expense) for fiscal year 2017 is USD114 million (see Exhibit 18). The income tax note disclosure in Exhibit 20 reconciles how the income tax provision was determined beginning with MU's reported income before taxes (shown in Exhibit 20 as USD5,196 million for fiscal year 2017). The note disclosure then denotes the income tax provision for 2017 that is current (USD153 million), which is then offset by the deferred tax benefit for foreign taxes (USD39 million), for a net income tax provision of USD114 million. Exhibit 20 further shows a reconciliation of how the income tax provision was derived from the US federal statutory rate. Many public companies comply with this required disclosure by displaying the information in percentage terms, but MU has elected to provide the disclosure in absolute dollar amounts. From this knowledge, for 2017, we can see that the dollar amount shown for US federal income tax provision at the statutory rate (USD1,819 million) was determined by multiplying MU's income before taxes by the 35 percent US federal statutory rate (USD5,196 × 0.35 = USD1,819).

In addition, the note disclosure in Exhibit 20 provides detailed information about the derivation of the deferred tax assets (USD766 million for 2017) and deferred tax liabilities (USD17 million for 2017). These deferred tax assets are shown separately on MU's consolidated balance sheet for fiscal year 2017 with noncurrent assets (see Exhibit 19), while the deferred tax liabilities are included in other noncurrent liabilities (also see Exhibit 19).

Exhibit 18: Micron Technology, Inc. Consolidated Statements of Operations (US dollar millions, except per share)

For the Year Ended	31 Aug. 2017	1 Sept. 2016	3 Sept. 2015
Net sales	20,322	USD12,399	USD16,192
Cost of goods sold	11,886	9,894	10,977
Gross margin	8,436	2,505	5,215
Selling, general and administrative	743	659	719
Research and development	1,824	1,617	1,540
Restructure and asset impairments	18	67	3
Other operating (income) expense, net	(17)	(6)	(45)
Operating income	5,868	168	2,998
Interest income (expense), net	(560)	(395)	(336)
Other non-operating income (expense), net	(112)	(54)	(53)
Income tax (provision) benefit	(114)	(19)	(157)
Equity in net income (loss) of equity method investees	8	25	447
Net income (loss) attributable to noncontrolling interests	(1)	(1)	—
Net income (loss) attributable to Micron	USD5,089	USD(276)	USD2,899
Earnings (loss) per share:			
Basic	USD4.67	USD(0.27)	USD2.71
Diluted	USD4.41	USD(0.27)	USD2.47
Number of shares used in per share calculations:			
Basic	1,089	1,036	1,070
Diluted	1,154	1,036	1,170

Exhibit 19: Micron Technology, Inc. Consolidated Balance Sheets (US dollar millions)

As of	31 Aug. 2017	1 Sept. 2016
Assets		
Cash and equivalents	USD5,109	USD4,140
Short-term investments	319	258
Receivables	3,759	2,068
Inventories	3,123	2,889
Other current assets	147	140
Total current assets	12,457	9,495
Long-term marketable investments	617	414
Property, plant and equipment, net	19,431	14,686
Equity method investments	16	1,364

As of	31 Aug. 2017	1 Sept. 2016
Intangible assets, net	387	464
Deferred tax assets	766	657
Other noncurrent assets	1,662	460
Total assets	USD35,336	USD27,540
Liabilities and shareholders' equity		
Accounts payable and accrued expenses	USD3,664	USD3,879
Deferred income	408	200
Current debt	1,262	756
Total current liabilities	5,334	4,835
Long-term debt	9,872	9,154
Other noncurrent liabilities	639	623
Total liabilities	15,845	14,612
Redeemable convertible notes	21	—
Micron shareholder's equity		
Common stock of USD0.10 par value, 3,000 shares authorized, 1,116 shares issued and 1,112 shares outstanding (1,094 issued and 1,040 outstanding as of September 1, 2016)	112	109
Additional capital	8,287	7,736
Retained earnings	10,260	5,299
Treasury stock, 4 shares held (54 as of 1 September 2016)	(67)	(1,029)
Accumulated other comprehensive income (loss)	29	(35)
Total Micron shareholders' equity	18,621	12,080
Noncontrolling interests in subsidiaries	849	848
Total equity	19,470	12,928
Total liabilities and shareholders' equity	35,336	USD27,540

Exhibit 20: Micron Technology, Inc. Income Taxes Note to the Consolidated Financial Statements

Income (loss) before taxes and the income tax (provision) benefit consisted of the following:

(USD millions)	2017	2016	2015
Income (loss) before income taxes, net income (loss) attributable to noncontrolling interests, and equity in net income (loss) of equity method investees			
Foreign	USD5,252	(USD353)	USD2,431
US	(56)	72	178
	USD5,196	(USD281)	USD2,609
Income tax (provision) benefit:			
Current:			
Foreign	(USD152)	(USD27)	(USD93)
State	(1)	(1)	(1)

(USD millions)	2017	2016	2015
US federal	—	—	6
	(153)	(28)	(88)
Deferred:			
US federal	—	39	15
State	—	2	1
Foreign	39	(32)	(85)
	39	9	(69)
Income tax (provision)	(USD114)	(USD19)	(USD157)

The company's income tax (provision) computed using the US federal statutory rate and the company's income tax (provision) benefit is reconciled as shown in Exhibit 21:

Exhibit 21: Company Income Tax (US dollar millions)

	2017	2016	2015
US federal income tax (provision) benefit at statutory rate	(USD1,819)	USD98	(USD913)
Foreign tax rate differential	1,571	(300)	515
Change in valuation allowance	64	63	260
Change in unrecognized tax benefits	12	52	(118)
Tax credits	66	48	53
Noncontrolling investment transactions	—	—	57
Other	(8)	20	(11)
Income tax (provision) benefit	(114)	(USD19)	(USD157)

State taxes reflect investment tax credits of USD233 million at 31 August 2017. Deferred income taxes reflect the net tax effects of temporary differences between the bases of assets and liabilities for financial reporting and income tax purposes. The company's deferred tax assets and liabilities consist of the following as of the end of the periods shown in Exhibit 22:

Exhibit 22: Deferred Tax Assets and Liabilities (US dollar millions)

	2017	2016
Deferred tax assets:		
Net operating loss and tax credit carryforwards	USD3,426	USD3,014
Accrued salaries, wages, and benefits	211	142
Other accrued liabilities	59	76
Other	86	65
Gross deferred assets	3,782	3,297
Less valuation allowance	(2,321)	(2,107)
Deferred tax assets, net of valuation allowance	1,461	1,190
Deferred tax liabilities:		

	2017	2016
Debt discount	(145)	(170)
Property, plant, and equipment	(300)	(135)
Unremitted earnings on certain subsidiaries	(123)	(121)
Product and process technology	(85)	(81)
Other	(59)	(28)
Deferred tax liabilities	(712)	(535)
Net deferred tax assets	USD749	USD655
Reported as:		
Current deferred tax assets (included in other current assets)	USD—	USD—
Deferred tax assets	766	657
Current deferred tax liabilities (included in accounts payable and accrued expenses)	—	—
Deferred tax liabilities (included in other noncurrent liabilities)	(17)	(2)
Net deferred tax assets	USD749	USD655

The company has a valuation allowance against substantially all of its US net deferred tax assets. As of 31 August 2017, the company had aggregate US tax net operating loss carryforwards of USD3.88 billion and unused US tax credit carryforwards of USD416 million. The company also has unused state tax net operating loss carryforwards of USD1.95 billion and unused state tax credits of USD233 million. The net operating loss carryforwards and the tax credit carryforwards expire between 2018 to 2037.

The changes in valuation allowance of USD64 million and USD63 million in 2017 and 2016, respectively, are primarily a result of uncertainties of realizing certain US and foreign net operating losses and certain tax credit carryforwards.

Provision has been made for deferred taxes on undistributed earnings of non-US subsidiaries to the extent that dividend payments from such companies are expected to result in additional tax liability. Remaining undistributed earnings of USD12.91 billion as of 31 August 2017 have been indefinitely reinvested. Determination of the amount of unrecognized deferred tax liability on these unremitted earnings is not practicable.

EXAMPLE 6

Financial Analysis

Use the financial statement information and disclosures provided by MU in Exhibit 18–Exhibit 20 to answer the following questions:

1. MU discloses a valuation allowance of USD2,321 million (see Exhibit 20) against gross deferred assets of USD3,782 million in 2017. Does the existence of this valuation allowance have any implications concerning MU's future earnings prospects?

   Solution:

   According to Exhibit 20, MU's deferred tax assets expire gradually until 2037 (2018 to 2037 for the net operating loss carryforwards and the tax credit carryforwards).

   Because the company is still relatively young, it is likely that most of these expirations occur toward the end of that period. Because cumulative US tax net operating loss carryforwards total USD3.88 billion, the valuation allowance could imply that MU is not reasonably expected to earn USD3.88 billion over the next 20 years. However, as we can see in Exhibit 18, MU earned a profit for 2017 and 2015, thereby showing that the allowance could be adjusted downward if the company continues to generate profits in the future and making it more likely than not that the deferred tax asset would be recognized.

2. How would MU's deferred tax assets and deferred tax liabilities be affected if the federal statutory tax rate was changed to 21 percent?

Solution:

MU's total deferred tax assets exceed total deferred tax liabilities by USD749 million. A change in the federal statutory tax rate to 21 percent from the current rate of 35 percent would make these net deferred assets less valuable. Also, because it is possible that the deferred tax asset valuation allowance could be adjusted downward in the future (see discussion to solution 1), the impact could be far greater in magnitude.

3. How would reported earnings have been affected if MU were not using a valuation allowance?

Solution:

The disclosure in Exhibit 20 shows that the increase in the valuation allowance increased the income tax provision as reported on the income statement by USD64 million in 2017. Additional potential reductions in the valuation allowance could similarly reduce reported income taxes (actual income taxes would not be affected by a valuation allowance established for financial reporting) in future years (see discussion to solution 1).

4. How would MU's USD3.88 billion in net operating loss carryforwards in 2017 (see Exhibit 20) affect the valuation that an acquiring company would be willing to offer?

Solution:

If an acquiring company is profitable, it may be able to use MU's tax loss carryforwards to offset its own tax liabilities. The value to an acquirer would be the present value of the carryforwards, based on the acquirer's tax rate and expected timing of realization. The higher the acquiring company's tax rate, and the more profitable the acquirer, the sooner it would be able to benefit. Therefore, an acquirer with a high current tax rate would theoretically be willing to pay more than an acquirer with a lower tax rate.

5. Under what circumstances should the analyst consider MU's deferred tax liability as debt or as equity? Under what circumstances should the analyst exclude MU's deferred tax liability from both debt and equity when calculating the debt-to-equity ratio?

Solution:

The analyst should classify the deferred tax liability as debt if the liability is expected to reverse with subsequent tax payment. If the liability is not expected to reverse, there is no expectation of a cash outflow and the liability should be treated as equity. By way of example, future company losses may preclude the payment of any income taxes, or changes in tax laws could result in taxes that are never paid. The deferred tax liability should be excluded from both debt and equity when both the amounts and timing of tax payments resulting from the reversals of temporary differences are uncertain.

QUESTION SET

1. Deferred tax liabilities should be treated as equity when:

   A. they are not expected to reverse.

   B. the timing of tax payments is uncertain.

   C. the amount of tax payments is uncertain.

   Solution:

   A is correct. If the liability will not reverse, there will be no required tax payment in the future and the "liability" should be treated as equity.

2. When both the timing and amount of tax payments are uncertain, analysts should treat deferred tax liabilities as:

   A. equity.

   B. liabilities.

   C. neither liabilities nor equity.

   Solution:

   C is correct. The deferred tax liability should be excluded from both debt and equity when both the amounts and timing of tax payments resulting from the reversals of temporary differences are uncertain.

Note I: Income Taxes

The components of earnings before income taxes are shown in Exhibit 23:

Exhibit 23: Earnings before Income Taxes (US dollar thousands)

	Year 3	Year 2	Year 1
Earnings before income taxes:			
United States	USD88,157	USD75,658	USD59,973
Foreign	116,704	113,509	94,760
Total	USD204,861	USD189,167	USD154,733

The components of the provision for income taxes are shown in Exhibit 24:

Exhibit 24: Provision for Income Taxes (US dollar thousands)

	Year 3	Year 2	Year 1
Income taxes			
Current:			
Federal	USD30,632	USD22,031	USD18,959
Foreign	28,140	27,961	22,263
	USD58,772	USD49,992	USD41,222
Deferred:			

	Year 3	Year 2	Year 1
Federal	(USD4,752)	USD5,138	USD2,336
Foreign	124	1,730	621
	(4,628)	6,868	2,957
Total	USD54,144	USD56,860	USD44,179

3. In Year 3, the company's US GAAP income statement recorded a provision for income taxes *closest* to:

   A. USD30,632.

   B. USD54,144.

   C. USD58,772.

   Solution:

   B is correct. The income tax provision in Year 3 was USD54,144, consisting of USD58,772 in current income taxes, of which USD4,628 were deferred.

4. The company's effective tax rate was *highest* in:

   A. Year 1.

   B. Year 2.

   C. Year 3.

   Solution:

   B is correct. The effective tax rate of 30.1 percent (USD56,860/USD189,167) was higher than the effective rates in Year 1 and Year 3.

5. Relative to the company's effective tax rate on US income, the company's effective tax rate on foreign income was:

   A. lower in each year presented.

   B. higher in each year presented.

   C. higher in some periods and lower in others.

   Solution:

   A is correct. In Year 3 the effective tax rate on foreign operations was 24.2 percent [(USD28,140 + USD124)/USD116,704], and the effective US tax rate was [(USD30,632 – USD4,752)/USD88,157] = 29.4 percent. In Year 2 the effective tax rate on foreign operations was 26.2 percent, and the US rate was 35.9 percent. In Year 1 the foreign rate was 24.1 percent, and the US rate was 35.5 percent.

A company's provision for income taxes resulted in effective tax rates attributable to loss from continuing operations before cumulative effect of change in accounting principles that varied from the statutory federal income tax rate of 34 percent, as summarized in Exhibit 25.

Exhibit 25: Effective Tax Rates

Year Ended 30 June	Year 3	Year 2	Year 1
Expected federal income tax expense (benefit) from continuing operations at 34 percent	(USD112,000)	USD768,000	USD685,000
Expenses not deductible for income tax purposes	357,000	32,000	51,000
State income taxes, net of federal benefit	132,000	22,000	100,000
Change in valuation allowance for deferred tax assets	(150,000)	(766,000)	(754,000)
Income tax expense	USD227,000	USD56,000	USD82,000

6. In Year 3, the company's net income (loss) was *closest* to:

   A. (USD217,000).

   B. (USD329,000).

   C. (USD556,000).

   Solution:

   C is correct. The income tax provision at the statutory rate of 34 percent is a benefit of USD112,000, suggesting that the pre-tax income was a loss of USD112,000/0.34 = (USD329,412). The income tax provision was USD227,000. (USD329,412) – USD227,000 = (USD556,412).

7. The USD357,000 adjustment in Year 3 *most likely* resulted in:

   A. an increase in deferred tax assets.

   B. an increase in deferred tax liabilities.

   C. no change to deferred tax assets and liabilities.

   Solution:

   C is correct. Accounting expenses that are not deductible for tax purposes result in a permanent difference, and thus do not give rise to deferred taxes.

8. Over the three years presented, changes in the valuation allowance for deferred tax assets were *most likely* indicative of:

   A. decreased prospect for future profitability.

   B. increased prospects for future profitability.

   C. assets being carried at a higher value than their tax base.

   Solution:

   B is correct. Over the three-year period, changes in the valuation allowance reduced cumulative income taxes by USD1,670,000. The reductions to the valuation allowance were a result of the company being "more likely than not" to earn sufficient taxable income to offset the deferred tax assets.

PRACTICE PROBLEMS

1. In the current year, Michaels Company has a carrying amount of USD3,500,000 and tax base of USD5,000,000 for accounts receivable. Michaels will most likely recognize:

   A. a deferred tax asset.

   B. a deferred tax liability.

   C. no deferred tax asset or liability.

2. James Company has received USD500,000 of tax credits from the recent installation of solar panels that will directly reduce their taxes. Which of the following *best* describes these tax credits?

   A. Permanent difference

   B. Taxable temporary difference

   C. Deductible temporary difference

3. Please use the selected data in Exhibit 1 for the Samuels Corporation.

Exhibit 1: Selected Data for Samuels Company (US dollar millions)

	Year 3	Year 2	Year 1
Equipment value for accounting purposes (*carrying amount*) (depreciation of USD1,000/year)	USD7,000	USD8,000	USD9,000
Equipment value for tax purposes (*tax base*) (depreciation of USD1,429/year)	USD5,714	USD7,143	USD8,571

   Assuming a 35 percent tax rate and the selected data below for the Samuels Company, the company's deferred tax liability in Year 3 is *closest* to:

   A. USD450.

   B. USD750.

   C. USD900.

4. Which of the following is added to income tax payable to determine the company's income tax expense as reported on the income statement?

   A. Deferred tax assets

   B. Deferred tax liabilities

   C. Changes in deferred tax assets and liabilities

5. Jamison Corp. is domiciled in the United States and has significant operations in the United Kingdom and Australia. The statutory tax rates are 21 percent in the United States, 19 percent in the United Kingdom, and 30 percent in Australia. The company generates Profit before tax of USD2,000,000 in the United States,

USD500,000 in the United Kingdom, and USD750,000 in Australia. There are no other differences between Jamison's effective and statutory tax rates. Jamison's combined effective tax rate is closest to:

A. 21.0 percent.

B. 22.8 percent.

C. 23.3 percent.

6. Which of the following statements about tax rates is correct?

A. The effective tax rate is typically used for forecasting cash flows.

B. The cash tax rate is relevant for projecting earnings on the income statement.

C. A company's income tax expense equals the sum of current taxes plus the change in deferred tax assets and liabilities.

The following information relates to questions 7-8

Please use the selected disclosure data in Exhibit 1 and Exhibit 2 for the Marcy Corporation.

Note I: Income Taxes

The components of earnings before income taxes are as shown in Exhibit 1:

Exhibit 1: Earnings before Income Taxes (US dollars thousands)

	Year 3	Year 2	Year 1
Earnings before income taxes:			
United States	USD117,758	USD107,053	USD97,321
Foreign	57,526	52,296	47,542
Total	USD175,284	USD159,349	USD144,863

The components of the provision for income taxes are as shown in Exhibit 2:

Exhibit 2: Provision for Income Taxes (US dollars thousands)

	Year 3	Year 2	Year 1
Income taxes			
Current:			
Federal	USD34,739	USD34,257	USD31,143
Foreign	14,382	13,074	17,591
	USD49,121	USD47,331	USD48,734
Deferred:			
Federal	(USD6,524)	(USD6,002)	(USD5,325)

	Year 3	Year 2	Year 1
Foreign	389	305	262
	(6,135)	(5,697)	(5,063)
Total	USD42,986	USD41,634	USD43,671

7. Marcy's effective tax rate was lowest in:
   A. Year 1.
   B. Year 2.
   C. Year 3.

8. Relative to Marcy's effective tax rate on foreign income, the company's effective tax rate on US income was:
   A. lower in each year presented.
   B. higher in each year presented.
   C. higher in some periods and lower in others.

SOLUTIONS

1. A is correct. Because the carrying amount is less than the tax base for this asset, this difference is a temporary difference that will result in a deferred tax asset. B is incorrect because a deferred tax liability would apply if the carrying amount was greater than the asset base. C is incorrect because this is not a permanent difference thus there will be either a deferred tax asset or deferred tax liability.

2. A is correct. Permanent differences are differences between tax laws and accounting standards that will not be reversed at some future date. Because they will not be reversed at a future date, these differences do not give rise to deferred tax. These items include tax credits for expenditures that directly reduce taxes, such as tax credits related to the purchase of solar power. B is incorrect because taxable temporary differences result in the recognition of deferred tax liabilities. C is incorrect because deductible temporary differences result in a deferred tax asset.

3. A is correct. USD450 is calculated as: (USD7,000 – USD5,714) × 0.35 = USD450. B is incorrect because it incorrectly sums the deferred tax liabilities from Years 2 and 3: (USD7,000 – USD5,714) × 0.35 + (USD8,000 – USD7,143) × 0.35 = USD750. C is incorrect because it incorrectly sums the deferred tax liabilities from Years 1, 2 and 3: (USD7,000 – USD5,714) × 0.35 + (USD8,000 – USD7,143) × 0.35 + (USD9,000 – USD8,571) × 0.35 = USD900.

4. C is correct. The changes in deferred tax assets and liabilities are added to income tax payable to determine the company's income tax expense (or credit) as it is reported on the income statement. A and B are incorrect because it is the changes in deferred tax assets and liabilities that are added to income tax payable.

5. B is correct. The combined effective tax rate is calculated as:

Country	Taxable Income	Statutory Rate	Taxes
U.S.	USD2,000,000	21%	USD420,000
U.K.	500,000	19	95,000
Australia	750,000	30	225,000
Total	USD3,250,000		740,000
Effective tax rate:		740,000/3,250,000	**22.8%**

The effective tax rate is a blend of the different tax rates of the countries in which the activities take place in relation to the profit generated in each country.

A is incorrect because 21.0 percent is the statutory tax rate in the US and does not incorporate statutory tax rates in the United Kingdom and Australia. C is incorrect because 23.3 percent is the simple average of all three statutory tax rates.

6. C is correct. A company's income tax expense equals the sum of current taxes (i.e., the amount currently payable) plus the change in deferred tax assets and liabilities. A is incorrect because the cash tax rate is typically used for forecasting cash flows. B is incorrect because the effective tax rate is relevant for projecting earnings on the income statement.

7. C is correct. The effective tax rate of 24.5 percent (USD42,986/USD175,284) in Year 3 was lower than the effective tax rates in Year 1 and Year 2. A is incorrect

because its effective tax rate of 30.1 percent is higher than that of Year 3. B is incorrect because its effective tax rate of 26.1 percent is higher than that of Year 3.

8. C is correct. In Year 1, the effective tax rate on foreign operations was 37.6 percent [(USD17,591 + USD262)/USD47,542], and the effective US tax rate was [(USD31,143 – USD5,325)/USD97,321] = 26.5 percent. In Year 2, the effective tax rate on foreign operations was 25.6 percent, and the US rate was 26.4 percent. In Year 3, the foreign rate was 25.7 percent, and the US rate was 24.0 percent.

LEARNING MODULE

10

Financial Reporting Quality

by Jack T. Ciesielski, CPA, CFA, Elaine Henry, PhD, CFA, and Thomas I. Selling, PhD, CPA.

Jack T. Ciesielski, CPA, CFA, is at R.G. Associates, Inc., former publisher of The Analyst's Accounting Observer (USA). Elaine Henry, PhD, CFA, is at Stevens Institute of Technology (USA). Thomas I. Selling, PhD, CPA, is at the Cox School of Business, Southern Methodist University (USA).

LEARNING OUTCOMES

Mastery	*The candidate should be able to:*
☐	compare financial reporting quality with the quality of reported results (including quality of earnings, cash flow, and balance sheet items)
☐	describe a spectrum for assessing financial reporting quality
☐	explain the difference between conservative and aggressive accounting
☐	describe motivations that might cause management to issue financial reports that are not high quality and conditions that are conducive to issuing low-quality, or even fraudulent, financial reports
☐	describe mechanisms that discipline financial reporting quality and the potential limitations of those mechanisms
☐	describe presentation choices, including non-GAAP measures, that could be used to influence an analyst's opinion
☐	describe accounting methods (choices and estimates) that could be used to manage earnings, cash flow, and balance sheet items
☐	describe accounting warning signs and methods for detecting manipulation of information in financial reports

The two major accounting standard setters are as follows: 1) the International Accounting Standards Board (IASB) who establishes International Financial Reporting Standards (IFRS) and 2) the Financial Accounting Standards Board (FASB) who establishes US GAAP. Throughout this learning module both standards are referred to and many, but not all, of these two sets of accounting rules are identified. Note: changes in accounting standards as well as new rulings and/or pronouncements issued after the publication of this learning module may cause some of the information to become dated.

1 INTRODUCTION

Financial reporting quality varies across companies. The ability to assess the quality of a company's financial reporting is an important skill for analysts. Indications of low-quality financial reporting can prompt an analyst to maintain heightened skepticism when reading a company's reports, to review disclosures critically when undertaking financial statement analysis, and to incorporate appropriate adjustments in assessments of past performance and forecasts of future performance.

LEARNING MODULE OVERVIEW

- Financial reporting quality can be thought of as spanning a continuum. Reporting of the highest quality contains information that is relevant, correct, complete, and unbiased, whereas the lowest quality reporting contains information that is not just biased or incomplete but possibly pure fabrication.
- Reporting quality, the focus of this module, pertains to the quality of the information disclosed. High-quality reporting represents the economic reality of the company's activities during the reporting period and the company's financial condition at the end of the period.
- Results quality (commonly referred to as earnings quality) pertains to the earnings and cash generated by the company's actual economic activities and the resulting financial condition, relative to expectations of current and future financial performance. Quality earnings can be regarded as more sustainable, providing a sound platform for forecasts.
- An aspect of financial reporting quality is the degree to which accounting choices are conservative or aggressive. "Aggressive" typically refers to choices that aim to enhance the company's reported performance and financial position by inflating the amount of revenues, earnings, and/or operating cash flow reported in the period; or by decreasing expenses for the period and/or the amount of debt reported on the balance sheet.
- Conservatism in financial reports can result from either (1) accounting standards that specifically require a conservative treatment of a transaction or an event or (2) judgments made by managers when applying accounting standards that result in conservative results.
- Managers may be motivated to issue less-than-high-quality financial reports to mask poor performance, boost the company's stock price, to increase personal compensation, and/or to avoid violation of debt covenants.
- Conditions that are conducive to the issuance of low-quality financial reports include a cultural environment that result in fewer or less transparent financial disclosures, book/tax conformity that shifts emphasis toward legal compliance and away from fair presentation, and limited capital markets regulation.
- Mechanisms that discipline financial reporting quality include open capital markets and incentives for companies to minimize cost of capital, independent auditors, contract provisions specifically tailored to penalize misreporting, and enforcement by regulatory entities.

- Pro forma earnings (also commonly referred to as non-GAAP or non-IFRS earnings) adjust earnings as reported on the income statement. Pro forma earnings that exclude negative items are a hallmark of aggressive presentation choices.
- Companies are required to make additional disclosures when presenting any non-GAAP or non-IFRS metric.
- Managers' considerable flexibility in choosing their companies' accounting policies and in formulating estimates provides opportunities for aggressive accounting.
- Examples of accounting choices that affect earnings and balance sheets include inventory cost flow assumptions, estimates of uncollectible accounts receivable, estimated realizability of deferred tax assets, depreciation method, estimated salvage value of depreciable assets, and estimated useful life of depreciable assets.
- Cash flow from operations is an important metric for investors that can be enhanced by management's operating choices, such as stretching accounts payable, and potentially by classification choices.

CONCEPTUAL OVERVIEW 2

☐ compare financial reporting quality with the quality of reported results (including quality of earnings, cash flow, and balance sheet items)

Ideally, analysts would always have access to financial reports that are based on sound financial reporting standards, such as those from the International Accounting Standards Board (IASB) and the Financial Accounting Standards Board (FASB), and that are free from manipulation. But, in practice, the quality of financial reports can vary greatly. High-quality financial reporting provides information that is useful to analysts in assessing a company's performance and prospects. Low-quality financial reporting contains inaccurate, misleading, or incomplete information.

Extreme lapses in financial reporting quality have given rise to high-profile scandals that resulted not only in investor losses but also in reduced confidence in the financial system. Financial statement users who were able to accurately assess financial reporting quality were better positioned to avoid losses. These lapses illustrate the challenges analysts face as well as the potential costs of failing to recognize practices that result in misleading or inaccurate financial reports.[1] Examples of misreporting can provide an analyst with insight into various signals that may indicate poor-quality financial reports.

This module addresses *financial reporting quality*, which pertains to the quality of information in financial reports, including disclosures in notes. High-quality reporting provides decision-useful information, which is relevant and faithfully represents the economic reality of the company's activities during the reporting period as well as the company's financial condition at the end of the period. A separate but interrelated

1 In this module, the examples of misleading or inaccurate financial reports occurred in prior years—*not* because there are no current examples of questionable financial reporting, but rather because it has been conclusively resolved that misreporting occurred in the historical examples.

attribute of quality is *quality of reported results* or *earnings quality*, which pertains to the earnings and cash generated by the company's actual economic activities and the resulting financial condition. The term "earnings quality" is commonly used in practice and will be used broadly to encompass the quality of earnings, cash flow, or balance sheet items. High-quality earnings result from activities that a company likely will be able to sustain in the future and provide a sufficient return on the company's investment. The concepts of earnings quality and financial reporting quality are interrelated because a correct assessment of earnings quality is possible only when there is some basic level of financial reporting quality. Beyond this basic level, as the quality of reporting increases, the ability of financial statement users to correctly assess earnings quality and to develop expectations for future performance also increases.

After providing a conceptual overview of reporting quality, this module discusses motivations that might cause, and conditions that might enable, management to issue financial reports that are not high quality and mechanisms that aim to provide discipline to financial reporting quality. We also describe choices made by management that can affect financial reporting quality—presentation choices, accounting methods, and estimates—as well as warning signs of poor-quality financial reporting.

Conceptual Overview

Financial reporting quality and results or earnings quality are interrelated attributes of quality. Exhibit 1 illustrates this interrelationship and its implications.

Exhibit 1: Relationships between Financial Reporting Quality and Earnings Quality

		Financial Reporting Quality	
		Low	**High**
Earnings (Results) Quality	High	LOW financial reporting quality impedes assessment of earnings quality and impedes valuation.	HIGH financial reporting quality enables assessment. HIGH earnings quality increases company value.
	Low		HIGH financial reporting quality enables assessment. LOW earnings quality decreases company value.

As shown in Exhibit 1, if financial reporting quality is low, the information provided is of little use in assessing the company's performance, and thus in making investment and other decisions.

Financial reporting quality varies across companies. High-quality reports contain information that is relevant, complete, neutral, and free from error. The lowest-quality reports contain information that is pure fabrication. Earnings (results) quality can range from high and sustainable to low and unsustainable. Providers of resources prefer high and sustainable earnings. Combining the two measures of quality—financial reporting and earnings—the overall quality of financial reports from a user perspective can be thought of as spanning a continuum from the highest to the lowest. Exhibit 2 presents a quality spectrum that provides a basis for evaluating better versus poorer quality reports. This spectrum ranges from reports that are of high financial reporting quality and reflect high and sustainable earnings quality to reports that are not useful because of poor financial reporting quality.

Exhibit 2: Quality Spectrum of Financial Reports

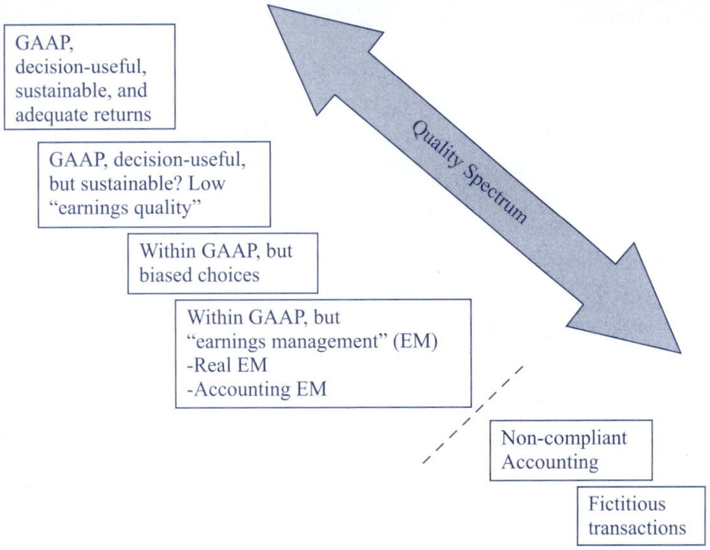

GAAP, DECISION USEFUL FINANCIAL REPORTING

3

☐ describe a spectrum for assessing financial reporting quality

At the top of the spectrum, labeled in Exhibit 2 as "GAAP, decision-useful, sustainable, and adequate returns," are high-quality reports that provide useful information about high-quality earnings.

- High-quality financial reports conform to the generally accepted accounting principles (GAAP) of the jurisdiction, such as International Financial Reporting Standards (IFRS), US GAAP, or other home-country GAAP. The exhibit uses the term GAAP to refer generically to the accounting standards accepted in a company's jurisdiction.
- In addition to conforming to GAAP, high-quality financial reports also embody the characteristics of decision-useful information, such as those defined in the *Conceptual Framework*.[2] Recall that the fundamental characteristics of useful information are relevance and faithful representation. Relevant information is defined as information that can affect a decision and encompasses the notion of materiality. (Information is considered material if

2 The characteristics of decision-useful information are identical under IFRS and US GAAP. In September 2010, the IASB adopted the *Conceptual Framework for Financial Reporting* in place of the *Framework for the Preparation and Presentation of Financial Statements* (1989). The *Conceptual Framework* represents the partial completion of a joint convergence project between the IASB and FASB on an updated framework. The *Conceptual Framework* (2010) contains two updated chapters: "The Objective of Financial Reporting" and "Qualitative Characteristics of Useful Financial Information." The remainder of the material in the *Conceptual Framework* is from the *Framework* (1989) and will be updated as the project is completed. Also in September 2010, the FASB issued Concepts Statement 8, "Conceptual Framework for Financial Reporting," to replace Concepts Statements 1 and 2.

"omitting it or misstating it could influence decisions that users make on the basis of the financial information of a specific reporting entity."[3]) Faithful representation of economic events is complete, neutral, and free from error.

The *Conceptual Framework* also enumerates enhancing characteristics of useful information: comparability, verifiability, timeliness, and understandability. Of course, the desirable characteristics for financial information require trade-offs. For example, financial reports must balance the aim of providing information that is produced quickly enough to be timely and thus relevant, and yet not so quickly that errors occur. Financial reports must balance the aim of providing information that is complete but not so exhaustive that immaterial information is included. High-quality information results when these and other trade-offs are made in an unbiased, skillful manner.

- High-quality earnings indicate an adequate level of return on investment and derive from activities that a company likely will be able to sustain in the future. An adequate level of return on investment exceeds the cost of the investment and also equals or exceeds the expected return. Sustainable activities and sustainable earnings are those expected to recur in the future. Sustainable earnings that provide a high return on investment contribute to higher valuation of a company and its securities.

GAAP, Decision-Useful, but Sustainable?

The next level down in Exhibit 2, "GAAP, decision-useful, but sustainable?" refers to circumstances in which high-quality reporting provides useful information, but that information reflects results or earnings that are not sustainable (lower earnings quality). The earnings may not be sustainable because the company cannot expect earnings that generate the same level of return on investment in the future or because the earnings, although replicable, will not generate sufficient return on investment to sustain the company. Earnings quality is low in both cases. Reporting can be high quality even when the economic reality being depicted is not of high quality. For example, consider a company that generates a loss, or earnings that do not provide an adequate return on investment, or earnings that resulted from non-recurring activities. The relatively undesirable economic reality could nonetheless be depicted in financial reporting that provides high-quality, decision-useful information.

Exhibit 3 presents an excerpt from the fiscal year 2014 first-quarter results of Toyota Motor Corporation, a Japanese automobile company. As highlighted by a *Wall Street Journal* article,[4] the company sold fewer cars but reported an 88 percent increase in operating profits compared with the prior year, primarily because of the change in exchange rates. The weaker yen benefited Toyota both because the company manufactures more cars in Japan (compared with its competitors) and because the company sells a significant number of cars outside of Japan. Exchange rate weakening is a less sustainable source of profits than manufacturing and selling cars. In summary, this example is a case of high-quality financial reporting coupled with lower earnings quality.

Exhibit 3: Excerpt from Toyota Motor Corporation's Consolidated Financial Results for FY2014 First Quarter Ending 30 June 2013

Consolidated vehicle unit sales in Japan and overseas decreased by 37 thousand units, or 1.6%, to 2,232 thousand units in FY2014 first quarter (the three months ended June 30, 2013) compared with FY2013 first quarter (the three months ended June 30, 2012). Vehicle unit sales in Japan decreased by 51 thousand units,

3 Text from conceptual frameworks referenced in Note 4.

4 Back Aaron 2013. "Toyota, What a Difference the Yen Makes." *Wall Street Journal* (4 August 2013).

or 8.8%, to 526 thousand units in FY2014 first quarter compared with FY2013 first quarter. Meanwhile, overseas vehicle unit sales increased by 14 thousand units, or 0.8%, to 1,706 thousand units in FY2014 first quarter compared with FY2013 first quarter.

As for the results of operations, net revenues increased by 753.7 billion yen, or 13.7%, to 6,255.3 billion yen in FY2014 first quarter compared with FY2013 first quarter, and operating income increased by 310.2 billion yen, or 87.9%, to 663.3 billion yen in FY2014 first quarter compared with FY2013 first quarter. The factors contributing to an increase in operating income were the effects of changes in exchange rates of 260.0 billion yen, cost reduction efforts of 70.0 billion yen, marketing efforts of 30.0 billion yen and other factors of 10.2 billion yen. On the other hand, the factors contributing to a decrease in operating income were the increase in expenses and others of 60.0 billion yen.

Source: Back Aaron 2013. "Toyota, What a Difference the Yen Makes." *Wall Street Journal* (4 August 2013).

BIASED ACCOUNTING CHOICES

4

☐ describe a spectrum for assessing financial reporting quality

The next level down in the spectrum shown in Exhibit 2 is "Within GAAP, but biased choices." Biased choices result in financial reports that do not faithfully represent the economic substance of what is being reported. The problem with bias in financial reporting, as with other deficiencies in reporting quality, is that it impedes an investor's ability to correctly assess a company's past performance, to accurately forecast future performance, and thus to appropriately value the company.

Choices are deemed to be "aggressive" if they increase a company's reported performance and financial position in the period under review. The choice can increase the amount of revenues, earnings, or operating cash flow reported for the period, or decrease expenses, or reduce the level of debt reported on the balance sheet. Aggressive choices may lead to a reduction in the company's reported performance and in its financial position in later periods. In contrast, choices are deemed "conservative" if they decrease a company's performance and financial position in the reporting period. This can include lowering the reported revenues, earnings, or operating cash flow reported or increasing expenses, or recording a higher level of debt on the balance sheet. Conservative choices may lead to a rise in the company's reported performance and financial position in later periods.

Another type of bias is understatement of earnings volatility, so-called earnings smoothing. Earnings smoothing can result from conservative choices to understate earnings in periods when a company's operations are performing well, building up (often hidden) reserves that allow aggressive choices in periods when its operations are struggling.

Biased choices can be made not only in the context of reported amounts but also in the context of how information is presented. For example, companies can disclose information transparently, which facilitates analysis, or they can disclose it in a manner that aims to obscure unfavorable or emphasize favorable information.

EXAMPLE 1

Quality of Financial Reports

PACCAR Inc. designs, manufactures, and distributes trucks and related aftermarket parts that are sold worldwide under the Kenworth, Peterbilt, and DAF nameplates. In 2013, the US SEC charged PACCAR for various accounting deficiencies that "clouded their financial reporting to investors in the midst of the financial crisis." The SEC complaint cites the company's 2009 segment reporting. Exhibit 4 presents an excerpt from the notes to PACCAR's financial statements and an excerpt from the management discussion and analysis (MD&A) of PACCAR's annual report.

Exhibit 4: PACCAR'S 2009 Financial Statements and Annual Report

A. Excerpt from Notes

S. SEGMENT AND RELATED INFORMATION

PACCAR operates in two principal segments, Truck and Financial Services.

The Truck segment includes the manufacture of trucks and the distribution of related aftermarket parts, both of which are sold through a network of independent dealers. . . . The Financial Services segment is composed of finance and leasing products and services provided to truck customers and dealers ... Included in All Other is PACCAR's industrial winch manufacturing business. Also within this category are other sales, income and expenses not attributable to a reportable segment, including a portion of corporate expense.

Pre-tax Income by Business Segment (USD millions)

	2009	2008	2007
Truck	USD25.9	USD1,156.5	USD1,352.8
All other	42.2	6.0	32.0
	68.1	1,162.5	1,384.8
Financial services	84.6	216.9	284.1
Investment income	22.3	84.6	95.4
	USD175.0	USD1,464.0	USD1,764.3

B. Excerpt from MD&A

Net sales and revenues and gross margins for truck units and aftermarket parts are provided below. The aftermarket parts gross margin includes direct revenues and costs, but excludes certain truck segment costs.

	2009	2008	Change (%)
Net Sales and Revenues			
Trucks	USD5,103.30	USD11,281.30	-55
Aftermarket parts	1,890.70	2,266.10	-17
	USD6,994.00	USD13,547.40	-48
Gross Margin			
Trucks	-USD46.6	USD1,141.70	-104

	2009	2008	Change (%)
Aftermarket parts	625.7	795.20	–21
	USD579.1	USD1,936.90	–70

1. Based on the segment data excerpted from the notes to the financial statements, was PACCAR's truck segment profitable in 2009?

   Solution:

   Yes, the segment data presented in the note to the financial statements indicates that the truck segment earned USD25.9 million in 2009.

2. Based on the data about the truck's gross margin presented in the MD&A, was PACCAR's truck segment profitable in 2009?

   Solution:

   No, the segment data presented in the MD&A indicates that the truck segment had a negative gross margin.

3. What is the main difference between the note presentation and the MD&A presentation?

   Solution:

   The main difference between the note presentation and the MD&A presentation is that the aftermarket parts business is combined with the trucks business in the notes but is separated in the MD&A. Although the data are not exactly comparable in the two disclosures (because the note shows income before taxes and the MD&A shows gross profit), the two disclosures present a different picture of PACCAR's profits from truck sales.

4. The SEC complaint stated that "PACCAR failed to report the operating results of its aftermarket parts business separately from its truck sales business as required under segment reporting requirements, which are in place to ensure that investors gain the same insight into a company as its executives." Is the PACCAR situation an example of issues with financial reporting quality, earnings quality, or both?

   Solution:

   The PACCAR situation appears to be an example of issues with both financial reporting quality and earnings quality. The substantial decrease in truck sales and the negative gross margin reflect poor earnings quality. The failure to disclose clear segment information is an instance of poor financial reporting quality.

Although choices exist within GAAP for the presentation of a desired economic picture, non-GAAP reporting adds yet another dimension of management discretion. Non-GAAP reporting of financial metrics not in compliance with generally accepted accounting principles, such as US GAAP and IFRS, includes both financial metrics and operating metrics.[5] Non-GAAP financial metrics relate directly to the financial statements. A common non-GAAP financial metric is "non-GAAP earnings," which are created by companies "that adjust standards-compliant earnings to *exclude items*

5 The term "non-GAAP" refers generally to all metrics that are non-compliant with GAAP and thus includes "non-IFRS" metrics.

required by accounting standards or to *include items not permitted* by accounting standards" (Ciesielski and Henry, 2017). In contrast, non-GAAP operating metrics do not relate directly to the financial statements and include metrics that are typically industry-driven, such as subscriber numbers, active users, and occupancy rates.

Non-GAAP financial reporting has become increasingly common, presenting challenges to analysts. An important challenge is that non-GAAP financial reporting diminishes comparability across financial statements. The adjustments that companies make to create non-GAAP earnings, for example, are generally ad hoc and thus differ significantly. When evaluating non-GAAP metrics, investors must decide the extent to which specific adjustments should be incorporated into their analyses and forecasts.[6]

Another challenge arises from differences in terminology. Non-GAAP earnings are sometimes referred to as underlying earnings, adjusted earnings, recurring earnings, core earnings, or similar. Exhibit 5 provides an example from Jaguar Land Rover Automotive plc (JLR), a subsidiary of Tata Motors Ltd. The company prepares its financial reports under IFRS. The exhibit is an excerpt from JLR's 2016/17 annual report and uses the term "alternative performance measures." Exhibit 6 is from Tata Motors Ltd.'s Form 6-K filed with the US SEC, containing supplemental information regarding JLR and using the term "non-IFRS Financial Measures." The information in the two exhibits is essentially identical, but the terminology and formatting differ.

Exhibit 5: Excerpt from JLR's 2016/17 Annual Report: Footnote 3

3) ALTERNATIVE PERFORMANCE MEASURES

Many companies use alternative performance measures (APMs) to provide helpful additional information for users of their financial statements, telling a clearer story of how the business has performed over the period. . . . These measures exclude certain items that are included in comparable statutory measures....

Reconciliations between these alternative performance measures and statutory reported measures are shown below.

Fiscal year ended 31 March 2017	GBP millions
EBITDA	**2,955**
Depreciation and amortization	−1,656
Share of profit/(loss) of equity accounted investments	159
EBIT	**1,458**
Foreign exchange (loss)/gain on derivatives	−11
Unrealised gain/(loss) on commodities	148
Foreign exchange loss on loans	−101
Finance income	33
Finance expense (net)	−68
Exceptional item	**151**
Profit before tax	**1,610**

6 A survey of non-GAAP earnings in the S&P 500 is presented in Ciesielski and Henry (2017) . Some observers even recommend that investors shift their focus from a company's earnings to a company's "strategic assets" and the contribution of these assets to its competitive edge (Gu and Lev, 2017).

Exhibit 6: Excerpt from Tata Motors Ltd. SEC Form 6-K

Non-IFRS Financial Measures

This Report includes references to certain non-IFRS measures, including EBITDA, EBIT . . . [These measures] and related ratios should not be considered in isolation and are not measures of JLR's financial performance or liquidity under IFRS and should not be considered as an alternative to profit or loss for the period or any other performance measures derived in accordance with IFRS or as an alternative to cash flow from operating, investing or financing activities or any other measure of JLR's liquidity derived in accordance with IFRS. . . . In addition, EBITDA, EBIT... as defined, may not be comparable to other similarly titled measures used by other companies.

Form 6-K Supplemental Information Regarding the Jaguar and Land Rover Business of Tata Motors Limited

The reconciliation of JLR's EBIT and EBITDA to profit for the period line item is:

Fiscal year ended 31 March 2017	GBP millions
Profit for the period	1,272
Add back taxation	338
Add/(less) back exceptional charge/(credit)	–151
Add back/(less) foreign exchange (gains)/loss – financing	101
Add back/(less) foreign exchange (gains)/loss – derivatives	11
Add back/(less) unrealized commodity losses/(gains) – unrealized derivatives	–148
Less finance income	–33
Add back finance expense (net)	68
EBIT	**1,458**
Add back depreciation and amortization	1,656
Add/(less) back share of loss/(profit) from equity accounted investees	–159
EBITDA	**2,955**

Management emphasis on non-GAAP financial measures to deflect attention from less-than-desirable GAAP financial results is an example of an aggressive presentation choice. Since 2003, if a company uses a non-GAAP financial measure[7] in an SEC filing, it is required to display the most directly comparable GAAP measure with equal prominence and to provide a reconciliation between the non-GAAP measure and the equivalent GAAP measure. In other words, a company is not allowed to give more prominence to a non-GAAP financial measure in an SEC filing.

Similarly, the IFRS Practice Statement "Management Commentary," issued December 2010, requires disclosures when non-IFRS measures are included in financial reports:

> If information from the financial statements has been adjusted for inclusion in management commentary, that fact should be disclosed. If financial performance measures that are not required or defined by IFRSs are included

7 Non-domestic private issuers can file financial statements prepared in accordance with IFRS without reconciliation to US GAAP. The SEC recognizes US GAAP and IFRS as GAAP.

within management commentary, those measures should be defined and explained, including an explanation of the relevance of the measure to users. When financial performance measures are derived or drawn from the financial statements, those measures should be reconciled to measures presented in the financial statements that have been prepared in accordance with IFRSs. (page 17)

The reconciliation between as-reported measures (GAAP financial measures presented in the financial statements) and as-adjusted measures (non-GAAP financial measures presented in places other than the financial statements) can provide important information.

The European Securities and Markets Authority (ESMA) published guidelines in October 2015 (*ESMA Guidelines on Alternative Performance Measures*) covering such points as the definition of APMs, reconciliation to GAAP, explanation of the metrics' relevance, and consistency over time. We discuss ESMA in more detail later in this module.

EXAMPLE 2

Presentation of Non-GAAP Financial Measures

Convatec Group PLC (Convatec), a global medical products manufacturer, raised USD1.8 billion through an initial public offering (IPO) on the London Stock Exchange in 2016. The company had been purchased by private equity firms from Bristol-Myers Squibb in 2008 for USD4.1 billion. Exhibit 7 presents excerpts from the company's regulatory filing at the London Stock Exchange announcing its full year 2016 results.

Exhibit 7: Excerpt from Convatec's Press Release for Full Year 2016 Results

A. Strong results, delivering on strategy

CEO Review

At constant currency, revenue grew 4% to $1,688 million and adjusted EBITDA was $508 million, up 6.5% at constant currency. . .

[Footnote] Constant currency growth 'CER' is calculated by restating 2016 results using 2015 foreign exchange rates for the relevant period.

Consolidated Statement of Profit or Loss for the year ended 31 December 2016 (USD millions)

	2016	2015
Revenue	1,688.3	1,650.4
Cost of goods sold	−821.0	−799.9
Gross profit	867.3	850.5
Selling and distribution expenses	−357.0	−346.7
General and administrative expenses	−318.2	−233.1
Research and development expenses	−38.1	−40.3
Operating profit	154.0	230.4
Finance costs	−271.4	−303.6
Other expense, net	−8.4	−37.1
Loss before income taxes	−125.8	−110.3

	2016	2015
Income tax (expense) benefit	−77.0	16.9
Net loss	−202.8	−93.4

B. Non-IFRS Financial Information

This release contains certain financial measures that are not defined or recognised under IFRS. These measures are referred to as "Adjusted" measures. . . . These measures are not measurements of financial performance or liquidity under IFRS and should not replace measures of liquidity or operating profit that are derived in accordance with IFRS.

C. Reconciliation to adjusted earnings

2016	Reported	(a)	(b)	(c)	(d)	(e)	(f)	(g)	Adjusted
Revenue	1,688.3	—	—	—	—	—	—	—	1,688.3
⋮									
Operating profit	**154.0**	**155.1**	**30.9**	**11.7**	**0.8**	—	**90.2**	**29.5**	**472.2**
⋮									
(Loss) profit before income taxes	−125.8	155.1	30.9	11.7	0.8	37.6	90.2	29.5	230.0
Income tax expense[(h)]	−77.0								−51.2
Net (loss) profit	−202.8								178.8

(a) Represents an adjustment to exclude (i) acquisition-related amortisation expense ... (ii) accelerated depreciation ... related to the closure of certain manufacturing facilities, and (iii) impairment charges and assets write offs related to property, plant and equipment and intangible assets ....

(b) Represents restructuring costs and other related costs ...

(c) Represents remediation costs which include regulatory compliance costs related to FDA activities, IT enhancement costs, and professional service fees associated with activities that were undertaken in respect of the Group's compliance function and to strengthen its control environment within finance.

(d) Represents costs primarily related to (i) corporate development activities and (ii) a settlement of ordinary course multi-year patent-related litigations in 2015 ....

(e) Represents adjustments to exclude (i) loss on extinguishment of debt and write off of deferred financing fees ... and (ii) foreign exchange related transactions.

(f) Represents an adjustment to exclude (i) share-based compensation expense ... arising from pre-IPO employee equity grants and (ii) pre-IPO ownership structure related costs, including management fees to Nordic Capital and Avista (refer to Note 6 Related Party Transactions for further information).

(g) Represents IPO related costs, primary advisory fees.

(h) Adjusted income tax expense/benefit is income tax (expense) benefit net of tax adjustments.

D. Adjusted EBITDA

Adjusted EBITDA is defined as Adjusted EBIT . . . further adjusted to exclude (i) software and R&D amortisation, (ii) depreciation and (iii) post-IPO share-based compensation.

The following table reconciles the Group's Adjusted EBIT to Adjusted EBITDA.

	2016 (USD millions)
Adjusted EBIT	472.2
Software and R&D amortization	6.7
Depreciation	27.9
Post-IPO share-based compensation	0.8
Adjusted EBITDA	507.6

1. Based on the information provided in Exhibit 7, explain the differences between the following two disclosures contained in Convatec's press release:

   A. CEO Review of 2016 results states that revenue grew 4 percent to USD1,688 million.

   B. Convatec's Consolidated Statement of Profit or Loss shows 2016 revenues of USD1,688.3 million and 2015 revenues of USD1,650.4 million.

   Solution:

   The amount of revenue reported on the company's income statement conforms to International Financial Reporting Standards (IFRS). Using the amounts from the income statement, the company's total revenue increased by 2.3% (= USD1,688.3/USD1,650.4 – 1). The revenue growth rate of 4 percent in the CEO review is a non-IFRS measure, calculated on a "constant currency" basis, which the footnote describes as a comparison using 2016 revenues restated at 2015 foreign exchange rates.

2. Based on the information provided, explain the differences between the following two disclosures contained in Convatecs's earnings release:

   A. The CEO Review of 2016 results states that adjusted EBITDA was USD508 million, up 6.5 percent at constant currency.

   B. Convatec's Consolidated Statement of Profit or Loss shows 2016 net loss of USD202.8 million and 2015 net loss of USD93.4 million.

   Solution:

   The amounts reported on the company's income statement conform to IFRS. Using amounts from the income statement, the company reported a loss in 2016 of USD202.8 million, which was more than twice as large a loss as the USD93.4 million loss reported in 2015. Also referring to the income statement, the company reported 2016 operating profit (referred to elsewhere as EBIT) of USD154.0 million, a decline of 33.2 percent from the USD230.4 million operating profit reported in 2016.

   In contrast, the adjusted EBITDA amount highlighted in the CEO Review is neither defined nor recognized under IFRS. It is a non-IFRS measure. To create the adjusted EBITDA, the company first begins with EBIT (called Operating profit in excerpts II and III) of USD154.0 and creates adjusted EBIT (USD472.2 million) by adding back eight different expenses that IFRS requires the company to recognize. These adjustments are listed beneath the first tabular reconciliation in items (a) through (g). After developing Adjusted EBIT, the company creates adjusted EBITDA (USD507.6 million) by adding back a further three different expenses that IFRS requires the company to recognize.

   Overall, there are three key differences between Disclosures A and B: (1) Most important, disclosure A refers to a non-IFRS metric rather than an IF-

RS-compliant metric; (2) Disclosure A refers to operating profit, which was positive, rather than to net income, which was negative; and (3) Disclosure A highlights a positive economic outcome—that is, an increase, on a currency-adjusted basis. An analyst should be aware of the alternative means by which earnings announcements can paint a positive picture of companies' results.

Often, poor reporting quality occurs simultaneously with poor earnings quality; for example, aggressive accounting choices are made to obscure poor performance. It is also possible, of course, for poor reporting quality to occur with high-quality earnings. Although a company with good performance would not require aggressive accounting choices to obscure poor performance, it might nonetheless produce poor-quality reports for other reasons. A company with good performance might not be able to produce high-quality reports because of inadequate internal systems.

Another scenario in which poor reporting quality might occur simultaneously with high-quality earnings is that a company with good performance might deliberately produce reports based on "conservative" rather than aggressive accounting choices—that is, choices that make current performance look worse. One motivation might be to avoid unwanted political attention. Another motivation could arise in a period in which management had already exceeded targets before the end of the period and thus made conservative accounting choices that would delay reporting profits until the following period (so-called hidden reserves). Similar motivations might also contribute to accounting choices that create the appearance that the trajectory of future results would appear more attractive. For example, a company might make choices to accelerate losses in the first year of an acquisition or the first year of a new CEO's tenure so that the trajectory of future results would appear more attractive.

Overall, *unbiased* financial reporting is optimal. Some investors may prefer conservative choices rather than aggressive ones, however, because a positive surprise is easier to tolerate than a negative surprise. Biased reporting, whether conservative or aggressive, adversely affects a user's ability to assess a company.

The quality spectrum considers the more intuitive situation in which less-than-desired underlying economics are the central motivation for poor reporting quality. In addition, it is necessary to have some degree of reporting quality in order to evaluate earnings quality. Proceeding down the spectrum, therefore, the concepts of reporting quality and earnings quality become progressively less distinguishable.

Within GAAP, but "Earnings Management"

The next level down on the spectrum shown in Exhibit 2 is labeled "Within GAAP, but 'earnings management.'" The term "earnings management" is defined as making intentional choices that create biased financial reports.[8] The distinction between earnings management and biased choices is subtle and, primarily, a matter of intent. Earnings management represents "deliberate actions to influence reported earnings and their interpretation" (Ronen and Yaari, 2008). Earnings can be "managed" upward (increased) by taking *real* actions, such as deferring research and development (R&D) expenses into the next reporting period. Alternatively, earnings can be increased by *accounting* choices, such as changing accounting estimates. For example, the amount of

8 Various definitions have appeared in academic research. Closest to the discussion is Schipper (1989), which uses the term "earnings management" to mean "'disclosure management' in the sense of a purposeful intervention in the external financial reporting process, with the intent of obtaining some private gain (as opposed to, say, merely facilitating the neutral operation of the process)."

estimated product returns, bad debt expense, or asset impairment could be decreased to create higher earnings. Because it is difficult to determine intent, we include earnings management under the biased choices discussion.

5 DEPARTURES FROM GAAP

☐ describe a spectrum for assessing financial reporting quality

The next levels down on the spectrum shown in Exhibit 2 mark departures from GAAP. Financial reporting that departs from GAAP generally can be considered to be low quality. In such situations, earnings quality is likely difficult or impossible to assess because comparisons with earlier periods and/or other entities cannot be made. An example of improper accounting was Enron (accounting issues revealed in 2001), whose inappropriate use of off-balance-sheet structures and other complex transactions resulted in vastly understated indebtedness as well as overstated profits and operating cash flow. Another notorious example of improper accounting was WorldCom (accounting issues discovered in 2002), a company that by improperly capitalizing certain expenditures dramatically understated its expenses and thus overstated its profits. New Century Financial (who accounting issues were revealed in 2007) issued billions of dollars of subprime mortgages and improperly reserved only minimal amounts for loan repurchase losses. Each of these companies subsequently filed for bankruptcy.

In the 1980s, Polly Peck International (PPI) reported currency losses, incurred in the normal course of operations, directly through equity rather than in its profit and loss statements. In the 1990s, Sunbeam improperly reported revenues from "bill-and-hold" sales and also manipulated the timing of expenses in an effort to falsely portray outstanding performance of its then-new chief executive.

At the bottom of the quality spectrum, fabricated reports portray fictitious events, either to deceive investors by misrepresenting the company's performance or to obscure fraudulent misappropriation of the company's assets. Examples of fraudulent reporting are unfortunately easy to find, although they were not necessarily easy to identify at the time. In the 1970s, Equity Funding Corp. created fictitious revenues and even fictitious policyholders. In the 1980s, Crazy Eddie's reported fictitious inventory as well as fictitious revenues supported by fake invoices. In 2004, Parmalat reported fictitious bank balances.

EXAMPLE 3

Spectrum for Assessing Quality of Financial Reports

Jake Lake, a financial analyst, has identified several items in the financial reports of several (hypothetical) companies. Describe each of these items in the context of the financial reporting quality spectrum.

1. ABC Co.'s 2018 earnings totaled USD233 million, including a USD100 million gain from selling one of its less profitable divisions. ABC's earnings for the prior three years totaled USD120 million, USD107 million, and USD111 million. The company's financial reports are extremely clear and detailed,

and the company's earnings announcement highlights the one-time nature of the USD100 million gain.

Solution:

ABC's 2018 total earnings quality can be viewed as low because nearly half of the earnings are derived from a non-sustainable activity, namely the sale of a division. ABC's quality of earnings in 2018 from continuing operations may be high because the amounts are fairly consistent from year to year, although an analyst would undertake further analysis to confirm earnings quality. In general, a user of financial reports should look beyond the bottom-line net income. The description provided suggests that the company's reporting quality is high; the reports are clear and detailed, and the one-time nature of the USD100 million gain is highlighted.

2. DEF Co. discloses that, in 2018, it changed the depreciable life of its equipment from 3 years to 15 years. Equipment represents a substantial component of the company's assets. The company's disclosures indicate that the change is permissible under the accounting standards of its jurisdiction, but it provides only limited explanation of the change.

Solution:

DEF's accounting choice appears to be within permissible accounting standards, but its effect is to substantially lower depreciation expense and thus to increase earnings for the year. The quality of reported earnings is questionable. Although the new level of earnings may be sustainable, similar increases in earnings for future periods might not be achievable, because increasing earnings solely by changing accounting estimates is likely not sustainable. In addition, the description provided suggests that the company's reporting quality is low because it offers only a limited explanation for the change.

3. GHI Co.'s R&D expenditures for the past five years have been approximately 3 percent of sales. In 2018, the company significantly reduced its R&D expenditures. Without the reduction in R&D expenditures, the company would have reported a loss. No explanation is disclosed.

Solution:

GHI's operational choice to reduce its R&D may reflect real earnings management because the change enabled the company to avoid reporting a loss. In addition, the description provided suggests that the company's reporting quality is low because it does not offer an explanation for the change.

DIFFERENTIATE BETWEEN CONSERVATIVE AND AGGRESSIVE ACCOUNTING 6

- [ ] explain the difference between conservative and aggressive accounting

This lesson returns to the implications of conservative and aggressive accounting choices. As mentioned earlier, *unbiased* financial reporting is ideal. But some investors may prefer or be perceived to prefer conservative rather than aggressive accounting choices, because a positive surprise is acceptable. In contrast, management may make, or be perceived to make, aggressive accounting choices because they increase the company's reported performance and financial position.

Aggressive accounting choices in the period under review may decrease the company's reported performance and financial position in later periods, which creates a sustainability issue. Conservative choices do not typically create a sustainability issue because they decrease the company's reported performance and financial position, and may increase them in later periods. In terms of establishing expectations for the future, however, financial reporting that is relevant and faithfully representative is the most useful.

A common presumption is that financial reports are typically biased upward, but that is not always the case. Although accounting standards ideally promote unbiased financial reporting, some accounting standards may specifically require a conservative treatment of a transaction or an event. Also, managers may choose to take a conservative approach when applying standards. It is important that an analyst consider the possibility of conservative choices and their effects.

At its most extreme, conservatism follows accounting practices that "anticipate no profit, but anticipate all losses" (Bliss, 1924). But in general, conservatism means that revenues may be recognized once a verifiable and legally enforceable receivable has been generated and that losses need not be recognized until it becomes "probable" that an actual loss will be incurred. Conservatism is not an absolute but is characterized by degrees, such as "the accountant's tendency to require a higher degree of verification to recognize good news as gains than to recognize bad news as losses" (Basu, 1997). From this perspective, "verification" (e.g., physical existence of inventories, evidence of costs incurred or to be incurred, or establishment of rights and obligations on legal grounds) drives the degree of conservatism. For recognition of revenues, a higher degree of verification would be required than for expenses.

Conservatism in Accounting Standards

The *Conceptual Framework* supports neutrality of information: "A neutral depiction is without bias in the selection or presentation of financial information."[9] Neutrality—lack of upward or downward bias—is considered a desirable characteristic of financial reporting. Conservatism directly conflicts with the characteristic of neutrality because the asymmetric nature of conservatism leads to bias in measuring assets and liabilities—and, ultimately, earnings.

Despite efforts to support neutrality in financial reporting, many conservatively biased standards remain. Standards across jurisdictions may differ on the extent of conservatism embedded within them. An analyst should be aware of the implications of accounting standards for the financial reports.

9 International Accounting Standards Board (IASB) and Financial Accounting Standards Board (FASB), *The Conceptual Framework for Financial Reporting* (2010): QC 14.

An example is the different treatment by IFRS and US GAAP of the impairment of long-lived assets.[10] Both IFRS and US GAAP specify an impairment analysis protocol that begins with an assessment of whether recent events indicate that the economic benefit from an individual or group of long-lived assets may be less than its carrying amount(s). From that point on, however, the two regimes diverge:

- Under IFRS, if the "recoverable amount" (the higher of fair value less costs to sell and value in use) is less than the carrying amount, then an impairment charge will be recorded.
- Under US GAAP, an impairment charge will be recorded only when the sum of the undiscounted future cash flows expected to be derived from the asset(s) is less than the carrying amount(s). If the undiscounted future cash flows are less than the carrying amount, the asset is written down to fair value.

To illustrate the difference in application, assume that a factory is the unit of account eligible for impairment testing. Its carrying amount is USD10,000,000; "fair value" and "recoverable amount" are both USD6,000,000; and the undiscounted future net cash flows associated with the factory total USD10,000,000. Under IFRS, an impairment charge of USD4,000,000 would be recorded; under US GAAP, however, no impairment charge would be recognized.

Thus, on its face, IFRS would be regarded as more conservative than US GAAP because impairment losses normally would be recognized earlier under IFRS than under US GAAP. But, taking the analysis one step further, such a broad generalization may not hold up. For example, if an asset is impaired under both IFRS and US GAAP, and the asset's value in use exceeds its fair value, the impairment loss under US GAAP will be greater. Also, IFRS permits the recognition of recoveries of the recoverable amount in subsequent periods if evidence indicates that the recoverable amount has subsequently increased. In contrast, US GAAP prohibits the subsequent write-up of an asset after an impairment charge has been taken; it would recognize the asset's increased value only when the asset is ultimately sold.

Common examples of conservatism in accounting standards include the following:

- *Research costs.* Because the future benefit of research costs is uncertain at the time the costs are incurred, both US GAAP and IFRS require immediate expensing instead of capitalization.
- *Litigation losses.* When it becomes "probable" that a cost will be incurred, both US GAAP and IFRS require expense recognition, even though a legal liability may not be incurred until a future date.
- *Insurance recoverables.* Generally, a company that receives payment on an insurance claim may not recognize a receivable until the insurance company acknowledges the validity of the claimed amount.

Watts (2003) reviews empirical studies of conservatism and identifies the following four potential benefits of conservatism:

- Given asymmetrical information, conservatism may protect the contracting parties with less information and greater risk. This protection is necessary because the contracting party may be at a disadvantage. For example, corporations that access debt markets have limited liability, and lenders thus have limited recourse to recover their losses from shareholders. As another

10 See International Accounting Standards (IAS) 36 and FASB, Accounting Standards Codification (ASC), Section 360-10-35.

example, executives who receive earnings-based bonuses might not be subject to having those bonuses "clawed back" if earnings are subsequently discovered to be overstated.

- Conservatism reduces the possibility of litigation and, by extension, litigation costs. Rarely, if ever, is a company sued because it understated good news or overstated bad news.
- Conservative rules may protect the interests of regulators and politicians by reducing the possibility that fault will be found with them if companies overstate earnings or assets.
- In many tax jurisdictions, financial and tax reporting rules are linked. For example, in Germany and Japan, only deductions taken against reported income can be deducted against taxable income. Hence, companies can reduce the present value of their tax payments by electing conservative accounting policies for certain types of events.

Analysts should consider possible conservative and aggressive biases and their consequences when examining financial reports. Current-period financial reports may be unbiased, upward biased through aggressive accounting choices, downward biased through conservative accounting choices, or biased through a combination of conservative and aggressive accounting choices.

Bias in the Application of Accounting Standards

Any application of accounting standards, whether or not the standard is neutral, often requires significant amounts of judgment. Characterizing the application of an accounting standard as conservative or aggressive is more a matter of intent than definition.

Careful analysis of disclosures, facts, and circumstances contributes to making an accurate inference of intent. Management seeking to manipulate earnings may take a longer view by sacrificing short-term profitability in order to ensure higher profits in later periods. One example of biased accounting in the guise of conservatism is the so-called big bath restructuring charge. Both US GAAP and IFRS provide for accrual of future costs associated with restructurings, and these costs are often associated with and presented along with asset impairments. But in some instances, companies use the accounting provisions to estimate "big" losses in the period under review so that performance in future periods will appear better. Having observed numerous instances of manipulative practices in the late 1990s, in which US companies set up opportunities to report higher profits in future periods that were not connected with performance in those periods, the SEC staff issued rules that narrowed the circumstances under which costs can be categorized as part of a "non-recurring" restructuring event and enhanced the transparency surrounding restructuring charges and asset impairments.[11]

A similar manifestation of big bath accounting is often referred to as "cookie jar reserve accounting." Both US GAAP and IFRS require accruals of estimates of future non-payments of loans. In his 1998 speech "The Numbers Game," SEC chair Arthur Levitt expressed the general concern that corporations were overstating loans and other forms of loss allowances for the purpose of smoothing income over time.[12] In 2003, the SEC issued interpretive guidance that essentially requires a company to provide a separate section in management discussion and analysis (MD&A) titled "Critical

---

11 SEC, "Restructuring and Impairment Charges," Staff Accounting Bulletin (SAB) No. 100 (1999), www.sec.gov/interps/account/sab100.htm.

12 Arthur Levitt, "The Numbers Game," Remarks given at NYU Center for Law and Business (28 September 1998), www.sec.gov/news/speech/speecharchive/1998/spch220.txt.

Accounting Estimates."[13] If the effects of subjective estimates and judgments of highly uncertain matters are material to stakeholders (investors, customers, suppliers, and other users of the financial statements), disclosures of their nature and exposure to uncertainty should be made in the MD&A. This requirement is in addition to required disclosures in the notes to the financial statements.

CONTEXT FOR ASSESSING FINANCIAL REPORTING QUALITY

7

☐ describe motivations that might cause management to issue financial reports that are not high quality and conditions that are conducive to issuing low-quality, or even fraudulent, financial reports

In assessing financial reporting quality, it is useful to consider whether a company's managers may be motivated to issue financial reports that are not high quality. If motivation exists, an analyst should consider whether the reporting environment is conducive to managers' misreporting. It is important to consider mechanisms within the reporting environment that discipline financial reporting quality, such as the regulatory regime.

Motivations

Managers may be motivated to issue financial reports that are not high quality to mask poor performance, such as a loss of market share or lower profitability than competitors. As Lewis (2012) stated, "A firm experiencing performance problems, particularly those it considers transient, may induce a response that inflates current earnings numbers in exchange for lower future earnings."

- Even when there is no need to mask poor performance, managers frequently have incentives to meet or beat market expectations as reflected in analysts' forecasts or management's own forecasts. Exceeding forecasts may increase the stock price, if only temporarily. Additionally, exceeding forecasts can increase management compensation that is linked to increases in stock price or to reported earnings. Graham, Harvey, and Rajgopal (2005) found that the chief financial officers (CFOs) they surveyed view earnings as the most important financial metric to financial markets. Achieving (or exceeding) particular benchmarks, including prior-year earnings and analysts' forecasts, is very important. The authors examined a variety of motivations for why managers might "exercise accounting discretion to achieve some desirable earnings goal." Motivations to meet earnings benchmarks include equity market effects (e.g., building credibility with market participants and positively affecting stock price) and trade effects (e.g., enhancing reputation with customers and suppliers). Equity market effects are the most powerful incentives, but trade effects are important, particularly for smaller companies.

13 SEC, "Commission Guidance Regarding Management's Discussion and Analysis of Financial Condition and Results of Operations," Financial Reporting Release (FRR) No. 72 (2003), www.sec.gov/rules/interp/33-8350.htm.

- Career concerns and incentive compensation may motivate accounting choices. For example, managers might be concerned that working for a company that performs poorly will limit their future career opportunities or that they will not receive a bonus based on exceeding a particular earnings target. In both cases, management might be motivated to make accounting choices to increase earnings. In a period of marginally poor performance, a manager might accelerate or inflate revenues or delay or under-report expenses. Conversely, in a period of strong performance, a manager might delay revenue recognition or accelerate expense recognition to increase the probability of exceeding the next period's targets (i.e., to "bank" some earnings for the next period.) The surveyed managers indicated a greater concern with career implications of reported results than with incentive compensation implications.

Avoiding debt covenant violations can motivate managers to inflate earnings. Graham, Harvey, and Rajgopal's survey indicates that avoidance of bond covenant violation is important to highly leveraged and unprofitable companies but relatively unimportant overall.

Conditions Conducive to Issuing Low-Quality Financial Reports

As discussed, deviations from a neutral presentation of financial results could be driven by management choices or by a jurisdiction's financial reporting standards. Ultimately, a decision to issue low-quality, or even fraudulent, financial reports is made by an individual or individuals. Why individuals make such choices is not always immediately apparent. For example, why would the newly appointed CEO of Sunbeam, who already had a net worth of more than USD100 million, commit accounting fraud by improperly reporting revenues from "bill-and-hold" sales and manipulating the timing of expenses, rather than admit to lower-than-expected financial results?

Typically, three conditions exist when low-quality financial reports are issued: opportunity, pressure or motivation, and rationalization—sometimes referred to as the **fraud triangle**. Opportunity can be the result of internal conditions, such as poor internal controls or an ineffective board of directors, or external conditions, such as accounting standards that provide scope for divergent choices or minimal consequences for an inappropriate choice. Motivation can result from pressure to meet some criteria for personal reasons, such as a bonus, or corporate reasons, such as concern about financing in the future. Rationalization is important because if a decision maker is concerned about a choice, that person needs to be able to justify it to him- or herself.

Former Enron CFO Andrew Fastow, speaking at the 2013 Association of Certified Fraud Examiners Annual Fraud Conference, indicated that he knew at the time he was doing something wrong but followed procedure to justify his decision (Pavlo, 2013). He made sure to get management and board approval, as well as legal and accounting opinions, and to include appropriate disclosures. The incentive and corporate culture was to create earnings rather than focus on long-term value. Clearly, as reflected in his prison sentence, he did something that was not only wrong but illegal.

MECHANISMS THAT DISCIPLINE FINANCIAL REPORTING QUALITY

8

☐ describe mechanisms that discipline financial reporting quality and the potential limitations of those mechanisms

Markets may discipline poor financial reporting quality. Companies and nations compete for capital, and the cost of capital is a function of perceived risk—including the risk that a company's financial statements will skew investors' expectations. Thus, in the absence of other conflicting economic incentives, a company seeking to minimize its long-term cost of capital should aim to provide high-quality financial reports. In addition to markets, other mechanisms that discipline financial reporting quality include market regulatory authorities, auditors, and private contracts.

Market Regulatory Authorities

Companies seeking to minimize the cost of capital should maximize reporting quality, but as discussed earlier, conflicting incentives often exist. For this reason, national regulations, and the regulators that establish and enforce rules, can play a significant role in financial reporting quality. Many of the world's securities regulators are members of the International Organization of Securities Commissions (IOSCO). IOSCO is recognized as the "global standard setter for the securities sector" although it does not actually set standards but rather establishes objectives and principles to guide securities and capital market regulation. IOSCO's membership includes more than 120 securities regulators and 80 other securities market participants, such as stock exchanges.[14]

One member of IOSCO is The European Securities and Markets Authority (ESMA), an independent EU authority with a mission to "enhance the protection of investors and reinforce stable and well-functioning financial markets in the European Union."[15] ESMA organizes financial reporting enforcement activities through a forum consisting of European enforcers from European Economic Area countries. Direct supervision and enforcement activities are performed at the national level. For example, the Financial Conduct Authority (FCA) is the IOSCO member with primary responsibility for securities regulation in the United Kingdom. ESMA reported that European enforcers examined the interim or annual financial statements of 1,141 issuers in 2017, which in turn led to enforcement actions for 328 issuers with the following outcomes: 12 required reissuances of financial statements, 71 required public corrective notes, and 245 required corrections to be made in future financial statements.[16]

Another member of IOSCO is the US regulatory authority, the Securities and Exchange Commission. The SEC is responsible for overseeing approximately 9,100 US public companies (along with investment advisers, broker/dealers, securities exchanges, and other entities) and reviews the disclosures of these companies at least once every three years with the aim of improving information available to investors

14 Visit www.iosco.org for more information.
15 Text from ESMA's mission statement on their website: www.esma.europa.eu.
16 ESMA, "Enforcement and Regulatory Activities of Accounting Enforcers in 2017," ESMA32-63-424, European Securities and Markets Authority (3 April 2018), www.esma.europa.eu.

and potentially uncovering possible violations of securities laws.[17] In 2017, the SEC reported that it had filed 754 total and 446 standalone enforcement actions, about 20 percent of which concerned issuer reporting or accounting and auditing.[18]

Examples of regulatory bodies in Asia include the Financial Services Agency in Japan, the China Securities Regulatory Commission, and the Securities and Exchange Board of India. Examples of regulatory bodies in South America include the Comisión Nacional de Valores in Argentina, Comissão de Valores Mobiliários in Brazil, and Comisión para el Mercado Financiero in Chile. A full list of IOSCO members can be found on the organization's website.

Typical features of a regulatory regime that most directly affect financial reporting quality include the following:

- *Registration requirements.* Market regulators typically require publicly traded companies to register securities before offering the securities for sale to the public. A registration document typically contains current financial statements, other relevant information about the risks and prospects of the company issuing the securities, and information about the securities being offered.
- *Disclosure requirements.* Market regulators typically require publicly traded companies to make public periodic reports, including financial reports and management comments. Standard-setting bodies, such as the IASB and FASB, are typically private sector, self-regulated organizations with board members who are experienced accountants, auditors, users of financial statements, and academics. Regulatory authorities, such as the Accounting and Corporate Regulatory Authority in Singapore, the Securities and Exchange Commission in the United States, the Securities and Exchange Commission in Brazil, and the Financial Reporting Council in the United Kingdom, have the legal authority to enforce financial reporting requirements and exert other controls over entities that participate in the capital markets within their jurisdiction. In other words, *generally*, standard-setting bodies set the standards, and regulatory authorities recognize and enforce those standards. Without the recognition of standards by regulatory authorities, the private-sector standard-setting bodies would have no authority. Regulators often retain the legal authority to establish financial reporting standards in their jurisdiction and can overrule the private-sector standard-setting bodies.
- *Auditing requirements.* Market regulators typically require companies' financial statements to be accompanied by an audit opinion attesting that the financial statements conform to the relevant set of accounting standards. Some regulators, such as the SEC in the United States, require an additional audit opinion attesting to the effectiveness of the company's internal controls over financial reporting.
- *Management commentaries.* Regulations typically require publicly traded companies' financial reports to include statements by management. For example, the FCA in the United Kingdom requires a management report containing "(1) a fair review of the issuer's business; and (2) a description of the principal risks and uncertainties facing the issuer" (Disclosure Guidance and Transparency Rules sourcebook).

17 SEC, "FY2013 Congressional Justification," Securities and Exchange Commission (February 2012), www.sec.gov/about/secfy13congbudgjust.pdf.

18 SEC, Securities and Exchange Commission Division of Enforcement Annual Report, "A Look Back at Fiscal Year 2017," www.sec.gov/report.

- *Responsibility statements.* Regulations typically require a statement from the person or persons responsible for the company's filings. Such statements require the responsible individuals to explicitly acknowledge responsibility and to attest to the correctness of the financial reports. Some regulators, such as the SEC in the United States, require formal certifications that carry specific legal penalties for false certifications.
- *Regulatory review of filings.* Regulators typically undertake a review process to ensure that the rules have been followed. The review process typically covers all initial registrations and a sample of subsequent periodic financial reports.
- *Enforcement mechanisms.* Regulators are granted various powers to enforce the securities market rules. Such powers can include assessing fines, suspending or permanently barring market participants, and bringing criminal prosecutions. Public announcements of disciplinary actions are also a type of enforcement mechanism.

In summary, market regulatory authorities play a central role in encouraging high-quality financial reporting.

Auditors

As noted, regulatory authorities typically require that publicly traded companies' financial statements be audited by an independent auditor. Private companies also obtain audit opinions for their financial statements, either voluntarily or because audit reports are required by an outside party, such as providers of debt or equity capital.

Audit opinions provide financial statement users with some assurance that the information complies with the relevant set of accounting standards and presents the company's information fairly. Exhibit 8 , Exhibit 9, Exhibit 10, and Exhibit 11 provide excerpts from the independent auditors' reports for GlaxoSmithKline plc, Alibaba Group Holding Limited, Apple Inc., and Tata Motors Limited, respectively. For each company, the auditor issued an unqualified opinion on the financial statements, indicating that the financial statements present fairly the company's performance in accordance with relevant standards. (Note: The term "unqualified opinion" means that the opinion did not include any qualifications or exceptions; the term is synonymous with the less formal term "clean opinion." Unqualified opinions are the most common opinions issued.) Other items in the audit reports reflect the specific requirements of the company's regulatory regime. For example, the audit report for GlaxoSmithKline spans nine pages and includes opinions on the company's financial statements as well as the Strategic Report and the Directors' Report. This audit report also includes disclosures about "Key audit matters," in accordance with International Standards on Auditing (ISAs) issued by the International Auditing and Assurance Standards Board (IAASB) in 2015 and effective for periods ending on or after 15 December 2016.

The excerpts for Alibaba, Apple, and Tata Motors show the auditors' opinions on the companies' financial statements and additionally the SEC-required opinions on the effectiveness of the companies' internal controls because these companies are listed in the United States. For Alibaba, a single report includes both unqualified opinions: (1) the financial statements present fairly the financial position, results of operations, and cash flows . . . in conformity with US GAAP; and (2) the company maintained effective control over financial reporting. For Apple, the first report includes the unqualified opinion on the financial statements, and the second report includes the unqualified opinion on the company's effective internal controls. For Tata Motors, the first report includes the unqualified opinion that the financial statements present the company's position and results fairly in accordance with IFRS. (The SEC permits non-US companies to report using US GAAP, IFRS as issued by the IASB, or home-country GAAP.) However, the second report includes an *adverse* opinion on the effectiveness of the company's internal controls: "In our opinion, because of the effect of the material weakness . . . the company has not maintained effective internal control." The report explains that the material weakness involved a third party's inappropriate access to the company's systems. The report further states that although the material weakness resulted in ineffective internal controls, it did not affect the audit opinion on the financial statements. Elsewhere in Tata Motors' annual report (not shown in the excerpt), the company discloses that the weakness did not result in misstatement and that it has undertaken remedial measures.

Exhibit 8: Excerpt from Audit Opinion of PricewaterhouseCoopers LLP from the 2017 Annual Report *(pages 149–157)* of GlaxoSmithKline plc

In our opinion, GlaxoSmithKline e Group financial statements (the "financial statements"):

- give a true and fair view of the state of the Group's affairs as at 31 December 2017 and of its profit and cash flows for the year then ended;
- have been properly prepared in accordance with International Financial Reporting Standards ("IFRSs") as adopted by the European Union; and
- have been prepared in accordance with the requirements of the Companies Act 2006 and Article 4 of the IAS Regulation.

...

In our opinion, the Group financial statements have been properly prepared in accordance with IFRSs as issued by the IASB.

...

Key audit matters

Key audit matters are those matters that, in the auditors' professional judgement, were of most significance in the audit of the financial statements of the current period and include the most significant assessed risks of material misstatement (whether or not due to fraud) identified by the auditors, including those which had the greatest effect on: the overall audit strategy; the allocation of resources in the audit; and directing the efforts of the engagement team. These matters, and any comments we make on the results of our procedures thereon, were addressed in the context of our audit of the financial statements as a whole, and in forming our opinion thereon, and we do not provide a separate opinion on these matters. This is not a complete list of all risks identified by our audit.

...

In our opinion, based on the work undertaken in the course of the audit, the information given in the Strategic Report and Directors' Report for the year ended 31 December 2017 is consistent with the financial statements and has been prepared in accordance with applicable legal requirements.

Exhibit 9: Excerpt from Audit Opinion of PricewaterhouseCoopers Hong Kong, SAR from the Annual Report *(SEC Form 20-F, pages F-2 and F-3)* of Alibaba Group Holding Limited for the year ended 31 March 2018

In our opinion, the consolidated financial statements referred to above present fairly, in all material respects, the financial position of the Company as of March 31, 2017 and 2018, and the results of their operations and their cash flows for each of the three years in the period ended March 31, 2018 in conformity with accounting principles generally accepted in the United States of America. Also in our opinion, the Company maintained, in all material respects, effective internal control over financial reporting as of March 31, 2018, based on criteria established in Internal Control — Integrated Framework (2013) issued by the COSO.

Exhibit 10: Excerpt from Audit Opinion of Ernst & Young from the Annual Report (*SEC Form 10-K, pages 70 and 71*) of Apple Inc. for the year ended 30 September 30 2017

[From the Financial Statement Opinion]

We have audited the accompanying consolidated balance sheets of Apple Inc. as of September 30, 2017 and September 24, 2016, and the related consolidated statements of operations, comprehensive income, shareholders' equity and cash flows for each of the three years in the period ended September 30, 2017.

...

In our opinion, the financial statements referred to above present fairly, in all material respects, the consolidated financial position of Apple Inc. at September 30, 2017 and September 24, 2016, and the consolidated results of its operations and its cash flows for each of the three years in the period ended September 30, 2017, in conformity with U.S. generally accepted accounting principles.

We also have audited, in accordance with the standards of the Public Company Accounting Oversight Board (United States), Apple Inc.'s internal control over financial reporting as of September 30, 2017, based on criteria established in Internal Control – Integrated Framework issued by the Committee of Sponsoring Organizations of the Treadway Commission (2013 framework) and our report dated November 3, 2017 expressed an unqualified opinion thereon.

[From the Internal Controls Opinion]

We have audited Apple Inc.'s internal control over financial reporting as of September 30, 2017, based on criteria established in Internal Control – Integrated Framework issued by the Committee of Sponsoring Organizations of the Treadway Commission (2013 framework) ("the COSO criteria").

...

In our opinion, Apple Inc. maintained, in all material respects, effective internal control over financial reporting as of September 30, 2017, based on the COSO criteria.

We also have audited, in accordance with the standards of the Public Company Accounting Oversight Board (United States), the 2017 consolidated financial statements of Apple Inc. and our report dated November 3, 2017 expressed an unqualified opinion thereon.

Exhibit 11: Excerpt from Audit Opinion of KPMG Mumbai, India from the Annual Report (*SEC Form 20-F, pages F2 to F4*) of Tata Motors Limited for the year ended 31 March 2018

Opinion on the Consolidated Financial Statements

We have audited the accompanying consolidated balance sheet of Tata Motors Limited and its subsidiaries (the "Company") as of March 31, 2018, the related consolidated income statement, statement of comprehensive income, statement of cash flows, and statement of changes in equity for the year ended March 31, 2018, and the related notes and financial statement schedule 1 (collectively, the consolidated financial statements).

In our opinion, the consolidated financial statements present fairly, in all material respects, the financial position of the Company as of March 31, 2018, and the results of its operations and its cash flows for the year ended March 31, 2018, in conformity with the International Financial Reporting Standards as issued by the International Accounting Standards Board ("IFRS").

We also have audited, in accordance with the standards of the Public Company Accounting Oversight Board (United States) (PCAOB), the Company's internal control over financial reporting as of March 31, 2018, based on criteria established in Internal Control – Integrated Framework (2013) issued by the Committee of Sponsoring Organizations of the Treadway Commission, and our report dated July, 31, 2018 expressed an adverse opinion on the effectiveness of the Company's internal control over financial reporting.

...

Opinion on Internal Control Over Financial Reporting

We have audited Tata Motors Limited's and subsidiaries' (the Company) internal control over financial reporting as of March 31, 2018, based on criteria established in Internal Control – Integrated Framework (2013) issued by the Committee of Sponsoring Organizations of the Treadway Commission. In our opinion, because of the effect of the material weakness described below, on the achievement of the objectives of the control criteria, the Company has not maintained effective internal control over financial reporting as of March 31, 2018, based on criteria established in *Internal Control – Integrated Framework (2013)* issued by the Committee of Sponsoring Organizations of the Treadway Commission.

...

A material weakness is a deficiency, or a combination of deficiencies, in internal control over financial reporting, such that there is a reasonable possibility that a material misstatement of the company's annual or interim financial statements will not be prevented or detected on a timely basis. A material weakness related to inappropriate system access restrictions at a third party logistics provider has been identified and included in management's assessment. The material weakness was considered in determining the nature, timing, and extent of audit tests applied in our audit of the 2018 consolidated financial statements, and this report does not affect our report on those consolidated financial statements.

Although audit opinions provide discipline for financial reporting quality, inherent limitations exist. First, an audit opinion is based on a review of information prepared by the company. If a company deliberately intends to deceive its auditor, a review of information might not uncover misstatements. Second, an audit is based on sampling, and the sample might not reveal misstatements. Third, an "expectations gap" may exist between the auditor's role and the public's expectation of auditors. An audit is not typically intended to detect fraud; it is intended to provide assurance that the financial reports are fairly presented. Finally, the company being audited pays the audit fees, often established through a competitive process. This situation could provide an auditor with an incentive to show leniency to the company being audited, particularly if the auditor's firm provides additional services to the company.

Private Contracting

Aspects of private contracts, such as loan agreements or investment contracts, can also serve as mechanisms to discipline poor financial reporting quality. Many parties that have a contractual arrangement with a company have an incentive to monitor that company's performance and to ensure that the company's financial reports are high quality. For example, loan agreements often contain loan covenants, which create specifically tailored financial reporting requirements that are legally binding for the issuer. As noted earlier, avoidance of debt covenant violation is a potential motivation for managers to inflate earnings. As another example, an investment contract could contain provisions giving investors the option to recover all or part of their investment if certain financial triggers occur. Such provisions could motivate the investee's managers to manipulate reported results to avoid the financial triggers.

Because the financial reports prepared by the investees or borrowers directly affect the contractual outcomes—potentially creating a motivation for misreporting—investors and lenders are motivated to monitor financial reports and to ensure that they are high quality.

EXAMPLE 4

Financial Reporting Manipulation: Motivations and Disciplining Mechanisms

For each of the following two scenarios, identify (1) factors that might motivate the company's managers to manipulate reported financial amounts and (2) applicable mechanisms that could discipline poor financial reporting quality.

1. ABC Co. is a private company. Bank NTBig has made a loan to ABC Co. ABC is required to maintain a minimum 2.0 interest coverage ratio. In its most recent financial reports, ABC reported earnings before interest and taxes of USD1,200 and interest expense of USD600. In the report's notes, the company discloses that it changed the estimated useful life of its property, plant, and equipment during the year. Depreciation was approximately USD150 lower as a result of this change in estimate.

   Solution:

   The need to maintain a minimum interest coverage ratio of 2.0 might motivate ABC's managers to manipulate reported financial amounts. The company's coverage ratio based on the reported amounts is exactly equal to 2.0. If ABC's managers had not changed the estimated useful life of the property, plant, and equipment, the coverage ratio would have fallen below the required level.

EBIT, as reported	USD1,200
Impact on depreciation expense of changed assumptions about useful life	150
EBIT, as adjusted	USD1,050
Interest expense	USD600
Coverage ratio, as reported	2.00
Coverage ratio, as adjusted	1.75

The potential disciplining mechanisms include the auditors, who will assess the reasonableness of the depreciable lives estimates. In addition, the lenders will carefully scrutinize the change in estimate because the company only barely achieved the minimum coverage ratio and would not have achieved the minimum without the change in accounting estimate.

2. DEF Co. is a publicly traded company. For the most recent quarter, the average of analysts' forecasts for earnings per share was USD2.50. In its quarterly earnings announcement, DEF reported net income of USD3,458,780. The number of common shares outstanding was 1,378,000. DEF's main product is a hardware device that includes a free two-year service contract in the selling price. Based on management estimates, the company allocates a portion of revenues to the hardware device, which it recognizes immediately, and a portion to the service contract, which it defers and recognizes over the two years of the contract. Based on the disclosures, a higher percentage of revenue was allocated to hardware than in the past, with an estimated after-tax impact on net income of USD27,000.

   Solution:

   The desire to meet or exceed the average of analysts' forecasts for earnings per share might motivate DEF Co.'s managers to manipulate reported financial amounts. As illustrated in the following calculations, the impact of allocating a greater portion of revenue to hardware enabled the company to exceed analysts' earnings per share forecasts by USD0.01.

Net income, as reported	USD3,458,780
Impact on gross profit of changed revenue recognition, net of tax	27,000
Net income, as adjusted	USD3,431,780
Weighted average number of shares	1,378,000
Earnings per share, as reported	USD2.51
Earnings per share, as adjusted	USD2.49

Potential disciplining mechanisms include the auditors, market regulators, financial analysts, and financial journalists.

9 DETECTION OF FINANCIAL REPORTING QUALITY ISSUES: INTRODUCTION AND PRESENTATION CHOICES

☐ describe presentation choices, including non-GAAP measures, that could be used to influence an analyst's opinion

Choices in the application of accounting standards abound, which is perhaps one reason why accounting literature and texts are so voluminous. Compounding the complexity, measurement often depends on estimates of economic phenomena. Two estimates might be justifiable, but they may have significantly different effects on the company's financial statements. As discussed earlier, the choice of a particular estimate may depend on the motivations of the reporting company's managers. With many choices available, and the inherent flexibility of estimates in the accounting process, managers have many tools for managing and meeting analysts' expectations through financial reporting.

An understanding of the choices that companies make in financial reporting is fundamental to evaluating the overall quality—both financial reporting and earnings quality—of the reports produced. Choices exist both in how information is presented (financial reporting quality) and in how financial results are calculated (earnings quality). Choices in presentation (financial reporting quality) may be transparent to investors. Choices in the calculation of financial results (earnings quality), however, are more difficult to discern because they can be deeply embedded in the construction of reported financial results.

The availability of accounting choices enables managers to affect the reporting of financial results. Some choices increase performance and financial position in the reporting period (aggressive choices), and others increase them in later periods (conservative choices). A manager who wants to increase performance and financial position in the reporting period could:

- recognize revenue prematurely;
- use non-recurring transactions to increase profits;
- defer expenses to later periods;
- measure and report assets at higher values; and/or
- measure and report liabilities at lower values.
- A manager who wants to increase performance and financial position in a later period could:
- defer current income to a later period (save income for a "rainy day"); and/or
- recognize future expenses in a current period, setting the table for improving future performance.

This lesson describes some of the potential choices for how information is presented and how accounting elements [assets, liabilities, owners' equity, revenue and gains (income), and expenses and losses] are recognized, measured, and reported. In addition to choices within GAAP, companies may prepare fraudulent reports. For example, these reports may include non-existent revenue or assets. Later lessons discuss warning signs that may indicate poor-quality financial reports.

Presentation Choices

The technology boom of the 1990s and the internet bubble of the early 2000s featured companies, popular with investors, that often shared the same characteristic: They could not generate enough current earnings to justify their stock prices using the traditional price-to-earnings ratio (P/E) approaches to valuation. Many investors chose to explain these apparent anomalies by rationalizing that the old focus on profits and traditional valuation approaches no longer applied to such companies. Strange new metrics for determining operating performance emerged. Website operators spoke of the "eyeballs" they had captured in a quarter, or the "stickiness" of their websites for web surfers' visits. Various versions of "pro forma earnings"—that is, "non-GAAP earnings measures"—became a financial reporting staple of the era.

Many technology companies were accomplished practitioners of pro forma reporting, but they were not the first to use it. In the early 1990s, downsizing of large companies was a commonplace event, and massive restructuring charges obscured the operating performance at many established companies. For example, as it learned to cope in a world that embraced the personal computer rather than mainframe computing, International Business Machines (IBM) reported massive restructuring charges in 1991, 1992, and 1993: USD3.7 billion, USD11.6 billion, and USD8.9 billion, respectively. IBM was not alone. Sears incurred USD2.7 billion of restructuring charges in 1993, and AT&T reported restructuring charges of USD7.7 billion in 1995. These events were not isolated; restructuring charges were a standard quarterly reporting event. To counter perceptions that their operations were floundering, and supposedly to assist investors in evaluating operating performance, companies often sanitized earnings releases by excluding restructuring charges in pro forma measures of financial performance.

Accounting principles for reporting business combinations also played a role in boosting the popularity of pro forma earnings. Before 2001, acquisitions of one company by another often resulted in goodwill amortization charges that made subsequent earnings reports look weak. Complicating matters, there were two accounting methods for recording acquisitions: pooling-of-interests and purchase methods. The now-extinct pooling-of-interests treatment was difficult for companies to achieve because of the many restrictive criteria for its use, but it was greatly desired because it did not result in goodwill amortization charges. In the technology boom period, acquisitions were common and many were reported as purchases, with consequential goodwill amortization dragging down earnings for as long as 40 years under the then-existing rules. Acquisitive companies reporting under purchase accounting standards perceived themselves to be at a reporting disadvantage compared with companies able to apply pooling-of-interests. They responded by presenting earnings adjusted for the exclusion of amortization of intangible assets and goodwill.

Because investors try to make intercompany comparisons on a consistent basis, earnings before interest, taxes, depreciation, and amortization (EBITDA) has become an extremely popular performance measure. EBITDA is widely viewed as eliminating noisy reporting signals. That noise may be introduced by different accounting methods among companies for depreciation, amortization of intangible assets, and restructuring charges. Companies may construct and report their own version of EBITDA, sometimes referring to it as "adjusted EBITDA," by adding to the list of items to exclude from net income. Items that analysts might encounter include the following:

- rental payments for operating leases, resulting in EBITDAR (earnings before interest, taxes, depreciation, amortization, and rentals);
- equity-based compensation, usually justified on the grounds that it is a non-cash expense;
- acquisition-related charges;
- impairment charges for goodwill or other intangible assets;
- impairment charges for long-lived assets;
- litigation costs; and
- loss/gain on debt extinguishments.

Among other incentives for the spread of non-GAAP earnings measures are loan covenants. Lenders may make demands on a borrowing company that require achieving and maintaining performance criteria that use GAAP net income as a starting point but arrive at a measure suitable to the lender. The company may use this measure as its preferred non-GAAP metric in earnings releases and also when describing its liquidity or solvency situation in the management commentary (called management discussion and analysis in the United States).

As mentioned earlier, if a company uses a non-GAAP financial measure in an SEC filing, it must display the most directly comparable GAAP measure with equal prominence and provide a reconciliation between the two. Management must explain why it believes that the non-GAAP financial measure provides useful information regarding the company's financial condition and operations. Management must also disclose additional purposes, if material, for which it uses the non-GAAP financial measures.

Similarly, IFRS requires a definition and explanation of any non-IFRS measures included in financial reports, including why the measure is potentially relevant to users. Management must provide reconciliations of non-IFRS measures with IFRS measures. The concern is that management may use non-GAAP measures to distract attention from GAAP measures.

The SEC intended that the definition of non-GAAP financial measures would capture all measures with the effect of depicting either:

- a measure of performance that differs from that presented in the financial statements, such as income or loss before taxes or net income or loss, as calculated in accordance with GAAP; or
- a measure of liquidity that differs from cash flow or cash flow from operations computed in accordance with GAAP.[19]

The SEC prohibits the exclusion of charges or liabilities requiring cash settlement from any non-GAAP liquidity measures, other than EBIT and EBITDA. Also prohibited is the calculation of a non-GAAP performance measure intended to eliminate or smooth items tagged as non-recurring, infrequent, or unusual when such items are very likely to occur again. The SEC views the period within two years of either before or after the reporting date as the relevant time frame for considering whether a charge or gain is a recurring item. Example 5 describes a case of misuse and misreporting of non-GAAP measures.

EXAMPLE 5

Misuse and Misreporting of Non-GAAP Measures

Groupon is an online discount merchant. In the company's initial S-1 registration statement in 2011, then-CEO Andrew Mason gave prospective investors an upfront warning in a section entitled "We don't measure ourselves in conventional ways", which described Groupon's adjusted consolidated segment operating income (adjusted CSOI) measure. Exhibit 12 provides excerpts from a section entitled "Non-GAAP Financial Measures," which offered a more detailed explanation. Exhibit 13, also from the initial registration statement, shows a reconciliation of CSOI to the most comparable US GAAP measure. In its review, the SEC took the position that online marketing expenses were a recurring cost of business. Groupon responded that the marketing costs were similar to acquisition costs, not recurring costs, and that "we'll ramp down marketing just as fast as we ramped it up, reducing the customer acquisition part of our marketing expenses" as time passes.[20]

Eventually, and after much negative publicity, Groupon changed its non-GAAP measure. Exhibit 14 shows an excerpt from the final prospectus filed in November, after the SEC's review. Use the three exhibits to answer the questions that follow.

Exhibit 12: Groupon's "Non-GAAP Financial Measures"

Disclosures from June S-1 Filing

19 SEC, "Final Rule: Conditions for Use of Non-GAAP Financial Measures," Securities and Exchange Commission, www.sec.gov/rules/final/33-8176.htm.

20 Correspondence between Groupon and SEC, filed in EDGAR on 16 September 2011.

Adjusted CSOI is operating income of our two segments, North America and International, adjusted for online marketing expense, acquisition-related costs and stock-based compensation expense. Online marketing expense primarily represents the cost to acquire new subscribers and is dictated by the amount of growth we wish to pursue. Acquisition-related costs are non-recurring non-cash items related to certain of our acquisitions. Stock-based compensation expense is a non-cash item. We consider Adjusted CSOI to be an important measure of the performance of our business as it excludes expenses that are non-cash or otherwise not indicative of future operating expenses. We believe it is important to view Adjusted CSOI as a complement to our entire consolidated statements of operations.

Our use of Adjusted CSOI has limitations as an analytical tool, and you should not consider this measure in isolation or as a substitute for analysis of our results as reported under GAAP. Some of these limitations are:

- Adjusted CSOI does not reflect the significant cash investments that we currently are making to acquire new subscribers;
- Adjusted CSOI does not reflect the potentially dilutive impact of issuing equity-based compensation to our management team and employees or in connection with acquisitions;
- Adjusted CSOI does not reflect any interest expense or the cash requirements necessary to service interest or principal payments on any indebtedness that we may incur;
- Adjusted CSOI does not reflect any foreign exchange gains and losses;
- Adjusted CSOI does not reflect any tax payments that we might make, which would represent a reduction in cash available to us;
- Adjusted CSOI does not reflect changes in, or cash requirements for, our working capital needs; and
- Other companies, including companies in our industry, may calculate Adjusted CSOI differently or may use other financial measures to evaluate their profitability, which reduces the usefulness of it as a comparative measure.

Because of these limitations, Adjusted CSOI should not be considered as a measure of discretionary cash available to us to invest in the growth of our business. When evaluating our performance, you should consider Adjusted CSOI alongside other financial performance measures, including various cash flow metrics, net loss and our other GAAP results.

Exhibit 13: Groupon's Adjusted CSOI

Excerpt from June S-1 Filing

The following is a reconciliation of CSOI to the most comparable US GAAP measure, "loss from operations," for the years ended December 31, 2008, 2009, and 2010 and the three months ended March 31, 2010 and 2011:

(in USD thousands)	Year Ended 31 December			Three Months Ended 31 March	
	2008	2009	2010	2010	2011
(Loss) Income from operations	(1,632)	(1,077)	(420,344)	8,571	(117,148)
Adjustments:					
Online marketing	162	4,446	241,546	3,904	179,903
Stock-based compensation	24	115	36,168	116	18,864
Acquisition-related	—	—	**203,183**	—	—
Total adjustments	186	4,561	480,897	4,020	198,767
Adjusted CSOI	(1,446)	3,484	60,553	12,591	81,619

Exhibit 14: Groupon's CSOI

Excerpt from Revised S-1 Filing

The following is a reconciliation of CSOI to the most comparable US GAAP measure, "loss from operations," for the years ended December 31, 2008, 2009, and 2010 and the nine months ended September 30, 2010 and 2011:

(in USD thousands)	Year Ended 31 December			Nine Months Ended 30 September	
	2008	2009	2010	2010	2011
Loss from operations	(1,632)	(1,077)	(420,344)	(84,215)	(218,414)
Adjustments:					
Stock-based compensation	24	115	36,168	8,739	60,922
Acquisition-related	—	—	203,183	37,844	(4,793)
Total adjustments	24	115	239,351	46,583	56,129
CSOI	(1,608)	(962)	(180,993)	(37,632)	(162,285)

1. What cautions did Groupon include along with its description of the adjusted CSOI metric?

Solution:

Groupon cautioned that the adjusted CSOI metric should not be considered in isolation, should not be considered as a substitute for analysis using GAAP results, and "should not be considered a measure of discretionary cash flow." The company lists numerous limitations, primarily citing items that adjusted CSOI did not reflect.

2. Groupon excludes "online marketing" from adjusted CSOI. How does the exclusion of this expense compare with the SEC's limits on non-GAAP performance measures?

   Solution:

   The SEC specifies that non-GAAP measures should not eliminate items tagged as non-recurring, infrequent, or unusual when such items may be very likely to occur again. Because the online marketing expense occurred in every period reported and is likely to occur again, exclusion of this item appears contrary to SEC requirements.

3. In the first quarter of 2011, what was the effect of excluding online marketing expenses on the calculation of adjusted CSOI?

   Solution:

   As shown in Exhibit 13, in the first quarter of 2011, the exclusion of the online marketing expense was enough to swing the company from a net loss under US GAAP reporting to a profit—at least, a profit as defined by adjusted CSOI. Using adjusted CSOI as a performance measure, the company showed results that were 35 percent higher for the first *quarter* of 2011 compared with the entire previous *year*.

4. For 2010, how did results under the revised non-GAAP metric compare with the originally reported metric?

   Solution:

   As shown in Exhibit 14, the revised metric is now called CSOI and no longer refers to adjusted CSOI. For 2010, results under the revised non-GAAP metric, which includes online marketing costs, shows a loss of USD180,993,000 instead of a profit of USD60,553,000.

In Example 5, Groupon changed its reporting and corrected the non-GAAP metric that the SEC had identified as misleading. In other cases, the SEC has pursued enforcement actions against companies for reporting misleading non-GAAP information. One such action was brought in 2009 against SafeNet Inc., in which the SEC charged the company with improperly classifying ordinary operating expenses as non-recurring. This related to the integration of an acquired company and exclusion of the expenses from non-GAAP earnings to exceed earnings targets. A second action was brought by the SEC in 2017 against MDC Partners Inc. (MDCA) for improper reconciliation of a non-GAAP measure and for improperly displaying the non-GAAP measure with greater prominence in its earnings releases. The case was brought after the company agreed to follow the rules but then failed to do so, as evidenced by the remark in the SEC's action: "Despite agreeing to comply with non-GAAP financial measure disclosure rules in December 2012 correspondence with the [SEC's] Division of Corporation Finance, MDCA continued to violate those rules for six quarters." Exhibit 15 presents the headline and subheadings for one of MDC Partners' earnings announcements that was the subject of the enforcement action.

Exhibit 15: Excerpt from MDC Partners Inc. Press Release

This excerpt shows the headline, subheads, and lead sentence of the company's press release announcing periodic earnings.

SEC Form 8-K filed 24 April 2014

MDC PARTNERS INC. REPORTS RECORD RESULTS FOR THE THREE MONTHS ENDED MARCH 31, 2014

ORGANIC REVENUE GROWTH OF 8.3%, EBITDA GROWTH OF 18.1% AND 90 BASIS POINTS OF MARGIN IMPROVEMENT

FREE CASH FLOW GROWTH OF 34.0%

INCREASED 2014 GUIDANCE IMPLIES YEAR-OVER-YEAR EBITDA GROWTH OF +13.5% TO +16.1%, MARGIN IMPROVEMENT OF 60 TO 70 BASIS POINTS, AND FREE CASH FLOW GROWTH OF +15.8% TO +20.2%

FIRST QUARTER HIGHLIGHTS

- Revenue increased to $292.6 million from $265.6 million, an increase of 10.1%
- Organic revenue increased 8.3%
- EBITDA increased to $36.4 million from $30.8 million, an increase of 18.1%
- EBITDA margin increased 90 basis points to 12.5% from 11.6%
- Free Cash Flow increased to $20.6 million from $15.4 million, an increase of 34.0%
- Net New Business wins totaled $24.4 million

NEW YORK, NY (April 24, 2014) – MDC Partners Inc. (NASDAQ: MDCA; TSX: MDZ.A) today announced financial results for the three months ended March 31, 2014.

...

In general, management may choose to construct non-GAAP financial measures not only to help investors better understand the company's performance but also to paint a more flattering picture of its performance. In some cases, management may attempt to present non-GAAP measures in a way that diverts attention from the standards-compliant financial information that it is required to present.

ACCOUNTING CHOICES AND ESTIMATES

10

☐ describe accounting methods (choices and estimates) that could be used to manage earnings, cash flow, and balance sheet items

Management's accounting policies and choices do not necessarily involve complex accounting standards. Something as simple as the shipping terms for goods delivered to customers can have a profound effect on the timing of revenue. On the last day of the first quarter, suppose a company ships USD10,000 of goods to a customer on the terms "free on board (FOB) shipping point," arriving the next day. This shipping term means that the customer takes title to the goods, and bears the risk of loss, at the time the goods leave the seller's loading dock. Barring any issues with collectability of the receivable, or a likelihood of a return, the seller would be able to recognize revenue on the sale along with the associated profit. That revenue and profit would be recognized in the first quarter of the year. If the point at which the goods' title transfers to the customer is changed to "FOB destination," then the revenue pattern will be completely different. Under these terms, the title—and risk of loss—transfers to the customer when the goods arrive at their destination, which is the customer's address. The seller cannot recognize the sale and profit until the shipment arrives the following day, which is the start of a new accounting period.

A simple change in shipping terms can make the difference between revenue and profits in the reporting period or postponing them until the next period. Shipping terms can also influence management behavior. To "make the numbers," managers might push product out the door prematurely under FOB shipping point arrangements to reflect as much revenue as possible in the reporting period. Alternatively, in the case of an over-abundance of orders, the company could run the risk of exceeding analysts' consensus estimates by a large margin. Management might be uncomfortable with this situation because investors might extrapolate too much from one reporting period in which expectations were exceeded. Management might want to prevent investors from becoming too optimistic and, if possible, delay revenue recognition until the next quarter. This result could be accomplished by fulfilling customer orders by initiating delivery on the last day of the quarter, with shipping terms set as FOB destination. By doing so, title would transfer in the next accounting period. Another possibility in this scenario is that if the customers insisted on FOB shipping point terms, the selling company could simply delay shipment until after the close of the quarter.

This illustration also highlights a difficult distinction for investors to make. A company may use accounting as a tool to aggressively promote earnings growth—as in the example with the premature shipment of goods with FOB shipping point terms—but it may be aggressively managing the business flow by slacking off on shipping goods when business is "too good," as in the second example. In either case, a desired management outcome is obtained by a simple change in shipping terms. Yet, many investors might be inclined to say that the second example is a conservative kind of earnings management and accept it, even though it artificially masks the actual economic activity that occurred at the time.

How Accounting Choices and Estimates Affect Earnings and Balance Sheets

Assumptions about inventory cost flows provide another example of how accounting choices can affect financial reporting. Companies may assume that their purchases of inventory items are sold to customers on a first-in, first-out (FIFO) basis, with the result that the remaining inventory reflects the most recent costs. Alternatively, they may assume that their purchases of inventory items are sold to customers on a weighted-average cost basis. Example 6 makes the point that merely choosing a cost flow assumption can affect profitability.

EXAMPLE 6

Effect of Cost Flow Assumption

A company starts operations with no inventory at the beginning of a fiscal year and makes purchases of a good for resale five times during the period at increasing prices. Each purchase is for the same number of units of the good. The purchases, and the cost of goods available for sale, appear in the following table. Notice that the price per unit has increased by 140 percent by the end of the period.

	Units	Price	Cost
Purchase 1	5	USD100	USD500
Purchase 2	5	150	750
Purchase 3	5	180	900
Purchase 4	5	200	1,000
Purchase 5	5	240	1,200
Cost of goods available for sale			USD4,350

During the period, the company sells, at USD250 each, all of the goods purchased except for five of them. Although the ending inventory consists of five units, the cost attached to those units can vary greatly.

1. What are the ending inventory and cost of goods sold if the company uses the FIFO method of inventory costing?

   Solution:

   The ending inventory and cost of goods sold if the company uses the FIFO method of inventory costing are USD1,200 and USD3,150.

2. What are the ending inventory and cost of goods sold if the company uses the weighted-average method of inventory costing?

   Solution:

   The ending inventory and cost of goods sold if the company uses the weighted-average method of inventory costing are USD870 and USD3,480.

3. Compare cost of goods sold and gross profit calculated under the two methods.

   Solution:

   The following table shows how the choice of inventory costing methods—FIFO versus weighted average—affects the cost of goods sold and gross profit.

Cost Flow Assumption	FIFO	Weighted Average
Cost of goods available for sale	USD4,350	USD4,350
Ending inventory (5 units)	(1,200)	(870)
Cost of goods sold	USD3,150	USD3,480
Sales	USD5,000	USD5,000
Cost of goods sold	3,150	3,480
Gross profit	USD1,850	USD1,520
Gross profit margin	37.0%	30.4%

Note: Average inventory cost is calculated as Cost of goods available for sale/Units purchased = \$4,350/25 = \$174. There are five units in ending inventory, yielding an inventory value of \$870.

Depending on which cost flow assumption the company uses, the end-of-period inventory is either USD870 (under the weighted-average method) or USD1,200 (under FIFO). The choice of method results in a difference of USD330 in gross profit and 6.6 percent in gross profit margin.

The previous example is simplified and extreme for purposes of illustration clarity, but the point is important: Management's choice among acceptable inventory assumptions and methods affects profit. The selection of an inventory costing method is a policy decision, and companies cannot arbitrarily switch from one method to another. The selection does matter to profitability, however, and it also matters to the balance sheet.

In periods of changing prices, the FIFO cost assumption will provide a more current picture of ending inventory value, because the most recent purchases will remain in inventory. The balance sheet will be more relevant to investors. Under the weighted-average cost assumption, however, the balance sheet will display a blend of old and new costs. During inflationary periods, the value of the inventory will be understated: The company will not be able to replenish its inventory at the value shown. At the same time, the weighted-average inventory cost method ensures that the more current costs are shown in cost of sales, making the income statement more relevant than under the FIFO assumption. Trade-offs exist, and investors should be aware of how accounting choices affect financial reports. High-quality financial reporting provides users with sufficient information to assess the effects of accounting choices.

Estimates abound in financial reporting because of the use of accrual accounting, which attempts to show the effects of all economic events on a company during a particular period. Accrual accounting stands in contrast to cash basis accounting, which shows only the cash transactions conducted by a company. Although a high degree of certainty exists with reporting only cash transactions, much information is hidden. For instance, a company with growing revenues that makes the majority of its sales on credit would be understating its revenues for each period if it reported only cash transactions. On an accrual basis, revenues reflect all transactions that occurred, whether they transacted on a cash basis or credit-extended basis. Estimates enter the process because some facts related to events occurring in a particular period might not yet be known. Estimates can be well grounded in reality and applied to present a complete picture of the events affecting a company, or they can be management tools for achieving a desired financial picture.

To illustrate how estimates can affect financial reporting, consider sales made on credit. A company sells USD1,000,000 of merchandise on credit and records the sale just before year end. Under accrual accounting, that amount is included in revenues and accounts receivable. The company's managers know from experience that they will never collect every dollar of the accounts receivable. Past experience is that, on average, only 97 percent of accounts receivable is collected. The company would estimate an amount of the uncollectible accounts at the time the sales occur and record an uncollectible accounts expense of USD30,000, lowering earnings. The other side of the entry would be to establish an allowance for uncollectible accounts of USD30,000. This allowance would be a contra asset account, presented as an offset to accounts receivable. The accounts receivable, net of the allowance for uncollectible accounts, would be stated at USD970,000, which is the amount of cash the company ultimately expects to receive. If cash-basis accounting had been used, no revenues or accounts receivable would have been reported even though sales of merchandise had occurred. Accrual accounting, which contains estimates about future events, provides a much fuller picture of what transpired in the period than pure cash-basis accounting.

Yet, accrual accounting poses temptations to managers to manage the numbers, rather than to manage the business. Suppose a company's managers realize that the company will not meet analysts' consensus estimates in a particular quarter, and further, their bonus pay is dependent on reaching specified earnings targets. By offering special payment terms, or discounts, the managers may induce customers to take delivery of products that they normally would not order, so they could ship the products on FOB shipping point terms and recognize the revenues in the current quarter. They could even be so bold as to ship the goods under those terms even if the customer did not order them, in the hope that the customer would keep them or, at worst, return them in the next accounting period. Their aim would be to move the product off the company's property with FOB shipping point terms.

To further improve earnings in order to meet the consensus estimates, the company's managers might revise their estimate of the uncollectible accounts. The company's collection history shows a typical non-collection rate of 3 percent of sales, but the managers might rationalize the use of a 2 percent non-collection rate. This change will reduce the allowance for uncollectible accounts and the expense reported for the period. The managers might be able to justify the reduction on the grounds that the sales occurred in a part of the country that was experiencing an improved economic outlook, or that the company's collection history had been biased by the inclusion of a prolonged period of economic downturn. Whatever the justification, it would be hard to prove that the new estimate was completely right or wrong until time had passed. Because proof of the reliability of estimates is rarely available at the time the estimate is recorded, managers have a readily available means for manipulating earnings at their discretion.

ConAgra Foods Inc. provides an example of how the allowance for uncollectible accounts may be manipulated to manage earnings.[21] A subsidiary, called United Agri-Products (UAP), engaged in several improper accounting practices, one of them being the understatement of uncollectible account expenses for several years. Exhibit 16 presents an excerpt from the SEC's Accounting and Auditing Enforcement Release.

Exhibit 16: SEC's Accounting and Auditing Enforcement Release Regarding United Agri-Products

Generally, UAP's policy required that accounts which were past due between 90 days and one year should be reserved at 50%, and accounts over one year past due were to be reserved at 100%.

... In FY 1999 and continuing through FY 2000, UAP had substantial bad debt problems. In FY 2000, certain former UAP senior executives were informed that UAP needed to record an additional $50 million of bad debt expense. Certain former UAP senior executives were aware that in FY 1999 the size of the bad debt at certain IOCs had been substantial enough that it could have negatively impacted those IOC's ability to achieve PBT (profits before taxes) targets. In addition, just prior to the end of UAP's FY 2000, the former UAP COO (chief operating officer), in the presence of other UAP employees, ordered that UAP's bad debt reserve be reduced by $7 million in order to assist the Company in meeting its PBT target for the fiscal year.

... At the end of FY 2000, former UAP senior executives reported financial results to ConAgra which they knew, or were reckless in not knowing, overstated UAP's income before income taxes because UAP had failed to record sufficient bad debt expense. The misconduct with respect to bad debt expense caused ConAgra to overstate its reported income before income taxes by $7 million, or 1.13%, in FY 2000. At the Agricultural Products' segment level, the misconduct caused that segment's reported operating profit to be overstated by 5.05%.

Deferred-tax assets provide a similar example of choices in estimates affecting the earnings outcome. Deferred-tax assets may arise when a company reports a net operating loss under tax accounting rules. A company may record a deferred-tax asset based on the expectation that losses in the reporting period will offset expected future

21 Accounting and Auditing Enforcement Release No. 2542, "SEC v. James Charles Blue, Randy Cook, and Victor Campbell,) United States District Court for the District of Colorado, Civ. Action No. 07-CV-00095 REB-MEH (17 January 2007).

profits and reduce the company's future income tax liability. Accounting standards require that the deferred tax asset be reduced by a "valuation allowance" to account for the possibility that the company will not be able to generate enough profit to use all of the available tax benefits.[22]

Assume a company loses EUR1 billion in 2012, generating a net operating loss of the same amount for tax purposes. The company's income tax rate is 25 percent, and it will be able to apply the net operating loss to its taxable income for the next 10 years. The net operating loss results in a deferred tax asset with a nominal value of EUR250 million (25% × EUR1,000,000,000). Initial recognition would result in a deferred tax asset of EUR250 million and a credit to deferred tax expense of EUR250 million. The company must address the question of whether or not the EUR250 million will ever be completely applied to future income. It may be experiencing increased competition and other circumstances that resulted in the EUR1 billion loss, and it may be unreasonable to assume it will have taxable income against which to apply the loss. In fact, the company's managers might believe it is reasonable to assume only that it will survive for five years, and with marginal profitability. The EUR250 million deferred tax asset is thus overstated if no valuation allowance is recorded to offset it.

The managers believe that only EUR100 million of the net operating losses actually will be applied to the company's taxable income. That belief implies that only EUR25 million of the tax benefits will ever be realized. The deferred tax assets reported on the balance sheet should not exceed this amount. The company should record a valuation allowance of EUR225 million, which would offset the deferred tax asset balance of EUR250 million, resulting in a net deferred tax asset balance of EUR25 million. There also would be a EUR225 million credit to the deferred tax provision. It is important to understand that the valuation allowance should be revised whenever facts and circumstances change.

The ultimate value of the deferred tax asset is driven by management's outlook for the future—and that outlook may be influenced by other factors. If the company needs to stay in compliance with debt covenants and needs every euro of value that can be justified by the outlook, its managers may take a more optimistic view of the future and keep the valuation allowance artificially low (in other words, the net deferred tax asset high).

PowerLinx Inc. provides an example of how over-optimism about the realizability of a deferred tax asset can lead to misstated financial reports. PowerLinx was a maker of security video cameras, underwater cameras, and accessories. Aside from fraudulently reporting 90 percent of its fiscal year 2000 revenue, PowerLinx had problems with valuation of its deferred tax assets. Exhibit 17 provides an excerpt from the SEC's Accounting and Auditing Enforcement Release with emphasis added.[23]

Exhibit 17: SEC's Accounting and Auditing Enforcement Release Regarding PowerLinx

PowerLinx improperly recorded on its fiscal year 2000 balance sheet a deferred tax asset of $1,439,322 without any valuation allowance. The tax asset was material, representing almost forty percent of PowerLinx's total assets of $3,841,944. PowerLinx also recorded deferred tax assets of $180,613, $72,907, and $44,921, respectively, in its financial statements for the first three quarters of 2000.

22 See Accounting Standards Codification (ASC) 740-10-30-16 to 25, *Establishment of a Valuation Allowance for Deferred Tax Assets.*

23 Accounting and Auditing Enforcement Release No. 2448, "In the Matter of Douglas R. Bauer, Respondent," SEC (27 June 2006), www.sec.gov/litigation/admin/2006/34-54049.pdf.

PowerLinx did not have a proper basis for recording the deferred tax assets. The company had accumulated significant losses in 2000 and had no historical operating basis from which to conclude that it would be profitable in future years. Underwater camera sales had declined significantly and the company had devoted most of its resources to developing its SecureView product. The sole basis for PowerLinx's "expectation" of future profitability was the purported $9 million backlog of SecureView orders, which management assumed would generate taxable income; however, this purported backlog, which predated Bauer's hiring, did not reflect actual demand for SecureView cameras and, consequently, was not a reasonable or reliable indicator of future profitability.

Another example of misstated financial results caused by improper reflection of the realizability of a deferred tax asset occurred with Hampton Roads Bankshares Inc. (HRBS), a commercial bank with deteriorating loan portfolio quality and commensurate losses in the years following the financial crisis. The company reported a deferred tax asset related to its loan losses; however, it did not establish a valuation allowance against its deferred tax asset. This decision was based on dubious projections indicating that the company would earn the necessary future taxable income "to fully utilize the [deferred tax asset] DTA over the applicable carry-forward period."[24] Over time, it became clear that the earnings projections were not realistic, and ultimately the company restated its financial results to include a valuation allowance against almost the entire deferred tax asset. Exhibit 18 presents an excerpt from the company's amended Form 10-Q/A containing the restatement.

Exhibit 18: Excerpt from Hampton Roads Bankshares, Inc. Form 10-Q/A filed August 13, 2010

NOTE B – RESTATEMENT OF CONSOLIDATED FINANCIAL STATEMENTS

Subsequent to filing the Company's annual report on Form 10-K for the year ended December 31, 2009 and its Form 10-Q for the three months ended March 31, 2010 the Company determined that a valuation allowance on its deferred tax assets should be recognized as of December 31, 2009. The Company decided to establish a valuation allowance against the deferred tax asset because it is uncertain when it will realize this asset.

Accordingly, the December 31, 2009 consolidated balance sheet and the March 31, 2010 consolidated financial statements have been restated to account for this determination. The effect of this change in the consolidated financial statements was as follows (in thousands, except per share amounts).

Consolidated Balance Sheet at 31 March 2010

	As Reported	Adjustment	As Restated
Deferred tax assets, net	USD70,323	USD(70,323)	—
Total assets	3,016,470	(70,323)	USD2,946,147
Retained earnings deficit	(158,621)	(70,323)	(228,944)
Total shareholder's equity	156,509	(70,323)	86,186
Total liabilities and shareholders' equity	3,016,470	(70,323)	2,946,147

24 Accounting and Auditing Enforcement Release No. 3600, "In the Matter of Hampton Roads Bankshares Inc., Respondent," SEC (5 December 2014), www.sec.gov/litigation/admin/2014/34-73750.pdf.

Consolidated Balance Sheet at 31 December 2009

	As Reported	Adjustment	As Restated
Deferred tax assets, net	USD56,380	USD(55,983)	USD397
Total assets	2,975,559	(55,983)	2,919,576
Retained earnings deficit	(132,465)	(55,983)	(188,488)
Total shareholder's equity	180,996	(55,983)	125,013
Total liabilities and shareholders' equity	2,975,559	(55,983)	2,919,576

Another example of how choices and estimates can affect reported results lies in the selection of a depreciation method for allocating the cost of long-lived assets to accounting periods subsequent to their acquisition. A company's managers may choose to depreciate long-lived assets (1) on a straight-line basis, with each year bearing the same amount of depreciation expense; (2) using an accelerated method, with greater depreciation expense recognition in the earlier part of an asset's life; or (3) using an activity-based depreciation method, which allocates depreciation expense based on units of use or production. Depreciation expense is affected by another set of choices and estimates regarding the salvage value of the assets being depreciated. A salvage value of zero will always increase depreciation expense under any method compared with the choice of a non-zero salvage value.

Assume a company invests USD1,000,000 in manufacturing equipment and expects it to have a useful economic life of 10 years. During its expected life, the equipment will produce 400,000 units of product, or USD2.50 depreciation expense per unit produced. When it is disposed of at the end of its expected life, the company's managers expect to realize no value for the equipment. Exhibit 19 shows the differences in the three alternative methods of depreciation: straight-line, accelerated on a double-declining balance basis, and units-of-production method, with no salvage value assumed at the end of the equipment's life.

Exhibit 19: Alternative Methods of Depreciation

	Straight-Line Method	Double-Declining Balance Method			Units-of-Production Method		
Year	Depreciation Expense	Balance	Declining Balance Rate	Depreciation Expense	Units Produced	Depreciation Rate/Unit	Depreciation Expense
1	USD100,000	USD1,000,000	20%	USD200,000	90,000	USD2.50	USD225,000
2	100,000	800,000	20%	160,000	80,000	USD2.50	200,000
3	100,000	640,000	20%	128,000	70,000	USD2.50	175,000
4	100,000	512,000	20%	102,400	60,000	USD2.50	150,000
5	100,000	409,600	20%	81,920	50,000	USD2.50	125,000
6	100,000	327,680	20%	65,536	10,000	USD2.50	25,000
7	100,000	262,144	20%	52,429	10,000	USD2.50	25,000
8	100,000	209,715	20%	41,943	10,000	USD2.50	25,000
9	100,000	167,772	20%	33,554	10,000	USD2.50	25,000
10	100,000	134,218	20%	26,844	10,000	USD2.50	25,000
Total	USD1,000,000			USD892,626	400,000		USD1,000,000

The straight-line method allocates the cost of the equipment evenly to all 10 years of the equipment's life. The double-declining balance method will have a higher allocation of cost to the earlier years of the equipment's life. As its name implies, the depreciation expense will decline in each succeeding year because it is based on a fixed rate applied to a declining balance. The rate used was double the straight-line rate, but it could have been any other rate that the company's managers believed was representative of the way the actual equipment depreciation occurred. Notice that the double-declining balance method also results in an incomplete depreciation of the machine at the end of 10 years; a balance of USD107,374 (= USD1,000,000 – USD892,626) remains at the end of the expected life, which will result in a loss upon the retirement of the equipment if the company's expectation of zero salvage value turns out to be correct. Some companies may choose to depreciate the equipment to its expected salvage value, zero in this case, in its final year of use. Some companies may use a policy of switching to straight-line depreciation after the midlife of its depreciable assets in order to fully depreciate them. That particular pattern is coincidentally displayed in the units-of-production example, in which the equipment is used most heavily in the earliest part of its useful life, and then levels off to much less utilization in the second half of the expected life.

Exhibit 20 shows the different expense allocation patterns of the methods over the same life. Each will affect earnings differently.

Exhibit 20: Expense Allocation Patterns of Different Depreciation Methods

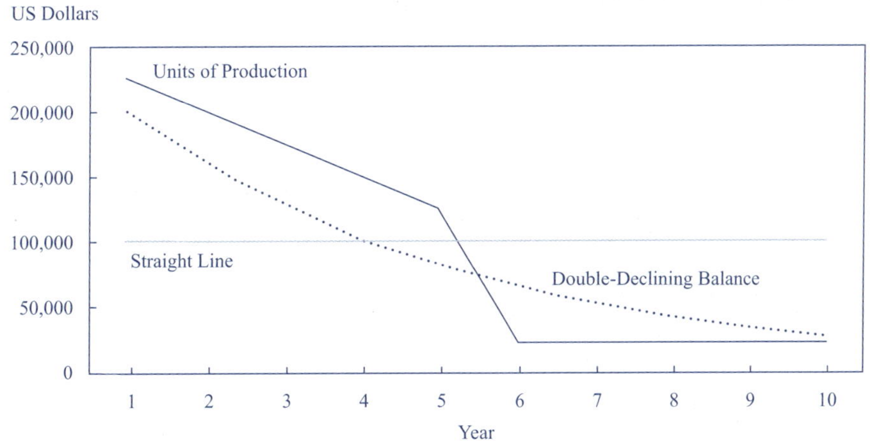

The company's managers could justify any of these methods. Each might fairly represent the way the equipment will be consumed over its expected economic life, which is a subjective estimate. The choices of methods and lives can profoundly affect reported income. These choices are not proven right or wrong until far into the future—but managers must estimate their effects in the present.

Exhibit 21 shows the effects of the three different methods on operating profit and operating profit margins, assuming that the production output of the equipment generates revenues of USD500,000 each year and USD200,000 of cash operating expenses are incurred, leaving USD300,000 of operating profit before depreciation expense.

Exhibit 21: Effects of Depreciation Methods on Operating Profit

	Straight Line		
Year	**Depreciation**	**Operating Profit**	**Operating Profit Margin**
1	USD100,000	USD200,000	40.0%
2	100,000	200,000	40.0%
3	100,000	200,000	40.0%
4	100,000	200,000	40.0%
5	100,000	200,000	40.0%
6	100,000	200,000	40.0%
7	100,000	200,000	40.0%
8	100,000	200,000	40.0%
9	100,000	200,000	40.0%
10	100,000	200,000	40.0%

	Double-Declining Balance		
Year	**Depreciation**	**Operating Profit**	**Operating Profit Margin**
1	USD200,000	USD100,000	20.0%
2	160,000	140,000	28.0%
3	128,000	172,000	34.4%
4	102,400	197,600	39.5%
5	81,920	218,080	43.6%
6	65,536	234,464	46.9%
7	52,429	247,571	49.5%
8	41,943	258,057	51.6%
9	33,554	266,446	53.3%
10	134,218*	165,782	33.2%

	Units of Production		
Year	**Depreciation**	**Operating Profit**	**Operating Profit Margin**
1	USD225,000	USD75,000	15.0%
2	200,000	100,000	20.0%
3	175,000	125,000	25.0%
4	150,000	150,000	30.0%
5	125,000	175,000	35.0%
6	25,000	275,000	55.0%
7	25,000	275,000	55.0%
8	25,000	275,000	55.0%
9	25,000	275,000	55.0%
10	25,000	275,000	55.0%

* *Includes $107,374 of undepreciated basis, treated as depreciation expense in final year of service.*

The straight-line method shows consistent operating profit margins, and the other two methods show varying degrees of increasing operating profit margins as the depreciation expense decreases over time.

Exhibit 21 shows the differences among alternative methods, but even more depreciation expense variation is possible by changing estimated lives and assumptions about salvage value. For instance, change the expected life assumption to 5 years from 10 and add an expectation that the equipment will have a 10 percent salvage value at the end of its expected life. Exhibit 22 shows the revised depreciation calculations. Notice that under the double-declining balance method, the depreciation rate is applied to the gross cost, unlike the other two methods. The straight-line method and the units-of-production method subtract the salvage value from the cost before depreciation expense is calculated. Also note that the assumption about the usage of the equipment is revised so that it is depreciated only to its salvage value of USD100,000 by the end of its estimated life. The total depreciation under each method is USD900,000.

Exhibit 22: Depreciation Calculations for Each Method in Changed Scenario

	Straight-Line Method	Double-Declining Balance Method			Units-of-Production Method		
Year	Depreciation Expense	Balance	Declining Balance Rate[1]	Depreciation Expense	Units Produced	Depreciation Rate/Unit	Depreciation Expense
1	**USD180,000**	USD1,000,000	40%	**USD400,000**	100,000	USD2.25	**USD225,000**
2	**180,000**	600,000	40%	**240,000**	90,000	USD2.25	**202,500**
3	**180,000**	360,000	40%	**144,000**	80,000	USD2.25	**180,000**
4	**180,000**	216,000	40%	**86,400**	70,000	USD2.25	**157,500**
5	**180,000**	129,600	40%	29,600[2]	60,000	USD2.25	**135,000**
Total	**USD900,000**			**USD900,000**	400,000		**USD900,000**

[1] *Declining balance rate of 20% calculated as 10-year life being equivalent to 10% annual depreciation rate, multiplied by 2 = 20%.*

[2] *Depreciation calculated as $29,600 instead of 40% × $129,600. Rote application of the declining-balance rate would have resulted in $51,840 of expense, which would have depreciated the asset below salvage value.*

Exhibit 23 shows the different expense allocation patterns of the methods over the five-year expected life, and assuming a 10 percent salvage value. Although each method is distinctly different in the timing of the cost allocation over time, the variation is less pronounced than over the longer life used in the previous example.

Exhibit 23: Expense Allocation Patterns of Depreciation Methods in Changed Scenario

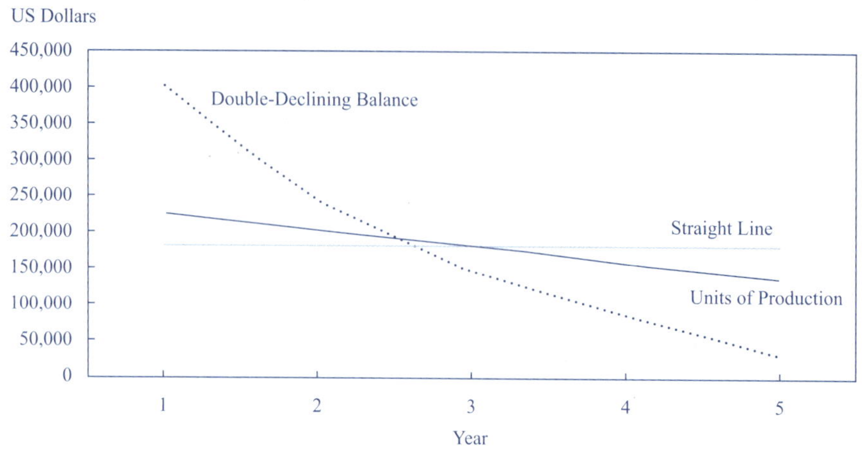

One of the clearest examples of how choices affect both the balance sheet and income statement can be found in capitalization practices. In classifying a payment made, management must determine whether the payment will benefit only the current period—making it an expense—or whether it will benefit future periods, leading to classification as a cost to be capitalized as an asset. This management judgment embodies an implicit forecast of how the item acquired by the payment will be used, or not used, in the future.

That judgment can be biased by the powerful effect a capitalization policy can have on earnings. Every amount capitalized on the balance sheet as a building, an item of inventory, a deferred cost, or any "other asset" is an amount that has not been recognized as an expense in the reporting period.

A real-life example can be found in the case of WorldCom Inc., a telecom concern that grew rapidly in the late 1990s. Much of WorldCom's financial reporting was eventually found to be fraudulent. An important part of the misreporting centered on its treatment of what is known in the telecom industry as "line costs." These are the costs of carrying a voice call or data transmission from its starting point to its ending point, and they represented WorldCom's largest expense. WorldCom's CFO decided to capitalize such costs instead of treating them as an operating expense. As a consequence, from the second quarter of 1999 through the first quarter of 2002, WorldCom increased its operating income by USD7 billion. In three of the five quarters in which the improper line cost capitalization took place, WorldCom would have recognized pre-tax losses instead of profits.[25]

Similarly, acquisitions are an area in which managers must exercise judgment. An allocation of the purchase price must be made to all of the different assets acquired based on their fair values, and those fair values are not always objectively verifiable. Management may have to make its own estimate of fair values for assets acquired, and it may be biased toward a low estimate for the values of depreciable assets in order to depress future depreciation expense. Another benefit to keeping depreciable asset values low is that the amount of the purchase price that cannot be allocated to specific assets is classified as goodwill, which is neither depreciated nor amortized in future reporting periods.

25 See Report of Investigation by the Special Investigative Committee of the Board of Directors of WorldCom, Inc., by Dennis R. Beresford, Nicholas deB. Katzenbach, and C.B. Rogers, Jr., (31 March 2003), pages 9–11, www.sec.gov/Archives/edgar/data/723527/000093176303001862/dex991.htm.

Goodwill reporting has choices of its own. Although goodwill has no effect on future earnings when unimpaired, annual testing of its fair value may reveal that the excess of price paid over the fair value of assets may not be recoverable, which should lead to a write-down of goodwill. The estimation process for the fair value of goodwill may depend heavily on projections of future performance. Those projections may be biased upward to avoid a goodwill write-down.

ACCOUNTING CHOICES THAT AFFECT THE CASH FLOW STATEMENT

11

☐ describe accounting methods (choices and estimates) that could be used to manage earnings, cash flow, and balance sheet items

The cash flow statement consists of three sections: the operating section, which shows the cash generated or used by operations; the investing section, which shows cash used for investments or provided by their disposal; and the financing section, which shows transactions attributable to financing activities.

The operating section is closely scrutinized by investors. Many of them consider it a reality check on reported earnings, on the grounds that earnings attributable to accrual accounting only and unsupported by actual cash flows may indicate earnings manipulation. Such investors believe that amounts shown for cash generated by operations is more insulated from managerial manipulation than the income statement. Cash generated by operations can be managed to an extent, however.

The operating section of the cash flow statement can be shown either under the direct method or the indirect method. Under the direct method, "entities are encouraged to report major classes of gross cash receipts and gross cash payments and their arithmetic sum—the net cash flow from operating activities."[26] In practice, companies rarely use the direct method. Instead, they use the indirect method, which shows a reconciliation of net income to cash provided by operations. The reconciliation shows the non-cash items affecting net income along with changes in working capital accounts affecting cash from operations. Exhibit 24 provides an example of the indirect presentation method.

Exhibit 24: Indirect Presentation Method

Cash Flows from Operating Activities (USD millions)	2018
Net income	USD3,000
Adjustments to reconcile net income to net cash provided by operating activities:	
Provision for doubtful receivables	10
Provision for depreciation and amortization	1,000
Goodwill impairment charges	35
Share-based compensation expense	100

26 Accounting Standards Codification (ASC), Section 230-10-45-25, *Reporting Operating, Investing, and Financing Activities*. The direct method and indirect method are similar in IFRS, as addressed in IAS 7, Paragraph 18.

Cash Flows from Operating Activities (USD millions)	2018
Provision for deferred income taxes	200
Changes in assets and liabilities:	
Trade, notes, and financing receivables related to sales	(2,000)
Inventories	(1,500)
Accounts payable	1,200
Accrued income taxes payable/receivable	(80)
Retirement benefits	90
Other	(250)
Net cash provided by operating activities	USD1,805

Whether the indirect method or direct method is used, simple choices exist for managers to improve the *appearance* of cash flow provided by operations without actually improving it. One such choice is in the area of accounts payable management, shaded in Exhibit 24. Assume that the accounts payable balance is USD5,200 million at the end of the period, an increase of USD1,200 million from its previous year-end balance of USD4,000 million. The USD1,200 million increase in accounts payable matched increased expenses or assets but did not require cash. If the company's managers had further delayed paying creditors USD500 million until the day *after* the balance sheet date, they could have increased the cash provided by operating activities by USD500 million. If the managers believe that cash generated from operations is a metric of focus for investors, they can impress them with artificially strong cash flow by simply stretching the accounts payable credit period.

What might alert investors to such machinations? They need to examine the composition of the operations section of the cash flow statement—if they do not, then *nothing* will ever alert them. Studying changes in the working capital can reveal unusual patterns that may indicate manipulation of the cash provided by operations.

Another practice that might lead an investor to question the quality of cash provided by operations is to compare a company's cash generation with an industry-wide level or with the cash operating performance of one or more similar competitors. Cash generation performance can be measured several ways. One way is to compare the relationship between cash generated by operations and net income. Cash generated by operations in excess of net income signifies better quality of earnings, whereas a chronic excess of net income over cash generated by operations should be a cause for concern; it may signal the use of accounting methods to simply raise net income instead of depicting financial reality. Another way to measure cash generation performance is to compare cash generated by operations with debt service, capital expenditures, and dividends (if any). When there is a wide variance between the company's cash generation performance and that of its benchmarks, investors should seek an explanation and carefully examine the changes in working capital accounts.

Because investors may focus on cash from operations as an important metric, managers may resort to managing the working capital accounts as described in order to present the most favorable picture. But this can be done in other ways. A company may misclassify operating uses of cash into either the investing or financing sections of the cash flow statement, which enhances the appearance of cash generated by operating activities.

Dynegy Inc. provides an example of manipulation of cash from operations through clever construction of contracts and assistance from an unconsolidated special purpose entity named ABG Gas Supply LLC (ABG). In April 2001, Dynegy entered into a contract for the purchase of natural gas from ABG. According to the contract, Dynegy would purchase gas at *below-market* rates from ABG for nine months and sell it at the current market rate. The nine-month term coincided with Dynegy's 2001 year-end and would result in gains backed by cash flows. Dynegy also agreed to buy gas at *above-market* rates from ABG for the following 51 months and sell it at the current market rate. The contract was reported at its fair value at the end of fiscal year 2001. It had no effect on net income for the year. The earlier portion of the contract resulted in a gain, supported by USD300 million of cash flow, but the latter portion of the contract resulted in non-cash losses that offset the profit. The mark-to-market rules required the recognition of both gains and losses from all parts of the contract, and hence the net effect on earnings was zero.

In April 2002, a *Wall Street Journal* article exposed the chicanery, thanks to leaked documents. The SEC required Dynegy to restate the cash flow statement by reclassifying USD300 million from the operating section of the cash flow statement to the financing section, on the grounds that Dynegy had used ABG as a conduit to effectively borrow USD300 million from Citigroup. The bank had extended credit to ABG, which it used to finance its losses on the contract (Lee, 2012).

Another area of flexibility in cash flow reporting is found in the area of interest capitalization, which creates differences between total interest payments and total interest costs.[27] Assume a company incurs total interest cost of USD30,000, composed of USD3,000 of discount amortization and USD27,000 of interest payments. Of the USD30,000, two-thirds of it (USD20,000) is expensed; the remaining third (USD10,000) is capitalized as plant assets. If the company uses the same interest expense/capitalization proportions to allocate the interest payments between operating and investing activities, then it will report USD18,000 (2/3 × USD27,000) as an operating outflow and USD9,000 (1/3 × USD27,000) as an investing outflow. The company might also choose to offset the entire USD3,000 of non-cash discount amortization against the USD20,000 treated as expense, resulting in an operating outflow as low as USD17,000, or as much as USD20,000 if it allocated all of the non-cash discount amortization to interest capitalized as investing activities. Similarly, the investing outflow could be as much as USD10,000 or as little as USD7,000, depending on the treatment of the non-cash discount amortization. There are choices within the choices, all in areas in which investors believe choices do not even exist. Nurnberg and Largay (1998) have noted that companies apparently favor the method that reports the lowest operating outflow, presumably to maximize reported cash from operations.

Investors and analysts need to be aware that presentation choices permitted in IAS 7, *Statement of Cash Flows*, offer flexibility in classification of certain items in the cash flow statement. This flexibility can drastically change the results in the operating section of the cash flow statement. An excerpt from IAS 7, Paragraphs 33 and 34, provides the background:

> 33. Interest paid and interest and dividends received are usually classified as operating cash flows for a financial institution. However, there is no consensus on the classification of these cash flows for other entities. Interest paid and interest and dividends received may be classified as operating cash flows because they enter into the determination of profit or loss. *Alternatively, interest paid and interest and dividends received may be classified as financing cash flows and investing cash flows respectively, because they are costs of obtaining financial resources or returns on investments.*
>
> 34. Dividends paid may be classified as a financing cash flow because they are a cost of obtaining financial resources. *Alternatively, dividends paid may be classified as a component of cash flows from operating activities in order to assist users to determine the ability of an entity to pay dividends out of operating cash flows.* [Emphasis added.]

27 See Nurnberg and Largay (1998) and Nurnberg (2006) .

By allowing a choice of operating or financing for the placement of interest and dividends received or paid, IAS 7 gives a company's managers the opportunities to select the presentation that gives the best-looking picture of operating performance. An example is Norse Energy Corp. ASA, a Norwegian gas explorer and producer, which changed its classifications of interest paid and interest received in 2007 (Gordon, Henry, Jorgensen, and Linthicum, 2017). Interest paid was switched to financing instead of decreasing cash generated from operations. Norse Energy also switched its classification of interest received to investing from operating cash flow. The net effect of these changes was to report positive, rather than negative, operating cash flows in both 2007 and 2008. With these simple changes, the company could also change the perception of its operations. The cash flow statement formerly presented the appearance of a company with operations that used more cash than it generated, and it possibly raised questions about the sustainability of operations. After the revision, the operating section of the cash flow statement depicted a much more viable operation.

Exhibit 25 shows the net effect of the reclassifications on Norse Energy's cash flows.

Exhibit 25: Reclassification of Cash Flows (amounts in USD millions)

	As Reported (following 2007 reclassification)		Adjustments (without reclassification*)		Pro forma (without reclassification)	
	2008	2007	2008	2007	2008	2007
Operating	**USD5.30**	**USD2.80**	**(USD13.70)**	**(USD14.40)**	**(USD8.40)**	**(USD11.60)**
Investing	USD0.90	(USD56.80)	(USD9.00)	(USD3.50)	(USD8.10)	(USD60.30)
Financing	(USD16.60)	USD34.50	USD22.70	USD17.90	USD6.10	USD52.40
Total	(USD10.40)	(USD19.50)	USD0	USD0	(USD10.40)	(USD19.50)

** The adjustments reverse the addition of interest received to investing and instead add it to operating. The adjustments also reverse the deduction of interest paid from financing and instead subtract it from operating.*

12 ACCOUNTING CHOICES THAT AFFECT FINANCIAL REPORTING

☐ describe accounting methods (choices and estimates) that could be used to manage earnings, cash flow, and balance sheet items

Exhibit 26 summarizes some of the areas in which choices can be made that affect financial reports.

Exhibit 26: Areas in Which Choices and Estimates Affect Financial Reporting

Area of Choice/Estimate	Analyst Concerns
Revenue recognition	▪ How is revenue recognized: upon shipment or upon delivery of goods? ▪ Is the company engaging in "channel stuffing"—the practice of overloading a distribution channel with more product than it is normally capable of selling? This can be accomplished by inducing customers to buy more through unusual discounts, the threat of near-term price increases, or both—or simply by shipping goods that were not ordered. These transactions may be corrected in a subsequent period and may result in restated results. Are accounts receivable relative to revenues abnormally high for relative to the company's history or to its peers? If so, channel stuffing may have occurred. ▪ Is there unusual activity in the allowance for sales returns relative to past history? ▪ Does the company's days sales outstanding show any collection issues that might indicate shipment of unneeded or unwanted goods to customers? ▪ Does the company engage in "bill-and-hold" transactions? This is when a customer purchases goods but requests that they remain with the seller until a later date. This kind of transaction makes it possible for a seller to manufacture fictitious sales by declaring end-of-period inventory as "sold but held," with a minimum of effort and phony documentation. ▪ Does the company use rebates as part of its marketing approach? If so, how significantly do the estimates of rebate fulfillment affect net revenues, and have any unusual breaks with history occurred? ▪ Does the company separate its revenue arrangements into multiple deliverables of goods or services? This area is one of great revenue recognition flexibility and also is one that provides little visibility to investors. They simply cannot examine a company's arrangements and decide for themselves whether or not revenue has been properly allocated to different components of a contract. If a company uses multiple deliverable arrangements with its customers as a routine matter, investors might be more sensitive to revenue reporting risks. In seeking a comfort level, they might ask the following questions: Does the company explain adequately how it determines the different allocations of deliverables and how revenue is recognized on each one? Do deferred revenues result? If not, does it seem reasonable that there are no deferred revenues for this kind of arrangement? Are there unusual trends in revenues and receivables, particularly with regard to cash conversion? If an investor is not satisfied with the answers to these questions, he or she might be more comfortable with other investment choices.

Area of Choice/Estimate	Analyst Concerns
Long-lived assets: Depreciation policies	▪ Do the estimated life spans of the associated assets make sense, or are they unusually low compared with others in the same industry? ▪ Have there been changes in depreciable lives that have a positive effect on current earnings? ▪ Do recent asset write-downs indicate that company policy on asset lives might need to be reconsidered?
Intangibles: Capitalization policies	▪ Does the company capitalize expenditures related to intangibles, such as software? Does its balance sheet show any R&D capitalized as a result of acquisitions? Or, if the company is an IFRS filer, has it capitalized any internally generated development costs? ▪ How do the company's capitalization policies compare with the competition? ▪ Are amortization policies reasonable?
Allowance for doubtful accounts/loan loss reserves	▪ Are additions to such allowances lower or higher than in the past? ▪ Does the collection experience justify any difference from historical provisioning? ▪ Is there a possibility that any lowering of the allowance may be the result of industry difficulties along with the difficulty of meeting earnings expectations?
Inventory cost methods	▪ Does the company use a costing method that produces fair reporting results in view of its environment? How do its inventory methods compare with others in its industry? Are there differences that will make comparisons uneven if there are unusual changes in inflation? ▪ Does the company use reserves for obsolescence in its inventory valuation? If so, are they subject to unusual fluctuations that might indicate adjusting them to arrive at a specified earnings result? ▪ If a company reports under US GAAP and uses last-in, first-out (LIFO) inventory accounting, does LIFO liquidation (the assumed sale of old, lower-cost layers of inventory) occur through inventory reduction programs? This inventory reduction may generate earnings without supporting cash flow, and management may intentionally reduce the layers to produce specific earnings benefits.

Area of Choice/Estimate	Analyst Concerns
Tax asset valuation accounts	▪ Tax assets, if present, must be stated at the value at which management expects to realize them, and an allowance must be set up to restate tax assets to the level expected to eventually be converted into cash. Determining the allowance involves an estimate of future operations and tax payments. Does the amount of the valuation allowance seem reasonable, overly optimistic, or overly pessimistic? ▪ Are there contradictions between the management commentary and the allowance level, or the tax note and the allowance level? There cannot be an optimistic management commentary and a fully reserved tax asset, or vice versa. One of them has to be wrong. ▪ Look for changes in the tax asset valuation account. It may be 100 percent reserved at first, and then "optimism" increases whenever an earnings boost is needed. Lowering the reserve decreases tax expense and increases net income.
Goodwill	▪ Companies must annually assess goodwill balances for impairment on a qualitative basis. If further testing appears necessary, it is based on estimates of the fair value of the reporting units (US GAAP issuers), or cash-generating units (IFRS issuers), associated with goodwill balances. The tests are based on subjective estimates, including future cash flows and the employment of discount rates. ▪ Do the disclosures on goodwill testing suggest that the exercise was skewed to avoid impairment charges?
Warranty reserves	▪ Have additions to the reserves been reduced, perhaps to make earnings targets? Examine the trend in the charges of actual costs against the reserves: Do they support or contradict the warranty provisioning activity? Do the actual costs charged against the reserve give the analyst any indication about the quality of the products sold?
Related-party transactions	▪ Is the company engaged in transactions that disproportionately benefit members of management? Does one company have control over another's destiny through supply contracts or other dealings? ▪ Do extensive dealings take place with *non-public* companies that are under management control? If so, those companies could absorb losses (e.g., through supply arrangements that are unfavorable to them) to make the public company's performance look good. This scenario may provide opportunities for an owner to cash out.

The most important lesson is that choices exist among accounting methods and estimates, and an analyst needs a working knowledge of these options to understand whether management may have made choices to achieve a desired result.

13 WARNING SIGNS

- [ ] describe accounting warning signs and methods for detecting manipulation of information in financial reports

The choices management makes to achieve desired results leave a trail, like tracks in sand or snow. The evidence, or warning signs, of information manipulation in financial reports is directly linked to the basic means of manipulation: biased revenue recognition and biased expense recognition. The bias may relate to timing or location of recognition. An example of the timing issue is that a company may choose to defer expenses by capitalizing them. Regarding location, it may recognize a loss in other comprehensive income or directly through equity, rather than through the profit and loss statement. The alert investor or analyst should do the following to identify the warning signs.

Pay Attention to Revenue

The single largest number on the income statement is revenue, and revenue recognition is a recurring source of accounting manipulation and even outright fraud. Answering the question, "Is revenue higher or lower than the previous comparable period?" is not sufficient. Many analytical procedures can be routinely performed to identify warning signals of malfeasance:

- *Examine the accounting policies note for a company's revenue recognition policies.*
- Consider whether the policies make it easier to prematurely recognize revenue, such as recognizing revenue immediately upon shipment of goods, or if the company uses bill-and-hold arrangements whereby a sale is recognized before goods actually are shipped to the customer.
- Barter transactions may exist, which can be difficult to value properly.
- Rebate programs involve many estimates, including forecasts of the amount of rebates that ultimately will be incurred, which can have significant effects on revenue recognition.
- Multiple-deliverable arrangements of goods and services are common, but clarity about the timing of revenue recognition for each item or service delivered is necessary for the investor to be comfortable with the reporting of revenues.

Although none of these decisions necessarily violates accounting standards, each involves significant judgement and warrants close attention if other warning signs are present.

- *Look at revenue relationships.* Compare a company's revenue growth with its primary competitors or its industry peer group.
- If a company's revenue growth is out of line with its competitors, its industry, or the economy, the investor or analyst needs to understand the reasons for the outperformance. It may be a result of superior management or products and services, but not all management is superior, nor are the products and services of their companies. Revenue quality might be suspect, and the investor should take additional analytical steps.
- Compare accounts receivable with revenues over several years.

- Examine the trend to determine whether receivables are increasing as a percentage of total revenues. If so, a company might be engaging in channel-stuffing activities, or worse, recording fictitious sales transactions.
- Calculate receivables turnover for several years:

- Examine the trend for unusual changes and seek an explanation if they exist.
- Compare a company's days sales outstanding (DSO) or receivables turnover with that of relevant competitors or an industry peer group and determine whether the company is an outlier.

An increase in DSO or decrease in receivables turnover could suggest that some revenues are recorded prematurely or are even fictitious, or that the allowance for doubtful accounts is insufficient.

- Examine asset turnover. If a company's managers make poor asset allocation choices, revenues may not be sufficient to justify the investment. Be particularly alert when asset allocation choices involve acquisitions of entire companies. If post-acquisition revenue generation is weak, managers might reach for revenue growth anywhere it can be found. That reach for growth might result in accounting abuses.

Revenues, divided by total assets, indicate the productivity of assets in generating revenues. If the company's asset turnover is continually declining, or lagging the asset turnover of competitors or the industry, it may portend future asset write-downs, particularly in the goodwill balances of acquisitive companies.

Pay Attention to Signals from Inventories

Although inventory is not a component of every company's asset base, its presence creates an opportunity for accounting manipulation.

- *Look at inventory relationships.* Because revenues involve items sold from inventory, the kind of examination an investor should perform on inventory is similar to that for revenues.
- Compare growth in inventories with competitors and industry benchmarks. If a company's inventory growth is out of line with its peers, without any concurrent sales growth, then it simply may be the result of poor inventory management—an operational inefficiency that might affect an investor's view of a company. It also may signal obsolescence problems in the company's inventory that have not yet been recognized through markdowns to the inventory's net realizable value. Reported gross and net profits could be overstated because of overstated inventory.
- Calculate the inventory turnover ratio. This ratio is the cost of sales divided by the average ending inventory. Declining inventory turnover could also suggest obsolescence problems that should be recognized.
- Companies reporting under US GAAP may use LIFO inventory cost flow assumptions. When this assumption is part of the accounting policies, and a company operates in an inflationary environment, investors should note whether old, low-cost inventory costs have been passed through current earnings and artificially improved gross, operating, and net profits.

Pay Attention to Capitalization Policies and Deferred Costs

In a study of enforcement actions over a five-year period, the SEC found that improper revenue recognition was the most prevalent accounting issue.[28] Suppression of expenses was the next most prevalent problem noted. As the earlier discussion of WorldCom showed, improper capitalization practices can result in a significant misstatement of financial results.

- *Examine the company's accounting policy note for its capitalization policy for long-term assets, including interest costs, and for its handling of other deferred costs.* Compare the company's policy with the industry practice. If the company is the only one capitalizing certain costs while other industry participants treat them as expenses, a red flag is raised. If an outlier company of this type is encountered, it would be useful to cross-check such a company's asset turnover and profitability margins with others in its industry. An investor might expect such a company to be more profitable than its competitors, but the investor might also have lower confidence in the quality of the reported numbers.

Pay Attention to the Relationship between Cash Flow and Net Income

Net income propels stock prices, but cash flow pays bills. Management can manipulate either one, but sooner or later, net income must be realized in cash if a company is to remain viable. When net income is higher than cash provided by operations, one possibility is that aggressive accrual accounting policies have shifted current expenses to later periods. Increasing earnings in the presence of declining cash generated by operations might signal accounting irregularities.

- *Construct a time series of cash generated by operations divided by net income.* If the ratio is consistently below 1.0 or has declined repeatedly, the company's accrual accounts may have problems.

Look for Other Potential Warnings Signs

Other areas that might suggest the need for further analysis include the following:

- *Depreciation methods and useful lives.* As discussed earlier, selection of depreciation methods and useful lives can greatly influence profitability. An investor should compare a company's policies with those of its peers to determine whether it is particularly lenient in its effects on earnings. Investors should likewise compare the length of depreciable lives used by a company with those used by its peers.
- *Fourth-quarter surprises.* An investor should be suspicious of possible earnings management if a company routinely disappoints investors with poor earnings or overachieves in the fourth quarter of the year when no seasonality exists in the business. The company may be over- or under-reporting profits in the first three quarters of the year.
- *Presence of related-party transactions.* Related-party transactions often arise when a company's founders are still very active in managing the company, with much of their wealth tied to the company's fortunes. They may be more

28 SEC, "Report Pursuant to Section 704 of the Sarbanes–Oxley Act of 2002," pages 5–6, www.sec.gov/news/studies/sox704report.pdf.

biased in their view of a company's performance because it relates directly to their own wealth and reputations, and they may be able to transact business with the company in ways that may not be detected. For instance, they may purchase unsellable inventory from the company for disposal in another company of their own to avoid markdowns.

- *Non-operating income or one-time sales included in revenue.* To disguise weakening revenue growth, or just to enhance revenue growth, a company might classify non-operating income items into revenues or fail to clarify the nature of revenues. In the first quarter of 1997, Sunbeam Corporation included one-time disposal of product lines in sales without indicating that such non-recurring sales were included in revenues. This inclusion gave investors a false impression of the company's sustainable revenue-generating capability.
- *Classification of expenses as "non-recurring."* To make operating performance look more attractive, managers might carve out "special items" in the income statement. Particularly when these items appear period after period, equity investors might find their interests best served by not accepting the carve-out of serial "special items" and instead focusing on the net income line in evaluating performance over long periods.
- *Gross/operating margins out of line with competitors or industry.* This disparity is an ambivalent warning sign. It might signal superior management ability. But it might also signal the presence of accounting manipulations to add a veneer of superior management ability to the company's reputation. Only the compilation and examination of other warning signals will enable an investor or analyst to decide which signal is being given.

Warning signals are just that: signals, not indisputable declarations of accounting manipulation guilt. Investors and analysts need to evaluate them cohesively, not on an isolated basis. When an investor finds a number of these signals, the investee company should be viewed with caution or even discarded in favor of alternatives.

Furthermore, as discussed earlier, context is important in judging the value of warning signals. A few examples of facts and circumstances to be aware of are as follows.

- *Younger companies with an unblemished record of meeting growth projections.* It is plausible, especially for a younger company with new and popular product offerings, to generate above-average returns for a period of time. But, as demand dissipates, products mature, and competitors challenge for market share, management may seek to extend its recent record of rapid growth in sales and profitability by unconventional means. At this point, the "earnings games" begin, including aggressive estimates, drawing down "cookie jar" reserves, selling assets for accounting gains, taking on excess leverage, or entering into financial transactions with no apparent business purpose other than financial statement "window dressing."
- *Management has adopted a minimalist approach to disclosure.* Confidence in accounting quality depends on disclosure. If management does not seem to take seriously its obligation to provide information, one needs to be concerned. For example, for a large company, management might claim that it has only one reportable segment, or its commentary might be similar from period to period. A plausible explanation for minimalist disclosure policies could be that management is protecting investors' interests by withholding valuable information from competitors. But, this is not necessarily the case. For example, after Sony Corporation acquired CBS Records and Columbia Pictures, it incurred substantial losses for a number of years. Yet, Sony chose to hide its negative trends and doubtful future prospects by

aggregating the results within a much larger "Entertainment Division." In 1998, after Sony ultimately wrote off much of the goodwill associated with these ill-fated acquisitions, the SEC sanctioned Sony and its CFO for failing to separately discuss them in the MD&A in a balanced manner.[29]

- *Management fixation on earnings reports.* Beware of companies whose management appears to be fixated on reported earnings, sometimes to the detriment of attending to real drivers of value. Indicators of excessive earnings fixation include the aggressive use of non-GAAP measures of performance, special items, or non-recurring charges. Another indicator of earnings fixation is highly decentralized operations in which division managers' compensation packages are heavily weighted toward the attainment of reported earnings or non-GAAP measures of performance.

Company Culture

A company's culture is an intangible that investors should bear in mind when they are evaluating financial statements for the possibility of accounting manipulation. A management's highly competitive mentality may serve investors well when the company conducts business (assuming that actions taken are not unethical, illegal, or harmfully myopic), but that kind of thinking should not extend to communications with the owners of the company: the shareholders. That mentality can lead to the kind of accounting gamesmanship seen in the early part of the century. In examining financial statements for warning signs of manipulation, the investor should consider whether that mindset exists in the preparation of the financial statements.

One notable example of this mindset comes from one of the most recognized corporate names in the world, General Electric. In the mid-1980s, GE acquired Kidder Peabody, and it was ultimately determined that much of the earnings that Kidder had reported were bogus. As a consequence, GE announced within two days of the acquisition that it would take a non-cash write-off of USD350 million. Here is how former CEO/Chair Jack Welsh described the ensuing meeting with senior management in his memoir, *Straight from the Gut*:

> The response of our business leaders to the crisis was typical of the GE *culture* [emphasis added]. Even though the books had closed on the quarter, many immediately offered to pitch in to cover the Kidder gap. Some said they could find an extra USD10 million, USD20 million, and even USD30 million from their businesses to offset the surprise. Though it was too late, their willingness to help was a dramatic contrast to the excuses I had been hearing from the Kidder people. (page 225)

It appears that the corporate governance apparatus fostered a GE culture that extended the concept of teamwork to the point of "sharing" profits to win one for the team as a whole, which is incompatible with the concept of neutral financial reporting. Although research is not conclusive on this question, it may be worth considering that predisposition to earnings manipulation is more likely to be present when the CEO and board chair positions are held by the same person, or when the audit committee of the board essentially serves at the pleasure of the CEO and lacks financial reporting sophistication. Finally, one could discuss whether the financial reporting environment today would reward or penalize a CEO who openly endorsed a view that he or she could legitimately exercise financial reporting discretion—albeit within limits—for the purpose of artificially smoothing earnings.

29 SEC, Accounting and Auditing Enforcement Release No. 1061, "In the Matter of Sony Corporation and Sumio Sano, Respondents" (5 August 1998).

Restructuring or Impairment Charges

At times, a company's stock price has been observed to rise after it recognized a big bath charge to reported earnings. The conventional wisdom explaining the stock price rise is that accounting recognition signals something positive: that management is now ready to part with the lagging portion of a company, so as to redirect its attention and talents to more profitable activities. Consequently, the earnings charge should be disregarded for being solely related to past events.

The analyst should also consider, however, that the events leading ultimately to the big bath on the financial statements did not happen overnight, even though the accounting for those events occurs at a subsequent point. Management may want to communicate that the accounting adjustments reflect the company's new path, but the restructuring charge also indicates that the old path of reported earnings was not real. In particular, expenses reported in prior years were very likely understated—even assuming that no improper financial statement manipulation had occurred. To extrapolate historical earnings trends, an analyst should consider making pro forma analytical adjustments to prior years' earnings to reflect a reasonable division of the latest period's restructuring and impairment charges.

Management Has a Merger and Acquisition Orientation

Tyco International Ltd. acquired more than 700 companies from 1996 to 2002. Even assuming the best of intentions regarding financial reporting, a growth-at-any-cost corporate culture poses a severe challenge to operational and financial reporting controls. In Tyco's case, the SEC found that it consistently and fraudulently understated assets acquired (lowering future depreciation and amortization charges) and overstated liabilities assumed (avoiding expense recognition and potentially increasing earnings in future periods).[30]

30 SEC, Accounting and Auditing Enforcement Release No. 2414, "SEC Brings Settled Charges Against Tyco International Ltd. Alleging Billion Dollar Accounting Fraud" (17 April 2006), www.sec.gov/litigation/litreleases/2006/lr19657.htm.

REFERENCES

Basu, Sudipta. December 1997. "The Conservatism Principle and the Asymmetric Timeliness of Earnings." *Journal of Accounting and Economics* 24 (1): 3–37. 10.1016/S0165-4101(97)00014-1

Bliss, James Harris. 1924. *Management through Accounts.* New York: Ronald Press Company.

Ciesielski, Jack T. and Henry Elaine. 2017. "Accounting's Tower of Babel: Key Considerations in Assessing Non-GAAP Earnings." *Financial Analysts Journal* 73 (2): 34–50. 10.2469/faj.v73.n2.5

Gordon, Elizabeth, Elaine Henry, Bjorn Jorgensen, and Cheryl Linthicum. 2017. "Flexibility in Cash-Flow Classification under IFRS: Determinants and Consequences." *Review of Accounting Studies* 22 (2): 839872.

Graham, John, Campbell Harvey, and Shiva Rajgopal. December 2005. "The Economic Implications of Corporate Financial Reporting." *Journal of Accounting and Economics* 40 (1-3): 3–73. 10.1016/j.jacceco.2005.01.002

Gu, Feng and Baruch Lev. 2017. "Time to Change Your Investment Model." *Financial Analysts Journal* 73 (4): 23–33. 10.2469/faj.v73.n4.4

Lewis, Craig M. "*Risk Modeling at the SEC: The Accounting Quality Model.*" Speech, the Financial Executives International Committee on Finance and Information Technology (13 December 2012), www.sec.gov/news/speech/2012/spch121312cml.htm.

Nurnberg, H. "*Perspectives on the Cash Flow Statement under FASB Statement No. 95.*" Center for Excellence in Accounting and Security Analysis Occasional Paper Series. Columbia Business School, 2006.

Nurnberg, H. and J. Largay. December 1998. "Interest Payments in the Cash Flow Statement." *Accounting Horizons* 12 (4): 407418.

Pavlo, Walter. "*Former Enron CFO Andrew Fastow Speaks At ACFE Annual Conference,*" *Forbes* (26 June 2013), www.forbes.com/sites/walterpavlo/2013/06/26/fmr-enron-cfo-andrew-fastow-speaks-at-acfe-annual-conference/.

Ronen, Joshua. 2008. *Yaari Varda. Earnings Management: Emerging Insights in Theory, Practice, and Research.* New York: Springer.

Schipper, Katherine. December 1989. "Commentary on Earnings Management." *Accounting Horizons* 3 (4): 91102.

Watts, Ross. September 2003. "Conservatism in Accounting Part I: Explanations and Implications." *Accounting Horizons* 17 (3): 207–221. 10.2308/acch.2003.17.3.207

PRACTICE PROBLEMS

1. In contrast to earnings quality, financial reporting quality *most likely* pertains to:

   A. sustainable earnings.

   B. relevant information.

   C. adequate return on investment.

2. The information provided by a low-quality financial report will *most likely*:

   A. decrease company value.

   B. indicate earnings are not sustainable.

   C. impede the assessment of earnings quality.

3. To properly assess a company's past performance, an analyst requires:

   A. high earnings quality.

   B. high financial reporting quality.

   C. both high earnings quality and high financial reporting quality.

4. Low quality earnings *most likely* reflect:

   A. low-quality financial reporting.

   B. company activities which are unsustainable.

   C. information that does not faithfully represent company activities.

5. Earnings that result from non-recurring activities *most likely* indicate:

   A. lower-quality earnings.

   B. biased accounting choices.

   C. lower-quality financial reporting.

6. Which attribute of financial reports would *most likely* be evaluated as optimal in the financial reporting spectrum?

   A. Conservative accounting choices

   B. Sustainable and adequate returns

   C. Emphasized pro forma earnings measures

7. Financial reports of the lowest level of quality reflect:

   A. fictitious events.

   B. biased accounting choices.

   C. accounting that is non-compliant with GAAP.

8. When earnings are increased by deferring research and development (R&D) investments until the next reporting period, this choice is considered:
   - **A.** non-compliant accounting.
   - **B.** earnings management as a result of a real action.
   - **C.** earnings management as a result of an accounting choice.

9. A high-quality financial report may reflect:
   - **A.** earnings smoothing.
   - **B.** low earnings quality.
   - **C.** understatement of asset impairment.

10. If a particular accounting choice is considered aggressive in nature, then the financial performance for the reporting period would *most likely*:
    - **A.** be neutral.
    - **B.** exhibit an upward bias.
    - **C.** exhibit a downward bias.

11. Conservative accounting choices will most likely lead to:
    - **A.** decreased reported earnings in later periods.
    - **B.** increased reported earnings in the period under review.
    - **C.** increased debt reported on the balance sheet at the end of the current period.

12. Which of the following is *most likely* to be considered a potential benefit of accounting conservatism?
    - **A.** A reduction in litigation costs
    - **B.** Less biased financial reporting
    - **C.** An increase in current period reported performance

13. Which of the following statements *most likely* describes a situation that would motivate a manager to issue low-quality financial reports? The manager has:
    - **A.** increased the market share of products significantly.
    - **B.** earned compensation that is linked to stock price performance.
    - **C.** brought the company's profitability to a level higher than competitors.

14. Which of the following concerns would *most likely* motivate a manager to make conservative accounting choices?
    - **A.** Attention to future career opportunities
    - **B.** Debt covenant violation risk in the current period
    - **C.** Unexpected strength in the business environment

15. Which of the following conditions *best* explains why a company's manager would obtain legal, accounting, and board level approval prior to issuing low-quality financial reports?

   A. Motivation

   B. Opportunity

   C. Rationalization

16. A company is experiencing a period of strong financial performance. To increase the likelihood of exceeding analysts' earnings forecasts in the next reporting period, the company would *most likely* undertake accounting choices for the period under review that:

   A. inflate reported revenue.

   B. delay expense recognition.

   C. accelerate expense recognition.

17. Which of the following situations represents a motivation, rather than an opportunity, to issue low-quality financial reports?

   A. Poor internal controls

   B. Search for a personal bonus

   C. Inattentive board of directors

18. Which of the following situations will *most likely* motivate managers to inflate reported earnings?

   A. Possibility of bond covenant violation

   B. Earnings that have exceeded analysts' forecasts

   C. Earnings that have grown from the prior-year period

19. Which of the following *best* describes an opportunity for management to issue low-quality financial reports?

   A. Ineffective board of directors

   B. Pressure to achieve some performance level

   C. Corporate concerns about financing in the future

20. An audit opinion of a company's financial reports is *most likely* intended to:

   A. detect fraud.

   B. reveal misstatements.

   C. ensure that financial information is presented fairly.

21. If a company uses a non-GAAP financial measure in an SEC filing, then the company must:

   A. give more prominence to the non-GAAP measure if it is used in earnings releases.

B. provide a reconciliation of the non-GAAP measure and equivalent GAAP measure.

C. exclude charges requiring cash settlement from any non-GAAP liquidity measures.

22. A company wishing to increase earnings in the reporting period may choose to:

A. decrease the useful life of depreciable assets.

B. lower estimates of uncollectible accounts receivables.

C. classify a purchase as an expense rather than a capital expenditure.

23. Which technique *most likely* increases the cash flow provided by operations?

A. Stretching the accounts payable credit period

B. Applying all non-cash discount amortization against interest capitalized

C. Shifting classification of interest paid from financing to operating cash flows

24. Bias in revenue recognition would *least likely* be suspected if:

A. the firm engages in barter transactions.

B. reported revenue is higher than the previous quarter.

C. revenue is recognized before goods are shipped to customers.

25. Which of the following is an indication that a company may be recognizing revenue prematurely? Relative to its competitors, the company's:

A. asset turnover is decreasing.

B. receivables turnover is increasing.

C. days sales outstanding is increasing.

26. Which of the following would *most likely* signal that a company may be using aggressive accrual accounting policies to shift current expenses to later periods? Over the last five-year period, the ratio of cash flow to net income has:

A. increased each year.

B. decreased each year.

C. fluctuated from year to year.

27. An analyst reviewing a firm with a large reported restructuring charge to earnings should:

A. view expenses reported in prior years as overstated.

B. disregard it because it is solely related to past events.

C. consider making pro forma adjustments to prior years' earnings.

SOLUTIONS

1. B is correct. Financial reporting quality pertains to the quality of information in financial reports. High-quality financial reporting provides decision-useful information, which is relevant and faithfully represents the economic reality of the company's activities. Earnings of high quality are sustainable and provide an adequate level of return. Highest-quality financial reports reflect both high financial reporting quality and high earnings quality.

2. C is correct. Financial reporting quality pertains to the quality of the information contained in financial reports. High-quality financial reports provide decision-useful information that faithfully represents the economic reality of the company. Low-quality financial reports impede assessment of earnings quality. Financial reporting quality is distinguishable from earnings quality, which pertains to the earnings and cash generated by the company's actual economic activities and the resulting financial condition. Low-quality earnings are not sustainable and decrease company value.

3. B is correct. Financial reporting quality pertains to the quality of the information contained in financial reports. If financial reporting quality is low, the information provided is of little use in assessing the company's performance. Financial reporting quality is distinguishable from earnings quality, which pertains to the earnings and cash generated by the company's actual economic activities and the resulting financial condition.

4. B is correct. Earnings quality pertains to the earnings and cash generated by the company's actual economic activities and the resulting financial condition. Low-quality earnings are likely not sustainable over time because the company does not expect to generate the same level of earnings in the future or because earnings will not generate sufficient return on investment to sustain the company. Earnings that are not sustainable decrease company value. Earnings quality is distinguishable from financial reporting quality, which pertains to the quality of the information contained in financial reports.

5. A is correct. Earnings that result from non-recurring activities are unsustainable. Unsustainable earnings are an example of lower-quality earnings. Recognizing earnings that result from non-recurring activities is neither a biased accounting choice nor indicative of lower quality financial reporting because it faithfully represents economic events.

6. B is correct. At the top of the quality spectrum of financial reports are reports that conform to GAAP, are decision useful, and have earnings that are sustainable and offer adequate returns. In other words, these reports have both high financial reporting quality and high earnings quality.

7. A is correct. Financial reports span a quality continuum from high to low based on decision-usefulness and earnings quality (see Exhibit 2). The lowest-quality reports portray fictitious events, which may misrepresent the company's performance or obscure fraudulent misappropriation of the company's assets.

8. B is correct. Deferring R&D investments into the next reporting period is an example of earnings management by taking a *real* action.

9. B is correct. High-quality financial reports offer useful information, meaning information that is relevant and faithfully represents actual performance. Although

low earnings quality may not be desirable, if the reported earnings are representative of actual performance, they are consistent with high-quality financial reporting. Highest-quality financial reports reflect both high financial reporting quality and high earnings quality.

10. B is correct. Aggressive accounting choices aim to enhance the company's reported performance by inflating the amount of revenues, earnings, or operating cash flow reported in the period. Consequently, the financial performance for that period would most likely exhibit an upward bias.

11. C is correct. Accounting choices are considered conservative if they decrease the company's reported performance and financial position in the current period under review. Conservative choices may increase the amount of debt reported on the balance sheet. They may decrease the revenues, earnings, or operating cash flow reported for the period and increase those amounts in later periods.

12. A is correct. Conservatism reduces the possibility of litigation and, by extension, litigation costs. Rarely, if ever, is a company sued because it understated good news or overstated bad news. Accounting conservatism is a type of bias in financial reporting that decreases a company's reported performance. Conservatism directly conflicts with the characteristic of neutrality.

13. B is correct. Managers often have incentives to meet or beat market expectations, particularly if management compensation is linked to increases in share prices or to reported earnings.

14. C is correct. Managers may be motivated to understate earnings in a period with unexpected strong performance by delaying revenue recognition or accelerating expense recognition to increase the probability of exceeding expectations in a subsequent period (referred to as "banking" some earnings for the next period.)

15. C is correct. Typically, conditions of opportunity, motivation, and rationalization exist when individuals issue low-quality financial reports. Rationalization occurs when an individual is concerned about a choice and needs to be able to justify it to herself or himself. If the manager is concerned about a choice in a financial report, the manager may ask for other opinions to convince herself or himself that it is okay.

16. C is correct. In a period of strong financial performance, managers may pursue accounting choices that increase the probability of exceeding earnings forecasts for the next period. By accelerating expense recognition or delaying revenue recognition, managers may reduce financial performance in the current period in order to inflate earnings in the next period and increase the likelihood of exceeding targets.

17. B is correct. Motivation can result from pressure to meet some criteria for personal reasons, such as a bonus, or corporate reasons, such as concern about future financing. Poor internal controls and an inattentive board of directors offer opportunities to issue low-quality financial reports.

18. A is correct. The possibility of bond covenant violations may motivate managers to inflate earnings in the reporting period. In so doing, the company may be able to avoid the consequences associated with violating bond covenants.

19. A is correct. Opportunities to issue low-quality financial reports include internal conditions, such as an ineffective board of directors, and external conditions, such as accounting standards that provide scope for divergent choices. Pressure

to achieve a certain level of performance and corporate concerns about future financing are examples of motivations to issue low-quality financial reports. Typically, three conditions exist when low-quality financial reports are issued: opportunity, motivation, and rationalization.

20. C is correct. An audit is intended to provide assurance that the company's financial reports are presented fairly, thus providing discipline regarding financial reporting quality. Regulatory agencies usually require that the financial statements of publicly traded companies be audited by an independent auditor to provide assurance that the financial statements conform to accounting standards. Privately held companies may also choose to obtain audit opinions either voluntarily or because an outside party requires it. An audit is not typically intended to detect fraud. An audit is based on sampling and it is possible that the sample might not reveal misstatements.

21. B is correct. If a company uses a non-GAAP financial measure in an SEC filing, it is required to provide the most directly comparable GAAP measure with equivalent prominence in the filing. In addition, the company is required to provide a reconciliation between the non-GAAP measure and the equivalent GAAP measure. Similarly, IFRS requires that any non-IFRS measures included in financial reports must be defined and their potential relevance explained. The non-IFRS measures must be reconciled with IFRS measures.

22. B is correct. If a company wants to increase reported earnings, the company's managers may reduce the allowance for uncollected accounts and the related expense reported for the period. Decreasing the useful life of depreciable assets would increase depreciation expense and decrease earnings in the reporting period. Classifying a purchase as an expense, rather than capital expenditure, would decrease earnings in the reporting period. The use of accrual accounting may result in estimates in financial reports, because all facts associated with events may not be known at the time of recognition. These estimates can be grounded in reality or managed by the company to present a desired financial picture.

23. A is correct. Managers can temporarily show a higher cash flow from operations by stretching the accounts payable credit period. In other words, the managers delay payments until the next accounting period. Applying all non-cash discount amortization against interest capitalized causes reported interest expenses and operating cash outflow to be higher, resulting in a lower cash flow provided by operations. Shifting the classification of interest paid from financing to operating cash flows lowers the cash flow provided by operations.

24. B is correct. Bias in revenue recognition can lead to manipulation of information presented in financial reports. Addressing the question as to whether revenue is higher or lower than the previous period is insufficient to determine if there is bias in revenue recognition. Additional analytical procedures must be performed to identify warning signals of accounting malfeasance. Barter transactions are difficult to value properly and may result in bias in revenue recognition. Policies that make it easier to prematurely recognize revenue, such as before goods are shipped to customers, may be a warning sign of accounting malfeasance.

25. C is correct. If a company's days sales outstanding (DSO) is increasing relative to competitors, this may be a signal that revenues are being recorded prematurely or are even fictitious. Numerous analytical procedures can be performed to provide evidence of manipulation of information in financial reporting. These warning signs are often linked to bias associated with revenue recognition and expense recognition policies.

26. B is correct. If the ratio of cash flow to net income for a company is consistently below 1 or has declined repeatedly over time, this may be a signal of manipulation of information in financial reports through aggressive accrual accounting policies. When net income is consistently higher than cash provided by operations, one possible explanation is that the company may be using aggressive accrual accounting policies to shift current expenses to later periods.

27. C is correct. To extrapolate historical earnings trends, an analyst should consider making pro forma analytical adjustments of prior years' earnings to reflect in those prior years a reasonable share of the current period's restructuring and impairment charges.

LEARNING MODULE

11

Financial Analysis Techniques

by Elaine Henry, PhD, CFA, Thomas R. Robinson, Phd, CAIA, CFA, and J. Hennie van Greuning, DCom, CFA.

Elaine Henry, PhD, CFA, is at Stevens Institute of Technology (USA). Thomas R. Robinson, Phd, CAIA, CFA, is at Robinson Global Investment Management LLC, (USA). J. Hennie van Greuning, DCom, CFA, is at BIBD (Brunei).

LEARNING OUTCOMES

Mastery	*The candidate should be able to:*
☐	describe tools and techniques used in financial analysis, including their uses and limitations
☐	calculate and interpret activity, liquidity, solvency, and profitability ratios
☐	describe relationships among ratios and evaluate a company using ratio analysis
☐	demonstrate the application of DuPont analysis of return on equity and calculate and interpret effects of changes in its components
☐	describe the uses of industry-specific ratios used in financial analysis
☐	describe how ratio analysis and other techniques can be used to model and forecast earnings

The two major accounting standard setters are as follows: 1) the International Accounting Standards Board (IASB) who establishes International Financial Reporting Standards (IFRS) and 2) the Financial Accounting Standards Board (FASB) who establishes US GAAP. Throughout this learning module both standards are referred to and many, but not all, of these two sets of accounting rules are identified. Note: changes in accounting standards as well as new rulings and/or pronouncements issued after the publication of this learning module may cause some of the information to become dated.

1 INTRODUCTION

Analysts convert financial statement and other data into metrics that assist in decision making and help answer questions such as the following: How successfully has a target company performed, relative to its own past performance and relative to its competitors? How is the company likely to perform in the future? Based on expectations about future performance, what is the value of this company or the securities it issues? This module describes various techniques used to answer these and other questions. These financial analysis techniques are crucial to a wide range of analytical tasks, including valuing equity securities, assessing credit risk, conducting due diligence related to an acquisition, and evaluating business performance.

LEARNING MODULE OVERVIEW

- There is no single approach to structuring the financial analysis process, but a general framework entails the following phases: articulate the purpose of the analysis, collect input data, process the data, analyze and interpret the processed data, develop and communicate conclusions and recommendations, follow-up periodically to determine if any changes are necessary to recommendations or holdings.
- The purpose of analysis is not simply to compile information and do computations, but to integrate these into a cohesive result that addresses not just what happened, but why it happened and whether it created value. An analyst must be able to understand the "why" behind the numbers and ratios, not just what the numbers and ratios are.
- Evaluations require comparisons. It is difficult to say that a company's financial performance was "good" or "bad" without clarifying the basis for comparison. Cross-sectional analysis compares multiple companies at the same point in time or over the same range of time, and trend or time-series analysis compares measures for a single company over a period of time.
- Ratios and common-size financial statements can remove size as a factor and enable more relevant comparisons. Financial statement ratios are helpful for valuing companies and securities, selecting investments, and predicting financial distress. The ratio is an indicator of some aspect of a company's performance, telling what happened but not why it happened.
- Common-size analysis involves expressing financial data, including entire financial statements, in relation to a single financial statement item, or base. A vertical common-size balance sheet divides each balance sheet item by the same period's total assets and expresses the results as percentages. A vertical common-size income statement divides each income statement item by revenue or by total assets. A horizontal common-size balance sheet divides the quantity of each item by a base year quantity of the same item to yield a percentage change in that item from the base year. Trend data generated by a horizontal common-size analysis can be compared across financial statements.

- Graphs facilitate comparison of performance and financial structure over time, provide a visual overview of changes and trends, and can be used to communicate the conclusions from financial analysis. Regression analysis can help identify relationships or correlation between variables.
- Activity ratios measure the efficiency of a company's operations, such as a collection of receivables or management of inventory. Major activity ratios include inventory turnover, days of inventory on hand, receivables turnover, days of sales outstanding, payables turnover, number of days of payables, working capital turnover, fixed asset turnover, and total asset turnover.
- Liquidity ratios measure the ability of a company to meet short-term obligations. Major liquidity ratios include the current ratio, quick ratio, cash ratio, and defensive interval ratio. The cash conversion cycle is a measure of liquidity that is not a simple ratio.
- Solvency ratios measure the ability of a company to meet long-term obligations. Major solvency ratios include debt ratios (including the debt-to-assets ratio, debt-to-capital ratio, debt-to-equity ratio, and financial leverage ratio) and coverage ratios (including interest coverage and fixed charge coverage).
- Profitability ratios measure the ability of a company to generate profits from revenue and assets. Major profitability ratios include return on sales ratios (including gross profit margin, operating profit margin, pretax margin, and net profit margin) and return on investment ratios (including operating return on assets [ROA], ROA, return on total capital, return on equity [ROE], and return on common equity).
- It is important to examine a variety of financial ratios—not a single ratio or category of ratios in isolation—to ascertain the overall position and performance of a company.
- DuPont analysis breaks ROE into components that are indicators of different aspects of company performance. Many levels of decomposition are possible.
- The five-component DuPont decomposition expresses a company's ROE as a function of its tax rate, interest burden, operating profitability, efficiency, and leverage.
- Because aspects of performance that are considered important in one industry may be irrelevant in another, industry-specific ratios are used that reflect these differences.
- Techniques such as sensitivity analysis, scenario analysis, and simulation are used to forecast future financial performance.

THE FINANCIAL ANALYSIS PROCESS 2

☐ describe tools and techniques used in financial analysis, including their uses and limitations

In financial analysis, it is essential to clearly identify and understand the final objective and the steps required to reach that objective. In addition, the analyst needs to know where to find relevant data, how to process and analyze the data (in other words, know the typical questions to address when interpreting data), and how to communicate the analysis and conclusions.

The Objectives of the Financial Analysis Process

Because of the variety of reasons for performing financial analysis, the numerous available techniques, and the often substantial amount of data, it is important that the analytical approach be tailored to the specific situation. Prior to beginning any financial analysis, the analyst should clarify the purpose and context, and clearly understand the following:

- What is the purpose of the analysis? What questions will this analysis answer?
- What level of detail will be needed to accomplish this purpose?
- What data are available for the analysis?
- What are the factors or relationships that will influence the analysis?
- What are the analytical limitations, and will these limitations potentially impair the analysis?

Having clarified the purpose and context of the analysis, the analyst can select the set of techniques (e.g., ratios) that will best assist in making a decision. Although there is no single approach to structuring the analysis process, a general framework is set forth in Exhibit 1. The steps in this process were discussed in more detail in an earlier module; the primary focus of this module is on Phases 3 and 4, processing and analyzing data.

Exhibit 1: A Financial Statement Analysis Framework

Phase		Sources of Information	Output
1.	Articulate the purpose and context of the analysis.	▪ The nature of the analyst's function, such as evaluating an equity or debt investment or issuing a credit rating. ▪ Communication with client or supervisor on needs and concerns. ▪ Institutional guidelines related to developing specific work product.	▪ Statement of the purpose or objective of analysis. ▪ A list (written or unwritten) of specific questions to be answered by the analysis. ▪ Nature and content of report to be provided. ▪ Timetable and budgeted resources for completion.
2.	Collect input data.	▪ Financial statements, other financial data, questionnaires, and industry/economic data. ▪ Discussions with management, suppliers, customers, and competitors. ▪ Company site visits (e.g., to production facilities or retail stores).	▪ Organized financial statements. ▪ Financial data tables. ▪ Completed questionnaires, if applicable.

Phase		Sources of Information	Output
3.	Process data.	▪ Data from the previous phase.	▪ Adjusted financial statements. ▪ Common-size statements. ▪ Ratios and graphs. ▪ Forecasts.
4.	Analyze/interpret the processed data.	▪ Input data as well as processed data.	▪ Analytical results.
5.	Develop and communicate conclusions and recommendations (e.g., with an analysis report).	▪ Analytical results and previous reports. ▪ Institutional guidelines for published reports.	▪ Analytical report answering questions posed in Phase 1. ▪ Recommendation regarding the purpose of the analysis, such as whether to make an investment or grant credit.
6.	Follow-up.	▪ Information gathered by periodically repeating above steps as necessary to determine whether changes to holdings or recommendations are necessary.	▪ Updated reports and recommendations.

Distinguishing between Computations and Analysis

An effective analysis encompasses both computations and interpretations. A well-reasoned analysis differs from a mere compilation of various pieces of information, computations, tables, and graphs by integrating the data collected into a cohesive whole. Analysis of past performance, for example, should address not only what happened but also why it happened and whether it created value. Some of the key questions to address include the following:

- What aspects of performance are critical for this company to successfully compete in this industry?
- How well did the company's performance meet these critical aspects? (Established through computation and comparison with appropriate benchmarks, such as the company's own historical performance or competitors' performance.)
- What were the key causes of this performance, and how does this performance reflect the company's strategy? (Established through analysis.)

If the analysis is forward looking, additional questions include the following:

- What is the likely impact of an event or trend? (Established through interpretation of analysis.)
- What is the likely response of management to this trend? (Established through evaluation of quality of management and corporate governance.)
- What is the likely impact of trends in the company, industry, and economy on future cash flows? (Established through assessment of corporate strategy and through forecasts.)
- What are the recommendations of the analyst? (Established through interpretation and forecasting of results of analysis.)
- What risks should be highlighted? (Established by an evaluation of major uncertainties in the forecast and in the environment within which the company operates.)

Example 1 demonstrates how a company's financial data can be analyzed in the context of its business strategy and changes in that strategy. An analyst must be able to understand the "why" behind the numbers and ratios, not just what the numbers and ratios are.

EXAMPLE 1

Strategy Reflected in Financial Performance

Apple Inc. engages in the design, manufacture, and sale of computer hardware, mobile devices, operating systems and related products, and services. It also operates retail and online stores. Microsoft develops, licenses, and supports software products, services, and technology devices through a variety of channels including retail stores in recent years. Selected financial data for 2015 through 2017 for these two companies are given in Exhibit 2 and Exhibit 3. Apple's fiscal year (FY) ends on the final Saturday in September (for example, FY2017 ended on 30 September 2017). Microsoft's fiscal year ends on 30 June (for example, FY2017 ended on 30 June 2017).

Exhibit 2: Selected Financial Data for Apple (US dollar millions)

Fiscal year	2017	2016	2015
Net sales (or Revenue)	229,234	215,639	233,715
Gross margin	88,186	84,263	93,626
Operating income	61,344	60,024	71,230

Exhibit 3: Selected Financial Data for Microsoft (US dollar millions)*

Fiscal year	2017	2016	2015
Net sales (or revenue)	89,950	85,320	93,580
Gross margin	55,689	52,540	60,542
Operating income	22,326	20,182	18,161

** Microsoft revenue for 2017 and 2016 were subsequently revised in the company's 2018 10-K report due to changes in revenue recognition and lease accounting standards.*

Source: 10-K reports for Apple and Microsoft.

Apple reported a 7.7 percent decrease in net sales from FY2015 to FY2016 and an increase of 6.3 percent from FY2016 to FY2017 for an overall slight decline over the three-year period. Gross margin decreased 10.0 percent from FY2015 to FY2016 and increased 4.7 percent from FY2016 to FY2017. This also represented an overall decline in gross margin over the three-year period. The company's operating income exhibited similar trends.

Microsoft reported an 8.8 percent decrease in net sales from FY2015 to FY2016 and an increase of 5.4 percent from FY2016 to FY2017 for an overall slight decline over the three-year period. Gross margin decreased 13.2 percent from FY2015 to FY2016 and increased 6.0 percent from FY2016 to FY2017. Similar to Apple, this represented an overall decline in gross margin over the three-year period. Microsoft's operating income, in contrast, exhibited growth each year and for the three-year period. Overall growth in operating income was 23 percent.

What caused Microsoft's growth in operating income while Apple and Microsoft had similar negative trends in sales and gross margin? Apple's decline in sales, gross margin, and operating income from FY2015 to FY2016 was caused by declines in iPhone sales and weakness in foreign currencies relative to the US dollar. FY2017 saw a rebound in sales of iPhones, Mac computers, and services offset somewhat by continued weaknesses in foreign currencies. Microsoft similarly had declines in revenue and gross margin from sales of its devices and Windows software in FY2016, as well as negative impacts from foreign currency weakness. Microsoft's increase in revenue and gross margin in FY2017 was driven by the acquisition of LinkedIn, higher sales of Microsoft Office software, and higher sales of cloud services. The driver in the continuous increase in operating income for Microsoft was a large decline over the three-year period in impairment, integration, and restructuring charges. Microsoft recorded a USD10 billion charge in FY2015 related to its phone business, and there were further charges of USD1.1 billion in FY2016 and USD306 million in FY2017. Absent these large write-offs, Microsoft would have had a trend similar to Apple's in operating income over the three-year period.

Analysts often need to communicate the findings of their analysis in a written report. Their reports should communicate how conclusions were reached and why recommendations were made. For example, a report might present the following:

- the purpose of the report, unless it is readily apparent;
- relevant aspects of the business context, including:
  - economic environment (country/region, macro economy, sector),
  - financial and other infrastructure (accounting, auditing, rating agencies), and
  - legal and regulatory environment (and any other material limitations on the company being analyzed);
- evaluation of corporate governance and assessment of management strategy, including the company's competitive advantage(s);
- assessment of financial and operational data, including key assumptions in the analysis; and
- conclusions and recommendations, including limitations of the analysis and risks.

An effective narrative and well supported conclusions and recommendations are normally enhanced by using 3–10 years of data as well as by analytic techniques appropriate to the purpose of the report.

ANALYTICAL TOOLS AND TECHNIQUES 3

☐ describe tools and techniques used in financial analysis, including their uses and limitations

The tools and techniques presented in this lesson facilitate evaluations of company data. Evaluations require comparisons. It is difficult to say that a company's financial performance was "good" or "bad" without clarifying the basis for comparison. In assessing a company's ability to generate and grow earnings and cash flow, and the risks related to those earnings and cash flows, the analyst draws comparisons to other companies at the same point in time or over the same range of time (cross-sectional analysis) and over time (trend or time-series analysis).

For example, an analyst may wish to compare the profitability of companies competing in a global industry. If the companies differ significantly in size or report their financial data in different currencies, comparing net income as reported is not useful. Ratios (which express one number in relation to another) and common-size financial statements can remove size as a factor and enable a more relevant comparison. To achieve comparability across companies reporting in different currencies, one approach is to translate all reported numbers into a common currency using average or period-end exchange rates. Alternatively, if the focus is primarily on ratios, comparability can be achieved without translating the currencies.

The analyst may also want to examine comparable performance over time. Again, the nominal currency amounts of sales or net income may not highlight significant changes. To address this challenge, horizontal financial statements (whereby quantities are stated in terms of a selected base year value) can make such changes more apparent. Another obstacle to comparison is differences in fiscal year end. To achieve comparability, one approach is to develop trailing 12 months of data. Finally, it should be noted that differences in accounting standards can limit comparability.

EXAMPLE 2

Ratio Analysis

An analyst is examining the profitability of two international companies with large shares of the global personal computer market: Acer Inc. and Lenovo Group Limited. Acer has pursued a strategy of selling its products at affordable prices. In contrast, Lenovo aims to achieve higher selling prices by stressing the high engineering quality of its personal computers for business use. Acer reports in New Taiwan dollars (TWD) and Lenovo reports in US dollars (USD). For Acer, fiscal year end is 31 December. For Lenovo, fiscal year end is 31 March; thus, FY2017 ended 31 March 2018.

The analyst collects the data shown in Exhibit 4. Use this information to answer the following questions:

Exhibit 4: Acer versus Lenova Profitability

Acer

TWD Millions	FY2013	FY2014	FY2015	FY2016	FY2017
Revenue	360,132	329,684	263,775	232,724	237,275
Gross profit	22,550	28,942	24,884	23,212	25,361
Net income	(20,519)	1,791	604	(4,901)	2,797

Lenovo

USD Millions	FY2013	FY2014	FY2015	FY2016	FY2017
Revenue	38,707	46,296	44,912	43,035	45,350
Gross profit	5,064	6,682	6,624	6,105	6,272
Net income (Loss)	817	837	(145)	530	(127)

Note: Fiscal years for Lenovo end 31 March. Thus, FY2017 represents the fiscal year ended 31 March 2018; the same applies respectively for prior years.

1. Which company is larger based on the amount of revenue, in US dollars, reported in fiscal year 2017? For FY2017, assume the relevant, average exchange rate was 30.95 TWD/USD.

   Solution:

   Lenovo is much larger than Acer based on FY2017 revenues in US dollar terms. Lenovo's FY2017 revenues of USD45.35 billion are considerably higher than Acer's USD7.67 billion (= TWD237.275 million/30.95).
   Acer: At the assumed average exchange rate of 30.95 TWD/USD, Acer's FY2017 revenues are equivalent to USD7.67 billion (= TWD237.275 million ÷ 30.95 TWD/USD).
   Lenovo: Lenovo's FY2017 revenues totaled USD45.35 billion.
   Note: Comparing the size of companies reporting in different currencies requires translating reported numbers into a common currency using exchange rates at some point in time. This solution converts the revenues of Acer to billions of US dollars using the average exchange rate of the fiscal period. It would be equally informative (and would yield the same conclusion) to convert the revenues of Lenovo to New Taiwan dollars.

2. Which company had the higher revenue growth from FY2016 to FY2017? FY2013 to FY2017?

   Solution:

   The growth in Lenovo's revenue was much higher than Acer's in the most recent fiscal year and for the five-year period.

	Change in Revenue FY2016 versus FY2017 (%)	Change in Revenue FY2013 to FY2017 (%)
Acer	1.96	(34.11)
Lenovo	5.38	17.16

   The table shows two growth metrics. Calculations are illustrated using the revenue data for Acer:

The change in Acer's revenue for FY2016 versus FY2017 is 1.96 percent calculated as (237,275 – 232,724) ÷ 232,724 or equivalently (237,275 ÷ 232,724) – 1. The change in Acer's revenue from FY2013 to FY2017 is a decline of 34.11 percent.

3. How do the companies compare, based on profitability?

Solution:

Profitability can be assessed by comparing the amount of gross profit to revenue and the amount of net income to revenue. The following table presents these two profitability ratios—gross profit margin (gross profit divided by revenue) and net profit margin (net income divided by revenue)—for each year.

Acer	FY2013 (%)	FY2014 (%)	FY2015 (%)	FY2016 (%)	FY2017 (%)
Gross profit margin	6.26	8.78	9.43	9.97	10.69
Net profit margin	(5.70)	0.54	0.23	(2.11)	1.18

Lenovo	FY2013 (%)	FY2014 (%)	FY2015 (%)	FY2016 (%)	FY2017 (%)
Gross profit margin	13.08	14.43	14.75	14.19	13.83
Net profit margin	2.11	1.81	(0.32)	1.23	(0.28)

The net profit margins indicate that both companies' profitability is relatively low. Acer's net profit margin is lower than Lenovo's in three out of the five years. Acer's gross profit margin increased each year but remains significantly below that of Lenovo. Lenovo's gross profit margin grew from FY2013 to FY2015 and then declined in FY2016 and FY2017. Overall, Lenovo is the more profitable company, likely attributable to its larger size and commensurate economies of scale. (Lenovo has the largest share of the personal computer market relative to other personal computer companies.)

4 FINANCIAL RATIO ANALYSIS

☐ describe tools and techniques used in financial analysis, including their uses and limitations

There are many relationships among financial accounts and various expected relationships from one point in time to another. Ratios are a useful way of expressing these relationships. Ratios express one quantity in relation to another, usually as a quotient.

Extensive academic research has examined the importance of ratios in predicting stock returns (Ou and Penman, 1989; Abarbanell and Bushee, 1998) or credit failure (Altman, 1968; Ohlson, 1980; Hopwood et al., 1994). This research has found that financial statement ratios are effective in selecting investments and in predicting financial distress. Practitioners routinely use ratios to derive and communicate the value of companies and securities.

Several aspects of ratio analysis are important to understand. First, the computed ratio is not "the answer." The ratio is an *indicator* of some aspect of a company's performance, telling what happened but not why it happened. For example, an analyst might want to answer the question: Which of two companies was more profitable? As demonstrated in the previous example, the net profit margin, which expresses profit relative to revenue, can provide insight into this question. Net profit margin is calculated by dividing net income by revenue:

$$\frac{\text{Net income}}{\text{Revenue}}.$$

Assume Company A has EUR100,000 of net income and Company B has EUR200,000 of net income. Company B generated twice as much income as Company A, but was it more profitable? Assume further that Company A has EUR2,000,000 of revenue, and thus a net profit margin of 5 percent, and Company B has EUR6,000,000 of revenue, and thus a net profit margin of 3.33 percent. Expressing net income as a percentage of revenue clarifies the relationship: For each EUR100 of revenue, Company A earns EUR5 in net income, whereas Company B earns only EUR3.33 for each EUR100 of revenue. So, we can now answer the question of which company was more profitable in percentage terms: Company A was more profitable, as indicated by its higher net profit margin of 5 percent. Note that Company A was more *profitable* despite the fact that Company B reported higher absolute amounts of net income and revenue. However, this ratio by itself does not tell us *why* Company A has a higher profit margin. Further analysis is required to determine the reason (perhaps higher relative sales prices or better cost control or lower effective tax rates).

Company size sometimes confers economies of scale, so the absolute amounts of net income and revenue are useful in financial analysis. However, ratios control for the effect of size, which enhances comparisons between companies and over time.

A second important aspect of ratio analysis is that differences in accounting policies (across companies and across time) can distort ratios, and a meaningful comparison, therefore, may involve adjustments to the financial data. Third, not all ratios are necessarily relevant to a particular analysis. The ability to select a relevant ratio or ratios to answer the research question is an analytical skill. Finally, as with financial analysis in general, ratio analysis does not stop with computation; interpretation of the result is essential. In practice, differences in ratios across time and across companies can be subtle, and interpretation is situation specific.

The Universe of Ratios

No authoritative bodies specify the exact formulas for computing ratios or provide a standard, comprehensive list of ratios. Formulas and even names of ratios often differ from analyst to analyst or from database to database. The number of different ratios that can be created is practically limitless. Several widely accepted ratios, however, have been found to be useful, which are the focus of this module. The analyst should be aware that different ratios may be used in practice and that certain industries have unique ratios tailored to the characteristics of that industry. When faced with an unfamiliar ratio, the analyst can examine the underlying formula to gain insight into what the ratio is measuring. For example, consider the following ratio formula:

$$\frac{\text{Operating income}}{\text{Average total assets}}.$$

Never having seen this ratio, an analyst might question whether a result of 12 percent is better than 8 percent. The answer can be found in the ratio itself. The numerator is operating income and the denominator is average total assets, so the ratio can be interpreted as the amount of operating income generated per unit of assets. For every EUR100 of average total assets, generating EUR12 of operating income is better than generating EUR8 of operating income. Furthermore, it is apparent that this particular ratio is an indicator of profitability (as well as efficiency in use of assets in generating operating profits). When encountering a ratio for the first time, the analyst should evaluate the numerator and denominator to assess what the ratio is attempting to measure and how it should be interpreted. This is demonstrated in Example 3.

EXAMPLE 3

Interpreting a Financial Ratio

A US insurance company reports that its "combined ratio" is determined by dividing losses and expenses incurred by net premiums earned. It reports the following combined ratios:

Exhibit 5: Combined Ratio

Fiscal Year	5	4	3	2	1
Combined ratio	90.1%	104.0%	98.5%	104.1%	101.1%

1. Explain what this ratio is measuring and compare the results reported for each of the years shown in the chart. What other information might an analyst want to review before making any conclusions on this information?

Solution:

The combined ratio is a profitability measure. The ratio is explaining how much costs (losses and expenses) were incurred for every dollar of revenue (net premiums earned). The underlying formula indicates that a *lower* value for this ratio is better. The year 5 ratio of 90.1 percent means that for every dollar of net premiums earned, the costs were USD0.901, yielding a gross profit of $0.099. Ratios greater than 100 percent indicate an overall loss. A review of the data indicates that there does not seem to be a consistent trend in this ratio. Profits were achieved in years 5 and 3. The results for years 4 and 2 show the most significant costs at approximately 104 percent.

The analyst would want to discuss this data further with management and understand the characteristics of the underlying business. He or she would want to understand why the results are so volatile. The analyst would also want to determine what should be used as a benchmark for this ratio.

The Operating income/Average total assets ratio is one of many versions of the **return on assets (ROA)** ratio. Note that there are other ways of specifying this formula based on how assets are defined. Some financial ratio databases compute ROA using the ending value of assets rather than average assets. In limited cases, one may also see beginning assets in the denominator. Which one is right? It depends on what you are trying to measure and the underlying company trends. If the company has a stable level of assets, the answer will not differ greatly under the three measures of assets (beginning, average, and ending). However, if the assets are growing (or shrinking), the results will differ among the three measures. When assets are growing, operating income divided by ending assets may not make sense because some of the income would have been generated before some assets were purchased, and this would understate the company's performance. Similarly, if beginning assets are used, some of the operating income later in the year may have been generated only because of the addition of assets; therefore, the ratio would overstate the company's performance. Because operating income occurs throughout the period, it generally makes sense to use some average measure of assets. A good general rule is that when an income statement or cash flow statement number is in the numerator of a ratio and a balance sheet number is in the denominator, then an average should be used for the denominator. It is generally not necessary to use averages when only balance sheet numbers are used in both the numerator and denominator because both are determined as of the same date. However, in some instances, even ratios that only use balance sheet data may use averages. For example, **return on equity (ROE)**, which is defined as net income divided by average shareholders' equity, can be decomposed into other ratios, some of which only use balance sheet data. In decomposing ROE into component ratios, if an average is used in one of the component ratios, then it should be used in the other component ratios. The decomposition of ROE is discussed further in a later lesson.

If an average is used, judgment is also required about what average should be used. For simplicity, most ratio databases use a simple average of the beginning and end-of-year balance sheet amounts. If the company's business is seasonal so that levels of assets vary by interim period (semiannual or quarterly), then it may be beneficial to take an average over all interim periods, if available. (If the analyst is working within a company and has access to monthly data, this can also be used.)

Value, Purposes, and Limitations of Ratio Analysis

The value of ratio analysis is that it enables a financial analyst to evaluate past performance, assess the current financial position of the company, and gain insights useful for projecting future results. As noted previously, the ratio itself is not "the answer" but is an indicator of some aspect of a company's performance. Financial ratios provide insights into the following:

- economic relationships within a company that help analysts project earnings and free cash flow;
- a company's financial flexibility, or ability to obtain the cash required to grow and meet its obligations, even if unexpected circumstances develop;
- management's ability;
- changes in the company or industry over time; and
- comparability with peer companies or the relevant industry(ies).

Ratio analysis also has limitations. Factors to consider include the following:

- *The heterogeneity or homogeneity of a company's operating activities.* Companies may have divisions operating in many different industries. This can make it difficult to find comparable industry ratios to use for comparison purposes.
- *The need to determine whether the results of the ratio analysis are consistent.* One set of ratios may indicate a problem, whereas another set may indicate that the potential problem is only short term in nature.
- *The need to use judgment.* A key issue is whether a ratio for a company is within a reasonable range. Although financial ratios are used to help assess the growth potential and risk of a company, they cannot be used alone to directly value a company or its securities, or to determine its

creditworthiness. The entire operation of the company must be examined, and the external economic and industry setting in which it is operating must be considered when interpreting financial ratios.

- *The use of alternative accounting methods.* Companies frequently have latitude when choosing certain accounting methods. Ratios taken from financial statements that employ different accounting choices may not be comparable unless adjustments are made. Some important accounting considerations include the following:

  - FIFO (first in, first out), LIFO (last in, first out), or average cost inventory valuation methods (International Financial Reporting Standards [IFRS] does not allow LIFO);
  - Cost or equity methods of accounting for unconsolidated affiliates;
  - Straight-line or accelerated methods of depreciation; and
  - Operating or finance lease treatment for lessors (under US GAAP, the type of lease affects classifications of expenses; under IFRS, operating lease treatment for lessors is not applicable).

Convergence efforts between IFRS and US GAAP make the financial statements of different companies more comparable and may overcome some of these difficulties. Nonetheless, there will remain accounting choices that the analyst must consider.

Sources of Ratios

Ratios may be computed using data obtained directly from companies' financial statements or from a database such as Bloomberg, Compustat, FactSet, or Thomson Reuters. The information provided by the database may include information as reported in companies' financial statements and ratios calculated based on the information. These databases are popular because they provide easy access to many years of historical data so that trends over time can be examined. They also allow for ratio calculations based on periods other than the company's fiscal year, such as for the trailing 12 months (TTM) or most recent quarter (MRQ).

EXAMPLE 4

Trailing 12 Months

1. On 15 July, an analyst is examining a company with a fiscal year ending on 31 December. Use the following data to calculate the company's TTM earnings (for the period ended 30 June 2018):

   - Earnings for the year ended 31 December 2017: USD1,200;
   - Earnings for the six months ended 30 June 2017: USD550; and
   - Earnings for the six months ended 30 June 2018: USD750.

   Solution:

   The company's TTM earnings is USD1,400, calculated as USD1,200 – USD550 + USD750.

Analysts should be aware that the underlying formulas for ratios may differ by vendor. The formula used should be obtained from the vendor, and the analyst should determine whether any adjustments are necessary. Furthermore, database providers often exercise judgment when classifying items. For example, operating income may not appear directly on a company's income statement, and the vendor may use judgment to classify income statement items as "operating" or "non-operating." Variation in such judgments would affect any computation involving operating income. It is therefore a good practice to use the same source for data when comparing different companies or when evaluating the historical record of a single company. Analysts should verify the consistency of formulas and data classifications by the data source. Analysts should also be mindful of the judgments made by a vendor in data classifications and refer to the source financial statements until they are comfortable that the classifications are appropriate.

Collection of financial data from regulatory filings and calculation of ratios can be automated. The eXtensible Business Reporting Language (XBRL) is a mechanism that attaches "smart tags" to financial information (e.g., total assets), so that software can automatically collect the data and perform desired computations. The organization developing XBRL (www.xbrl.org) is an international nonprofit consortium of more than 600 members from companies, associations, and agencies, including the International Accounting Standards Board (IASB). Many stock exchanges and regulatory agencies around the world now use XBRL for receiving and distributing public financial reports from listed companies.

Analysts can compare a subject company to similar (peer) companies in vendor databases or use aggregate industry data. For non-public companies, aggregate industry data can be obtained from such sources as Annual Statement Studies by the Risk Management Association or Dun & Bradstreet. These publications typically provide industry data with companies sorted into quartiles. By definition, 25 percent of companies' ratios fall within the lowest quartile, 25 percent have ratios between the lower quartile and median value, and so on. Analysts can then determine a company's relative standing in the industry.

COMMON SIZE BALANCE SHEETS AND INCOME STATEMENTS 5

☐ describe tools and techniques used in financial analysis, including their uses and limitations

Common-size analysis involves expressing financial data, including entire financial statements, in relation to a single financial statement item, or base. Items used most frequently as the bases are total assets or revenue. In essence, common-size analysis creates a ratio between every financial statement item and the base item. Common-size analysis was demonstrated in earlier modules for the income statement, balance sheet, and cash flow statement. In this lesson, we present common-size analysis of financial statements in greater detail and include further discussion of their interpretation.

Common-Size Analysis of the Balance Sheet A vertical common-size balance sheet, prepared by dividing each item on the balance sheet by the same period's total assets and expressing the results as percentages, highlights the composition of the balance sheet. What is the mix of assets being used? How is the company financing itself? How does one company's balance sheet composition compare with that of peer companies, and what are the reasons for any differences? A horizontal common-size balance sheet, prepared by computing the increase or decrease in percentage terms of each balance sheet item from the prior year or prepared by dividing the quantity of each item by a base year quantity of the item, highlights changes in items. These changes can be compared to expectations.

Exhibit 6 presents a vertical common-size (partial) balance sheet for a hypothetical company in two time periods. In this example, receivables have increased from 35 percent to 57 percent of total assets and the ratio has increased by 63 percent from Period 1 to Period 2. What are possible reasons for such an increase? The increase might indicate that the company is making more of its sales on a credit basis rather than a cash basis, perhaps in response to some action taken by a competitor. Alternatively, the increase in receivables as a percentage of assets may have occurred because of a change in another current asset category, for example, a decrease in the level of inventory; the analyst would then need to investigate why that asset category has changed. Another possible reason for the increase in receivables as a percentage of assets is that the company has lowered its credit standards, relaxed its collection procedures, or adopted more aggressive revenue recognition policies. The analyst can turn to other comparisons and ratios (e.g., comparing the rate of growth in accounts receivable with the rate of growth in sales) to help determine which explanation is most likely.

Exhibit 6: Vertical Common-Size (Partial) Balance Sheet for a Hypothetical Company

	Period 1 Percent of Total Assets	Period 2 Percent of Total Assets
Cash	25	15
Receivables	35	57
Inventory	35	20
Fixed assets, net of depreciation	5	8
Total assets	100	100

Common-Size Analysis of the Income Statement

A vertical common-size income statement divides each income statement item by revenue, or sometimes by total assets (especially in the case of financial institutions). If there are multiple revenue sources, a decomposition of revenue in percentage terms is useful. Exhibit 7 presents a hypothetical company's vertical common-size income statement in two time periods. Revenue is separated into the company's four services, each shown as a percentage of total revenue.

In this example, revenues from Service A have become a far greater percentage of the company's total revenue (30 percent in Period 1 and 45 percent in Period 2). What are possible reasons for and implications of this change in business mix? Did the company make a strategic decision to sell more of Service A, perhaps because it is more profitable? Apparently not, because the company's earnings before interest, taxes, depreciation, and amortization (EBITDA) declined from 53 percent of sales to 45 percent, so other possible explanations should be examined. In addition, we note from the composition of operating expenses that the main reason for this decline in profitability is that salaries and employee benefits have increased from 15 percent to 25 percent of total revenue. Are more highly compensated employees required for Service A? Were higher training costs incurred to increase revenues from Service A? If the analyst wants to predict future performance, the causes of these changes must be understood.

In addition, Exhibit 7 shows that the company's income tax as a percentage of sales has declined dramatically (from 15 percent to 8 percent). Furthermore, taxes as a percentage of earnings before tax (EBT) (the effective tax rate, which is usually the more relevant comparison), have decreased from 36 percent (= 15/42) to 24 percent

(= 8/34). Is Service A, which in Period 2 is a greater percentage of total revenue, provided in a jurisdiction with lower tax rates? If not, what is the explanation for the change in effective tax rate?

The observations based on Exhibit 7 summarize the issues that can be raised through analysis of the vertical common-size income statement.

Exhibit 7: Vertical Common-Size Income Statement for Hypothetical Company

	Period 1Percent of Total Revenue	Period 2Percent of Total Revenue
Revenue source: Service A	30	45
Revenue source: Service B	23	20
Revenue source: Service C	30	30
Revenue source: Service D	17	5
Total revenue	**100**	**100**
Operating expenses (excluding depreciation)		
Salaries and employee benefits	15	25
Administrative expenses	22	20
Rent expense	10	10
EBITDA	**53**	**45**
Depreciation and amortization	4	4
EBIT	**49**	**41**
Interest paid	7	7
EBT	**42**	**34**
Income tax provision	15	8
Net income	**27**	**26**

EBIT = earnings before interest and tax.

6 CROSS-SECTIONAL, TREND ANALYSIS, AND RELATIONSHIPS IN FINANCIAL STATEMENTS

☐ describe tools and techniques used in financial analysis, including their uses and limitations

As noted previously, ratios and common-size statements derive their utility through comparison. **Cross-sectional analysis** (sometimes called "relative analysis") compares a specific metric for one company with the same metric for another company or group of companies measured at the same point in time or over the same range of time, allowing comparisons even though the companies might be of significantly different sizes or operate in different currencies. This is illustrated in Exhibit 8.

Exhibit 8: Vertical Common-Size (Partial) Balance Sheet for Two Hypothetical Companies

Assets	Company 1 Percent of Total Assets	Company 2 Percent of Total Assets
Cash	38	12
Receivables	33	55
Inventory	27	24
Fixed assets net of depreciation	1	2
Investments	1	7
Total Assets	**100**	**100**

Exhibit 8 presents a vertical common-size (partial) balance sheet for two hypothetical companies at the same point in time. Company 1 is clearly more liquid (liquidity is a function of how quickly assets can be converted into cash) than Company 2, which has only 12 percent of assets available as cash, compared with the highly liquid Company 1, which has 38 percent of assets available as cash. Given that cash is generally a relatively low-yielding asset and thus not a particularly efficient use of excess funds, why does Company 1 hold such a large percentage of total assets in cash? Perhaps the company is preparing for an acquisition, or maintains a large cash position as insulation from a particularly volatile operating environment. Another issue highlighted by the comparison in this example is the relatively high percentage of receivables in Company 2's assets, which may indicate a greater proportion of credit sales, overall changes in asset composition, lower credit or collection standards, or aggressive accounting policies.

Trend Analysis

When looking at financial statements and ratios, trends in the data, whether they are improving or deteriorating, are as important as the current absolute or relative levels. Trend analysis provides important information regarding historical performance and growth and, given a sufficiently long history of accurate seasonal information, can be of great assistance as a planning and forecasting tool for management and analysts.

Exhibit 9 presents a partial balance sheet for a hypothetical company over five periods. The last two columns of the table show the changes for Period 5 compared with Period 4, expressed both in absolute currency (in this case, dollars) and in percentages. A small percentage change could hide a significant currency change and vice versa, prompting the analyst to investigate the reasons despite one of the changes being relatively small. In this example, the largest percentage change was in investments, which decreased by 33.3 percent. However, an examination of the absolute currency amount of changes shows that investments changed by only USD2 million, and the more significant change was the USD12 million increase in receivables.

Another way to present data covering a period of time is to show each item in relation to the same item in a base year (i.e., a horizontal common-size balance sheet). Exhibit 10 and Exhibit 11 illustrate alternative presentations of horizontal common-size balance sheets. Exhibit 10 presents the information from the same partial balance sheet as in Exhibit 9, but indexes each item relative to the same item in Period 1. For example, in Period 2, the company had USD29 million cash, which is 74 percent or 0.74 of the amount of cash it had in Period 1. Expressed as an index relative to Period 1, where each item in Period 1 is given a value of 1.00, the value in Period 2 would be 0.74 (USD29/USD39 = 0.74). In Period 3, the company had USD27 million cash, which is 69 percent of the amount of cash it had in Period 1 (USD27/USD39 = 0.69).

Exhibit 11 presents the percentage change in each item, relative to the previous year. For example, the change in cash from Period 1 to Period 2 was −25.6 percent (USD29/USD39 − 1 = −0.256), and the change in cash from Period 2 to Period 3 was −6.9 percent (USD27/USD29 − 1 = −0.069). An analyst will select the horizontal common-size balance that addresses the particular period of interest. Exhibit 10 clearly highlights that in Period 5 compared to Period 1, the company has less than half the amount of cash, four times the amount of investments, and eight times the amount of property, plant, and equipment. Exhibit 11 highlights year-to-year changes: For example, cash has declined in each period. Presenting data this way highlights significant changes. Again, note that a mathematically big change is not necessarily an important change. For example, fixed assets increased 100 percent (i.e., doubled between Period 1 and 2); however, as a proportion of total assets, fixed assets increased from 1 percent of total assets to 2 percent of total assets. The company's working capital assets (receivables and inventory) are a far higher proportion of total assets and would likely warrant more attention from an analyst.

An analysis of horizontal common-size balance sheets highlights structural changes that have occurred in a business. Past trends are obviously not necessarily an accurate predictor of the future, especially when the economic or competitive environment changes. An examination of past trends is more valuable when the macroeconomic and competitive environments are relatively stable and when the analyst is reviewing a stable or mature business. However, even in less stable contexts, historical analysis can serve as a basis for developing expectations. Understanding of past trends is helpful in assessing whether these trends are likely to continue or if the trend is likely to change direction.

Exhibit 9: Partial Balance Sheet for a Hypothetical Company over Five Periods

	Period					Change 4 to 5 (US dollar millions)	Change 4 to 5 (%)
Assets (US dollar millions)	**1**	**2**	**3**	**4**	**5**		
Cash	39	29	27	19	16	−3	−15.8
Investments	1	7	7	6	4	−2	−33.3
Receivables	44	41	37	67	79	12	17.9
Inventory	15	25	36	25	27	2	8.0
Fixed assets net of depreciation	1	2	6	9	8	−1	−11.1
Total assets	100	104	113	126	134	8	6.3

Exhibit 10: Horizontal Common-Size (Partial) Balance Sheet for a Hypothetical Company over Five Periods, with Each Item Expressed Relative to the Same Item in Period One

	Period				
Assets	**1**	**2**	**3**	**4**	**5**
Cash	1.00	0.74	0.69	0.49	0.41
Investments	1.00	7.00	7.00	6.00	4.00
Receivables	1.00	0.93	0.84	1.52	1.80

Assets	Period 1	2	3	4	5
Inventory	1.00	1.67	2.40	1.67	1.80
Fixed assets net of depreciation	1.00	2.00	6.00	9.00	8.00
Total assets	1.00	1.04	1.13	1.26	1.34

Exhibit 11: Horizontal Common-Size (Partial) Balance Sheet for a Hypothetical Company over Five Periods, with Percent Change in Each Item Relative to the Prior Period

	Period			
Assets	**2 (%)**	**3 (%)**	**4 (%)**	**5 (%)**
Cash	−25.6	−6.9	−29.6	−15.8
Investments	600.0	0.0	−14.3	−33.3
Receivables	−6.8	−9.8	81.1	17.9
Inventory	66.7	44.0	−30.6	8.0
Fixed assets net of depreciation	100.0	200.0	50.0	−11.1
Total assets	4.0	8.7	11.5	6.3

One measure of success is for a company to grow at a rate greater than the rate of the overall market in which it operates. Companies that grow slowly may find themselves unable to attract equity capital. Conversely, companies that grow too quickly may find that their administrative and management information systems cannot keep up with the rate of expansion.

Relationships Among Financial Statements

Trend data generated by a horizontal common-size analysis can be compared across financial statements. For example, the growth rate of assets for the hypothetical company in Exhibit 12 can be compared with the company's growth in revenue over the same period of time. If revenue is growing more quickly than assets, the company may be increasing its efficiency (i.e., generating more revenue for every dollar invested in assets).

As another example, consider the following year-over-year percentage changes for a hypothetical company:

Exhibit 12: Year-over-Year Percentage Changes

Revenue	**+20%**
Net income	+25%
Operating cash flow	−10%
Total assets	+30%

Net income is growing faster than revenue, which indicates increasing profitability. However, the analyst would need to determine whether the faster growth in net income resulted from continuing operations or from non-operating, non-recurring items. In addition, the 10 percent decline in operating cash flow despite increasing revenue and net income clearly warrants further investigation because it could indicate a problem with earnings quality (perhaps aggressive reporting of revenue). Lastly, the fact that assets have grown faster than revenue indicates the company's efficiency may be declining. The analyst should examine the composition of the increase in assets and the reasons for the changes. Example 5 illustrates a historical example of a company for which comparisons of trend data from different financial statements were actually indicative of aggressive accounting policies.

EXAMPLE 5

Use of Comparative Growth Information[1]

In July 1996, Sunbeam, a US company, brought in new management to turn the company around. In the following year, 1997, using 1996 as the base, the following was observed based on reported numbers:

Exhibit 13: Sunbeam Revenue

Revenue	**+19 percent**
Inventory	+58 percent
Receivables	+38 percent

It is generally more desirable to observe inventory and receivables growing at a slower (or similar) rate than revenue growth. Receivables growing faster than revenue can indicate operational issues, such as lower credit standards or aggressive accounting policies for revenue recognition. Similarly, inventory growing faster than revenue can indicate an operational problem with obsolescence or aggressive accounting policies, such as an improper overstatement of inventory to increase profits.

In this case, the explanation lay in aggressive accounting policies. Sunbeam was later charged by the US Securities and Exchange Commission with improperly accelerating the recognition of revenue and engaging in other practices, such as billing customers for inventory prior to shipment.

THE USE OF GRAPHS AND REGRESSION ANALYSIS 7

☐ describe tools and techniques used in financial analysis, including their uses and limitations

1 Adapted from Robinson and Munter (2004, p. 2–15).

Graphs facilitate comparison of performance and financial structure over time, highlighting changes in significant aspects of business operations. In addition, graphs provide the analyst (and management) with a visual overview of risk trends in a business. Graphs may also be used effectively to communicate the analyst's conclusions regarding financial condition and risk management aspects.

Exhibit 14 presents the information from Exhibit 9 in a stacked column format. The graph makes the significant decline in cash and growth in receivables (both in absolute terms and as a percentage of assets) readily apparent. In Exhibit 14, the vertical axis shows US dollar millions and the horizontal axis denotes the period.

Choosing the appropriate graph to communicate the most significant conclusions of a financial analysis is a skill. In general, pie graphs are most useful to communicate the composition of a total value (e.g., assets over a limited amount of time, say one or two periods). Line graphs are useful when the focus is on the change in amount for a limited number of items over a relatively longer time period. When the composition and amounts, as well as their change over time, are all important, a stacked column graph can be useful.

Exhibit 14: Stacked Column Graph of Asset Composition of Hypothetical Company over Five Periods

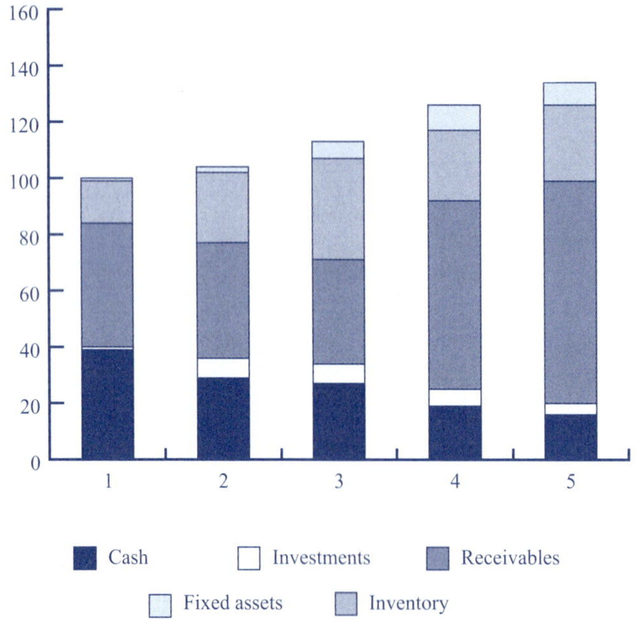

When comparing Period 5 with Period 4, the growth in receivables appears to be within normal bounds; but when comparing Period 5 with earlier periods, the dramatic growth becomes apparent. In the same manner, a simple line graph will also illustrate the growth trends in key financial variables. Exhibit 15 presents the information from Exhibit 9A as a line graph, illustrating the growth of assets of a hypothetical company over five periods. The steady decline in cash, volatile movements of inventory, and dramatic growth of receivables is clearly illustrated. Again, the vertical axis is shown in US dollar millions and the horizontal axis denotes periods.

Exhibit 15: Line Graph of Growth of Assets of Hypothetical Company over Five Periods

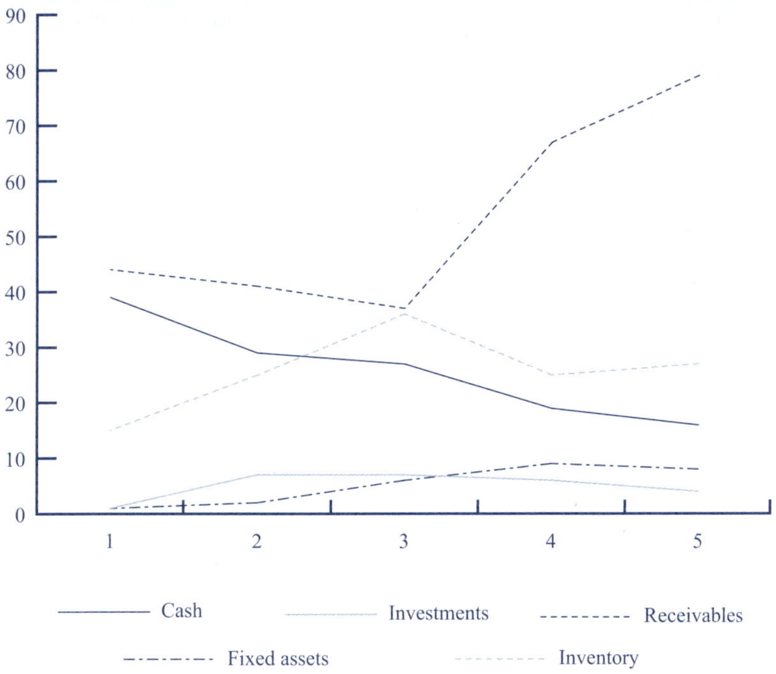

Regression Analysis

When analyzing the trend in a specific line item or ratio, frequently it is possible simply to visually evaluate the changes. For more complex situations, regression analysis can help identify relationships (or correlation) between variables. For example, a regression analysis could relate a company's sales to GDP over time, providing insight into whether the company is cyclical. In addition, the statistical relationship between sales and GDP could be used as a basis for forecasting sales.

Other examples in which regression analysis may be useful include the relationship between a company's sales and inventory over time, or the relationship between hotel occupancy and a company's hotel revenues. In addition to providing a basis for forecasting, regression analysis facilitates identification of items or ratios that are not behaving as expected, given historical statistical relationships.

COMMON RATIO CATEGORIES, INTERPRETATION, AND CONTEXT 8

- [ ] calculate and interpret activity, liquidity, solvency, and profitability ratios

In the previous lesson, we focused on ratios resulting from common-size analysis. In this lesson, we expand the discussion to include other commonly used financial ratios and the broad classes into which they are categorized. There is some overlap with common-size financial statement ratios. For example, a common indicator of profitability is the net profit margin, which is calculated as net income divided by sales. This ratio appears on a vertical common-size income statement. Other ratios involve information from multiple financial statements or even data from outside the financial statements.

Because of the large number of ratios, it is helpful to think about ratios in terms of broad categories based on what aspects of performance a ratio is intended to detect. Financial analysts and data vendors use a variety of categories to classify ratios. The category names and the ratios included in each category can differ. Common ratio categories include activity, liquidity, solvency, and profitability, which were introduced in earlier modules in Corporate Issuers. These categories are summarized in Exhibit 16. Each category measures a different aspect of the company's business, but all are useful in evaluating a company's overall ability to generate cash flows from operating its business and the associated risks.

Exhibit 16: Categories of Financial Ratios

Category	Description
Activity	**Activity ratios** measure the efficiency of a company's operations, such as the collection of receivables and management of inventory.
Liquidity	**Liquidity ratios** measure the company's ability to meet its short-term obligations.
Solvency	**Solvency ratios** measure a company's ability to meet long-term obligations. Subsets of these ratios are also known as "leverage" and "long-term debt" ratios.
Profitability	**Profitability ratios** measure the company's ability to generate profits from its resources (assets) or sales.

Interpretation and Context

Financial ratios can be interpreted only in the context of other information. In general, the financial ratios of a company are compared with those of its major competitors (cross-sectional and trend analysis) and to the company's prior periods (trend analysis). The goal is to understand the underlying causes of divergence between a company's ratios and those of the industry. Even ratios that remain consistent require understanding because consistency can sometimes indicate accounting policies selected to smooth earnings. An analyst should evaluate financial ratios in the context of the following:

1. *Prior period results.* Trend analysis can reveal whether a company's performance and position are weakening or strengthening.
2. *Expectations.* These are point or range estimates for key values, such as sales growth, profit margins, and leverage ratios, that are specified by the analyst or external analysts before results are published. Differences from expectations should be scrutinized for setting expectations in subsequent periods.
3. *Industry peers and competitors* (*cross-sectional analysis*). A company can be compared with others in its industry by relating its financial ratios to industry norms or to a subset of the companies in an industry. When industry norms are used to make judgments, care must be taken for the following reasons:

- Companies may have several different lines of business. This will cause aggregate financial ratios to be distorted. It is better to examine industry-specific ratios by lines of business.
- Differences in business model and corporate strategies can affect certain financial ratios.
- Some ratios are industry specific, and not all ratios are important to all industries.
- Differences in accounting methods used by companies can distort financial ratios.

4. *Company goals and strategy.* Actual ratios can be compared with company objectives to determine whether objectives are being attained and whether the results are consistent with the company's strategy.
5. *Economic conditions.* For cyclical companies, financial ratios tend to improve when the economy is strong and weaken during recessions. Therefore, financial ratios should be examined in light of the current phase of the business cycle.

The following lessons discuss the calculation and interpretation of activity, liquidity, solvency, and profitability ratios using a company's financial statements.

ACTIVITY RATIOS

9

☐ calculate and interpret activity, liquidity, solvency, and profitability ratios

Activity ratios, also known as **asset utilization ratios** or **operating efficiency ratios**, are measures of operational performance—how effectively the company is using working capital and longer term assets. Since working capital efficiency has a direct impact on liquidity, some activity ratios are also useful in assessing liquidity.

Calculation of Activity Ratios

Exhibit 17 presents commonly used activity ratios.

Exhibit 17: Definitions of Commonly Used Activity Ratios

Activity Ratios	Numerator	Denominator
Inventory turnover	Cost of sales or cost of goods sold	Average inventory
Days of inventory on hand (DOH)	Number of days in period	Inventory turnover
Receivables turnover	Revenue	Average receivables
Days of sales outstanding (DSO)	Number of days in period	Receivables turnover
Payables turnover	Cost of sales or cost of goods sold	Average trade payables
Number of days of payables	Number of days in period	Payables turnover

Activity Ratios	Numerator	Denominator
Working capital turnover	Revenue	Average working capital
Fixed asset turnover	Revenue	Average net fixed assets
Total asset turnover	Revenue	Average total assets

Activity ratios generally combine information from the income statement in the numerator with balance sheet items in the denominator. Because the income statement measures what happened *during* a period, whereas the balance sheet shows the condition only at the end of the period, average balance sheet figures are normally used for consistency.

Activity ratios can be computed for any annual or interim period, but care must be taken in the interpretation and comparison across periods. For example, if the same company had cost of goods sold for the first quarter (90 days) of the following year of EUR35,000 and average inventory of EUR11,000, the inventory turnover would be 3.18 times. However, this turnover rate is 3.18 times per quarter, which is not directly comparable to the 12 times per year in the preceding year. In this case, we can annualize the quarterly inventory turnover rate by multiplying the quarterly turnover by 4 (12 months/3 months; or by 4.06, using 365 days/90 days) for comparison to the annual turnover rate. So, the quarterly inventory turnover is equivalent to a 12.72 annual inventory turnover (or 12.90 if we annualize the ratio using a 90-day quarter and a 365-day year). To compute the DOH using quarterly data, we can use the quarterly turnover rate and the number of days in the quarter for the numerator—or, we can use the annualized turnover rate and 365 days; either results in DOH of around 28.3, with slight differences due to rounding (90/3.18 = 28.30 and 365/12.90 = 28.29). Another time-related computational detail is that for companies using a 52/53-week annual period and for leap years, the actual days in the year should be used rather than 365.

In some cases, an analyst may want to know how many days of inventory are on hand at the end of the year rather than the average for the year. In this case, it would be appropriate to use the year-end inventory balance in the computation rather than the average. If the company is growing rapidly or if costs are increasing rapidly, analysts should consider using cost of goods sold just for the fourth quarter in this computation because the cost of goods sold of earlier quarters may not be relevant. Example 6 further demonstrates computation of activity ratios using Hong Kong Stock Exchange (HKEX)–listed Lenovo Group Limited.

EXAMPLE 6

Computation of Activity Ratios

1. An analyst would like to evaluate Lenovo Group's efficiency in collecting its trade accounts receivable during the fiscal year ended 31 March 2018 (FY2017). The analyst gathers the following information in Exhibit 18 from Lenovo's annual and interim reports:

Exhibit 18: Lenovo

	US dollar thousands
Trade receivables as of 31 March 2017	4,468,392
Trade receivables as of 31 March 2018	4,972,722
Revenue for year ended 31 March 2018	45,349,943

Calculate Lenovo's receivables turnover and number of days of sales outstanding (DSO) for the fiscal year ended 31 March 2018.

Solution:

Receivables turnover	=	Revenue/Average receivables
	=	45,349,943/[(4,468,392 + 4,972,722)/2]
	=	45,349,943/4,720,557
	=	9.6069 times, or 9.6 rounded
DSO	=	Number of days in period/Receivables turnover
	=	365/9.6
	=	38.0 days

On average, it took Lenovo 38 days to collect receivables during the fiscal year ended 31 March 2018.

Interpretation of Activity Ratios

Inventory Turnover and DOH

Inventory turnover indicates the resources tied up in inventory (i.e., the carrying costs) and, therefore, can be used to indicate inventory management effectiveness. In general, inventory turnover and DOH (days of inventory on hand) should be benchmarked against industry norms.

A high inventory turnover ratio relative to industry norms might indicate highly effective inventory management. Alternatively, a high inventory turnover ratio (and commensurately low DOH) could possibly indicate the company does not carry adequate inventory, so shortages could potentially hurt revenue. To assess which explanation is more likely, the analyst can compare the company's revenue growth with that of the industry. Slower growth combined with higher inventory turnover could indicate inadequate inventory levels. Revenue growth at or above the industry's growth supports the interpretation that the higher turnover reflects greater inventory management efficiency.

A low inventory turnover ratio (and commensurately high DOH) relative to the rest of the industry could be an indicator of slow-moving inventory, perhaps because of technological obsolescence or a change in fashion. Again, comparing the company's sales growth with the industry can offer insight.

Receivables Turnover and DSO

The number of DSO (days of sales outstanding) reflects how fast the company collects cash from customers to whom it offers credit. Although limiting the numerator to sales made on credit in the receivables turnover would be more appropriate, credit sales information is usually not available to analysts; therefore, revenue as reported in the income statement is generally used.

As with inventory management, comparison of the company's sales growth relative to the industry can help the analyst assess whether sales are being lost due to stringent credit policies. In addition, comparing the company's estimates of uncollectible accounts receivable and actual credit losses with past experience and with peer companies can help assess whether low turnover reflects credit management issues. Companies often provide details of receivables aging (how much receivables have been outstanding by age). This can be used along with DSO to understand trends in collection, as demonstrated in Example 7.

EXAMPLE 7

Evaluation of an Activity Ratio

An analyst has computed the average DSO for Lenovo for fiscal years ended 31 March 2018 and 2017:

Exhibit 19: Average DSO

	FY2017	FY2016
Days of sales outstanding	38.0	37.6

Revenue increased from USD43.035 billion for fiscal year ended 31 March 2017 (FY2016) to USD45.350 billion for fiscal year ended 31 March 2018 (FY2017). The analyst would like to better understand the change in the company's DSO from FY2016 to FY2017 and whether the increase is indicative of any issues with the customers' credit quality. The analyst collects accounts receivable aging information from Lenovo's annual reports and computes the percentage of accounts receivable by days outstanding. This information is presented in Exhibit 20:

Exhibit 20: Accounts Receivable

	FY2017		FY2016		FY2015	
	USD000	Percent	USD000	Percent	USD000	Percent
Accounts receivable						
0–30 days	3,046,240	59.95	2,923,083	63.92	3,246,600	71.99
31–60 days	1,169,286	23.01	985,251	21.55	617,199	13.69
61–90 days	320,183	6.30	283,050	6.19	240,470	5.33
Over 90 days	545,629	10.74	381,387	8.34	405,410	8.99
Total	5,081,338	100.00	4,572,771	100.00	4,509,679	100.00

	FY2017		FY2016		FY2015	
	USD000	Percent	USD000	Percent	USD000	Percent
Less: Provision for impairment	−108,616	−2.14	−104,379	−2.28	−106,172	−2.35
Trade receivables, net	4,972,722	97.86	4,468,392	97.72	4,403,507	97.65
Total sales	*45,349,943*		*43,034,731*		*44,912,097*	

Note: Lenovo's footnotes disclose that general trade customers are provided with credit terms ranging from 0 to 120 days.

These data indicate that total accounts receivable increased by 11 percent (net, after impairment) in FY2017 versus FY2016, while total sales increased by only 5.4 percent. Further, the percentage of receivables in all categories older than 30 days has increased over the three-year period, indicating that customers are indeed taking longer to pay. Conversely, the provision for impairment (estimate of uncollectible accounts) has declined as a percent of total receivables. Considering all this information, the company may be increasing customer financing purposely to drive its sales growth. They also may be underestimating the impairment. This should be investigated further by the analyst.

Payables Turnover and the Number of Days of Payables

The number of days of payables reflects the average number of days the company takes to pay its suppliers, and the payables turnover ratio measures how many times per year the company theoretically pays off all its creditors. A payables turnover ratio that is high (low days payable) relative to the industry could indicate that the company is not making full use of available credit facilities; alternatively, it could result from a company taking advantage of early payment discounts. An excessively low turnover ratio (high days payable) could indicate trouble making payments on time, or alternatively, exploitation of lenient supplier terms. This is another example in which it is useful to look simultaneously at other ratios. If liquidity ratios indicate that the company has sufficient cash and other short-term assets to pay obligations and yet the days payable ratio is relatively high, the analyst would favor the lenient supplier credit and collection policies as an explanation.

Working Capital Turnover

Working capital turnover indicates how efficiently the company generates revenue with its working capital. For example, a working capital turnover ratio of 4.0 indicates that the company generates EUR4 of revenue for every EUR1 of working capital. A high working capital turnover ratio indicates greater efficiency (i.e., the company is generating a high level of revenues relative to working capital). For some companies, working capital can be near zero or negative, rendering this ratio incapable of being interpreted. The following two ratios are more useful in those circumstances.

Fixed Asset Turnover

This ratio measures how efficiently the company generates revenues from its investments in fixed assets. Generally, a higher fixed asset turnover ratio indicates more efficient use of fixed assets in generating revenue. A low ratio can indicate inefficiency, a capital-intensive business environment, or a new business not yet operating at full capacity—in which case the analyst will not be able to link the ratio directly to efficiency. In addition, asset turnover can be affected by factors other than a company's efficiency. The fixed asset turnover ratio would be lower for a company whose assets are newer (and, therefore, less depreciated and so reflected in the financial statements at a higher carrying value) than the ratio for a company with older assets (that are thus more depreciated and so reflected at a lower carrying value). The fixed asset ratio can be erratic because, although revenue may have a steady growth rate, increases in fixed assets may not follow a smooth pattern; so, every year-to-year change in the ratio does not necessarily indicate important changes in the company's efficiency.

Total Asset Turnover

The total asset turnover ratio measures the company's overall ability to generate revenues with a given level of assets. A ratio of 1.20 would indicate that the company is generating EUR1.20 of revenues for every EUR1 of average assets. A higher ratio indicates greater efficiency. Because this ratio includes both fixed and current assets, inefficient working capital management can distort overall interpretations. It is therefore helpful to analyze working capital and fixed asset turnover ratios separately.

A low asset turnover ratio can be an indicator of inefficiency or of relative capital intensity of the business. The ratio also reflects strategic decisions by management—for example, the decision whether to use a more labor-intensive (and less capital-intensive) approach to its business or a more capital-intensive (and less labor-intensive) approach.

When interpreting activity ratios, the analysts should examine not only the individual ratios but also the collection of relevant ratios to determine the overall efficiency of a company. Example 8 demonstrates the evaluation of activity ratios, both narrow (e.g., days of inventory on hand) and broad (e.g., total asset turnover) for a hypothetical manufacturer.

EXAMPLE 8

Evaluation of Activity Ratios

ZZZ Company is a hypothetical manufacturing company. As part of an analysis of management's operating efficiency, an analyst collects the following activity ratios from a data provider:

Exhibit 21: Operating Efficiency

Ratio	2018	2017	2016	2015
DOH	35.68	40.70	40.47	48.51
DSO	45.07	58.28	51.27	76.98
Total asset turnover	0.36	0.28	0.23	0.22

These ratios indicate that the company has improved on all three measures of activity over the four-year period. The company appears to be managing its inventory more efficiently, is collecting receivables faster, and is generating a higher level of revenues relative to total assets. The overall trend appears good, but thus far, the analyst has only determined *what* happened. A more important question is *why* the ratios improved, because understanding good changes as well as bad ones facilitates judgments about the company's future performance. To answer this question, the analyst examines company financial reports as well as external information about the industry and economy. In examining the annual report, the analyst notes that in the fourth quarter of 2018, the company experienced an "inventory correction" and that the company recorded an allowance for the decline in market value and obsolescence of inventory of about 15 percent of year-end inventory value (compared with about a 6 percent allowance in the prior year). This reduction in the value of inventory accounts for a large portion of the decline in DOH from 40.70 in 2017 to 35.68 in 2018. Management claims that this inventory obsolescence is a short-term issue; analysts can watch DOH in future interim periods to confirm this assertion. In any event, all else being equal, the analyst would likely expect DOH to return to a level closer to 40 days going forward.

More positive interpretations can be drawn from the total asset turnover. The analyst finds that the company's revenues increased more than 35 percent, whereas total assets increased only by about 6 percent. Based on external information about the industry and economy, the analyst attributes the increased revenues both to overall growth in the industry and to the company's increased market share. Management was able to achieve growth in revenues with a comparatively modest increase in assets, leading to an improvement in total asset turnover. Note further that part of the reason for the increase in asset turnover is lower DOH and DSO.

LIQUIDITY RATIOS

10

☐ calculate and interpret activity, liquidity, solvency, and profitability ratios

Liquidity analysis measures a company's ability to meet its short-term obligations. In the short run, a company's sources of liquidity typically include cash and marketable securities on hand and debt issuance. In the longer run, for non-financial companies, liquidity is addressed by cash flows from operations and managing the structure of liabilities, such as the timing of debt maturities (see the following discussion on the financial sector).

The level of liquidity needed differs from one industry to another. A particular company's liquidity position may vary according to the anticipated need for funds at any given time. Judging whether a company has adequate liquidity requires analysis of its historical funding requirements, current liquidity position, anticipated future funding needs, and options for reducing funding needs or attracting additional funds (including actual and potential sources of such funding).

Larger companies are usually better able to control the level and composition of their liabilities than smaller companies. Therefore, they may have more potential funding sources, including public capital and money markets. Greater discretionary access to capital markets also reduces the size of the liquidity buffer needed relative to companies without such access.

Contingent liabilities, such as letters of credit or financial guarantees, can also be relevant when assessing liquidity. The importance of contingent liabilities varies for the non-banking and banking sector. In the non-banking sector, contingent liabilities (usually disclosed in the footnotes to the company's financial statements) represent potential cash outflows, and when appropriate, should be included in an assessment of a company's liquidity. In the banking sector, contingent liabilities represent potentially significant cash outflows that are not dependent on the bank's financial condition. Although outflows in normal market circumstances typically may be low, a general macroeconomic or market crisis can trigger a substantial increase in cash outflows related to contingent liabilities because of the increase in defaults and business bankruptcies that often accompany such events. In addition, such crises are usually characterized by diminished levels of overall liquidity, which can further exacerbate funding shortfalls. Therefore, for the banking sector, the effect of contingent liabilities on liquidity warrants particular attention.

Calculation of Liquidity Ratios

Common liquidity ratios, introduced in earlier modules in Corporate Issuers, are presented in Exhibit 22. These liquidity ratios reflect a company's position at a point in time and, therefore, typically use data from the ending balance sheet rather than averages.

Exhibit 22: Definitions of Commonly Used Liquidity Ratios

Liquidity Ratios	Numerator	Denominator
Current ratio	Current assets	Current liabilities
Quick ratio	Cash + Short-term marketable investments + Receivables	Current liabilities
Cash ratio	Cash + Short-term marketable investments	Current liabilities
Defensive interval ratio	Cash + Short-term marketable investments + Receivables	Daily cash expenditures
Additional Liquidity Measure		
Cash conversion cycle (net operating cycle)	DOH + DSO − Number of days of payables	

The **defensive interval ratio** measures how long a company can pay its daily cash expenditures using only its existing liquid assets, without additional cash flow coming in. This ratio is similar to the "burn rate" often computed for early-stage companies that are funded by venture capital funds and company insiders. The numerator of this ratio includes the same liquid assets used in the quick ratio, and the denominator is an estimate of daily cash expenditures. To obtain daily cash expenditures, the total of cash expenditures for the period is divided by the number of days in the period. Total cash expenditures for a period can be approximated by summing all expenses on the income statement—such as cost of goods sold; selling, general, and administrative expenses; and research and development expenses—and then subtracting any non-cash expenses, such as depreciation and amortization (typically, taxes are not included).

Interpretation of Liquidity Ratios

In the following, we discuss the interpretation of the five basic liquidity measures presented in Exhibit 22.

Current Ratio

A higher current ratio indicates a higher level of liquidity (i.e., a greater ability to meet short-term obligations). A lower ratio indicates less liquidity, implying a greater reliance on operating cash flow and outside financing to meet short-term obligations. The current ratio implicitly assumes that inventories and accounts receivable are indeed liquid (which is presumably not the case when related turnover ratios are low).

Quick Ratio

The quick ratio is more conservative than the current ratio because it includes only the more liquid current assets (sometimes referred to as "quick assets") in relation to current liabilities. Like the current ratio, a higher quick ratio indicates greater liquidity.

The quick ratio reflects the fact that certain current assets—such as prepaid expenses, some taxes, and employee-related prepayments—represent costs of the current period that have been paid in advance and cannot usually be converted back into cash. This ratio also reflects the fact that inventory might not be easily and quickly converted into cash, and furthermore, that a company probably would not be able to sell all of its inventory for an amount equal to its carrying value, especially if it were required to sell the inventory quickly. In situations in which inventories are illiquid (as indicated, for example, by low inventory turnover ratios), the quick ratio may be a better indicator of liquidity than the current ratio.

Cash Ratio

The cash ratio normally represents a reliable measure of an entity's liquidity in a crisis situation. Only highly marketable short-term investments and cash are included. In a general market crisis, the fair value of marketable securities could decrease significantly as a result of market factors, in which case even this ratio might not provide reliable information.

Defensive Interval Ratio

The defensive interval ratio measures how long the company can continue to pay its expenses from its existing liquid assets without receiving any additional cash inflow. A defensive interval ratio of 50 would indicate that the company can continue to pay its operating expenses for 50 days before running out of quick assets, assuming no additional cash inflows. A higher defensive interval ratio indicates greater liquidity. If a company's defensive interval ratio is very low relative to peer companies or to the company's own history, the analyst would want to ascertain whether there is sufficient cash inflow expected to mitigate the low defensive interval ratio.

Cash Conversion Cycle (Net Operating Cycle)

This cash conversion cycle metric indicates the amount of time that elapses from the point when a company invests in working capital until the point at which the company collects cash. A shorter cash conversion cycle indicates greater liquidity. A short cash conversion cycle implies that the company only needs to finance its inventory and accounts receivable for a short period of time. A longer cash conversion cycle indicates lower liquidity; it implies that the company must finance its inventory and accounts receivable for a longer period of time, possibly indicating a need for a higher level of capital to fund current assets. Example 9 demonstrates the advantages of a short cash conversion cycle as well as how a company's business strategies are reflected in financial ratios.

EXAMPLE 9

Evaluation of Liquidity Measures

An analyst is evaluating the liquidity of Apple and calculates the number of days of receivables, inventory, and accounts payable, as well as the overall cash conversion cycle, as shown in Exhibit 23:

Exhibit 23: Liquidity of Apple

	FY2017	FY2016	FY2015
DSO	27	28	27
DOH	9	6	6
Less: Number of days of payables	112	101	86
Equals: Cash conversion cycle	(76)	(67)	(53)

The minimal DOH indicates that Apple maintains lean inventories, which is attributable to key aspects of the company's business model where manufacturing is outsourced. In isolation, the increase in number of days payable (from 86 days in FY2015 to 112 days in FY2017) might suggest an inability to pay suppliers; however, in Apple's case, the balance sheet (not shown here) indicates that the company has more than USD70 billion of cash and short-term investments, which would be more than enough to pay suppliers sooner if Apple chose to do so. Instead, Apple takes advantage of the favorable credit terms granted by its suppliers. The overall effect is a negative cash cycle, a somewhat unusual result. Instead of requiring additional capital to fund working capital as is the case for most companies, Apple has excess cash to invest for over 50 days during that three-year period (reflected on the balance sheet as short-term investments) on which it is earning, rather than paying, interest.

EXAMPLE 10

Bounds and Context of Financial Measures

The previous example focused on the cash conversion cycle, which many companies identify as a key performance metric. The less positive the number of days in the cash conversion cycle, typically, the better it is considered to be. However, is this always true?

This example considers the following question: If a larger negative number of days in a cash conversion cycle is considered to be a desirable performance metric, does identifying a company with a large negative cash conversion cycle necessarily imply good performance?

Using a historical example, National Datacomputer, a technology company, had large negative number of days in its cash conversion cycle during the 2005 to 2009 period. In 2008, its cash conversion cycle was –275.5 days.

Exhibit 24: National Datacomputer Inc. (US dollar millions)

Fiscal year	2004	2005	2006	2007	2008	2009
Sales	3.248	2.672	2.045	1.761	1.820	1.723
Cost of goods sold	1.919	1.491	0.898	1.201	1.316	1.228
Receivables, Total	0.281	0.139	0.099	0.076	0.115	0.045
Inventories, Total	0.194	0.176	0.010	0.002	0.000	0.000
Accounts payable	0.223	0.317	0.366	1.423	0.704	0.674
DSO		28.69	21.24	18.14	19.15	16.95

Fiscal year	2004	2005	2006	2007	2008	2009
DOH		45.29	37.80	1.82	0.28	0.00
*Less: Number of days of payables**		66.10	138.81	271.85	294.97	204.79
Equals: Cash conversion cycle		7.88	−79.77	−251.89	−275.54	−187.84

**Calculated using Cost of goods sold as an approximation of purchases. Ending inventories 2008 and 2009 are reported as $0 million; therefore, inventory turnover for 2009 cannot be measured. However, given inventory and average sales per day, DOH in 2009 is 0.00.*

Source: Raw data from Compustat. Ratios calculated."

National Datacomputer had a negative cash conversion cycle because the company's accounts payable increased substantially over the period. An increase from approximately 66 days in 2005 to 295 days in 2008 to pay trade creditors is clearly a negative signal. In addition, the company's inventories disappeared, most likely because the company did not have enough cash to purchase new inventory and was unable to get additional credit from its suppliers.

Of course, an analyst would have immediately noted the negative trends in these data, as well as additional data throughout the company's financial statements. In its management discussion and analysis (MD&A), the company clearly reports the risks as follows:

> Because we have historically had losses and only a limited amount of cash has been generated from operations, we have funded our operating activities to date primarily from the sale of securities and from the sale of a product line in 2009. In order to continue to fund our operations, we may need to raise additional capital, through the sale of securities. We cannot be certain that any such financing will be available on acceptable terms, or at all. Moreover, additional equity financing, if available, would likely be dilutive to the holders of our common stock, and debt financing, if available, would likely involve restrictive covenants and a security interest in all or substantially all of our assets. If we fail to obtain acceptable financing when needed, we may not have sufficient resources to fund our normal operations which would have a material adverse effect on our business.
>
> IF WE ARE UNABLE TO GENERATE ADEQUATE WORKING CAPITAL FROM OPERATIONS OR RAISE ADDITIONAL CAPITAL THERE IS SUBSTANTIAL DOUBT ABOUT THE COMPANY'S ABILITY TO CONTINUE AS A GOING CONCERN. (emphasis added by company)

Subsequently, the company's 2010 Form 10-K reported:

> In January 2011, due to our inability to meet our financial obligations and the impending loss of a critical distribution agreement granting us the right to distribute certain products, our secured lenders ("Secured Parties") acting upon an event of default, sold certain of our assets (other than cash and accounts receivable) to Micronet, Ltd. ("Micronet"), an unaffiliated corporation pursuant to the terms of an asset purchase agreement between the Secured Parties and Micronet dated January 10, 2010 (the "Asset Purchase Agreement"). In order to induce Micronet to enter into the agreement, the Company also provided certain representations and warranties regarding certain business matters.

In summary, it is always necessary to consider ratios within bounds of reasonability and to understand the reasons underlying changes in ratios. Ratios must not only be calculated but also must be interpreted by an analyst.

Source: Form 10-K, National Datacomputer Inc., 2009, p. 7.

Source: Form 10-K, National Datacomputer Inc., 2010.

11 SOLVENCY RATIOS

☐ calculate and interpret activity, liquidity, solvency, and profitability ratios

Solvency refers to a company's ability to fulfill its long-term debt obligations. Assessment of a company's ability to pay its long-term obligations (i.e., to make interest and principal payments) generally includes an in-depth analysis of the components of its financial structure. Solvency ratios, introduced in earlier modules in Corporate Issuers, provide information regarding the relative amount of debt in the company's capital structure and the adequacy of earnings and cash flow to cover interest expenses and other fixed charges (such as lease payments) as they come due.

By analyzing financial statements, an analyst aims to understand levels and trends in a company's use of financial leverage in relation to past practices and the practices of peer companies. Analysts also need to be aware that the greater a company's operating leverage, the greater the risk of the operating income stream available to cover debt payments; operating leverage can thus limit a company's capacity to use financial leverage.

A company's relative solvency is fundamental to valuation of its debt securities and its creditworthiness. Understanding a company's use of debt can provide analysts with insight into the company's future business prospects because management's decisions about financing may signal their beliefs about a company's future. For example, the issuance of long-term debt to repurchase common shares may indicate that management believes the market is underestimating the company's prospects and that the shares are undervalued.

Calculation of Solvency Ratios

The two primary types of solvency ratios are debt ratios and coverage ratios. Debt ratios focus on the balance sheet and measure the amount of debt capital relative to equity capital. Coverage ratios focus on the income statement and measure the ability of a company to cover its debt payments. These ratios are useful in assessing a company's solvency and, therefore, in evaluating the quality of a company's bonds and other debt obligations.

Exhibit 25 describes commonly used solvency ratios. The first three of the debt ratios presented use total debt in the numerator. The definition of total debt used in these ratios varies, with some market participants using the sum of interest-bearing short-term and long-term debt, excluding liabilities such as accrued expenses, accounts payable, and leases. (For calculations in this module, we use this definition.) Other market participants use definitions that are more inclusive (e.g., all liabilities) or restrictive (e.g., long-term debt only, in which case the ratio is sometimes qualified as "long-term," as in "long-term debt-to-equity ratio"). Finally, analysts also use solvency ratios that deduct cash, cash equivalents, and marketable securities from interest-bearing short-term and long-term debt to calculate **net debt** (or **net cash** if the former exceeds the latter). The assumption is that cash, cash equivalents, and marketable securities could be used to pay debt obligations, so it is only debt in excess of this amount that must be covered by future operating cash flows. Analysts should be transparent about their calculation methodologies and closely scrutinize ratios reported by issuers.

Exhibit 25: Definitions of Commonly Used Solvency Ratios

Solvency Ratios	Numerator	Denominator
Debt Ratios		
Debt-to-assets ratio[a]	Total debt[b]	Total assets
Debt-to-capital ratio	Total debt[b]	Total debt[b] + Total shareholders' equity
Debt-to-equity ratio	Total debt[b]	Total shareholders' equity
Financial leverage ratio[c]	Average total assets	Average total equity
Debt-to-EBITDA	Total or net debt	EBITDA
Coverage Ratios		
Interest coverage	EBIT	Interest payments
Fixed charge coverage	EBIT + Lease payments	Interest payments + Lease payments

[a] *"Total debt ratio" is another name sometimes used for this ratio.*
[b] *In this reading, total debt is the sum of interest-bearing short-term and long-term debt.*
[c] *Average total assets divided by average total equity is used for the purposes of this reading (in particular, Dupont analysis covered later). In practice, period-end total assets divided by period-end total equity is often used."*

Interpretation of Solvency Ratios

In the following, we discuss the interpretation of the basic solvency ratios presented in Exhibit 25.

Debt-to-Assets Ratio

This ratio measures the percentage of total assets financed with debt. For example, a **debt-to-assets ratio** of 0.40 or 40 percent indicates that 40 percent of the company's assets are financed with debt. Generally, higher debt means higher financial risk and thus weaker solvency.

Debt-to-Capital Ratio

The **debt-to-capital ratio** measures the percentage of a company's capital (debt plus equity) represented by debt. As with the previous ratio, a higher ratio generally means higher financial risk and thus indicates weaker solvency.

Debt-to-Equity Ratio

The **debt-to-equity ratio** measures the amount of debt capital relative to equity capital. Interpretation is similar to the preceding two ratios (i.e., a higher ratio indicates weaker solvency). A ratio of 1.0 would indicate equal amounts of debt and equity, which is equivalent to a debt-to-capital ratio of 50 percent. Alternative definitions of this ratio use the market value of stockholders' equity rather than its book value (or use the market values of both stockholders' equity and debt).

Financial Leverage Ratio

The **financial leverage ratio** (often called simply the "leverage ratio") measures the amount of total assets supported for each one money unit of equity. For example, a value of 3 for this ratio means that each EUR1 of equity supports EUR3 of total assets. The higher the financial leverage ratio, the more leveraged the company is in the sense of using debt and other liabilities to finance assets. This ratio is often defined in terms of average total assets and average total equity.

Debt-to-EBITDA Ratio

The debt-to-EBITDA ratio estimates how many years it would take to repay total debt based on earnings before income taxes, depreciation, and amortization (an approximation of operating cash flow). This ratio is commonly used in debt covenants between issuers and debt investors.

Interest Coverage

The **interest coverage ratio** measures the number of times a company's EBIT could cover its interest payments. Thus, it is sometimes referred to as "times interest earned." A higher **interest coverage** ratio indicates stronger solvency, offering greater assurance that the company can service its debt (i.e., bank debt, bonds, notes) from operating earnings. This ratio is commonly used in debt covenants between issuers and lenders or fixed income investors.

Fixed Charge Coverage

The **fixed charge coverage ratio** relates fixed charges, or obligations, to the cash flow generated by the company. It measures the number of times a company's earnings (before interest, taxes, and lease payments) can cover the company's interest and lease payments. Similar to the interest coverage ratio, a higher **fixed charge coverage** ratio implies stronger solvency, offering greater assurance that the company can service its debt (i.e., bank debt, bonds, notes, and leases) from normal earnings. The ratio is sometimes used as an indication of the quality of the preferred dividend, with a higher ratio indicating a more secure preferred dividend.

Example 11 demonstrates the use of solvency ratios in evaluating the creditworthiness of a company.

EXAMPLE 11

Evaluation of Solvency Ratios

A credit analyst is evaluating the solvency of Eskom, a South African public utility based on financial statements for the year ended 31 March 2017. The data in Exhibit 26 are gathered from the company's 2017 annual report:

Exhibit 26: Eskom 2017 Annual Report

South African rand, millions	2017	2016	2015
Total Assets	710,009	663,170	559,688
Short-Term Debt	18,530	15,688	19,976
Long-Term Debt	336,770	306,970	277,458
Total Liabilities	534,067	480,818	441,269
Total Equity	175,942	182,352	118,419

1. Calculate the company's financial leverage ratios for 2016 and 2017.

   Solution:

   (Amounts are millions of Rand.)
   For 2017, average total assets were (710,009 + 663,170)/2 = 686,590, and average total equity was (175,942 + 182,352)/2 = 179,147. Thus, financial leverage was 686,590/179,942 = 3.83. For 2016, financial leverage was 4.07.

	2017	2016
Average Assets	686,590	611,429
Average Equity	179,147	150,386
Financial Leverage	3.83	4.07

2. Interpret the financial leverage ratio calculated in question 1.

   Solution:

   For 2017, every South African rand in total equity supported ZAR3.83 in total assets, on average. Financial leverage decreased from 2016 to 2017 on this measure.

3. What are the company's debt-to-assets, debt-to-capital, and debt-to-equity ratios for the three years?

   Solution:

   (Amounts are millions of South African rand other than ratios.)

	2017	2016	2015
Total Debt	355,300	322,658	297,434
Total Capital	531,242	505,010	415,853
Debt/Assets	50.0%	48.7%	53.1%
Debt/Capital	66.9%	63.9%	71.5%
Debt/Equity	2.02	1.77	2.51

4. What is the discernable trend over the three years?

   Solution:

   On all three metrics, the company's leverage decreased from 2015 to 2016 and increased from 2016 to 2017. For 2016 the decrease in leverage resulted from a conversion of subordinated debt into equity as well as additional issuance of equity. However, in 2017 debt levels increased again relative to assets, capital, and equity indicating that the company's solvency has weakened. From a creditor's perspective, lower solvency (higher debt) indicates higher risk of default on obligations.

As with all ratio analysis, it is important to consider leverage ratios in a broader context. In general, companies with lower business risk and operations that generate steady cash flows are better positioned to take on more leverage without a commensurate increase in the risk of insolvency. In other words, a higher proportion of debt financing poses less risk of non-payment of interest and debt principal to a company with steady cash flows than to a company with volatile cash flows.

12 PROFITABILITY RATIOS

☐ calculate and interpret activity, liquidity, solvency, and profitability ratios

The ability to generate profit on capital invested is a key determinant of a company's overall value and the value of the securities it issues. Consequently, many equity analysts consider profitability to be a key focus of their analytical efforts.

Profitability reflects a company's competitive position in the market, and by extension, the quality of its management. The income statement reveals the sources of earnings and the components of revenue and expenses. Earnings can be distributed to shareholders or reinvested in the company.

Calculation of Profitability Ratios

Profitability ratios measure the return earned by the company during a period. Exhibit 27 provides the definitions of a selection of commonly used profitability ratios, some of which were introduced in earlier modules in Corporate Issuers. Return-on-sales profitability ratios express various subtotals on the income statement (e.g., gross profit, operating profit, net profit) as a percentage of revenue. Essentially, these ratios constitute part of a common-size income statement discussed earlier. Return on investment profitability ratios measure income relative to assets, equity, or total capital employed by the company. For operating ROA, returns are measured as operating income, that is, prior to deducting interest on debt capital. For ROA and ROE, returns are measured as net income, that is, after deducting interest paid on debt capital. For return on common equity, returns are measured as net income minus preferred dividends (because preferred dividends are a return to preferred equity).

Exhibit 27: Definitions of Commonly Used Profitability Ratios

Profitability Ratios	Numerator	Denominator
Return on Sales[a]		
Gross profit margin	Gross profit	Revenue
Operating profit margin	Operating income[b]	Revenue
Pretax margin	EBT (earnings before tax but after interest)	Revenue
Net profit margin	Net income	Revenue
Return on Investment		
Operating ROA	Operating income	Average total assets
ROA	Net income	Average total assets
Return on invested capital	EBIT × (1 - Effective Tax Rate)	Average total short- and long-term debt and equity
ROE	Net income	Average total equity
Return on common equity	Net income – Preferred dividends	Average common equity

[a] *"Sales" is being used as a synonym for "revenue."*
[b] *Some analysts use EBIT as a shortcut representation of operating income. Note that EBIT, strictly speaking, includes non-operating items such as dividends received and gains and losses on investment*

securities. Of utmost importance is that the analyst compute ratios consistently whether comparing different companies or analyzing one company over time."

Interpretation of Profitability Ratios

In the following, we discuss the interpretation of the profitability ratios presented in Exhibit 27. For each of the profitability ratios, a higher ratio indicates greater profitability.

Gross Profit Margin

Gross profit margin indicates the percentage of revenue available to cover operating and other expenses and to generate profit. Higher gross profit margin indicates some combination of higher product pricing and lower product costs. The ability to charge a higher price is constrained by competition, so gross profits are affected by (and usually inversely related to) competition. If a product has a competitive advantage (e.g., superior branding, better quality, or exclusive technology), the company is better able to charge more for it. On the cost side, higher gross profit margin can also indicate that a company has a competitive advantage in product costs.

Operating Profit Margin

Operating profit is calculated as gross profit minus operating costs. So, an **operating profit margin** increasing faster than the gross profit margin can indicate improvements in controlling operating costs, such as administrative overheads. In contrast, a declining operating profit margin could be an indicator of deteriorating control over operating costs.

Pretax Margin

Pretax income (also called "earnings before tax" or EBT) is calculated as operating profit minus interest, and the **pretax margin** is the ratio of pretax income to revenue. The pretax margin reflects the effects on profitability of leverage and other (non-operating) income and expenses. If a company's pretax margin is increasing primarily as a result of increasing amounts of non-operating income, the analyst should evaluate whether this increase reflects a deliberate change in a company's business focus and, therefore, the likelihood that the increase will continue.

Net Profit Margin

Net profit, or net income, is calculated as revenue minus all expenses. Net income includes both recurring and non-recurring components. Generally, the net income used in calculating the net profit margin is adjusted for non-recurring items to offer a better view of a company's potential future profitability.

ROA

ROA measures the return earned by a company on its assets. The higher the ratio, the more income is generated by a given level of assets. Most databases compute this ratio as follows:

$$\frac{\text{Net income}}{\text{Average total assets}}.$$

An issue with this computation is that net income is the return to equity holders, whereas assets are financed by both equity holders and creditors. Interest expense (the return to creditors) has already been subtracted in the numerator. Some analysts, therefore, prefer to add back interest expense in the numerator. In such cases, interest must be adjusted for income taxes because net income is determined after taxes. With this adjustment, the ratio would be computed as follows:

$$\frac{\text{Net income} + \text{Interest expense}(1 - \text{Tax rate})}{\text{Average total assets}}.$$

Alternatively, some analysts elect to compute ROA on a pre-interest and pre-tax basis (operating ROA in Exhibit 27) as follows:

$$\frac{\text{Operating income or EBIT}}{\text{Average total assets}}.$$

In this ROA calculation, returns are measured prior to deducting interest on debt capital (i.e., as operating income or EBIT). This measure reflects the return on all assets invested in the company, whether financed with liabilities, debt, or equity. Whichever form of ROA is chosen, the analyst must use it consistently in comparisons to other companies or time periods.

Return on Invested Capital

Return on invested capital (ROIC) measures the after-tax profitability a company earns on all of the capital that it employs (short-term debt, long-term debt, and equity). As with operating ROA, returns are measured prior to deducting interest on debt capital (i.e., as operating income or EBIT).

ROE

ROE measures the return earned by a company on its equity capital, including minority equity, preferred equity, and common equity. As noted, return is measured as net income (i.e., interest on debt capital is not included in the return on equity capital). A variation of ROE is return on common equity, which measures the return earned by a company only on its common equity.

Both ROA and ROE are important measures of profitability and will be explored in more detail later. As with other ratios, profitability ratios should be evaluated individually and as a group to gain an understanding of what is driving profitability (operating versus non-operating activities). Example 12 demonstrates the evaluation of profitability ratios and the use of the management report (sometimes called management discussion and analysis or management commentary) that accompanies financial statements to explain the trend in ratios.

EXAMPLE 12

Evaluation of Profitability Ratios

Recall from Example 1 that an analysis found that Apple's gross margin declined over the three-year period FY2015 to FY2017. An analyst would like to further explore Apple's profitability using a five-year period. He gathers the following revenue data and calculates the following profitability ratios from information in Apple's annual reports, as shown in Exhibit 28:

Exhibit 28: Profitability Ratios for Apple (US dollar millions)

	2017	2016	2015	2014	2013
Sales	229,234	215,639	233,715	182,795	170,910
Gross profit	88,186	84,263	93,626	70,537	64,304
Operating income	61,344	60,024	71,230	52,503	48,999

	2017	2016	2015	2014	2013
Pre-tax income	64,089	61,372	72,515	53,483	50,155
Net income	48,351	45,687	53,394	39,510	37,037
Gross profit margin	38.47%	39.08%	40.06%	38.59%	37.62%
Operating income margin	26.76%	27.84%	30.48%	28.72%	28.67%
Pre-tax margin	27.96%	28.46%	31.03%	29.26%	29.35%
Net profit margin	21.09%	21.19%	22.85%	21.61%	21.67%

1. Evaluate the overall trend in Apple's profitability ratios for the five-year period.

   Solution:

   Sales had increased steadily through 2015, dropped in 2016, and rebounded somewhat in 2017. As noted in Example 1, the sales decline in 2016 was related to a decline in iPhone sales and weakness in foreign currencies. Margins also rose from 2013 to 2015 and declined in 2016. However, in spite of the increase in sales in 2017, all margins declined slightly indicating costs were rising faster than sales. In spite of the fluctuations, Apple's bottom line net profit margin was relatively stable over the five-year period.

QUESTION SET

1. Which ratio would a company *most likely* use to measure its ability to meet short-term obligations?

   A. Current ratio

   B. Payables turnover

   C. Gross profit margin

   Solution:

   A is correct. The current ratio is a liquidity ratio. It compares the net amount of current assets expected to be converted into cash within the year with liabilities falling due in the same period. A current ratio of 1.0 would indicate that the company would have just enough current assets to pay current liabilities.

2. Which of the following ratios would be *most* useful in determining a company's ability to cover its lease and interest payments?

   A. ROA

   B. Total asset turnover

   C. Fixed charge coverage

   Solution:

   C is correct. The fixed charge coverage ratio is a coverage ratio that relates known fixed charges or obligations to a measure of operating profit or cash flow generated by the company. Coverage ratios, a category of solvency ratios, measure the ability of a company to cover its payments related to debt and leases.

3. Assuming no changes in other variables, which of the following would decrease ROA?

   A. An increase in average assets

   B. A decrease in interest expense

   C. A decrease in the effective tax rate

   Solution:

   A is correct. Assuming no changes in other variables, an increase in average assets (an increase in the denominator) would decrease ROA. A decrease in either the effective tax rate or interest expense, assuming no changes in other variables, would increase ROA.

13 INTEGRATED FINANCIAL RATIO ANALYSIS

☐ describe relationships among ratios and evaluate a company using ratio analysis

In prior lessons, the text presented separately activity, liquidity, solvency, and profitability ratios. Before discussing valuation ratios, this lesson demonstrates the importance of examining a variety of financial ratios—not a single ratio or category of ratios in isolation—to ascertain the overall position and performance of a company. Experience shows that the information from one ratio category can be helpful in answering questions raised by another category and that the most accurate overall picture comes from integrating information from all sources.

The Overall Ratio Picture: Examples

We present two simple examples to introduce the use of a variety of ratios to address an analytical task. Example 13 shows how the analysis of a pair of activity ratios resolves an issue concerning a company's liquidity. Example 14 shows that examining the overall ratios of multiple companies can assist an analyst in drawing conclusions about their relative performances.

EXAMPLE 13

A Variety of Ratios

An analyst is evaluating the liquidity of a Canadian manufacturing company and obtains the liquidity ratios shown in Exhibit 29:

Exhibit 29: Liquidity Ratios

Fiscal Year	10	9	8
Current ratio	2.1	1.9	1.6
Quick ratio	0.8	0.9	1.0

The ratios present a contradictory picture of the company's liquidity. Based on the increase in its current ratio from 1.6 to 2.1, the company appears to have strong and improving liquidity; however, based on the decline of the quick ratio from 1.0 to 0.8, its liquidity appears to be deteriorating. Because both ratios have exactly the same denominator, current liabilities, the difference must be the result of changes in some asset that is included in the current ratio but not in the quick ratio (e.g., inventories). The analyst collects the activity ratios in Exhibit 30:

Exhibit 30: Activity Ratios

DOH	55	45	30
DSO	24	28	30

The company's DOH has deteriorated from 30 days to 55 days, meaning that the company is holding increasingly larger amounts of inventory relative to sales. The decrease in DSO implies that the company is collecting receivables faster. If the proceeds from these collections were held as cash, there would be no effect on either the current ratio or the quick ratio. However, if the proceeds from the collections were used to purchase inventory, there would be no effect on the current ratio and a decline in the quick ratio (i.e., the pattern shown in this example). Collectively, the ratios suggest that liquidity is declining and that the company may have an inventory problem that needs to be addressed.

EXAMPLE 14

A Comparison of Two Companies (1)

An analyst collects the information in Exhibit 31 for two hypothetical companies.

Exhibit 31: Company Comparison

	Fiscal Year			
Anson Industries	**5**	**4**	**3**	**2**
Inventory turnover	76.69	89.09	147.82	187.64
DOH	4.76	4.10	2.47	1.95
Receivables turnover	10.75	9.33	11.14	7.56
DSO	33.95	39.13	32.77	48.29
Accounts payable turnover	4.62	4.36	4.84	4.22
Days payable	78.97	83.77	75.49	86.56
Cash from operations/Total liabilities	31.41%	11.15%	4.04%	8.81%
ROE	5.92%	1.66%	1.62%	−0.62%
ROA	3.70%	1.05%	1.05%	−0.39%
Net profit margin (Net income/Revenue)	3.33%	1.11%	1.13%	−0.47%
Total asset turnover (Revenue/Average assets)	1.11	0.95	0.93	0.84
Leverage (Average assets/Average equity)	1.60	1.58	1.54	1.60

	Fiscal Year			
Anson Industries	**5**	**4**	**3**	**2**
	Fiscal Year			
Clarence Corporation	**5**	**4**	**3**	**2**
Inventory turnover	9.19	9.08	7.52	14.84
DOH	39.73	40.20	48.51	24.59
Receivables turnover	8.35	7.01	6.09	5.16
DSO	43.73	52.03	59.92	70.79
Accounts payable turnover	6.47	6.61	7.66	6.52
Days payable	56.44	55.22	47.64	56.00
Cash from operations/Total liabilities	13.19%	16.39%	15.80%	11.79%
ROE	9.28%	6.82%	−3.63%	−6.75%
ROA	4.64%	3.48%	−1.76%	−3.23%
Net profit margin (Net income/ Revenue)	4.38%	3.48%	−1.60%	−2.34%
Total asset turnover (Revenue/ Average assets)	1.06	1.00	1.10	1.38
Leverage (Average assets/Average equity)	2.00	1.96	2.06	2.09

Note: Ratios are expressed in terms of two decimal places and are rounded. Therefore, expected relationships may not hold perfectly.

1. Which of the following choices best describes reasonable conclusions an analyst might make about the companies' efficiency?

   A. In FY5, Anson's DOH of only 4.76 indicated that it was less efficient at inventory management than Clarence, which had DOH of 39.73.

   B. Over the past four years, Anson has shown greater improvement in efficiency than Clarence, as indicated by its total asset turnover ratio increasing from 0.84 to 1.11.

   C. In FY5, Clarence's receivables turnover of 8.35 times indicated that it was more efficient at receivables management than Anson, which had receivables turnover of 10.75.

   Solution:

   B is correct. Over the past four years, Anson has shown greater improvement in efficiency than Clarence, as indicated by its total asset turnover ratio increasing from 0.84 to 1.11. Over the same period of time, Clarence's total asset turnover ratio has declined from 1.38 to 1.06. Choices A and C are incorrect because DOH and receivables turnover are misinterpreted.

14 DUPONT ANALYSIS—THE DECOMPOSITION OF ROE

☐ demonstrate the application of DuPont analysis of return on equity and calculate and interpret effects of changes in its components

As noted earlier, ROE measures the return a company generates on its equity capital. To understand what drives a company's ROE, a useful technique is to decompose ROE into its component parts. (Decomposition of ROE is sometimes referred to as **DuPont analysis** because it was developed originally at that company.) Decomposing ROE involves expressing the basic ratio (i.e., net income divided by average shareholders' equity) as the product of component ratios. Because each of these component ratios is an indicator of a distinct aspect of a company's performance that affects ROE, the decomposition allows us to evaluate how these different aspects of performance affected the company's profitability as measured by ROE.

Decomposing ROE is useful in determining the reasons for changes in ROE over time for a given company and for differences in ROE for different companies in a given time period. The information gained can also be used by management to determine which areas they should focus on to improve ROE. This decomposition will also show why a company's overall profitability, measured by ROE, is a function of its efficiency, operating profitability, taxes, and use of financial leverage. DuPont analysis shows the relationship between the various categories of ratios discussed in this module and how they all influence the return to the investment of the owners.

Analysts have developed several different methods of decomposing ROE. The decomposition presented here is one of the most commonly used and the one found in popular research databases, such as Bloomberg. Return on equity is calculated as follows:

ROE = Net income/Average shareholders' equity.

The decomposition of ROE makes use of simple algebra and illustrates the relationship between ROE and ROA. Expressing ROE as a product of only two of its components, we can write:

$$\begin{aligned} \text{ROE} &= \frac{\text{Net income}}{\text{Average shareholders' equity}} \\ &= \frac{\text{Net income}}{\text{Average total assets}} \times \frac{\text{Average total assets}}{\text{Average shareholders' equity}} \end{aligned} \qquad (1)$$

which can be interpreted as follows:

ROE = ROA × Leverage.

In other words, ROE is a function of a company's ROA and its use of financial leverage ("leverage" for short, in this discussion). A company can improve its ROE by improving ROA or by increasing leverage. Consistent with the definition given earlier, leverage is measured as average total assets divided by average shareholders' equity. If a company had no leverage (no liabilities), its leverage ratio would equal 1.0 and ROE would exactly equal ROA. As a company takes on liabilities, its leverage increases. As long as a company is able to borrow at a rate lower than the marginal rate it can earn investing the borrowed money, the company is making an effective use of leverage and ROE would increase as leverage increases. If a company's borrowing cost exceeds the marginal rate it can earn on investing in the business, ROE would decline as leverage increased because the effect of borrowing would be to depress ROA.

Using the data from Example 14 for Anson Industries, an analyst can examine the trend in ROE and determine whether the increase from an ROE of –0.625 percent in FY2 to 5.925 percent in FY5 is a function of ROA or the use of leverage:

Exhibit 32: Anson Industries

	ROE	=	ROA	×	Leverage
FY5	5.92%		3.70%		1.60
FY4	1.66%		1.05%		1.58
FY3	1.62%		1.05%		1.54
FY2	−0.62%		−0.39%		1.60

Over the four-year period, the company's leverage factor was relatively stable. The primary reason for the increase in ROE is the increase in profitability measured by ROA.

Just as ROE can be decomposed, the individual components such as ROA can be decomposed. Further decomposing ROA, we can express ROE as a product of three component ratios:

$$\frac{\text{Net income}}{\text{Average shareholders' equity}} = \frac{\text{Net income}}{\text{Revenue}} \times \frac{\text{Revenue}}{\text{Average total assets}} \times \frac{\text{Average total assets}}{\text{Average shareholders' equity}} \quad (2)$$

which can be interpreted as follows:

ROE = Net profit margin × Total asset turnover × Leverage.

The first term on the right-hand side of this equation is the net profit margin, an indicator of profitability: how much income a company derives per one monetary unit (e.g., euro or US dollar) of sales. The second term on the right is the asset turnover ratio, an indicator of efficiency: how much revenue a company generates per one money unit of assets. Note that ROA is decomposed into these two components: net profit margin and total asset turnover. A company's ROA is a function of profitability (net profit margin) and efficiency (total asset turnover). The third term on the right-hand side of the equation is a measure of financial leverage, an indicator of solvency: the total amount of a company's assets relative to its equity capital. This decomposition illustrates that a company's ROE is a function of its net profit margin, its efficiency, and its leverage. Again, using the data from Example 14 for Anson Industries, the analyst can evaluate in more detail the reasons behind the trend in ROE:

Exhibit 33: Anson Industries

	ROE	=	Net profit margin	×	Total asset turnover	×	Leverage
FY5	5.92%		3.33%		1.11		1.60
FY4	1.66%		1.11%		0.95		1.58
FY3	1.62%		1.13%		0.93		1.54
FY2	−0.62%		−0.47%		0.84		1.60

This further decomposition confirms that increases in profitability (measured here as net profit margin) are indeed an important contributor to the increase in ROE over the four-year period. However, Anson's asset turnover has also increased steadily. The increase in ROE is, therefore, a function of improving profitability and improving efficiency. As noted earlier, ROE decomposition can also be used to compare the ROEs of peer companies, as demonstrated in Example 15.

EXAMPLE 15

A Comparison of Two Companies (2)

1. Referring to the data for Anson Industries and Clarence Corporation in Example 14, which of the following choices best describes reasonable conclusions an analyst might make about the companies' ROE?

   A. Anson's inventory turnover of 76.69 indicates it is more profitable than Clarence.

   B. The main driver of Clarence's superior ROE in FY5 is its more efficient use of assets.

   C. The main drivers of Clarence's superior ROE in FY5 are its greater use of debt financing and higher net profit margin.

   Solution:

   C is correct. The main driver of Clarence's superior ROE (9.28 percent compared with only 5.92 percent for Anson) in FY5 is its greater use of debt financing (leverage of 2.00 compared with Anson's leverage of 1.60) and higher net profit margin (4.38 percent compared with only 3.33 percent for Anson).

   A is incorrect because inventory turnover is not a direct indicator of profitability. An increase in inventory turnover may indicate more efficient use of inventory which in turn could affect profitability; however, an increase in inventory turnover would also be observed if a company was selling more goods even if it was not selling those goods at a profit. B is incorrect because Clarence has less efficient use of assets than Anson, indicated by turnover of 1.06 for Clarence compared with Anson's turnover of 1.11.

To separate the effects of taxes and interest, we can further decompose the net profit margin and write:

$$\frac{\text{Net income}}{\text{Average shareholders' equity}} = \frac{\text{Net income}}{\text{EBT}} \times \frac{\text{EBT}}{\text{EBIT}} \times \frac{\text{EBIT}}{\text{Revenue}} \times \frac{\text{Revenue}}{\text{Average total assets}} \times \frac{\text{Average total assets}}{\text{Average shareholders' equity}} \quad (3)$$

which can be interpreted as follows:

ROE = Tax burden × Interest burden × EBIT margin × Total asset turnover × Leverage.

This five-way decomposition is the one found in financial databases such as Bloomberg. The first term on the right-hand side of this equation measures the effect of taxes on ROE. Essentially, it reflects one minus the average tax rate, or how much of a company's pretax profits it gets to keep. This can be expressed in decimal or percentage form. So, a 30 percent tax rate would yield a factor of 0.70 or 70 percent. A higher value for the tax burden implies that the company can keep a higher percentage of its pretax profits, indicating a lower tax rate. A decrease in the tax burden ratio implies the opposite (i.e., a higher tax rate leaving the company with less of its pretax profits).

The second term on the right-hand side captures the effect of interest on ROE. Higher borrowing costs reduce ROE. Some analysts prefer to use operating income instead of EBIT for this term and the following term. Either operating income or EBIT is acceptable as long as it is applied consistently. In such a case, the second term would measure both the effect of interest expense and non-operating income on ROE.

The third term on the right-hand side captures the effect of operating margin (if operating income is used in the numerator) or EBIT margin (if EBIT is used) on ROE. In either case, this term primarily measures the effect of operating profitability on ROE.

The fourth term on the right-hand side is again the total asset turnover ratio, an indicator of the overall efficiency of the company (i.e., how much revenue it generates per unit of total assets). The fifth term on the right-hand side is the financial leverage ratio described above—the total amount of a company's assets relative to its equity capital.

This decomposition expresses a company's ROE as a function of its tax rate, interest burden, operating profitability, efficiency, and leverage. An analyst can use this framework to determine what factors are driving a company's ROE. The decomposition of ROE can also be useful in forecasting ROE based upon expected efficiency, profitability, financing activities, and tax rates. The relationship of the individual factors, such as ROA to the overall ROE, can also be expressed in the form of an ROE tree to study the contribution of each of the five factors, as shown in Exhibit 34 for Anson Industries.

Exhibit 34 shows that Anson's ROE of 5.92 percent in FY5 can be decomposed into ROA of 3.70 percent and leverage of 1.60. ROA can further be decomposed into a net profit margin of 3.33 percent and total asset turnover of 1.11. Net profit margin can be decomposed into a tax burden of 0.70 (an average tax rate of 30 percent), an interest burden of 0.90, and an EBIT margin of 5.29 percent. Overall ROE is decomposed into five components.

Exhibit 34: DuPont Analysis of Anson Industries' ROE: Fiscal Year 5

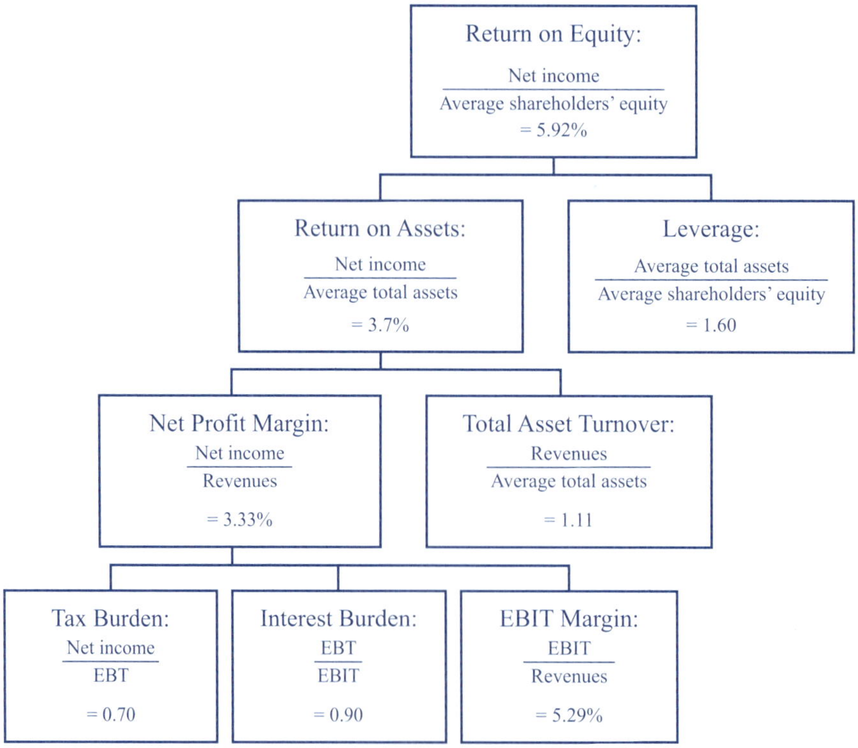

Example 16 demonstrates how the five-component decomposition can be used to determine reasons behind the trend in a company's ROE.

EXAMPLE 16

Five-Way Decomposition of ROE

An analyst examining Amsterdam PLC (a hypothetical company) wishes to understand the factors driving the trend in ROE over a four-year period. The analyst obtains and calculates the following data from Amsterdam's annual reports:

Exhibit 35: Amsterdam's Annual Reports

	2017	2016	2015	2014
ROE	9.53%	20.78%	26.50%	24.72%
Tax burden	60.50%	52.10%	63.12%	58.96%
Interest burden	97.49%	97.73%	97.86%	97.49%
EBIT margin	7.56%	11.04%	13.98%	13.98%
Asset turnover	0.99	1.71	1.47	1.44
Leverage	2.15	2.17	2.10	2.14

1. What might the analyst conclude?

Solution:

The tax burden measure has varied, with no obvious trend. In the most recent year, 2017, taxes declined as a percentage of pretax profit. (Because the tax burden reflects the relation of after-tax profits to pretax profits, the increase from 52.10 percent in 2016 to 60.50 percent in 2017 indicates that taxes declined as a percentage of pretax profits.) This decline in average tax rates could be a result of lower tax rates from new legislation or revenue in a lower tax jurisdiction. The interest burden has remained fairly constant over the four-year period indicating that the company maintains a fairly constant capital structure. Operating margin (EBIT margin) declined over the period, indicating the company's operations were less profitable. This decline is generally consistent with declines in oil prices in 2017 and declines in refining industry gross margins in 2016 and 2017. The company's efficiency (asset turnover) decreased in 2017. The company's leverage remained constant, consistent with the constant interest burden. Overall, the trend in ROE (declining substantially over the recent years) resulted from decreases in operating profits and a lower asset turnover. Additional research on the causes of these changes is required to develop expectations about the company's future performance.

The most detailed decomposition of ROE that we have presented is a five-way decomposition. Nevertheless, an analyst could further decompose individual components of a five-way analysis. For example, EBIT margin (EBIT/Revenue) could be further decomposed into a non-operating component (EBIT/Operating income) and an operating component (Operating income/Revenue). The analyst can also examine which other factors contributed to these five components. For example, an improvement in efficiency (total asset turnover) may have resulted from better management of inventory (DOH) or better collection of receivables (DSO).

15 INDUSTRY-SPECIFIC FINANCIAL RATIOS

☐ describe the uses of industry-specific ratios used in financial analysis

As stated earlier, a universally accepted definition and classification of ratios does not exist. The purpose of ratios is to serve as indicators of important aspects of a company's performance and value. Aspects of performance that are considered important in one industry may be irrelevant in another, and industry-specific ratios reflect these differences. For example, companies in the retail industry may report same-store sales changes because, in the retail industry, it is important to distinguish between growth that results from opening new stores and growth that results from generating more sales at existing stores. Industry-specific metrics can be especially important to the value of equity in early-stage industries, where companies are not yet profitable.

In addition, regulated industries—especially in the financial sector—often are required to comply with specific regulatory ratios. For example, the banking sector's liquidity and cash reserve ratios provide an indication of banking liquidity and reflect monetary and regulatory requirements. Banking capital adequacy requirements attempt to relate banks' solvency requirements directly to their specific levels of risk exposure.

Exhibit 36 presents, for illustrative purposes only, some industry-specific ratios.

Exhibit 36: Definitions of Some Common Industry-Specific Ratios

Ratio	Numerator	Denominator
Business Risk		
Coefficient of variation of operating income	Standard deviation of operating income	Average operating income
Coefficient of variation of net income	Standard deviation of net income	Average net income
Coefficient of variation of revenues	Standard deviation of revenue	Average revenue

Financial Sector Ratios	Numerator	Denominator
Capital adequacy—banks	Various components of capital	Various measures such as risk-weighted assets, market risk exposure, or level of operational risk assumed
Monetary reserve requirement (Cash reserve ratio)	Reserves held at central bank	Specified deposit liabilities

Financial Sector Ratios	Numerator	Denominator
Liquid asset requirement	Approved "readily marketable" securities	Specified deposit liabilities
Net interest margin	Net interest income	Total interest-earning assets

Retail Ratios	Numerator	Denominator
Same (or comparable) store sales	Average revenue growth year over year for stores open in both periods	Not applicable
Sales per square meter (or square foot)	Revenue	Total retail space in square meters (or square feet)

Service Companies	Numerator	Denominator
Revenue per employee	Revenue	Total number of employees
Net income per employee	Net income	Total number of employees

Hotel	Numerator	Denominator
Average daily rate	Room revenue	Number of rooms sold
Occupancy rate	Number of rooms sold	Number of rooms available

Subscription or Relationship-Based Businesses	Numerator	Denominator
Average revenue per user (ARPU)	Revenue	Average number of subscribers or users

Note: Many other industry-specific ratios are outside the scope of this module. Resources such as Standard and Poor's Industry Surveys present useful ratios for each industry. Industry organizations may present useful ratios for the industry or a task specific to the industry.

MODEL BUILDING AND FORECASTING

16

☐ describe how ratio analysis and other techniques can be used to model and forecast earnings

Analysts often need to forecast future financial performance. For example, analysts' EPS forecasts and related equity valuations are widely followed by Wall Street. Analysts use data about the economy, industry, and company in arriving at a company's forecast. The results of an analyst's financial analysis, including common-size and ratio analyses, are integral to this process, along with the judgment of the analysts.

Based upon forecasts of growth and expected relationships among the financial statement data, the analyst can build a model to forecast future performance, which will be covered in later modules. In addition to budgets, pro forma financial statements are widely used in financial forecasting within companies, especially for use by senior executives and boards of directors. Last but not least, these budgets and forecasts are also used in presentations to credit analysts and others in obtaining external financing.

For example, based on a revenue forecast, an analyst may budget expenses based on expected common-size data. Forecasts of balance sheet and cash flow statements can be derived from expected ratio data, such as DSO. Forecasts are not limited to a single point estimate but should involve a range of possibilities. This can involve several techniques:

- **Sensitivity analysis**: Also known as "what if" analysis, sensitivity analysis shows the range of possible outcomes as specific assumptions are changed; this could, in turn, influence financing needs or investment in fixed assets.
- **Scenario analysis**: This type of analysis shows the changes in key financial quantities that result from given (economic) events, such as the loss of customers, the loss of a supply source, or a catastrophic event. If the list of events is mutually exclusive and exhaustive and the events can be assigned probabilities, the analyst can evaluate not only the range of outcomes but also standard statistical measures such as the mean and median value for various quantities of interest.
- **Simulation**: This is computer-generated sensitivity or scenario analysis based on probability models for the factors that drive outcomes. Each event or possible outcome is assigned a probability. Multiple scenarios are then run using the probability factors assigned to the possible values of a variable to determine an expected outcome for that variable.

REFERENCES

Abarbanell, J. S. and B. J. Bushee. 1998. "Abnormal Returns to a Fundamental Analysis Strategy." *Accounting Review* 73 (1): 19–45.

Altman, E. 1968. "Financial Ratios, Discriminant Analysis and the Prediction of Corporate Bankruptcy." *Journal of Finance* 23 (4): 589–609. doi:10.2307/2978933

Hopwood, William, James C. McKeown, and Jane F. Mutchler. 1994. "A Reexamination of Auditor versus Model Accuracy within the Context of the Going-Concern Opinion Decision." *Contemporary Accounting Research* 10 (2): 409–31.

Ohlson, James A. 1980. "Financial Ratios and the Probabilistic Prediction of Bankruptcy." *Journal of Accounting Research* 18 (1): 109–31.

Ou, J. A. and S. H. Penman. 1989. "Financial Statement Analysis and the Prediction of Stock Returns." *Journal of Accounting and Economics* 11 (4): 295–329. doi:10.1016/0165-4101(89)90017-7

Robinson, T. and P. Munter. 2004. "Financial Reporting Quality: Red Flags and Accounting Warning Signs." *Commercial Lending Review* 19 (1): 2–15.

PRACTICE PROBLEMS

1. Comparison of a company's financial results to other peer companies for the same time period is called:

   A. time-series analysis.

   B. common-size analysis.

   C. cross-sectional analysis.

2. An analyst observes a decrease in a company's inventory turnover. Which of the following would *most likely* explain this trend?

   A. The company installed a new inventory management system, allowing more efficient inventory management.

   B. Due to problems with obsolescent inventory last year, the company wrote off a large amount of its inventory at the beginning of the period.

   C. The company installed a new inventory management system but experienced some operational difficulties resulting in duplicate orders being placed with suppliers.

3. Which of the following would *best* explain an increase in receivables turnover?

   A. The company adopted new credit policies last year and began offering credit to customers with weak credit histories.

   B. Due to problems with an error in its old credit scoring system, the company had accumulated a substantial amount of uncollectible accounts and wrote off a large amount of its receivables.

   C. To match the terms offered by its closest competitor, the company adopted new payment terms now requiring net payment within 30 days rather than 15 days, which had been its previous requirement.

4. Brown Corporation had average days of sales outstanding of 19 days in the most recent fiscal year. Brown wants to improve its credit policies and collection practices and decrease its collection period in the next fiscal year to match the industry average of 15 days. Credit sales in the most recent fiscal year were $300 million, and Brown expects credit sales to increase to $390 million in the next fiscal year. To achieve Brown's goal of decreasing the collection period, the change in the average accounts receivable balance that must occur is *closest* to:

   A. +USD0.41 million.

   B. –USD0.41 million.

   C. –USD1.22 million.

The following information relates to questions 5-5

An analyst is interested in assessing both the efficiency and liquidity of Spherion PLC. The analyst has collected the data in Exhibit 1 for Spherion:

Exhibit 1: Spherion Data

	FY3	FY2	FY1
Days of inventory on hand	32	34	40
Days sales outstanding	28	25	23
Number of days of payables	40	35	35

5. Based on the data in Exhibit 1, what is the analyst *least likely* to conclude?
   - **A.** Inventory management has contributed to improved liquidity.
   - **B.** Management of payables has contributed to improved liquidity.
   - **C.** Management of receivables has contributed to improved liquidity.

6. To assess a company's ability to fulfill its long-term obligations, an analyst would *most likely* examine:
   - **A.** activity ratios.
   - **B.** liquidity ratios.
   - **C.** solvency ratios.

The following information relates to questions 7-8

An analyst is evaluating the solvency and liquidity of Apex Manufacturing and has collected the data in Exhibit 1:

Exhibit 1: Solvency and Liquidity of Apex Manufacturing (euro millions)

	FY5	FY4	FY3
Total debt	2,000	1,900	1,750
Total equity	4,000	4,500	5,000

7. Which of the following would be the analyst's *most likely* conclusion?
   - **A.** The company is becoming less liquid, as evidenced by the increase in its debt-to-equity ratio from 0.35 to 0.50 from FY3 to FY5.

B. The company is becoming increasingly more liquid, as evidenced by the increase in its debt-to-equity ratio from 0.35 to 0.50 from FY3 to FY5.

C. The company is becoming increasingly less solvent, as evidenced by the increase in its debt-to-equity ratio from 0.35 to 0.50 from FY3 to FY5.

8. What would be the *most* reasonable explanation of the financial data?

A. The decline in the company's equity results from a decline in the market value of this company's common shares.

B. The EUR250 increase in the company's debt from FY3 to FY5 indicates that lenders are viewing the company as increasingly creditworthy.

C. The decline in the company's equity indicates that the company may be incurring losses, paying dividends greater than income, or repurchasing shares.

---

9. An analyst observes the data in Exhibit 1 for two companies:

Exhibit 1: Data Comparison (US dollars)

	Company A	Company B
Revenue	4,500	6,000
Net income	50	1,000
Current assets	40,000	60,000
Total assets	100,000	700,000
Current liabilities	10,000	50,000
Total debt	60,000	150,000
Shareholders' equity	30,000	500,000

Which of the following choices *best* describes reasonable conclusions that the analyst might make about the two companies' ability to pay their current and long-term obligations?

A. Company A's current ratio of 4.0 indicates it is more liquid than Company B, whose current ratio is only 1.2, but Company B is more solvent, as indicated by its lower debt-to-equity ratio.

B. Company A's current ratio of 0.25 indicates it is less liquid than Company B, whose current ratio is 0.83, and Company A is also less solvent, as indicated by a debt-to-equity ratio of 200 percent compared with Company B's debt-to-equity ratio of only 30 percent.

C. Company A's current ratio of 4.0 indicates it is more liquid than Company B, whose current ratio is only 1.2, and Company A is also more solvent, as indicated by a debt-to-equity ratio of 200 percent compared with Company B's debt-to-equity ratio of only 30 percent.

The following information relates to questions 10-13

The following data appear in the five-year summary of a major international company. A business combination with another major manufacturer took place in FY13.

Exhibit 1: Five-Year Summary of a Major International Company

	FY10	FY11	FY12	FY13	FY14
Financial statements	GBP millions	GBP millions	GBP millions	GBP millions	GBP millions
Income statements					
Revenue	4,390	3,624	3,717	8,167	11,366
Profit before interest and taxation (EBIT)	844	700	704	933	1,579
Net interest expense	–80	–54	–98	–163	–188
Taxation	–186	–195	–208	–349	–579
Minorities	–94	–99	–105	–125	–167
Profit for the year	484	352	293	296	645
Balance sheets					
Fixed assets	3,510	3,667	4,758	10,431	11,483
Current asset investments, cash at bank and in hand	316	218	290	561	682
Other current assets	558	514	643	1,258	1,634
Total assets	4,384	4,399	5,691	12,250	13,799
Interest bearing debt (long term)	–602	–1,053	–1,535	–3,523	–3,707
Other creditors and provisions (current)	–1,223	–1,054	–1,102	–2,377	–3,108
Total liabilities	–1,825	–2,107	–2,637	–5,900	–6,815
Net assets	2,559	2,292	3,054	6,350	6,984
Shareholders' funds	2,161	2,006	2,309	5,572	6,165
Equity minority interests	398	286	745	778	819
Capital employed	2,559	2,292	3,054	6,350	6,984
Cash flow					

	FY10	FY11	FY12	FY13	FY14
Working capital movements	–53	5	71	85	107
Net cash inflow from operating activities	864	859	975	1,568	2,292

10. The company's total assets at year-end FY9 were GBP3,500 million. Which of the following choices *best* describes reasonable conclusions an analyst might make about the company's efficiency?

    A. Comparing FY14 with FY10, the company's efficiency deteriorated, as indicated by its current ratio.

    B. Comparing FY14 with FY10, the company's efficiency deteriorated due to asset growth faster than turnover revenue growth.

    C. Comparing FY14 with FY10, the company's efficiency improved, as indicated by a total asset turnover ratio of 0.86 compared with 0.64.

11. Which of the following choices *best* describes reasonable conclusions an analyst might make about the company's solvency?

    A. Comparing FY14 with FY10, the company's solvency improved, as indicated by the growth in its profits to GBP 645 million.

    B. Comparing FY14 with FY10, the company's solvency deteriorated, as indicated by a decrease in interest coverage from 10.6 to 8.4.

    C. Comparing FY14 with FY10, the company's solvency improved, as indicated by an increase in its debt-to-assets ratio from 0.14 to 0.27.

12. Which of the following choices *best* describes reasonable conclusions an analyst might make about the company's liquidity?

    A. Comparing FY14 with FY10, the company's liquidity improved, as indicated by an increase in its current ratio from 0.71 to 0.75.

    B. Comparing FY14 with FY10, the company's liquidity deteriorated, as indicated by a decrease in interest coverage from 10.6 to 8.4.

    C. Comparing FY14 with FY10, the company's liquidity improved, as indicated by an increase in its debt-to-assets ratio from 0.14 to 0.27.

13. Which of the following choices *best* describes reasonable conclusions an analyst might make about the company's profitability?

    A. Comparing FY14 with FY10, the company's profitability improved, as indicated by an increase in its debt-to-assets ratio from 0.14 to 0.27.

    B. Comparing FY14 with FY10, the company's profitability improved, as indicated by the growth in its shareholders' equity to GBP6,165 million.

    C. Comparing FY14 with FY10, the company's profitability deteriorated, as indicated by a decrease in its net profit margin from 11.0 percent to 5.7 percent.

14. An analyst compiles the data in Exhibit 1 for a company:

Exhibit 1: Net Profit Margin

	FY13	FY14	FY15
ROE	19.8%	20.0%	22.0%
Return on total assets	8.1%	8.0%	7.9%
Total asset turnover	2.0	2.0	2.1

Based only on the information above, the *most* appropriate conclusion is that, over the period FY13 to FY15, the company's:

A. net profit margin and financial leverage have decreased.

B. net profit margin and financial leverage have increased.

C. net profit margin has decreased but its financial leverage has increased.

15. A decomposition of ROE for Integra SA is as follows:

Exhibit 1: Integra SA ROE

	FY12	FY11
ROE	18.90%	18.90%
Tax burden	0.70	0.75
Interest burden	0.90	0.90
EBIT margin	10.00%	10.00%
Asset turnover	1.50	1.40
Leverage	2.00	2.00

Which of the following choices *best* describes reasonable conclusions an analyst might make based on this ROE decomposition?

A. Profitability and the liquidity position both improved in FY12.

B. The higher average tax rate in FY12 offset the improvement in profitability, leaving ROE unchanged.

C. The higher average tax rate in FY12 offset the improvement in efficiency, leaving ROE unchanged.

16. A decomposition of ROE for Company A and Company B is as follows:

Exhibit 1: ROE for Company A and Company B

	Company A		Company B	
	FY15	FY14	FY15	FY14
ROE	26.46%	18.90%	26.33%	18.90%
Tax burden	0.7	0.75	0.75	0.75
Interest burden	0.9	0.9	0.9	0.9
EBIT margin	7.00%	10.00%	13.00%	10.00%
Asset turnover	1.5	1.4	1.5	1.4
Leverage	4	2	2	2

An analyst is *most likely* to conclude that:

A. Company A's ROE is higher than Company B's in FY15, and one explanation consistent with the data is that Company A may have purchased new, more efficient equipment.

B. the difference between the two companies' ROE in FY15 is very small and Company A's ROE remains similar to Company B's ROE mainly due to Company A increasing its financial leverage.

C. Company A's ROE is higher than Company B's in FY15, and one explanation consistent with the data is that Company A has made a strategic shift to a product mix with higher profit margins.

17. When developing forecasts, analysts should *most likely*:

A. develop possibilities relying exclusively on the results of financial analysis.

B. aim to develop extremely precise forecasts using the results of financial analysis.

C. use the results of financial analysis, analysis of other information, and judgment.

SOLUTIONS

1. C is correct. Cross-sectional analysis involves the comparison of companies with each other for the same time period. Time-series or trend analysis is the comparison of financial data across different time periods. Common-size analysis involves expressing financial data in relation to a single financial statement item, or base.

2. C is correct. The company's problems with its inventory management system causing duplicate orders would likely result in a higher amount of inventory and, therefore, would result in a decrease in inventory turnover. A more efficient inventory management system and a write-off of inventory at the beginning of the period would both likely decrease the average inventory for the period (the denominator of the inventory turnover ratio), thus increasing the ratio rather than decreasing it.

3. B is correct. A write-off of receivables would decrease the average amount of accounts receivable (the denominator of the receivables turnover ratio), thus increasing this ratio. Customers with weaker credit are more likely to make payments more slowly or to pose collection difficulties, which would likely increase the average amount of accounts receivable and thus decrease receivables turnover. Longer payment terms would likely increase the average amount of accounts receivable and thus decrease receivables turnover.

4. A is correct. The average accounts receivable balances (actual and desired) must be calculated to determine the desired change. The average accounts receivable balance can be calculated as an average day's credit sales times the DSO. For the most recent fiscal year, the average accounts receivable balance is USD15.62 million [= (USD300,000,000/365) × 19]. The desired average accounts receivable balance for the next fiscal year is USD16.03 million (= (USD390,000,000/365) × 15). This is an increase of USD0.41 million (= 16.03 million – 15.62 million). An alternative approach is to calculate the turnover and divide sales by turnover to determine the average accounts receivable balance. Turnover equals 365 divided by DSO. Turnover is 19.21 (= 365/19) for the most recent fiscal year and is targeted to be 24.33 (= 365/15) for the next fiscal year. The average accounts receivable balances are USD15.62 million (= USD300,000,000/19.21), and USD16.03 million (= USD390,000,000/24.33). The change is an increase in receivables of USD0.41 million

5. C is correct. The analyst is *unlikely* to reach the conclusion given in Statement C because days of sales outstanding increased from 23 days in FY1 to 25 days in FY2 to 28 days in FY3, indicating that the time required to collect receivables has increased over the period. This is a negative factor for Spherion's liquidity. By contrast, days of inventory on hand dropped over the period FY1 to FY3, a positive for liquidity. The company's increase in days payable, from 35 days to 40 days, shortened its cash conversion cycle, thus also contributing to improved liquidity.

6. C is correct. Solvency ratios are used to evaluate the ability of a company to meet its long-term obligations. An analyst is more likely to use activity ratios to evaluate how efficiently a company uses its assets. An analyst is more likely to use liquidity ratios to evaluate the ability of a company to meet its short-term obligations.

7. C is correct. The company is becoming increasingly less solvent, as evidenced by its debt-to-equity ratio increasing from 0.35 to 0.50 from FY3 to FY5. The

amount of a company's debt and equity do not provide direct information about the company's liquidity position.

Debt to equity:

FY5: 2,000/4,000 = 0.5000

FY4: 1,900/4,500 = 0.4222

FY3: 1,750/5,000 = 0.3500

8. C is correct. The decline in the company's equity indicates that the company may be incurring losses, paying dividends greater than income, or repurchasing shares. Recall that Beginning equity – Shares repurchased + Comprehensive income – Dividends = Ending equity. The book value of a company's equity is not affected by changes in the market value of its common stock. An increased amount of lending does not necessarily indicate that lenders view a company as increasingly creditworthy. Creditworthiness is not evaluated based on how much a company has increased its debt but rather on its willingness and ability to pay its obligations. (Its financial strength is indicated by its solvency, liquidity, profitability, efficiency, and other aspects of credit analysis.)

9. A is correct. Company A's current ratio of 4.0 (= USD40,000/USD10,000) indicates it is more liquid than Company B, whose current ratio is only 1.2 (=USD60,000/USD50,000). Company B is more solvent, as indicated by its lower debt-to-equity ratio of 30 percent (= USD150,000/USD500,000) compared with Company A's debt-to-equity ratio of 200 percent (= USD60,000/USD30,000).

10. B is correct. The company's efficiency deteriorated, as indicated by the decline in its total asset turnover ratio from 1.11 {= 4,390/[(4,384 + 3,500)/2]} for FY10 to 0.87 {= 11,366/[(12,250 + 13,799)/2]} for FY14. The decline in the total asset turnover ratio resulted from an increase in average total assets from GBP3,942 [= (4,384 + 3,500)/2] for FY10 to GBP13,024.5 for FY14, an increase of 230 percent, compared with an increase in revenue from GBP4,390 in FY10 to GBP11,366 in FY14, an increase of only 159 percent. The current ratio is not an indicator of efficiency.

11. B is correct. Comparing FY14 with FY10, the company's solvency deteriorated, as indicated by a decrease in interest coverage from 10.6 (= 844/80) in FY10 to 8.4 (= 1,579/188) in FY14. The debt-to-asset ratio increased from 0.14 (= 602/4,384) in FY10 to 0.27 (= 3,707/13,799) in FY14. This is also indicative of deteriorating solvency. In isolation, the amount of profits does not provide enough information to assess solvency.

12. A is correct. Comparing FY14 with FY10, the company's liquidity improved, as indicated by an increase in its current ratio from 0.71 [= (316 + 558)/1,223] in FY10 to 0.75 [= (682 + 1,634)/3,108] in FY14. Note, however, comparing only the cash ratio shows a decline in liquidity from 0.26 (= 316/1,223) in FY10 to 0.22 (= 682/3,108) in FY14. Debt-to-assets ratio and interest coverage are measures of solvency not liquidity.

13. C is correct. Comparing FY14 with FY10, the company's profitability deteriorated, as indicated by a decrease in its net profit margin from 11.0 percent (= 484/4,390) to 5.7 percent (= 645/11,366). Debt-to-assets ratio is a measure of solvency not an indicator of profitability. Growth in shareholders' equity, in isolation, does not provide enough information to assess profitability.

14. C is correct. The company's net profit margin has decreased and its financial

leverage has increased. ROA = Net profit margin × Total asset turnover. ROA decreased over the period despite the increase in total asset turnover; therefore, the net profit margin must have decreased.

ROE = Return on assets × Financial leverage. ROE increased over the period despite the drop in ROA; therefore, financial leverage must have increased.

15. C is correct. The increase in the average tax rate in FY12, as indicated by the decrease in the value of the tax burden (the tax burden equals one minus the average tax rate), offset the improvement in efficiency indicated by higher asset turnover) leaving ROE unchanged. The EBIT margin, measuring profitability, was unchanged in FY12 and no information is given on liquidity.

16. B is correct. The difference between the two companies' ROE in FY15 is very small and is mainly the result of Company A's increase in its financial leverage, indicated by the increase in its Assets/Equity ratio from 2 to 4. The impact of efficiency on ROE is identical for the two companies, as indicated by both companies' asset turnover ratios of 1.5. Furthermore, if Company A had purchased newer equipment to replace older, depreciated equipment, then the company's asset turnover ratio (computed as sales/assets) would have declined, assuming constant sales. Company A has experienced a significant decline in its operating margin, from 10 percent to 7 percent which, all else equal, would not suggest that it is selling more products with higher profit margins.

17. C is correct. The results of an analyst's financial analysis are integral to the process of developing forecasts, along with the analysis of other information and judgment of the analysts. Forecasts are not limited to a single point estimate but should involve a range of possibilities.

LEARNING MODULE

12

Introduction to Financial Statement Modeling

LEARNING OUTCOMES

Mastery	The candidate should be able to:
☐	demonstrate the development of a sales-based pro forma company model
☐	explain how behavioral factors affect analyst forecasts and recommend remedial actions for analyst biases
☐	explain how the competitive position of a company based on a Porter's five forces analysis affects prices and costs
☐	explain how to forecast industry and company sales and costs when they are subject to price inflation or deflation
☐	explain considerations in the choice of an explicit forecast horizon and an analyst's choices in developing projections beyond the short-term forecast horizon

The two major accounting standard setters are as follows: 1) the International Accounting Standards Board (IASB) who establishes International Financial Reporting Standards (IFRS) and 2) the Financial Accounting Standards Board (FASB) who establishes US GAAP. Throughout this learning module both standards are referred to and many, but not all, of these two sets of accounting rules are identified. Note: changes in accounting standards as well as new rulings and/or pronouncements issued after the publication of this learning module may cause some of the information to become dated.

1 INTRODUCTION

Financial statement modeling is a key step in the process of valuing companies and the securities they have issued. We begin our discussion with an overview of developing a revenue forecast. We then describe the general approach to forecasting each of the financial statements and demonstrate the construction of a financial statement model, including forecasted income statements, balance sheets, and statements of cash flows. Then, we describe key behavioral biases that can influence the modeling process and strategies to mitigate them. We then turn to several important topics on the effects of micro- and macroeconomic conditions on financial statement models: the impact of competitive factors on prices and costs, the effects of inflation and deflation, technological developments, and long-term forecasting considerations.

Most of the examples and exhibits used throughout the reading can be downloaded as a Microsoft Excel workbook. Each worksheet in the workbook is labeled with the corresponding example or exhibit number in the text.

LEARNING MODULE OVERVIEW

- A financial statement model is the starting point for most valuation models, and valuation estimates can be made based on a variety of metrics, including free cash flow, EPS, EBITDA, and EBIT.
- Some balance sheet line items, such as retained earnings, flow directly from the income statement, whereas accounts receivable, accounts payable, and inventory are very closely linked to income statement projections.
- Working capital accounts are modeled by projecting working capital ratios (e.g., days of inventory, days sales outstanding, days payable outstanding) which are combined with the sales and cost of sales forecast to produce projected working capital accounts on the balance sheet.
- Five key behavioral biases that influence analyst forecasts are overconfidence, illusion of control, conservatism, representativeness, and confirmation bias.
- Illusion of control, a bias linked to overconfidence, is a tendency to overestimate the ability to control what cannot be controlled and to take ultimately fruitless actions in pursuit of control.
- A common manifestation of confirmation bias among investment analysts is to structure the research process in pursuit of only positive news or certain criteria, or with a narrow scope.
- Competitive factors affect a company's ability to negotiate lower input prices with suppliers and to raise prices for products and services. Porter's five forces framework can be used as a basis for identifying such factors.
- Porter's five forces are Threat of substitutes, Rivalry, Bargaining power of suppliers, Bargaining power of buyers, and Threat of new entrants.
- Return on invested capital, ROIC, defined as net operating profit less adjusted taxes divided by the difference between operating assets and operating liabilities, is an after-tax measure of profitability. High and persistent levels of ROIC are often associated with having a competitive advantage.
- Inflation and deflation can significantly affect the accuracy of forecasts for a company's future revenue, profit, and cash flow.

- Forecasting revenue for a company faced with inflation in input costs requires an understanding of the price elasticity of the products, the different rates of cost inflation in the countries where the company is active, and the likely inflation in costs relevant to a company's individual product categories.
- Faced with rising input prices, a company might decide to preserve its margins by passing on the costs to its customers, or it might decide to accept some margin reduction to increase its market share.
- The choice of the forecast time horizon can be influenced by certain factors, including the investment strategy for which the security is being considered, the cyclicality of the industry, company-specific factors, and the analyst's employer's preferences.
- Normalized earnings are the expected level of mid-cycle earnings for a company in the absence of any unusual or temporary factors that affect profitability.
- One of the greatest challenges facing the analyst is anticipating inflection points, such as from economic disruption, regulation, and technology, when the future will look significantly different from the recent past.

BUILDING A FINANCIAL STATEMENT MODEL 2

☐ demonstrate the development of a sales-based pro forma company model

In this module, we apply the principles covered in earlier modules in Financial Statement Analysis and Corporate Issuers in a demonstration of building a financial statement model. The subject company is the Rémy Cointreau Group (Rémy), a French company that primarily sells spirits. After providing a brief overview of the company, we will focus primarily on the mechanics of constructing pro forma income statements, statements of cash flows, and balance sheets. Data sources for this example include the company's fiscal year ended 31 March 2021 and 2020 annual reports, the company's interim reports, and corresponding investor presentations for additional information on the underlying results of the respective divisions. While forecasts are described in some detail here, later modules in company analysis in the Equity topic area will discuss forecasting in much greater detail.

Company Overview

Rémy, whose reporting year ends 31 March, operates and reports three business segments:

1. Cognac. This division, composed primarily of Rémy Martin brand cognac, represented approximately 73 percent of FY2021 (year-end 31 March 2021) revenue and 94 percent of total current operating profit. Current operating profit is a non-IFRS measure reported by Rémy equal to IFRS operating profit excluding items related to discontinued brands or items deemed infrequent or immaterial, such as impairment or litigation provisions.

2. Liqueurs & Spirits. A diverse portfolio of spirits brands, the main brands in this segment are Cointreau, Metaxa, St-Rémy, Mount Gay, Bruichladdich, and The Botanist. The segment represented approximately 25 percent of FY2021 revenue and 14 percent of current operating profits.
3. Partner Brands. This segment includes other companies' brands that are marketed through Rémy's distribution network. They represented approximately 3 percent of FY2021 revenue and just under 0 percent of current operating profit, earning a slight operating loss in FY2021 of –EUR0.8 million. This division's importance has declined significantly over time as the company discontinued distribution ("partner brand") contracts.

Segment financial information is summarized in Exhibit 1. As shown, the company's largest business segment is also its most profitable: The Cognac segment earned a current operating profit margin of approximately 30 percent (= EUR221 million/EUR735 million) in fiscal year 2021. Exhibits are in the downloadable Microsoft Excel workbook in a single worksheet titled "Rémy." We strongly recommend following along with the Excel workbook and exploring the model construction in detail.

Exhibit 1: Analysis of Rémy's Turnover and Operating Profit

Revenue (euro millions)	**FY2019**	**FY2020**	**FY2021**
Cognac	774	736	735
Liqueurs and spirits	264	262	248
Partner brands	87	28	27
Total revenues	1,126	1,025	1,010
Current Operating Profit (euro millions)			
Cognac	236	200	221
Liqueurs and spirits	39	38	33
Partner brands	5	–2	–1
Holding/Corporate-level costs	–15	–20	–17
Total current operating profit	264	215	236
Current Operating Profit Margins			
Cognac	30.4%	27.1%	30.1%
Liqueurs and spirits	14.7%	14.3%	13.3%
Partner brands	5.6%	–6.2%	–3.0%
Holding/Corporate-level costs (percent of total revenue)	–1.3%	–2.0%	–1.7%
Total current operating margin	23.5%	21.0%	23.4%

Construction of pro forma income statements, as Exhibit 2 illustrates, is composed of four forecasting steps: revenue, COGS, other operating expenses, and, finally, non-operating items.

Exhibit 2: Income Statement Forecast Process

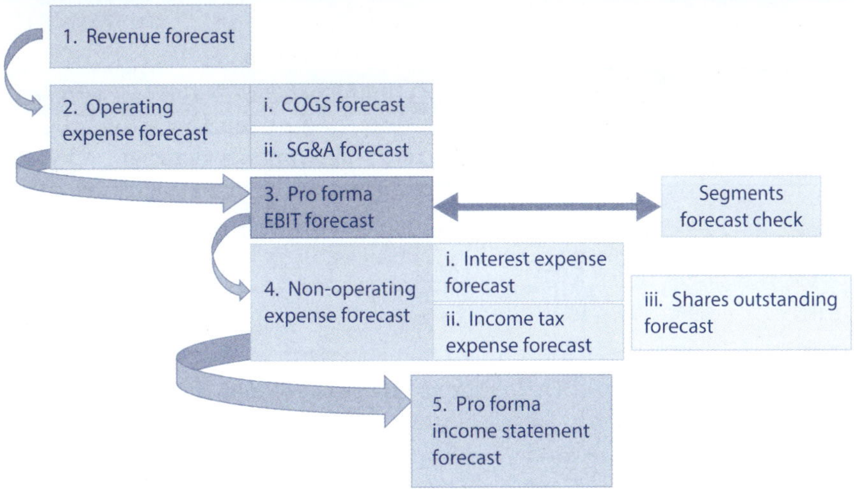

Revenue Forecast

For each segment, the change in revenue is driven by volume, price, and foreign currency estimates that are based on historical trends as adjusted for expected deviations from trend. Price changes refer not only to price changes for a single product but also to changes in mix, which are defined as changes resulting from selling varying quantities of higher- and lower-priced products. Changes in revenue attributable to volume or price/mix are organic growth and are shown separately from the impact of acquisitions and divestitures (scope change) and foreign exchange (forex impact in the model).

In the Cognac segment, historical volume growth is usually in the 4 to –6 percent range. For future years, volume growth is expected to remain robust but slower than the 9.1 percent achieved in 2021 as the global recovery from the COVID-19 pandemic and associated recession fades (volumes were down 10.1 percent in FY2020). The growing number of affluent Asian consumers will likely keep demand high, while developed market consumption is likely to be rather flat. In the model, the assumption is for 7 percent volume growth in 2022, declining to 6 percent in 2023 and 2024.

Price/mix contributed approximately 6.0 percent, 2.6 percent, and –5.4 percent to the Cognac segment revenue growth in FY2019, FY2020, and FY2021, respectively. Although the impact of price/mix on revenue growth has fluctuated in recent years, price/mix will likely remain a relatively significant contributor to revenue growth in the future given the favorable structure of the industry and the company's efforts to increase the share of revenues accounted for by what it calls "exceptional spirits" (those that cost more than USD50 per bottle and are seeing a 10 percent annual demand growth). A 4 percent price/mix contribution to revenue growth is assumed in 2022, with the trend maintained into 2023 and 2024. The combined projections for 2022 of 7 percent volume growth and 4 percent price/mix impact results in overall organic revenue growth of 11.3 percent, calculated as $[(1 + 0.07) \times (1 + 0.04)] - 1$.

In addition to the impact of volume and price/mix, Rémy's revenues are affected by movements in exchange rates. Company disclosures indicate that more than 70 percent of revenues are realized outside the eurozone, whereas most of Rémy's production occurs within the eurozone. The model forecasts no foreign currency impact on revenue in the 2022–24 forecast period.

Exhibit 3 summarizes historical and projected information for the Cognac segment's revenue.

Exhibit 3: Historical and Projected Information for Cognac Segment Revenue

	FY2018	FY2019	FY2020	FY2021	FY2022E	FY2023E	FY2024E
Cognac Segment Revenues (euro millions)	760	774	736	735	818	902	994
YoY%	7.4%	1.9%	−5.0%	−0.1%	11.3%	10.2%	10.2%
Volume growth (%)	6.0%	5.9%	−10.1%	9.1%	7.0%	6.0%	6.0%
Price/mix (%)	7.2%	6.0%	2.6%	−5.4%	4.0%	4.0%	4.0%
Organic growth (%)	13.6%	12.3%	−7.8%	3.2%	11.3%	10.2%	10.2%
Forex impact and scope change (%)	−5.8%	−4.0%	2.5%	−3.8%	0.0%	0.0%	0.0%
Effect of IFRS 15 adoption	0.0%	−6.0%	0.0%	0.0%	0.0%	0.0%	0.0%
YoY%	7.8%	2.3%	−5.3%	−0.6%	11.3%	10.2%	10.2%

A similar analysis can be performed to project revenue for the other segments. Then, the amounts can be summed to derive projected consolidated revenue.

COGS

Rémy's gross margin has remained roughly flat from FY2018 (67.5 percent) to FY2021 (67.3 percent) as total sales have decreased modestly. Going forward, we project gross margin to increase by 100 bps in each of the next three years based on increasing total revenues, particularly from price/mix, which is strongly accretive to gross margin (see the previous section on "Revenue Forecast"). Management has set a FY2030 objective of a 72.0 percent gross margin, largely in line with our forecasts. Should revenue growth prove more (less) robust than our forecast, we expect more (less) gross margin accretion.

SG&A Expenses and Other Operating Expenses

Distribution costs increased significantly over time, from 26.1 percent of revenue in FY2009 (not shown in the exhibits) to 38 percent in FY2018, and thereafter decreasing to 33.8 percent in FY2021. In particular, the setup of Rémy's distribution network in Asia increased the cost base. Rémy is very committed to its brand building and is also diversifying geographically. We estimate modest increases in distribution costs as a percentage of revenue, of 20 bps per year. Administrative costs as a percentage of revenue have increased from 8.1 percent to 10.1 percent as revenues have fallen, owing to the COVID-19 pandemic. However, the growth in absolute euro amounts has been modest, with costs of approximately EUR100 million in FY2019–FY2021. We expect 1 percent growth in administrative costs per year through FY2024E.

Other operating expenses (income), composed primarily of provisions for impairments of intangible assets, restructurings, and divestiture gains, has fluctuated from −EUR2 million to EUR20 million from FY2018 to FY2021. Because we do not anticipate any transactions that would result in other operating expenses or income, we forecast zero for this line in the model.

Exhibit 4 provides a consolidated income statement for Rémy through the EBIT and EBIT margin line.

Exhibit 4: Consolidated Historical and Projected Income Statement (Operating) for Rémy Cointreau Group (euro millions, unless noted)

	FY2018	FY2019	FY2020	FY2021	FY2022E	FY2023E	FY2024E
Sales	1,127	1,126	1,025	1,010	1,095	1,181	1,275
Cost of sales	366	415	348	330	347	362	379
Gross profit	761	711	677	680	748	819	897
Gross margin	67.5%	63.1%	66.1%	67.3%	68.3%	69.3%	70.3%
Change in gross margin	0.8%	–4.4%	2.9%	1.3%	1.0%	1.0%	1.0%
Distribution costs	433	346	355	342	373	404	439
Distribution costs as percent of sales	38.4%	30.7%	34.6%	33.8%	34.0%	34.2%	34.4%
Administrative expenses	92	101	107	103	104	105	106
Administrative expenses as % of sales	8.1%	8.9%	10.4%	10.1%	9.5%	8.9%	8.3%
Other operating expenses (income)	13	–2	20	0	0	0	0
EBIT	223	266	196	236	272	310	352
EBIT margin	19.8%	23.6%	19.1%	23.3%	24.8%	26.2%	27.6%

Operating Profit by Segment

In this section, we alternatively estimate operating profit and margin using a segment approach. Rémy discloses current operating profit for each of its segments as well as an operating cost at the corporate or holding company level. Recall that current operating profit is a non-IFRS measure that excludes certain items. These certain items are disclosed on Rémy's income statement as "Other operating expenses (income)." Therefore, the sum of the segment current operating profit equals consolidated EBIT before other operating expenses (income).

For the Cognac segment, the forecast of higher revenue growth, based partially on strong price/mix growth, assumes an improving product mix that will also result in a higher gross margin. But the benefit to gross margin will be somewhat mitigated by higher distribution costs. Thus, the expectation is that the Cognac segment's operating margin will increase to 33.4 percent by FY2024. As a benchmark, this forecast can be compared with the financial results reported by Hennessy (part of LVMH), another cognac brand. That company's operating margin in its Wine & Spirits segment in FY2017–2019 was 30–32 percent, though that business has a significantly higher mix of lower-priced products with lower gross margins.

For the other segments, there is not much upside. In the Liqueurs & Spirits division, we assume operating margin to increase modestly to 13.6 percent. In total, Rémy Cointreau Group's consolidated operating margin is forecast to improve from 23.4 percent in FY2021 to 27.6 percent in FY2024, largely because of growth and margin improvement in the Cognac segment, the most profitable division, and leverage from that sales growth on corporate-level costs.

While a segment approach like Exhibit 5 can be used instead of a consolidated approach to forecasting revenue and operating profit, it is also commonly used as a "check" on the consolidated forecasts. This analysis revealed, for example, that the model relies significantly on margin improvement in the Cognac segment.

Exhibit 5: Historical and Projected Operating Profit by Segment for Rémy Cointreau Group

Revenue (euro millions)	FY2018	FY2019	FY2020	FY2021	FY2022E	FY2023E	FY2024E
Cognac	760	774	736	735	818	902	994
Liqueurs and spirits	267	264	262	248	251	253	256
Partner brands	100	87	28	27	26	26	26
Total revenues	1,127	1,126	1,025	1,010	1,095	1,181	1,275

Current Operating Profit (euro millions)	FY2018	FY2019	FY2020	FY2021	FY2022E	FY2023E	FY2024E
Cognac	204	236	200	221	255	291	332
Liqueurs and spirits	43	39	38	33	34	34	35
Partner brands	5	5	−2	−1	−1	−1	−1
Holding/Corporate-level costs	−16	−15	−20	−17	−16	−15	−14
Total current operating profit	237	264	215	236	271	309	352

Current Operating Profit Margins	FY2018	FY2019	FY2020	FY2021	FY2022E	FY2023E	FY2024E
Cognac	26.9%	30.4%	27.1%	30.1%	31.2%	32.3%	33.4%
Liqueurs and spirits	16.0%	14.7%	14.3%	13.3%	13.4%	13.5%	13.6%
Partner brands	5.3%	5.6%	−6.2%	−3.0%	−3.0%	−3.0%	−3.0%
Holding/Corporate-level costs	−1.4%	−1.3%	−2.0%	−1.7%	−1.5%	−1.3%	−1.1%
Total current operating profit	21.0%	23.5%	21.0%	23.4%	24.8%	26.2%	27.6%

Non-Operating Items

Three types of non-operating line items are included in the model: finance expenses (i.e., interest expenses), income taxes, and shares outstanding.

Net finance cost on Rémy's income statement is interest expense on debt less interest income earned on cash and investments. Forecasting net finance cost, therefore, requires estimating the debt and cash positions and interest rates paid and earned.

Companies pay a fixed or variable interest rate on debt. If the interest rate is variable, the rate is typically determined by a market reference rate plus a credit spread. As shown in Exhibit 6, Rémy's interest expenses are fixed and calculated as 1.7 percent incurred on gross debt at the beginning of the period (EUR720 million at end of FY2020). Other financial expenses are assumed to be zero. Gross debt and the interest rate paid on it are estimated to remain flat from the year ended FY2021 level

Although interest income is typically forecasted after forecasting the cash position from the forecasted statement of cash flows, in this case we have simply estimated EUR0 in interest income through the model period; in each of FY2018–FY2021, annual interest income was EUR0, EUR0, EUR0.1, and EUR0.2 million, respectively, because Rémy maintains its liquidity in assets with zero or very low yields. For companies that own liquid assets with higher interest rates, or in higher interest rate environments, interest income should be forecast in the same manner as interest expense: forecasted cash and investments multiplied by a forecasted interest rate.

Exhibit 6: Debt Position and Financial Costs and Income for Rémy (EUR millions, unless noted)

	FY2018	FY2019	FY2020	FY2021	FY2022E	FY2023E	FY2024E
Long-term financial debt	397	424	452	424	424	424	424
Short-term financial debt and accrued interest	73	98	268	92	92	92	92
Gross debt	470	522	720	515	515	515	515
Interest expense	14.5	13.7	12.9	12.1	8.7	8.7	8.7
Interest rate (on beginning balance)		2.9%	2.5%	1.7%	1.7%	1.7%	1.7%
Interest income	0.0	0.0	0.1	0.2	0.0	0.0	0.0
Net finance cost	14.5	13.7	12.8	11.9	8.7	8.7	8.7

Corporate Income Tax Forecast

The French statutory corporate income tax rate at the time of analysis is 32 percent. Rémy Cointreau Group's effective tax rate has, over the longer run, been close to the statutory rate. Therefore, an estimated 32 percent effective tax rate is used in the forecast period. Rémy has no material minority interests in any of its subsidiaries.

Shares Outstanding

Shares outstanding to compute earnings per share (EPS) on the income statement are disclosed in two ways, both weighted averages throughout the fiscal year: basic and diluted. Basic shares outstanding includes common equity securities outstanding, while diluted shares outstanding is a type of what-if analysis; it is basic shares outstanding plus the number of shares from the exercise or conversion of in-the-money instruments, less an assumed repurchase of those if-issued shares.

Typically, the two major factors that affect shares outstanding over time are share issuance related to equity-based compensation of employees (increases shares outstanding) and share repurchases (decreases shares outstanding). Less common but sometimes significant transactions that also affect shares outstanding include acquisitions financed with stock, secondary issuance, and conversions of preferred stock or other instruments to common stock.

Exhibit 7 shows beginning and ending basic shares outstanding for the past six fiscal years as well as the annual net amount of share repurchases and issuance, which were gathered from the statements of stockholders' equity and notes to financial statements. Additionally, the basic and diluted shares outstanding on the income statement used to calculate basic and diluted EPS (weighted averages) are shown and differed by approximately 2.6 million shares in each of the past five years.

Exhibit 7: Shares Outstanding for Rémy (euro millions, unless noted)

	FY2016	FY2017	FY2018	FY2019	FY2020	FY2021
Beginning basic shares outstanding	48.6	48.6	49.6	50.0	49.8	49.8
Share repurchases	–0.0	0.0	–0.3	–1.0	–0.0	0.0
Share issuance	0.0	1.0	0.7	0.8	0.1	0.4
Ending basic shares outstanding	48.6	49.6	50.0	49.8	49.8	50.3
Weighted average basic shares	48.6	49.1	49.8	50.1	49.8	50.1
Dilutive securities	0.1	2.7	2.6	2.6	2.6	2.6
Weighted average diluted shares	48.7	51.8	52.4	52.7	52.4	53.1

As evident in Exhibit 7, shares outstanding for Rémy have not changed materially in six years because the company does not pay significant share-based compensation nor has it repurchased shares. Additionally, management has not disclosed an intention to repurchase shares in the near term. Therefore, the model assumes that weighted average basic and diluted shares outstanding on the income statement remain flat at the FY2021 level.

Pro Forma Income Statement

Now with the forecast components in place, a consolidated pro forma income statement can be constructed, as shown in Exhibit 8. Although not presented on the face of the income statement as disclosed by the company, the calculation of EBITDA is shown after EBIT by adding depreciation and amortization expense from the statement of cash flows. It is not linked to other quantities on the income statement but merely shown as a useful profitability measure.

Exhibit 8: Consolidated Historical and Projected Income Statement for Rémy Cointreau Group (euro millions, unless noted)

	FY2018	FY2019	FY2020	FY2021	FY2022E	FY2023E	FY2024E
Sales	1,127	1,126	1,025	1,010	1,095	1,181	1,275
Cost of sales	366	415	348	330	347	362	379
Gross profit	761	711	677	680	748	819	897
Gross margin	67.5%	63.1%	66.1%	67.3%	68.3%	69.3%	70.3%
Change in gross margin	0.8%	–4.4%	2.9%	1.3%	1.0%	1.0%	1.0%
Distribution costs	433	346	355	342	373	404	439
Distribution costs as percent of sales	38.4%	30.7%	34.6%	33.8%	34.0%	34.2%	34.4%

	FY2018	FY2019	FY2020	FY2021	FY2022E	FY2023E	FY2024E
Administrative expenses	92	101	107	103	104	105	106
Administrative expenses as percent of sales	8.1%	8.9%	10.4%	10.1%	9.5%	8.9%	8.3%
Other operating expenses (income)	13	–2	20	0	0	0	0
EBIT	223	266	196	236	272	310	352
EBIT margin	19.8%	23.6%	19.1%	23.3%	24.8%	26.2%	27.6%
Depreciation and amortization (add-back)	22	30	33	34			
Depreciation and amortization as percent of sales	1.9%	2.7%	3.3%	3.4%			
EBITDA	245	296	229	270			
EBITDA margin	21.7%	26.3%	22.3%	26.7%			
Net finance costs	15	14	13	12	9	9	9
Other financial expenses	8	19	15	3	0	0	0
Total financial expenses	22	33	28	15	9	9	9
Profit before tax	201	233	167	221	263	301	344
Income tax	54	68	61	78	84	96	110
Effective tax rate	26.6%	29.0%	36.4%	35.1%	32.0%	32.0%	32.0%
Income from associates	1	–7	0	1	0	0	0
Profit from continuing operations	148	159	107	144	179	205	234
Profit from discontinued operations	0	0	6	0	0	0	0
Net profit for the year	148	159	113	144	179	205	234
YoY%		8%	–29%	27%	24%	14%	14%
EPS basic continuing operations	2.97	3.18	2.14	2.88	3.58	4.09	4.67
EPS diluted continuing operations	2.82	3.02	2.04	2.74	3.40	3.89	4.44
EPS basic total	2.97	3.18	2.27	2.88	3.58	4.09	4.67
EPS diluted total	2.82	3.02	2.16	2.74	3.40	3.89	4.44
Average number of shares, basic (millions)	49.8	50.1	49.8	50.1	50.1	50.1	50.1
Average number of shares, diluted (millions)	52.4	52.7	52.4	52.6	52.6	52.6	52.6

Pro Forma Statement of Cash Flows

The forecast statements of cash flows begin with forecasted net income and other amounts from the forecast income statement, and then typically require estimates for capital expenditures, depreciation and amortization, working capital, share-based compensation, dividends, and share repurchases. Once the forecasted income statements and statements of cash flows are completed, forecasting the balance sheet is largely a matter of properly linking the spreadsheet, as illustrated in Exhibit 9.

Exhibit 9: Statement of Cash Flows Projection Process

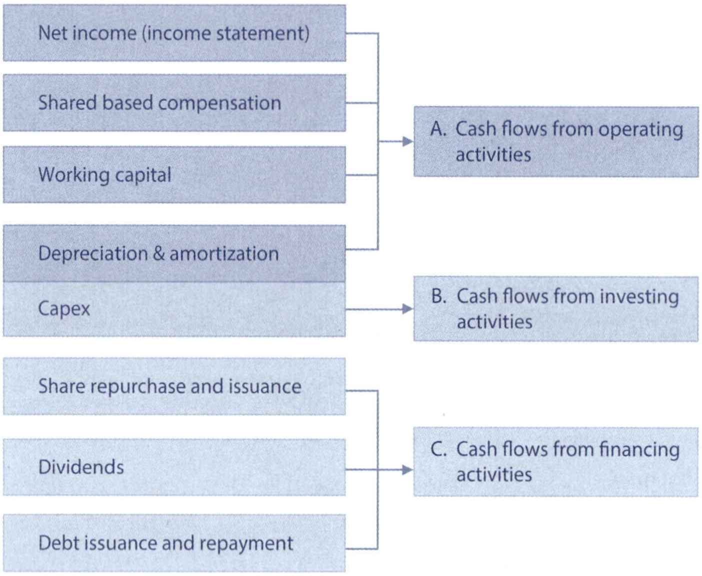

Capital Investments and Depreciation Forecasts

Capital investment, or capex, as a percentage of revenue was 5.3 percent in FY2021. Given the healthy volume growth prospects, we expect capex to remain at a modestly above historical average level of 5.0 percent of sales through FY2024. With Rémy's growing fixed asset base, it is logical that depreciation will increase. The model assumes that depreciation and amortization (D&A) is equal to 4.2 percent of prior year fixed assets, the average of the past three years. The breakdowns of capex and D&A are shown in Exhibit 10.

Exhibit 10: Capex, D&A Breakdowns

	2018	2019	2020	2021	2022E	2023E	2024E
D&A (euro millions)	22	30	33	34	36	36	37
As percent of prior year fixed assets		4.0%	4.3%	4.2%	4.2%	4.2%	4.2%
Capex, PP&E, and intangibles (euro millions)	34	45	65	54	55	59	64

	2018	2019	2020	2021	2022E	2023E	2024E
Capex as % of sales	3.0%	4.0%	6.3%	5.3%	5.0%	5.0%	5.0%
Capex/D&A ratio	1.6	1.5	1.9	1.6	1.5	1.6	1.7

Working Capital Forecasts

We have assumed that working capital ratios will remain similar to what the company experienced in the FY2018–21 period. In Exhibit 11, we include only the relevant balance sheet items related to revenues and costs (i.e., inventories, accounts receivable, and accounts payable) and keep the other items constant. Rémy Cointreau Group had positive net working capital of 105 percent of its sales in fiscal year 2021. The largest working capital component is inventory because much of Rémy's cognac requires years of aging. Inventory days on hand in FY2021 was 1,493, which reflects an approximate 300-day increase owing to the volume slowdown during the COVID-19 pandemic. Inventory days are partially mitigated by extended payment terms to suppliers; days payable outstanding has averaged around 500 days since FY2018.

We model the working capital accounts by projecting working capital ratios (days of inventory, days sales outstanding, days payable outstanding) which are combined with the sales and cost of sales forecast to produce projected working capital accounts on the balance sheet. We expect inventory days to decline through FY2024 as the inventory increase that occurred during the COVID-19 pandemic is worked through, days sales outstanding to remain at FY2021 levels, and for model days payable outstanding to decline back to an average level, again reflecting a normalization after the COVID-19 pandemic. As a result of the decrease in inventory days, the model projects a net positive contribution from working capital to the reconciliation of net income to cash flows from operations on the statement of cash flows, which is in stark contrast to prior years' negative contribution.

Exhibit 11: Working Capital Development for Rémy

	FY2018	FY2019	FY2020	FY2021	FY2022E	FY2023E	FY2024E
Inventories (euro millions)	1,170	1,246	1,364	1,493	1,426	1,340	1,245
Accounts receivable	210	271	199	158	171	185	200
Accounts payable	517	544	534	586	597	604	610
Working capital, net	863	973	1,029	1,065	1,000	922	835
Percent of sales	77%	86%	100%	105%	91%	78%	65%
Change in working capital		−110	−56	−36	64	79	87
Days inventories on hand	1,166	1,095	1,431	1,650	1,500	1,350	1,200
Days sales outstanding	68	88	71	57	57	57	57
Days payable outstanding	515	478	561	648	628	608	588

Forecasted Cash Flow Statement

With net income, D&A, change in working capital, capex, and debt estimates already in place, the cash flow statement shown in Exhibit 12 is almost automatically generated by linking the relevant lines on a spreadsheet. The three significant items left to forecast are share-based compensation, share repurchases or issuance, and dividends. Going forward, the model assumes flat share-based compensation, no share repurchases or issuance, and dividends paid equal to the FY2021 level through FY2024. Lines labeled "other" are aggregated and zeroed out going forward because they are immaterial, difficult to forecast, or both.

Exhibit 12: Projected Statement of Cash Flows for Rémy (euro millions)

	FY2018	FY2019	FY2020	FY2021	FY2022E	FY2023E	FY2024E
Net income (loss)	148	159	113	144	179	205	234
D&A	22	30	33	34	36	36	37
Share-based compensation	3	3	4	2	2	2	2
Investment in working capital	−7	−162	−72	−13	64	79	87
Other non-cash amounts	20	22	3	10	0	0	0
Cash flows from operations	185	53	81	177	281	322	360
Capex (PP&E and intangibles)	−34	−45	−65	−54	−55	−59	−64
Other investing activities	2	92	12	62	0	0	0
Cash flows from investments	−32	47	−53	8	−55	−59	−64
Debt issuance (repayment)	0	11	196	−246	0	0	0
Share issuance (repurchases)	−27	−104	−2	2	0	0	0
Dividends paid	−25	−9	−132	−10	−10	−10	−10
Cash flows from financing	−52	−102	62	−253	−10	−10	−10
FX translation effects	8	−6	1	−1	0	0	0
Net change in cash	109	−8	91	−68	217	254	287

	FY2018	FY2019	FY2020	FY2021	FY2022E	FY2023E	FY2024E
Cash and equivalents, beginning	78	187	179	269	201	418	671
Cash and equivalents, end	187	179	269	201	418	671	958

Forecasted Balance Sheet

The forecasted balance sheet is given in Exhibit 13 and is based on the combination of the projected income statement (Exhibit 8), the projected statement of cash flows (Exhibit 12), and the historical starting balance sheet. The balance sheet items that were not specifically discussed are held constant, which preserves the accounting identity. For ease of presentation, the stockholders' equity lines (e.g., common stock, additional paid in capital, retained earnings, treasury shares, accumulated other comprehensive income) are aggregated. For each forecast period, common stockholders' equity is the prior year value plus net income and share-based compensation less dividends.

If each of the discussed lines is linked properly—and other lines are held constant from FY2021—the forecasted balance sheet should balance each year. Consult the Rémy worksheet in the downloadable Microsoft Excel workbook for greater detail.

Exhibit 13: Projected Balance Sheet for Rémy (euro millions)

	FY2018	FY2019	FY2020	FY2021	FY2022E	FY2023E	FY2024E
Cash and equivalents	186.8	178.6	269.4	201.0	418	671	958
Accounts receivable	210	271	199	158	171	185	200
Inventories	1,170	1,246	1,364	1,493	1,426	1,340	1,245
Other current assets	16	5	16	10	10	10	10
Total current assets	1,583	1,700	1,848	1,861	2,025	2,206	2,412
PP&E, intangibles, goodwill, net	752	785	808	845	864	887	913
Investment in associates	20	1	1	2	2	2	2
Other non-current assets	186	139	131	73	73	73	73
Total assets	2,542	2,625	2,789	2,781	2,964	3,168	3,400
Short-term/current debt	73	98	268	92	92	92	92
Accounts payable	517	544	534	586	597	604	610
Other current liabilities and accrued expenses	26	31	39	42	42	42	42
Total current liabilities	616	673	842	720	731	737	744
Long-term/non-current debt	397	424	452	424	424	424	424
Other non-current liabilities	121	102	92	88	88	88	88
Total common equity	1,407	1,425	1,403	1,548	1,720	1,918	2,144
NCI (Non-Controlling Interest)	1	1	1	1	1	1	1
Total equity and liabilities	2,542	2,625	2,789	2,781	2,964	3,168	3,400

Valuation Model Inputs

A financial statement model is the starting point for most valuation models. Valuation estimates can be made based on a variety of metrics, including free cash flow, EPS, EBITDA, and EBIT. The company-specific inputs needed to build a discounted cash flow (DCF) to the firm model (to estimate enterprise value) are shown in Exhibit 14. All the variables are sourced from the forecasted income statements and statements of cash flows.

Exhibit 14: Calculating Free Cash Flow to the Firm as Basis for a DCF Valuation Model (euro millions)

	FY2021	FY2022E	FY2023E	FY2024E
EBIT	236	272	310	352
Taxes (32% tax rate)	−75	−87	−99	−113
After-tax EBIT	160	185	211	240
D&A	34	36	36	37
Change in working capital	−13	64	79	87
Capital expenditures	−54	−55	−59	−64
Free cash flow to the firm	127	230	267	300

3 BEHAVIORAL FINANCE AND ANALYST FORECASTS

☐ explain how behavioral factors affect analyst forecasts and recommend remedial actions for analyst biases

Studies have shown that experts in many fields persistently make forecasting errors arising from behavioral biases, and investment analysts' models of financial statements are in no way immune. To improve forecasts and the investment decisions based on them, analysts must be aware of the impact of biases and potential remedies for them. Five key behavioral biases that influence analyst forecasts are overconfidence, illusion of control, conservatism, representativeness, and confirmation bias.

Overconfidence in Forecasting

Overconfidence bias occurs when people demonstrate unwarranted faith in their own abilities. Studies have identified that 90 percent *confidence intervals* for forecasts, which should leave only 10 percent error rates, turn out to be wrong as much as 40 percent of the time (Russo and Schoemaker 1992). Studies have also suggested that individuals are more confident when making contrarian predictions that counter the consensus. That is, overconfidence arises more frequently when forecasting what others do not expect (Dunning, Griffin, Milojkovic, and Ross 1990).

To mitigate overconfidence bias, analysts should record and share their forecasts and review them regularly, identifying *both* the correct and incorrect forecasts they have made. Given the wide range of outcomes for most financial variables, an analyst will likely find that they have been wrong as much or more often than they have been right. The goal is to recognize that forecast error rates are high, so mitigating actions that widen the confidence interval of forecasts should be taken. One such action is **scenario analysis**. By asking, "Where could I be wrong and by how much?," an analyst can generate different forecast scenarios.

EXAMPLE 1

Mitigating Overconfidence: Scenario Analysis for Rémy

In the prior lesson, a financial statement model was constructed for Rémy Cointreau Group that includes only one set of forecasted numbers, or one scenario. Creating several more scenarios is an important modeling step because the range of outcomes for the most important variable is wider than a single point.

Three important variables in the forecast of free cash flow are organic sales growth in the Cognac segment, EBIT margin, and net working capital as a percentage of sales. A benefit of the spreadsheet-driven model is that the forecasts can be easily modified to calculate different free cash flow estimates. The base case inputs and forecast for 2024E free cash flow to the firm, as well as figures for two different scenarios, are shown in Exhibit 15.

Alternative Scenario 1 assumes that the Cognac segment's organic growth remains the same as its FY2021 rate, an EBIT margin of 23.6 percent, where it was before the COVID-19 pandemic, and working capital of 86 percent of sales, also the pre-pandemic level from FY2019. Alternative Scenario 2 assumes the same Cognac segment organic growth rate as the base case but an EBIT margin of 25.0 percent and working capital of 90 percent of sales. This scenario reflects strong growth but a high level of reinvestment in sales and marketing costs and aged cognac inventory to support that growth.

As Exhibit 15 demonstrates, there is a wide range of free cash flow estimates for 2022E–2024E because of a wide range of reasonable inputs for key variables.

Exhibit 15: Calculating Free Cash Flow to the Firm as Basis for a DCF Valuation Model (euro millions)

Base Case	2022E	2023E	2024E
Cognac segment organic growth	11.3%	10.2%	10.2%
EBIT margin	24.8%	26.2%	27.6%
Working capital as percent of sales	91%	78%	65%
Free cash flow to the firm est.	230	267	300
Alternative Scenario 1	**2022E**	**2023E**	**2024E**
Cognac segment organic growth	4.0%	4.0%	4.0%
EBIT margin	23.6%	23.6%	23.6%
Working capital as percent of sales	86%	86%	86%
Free cash flow to the firm est.	318	133	129
Alternative Scenario 2	**2022E**	**2023E**	**2024E**
Cognac segment organic growth	11.3%	10.2%	10.2%
EBIT margin	25.0%	25.0%	25.0%
Working capital as percent of sales	90%	90%	90%
Free cash flow to the firm est.	240	109	105

Illusion of Control

A bias often linked to overconfidence, illusion of control is a tendency to overestimate the ability to control what cannot be controlled and to take ultimately fruitless actions in pursuit of control. This bias often manifests in analysts' beliefs that forecasts can be rendered more accurate in two ways: by acquiring more information and opinions from experts and by creating more granular and complex models. Although additional information and complexity in model specification can improve forecasting accuracy, there are diminishing marginal returns. The amount of material information available for an investment is finite and adding immaterial information will mislead. Complex models tend to be overfitted to historical data sets which do not prove robust in a range of environments that include never-before-seen outliers. Excessive breadth of data and model complexity can also conceal assumptions and make updating forecasts upon the receipt of new information difficult. Finally, analysts face significant opportunity costs; additional hours modeling one company could mean that the analyst will examine fewer opportunities in total.

Beyond awareness of the bias and the recognition that uncertainty is an inherent characteristic in investments, illusion of control can be mitigated by restricting modeling variables to those that are regularly disclosed by the company, focusing on the most important or impactful variables, and speaking only with those who are likely to have unique or significant perspectives.

EXAMPLE 2

Illusion of Control: How Much Model Complexity?

Rémy Cointreau Group regularly reports revenues by segment and by geographic region (Europe/Middle East/Africa, the Americas, and Asia Pacific). It does not disclose segment revenue by geographic region (e.g., the Cognac segment revenue in the Asia Pacific region), nor does it disclose revenue by sales channel, such as retailers versus bars and restaurants, travel retail, and so on. In its quarterly earnings calls, however, the company often makes numerous references to segment growth rates in specific regions and growth rates of specific channels, even though the actual numbers are not disclosed. Such a practice is common, especially during the COVID-19 pandemic because large sales channel shifts occurred: travel retail in most regions experienced declines >90 percent, sales shifted from bars and restaurants to retailers for at-home consumption, and different geographies were affected by the pandemic at different times.

An analyst might be tempted to collect all these growth rates and other anecdotal figures that management discloses on its earnings calls and, perhaps by combining them with third-party estimates of sales, to build an extensive revenue model for Rémy in which each segment is broken out into geographic regions and sales channels.

Although such an endeavor might be useful to set expectations and to monitor over time, building the revenue forecast in this way would introduce several problems and probably not materially improve accuracy. First, because the data used in the model are not regularly disclosed, there is no way to check actuals versus estimates. Second, model construction would take dozens of hours. Finally, and perhaps most importantly, whether the constituent small parts of such a model would be accurate is unclear, which would not make the consolidated revenue forecast any more accurate than a simpler model.

Conservatism Bias

Conservatism bias is a bias in which people maintain their prior views or forecasts by inadequately incorporating new information. This often happens in forecasting when an analyst does not update their forecasting after receiving conflicting information, such as disappointing earnings results or a competitor action. Although the most common form of conservatism is the reluctance to incorporate new negative information into a forecast, analysts could also fail to adequately incorporate positive information and thus have estimates that are too low. A different name for conservatism bias in this context is anchoring and adjustment, referring to an analyst using their prior estimates as an "anchor" that is subsequently adjusted. Although nothing is wrong with modifying a previous forecast, the previous forecast or anchor tends to exert significant influence; in other words, the adjustment is too small, and the updated forecast is too close to the previous forecast.

Conservatism bias can be mitigated by reviews of forecasts and models by an investment team at a regular interval, such as each quarter, and by creating flexible models with fewer variables, to make changing assumptions easier. Because conservatism bias is related to overconfidence and the illusion of control, mitigating those biases can also serve to mitigate conservatism.

EXAMPLE 3

Conservatism Bias: Rémy Management Guidance for FY2022

The base case forecasts in the Rémy Cointreau Group model call for organic revenue growth of 11.3 percent and net income growth of 24 percent in FY2022E over FY2021. However, during the earnings call for the fourth quarter of FY2021, Rémy management gave the following guidance for FY2022:

- "Fiscal year 2022 will be a strong year of growth and investment, and we are on track to achieve our 2030 [objectives of a 72% gross margin and 33% operating margin]."
- "Being ahead of [our] 2030 strategic plan and given the favorable environment, [we] have decided to revise up [our] strategic investments [in sales and marketing] to support brands through the recovery and boost their medium-term growth potential by developing brand awareness and attractiveness."
- Fiscal year 2022 will have "top-line and bottom-line growth in the mid-teens in organic terms."

Based on these comments, your colleague suggests revising the Rémy model slightly by reducing the operating margin forecast to reduce net income growth from 24 percent to 20 percent.

1. What behavioral bias does your colleague's suggestion exhibit, and what research or steps should be taken, if any, with respect to revising the Rémy model? Explain your answer.

   Solution:

   Your colleague is exhibiting conservatism bias or anchoring and adjustment; they are anchored to the prior forecast of 24 percent net income growth and not fully considering management's guidance on profitability.
   Changing the model to follow the guidance without further consideration is not necessarily appropriate because results can and often do under- or

outperform guidance. However, in this case, management guidance differs quite significantly from the FY2022E forecast on both sales growth and net income growth. As a first step, management's credibility should be assessed by examining the company's performance against management guidance in the past. Second, the guidance should be considered as a scenario in the scenario analysis, and the investment implications of that scenario should be examined; for example, if the company will in fact increase sales and profits at a mid-teens rate in FY2022, does that result in an investment decision? Finally, the performance of, and guidance provided by, other alcohol and spirits companies should be compared to these figures as a check for reasonableness.

Representativeness Bias

Representativeness bias refers to the tendency to classify information based on past experiences and known classifications. New information might resemble or seem representative of familiar elements already classified but can in fact be very different and is better viewed from a different perspective. In these instances, the classification reflex can deceive, producing an incorrect understanding that biases all future thinking about the information. Base-rate neglect is a common form of representativeness bias in forecasting. In base-rate neglect, a phenomenon's rate of incidence in a larger population, or characteristics of a larger class to which a specific member belongs—its base rate—is neglected in favor of situation- or member-specific information. Considering the base rate is sometimes known as the "outside view," while the situation-specific is known as the "inside view."

For example, an analyst is modeling operating costs and margins for a biopharmaceutical company. The "inside view" approach would consider company-specific factors such as the types of drugs the company sells, the number of salespeople needed in each geographic region for each drug, and so on. The "outside view" approach would view the company as a member of the "biopharmaceuticals" industry, of which there are many others, and use industry or sector averages for gross margin, R&D expense as percentage of sales, and so on in the model.

Neither the outside nor inside view is superior; what makes for a superior forecast is considering both. One way of doing so is by starting with the base rate but determining which factors make the target company different from the base rate or class average and what the implications of those differences are, if any. For example, the analyst modeling the biopharmaceuticals company might start with industry averages in the model but change some of the variables to account for factors such as royalties versus product sales revenues, geographic composition of revenues, and whether the company is likely to face patent expirations on its products over the forecast period.

EXAMPLE 4

Considering Base Rates for Rémy

While constructing the Rémy model in the prior lesson, little attention was given to comparable companies or to the broader industry to which Rémy belongs. In other words, the model was constructed primarily with the "inside view." In this example, Rémy is put in the context of six other spirits-focused alcohol companies: Brown-Forman Corporation, Pernod Ricard SA, Davide Campari-Milano N.V., Diageo plc, Becle S.A.B de C.V. (Cuervo), and the Wine & Spirits segment of LVMH (LVMH W&S) for the five most recently reported fiscal years at the time of analysis. The variable used for the industry comparison is the five-year average of EBIT margin because it is a key model input, and the profitability of an individual company is strongly influenced by industry profitability. Many of these peer companies are significantly larger by revenue than Rémy, which is useful because we have modeled Rémy becoming larger over time. The analysis for Exhibit 16 is included in the Exhibit 16 worksheet in the downloadable Microsoft Excel workbook.

Exhibit 16: EBIT Margin Comparison of Spirits Companies, Last Five Reported Fiscal Years (euro millions)

EBIT margin	MRY-4	MRY-3	MRY-2	MRY-1	Most Recent Year (MRY)
Rémy	20%	20%	24%	19%	23%
Brown Forman	34%	32%	34%	32%	34%
Pernod	24%	25%	26%	26%	12%
Campari	22%	26%	25%	25%	17%
Diageo	27%	30%	30%	31%	18%
Cuervo	23%	26%	20%	18%	20%
LVMH W&S	31%	31%	32%	31%	29%
Peer average (ex Rémy)	27%	28%	28%	27%	22%
Peer five-year average (ex Rémy)	26%				

1. Evaluate the base case forecasts in the Rémy model as well as Rémy's management's FY2030 objective of a 33 percent operating margin considering the analysis in Exhibit 16.

   Solution:

   The base case forecasts in the Rémy model are for EBIT margins of 24.8 percent, 26.2 percent, and 27.6 percent in FY2022E, FY2023E, and FY2024E, respectively. The most recently reported fiscal year(s) for most of the peer companies include the effect of deleveraging from sales declines associated with the COVID-19 pandemic. Aside from that, the base case forecasts are close to the peer average and by that measure appear reasonable, though they are substantially higher than the past five years of profitability for Rémy itself.

   Rémy management's objective of 33 percent operating margin in 2030 appears high relative to those of its peers; only one company, Brown Forman, has achieved that level of profitability, on annual revenues ~3.0× that of Rémy. Industry-leading growth and profitability of Rémy's Cognac segment will be required to meet this objective.

Confirmation Bias

Confirmation bias is the tendency to look for and notice what confirms prior beliefs and to ignore or undervalue whatever contradicts them. A common manifestation of this bias among investment analysts is to structure the research process in pursuit of only positive news or certain criteria, or with a narrow scope. For example, an analyst might research a particular company but conduct only cursory research on its competitors and companies that offer substitute products. An analyst who has a positive view on a company might speak only to other analysts who share that view and the company's management, all of whom will likely tell the analyst what they want to hear and already know. Confirmation bias is closely related to overconfidence and representativeness biases.

The extent to which company management can be excessively optimistic is shown in Exhibit 17, which analyzes the annual report of a major European bank for 2007, published mere months before it entered bankruptcy and was nationalized.

Speaking with management is valuable given their role and should not be excluded from the research process, but analysts must be aware of management's inherent bias and seek differing perspectives, especially when examining a company with significant controversy. Two approaches to mitigating confirmation bias in the forecasting process are to speak to or read research from analysts with a negative opinion on the security under scrutiny and to seek perspectives from colleagues who are not economically or psychologically invested in the subject security.

EXAMPLE 5

Management Optimism

Consider this text analysis of the chairman's statement and business review in the 2007 annual report of a major European bank published in 2008, a few months before the bank was rescued by the government.

Exhibit 17: Text Analysis

Occurrences of ...			
Negative words		**Positive words**	
Disappoint/disappointed	0	Good	55
Bad/badly	0	Excellent	12
Poor	0	Success/successful	35
Weaker/weakening	7	Improvement	23
Slowdown	6	Strong/stronger/strongly	78

4 THE IMPACT OF COMPETITIVE FACTORS IN PRICES AND COSTS

☐ explain how the competitive position of a company based on a Porter's five forces analysis affects prices and costs

One of the tools that analysts can use to think about how competition will affect financial results is Michael Porter's widely used "five forces" framework (see Porter 1980) introduced in earlier learning modules.

Cognac Industry Overview

The cognac segment is Rémy Cointreau Group's most important business segment, accounting for over 90 percent of total operating profit. An important feature of the cognac market is that supply is limited and demand is growing. Supply is limited because the production of cognac, like that of champagne, is highly regulated, in this case through The Bureau National Interprofessionnel du Cognac. By regulation, cognac can be produced only in a limited geographic area, in and around the town of Cognac in southwest France. Furthermore, within the region, production volume is capped each year. Approximately 98 percent of production is exported. The cognac market is highly concentrated, with the top four players controlling 78 percent of world volume and 84 percent of global value. Rémy's market share is approximately 16 percent and 18 percent of global volume and value, respectively (*The Spirits Business,* June 2018). Demand for cognac has been growing because of increasing demand from Asia, particularly China and Singapore, more than offsetting a weakening European market. The global spirits market has grown more than 5 percent annually during the 2000–17 period (*Source:* IWSR drinks market analysis). Simultaneously, Rémy has also seen a product mix improvement because consumers increasingly prefer superior quality and more expensive cognac. Exhibit 18 summarizes Porter's five forces analysis of the cognac industry.

Exhibit 18: Porter's Five Forces Analysis of the Cognac Industry

Force	Degree	Factors to Consider
Threat of substitutes	Low	▪ Cognac consumers show brand loyalty and do not easily shift to other beverages or high-end spirits.
Rivalry	Low	▪ The market is consolidated, with four players controlling 78 percent of the world market in volume and 84 percent of global value. ▪ Only the European market is fragmented, with less than half of the market controlled by the top four.
Bargaining power of suppliers	Low/medium	▪ A large number of small independent vineyards supply inputs. ▪ Most of the distillation is carried out by a large body of independent distillers that sell to the big houses.
Bargaining power of buyers	Low	▪ Premium beverages are sold primarily to wine and spirits retail outlets that do not coordinate purchasing. ▪ Premium beverages are consumed primarily in small and fragmented on-premises outlets (restaurants, etc.).
Threat of new entrants	Low	▪ Producers have long-term contracts with suppliers in the Cognac area. ▪ Barriers to entry are high. • Building brands is difficult because they must have heritage/pedigree. • A large capital investment is required to build an inventory with "aged" cognac and set up a distribution network.

In summary, the cognac market, Rémy's largest and most profitable operating segment, exhibits a favorable profitability profile. In addition to limited supply and growing demand, the industry faces a generally favorable situation with respect to substitutes, rivalry, suppliers, buyers, and potential new entrants.

EXAMPLE 6

Analysis of Anheuser-Busch InBev Using Porter's Five Forces

The competitive structure a company faces can vary among countries, with implications for modeling revenue growth, profit margins, capital expenditures, and return on investments. For example, Anheuser-Busch (AB) InBev, the largest global brewer, operates in many countries, two of which are the United Kingdom and Brazil, the world's third largest beer market. AB InBev's competitive position and prospects in the highly consolidated and growing Brazilian market are much more favorable than in the fragmented and declining UK market.

The Brazilian beer market is divided among four players. AmBev (AB InBev's subsidiary in Brazil, of which it owns a 61.9 percent stake) is the dominant brewer with an estimated 65 percent market share in 2018 versus 20 percent for Heineken and 12 percent for Petropolis, Brazil's largest privately owned brewing group. Helped by its dominant market position and strong distribution network, AmBev was able to report an EBITDA margin of nearly 50.4 percent in 2018 (ri.ambev.com.br), the highest in the global beer industry. The industry participants focus less on price competition and more on expanding distribution and "premiumization" (i.e., selling more expensive beers.) Although the 2015–18 time period saw challenging trading conditions due to subdued consumer demand, causing years of decline in the market by volume, Brazil is still considered a promising market. In this environment, an analyst would likely forecast solid revenue growth for AmBev. Exhibit 19 presents an analysis of the Brazilian beer market using Porter's five forces framework. Most of the competitive forces represent a low threat to profitability (consistent with AmBev's historical profitability), implying that analysts would most likely forecast continued above-average profitability.

Exhibit 19: Analysis of the Brazilian Beer Market Using Porter's Five Forces

Force	Degree	Factors to Consider
Threat of substitutes	Medium	▪ Beer consumers do not easily shift to other beverages, but such alternatives as wine and spirits are available. ▪ Unlike in many other countries, the range of beers is relatively limited.
Rivalry	Low	▪ AmBev dominates the market with a 65% market share. Its economies of scale in production and distribution yield significant cost advantages relative to competition. ▪ Price competition is limited because of AmBev's cost advantages and because of typically increasing beer volumes.
Bargaining power of suppliers	Low	▪ The primary inputs (water, hops, barley, and packaging) are basically commodities.

Force	Degree	Factors to Consider
Bargaining power of buyers	Low	▪ Beer is mostly consumed in bars and restaurants. The owners of these outlets represent a large and highly fragmented group of beer buyers. ▪ The supermarket industry in Brazil is relatively fragmented, and supermarkets are less likely to offer alternatives, such as private labels.
Threat of new entrants	Low	▪ New entrants face relatively high barriers to entry because of the high costs of building a brewery, establishing a national distribution network, and establishing a nationally known brand name.

The UK beer market is also divided among four players, but the competitive structure is totally different than in Brazil. The market is more fragmented, with smaller market shares held by the largest players. Heineken, MolsonCoors, AB InBev, and Carlsberg had market shares of 24 percent (adbrands.net), 18 percent, 18 percent (www.ab-inbev.com), and 11 percent (carlsberggroup.com), respectively, in 2018. Consequently, the British market has no dominant brewer. Given the high fixed costs of a brewery, declining volumes of UK beer consumption, and the highly consolidated customer base, which provides the clients with substantial purchasing power (particularly in the retail channels), price competition is usually intense. A gradual switch from drinking beer in pubs and restaurants ("on-trade") to consumption at home ("off-trade") is making brewers even more exposed to the bargaining power of the dominant retail supermarket (grocers) chains. Increasing taxes on beer and rents faced by pub landlords add to the burden faced by the industry, leading to a steady decline of Britain's pub industry. Profitability has been lower than the beer industry's global average; operating margins are believed to be less than 10 percent. In this kind of environment, analysts would most likely forecast only very cautious revenue growth, if any. Exhibit 20 presents an analysis of the UK beer market using Porter's five forces framework.

Exhibit 20: Analysis of the UK Beer Market Using Porter's Five Forces

Force	Degree	Factors to Consider
Threat of substitutes	Medium	Beer consumers do not easily shift to other beverages, but such alternatives as wine, spirits, and cider are available.
Rivalry	High	The market is relatively fragmented with no dominant market leader and large numbers of small breweries. Declining beer volumes make price wars more likely. Brand loyalty is less developed because of the extensive range of alternative beers.
Bargaining power of suppliers	Low	The primary inputs (water, hops, barley, and packaging) are basically commodities.

Force	Degree	Factors to Consider
Bargaining power of buyers	High	The large supermarket chains that dominate the grocery sector have significant bargaining power. Large pub chains in the "on-trade" business (where beer is sold in pubs and restaurants) also have strong bargaining power.
Threat of new entrants	Low	Barriers to entry are relatively high because of the high costs of building a brewery, establishing a national distribution network (particularly given the history of brewers owning pubs and bars), and establishing a nationally known brand. Because the United Kingdom consists of islands, companies with breweries in other countries face higher transportation costs than existing participants.

There is a distinction between Porter's five forces and other factors that can affect profitability, such as government regulation and taxes:

> Industry structure, as manifested in the strength of the five competitive forces, determines the industry's long-run profit potential because it determines how the economic value created by the industry is divided. Government is not best understood as a sixth force because government involvement is neither inherently good nor bad for industry profitability. The best way to understand the influence of government on competition is to analyze how specific government policies affect the five competitive forces. (Porter 2008, page 10)

EXAMPLE 7

EuroAlco Case

In 20X2, EuroAlco was the beer market leader in Eurolandia (a fictional country) with 35 percent market share. The other four large brewers held 15 percent, 15 percent, 10 percent, and 7 percent share, respectively. The Eurolandia market is considered a growth market. It historically had high overall alcohol consumption but a relatively low per capita consumption of beer, a product that is attracting interest from the growing, younger population and is further supported by increasing disposable incomes.

At the start of year 20X1, the Eurolandia government, in its fight to curb alcohol consumption, tripled the excise duty (a special tax) on beer from EUR0.3 per liter to EUR0.9 and announced that excise duty will further increase by EUR0.1 per liter.

In the following year, 20X2, EuroAlco made efforts to strengthen the position of the more expensive brands in its portfolio. These efforts led to a 20 percent increase in selling costs. Similar to most consumer staple companies, EuroAlco experienced higher production costs. Poor grain harvests put price pressure on buyers of almost all feedstocks, and rising oil prices resulted in higher packaging costs. In 20X2, competing companies were much more cautious with A&P spending than EuroAlco.

Two analysts research EuroAlco at the start of year 20X3. In making their EuroAlco forecasts, both analysts use market data and the published annual report from EuroAlco (see Exhibit 21 and/or the Example 7 worksheet in the downloadable Microsoft Excel workbook). Based on the published data, they consider a number of scenarios and reach different conclusions.

Exhibit 21: EuroAlco Key Financial and Operational Data

				% change	
€ millions	**20X2**	**20X1**	**20X0**	**20X2/20X1**	**20X1/20X0**
Retailer gross sales	11,504	10,248	9,180	12%	12%
Excise duty	2,900	2,520	900	15%	180%
As % of retail revenues	25%	25%	10%		
Value-Added-Tax, VAT (20%)	1,434	1,288	1,380	11%	–7%
Retailer net sales	7,170	6,440	6,900	11%	–7%
Typical retailer profit	935	840	900	11%	–7%
As % of retailer net sales	13%	13%	13%		
Brewer net sales	6,235	5,600	6,000	11%	–7%

				% change	
Key Financial Indicators	**20X2**	**20X1**	**20X0**	**20X2/20X1**	**20X1/20X0**
Volume (mln hectoliters)	29	28	30	4%	–7%
Net sales	6,235	5,600	6,000	11%	–7%
Cost of sales	3,190	2,800	3,150	14%	–11%
Gross profit	3,045	2,800	2,850	9%	–2%
Selling expenses	2,088	1,680	1,650	24%	2%
Administrative expenses	145	140	150	4%	–7%
Operating profit	812	980	1,050	–17%	–7%
Average invested capital	3,000	3,000	3,100	0%	–3%
Gross margin	48.8%	50.0%	47.5%		
Selling expense %	33.5%	30.0%	27.5%		
Operating margin	13.0%	17.5%	17.5%		
Return on invested capital (pre-tax)	27%	33%	34%		

				% change	
€ per hectoliter (hl)	**20X2**	**20X1**	**20X0**	**20X2/20X1**	**20X1/20X0**
Retail price	397	366	306	8%	20%
Excise duty	100	90	30	11%	200%
VAT	49	46	46	7%	0%
Typical distributor profit	32	30	30	7%	0%

€ per hectoliter (hl)	20X2	20X1	20X0	% change 20X2/20X1	% change 20X1/20X0
Brewer net sales	215	200	200	8%	0%
Cost of sales	110	100	105	10%	–5%
Gross profit	105	100	95	5%	5%
Selling expenses	72	60	55	20%	9%
Administrative expenses	5	5	5	0%	0%
Operating profit	28	35	35	–20%	0%

Both analysts assume that the government will impose a further increase in the excise duty (special tax on beer). They also assume that the excise duty increase will be borne by the consumers, who will face a 10 percent price increase that will allow the brewers to maintain their net (after-tax) revenues per hectoliter (hl). They assume that half the cost of sales is fixed per hectoliter and half is variable based on volume, that selling expenses will remain unchanged as a percentage of sales, and that administrative expenses are fixed.

1. Analyst A expects price elasticity of 0.8, indicating that volume will fall by 8 percent given the 10 percent retail price increase. Calculate the impact on operating profit and operating profit margin in 20X3 using Exhibit 22, which is also in the Example 7 sheet in the downloadable Microsoft Excel workbook.

Exhibit 22: EuroAlco's Costs Structure for 20X2–20X3E (euro millions, unless noted)

		Analyst A		Analyst B	
	20X2	20X3E	YoY%	20X3E	YoY%
Volume (millions of hl)	29	26.7	–8.0%	27.6	–5.0%
Brewer net sales (€ per hl)	215				
Net sales	6,235				
Cost of sales	3,190				
Gross profit	3,045				
Gross margin	48.8%				
Selling expenses	2,088				
Administrative expenses	145	145		145	
Operating profit	812				
Operating profit margin	13.0%				
Cost of sales (fixed)	1,595	1,595		1,595	
Cost of sales (variable)	1,595				
Cost of sales (variable) per hl	55	55		55	
Selling expenses as % of sales	33.5%	33.5%		33.5%	

Solution:

Exhibit 23 (see the Example 7 worksheet in the downloadable Microsoft Excel workbook) shows the results for both analysts' projections. Analyst A predicts that operating profit will decrease by 25 percent to EUR608 in

20X3, resulting in an operating margin decline from 13.0 percent in 20X2 to 10.6 percent in 20X3. Analyst A calculates a revenue decline of 8 percent to EUR5,736 based on volume dropping by 8 percent and a constant price per hectoliter of EUR215. The decrease in volume reflects the price elasticity of 0.8 and the price increase of 10 percent as a result of the excise duty increase. COGS sold fell only 4 percent because part of the costs are fixed. COGS as the sum of fixed and variable costs is EUR1,595 + [26.68 (hl volume) × 55 (hl cost)] = EUR1,595 + 1,467 (ignoring rounding error) or EUR3,062. Analyst A predicts selling expenses will decline in line with sales by 8 percent and administrative costs will remain unchanged because of their fixed character in the short term.

2. Analyst B expects price elasticity of 0.5, indicating that volume will fall by 5 percent given the 10 percent retail price increase. Calculate the impact on operating profit and operating profit margin in 20X3 using Exhibit 22, which is also in the Example 7 sheet in the downloadable Microsoft Excel workbook.

Solution:

Analyst B forecasts that operating profit will decline by 16 percent to EUR684. Analyst B's calculations follow the same pattern as those of Analyst A, but Analyst B predicts a smaller, 5 percent, decline in volume. Analyst A's estimates are more pessimistic than those of Analyst B. Note that the net price per hectoliter for the brewer is held constant while the price for the consumer increased 10 percent as a result of the excise duty increase. Because of Analyst B's more optimistic volume forecast, fixed costs are spread over a higher level of sales than is the case for Analyst A. Consequently, Analyst B will have a higher operating margin estimate than Analyst A. However, both analysts are predicting a decline in operating margin in 20X3.

Exhibit 23: Analysts' Results for EuroAlco's Cost Structure and Projection (euro millions, unless noted)

		Analyst A		Analyst B	
	20X2	20X3E	YoY%	20X3E	YoY%
Volume (millions of hl)	29	26.7	−8%	27.6	−5%
Brewer net sales per hl	215	215	0%	215	0%
Net sales	6,235	5,736	−8%	5,923	−5%
Cost of sales	3,190	3,062	−4%	3,110	−3%
Gross profit	3,045	2,674	−12%	2,813	−8%
Gross margin	48.8%	46.6%	−5%	47.5%	−3%
Selling expenses	2,088	1,921	−8%	1,984	−5%
Administrative expenses	145	145	0%	145	0%
Operating profit	812	608	−25%	684	−16%
Operating profit margin	13.0%	10.6%	−19%	11.6%	−11%
Cost of sales (fixed)	1,595	1,595	0%	1,595	0%
Cost of sales (variable)	1,595	1,467	−8%	1,515	−5%

		Analyst A		Analyst B	
	20X2	20X3E	YoY%	20X3E	YoY%
Cost of sales (variable) per hl	55	55	0%	55	0%
Selling expenses as % of net sales	33.5%	33.5%	0%	33.5%	0%

3. Gross margin improved in 20X1 (50.0 percent) but fell in 20X2 (48.8 percent). Cost of sales was relatively high in 20X2 because of high barley costs, an important ingredient for brewing beer. Assume that in 20X2, half of the cost of sales is fixed and half is based on volume. Of the variable part of the cost of sales, assume that half the amount is related to the barley price in 20X2. Barley prices increased 25 percent in 20X2. Consider a scenario where no additional taxes are imposed in 20X3, revenues and volumes remain stable, and barley prices return to their 20X1 level. Calculate EuroAlco's estimated gross margin for 20X3.

Solution:

If barley prices return to their 20X1 level, they will decline 20 percent in 20X3. Because volumes are assumed to remain constant, other variable costs will not change. Gross profit in 20X2 was 48.8 percent of sales, which indicates the cost of sales was 51.2 percent (100% – 48.8%). Barley is 25 percent of the cost of sales (because barley represents half of variable costs, and variable cost of sales represents half of total cost of sales). Cost of sales is predicted to decline by 25% × 20% = 5%. New cost of sales will be 51.2% – (5% × 51.2%) or 48.6 percent. Consequently, gross margin is predicted to be 100% – 48.6% = 51.4% in 20X3. Compared with the gross margin of 48.8 percent in 20X2, gross margin is predicted to increase by 260 bps.

Exhibit 24: Gross Margin Analysis

	20X3	20X2	YoY%
Volume	29	29	0%
Revenue	6,235	6,235	0%
Cost of sales	3,031	3,190	–5%
Variable	1,436	1,595	–10%
Barley related	638	798	–20%
Not barley related	798	798	0%
Fixed	1,595	1,595	0%
Gross profit	3,205	3,045	5%
Gross margin	51.4%	48.8%	5%

4. EuroAlco's selling expenses increased from 30 percent of sales in 20X1 to 33.5 percent of sales in 20X2. Which competitive forces most likely influenced EuroAlco's significant increase in selling expenses?

Solution:

Intra-industry rivalry and threat of substitutes most likely influenced EuroAlco's significant increase in selling costs. By spending more on advertising, EuroAlco wanted to enhance the brand loyalty of its products, thus improving its competitive position versus its brewer rivals and makers of other alcoholic beverages. Furthermore, buyers' bargaining power probably also influenced EuroAlco's increased spending to the extent that advertising creates demand by the ultimate consumer. Strong demand at the ultimate consumer level for EuroAlco's specific brands could enhance the company's bargaining position with its direct customers, the distributors who serve as intermediaries.

5. Retailers are the direct customers of brewers. They buy directly from the brewer and sell to the ultimate consumer. Analyst A expects that the increase in mass retailers in Eurolandia will cause brewers' margins to decline. He expects EuroAlco's operating margin will decrease from 13 percent in 20X2 to 8 percent in 20X6, with stable sales (EUR6,235 million) and an unchanged amount of average invested capital (EUR3,000 million). Analyst B also sees the increasing importance of the larger food retailers but expects that EuroAlco can offset potential pricing pressure by offering more attractive trade credit (e.g., allowing the retailers longer payment terms). He thinks operating margin can remain stable at 13 percent with no sales growth. Average invested capital (EUR3,000 million), however, will double because of the extra investments in inventory and receivables. Describe the analysts' expectations about the impact of large retailers on brewers in terms of Porter's five forces and return on invested capital (ROIC; pre-tax). Which of the two scenarios would be better for EuroAlco?

Solution:

The increase in mass retailers in EuroAlco is expected to strengthen the bargaining power of buyers relative to brewers. According to Analyst A, this will lead to a lower operating margin of 8 percent, while Analyst B believes margins can be maintained if the company offers much more favorable credit terms reflected in doubling of invested capital. Analyst A expects operating profit on invested capital to fall from 27.1 percent (13 percent × EUR6,235/EUR3,000) to 16.6 percent (8 percent × EUR6,235/EUR3,000). Analyst B's assumptions indicate that the ROIC (operating profit divided by invested capital) in 20X2 of 27 percent will fall by half to 13.5 percent as the operating profit is earned on double the amount of invested capital (i.e., 13 percent × EUR6,235/EUR6,000). The scenario envisioned by Analyst A is better for EuroAlco. Full supporting calculations are in the Example 7 worksheet in the downloadable Microsoft Excel workbook.

Porter's five forces framework and similar analytical tools can help analysts assess the relative profit potential of a company by helping them understand the company's industry and its position within that industry. Understanding the industry and competitive contexts of a company helps analysts estimate whether, for example, sales growth is likely to be relatively high or low (relative to history, relative to the overall growth in the economy or a sector, and/or relative to competing companies) and whether profit margins are likely to be relatively high or low (relative to historical profit margins and relative to competing companies). The process of incorporating an industry and competitive analysis into expectations for future financial performance requires judgment. Suppose analysts observe that a given company is the market leader in a moderately competitive industry with limited buyer and supplier power and relatively high barriers to entry. In broad terms, analysts might project that the company's future revenue growth will be in line with that of the overall industry and that its profit margins and ROIC might be somewhat higher than those of other companies in the industry. But there is no mechanical link between the analysts' observations and projecting the company's future sales growth and profit margin. Instead, the link is more subjective and probabilistic.

5 MODELING INFLATION AND DEFLATION

- [ ] explain how to forecast industry and company sales and costs when they are subject to price inflation or deflation

Inflation and deflation (i.e., general increase and decrease in the prices of goods and services) can significantly affect the accuracy of forecasts for a company's future revenue, profit, and cash flow. The impact of inflation or deflation on revenue and expenses differs from company to company. Even within a single company, the impact of inflation or deflation is generally different for revenue and expenses categories.

Some companies are better able to pass on higher input costs by raising the prices at which they sell their output. The ability to pass on price increases can be the result of, for example, strong branding (Coca-Cola) or proprietary technology (Apple). Companies that are well positioned to pass on price increases are, in turn, more likely to have higher and more stable profits and cash flow, relative to competitors.

We first consider the impact of inflation on sales and then on costs.

Sales Projections with Inflation and Deflation

The following analysis addresses the projection of industry sales and company sales in the presence of inflation.

Industry Sales and Inflation or Deflation

Most increases in the cost of inputs, such as commodities or labor, will eventually result in higher prices for end products. Industry structure can be an important factor in determining the relationship between increases in input costs and increases in the price of end products. For example, in the United States, the beer market is an oligopoly, with one player, AB InBev, controlling almost half of the market. Moreover, the three-tier structure of the US beer market, in which the producers (the brewers) must use a third party (the wholesalers) to get their products (beer) to the consumers (bars, restaurants, and retailers) results in a fragmented customer base because brewers are not allowed to deliver directly to the end consumer but rather must use wholesale distributors. These wholesalers often differ state by state. Large nationwide retailers, such as Walmart, still must negotiate with several different wholesalers instead of using their dominant national market position to negotiate directly with the brewers. The industry structure in the United States has likely contributed to increases in beer prices roughly in line with the US Consumer Price Index. In other words, beer prices have generally risen during years of inflation in input costs and decreased when costs have eased (though there have been brief exceptional periods where the opposite has occurred). If necessary, US brewers have been able to increase prices to compensate for costs of inflation. In contrast, European beer companies distribute through a more concentrated customer base—namely, such dominant retail outlets as Carrefour, Tesco, and Ahold—which results in a weaker pricing position for the brewers. Also, the European market lacks an overall dominant brewer. As a result of the industry structure and the lack of underlying volume growth, changes in beer prices in Europe have been on average 100 bps less than customer inflation.

Exhibit 25: US General Inflation and Inflation in Beer Prices

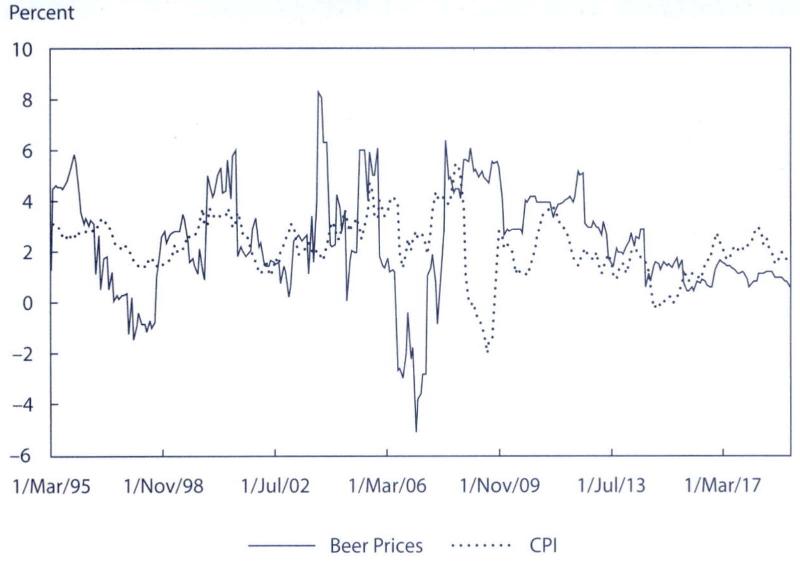

Source: US Bureau of Labor Statistics.

A company's efforts to pass on inflation through higher prices can have a negative impact on volume if the demand is price elastic, which is the case if cheaper substitutes are available. If selling prices could be increased 10 percent while maintaining unit sales volume to offset an increase of 10 percent in input costs, gross profit margin percentage would be the same but the absolute amount of gross profit would increase. In the short term, however, volumes will usually decline as result of a price increase. The decline would depend not only on the price elasticity of demand but also on the reaction of competitors and the availability of substitutes. Lower input costs also make lower consumer prices possible. The first competitor to lower prices will usually benefit with an uptick in volume. Competitors react quickly, however, resulting in a short-term benefit. The price–volume trade-off can make accurate revenue projections difficult. In an inflationary environment, raising prices too late will result in a profit margin squeeze but acting too soon could result in volume losses. In a deflationary environment, lowering prices too soon will result in a lower gross margin, but waiting too long will result in volume losses.

In the highly competitive consumer goods market, pricing is strongly influenced by movements in input prices, which can account for half of the COGS. In some time periods, customers' price sensitivity has resulted in a strong inverse relationship between volume and pricing. For example, Exhibit 26 illustrates Unilever's annual underlying volume and price growth from 2001 to 2020. Increased input prices for packaging, wheat, and milk forced Anglo-Dutch consumer staple company Unilever to increase prices for its products significantly in 2008. Consequently, volumes deteriorated. But as raw material prices fell in 2009–2010, the company's prices were lowered and volumes recovered strongly. As the company started to increase prices in 2011, volume growth once again slowed. In 2016, the company faced challenging conditions in several emerging markets as currency-devaluation-led cost increases led to weaker volumes. Both volume and price growth have moderated to low-single digit growth rates, also exhibiting lower volatility.

Exhibit 26: Unilever Overall Revenue Growth by Percentage Change in Volume and Price

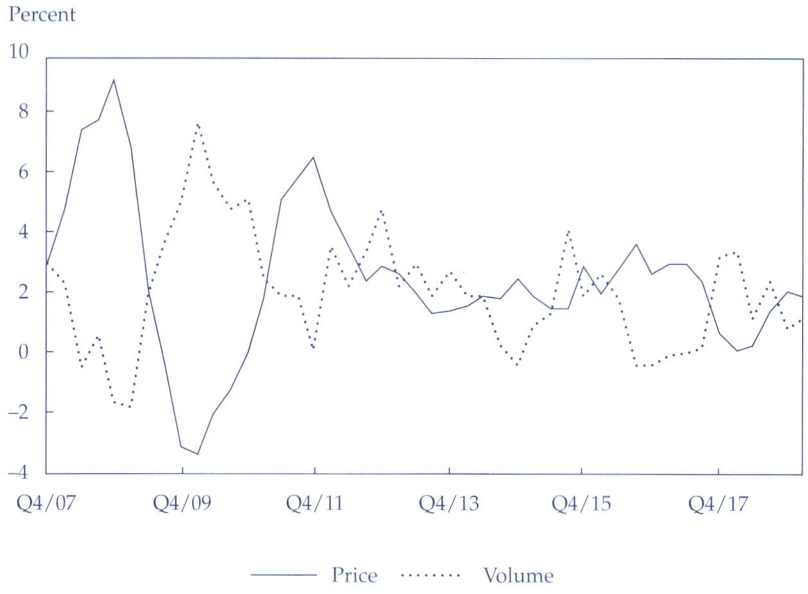

Sources: Unilever PLC filings.

Company Sales and Inflation or Deflation

Revenue projections in a model are based on the expected volume and price development. Forecasting revenue for a company faced with inflation in input costs requires some understanding of the price elasticity of the products, the different rates of cost inflation in the countries where the company is active, and, if possible, the likely inflation in costs relevant to a company's individual product categories. Pricing strategy and market position are also important.

The impact of higher prices on volume depends on the price elasticity of demand (i.e., how the quantity demanded varies with price). If demand is relatively price inelastic, revenues will benefit from inflation. If demand is relatively price elastic (i.e., elasticity is greater than unit price elasticity), revenue can decline even if unit prices are raised. For example, a regression of volume on food inflation in UK food stores from 1989 to 2012 (shown in Exhibit 27) gives a regression slope coefficient of –0.398. (For every increase by 1 percentage point in year-on-year food prices, year-on-year sales decreased by approximately 0.4 percent.)

An analyst covering UK food retailers can use this information when building forecast profit models. By assuming an expected level of food inflation, volume growth can be estimated and revenue calculated.

Exhibit 27: UK Relationship between Food Inflation and Volume, January 1989–February 2012

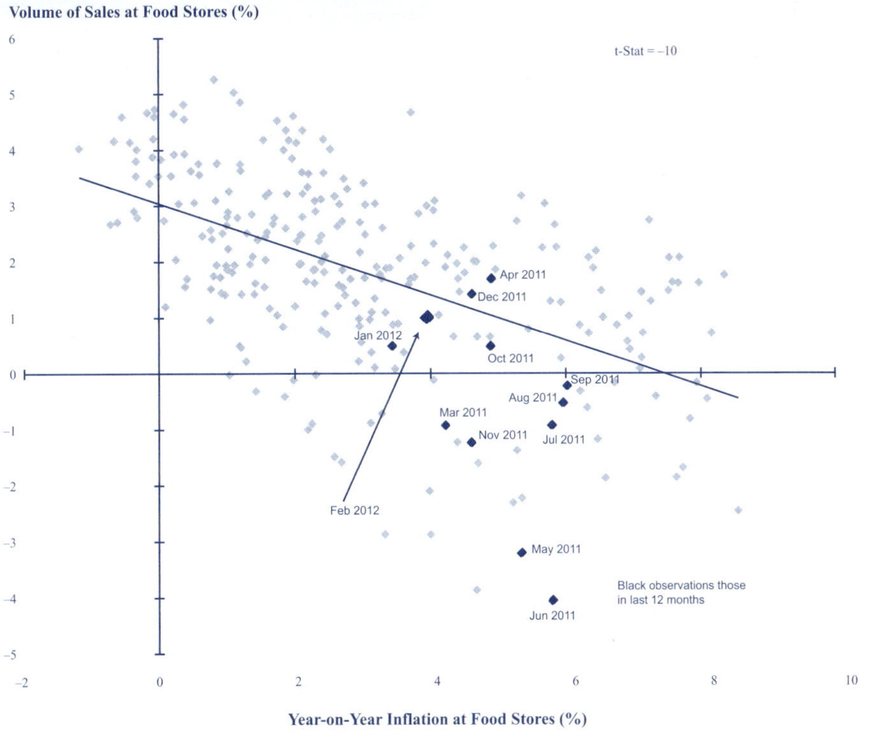

Source: Based on data from Datastream. Analysis is the authors'.

The expected pricing component for an international company should consider the geographic mix of its revenues to reflect different rates of inflation among countries. Of course, strategy and competitive factors, in addition to inflation in input costs, play roles in price setting.

AB InBev's volume growth and pricing have been more robust in emerging markets, for example, thanks to strong demand for its new beer products. The impact of inflation is also an important factor. In its Latin America South division, which then mainly consisted of Argentina, the brewer reported strong 24.7 percent organic revenue growth in 2011, of which only 2.1 percent was driven by volume and the remainder by price. As costs increased in line with revenues, operating margin remained more or less stable, and organic operating profit growth was high at 27 percent. With only a limited negative currency impact, reported operating profit increased 24 percent in US dollars.

High inflation in a company's export market relative to a company's domestic inflation rate generally implies that the export country's currency will come under pressure and any pricing gain could be wiped out by the currency losses. The strong pricing increases AB InBev reported in its Latin America South division were clearly driven by input price inflation. The absence of a negative currency impact should be seen as a positive surprise but not as a typical outcome. A country's currency will usually come under pressure and depreciate if high rates of inflation persist for an extended period.

Most analysts adjust for recent high inflation in foreign countries by assuming a normalized growth rate for both revenues and costs after one or two years. This constant currency growth rate is based on an underlying growth rate assumption for the business. This approach can understate revenues in the short term. Other analysts reflect in their forecasts the high impact of inflation on revenues and expenses and adjust growth rates for the expected currency (interest rate parity) impact. This approach is also imperfect given the difficulty in projecting currency rates.

Identifying a company's major input costs provides an indication of likely pricing. For a specialist retail bakery chain, for example, the impact of increased grain prices will be more significant than for a diversified standard supermarket chain. Consequently, it seems logical that the bakery is likely to increase its prices by a higher percentage than the grocer in response to increased grain prices.

Company strategy is also an important factor. Faced with rising input prices, a company might decide to preserve its margins by passing on the costs to its customers, or it might decide to accept some margin reduction to increase its market share. In other words, the company could try to gain market share by not fully increasing prices to reflect increased costs. On the one hand, Sysco Company (the largest food distributor to restaurants and institutions in North America) has sometimes not passed on food price increases in recessionary conditions out of concern of not financially weakening already recession-affected customers (e.g., restaurants, private clubs, schools, nursing homes). On the other hand, in 2011 and 2012, the large French cognac houses substantially increased the prices of their products in China to reduce strong demand. Because older cognac generates a higher price, it can be more profitable to build an inventory of vintage cognac rather than maximizing short-term volumes.

EXAMPLE 8

Passing on Input Cost Increases or Not

Four food retail analysts are assessing the impact of a potential increase in input costs on the global supermarket chain Carrefour. In this hypothetical scenario, they believe that rising oil prices and packaging prices will affect many of the company's suppliers. They believe that Carrefour is likely to be confronted with 4 percent inflation in its COGS (with stable volume). The analysts have their own expectations about how the company will react. Exhibit 28 shows Carrefour's 2020 results, and Exhibit 29 shows the four analysts' estimates of input prices, volume growth, and pricing for the following year. Both exhibits are in the Example 8 worksheet in the downloadable Microsoft Excel workbook.

Exhibit 28: Carrefour Data (euro millions, unless noted)

	2020
Total revenue	72,150
COGS	56,705
Gross profit	15,445
Gross margin	21.4%

Exhibit 29: Four Analysts' Estimates of Carrefour's Reaction to Inflation

	A	B	C	D
Price increase for revenues	0.00%	2.00%	3.00%	4.00%
Volume growth	5.00%	2.00%	1.00%	–4.00%

	A	B	C	D
Total revenue growth	5.00%	4.04%	4.03%	−0.16%
Input costs increase	4.00%	4.00%	4.00%	4.00%

1. What are each analyst's predictions for gross profit and gross margin?

   Solution:

   The results for each analyst are shown in Exhibit 30 and the Example 8 worksheet in the downloadable Microsoft Excel workbook. For Analyst B, revenues increase 4 percent [= (1.02 × 1.02) − 1] and COGS 6.1 percent [= (1.02 × 1.04) − 1]. The difference between the calculated revenue and COGS is the new gross profit and gross margin is gross profit as a percentage of revenue.

Exhibit 30: Results for Analysts' Predictions (EUR millions, unless noted)

	2020	Analyst A 2021E	YoY%	Analyst B 2021E	YoY%	Analyst C 2021E	YoY%	Analyst D 2021E	YoY%
Total revenue	72,150	75,758	5.0%	75,065	4%	75,058	4.0%	72,035	−0.2%
COGS	56,705	61,922	9.2%	60,153	6%	59,563	5.0%	56,614	−0.2%
Gross profit	15,445	13,836	−10%	14,912	−3%	15,495	0%	15,420	−0.2%
Gross margin	21.4%	18.3%		19.9%		20.6%		21.4%	

2. Which analyst has the highest forecast for gross margin?

   Solution:

   The highest gross margin is projected by Analyst D, who assumes that selling prices would increase by 4 percent to offset rising input costs and keep gross margin stable from the 2020 level.

3. Which analyst has the highest forecast for gross profit?

   Solution:

   The highest gross profit is projected by Analyst C.

Cost Projections with Inflation and Deflation

The following analysis addresses the forecasting of industry and company costs in the presence of inflation and deflation.

Industry Costs and Inflation or Deflation

Familiarity with the specific purchasing characteristics of an industry can also be useful in forecasting costs. For example, long-term price-fixed forward contracts and hedges can delay the impact of price increases. Thus, an analyst forecasting costs for an industry in which companies customarily use such purchasing practices would incorporate any expected input price fluctuations more slowly than they would for an industry in which the participants do not use long-term contracts or hedges.

Monitoring the underlying drivers of input prices can also be useful in forecasting costs. For example, weather conditions can have a dramatic impact on the price of agricultural products and consequently on the cost base of industries that rely on them. An analyst observing a particular weather pattern might thus be able to incorporate this information into forecasts of costs.

How inflation or deflation affects an industry's cost structure depends on its competitive environment. For example, if the participants within the industry have access to alternative inputs or are vertically integrated, the impact of volatility in input costs can be mitigated. Jacobs Douwe Egberts (JDE) is a coffee company that has been facing high and volatile coffee prices. However, its coffee is a blend of different kinds of beans. By shifting the mix slightly, JDE can keep both taste and costs constant by reducing the amount of the more expensive types of coffee beans in the blend. But if all supplier countries significantly increase the price of coffee simultaneously, JDE cannot use blending as an offset and will be confronted with overall higher input costs. To sustain its profitability, JDE will have to increase its prices to its clients. But if competition from other companies, such as Nestlé (Nespresso, Dolce Gusto, Nescafe) makes it difficult to increase prices, JDE will have to look for alternatives if it wants to keep its profit margins stable. An easy solution for the short term could be reducing advertising and promotional (A&P) spending, which usually improves profit. For the longer term, however, it could be harmful for revenues because the company's brand position could be weakened.

For example, in 2010, Russia experienced a heat wave that destroyed large parts of its grain harvest, causing prices for malting barley, a major input for beer, to increase significantly. Carlsberg, as the largest Russian brewer at that time, was particularly hard hit because it had to pay more for its Russian barley and also needed to import grain into the country, incurring additional transportation costs. By increasing imports from Western Europe, Carlsberg also pushed up barley prices in this region, affecting the cost base of other Western European brewers.

Company Costs and Inflation or Deflation

In forecasting a company's costs, it is often helpful to segment the cost structure by category and geography. For each item of cost, an assessment should be made about the impact of potential inflation and deflation on input prices. This assessment should take into account the company's ability to substitute cheaper alternatives for expensive inputs or to increase efficiency to offset the impact of increases in input prices. For example, although a jump in raw material prices in 2011 caused Unilever's and Nestlé's gross margins to fall sharply (by 110–170 bps), increases in operational efficiencies, such as reducing advertising spending, enabled both companies to achieve slightly higher overall operating profit margins that year. Example 9 shows the use of common size (percent-of-sales) analysis of inflation in input costs.

EXAMPLE 9

Inflation in Input Costs

Two fictional consumer staple companies—chocolate and sweets specialist "Choco A" and a food producer "Sweet B"—have costs that are constantly affected by inflation and deflation. Exhibit 31 (see the Example 9 worksheet in the downloadable Microsoft Excel workbook) presents a common size analysis.

Exhibit 31: Common Size Analysis for Sweet B and Choco A

	Sweet B	Choco A
Net sales	100%	100%
COGS	50%	36%
Gross margin	50%	64%
SG&A	31%	47%
Depreciation	3%	4%
EBIT	16%	13%
Raw materials	22%	22%
Packaging	12%	10%
Other COGS	16%	4%
Total COGS	50%	36%

Assume inflation of 10 percent for all costs (except depreciation) and that the companies are not able to pass on this increase through higher prices (total revenues will remain constant).

1. Calculate the gross profit margin for each company. Which company will experience the greater reduction in gross profit margin?

   Solution:

   The company with the higher COGS as a percent of net sales—equivalently, the lower gross margin—will experience the greater negative impact. Sweet B has a lower gross margin than Choco A: 50 percent compared with 64 percent, as shown in Exhibit 31. After the 10 percent increase in COGS to 1.10 × 50% = 55%, Sweet B's gross margin will fall to 45 percent, as shown in Exhibit 32. Sweet B's resulting gross margin of 45 percent represents a proportional decline of 10 percent from the initial value of 50 percent. In contrast, the proportional decline in Choco A's gross margin is approximately 4%/64% = 6%.

Exhibit 32: Effect of Cost Inflation

	All Costs (Except Depreciation) + 10%		Raw Materials + 10%	
	Sweet B	Choco A	Sweet B	Choco A
Net sales	100%	100%	100%	100%
COGS	55%	40%	52%	38%
Gross margin	45%	60%	48%	62%
SG&A	34%	52%	31%	47%
Depreciation	3%	4%	3%	4%
EBIT	8%	5%	14%	11%

2. Calculate the operating profit margin for each company. Which company will experience the greater reduction in operating profit (EBIT) margin?

Solution:

Choco A has higher overall costs than Sweet B, primarily as a consequence of its high SG&A expenses. Choco A's operating profit margin will drop to approximately 5 percent, as shown in Exhibit 32, representing a proportional decline of approximately 62 percent compared with a proportional decline of approximately 8%/16% = 50% for Sweet B.

3. Assume inflation of 10 percent only for the raw material costs (reflected in COGS) and that the companies are not able to pass on this increase through higher prices. Which company will be more affected negatively in terms of gross profit margin and operating profit margin?

Solution:

The company with the higher raw material expense component will experience the more negative effect. In this case, raw materials represent 22 percent of net sales for both Sweet B and Choco A. Gross margin and operating margin will decline by 220 bps for both. This impact is more severe on gross margin on a relative basis for Sweet B (2.2%/50% = 4.4% decline) than for Choco A (2.2%/64% = 3.4% decline). But the relative effect on operating margin will be more severe for Choco A (2.2%/13% = 16.9% decline) than for Sweet B (2.2%/16% = 13.8%).

6 THE FORECAST HORIZON AND LONG-TERM FORECASTING

☐ explain considerations in the choice of an explicit forecast horizon and an analyst's choices in developing projections beyond the short-term forecast horizon

The choice of the forecast time horizon can be influenced by certain factors, including the investment strategy for which the security is being considered, the cyclicality of the industry, company-specific factors, and the analyst's employer's preferences. Most professionally managed investment strategies describe the investment time frame, or average holding period, in the stated investment objectives of the strategy; the time frame should ideally correspond with average annual turnover of the portfolio. For example, a stated investment time horizon of three to five years would imply average annual portfolio turnover between 20 percent and 33 percent (average holding period is calculated as one/portfolio turnover). The cyclicality of the industry could also influence the analyst's choice of time frame because the forecast period should be long enough to allow the business to reach an expected mid-cycle level of sales and profitability. Similar to cyclicality, various company-specific factors, including recent acquisition or restructuring activity, can influence the selection of the forecast period to allow enough time for the realization of the expected benefits from such activity to be reflected in the financial statements. In other cases, there might be no individual analyst choice in the sense that the analyst's employer has specified more or less fixed parameters. Much of the discussion so far has focused on various methods of forecasting a company's income statement, balance sheet, and cash flow for an explicit short-term forecast period. Although the underlying principles remain the same if one extends the time horizon, certain considerations and choices are available to the analyst when developing longer-term projections.

Longer-term projections often provide a better representation of the normalized earnings potential of a company than a short-term forecast, especially when certain temporary factors are present. **Normalized earnings** are the expected level of mid-cycle earnings for a company in the absence of any unusual or temporary factors that affect profitability (either positively or negatively). For example, at any given point in time, a company's profitability can be influenced by a number of temporary factors, including the stage in the business cycle, recent merger and acquisition activity, and restructuring activity. Similarly, normalized free cash flow can be defined as the expected level of mid-cycle cash flow from operations adjusted for unusual items just described less recurring capital expenditures. By extending the forecast period, an analyst is able to adjust for these unusual or temporary factors and derive an estimate of earnings that the company is likely to earn in a normal year. We will consider various alternatives for two aspects of long-term forecasting: revenue forecasts and terminal value.

As with most income statement projections, a long-term forecast begins with a revenue projection, with most of the remaining income statement items subsequently derived from the level or change in revenue. Revenue projection methods were covered earlier.

Case Study: Estimating Normalized Revenue

Exhibit 33 contains 10 years of historical revenue data and four years of estimated normalized data for Continental AG, a global automotive supplier. The accompanying bar chart in Exhibit 34 graphically depicts the data and includes a trend line based on a linear regression of the data. The numerical values for each point along the trend line can be found by using the TREND formula in Microsoft Excel. The TREND formula uses observations on the dependent variable (in this case revenue) and observations on the explanatory (time) variable to perform a linear regression by using least squares criterion to find the best fit. After computing the best fit regression model, the TREND formula returns predicted values associated with new points in time. The worksheet for Exhibit 33 and Exhibit 34 in the downloadable Microsoft Excel workbook demonstrates the calculations used in the exhibits.

Exhibit 33: Historical and Estimated Revenue Data for Continental AG, 2011–2024E (euro billions)

	2011	2012	2013	2014	2015	2016	2017	2018	2019	2020	2021	2022	2023	2024
Revenue	30.5	32.7	33.3	34.5	39.2	40.6	44.0	44.4	44.5	37.7				
Normalized revenue	31.8	33.2	34.6	36.0	37.4	38.9	40.3	41.7	43.1	44.5	45.9	47.3	48.7	50.1
Percent above/below trend	−4.1%	−1.4%	−3.7%	−4.2%	4.8%	4.4%	9.3%	−6.6%	3.3%	−15.2%				

Exhibit 34: Historical and Estimated Revenue for Continental AG, 2011–2024E

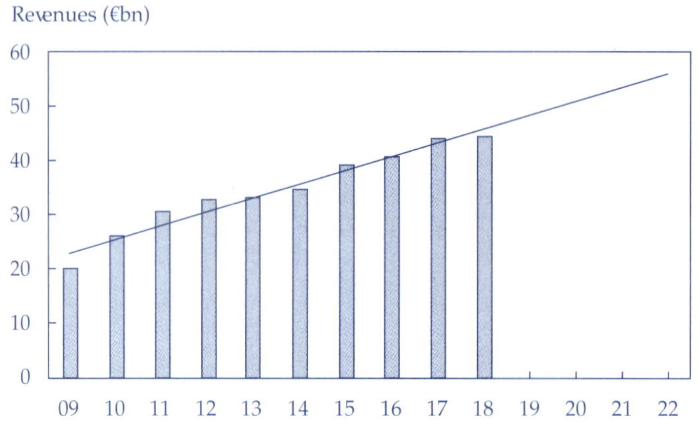

The "growth relative to GDP growth" and "market growth and market share" methods discussed earlier can also be applied to developing longer-term projections. Once a revenue projection has been established, previously described methods of forecasting costs can be used to complete the income statement, balance sheet, and cash flow statement.

If an analyst is creating a valuation model such as a DCF model, estimating a terminal value is required to capture the going-concern value of the company after the explicit forecast period. Certain considerations should be kept in mind when deriving the terminal value based on long-term projections.

First, an analyst should consider whether the terminal year free cash flow projection should be normalized before that cash flow is incorporated into a long-term projection. For example, if the explicitly forecasted terminal year free cash flow is "low" (e.g., because of business cycle reasons or capital investment projects), an adjustment to normalize the amount might be warranted. Second, an analyst should consider whether and how the future long-term growth rate will differ from the historical growth rate. For example, even some mature companies might be able to accelerate their long-term growth rate through product innovation and/or market expansion (e.g., Apple), whereas other seemingly well-protected "growers" could experience an unanticipated decline in their business as a result of technological change (e.g., Eastman Kodak Company, a global commercial printing and imaging company).

One of the greatest challenges facing the analyst is anticipating inflection points, when the future will look significantly different from the recent past. Most DCF models rely on a perpetuity calculation, which assumes that the cash flows from the last year of an explicit forecast grow at a constant rate forever. Because the perpetuity can account for a relatively large portion of the overall valuation of the company, it is critical that the cash flow used is representative of a "normalized" or "mid-cycle" result. If the analyst is examining a cyclical company, using a boom year as the starting point for the perpetuity could result in a grossly overstated valuation. Similarly, using a trough year could result in a valuation that is much too low.

Another important consideration is economic disruption. The economy can occasionally experience sudden, unprecedented changes that affect a wide variety of companies, such as the 2008 global financial crisis or the COVID-19 pandemic. Even a company with a sound strategy and solid operations can be thrown far off course by a sudden economic disruption, particularly if the company has a high degree of financial leverage.

Regulation and technology are also potential drivers of inflection points, and it is important for the analyst to keep a close eye on both. Government actions can have extreme, sudden, and unpredictable impacts on some businesses. Technological advances can turn fast-growing innovators obsolete in a matter of months. Both regulation and technology affect some industries more than others. Utilities experience intense regulation but might not see a significant technological change for decades. Semiconductor manufacturers must constantly keep up with new technology but experience relatively light regulation. Pharmaceutical manufacturers are heavily exposed to both regulation and technological advances.

Finally, long-term growth is a key input in the perpetuity calculation. Some companies and industries can grow faster than the overall economy for long periods of time, causing them to account for an increasing share of overall output. Examples include some technology companies, such as Tencent, Amazon, and Google. Other companies, such as those in the print media sector, are likely to grow slower than the overall economy or even shrink over time. Using an unrealistic long-term growth rate can put the analyst's valuation far off the mark.

EXAMPLE 10

Important Considerations When Making Assumptions

1. Turkish Airlines (THYAO.IS) operates in the highly cyclical global airline industry. Operating margins for 2011–2019 are shown in the following table and in the Example 10 worksheet in the downloadable Microsoft Excel workbook.

	2011	2012	2013	2014	2015	2016	2017	2018	2019
Operating margin	1.0%	10.8%	6.5%	5.6%	8.6%	−2.9%	9.0%	9.9%	7.9%

On the basis of only the information in the table, which of the following operating margins would *most likely* be appropriate to use in a perpetuity calculation for Turkish Airlines to arrive at a reasonable intrinsic value estimate?

A. 6.0 percent

B. 9.0 percent

C. 9.9 percent

Solution:

A is correct. Because the airline industry is cyclical, an estimate of "mid-cycle" or "normalized" operating margin is necessary to estimate a perpetuity value. The nine-year average operating margin was 6.3 percent.

For each of the companies in the following problems, indicate which of the choices is *least likely* to cause a change in the company's outlook.

2. ABC Diesel (hypothetical company), a manufacturer of diesel-power trucks

A. Consumers have started switching to trucks with electric engines, threatening ABC's historic strength in diesel engine trucks.

B. ABC Diesel has formed a partnership with Electrico (hypothetical), a company involved in research and innovation in electric engines.

C. Environmental regulations have been getting tighter in most regions, and consistent with prior experience, this need to make the engines less polluting is expected to continue over the next several years.

Solution:

C is correct. Although it is important that environmental regulations have been getting stricter, this is consistent with past experience and so does not represent a turning point.

---

3. Abbott Laboratories, a diversified manufacturer of health care products, including medical devices

A. Management reiterates its long-standing approach to capital deployment.

B. A competitor has demonstrated favorable efficacy data on a medical device candidate that will compete with an important Abbott product.

C. It has become more difficult for medical device manufacturers to receive regulatory approval for new products because of heightened safety concerns.

Solution:

A is correct. Management is sticking with its historical approach to capital deployment, so this does not represent a turning point.

---

4. Grupo Aeroportuario del Sureste, operator of nine airports in Mexico, especially in the tourist-heavy southeast

A. Global economic disruption has caused a sharp decline in international travel.

B. Regulators will allow the construction of a new airport by a competitor in Grupo Aeroportuario del Sureste's service territory.

C. A technological advance will allow airlines to save 5 percent on fuel costs, but it is not expected to meaningfully alter passenger volumes. Similar developments in the past have benefited airlines but not airports, whose price per passenger is regulated.

Solution:

C is correct. Although the technological advance is good for the airlines, it will not have a meaningful effect on passenger volumes, which will likely prevent the airports from sharing in that benefit. In contrast, both A and B could have a significant impact on the long-run earnings power of Mexican airports.

---

5. LinkedIn, operator of an online social network for professionals and part of Microsoft Corporation, with limited investment needs and no debt

A. Facebook, another online social network, announces a plan to enhance its offerings in the professional category.

B. Regulators announce an investigation of LinkedIn's privacy practices, which could result in significant changes to the service.

C. The US Federal Reserve has just increased interest rates. Although this will raise borrowing costs, the rate increase is not expected to have a negative impact on the economy.

Solution:

C is correct. Because LinkedIn carries no debt, it is unlikely that higher interest rates will cause a change in the company's outlook.

REFERENCES

Dunning, D., D. W. Griffin, J. D. Milojkovic, and L. Ross. 1990. "The Overconfidence Effect in Social Prediction." *Journal of Personality and Social Psychology* 58 (4): 568–81. https://psycnet.apa.org/record/1990-22524-00110.1037/0022-3514.58.4.568

Porter, Michael E. 1980. *Competitive Strategy: Techniques for Analyzing Industries and Competitors.* New York: Free Press.

Porter, Michael E. 2008. "*The Five Competitive Forces That Shape Strategy.*" (January). https://hbr.org/2008/01/the-five-competitive-forces-that-shape-strategy

Russo, J. Edward and Paul J. H. Schoemaker. 1992. "Managing Overconfidence." *MIT Sloan Management Review* 15 (January). https://sloanreview.mit.edu/article/managing-overconfidence/

PRACTICE PROBLEMS

The following information relates to questions 1-7

Nigel French, an analyst at Taurus Investment Management, is analyzing Archway Technologies, a manufacturer of luxury electronic auto equipment, at the request of his supervisor, Lukas Wright. French is asked to evaluate Archway's profitability over the past five years relative to its two main competitors, which are located in different countries with significantly different tax structures.

French begins by assessing Archway's competitive position within the luxury electronic auto equipment industry using Porter's five forces framework. A summary of French's industry analysis is presented in Exhibit 1.

Exhibit 1: Analysis of Luxury Electronic Auto Equipment Industry Using Porter's Five Forces Framework

Force	Factors to Consider
Threat of substitutes	Customer switching costs are high
Rivalry	Archway holds 60 percent of world market share; each of its two main competitors holds 15 percent
Bargaining power of suppliers	Primary inputs are considered basic commodities, and there are a large number of suppliers
Bargaining power of buyers	Luxury electronic auto equipment is very specialized (non-standardized)
Threat of new entrants	High fixed costs to enter industry

French notes that for the year just ended (2019), Archway's COGS was 30 percent of sales. To forecast Archway's income statement for 2020, French assumes that all companies in the industry will experience an inflation rate of 8 percent on the COGS. Exhibit 2 shows French's forecasts relating to Archway's price and volume changes.

Exhibit 2: Archway's 2020 Forecasted Price and Volume Changes

Average price increase per unit	5.00%
Volume growth	–3.00%

After putting together income statement projections for Archway, French forecasts Archway's balance sheet items. He uses Archway's historical efficiency ratios to forecast the company's working capital accounts.

Based on his financial forecast for Archway, French estimates a terminal value using a valuation multiple based on the company's average price-to-earnings multiple (P/E) over the past five years. Wright discusses with French how the terminal value estimate is sensitive to key assumptions about the company's future prospects. Wright asks French:

"What change in the calculation of the terminal value would you make if a technological development that would adversely affect Archway was forecast to occur sometime beyond your financial forecast horizon?"

1. Which profitability metric should French use to assess Archway's five-year historic performance relative to its competitors?

   A. Current ratio

   B. Operating margin

   C. Return on invested capital

2. Based on the current competitive landscape presented in Exhibit 1, French should conclude that Archway's ability to:

   A. pass along price increases is high.

   B. demand lower input prices from suppliers is low.

   C. generate above-average returns on invested capital is low.

3. Based on the current competitive landscape presented in Exhibit 1, Archway's operating profit margins over the forecast horizon are *least likely* to:

   A. decrease.

   B. remain constant.

   C. increase.

4. Based on Exhibit 2, Archway's forecasted gross profit margin for 2020 is *closest* to:

   A. 62.7 percent.

   B. 67.0 percent.

   C. 69.1 percent.

5. French's approach to forecasting Archway's working capital accounts would be *most likely* classified as a:

   A. hybrid approach.

   B. top-down approach.

   C. bottom-up approach.

6. The *most appropriate* response to Wright's question about the technological development is to:

   A. increase the required return.

   B. decrease the perpetual growth rate.

   C. decrease the price-to-earnings multiple.

7. If the luxury electronic auto equipment industry is subject to rapid technological changes and market share shifts, how should French *best* adapt his approach to

modeling?

A. Examine base rates

B. Forecast multiple scenarios

C. Speak to analysts who hold diverse opinions on the stock

The following information relates to questions 8-14

Gertrude Fromm is a transportation sector analyst at Tucana Investments. She is conducting an analysis of Omikroon, N.V., a hypothetical European engineering company that manufactures and sells scooters and commercial trucks.

Omikroon's petrol scooter division is the market leader in its sector and has two competitors. Omikroon's petrol scooters have a strong brand name and a well-established distribution network. Given the strong branding established by the market leaders, the cost of entering the industry is high. But Fromm anticipates that small, inexpensive, imported petrol-fueled motorcycles could become substitutes for Omikroon's petrol scooters.

Fromm uses ROIC as the metric to assess Omikroon's performance.

Omikroon has just introduced the first electric scooter to the market at year-end 2019. The company's expectations are as follows:

- Competing electric scooters will reach the market in 2021.
- Electric scooters will not be a substitute for petrol scooters.
- The important research costs in 2020 and 2021 will lead to more efficient electric scooters.

Fromm decides to use a five-year forecast horizon for Omikroon after considering the following three factors:

Factor 1 The annual portfolio turnover at Tucana Investments is 30 percent.

Factor 2 The electronic scooter industry is expected to grow rapidly over the next 10 years.

Factor 3 Omikroon has announced it would acquire a light truck manufacturer that will be fully integrated into its truck division by 2021 and will add 2 percent to the company's total revenues.

Fromm uses the base case forecast for 2020 shown in Exhibit 1 to perform the following sensitivity analysis:

- The price of an imported specialty metal used for engine parts increases by 20 percent.
- This metal constitutes 4 percent of Omikroon's cost of sales.
- Omikroon will not be able to pass on the higher metal expense to its customers.

Exhibit 1: Omikroon's Selected Financial Forecasts for 2020 Base Case (euro millions)

	Petrol Scooter Division	Commercial Truck Division	Electric Scooter Division	Total
Sales	99.05	45.71	7.62	152.38
Cost of sales				105.38
Gross profit				47.00
Operating profit				9.20

Omikroon will initially outsource its electric scooter parts. But manufacturing these parts in-house beginning in 2021 will imply changes to an existing factory. This factory cost EUR7 million three years ago and had an estimated useful life of 10 years. Fromm is evaluating two scenarios:

Scenario 1	Refit the existing factory for EUR27 million.
Scenario 2	Sell the existing factory for EUR5 million. Build a new factory costing EUR30 million with a useful life of 10 years.

8. Using Porter's five forces analysis, which of the following competitive factors is *most likely* to have the greatest impact on Omikroon's petrol scooter pricing power?

   A. Rivalry

   B. Threat of substitutes

   C. Threat of new entrants

9. The metric used by Fromm to assess Omikroon's performance incorporates:

   A. the degree of financial leverage.

   B. operating liabilities relative to operating assets.

   C. the firm's competitiveness relative to companies in other tax regimes.

10. Based on Omikroon's expectations, the gross profit margin of Omikroon's electric scooter division in 2021 is *most likely* to be affected by:

    A. competition.

    B. research costs.

    C. cannibalization by petrol scooters.

11. Which factor *best* justifies the five-year forecast horizon for Omikroon selected by Fromm?

    A. Factor 1

    B. Factor 2

    C. Factor 3

12. Fromm's sensitivity analysis will result in a decrease in the 2020 base case gross

profit margin *closest to*:

A. 0.55 percent.

B. 0.80 percent.

C. 3.32 percent.

13. Fromm's estimate of growth capital expenditures included in Omikroon's PP&E under Scenario 1 should be:

    A. lower than under Scenario 2.

    B. the same as under Scenario 2.

    C. higher than under Scenario 2.

14. To validate the forecast for rapid growth in the electronic scooter market over the next 10 years, Fromm speaks to the management of Omikroon and investor relations of ZeroWheel, a competitor. Which behavioral bias is Fromm *most likely* subject to?

    A. Confirmation

    B. Conservatism

    C. Overconfidence

The following information relates to questions 15-21

Angela Green, an investment manager at Horizon Investments, intends to hire a new investment analyst. After conducting initial interviews, Green has narrowed the pool to three candidates. She plans to conduct second interviews to further assess the candidates' knowledge of industry and company analysis.

Prior to the second interviews, Green asks the candidates to analyze Chrome Network Systems, a company that manufactures internet networking products. Each candidate is provided Chrome's financial information presented in Exhibit 1.

Exhibit 1: Chrome Network Systems Selected Financial Information (US dollar millions)

	Year-End		
	2017	**2018**	**2019**
Net sales	46.8	50.5	53.9
Cost of sales	18.2	18.4	18.8
Gross profit	28.6	32.1	35.1
SG&A expenses	19.3	22.5	25.1
Operating income	9.3	9.6	10.0
Interest expense	0.5	0.7	0.6

	Year-End		
	2017	2018	2019
Income before provision for income tax	8.8	8.9	9.4
Provision for income taxes	2.8	2.8	3.1
Net income	6.0	6.1	6.3

Green asks each candidate to forecast the 2020 income statement for Chrome and to outline the key assumptions used in their analysis. The job candidates are told to include Horizon's economic outlook for 2020 in their analysis, which assumes nominal GDP growth of 3.6 percent, based on expectations of real GDP growth of 1.6 percent and inflation of 2.0 percent.

Green receives the models from each of the candidates and schedules second interviews. To prepare for the interviews, Green compiles a summary of the candidates' key assumptions in Exhibit 2.

Exhibit 2: Summary of Key Assumptions Used in Candidates' Models

Metric	Candidate A	Candidate B	Candidate C
Net sales	Net sales will grow at the average annual growth rate in net sales over the 2017–19 time period.	Industry sales will grow at the same rate as nominal GDP, but Chrome will have a two-percentage-point decline in market share.	Net sales will grow 50 bps slower than nominal GDP.
Cost of sales	The 2020 gross margin will be the same as the average annual gross margin over the 2017–19 time period.	The 2020 gross margin will decline as costs increase by expected inflation.	The 2020 gross margin will increase by 20 bps from 2019.
SG&A expenses	The 2020 SG&A/net sales ratio will be the same as the average ratio over the 2017–19 time period.	The 2020 SG&A will grow at the rate of inflation.	The 2020 SG&A/net sales ratio will be the same as the 2019 ratio.
Interest expense	The 2020 interest expense assumes the effective interest rate will be the same as the 2019 rate.	The 2020 interest expense will be the same as the 2019 interest expense.	The 2020 interest expense will be the same as the average expense over the 2017–19 time period.
Income taxes	The 2020 effective tax rate will be the same as the 2019 rate.	The 2020 effective tax rate will equal the blended statutory rate of 30%.	The 2020 effective tax rate will be the same as the average effective tax rate over the 2017–19 time period.

15. Based on Exhibit 1, which of the following provides the strongest evidence that Chrome displays economies of scale?

A. Increasing net sales

B. Profit margins that are increasing with net sales

C. Gross profit margins that are increasing with net sales

16. Based on Exhibit 2, the job candidate *most likely* using a bottom-up approach to model net sales is:

    A. Candidate A.

    B. Candidate B.

    C. Candidate C.

17. Based on Exhibit 2, the modeling approach used by Candidate B to project future net sales is *most accurately* classified as a:

    A. hybrid approach.

    B. top-down approach.

    C. bottom-up approach.

18. Based on Exhibits 1 and 2, Candidate C's forecast for cost of sales in 2020 is *closest* to:

    A. USD18.3 million.

    B. USD18.9 million.

    C. USD19.3 million.

19. Based on Exhibits 1 and 2, Candidate A's forecast for SG&A expenses in 2020 is *closest* to:

    A. USD23.8 million.

    B. USD25.5 million.

    C. USD27.4 million.

20. Based on Exhibit 2, forecasted interest expense will reflect changes in Chrome's debt level under the forecast assumptions used by:

    A. Candidate A.

    B. Candidate B.

    C. Candidate C.

21. Candidate B asks Green if she had additional information on Horizon's industry peers and competitors, to put the profitability estimates in a richer context. By asking for this additional information for their analysis, Candidate B is *most likely* seeking to mitigate which behavioral bias?

    A. Conservatism

    B. Base rate neglect

    C. illusion of control

SOLUTIONS

1. B is correct. Operating (EBIT) margin is a pre-tax profitability measure that can be useful in the peer comparison of companies in countries with different tax structures. Archway's two main competitors are located in different countries with significantly different tax structures; therefore, a pre-tax measure is better than an after-tax measure, such as ROIC. The current ratio is a liquidity measure, not a profitability measure.

2. A is correct. Porter's five forces framework in Exhibit 1 describes an industry with high barriers to entry, high customer switching costs (suggesting a low threat of substitutes), and a specialized product (suggesting low bargaining power of buyers). Furthermore, the primary production inputs from the large group of suppliers are considered basic commodities (suggesting low bargaining power of suppliers). These favorable industry characteristics will likely enable Archway to pass along price increases and generate above-average returns on invested capital.

3. A is correct. The current favorable characteristics of the industry (high barriers to entry, low bargaining power of suppliers and buyers, low threat of substitutes), coupled with Archway's dominant market share position, will likely lead to Archway's profit margins being at least equal to or greater than current levels over the forecast horizon.

4. C is correct. The calculation of Archway's gross profit margin for 2020, which reflects the industry-wide 8% inflation on COGS, is calculated as follows:

Revenue growth	1.85%
COGS increase	4.76%
Forecasted revenue (Base revenue = 100)	101.85
Forecasted COGS (Base COGS = 30)	31.43
Forecasted gross profit	70.42
Forecasted gross profit margin	69.14%

Revenue growth = (1 + Price increase for revenue) × (1 + Volume growth) – 1

= (1.05) × (0.97) – 1

= 1.85%.

COGS increase = (1 + Price increase for COGS) × (1 + Volume growth) – 1

= (1.08) × (0.97) – 1

= 4.76%.

Forecasted revenue = Base revenue × Revenue growth increase

= 100 × 1.0185

= 101.85.

Forecasted COGS = Base COGS × COGS increase

$= 30 \times 1.0476$

$= 31.43.$

Forecasted gross profit = Forecasted revenue – Forecasted COGS

$= 101.85 - 31.43$

$= 70.42.$

Forecasted gross profit margin = Forecasted gross profit/Forecasted revenue

$= 70.42/101.85$

$= 69.14\%.$

5. C is correct. French is using a bottom-up approach to forecast Archway's working capital accounts by using the company's historical efficiency ratios to project future performance.

6. C is correct. If the future growth or profitability of a company is likely to be lower than the historical average (in this case, because of a potential technological development), then the target multiple should reflect a discount to the historical multiple to reflect this difference in growth and/or profitability. If a multiple is used to derive the terminal value of a company, the choice of the multiple should be consistent with the long-run expectations for growth and required return. French tells Wright he believes that such a technological development could have an adverse impact on Archway beyond the forecast horizon.

7. B is correct. Forecasting a single scenario would not be appropriate given the high degree of uncertainty and range of potential outcomes for companies in this industry.

8. B is correct. Small, inexpensive, imported petrol-fueled motorcycles are substitutes for petrol scooters and could increasingly have an impact on Omikroon's petrol scoter pricing power.

9. B is correct. Return on invested capital is net operating profit minus adjusted taxes divided by invested capital, where invested capital is defined as operating assets minus operating liabilities.

10. A is correct. Competition from other electric scooter manufacturers is expected to begin in one year. After this time, competing electric scooters could lead to lower demand for Omikroon's electric scooters and affect Omikroon's gross profit margin.

11. B is correct. The electric scooter market is expected to grow rapidly, so the contribution of Omikroon's new electric scooter division is forecast to expand significantly over the next 10 years. A is incorrect because the investment company's portfolio turnover is not relevant for forecasting Omrikoon's future results. C is incorrect because the light truck division is expected to add only 2% to total revenues in the future.

12. A is correct. The sensitivity analysis consists of an increase of 20 percent in the price of an input that constitutes 4 percent of cost of sales. Change in gross profit margin because of that increase is calculated as the change in cost of sales because of price increase divided by sales:

= (Cost of sales × 0.04 × 0.2)/Sales

= (105.38 × 0.04 × 0.2)/152.38

= 0.0055 or 0.55%

13. C is correct. In Scenario 1, growth capital expenditures of EUR27 million for the refit of the existing idle factory is higher than the growth capital expenditures in Scenario 2 of EUR25 million. The EUR25 million is the cost of building a new factory for EUR30 million less the proceeds from the sale of the existing idle factory of EUR5 million.

14. A is correct. The management of Omikroon and investor relations of ZeroWheel are almost certainly biased in favor of expecting strong growth for the markets they participate in. To evaluate the forecast, Fromm should seek more independent sources and balance the biased sources with sources biased in the opposite direction or an analyst who is more skeptical.

15. C is correct. Economies of scale are a situation in which average costs decrease with increasing sales volume. Chrome's gross margins have been increasing with net sales. Gross margins that increase with sales levels provide evidence of economies of scale, assuming that higher levels of sales reflect increased unit sales. Gross margin more directly reflects the cost of sales than does profit margin.

Metric	2017	2018	2019
Net sales	$46.8	$50.5	$53.9
Gross profit	28.6	32.1	35.1
Gross margin (gross profit/ net sales)	61.11%	63.56%	65.12%

16. A is correct. A bottom-up approach for developing inputs to equity valuation models begins at the level of the individual company or a unit within the company. By modeling net sales using the average annual growth rate, Candidate A is using a bottom-up approach. B and C are incorrect because both Candidate B and Candidate C are using a top-down approach, which begins at the level of the overall economy.

17. B is correct. A top-down approach usually begins at the level of the overall economy. Candidate B assumes industry sales will grow at the same rate as nominal GDP but that Chrome will have a 2-percentage-point decline in market share. A and C are incorrect because Candidate B is not using any elements of a bottom-up approach; therefore, a hybrid approach is not being employed.

18. C is correct. Candidate C assumes that the 2020 gross margin will increase by 20 bps from 2019 and that net sales will grow at 50 bps slower than nominal GDP (nominal GDP = Real GDP + Inflation = 1.6% + 2.0% = 3.6%). Accordingly, the 2020 forecasted cost of sales is USD19.27 million, rounded to USD19.3 million.

Metric	Calculation	Result
2020 gross margin = 2019 gm + 20 bps	USD35.1/USD53.9 = 65.12% + 0.20% =	65.32%
2020 CoS/net sales = 100% – gross margin	100% – 65.32% =	34.68%

Metric	Calculation	Result
2020 net sales = 2019 net sales × (1 + Nominal GDP – 0.50%)	USD53.9 million × (1 + 0.036 – 0.005) = USD53.9 million × 1.031 =	USD55.57 million
2020 cost of sales = 2020 net sales × CoS/net sales	USD55.57 × 34.68% =	USD19.27 million

19. B is correct. Candidate A assumes that the 2020 SG&A/net sales will be the same as the average SG&A/net sales over the 2017–19 time period and that net sales will grow at the annual average growth rate in net sales over the 2017–19 time period. Accordingly, the 2020 forecasted SG&A expenses are USD25.5 million.

Metric	Calculation	Result
Average SG&A/net sales, 2017–2019*	(41.24% + 44.55% + 46.57%)/3 =	44.12%
Average annual growth sales in net sales, 2017–2019**	(7.91% + 6.73%)/2 =	7.32%
2020 net sales = 2019 net sales × (1 + Average annual growth rate in net sales)	USD53.9 million × 1.0732 =	$57.85 million
2020 SG&A = 2020 net sales × Average SG&A/net sales	USD57.85 million × 44.12% =	$25.52 million

	2017	2018	2019
Net Sales	USD46.8	USD50.5	USD53.9
SG&A expenses	USD19.3	USD22.5	USD25.1
SG&A-to-sales ratio	41.24%	44.55%	46.57%

Year	Calculation
2018	(USD50.5/USD46.8) – 1 = 7.91%
2019	(USD53.9/USD50.5) – 1 = 6.73%

20. A is correct. In forecasting financing costs, such as interest expense, the debt/equity structure of a company is a key determinant. Accordingly, a method that recognizes the relationship between the income statement account (interest expense) and the balance sheet account (debt) would be a preferable method for forecasting interest expense when compared with methods that forecast based solely on the income statement account. By using the effective interest rate (interest expense divided by average gross debt), Candidate A is taking the debt/equity structure into account. B and C are incorrect because Candidate B (who forecasts 2020 interest expense to be the same as 2019 interest expense) and Candidate C (who forecasts 2020 interest expense to be the same as the 2017–19 average interest expense) are not taking the balance sheet into consideration.

21. B is correct. Base rates refer to attributes of a reference class and base rate neglect is ignoring such class information in favor of specific information. By incorporating industry data, Candidate B is seeking to mitigate this behavioral bias.

Glossary

Abandonment option The option to terminate an investment at some future time if the financial results are disappointing.

Abnormal return The amount by which a security's actual return differs from its expected return, given the security's risk and the market's return.

Absolute dispersion The amount of variability present without comparison to any reference point or benchmark.

Accelerated book build An offering of securities by an investment bank acting as principal that is accomplished in only one or two days.

Accounting profit Income as reported on the income statement, in accordance with prevailing accounting standards, before the provisions for income tax expense. Also called *income before taxes* or *pretax income*.

Accredited investors Investors that meet certain minimum regulatory net worth or other requirements in order to invest in certain types of alternative assets.

Accrued interest The amount of interest in currency or par value terms of a fixed-income instrument that accumulates from the last coupon payment until the trade settlement date. The amount is paid by the buyer to the seller.

Action lag Delay from policy decisions to implementation.

Active investment An approach to investing in which the investor seeks to outperform a given benchmark.

Active return The return on a portfolio minus the return on the portfolio's benchmark.

Activist Short for "activist shareholder." Managers secure sufficient equity holdings to allow them to seek a position in a company's board and influence corporate policies or direction.

Activity ratios Ratios that measure how well a company is managing key current assets and working capital over time.

Ad hoc committee A small group of lenders or bondholders who negotiate with an issuer on debt restructuring and refinancing before the issuer submits a final proposal to the wider group of all lenders and bondholders.

Add-on pricing A pricing approach based on high-margin optional features, customizations, and additional content.

Add-on rate A yield or pricing convention for money market instrument quotations. It is the interest earned on an instrument, derived from the difference between the price and face value, expressed as a percentage of the price and multiplied by the periodicity of the annual rate.

Agency costs Direct and indirect costs borne by the principal in a principal-agent relationship owing primarily to information asymmetries. Agency costs include the costs of monitoring and assessing the agent as well as missed opportunities.

Agency RMBS Securities created by the pooling of residential mortgage-backed securities in the United States by either the Federal National Mortgage Association (Fannie Mae) or the Federal Home Loan Mortgage Corporation (Freddie Mac). These RMBS carry the full faith and credit of the government, essentially a guarantee with respect to timely payment of interest and repayment of principal.

All-or-nothing (AON) orders An order that includes the instruction to trade only if the trade fills the entire quantity (size) specified.

Allocationally efficient A characteristic of a market, a financial system, or an economy that promotes the allocation of resources to their highest value uses.

Altcoin A cryptocurrency other than Bitcoin.

Alternative data Data that are generated from non-traditional sources, such as social media and sensor networks.

Alternative hypothesis The hypothesis that is accepted if the null hypothesis is rejected.

Alternative investment markets Market for investments other than traditional securities investments (i.e., traditional common and preferred shares and traditional fixed income instruments). The term usually encompasses direct and indirect investment in real estate (including timberland and farmland) and commodities (including precious metals); hedge funds, private equity, and other investments requiring specialized due diligence.

Alternative trading systems Trading venues that function like exchanges but that do not exercise regulatory authority over their subscribers except with respect to the conduct of the subscribers' trading in their trading systems. Also called *electronic communications networks* or *multilateral trading facilities*.

American depository receipt A US dollar-denominated security that trades like a common share on US exchanges.

American depository share The underlying shares on which American depository receipts are based. They trade in the issuing company's domestic market.

American options Options that may be exercised at any time from contract inception until maturity.

American-style Type of option contract that can be exercised at any time up to the option's expiration date.

Amortization The process of allocating the cost of intangible long-term assets having a finite useful life to accounting periods; the allocation of the amount of a bond premium or discount to the periods remaining until bond maturity.

Amortizing debt A loan or bond with a payment schedule that calls for the complete repayment of principal over the instrument's time to maturity.

Analysis of variance (ANOVA) A table that presents the sums of squares, degrees of freedom, mean squares, and F-statistic for a regression model.

Analytical duration Estimates of duration using mathematical formulas. Estimates of the impact of yield changes on bond prices using analytical duration implicitly assume that benchmark yields and spreads are independent variables and are uncorrelated.

Anchoring and adjustment bias An information-processing bias in which the use of a psychological heuristic influences the way people estimate probabilities.

Annual general meeting (AGM) A yearly meeting of the corporate board of directors and shareholders, typically held in person and digitally, during which votes on directors, compensation plans, shareholder resolutions, and any other matters properly brought forward at the meeting are held. Issuer management may also make presentations and hold events.

Anomalies Apparent deviations from market efficiency.

Antidilutive With reference to a transaction or a security, one that would increase earnings per share (EPS) or result in EPS higher than the company's basic EPS—antidilutive securities are not included in the calculation of diluted EPS.

Arbitrage (1) The simultaneous purchase of an undervalued asset or portfolio and sale of an overvalued but equivalent asset or portfolio in order to obtain a riskless profit on the price differential. Taking advantage of a market inefficiency in a risk-free manner. (2) The condition in a financial market in which equivalent assets or combinations of assets sell for two different prices, creating an opportunity to profit at no risk with no commitment of money. In a well-functioning financial market, few arbitrage opportunities are possible. (3) A risk-free operation that earns an expected positive net profit but requires no net investment of money.

Arbitrageurs Traders who engage in arbitrage. See *arbitrage*.

Arithmetic mean The sum of the observations divided by the number of observations.

Artificial intelligence (AI) Computer systems that are capable of performing tasks that previously required human intelligence. AI methods are sometimes better suited to identify complex, non-linear relationships than are traditional quantitative and statistical methods.

Ask The price at which a dealer or trader is willing to sell an asset, typically qualified by a maximum quantity (ask size). See *offer*.

Ask size The maximum quantity of an asset that pertains to a specific ask price from a trader. For example, if the ask for a share issue is $30 for a size of 1,000 shares, the trader is offering to sell at $30 up to 1,000 shares.

Asset allocation The process of determining how investment funds should be distributed among asset classes.

Asset class A group of assets that have similar characteristics, attributes, and risk–return relationships.

Asset utilization ratios Ratios that measure how efficiently a company performs day-to-day tasks, such as the collection of receivables and management of inventory.

Asset-backed commercial paper Secured form of commercial paper issuance. Loans or receivables are sold to a special purpose entity that issues the ABCP and makes interest and principal payments to investors from asset cash flows.

Asset-backed securities (ABS) A type of bond issued by a legal entity called a special purpose entity created solely to own assets such as loans, receivables, and mortgages and to distribute cash flows to ABS investors. Generally, ABS backed by mortgages are known as mortgage-backed securities (MBS) while ABS refer to non-mortgage ABS.

Asset-backed token A token that represents the ownership of a physical asset that does not exist on the blockchain and whose value is based on the underlying asset.

Asset-based valuation models Valuation based on estimates of the market value of a company's assets.

Asymmetric information Also known as *information asymmetry*; the differential of information between corporate insiders and outsiders regarding the company's performance and prospects. Managers typically have more information about the company's performance and prospects than owners and creditors.

At-the-money Describes a unique situation in which the price of the underlying is equal to an option's exercise price. Like an out-of-the-money option, the intrinsic value is zero.

Auction/reverse auction models Pricing models that establish prices through bidding (by sellers in the case of reverse auctions).

Autarky Countries seeking political self-sufficiency with little or no external trade or finance. State-owned enterprises control strategic domestic industries.

Automatic stabilizer A countercyclical factor that automatically comes into play as an economy slows and unemployment rises.

Availability bias An information-processing bias in which people take a heuristic approach to estimating the probability of an outcome based on how easily the outcome comes to mind.

Available-for-sale Under US GAAP, debt securities not classified as either held-to-maturity or held-for-trading securities. The investor is willing to sell but not actively planning to sell. In general, available-for-sale debt securities are reported at fair value on the balance sheet, with unrealized gains included as a component of other comprehensive income.

Average revenue (AR) Total revenue divided by quantity sold.

Backfill Bias A problem whereby certain surviving hedge funds may be added to databases and various hedge fund indexes only after they are initially successful and start to report their returns. Also see *survivorship bias*.

Backup line of credit A type of credit enhancement provided by a bank to an issuer of commercial paper to ensure that the issuer will have access to sufficient liquidity to repay maturing commercial paper if issuing new paper is not a viable option.

Backwardation A downward-sloping, or inverted, forward curve in a futures market.

Balance sheet ratios Financial ratios involving balance sheet items only.

Balanced With respect to a government budget, one in which spending and revenues (taxes) are equal.

Balloon payment A large payment required at maturity to retire a bond's outstanding principal amount.

Base rates The reference rate on which a bank bases lending rates to all other customers.

Base-rate neglect A type of representativeness bias in which the base rate or probability of the categorization is not adequately considered.

Basic EPS Net earnings available to common shareholders (i.e., net income minus preferred dividends) divided by the weighted average number of common shares outstanding.

Basis risk The possibility that the expected value of a derivative differs unexpectedly from that of the underlying.

Basket of listed depository receipts (BLDR) An exchange-traded fund (ETF) that represents a portfolio of depository receipts.

Bayes' formula The rule for updating the probability of an event of interest—given a set of prior probabilities for the event, information, and information given the event—if you receive new information.

Bearer bonds Bonds for which ownership is not recorded; only the clearing system knows who the bond owner is.

Behavioral finance A field of finance that examines the psychological variables that affect and often distort the investment decision making of investors, analysts, and portfolio managers.

Behind the market Said of prices specified in orders that are worse than the best current price; e.g., for a limit buy order, a limit price below the best bid.

Benchmark A bond used to compare against another bond to discern attributes, often a government bond with the same or similar time-to-maturity as the bond under analysis.

Benchmark spread The difference in yield-to-maturity between a bond and that of a benchmark bond.

Best bid The highest bid in the market.

Best effort offering An offering of a security using an investment bank in which the investment bank, as agent for the issuer, promises to use its best efforts to sell the offering but does not guarantee that a specific amount will be sold.

Best offer The lowest offer (ask price) in the market.

Best-in-class An ESG implementation approach that seeks to identify the most favorable companies and sectors based on ESG considerations. Also called *positive screening.*

Beta A measure of the sensitivity of a given investment or portfolio to movements in the overall market.

Bid The price at which a dealer or trader is willing to buy an asset, typically qualified by a maximum quantity.

Bid size The maximum quantity of an asset that pertains to a specific bid price from a trader.

Big data The vast amount of information being generated by both traditional sources—for example, stock exchanges, companies, governments—and non-traditional sources—for example, electronic devices, social media, sensor networks, and company exhaust.

Bilateralism The conduct of political, economic, financial, or cultural cooperation between two countries. Countries engaging in bilateralism may have relations with many different countries but in one-at-a-time agreements without multiple partners. Typically, countries exist on a spectrum between bilateralism and multilateralism.

Bimodal A distribution that has two most frequently occurring values.

Bitcoin A cryptocurrency using blockchain technology that was created in 2009.

Bivariate correlation Also known as Pearson correlation. A parametric measure of the relationship between two variables.

Black swan risk An event that is rare and difficult to predict but has an important impact.

Block brokers A broker (agent) that provides brokerage services for large-size trades.

Blockchain A type of digital ledger in which information is recorded sequentially and then linked together and secured using cryptographic methods.

Blue chip Widely held large market capitalization companies that are considered financially sound and are leaders in their respective industry or local stock market.

Board of directors A body or individual selected by a limited company's member(s) or shareholder(s), in a manner determined by the company's charter, that manages the company. Typically, for larger companies, boards of directors appoint and oversee executive management.

Bond equivalent yield A money market interest rate quoted on a 365-day add-on rate basis.

Bond indenture A legal document between a bond issuer and investors that governs each party's rights and responsibilities.

Bond market vigilantes Bond market participants who might reduce their demand for long-term bonds, thus pushing up their yields.

Bondholders Investors in an entity's securitized debt claims, such as commercial paper, notes, and bonds. Common types of bondholders include investment funds and institutional investors.

Bonds Contractual agreements between an issuer and bondholders.

Bonus issue of shares A type of dividend in which a company distributes additional shares of its common stock to shareholders instead of cash.

Book building Investment bankers' process of compiling a "book" or list of indications of interest to buy part of an offering.

Book value Shareholders' equity (total assets minus total liabilities) minus the value of preferred stock; common shareholders' equity.

Boom An expansionary phase characterized by economic growth "testing the limits" of the economy.

Bootstrap A resampling method that repeatedly draws samples with replacement of the selected elements from the original observed sample. Bootstrap is usually conducted by using computer simulation and is often used to find standard error or construct confidence intervals of population parameters.

Bottom-up analysis An investment selection approach that focuses on company-specific circumstances rather than emphasizing economic cycles or industry analysis.

Box and whisker plot A graphic for visualizing the dispersion of data across quartiles. It consists of a box with "whiskers" connected to the box.

Breakeven point Represents the price of the underlying in a derivative contract in which the profit to both counterparties would be zero.

Bridge financing Interim financing that provides funds until permanent financing can be arranged.

Broker An agent who executes orders to buy or sell securities on behalf of a client in exchange for a commission.

Brokered market A market in which brokers arrange trades among their clients.

Broker–dealer A financial intermediary (often a company) that may function as a principal (dealer) or as an agent (broker) depending on the type of trade.

Brownfield investments The third stage of development of an infrastructure asset. Brownfield investments involve expanding existing facilities and may involve privatization of public assets or a sale leaseback of completed greenfield projects. They are characterized by a shorter investment period with immediate cash flows and an operating history.

Budget surplus/deficit The difference between government revenue and expenditure for a stated fixed period of time.

Bullet bond A bond whose principal repayment is made entirely at maturity.

Bundling A pricing approach that refers to combining multiple products or services so that customers are incentivized or required to buy them together.

Business cycles Are recurrent expansions and contractions in economic activity affecting broad segments of the economy.

Business model A concise description of how a business works and makes revenues and profits, including its customers, products or services, channels for reaching customers, and pricing.

Businesses Organization entities formed and managed for the purpose of providing a return or economic benefits to its investors and owners.

Buy-side firm An investment management company or other investor that uses the services of brokers or dealers (i.e., the client of the sell side firms).

Buyback A transaction in which a company buys back its own shares. Unlike stock dividends and stock splits, share repurchases use corporate cash.

Cabotage The right to transport passengers or goods within a country by a foreign firm. Many countries—including those with multilateral trade agreements—impose restrictions on cabotage across transportation subsectors, meaning that shippers, airlines, and truck drivers are not allowed to transport goods and services within another country's borders.

Call market A market in which trades occur only at a particular time and place (i.e., when the market is called).

Call money rate The interest rate that buyers pay for their margin loan.

Call option The right to buy an underlying.

Call period The time during which the issuer of a callable bond can exercise the call option.

Call price The price at which the issuer of a callable bond has the right to purchase the bond from investors.

Call protection period The time during which the issuer of a callable bond is not allowed to exercise the call option.

Call risk The uncertain maturity and limited price appreciation associated with callable bonds.

Callable bond A bond containing an embedded call option that gives the issuer the right to buy the bond back from the investor at specified prices on predetermined dates.

Cannibalization A transfer of sales or market share from one product to another product owned by the same company. It tends to occur when the two products are actual or perceived substitutes.

Capacity The ability of the borrower to make its debt payments on time.

Capital Other company resources available that reduce reliance on debt.

Capital allocation The process that companies use for decision making on capital investments—those projects with a life of one year or longer.

Capital allocation line (CAL) A graph line that describes the combinations of expected return and standard deviation of return available to an investor from combining the optimal portfolio of risky assets with the risk-free asset.

Capital asset pricing model (CAPM) An equation describing the expected return on any asset (or portfolio) as a linear function of its beta relative to the market portfolio.

Capital expenditure Expenditure on physical capital (fixed assets).

Capital investments An expenditure for an asset or resource with a useful life of more than one year.

Capital market expectations (CME) Expectations concerning the risk and return prospects of asset classes.

Capital market line (CML) The line with an intercept point equal to the risk-free rate that is tangent to the efficient frontier of risky assets; represents the efficient frontier when a risk-free asset is available for investment.

Capital market securities Fixed-income securities with original maturities greater than one year.

Capital markets Financial markets that trade securities of longer duration, such as bonds and equities.

Capital restrictions Controls placed on foreigners' ability to own domestic assets and/or domestic residents' ability to own foreign assets.

Capital structure The mix of debt and equity that a company uses to finance its business; a company's specific mix of long-term financing.

Capital-indexed bond A type of index-linked bond for which changes in the index are captured with adjustments to the principal. A common example is Treasury Inflation Protected Securities (TIPS) issued by the United States government.

Capital-intensive businesses Companies or business activities that are characterized by a relatively low fixed asset turnover, a high percentage of capital expenditures to sales, or a high net-working-capital-to-sales ratio.

Capital-light businesses Also known as *asset light businesses*, companies or business activities characterized by relatively high fixed asset turnover, a low percentage of capital expenditures to sales, or a low net-working-capital-to-sales ratio.

Carried interest A performance fee (also referred to as an incentive fee, or carry) that is applied based on excess returns above a hurdle rate.

Carrying Investing and holding an asset for a period of time.

Carrying amount The amount at which an asset or liability is valued according to accounting principles.

Carrying value Of a fixed-income instrument is the purchase price plus (minus) the amortized amount of the discount (premium) if the bond is purchased at a price below (above) par value.

Cartel Participants in collusive agreements that are made openly and formally.

Cash conversion cycle The amount of time between an issuer paying its suppliers in cash and receiving cash from its customers.

Cash flow additivity principle The principle that dollar amounts indexed at the same point in time are additive.

Cash flow from operations A cash profit measure over a period for an issuer's primary business activities. It includes cash from customers as well as interest and dividends received from financial investments, less cash paid to employees and suppliers as well as taxes paid to governments and interest paid to lenders.

Cash flow hedge Refers to a specific **hedge accounting** classification in which a derivative is designated as absorbing the variable cash flow of a floating-rate asset or liability, such as foreign exchange, interest rates, or commodities.

Cash markets Markets in which specific assets are exchanged at current prices. Cash markets are often referred to as **spot markets**.

Cash prices The current prices prevailing in **cash markets**.

Cash ratio A measure of liquidity that is the ratio of cash and marketable securities to current liabilities.

Catch-up clause A clause in an agreement that favors the GP. For a GP who earns a 20% performance fee, a catch-up clause allows the GP to receive 100% of the distributions above the hurdle rate *until* she receives 20% of the profits generated, and then every excess dollar is split 80/20 between the LPs and GP.

CDS credit spread Reflects the credit spread of a credit default swap (CDS) derivative contract. As with cash bonds, CDS credit spreads depend on the probability of default (POD) and the loss given default (LGD).

Central bank digital currencies (CBDCs) A tokenized version of the currency issued by the central bank, such as a digital bank note or coin, and a digital liability of the central bank.

Central bank funds market The market in which deposit-taking banks that have an excess reserve with their national central bank can lend money to banks that need funds for maturities ranging from overnight to one year. Called the federal or fed funds market in the United States.

Central bank funds rate The interest rate at which central bank funds are bought (borrowed) and sold (lent) for maturities ranging from overnight to one year. Called federal or fed funds rate in the United States.

Central clearing mandate A requirement instituted by global regulatory authorities following the 2008 global financial crisis that most **over-the-counter (OTC)** derivatives be **cleared** by a **central counterparty (CCP)**.

Central counterparty (CCP) An economic entity that assumes the **counterparty credit risk** between derivative **counterparties**, one of which is typically a financial intermediary. CCPs provide **clearing** and **settlement** for most **derivative contracts**.

Central limit theorem The theorem that states the sum (and the mean) of a set of independent, identically distributed random variables with finite variances is normally distributed, whatever distribution the random variables follow.

Certificate of deposit (CD) An instrument that represents a specified amount of funds on deposit with a bank for a specified maturity and interest rate. CDs are issued in various denominations and can be negotiable or non-negotiable.

Channels Venues where a company markets and/or delivers its products and services.

Character The quality of a debt issuer's management.

Checking accounts Bank deposits with no stated maturity available for transactional purposes that pay little or no interest. Also known as a *demand deposit*.

Circuit breaker A pause in intraday trading for a brief period if a price limit is reached.

Classical cycle Refers to fluctuations in the level of economic activity when measured by GDP in volume terms.

Clawback A requirement that the general partner return any funds distributed as incentive fees until the limited partners have received their initial investment and a percentage of the total profit.

Clearing An exchange's process of verifying the execution of a transaction, exchange of payments, and recording of participants.

Clearing instructions Instructions that indicate how to arrange the final settlement ("clearing") of a trade.

Clearinghouse An entity associated with a futures market that acts as middleman between the contracting parties and guarantees to each party the performance of the other.

Closed-end fund A mutual fund in which no new investment money is accepted. New investors invest by buying existing shares, and investors in the fund liquidate by selling their shares to other investors.

Cluster sampling A procedure that divides a population into subpopulation groups (clusters) representative of the population and then randomly draws certain clusters to form a sample.

Co-investing In co-investing, the investor invests in assets *indirectly* through the fund but also possesses rights (known as co-investment rights) to invest *directly* in the same assets. Through co-investing, an investor is able to make an investment *alongside* a fund when the fund identifies deals.

Code of ethics An established guide that communicates an organization's values and overall expectations regarding member behavior. A code of ethics serves as a general guide for how community members should act.

Coefficient of determination (R^2) The percentage of the variation of the dependent variable that is explained by the independent variable. It is a measure of goodness of fit of a regression model.

Coefficient of variation The ratio of a set of observations' standard deviation to the observations' mean value.

Cognitive cost The effort involved in processing new information and updating beliefs.

Cognitive dissonance The mental discomfort that occurs when new information conflicts with previously held beliefs or cognitions.

Cognitive errors Behavioral biases resulting from faulty reasoning; cognitive errors stem from basic statistical, information-processing, or memory errors.

Coincident economic indicators Turning points that are usually close to those of the overall economy; they are believed to have value for identifying the economy's present state.

Collateral Assets or financial guarantees underlying a debt obligation that are above and beyond the issuer's promise to pay.

Collateral manager Buys and sells debt obligations for and from the CDO's collateral pool to generate sufficient cash flows to meet the obligations to the CDO bondholders.

Collateralized bond obligations (CBOs) CDOs backed by high-yield corporate and emerging market bonds.

Collateralized debt obligations (CDOs) Securities backed by a diversified pool of one or more debt obligations. CDOs can be backed by a broad range of debt.

Collateralized loan obligations (CLOs) Investment vehicle with exposure to a portfolio of leveraged loans separated into tranches with different cash flow claims and exposure to losses based on a waterfall.

Collateralized mortgage obligations Securitize mortgage pass-through securities or multiple pools of loans. CMOs are structured to redistribute the cash flows to different bond classes or tranches and create securities that have different exposures to prepayment risk.

Commercial paper (CP) Short-term, negotiable, unsecured promissory note that represents a debt obligation of the issuer.

Committed (regular) lines of credit Bank commitments to extend credit; the commitment is considered a short-term liability and is usually in effect for 364 days (one day short of a full year).

Committed capital The amount that the limited partners have agreed to provide to the private equity fund.

Commodities A product or service from a firm that is indistinguishable from products or services of competing firms, usually conforming to a common standard or grade imposed by convention or regulation.

Commoditization A process by which competing products become less differentiated over time and become interchangeable "commodities" in the eyes of customers. This process is typically associated with declining profitability for the selling firms.

Commodity producers A firm that makes and/or sells commodities.

Commodity swap A type of swap involving the exchange of payments over multiple dates as determined by specified reference prices or indexes relating to commodities.

Common market Level of economic integration that incorporates all aspects of the customs union and extends it by allowing free movement of factors of production among members.

Common shares A type of security that represents an ownership interest in a company. Also called *common stock*.

Common stock A type of security that represents an ownership interest in a company. Also called *common shares.*

Common-size analysis The restatement of financial statement items using a common denominator or reference item that allows one to identify trends and major differences; an example is an income statement in which all items are expressed as a percent of revenue.

Companies Organization entities formed and managed for the purpose of providing a return or economic benefits to its investors and owners.

Company research report A document that presents an analyst's investment recommendation on an issuer and its securities, supported by financial modeling, industry overviews and competitive analyses, valuation scenarios, ESG considerations, and investment risks.

Complete markets Informally, markets in which the variety of distinct securities traded is so broad that any desired payoff in a future state-of-the-world is achievable.

Concession agreement A contractual arrangement under which an entity (also known as a grantor) establishes terms and conditions with a developer or operator (referred to as a concessionaire) to plan, build, operate, finance, and maintain an infrastructure asset for a specific period.

Conditional expected value The expected value of a stated event given that another event has occurred.

Conditional pass-through covered bonds Convert to pass-through securities after the original maturity date if all bond payments have not yet been made.

Conditional variances The variance of one variable, given the outcome of another.

Conditions The general economic, competitive, and business environment faced by all borrowers that may affect their ability to service or refinance debt.

Confidence level The complement of the level of significance.

Confirmation bias A type of cognitive bias that makes individuals view information that confirms beliefs they already hold as more salient.

Consensus protocol A set of rules governing how blocks can join the blockchain that is designed to resist attempts at malicious manipulation up to a certain level of security; it can be either a proof of work or a proof of stake.

Conservatism bias A belief perseverance bias in which people maintain their prior views or forecasts by inadequately incorporating new information.

Constant yield-price trajectory A graphical depiction of the relationship between time to maturity and a bond price, assuming no default, that shows that a bond price approaches par as time passes.

Constituent securities With respect to an index, the individual securities within an index.

Contango Refers to spot price below forward price in a futures market.

Contingency provision Clause in a legal document that allows for some action if a specific event or circumstance occurs.

Contingency table A table of the frequency distribution of observations classified on the basis of two discrete variables.

Contingent claim A type of derivative in which one of the *counterparties* determines whether and when the trade will settle. An *option* is a common type of contingent claim.

Contingent convertible bonds Bonds that automatically convert to equity if a specific event or circumstance occurs, such as the issuer's equity capital falling below the minimum requirement set by regulators.

Continuous trading market A market in which trades can be arranged and executed any time the market is open.

Continuously compounded return The natural logarithm of 1 plus the holding period return, or equivalently, the natural logarithm of the ending price over the beginning price.

Contract manufacturers Companies that make products for other companies that meet specific terms and specifications.

Contract size Amount(s) used for calculation to price and value the derivative. The contract size is often referred to as "notional amount or notional principal."

Contraction The period of a business cycle after the peak and before the trough; often called a *recession* or, if exceptionally severe, called a *depression*.

Contraction risk The risk of earlier repayment of a mortgage-backed security than expected.

Contractionary Tending to cause the real economy to contract.

Contractionary fiscal policy A fiscal policy that has the objective to make the real economy contract.

Contribution margin A profitability measure using variable costs: unit price less unit variable cost. It can also be expressed as a percentage of price or sales.

Controlling shareholder An individual or entity that owns a majority of the voting rights in a corporation.

Convenience sampling A procedure of selecting an element from a population on the basis of whether or not it is accessible to a researcher or how easy it is for a researcher to access the element.

Convenience yield A non-cash benefit of holding a physical commodity versus a derivative.

Conversion price Predetermined share price at which convertible debt may be fully exchanged for common shares during the conversion period.

Conversion ratio The number of common shares a convertible bond or noteholder may receive in exchange for a specific bond par value.

Conversion value The current contingency feature value derived by comparing a convertible bond's price with its value if a bondholder were to exchange bonds for shares.

Convertible bond A bond that gives the bondholder the right to exchange the bond for a specified number of common shares in the issuing company.

Convertible debt A fixed-income instrument which combines the features of debt with equity via a contingent feature, allowing debtholders to exchange their claim for common shares at a predetermined fixed price in the future.

Convertible preference shares A type of equity security that entitles shareholders to convert their shares into a specified number of common shares.

Convexity The second order, usually a positive change in the price of a bond for a given change in yield, which can be negative for a callable bond such as a high-yield bond.

Convexity adjustment A measure that is used to complement modified duration to capture the second-order effect of yield changes on a bond's price. It is equal to the annual convexity statistic times one-half times the given change in the yield-to-maturity squared.

Convexity bias Refers to the difference in price changes for a given change in yield between interest rate futures and interest rate forward contracts. That is, interest rate forwards exhibit a non-linear or convex relationship between price and yield, while the price–yield relationship is linear for interest rate futures.

Cooperation The process by which countries work together toward some shared goal or purpose. These goals may, and often do, vary widely—from strategic or military concerns, to economic influence, to cultural preferences.

Cooperative country A country that engages and reciprocates in rules standardization; harmonization of tariffs; international agreements on trade, immigration, or regulation; and allowing the free flow of information, including technology transfer.

Core real estate strategies Strategies with exposure to well-leased, high-quality commercial and residential real estate in the best markets, generally offered by open-end funds. Investors expect core real estate to deliver stable returns, primarily from income from the property.

Core-plus real estate strategies Value-add investments that require modest redevelopment or upgrades to lease any vacant space together with possible alternative use of the underlying properties. Compared to core real estate strategies, these may be appealing for investors seeking higher returns and willing to accept additional risks from development, redevelopment, repositioning, and leasing.

Corporate issuers Limited companies or corporations that seek financing in financial markets by, for example, issuing debt or equity securities.

Corporations Another term for limited companies, though often used to refer to public limited companies. See *limited company*, *private limited company*, and *public limited company*.

Correlation A measure of the linear relationship between two random variables.

Correlation coefficient A number between −1 and +1 that measures the consistency or tendency for two investments to act in a similar way. It is used to determine the effect on portfolio risk when two assets are combined.

Cost averaging The periodic investment of a fixed amount of money.

Cost of capital The cost of financing for a company; the rate of return that suppliers of capital require as compensation for their contribution of capital (also called *opportunity cost of funds*).

Cost of carry The net of the costs and benefits related to owning an underlying asset for a specific period.

Cost of debt The required return on debt financing for a company, such as when it issues a bond, takes out a bank loan, or leases an asset through a finance lease.

Cost of equity The return required by equity investors to compensate for both the time value of money and the risk. Also referred to as the required rate of return on common stock or the required return on equity.

Counterparty Legal entities entering a **derivative contract**.

Counterparty credit risk The likelihood that a **counterparty** is unable to meet its financial obligations under the contract.

Counterparty risk The risk that the other party to a contract will fail to honor the terms of the contract.

Country The geopolitical environment as well as the legal and political system faced by all issuers in a jurisdiction that may affect debt payment.

Coupon Periodic interest payments paid by a bond issuer to investors, typically expressed as a percentage of par on an annual basis.

Cournot assumption Assumption in which each firm determines its profit-maximizing production level assuming that the other firms' output will not change.

Covariance A measure of the co-movement (linear association) between two random variables.

Covenants The terms and conditions of lending agreements that the issuer must comply with; they specify the actions that an issuer is obligated to perform (affirmative covenant) or prohibited from performing (negative covenant).

Credit default swap (CDS) A type of credit derivative in which one party, the credit protection buyer who is seeking credit protection against a third party, makes a series of regularly scheduled payments to the other party, the credit protection seller. The seller makes no payments until a credit event occurs.

Credit enhancements Provisions or methods that allow a borrower improve their creditworthiness in a structured transaction.

Credit event An occurrence that triggers the settlement of a CDS contract, including failure to make a debt payment, debt restructuring, or a bankruptcy filing.

Credit facilities Loan agreements with pre-specified terms and limits but with fluctuating balances based on borrower-specific needs at different points in time, analogous to a credit card.

Credit migration risk The risk that a bond issuer's creditworthiness deteriorates, or migrates lower, leading investors to believe the risk of default is higher. Also called **downgrade risk**.

Credit rating Letter-grade, qualitative measures of an issuer's ability to meet its debt obligations based on both the probability of default and the expected loss under a default scenario.

Credit rating agencies Institutions that issue and maintain credit ratings. The three largest are Standard & Poor's, Moody's, and Fitch Ratings.

Credit risk The expected economic loss under a potential borrower default over the life of the contract.

Credit spread The compensation for the risk of default in a debt security, typically measured by the yield-to-maturity difference between a bond and a comparable government benchmark security.

Credit spread risk The risk of greater expected loss due to changes in credit conditions as a result of macroeconomic, market, and/or issuer-related factors.

Credit tranching Internal credit enhancement where cash flows into a senior/subordinate structure.

Credit-linked notes Bonds whose coupon changes when the bonds' credit rating changes.

Critical values Values of the test statistic at which the decision changes from fail to reject the null hypothesis to reject the null hypothesis.

Cross-default clause Covenant or contract clause that specifies borrowers are considered in default if they default on another debt obligation.

Cross-sectional analysis Analysis over a group as of a given time.

Crossing networks Trading systems that match buyers and sellers who are willing to trade at prices obtained from other markets.

Crowdsourcing A business model that enables users to contribute directly to a product, service, or online content.

Cryptocurrency An electronic medium of exchange that lacks physical form.

Cryptocurrency wallet A storage unit for public and/or private keys for cryptocurrency transactions. These wallets may be a physical device, program, or service.

Cryptography An algorithmic process to encrypt data, making the data unusable if received by unauthorized parties.

Cumulative preference shares Preference shares for which any dividends that are not paid accrue and must be paid in full before dividends on common shares can be paid.

Cumulative voting A voting process whereby shareholders can accumulate and vote all their shares for a single candidate in an election, as opposed to having to allocate their voting rights evenly among all candidates.

Currencies Monies issued by national monetary authorities.

Currency Money issued by national monetary authorities.

Currency swap A swap in which each party makes interest payments to the other in different currencies.

Current government spending With respect to government expenditures, spending on goods and services that are provided on a regular, recurring basis including health, education, and defense.

Current ratio A measure of liquidity that is the ratio of current assets to current liabilities.

Current yield The sum of the coupon payments received over the year divided by the flat price. Also called the income, interest yield, or running yield.

Customs union Extends the free trade area (FTA) by not only allowing free movement of goods and services among members, but also creating a common trade policy against nonmembers.

CVaR Conditional VaR, a tail loss measure. The weighted average of all loss outcomes in the statistical distribution that exceed the VaR loss.

Daily settlement A specific process of *mark-to-market* by a central clearing party in which the profits and losses of all counterparties to derivatives contracts are determined using settlement prices for each contract.

Dark pools Alternative trading systems that do not display the orders that their clients send to them.

Data mining The practice of determining a model by extensive searching through a dataset for statistically significant patterns. Also called *data snooping*.

Data science An interdisciplinary field that harnesses advances in computer science, statistics, and other disciplines for the purpose of extracting information from big data (or data in general).

Data snooping The subconscious or conscious manipulation of data in a way that produces a statistically significant result (i.e., the p-value is sufficiently small or the t-statistic sufficiently large to indicate statistical significance), such as by running multiple simulations and naively accepting the best result. Also known as p-hacking.

Day order An order that is good for the day on which it is submitted. If it has not been filled by the close of business, the order expires unfilled.

Days of inventory on hand (DOH) The average number of days it would take to sell the amount of inventory on hand. It is calculated as either the ending or average balance of inventories divided by (cost of goods sold/days in the period).

Days payable outstanding (DPO) The average number of days it takes a company to pay its suppliers. It is calculated as either the ending or average balance of accounts payable divided by (cost of goods sold/days in the period).

Days sales outstanding (DSO) The average number of days it takes for a company to receive payment from customers who purchase goods or services on credit. It is calculated as either the ending or average balance of accounts receivable divided by (revenues/days in the period).

Dealers Financial intermediaries, such as commercial banks or investment banks, who transact as **counterparties** with derivative end users.

Debt A claim against an entity to receive cash, stock, or other assets at a future date. From the perspective of the debtor or borrower, an obligation to pay cash, stock, or other assets at a future date. Generally, debt claims are unconditional and are senior to equity claims.

Debt service coverage ratio A key indicator of credit performance equal to the ratio of net operating income to debt service.

Debt tax shield The tax benefit from interest paid on debt being tax deductible from income, equal to the marginal tax rate multiplied by the value of the debt.

Debt-to-assets ratio A solvency ratio calculated as total debt divided by total assets.

Debt-to-capital ratio A solvency ratio calculated as total debt divided by total debt plus total shareholders' equity.

Debt-to-equity ratio A solvency ratio calculated as total debt divided by total shareholders' equity.

Debt-to-income ratio (DTI) Residential lending metric that compares an individual's monthly debt payments to their monthly pre-tax, gross income.

Debut issuer An issuer approaching the bond market for the first time.

Deciles Values that divide a distribution ranked smallest to largest into 10 equal parts.

Declaration date The day that the corporation issues a statement declaring a specific dividend.

Decreasing returns to scale When a production process leads to increases in output that are proportionately smaller than the increase in inputs.

Deductible temporary differences Temporary differences that result in a reduction of or deduction from taxable income in a future period when the balance sheet item is recovered or settled.

Deep learning An area of artificial intelligence in which a system uses neural networks to perform multistage, non-linear data processing to identify patterns. Also called *deep learning nets*.

Deep learning nets See *Deep learning*.

Deep-in-the-money option An option that is highly likely to be exercised.

Deep-out-of-the-money option An option that is highly unlikely to be exercised.

Default When a borrower on a mortgage loan fails to meet the obligations of the loan.

Default risk premium An extra return that compensates investors for the possibility that the borrower will fail to make a promised payment at the contracted time and in the contracted amount.

Defeasance Mechanism that allows prepayment on mortgage, but the borrower must purchase a portfolio of government securities that fully replicates the cash flows of the remaining scheduled principal and interest payments, including the balloon loan balance, on the loan.

Defensive interval ratio A liquidity ratio that estimates the number of days that an entity could meet cash needs from liquid assets; calculated as (cash + short-term marketable investments + receivables) divided by daily cash expenditures.

Deferred coupon bonds Bonds that pay no coupons for their first few years but then pay a higher coupon than they otherwise normally would for the remainder of their life. Also called *split coupon bonds*.

Deferred tax assets A balance sheet asset that arises when an excess amount is paid for income taxes relative to accounting profit. The taxable income is higher than accounting profit and income tax payable exceeds tax expense. The company expects to recover the difference during the course of future operations when tax expense exceeds income tax payable.

Deferred tax liabilities A balance sheet liability that arises when a deficit amount is paid for income taxes relative to accounting profit. The taxable income is less than the accounting profit and income tax payable is less than tax expense. The company expects to eliminate the liability over the course of future operations when income tax payable exceeds tax expense.

Defined benefit pension plans (DB plans) Plans in which the company promises to pay a certain annual amount (defined benefit) to the employee after retirement. The company bears the investment risk of the plan assets.

Defined contribution pension plans Individual accounts to which an employee and typically the employer makes contributions during their working years and expect to draw on the accumulated funds at retirement. The employee bears the investment and inflation risk of the plan assets.

Deflation Negative inflation.

Degree of financial leverage The ratio of percentage change in net income to percentage change in operating income over a period. It is a measure of how sensitive net income is to changes in operating income, driven by the firm's use of debt in its capital structure.

Degree of operating leverage The ratio of percentage change in operating income to percentage change in sales over a period. It is a measure of how sensitive operating income is to changes in sales, driven by the fixed and variable cost composition of operating expenses.

Delta The sensitivity of the derivative price to a small change in the value of the underlying asset.

Demand shock A typically unexpected disturbance to demand, such as an unexpected interruption in trade or transportation.

Dependent variable The variable that is explained by a regression model.

Depository bank A bank that raises funds from depositors and other investors and lends it to borrowers.

Depository institutions Commercial banks, savings and loan banks, credit unions, and similar institutions that raise funds from depositors and other investors and lend it to borrowers.

Depository receipt A security that trades like an ordinary share on a local exchange and represents an economic interest in a foreign company.

Depreciation The process of systematically allocating the cost of long-lived (tangible) assets to the periods during which the assets are expected to provide economic benefits.

Derivative A financial instrument that derives its value from the performance of an underlying asset or factor (e.g., stock price, interest rate, or exchange rate).

Derivative contract A legal agreement between counterparties with a specific **maturity**, or length of time, until the closing of the transaction, or **settlement**.

Derivative pricing rule A pricing rule used by crossing networks in which a price is taken (derived) from the price that is current in the asset's primary market.

Differentiated products A product or service from a firm that is distinguishable or distinct from those of competing firms. It is customers who determine and value whether a product is differentiated.

Diffuse prior The assumption of equal prior probabilities.

Diffusion index Reflects the proportion of the index's components that are moving in a pattern consistent with the overall index.

Digital assets The umbrella term covering assets that can be created, stored, and transmitted electronically and have associated ownership or use rights. Digital assets include a variety of assets, such as cryptocurrencies, tokens (security and utility), and digital collectables.

Diluted EPS The EPS that would result if all dilutive securities were converted into common shares.

Dilution An increase in the number of shares outstanding from share issuance that decreases the percentage of shares owned by existing shareholders.

Direct investing Occurs when an investor makes a direct investment in an asset without the use of an intermediary.

Direct lending Providing capital directly from private debt investors.

Direct listing Where the equity of a security is floated on the public markets directly, without underwriters, reducing the complexity and cost of the transaction.

Direct sales Marketing and/or delivering products and services to customers without an intermediary or third party between the customer and seller.

Direct taxes Taxes levied directly on income, wealth, and corporate profits.

Discount factor The price equivalent of a zero rate. Also may be stated as the present value of a currency unit on a future date.

Discount rate A yield or pricing convention for money market instrument quotations. It is the interest earned on an instrument, derived from the difference between the price and face value, expressed as a percentage of the face value and multiplied by the periodicity of the annual rate.

Discounted cash flow models Valuation models that estimate the intrinsic value of a security as the present value of the future benefits expected to be received from the security.

Discriminatory pricing rule A pricing rule used in continuous markets in which the limit price of the order or quote that first arrived determines the trade price.

Diseconomies of scale Increase in cost per unit resulting from increased production.

Dispersion The variability of a population or sample of observations around the central tendency.

Display size The size of an order displayed to public view.

Disposition effect A type of cognitive bias that makes individuals unwilling to sell their possessions at a loss.

Distressed debt Debt of mature companies in financial difficulty, in bankruptcy, or likely to default on debt.

Distressed/restructuring These strategies focus on securities of companies either in or perceived to be near bankruptcy. In one approach, hedge funds simply purchase fixed-income securities trading at a significant discount to par but that are still senior enough to be backed by sufficient corporate assets.

Distributed ledger A type of database that can be shared among entities in a network.

Distributed ledger technology (DLT) Technology based on a distributed ledger.

Diversification ratio The ratio of the standard deviation of an equally weighted portfolio to the standard deviation of a randomly selected security.

Dividend discount model (DDM) The model of the value of stock that is the present value of all future dividends, discounted at the required return on equity.

Dividend payout ratio The ratio of cash dividends paid to earnings for a period.

Dividends Distributions of profits and/or net assets from a corporation to its shareholders. While often in cash, dividends can be also be paid in stock or assets, such as property.

Divisor A number (denominator) used to determine the value of a price return index. It is initially chosen at the inception of an index and subsequently adjusted by the index provider, as necessary, to avoid changes in the index value that are unrelated to changes in the prices of its constituent securities.

Domestic bonds A type of bond for which the issuer's domicile and jurisdiction of issuance are the same.

Domestic content provisions Stipulate that some percentage of the value added or components used in production should be of domestic origin.

Double taxation Income is taxed twice.

Downside risk The potential for loss.

Drag on liquidity An action or event that reduces available funds or delays cash inflows.

Drivers Causative factors that explain the level of and changes in an output variable.

DSC ratio A property's annual net operating income (NOI) divided by the debt service.

Dual-class structure A capital structure that includes at least two classes of equity shares with unequal voting rights.

Dupont analysis An approach to decomposing return on investment, e.g., return on equity, as the product of other financial ratios.

Duration The first-order, linear change in a bond's price for a given yield change in yield, which is a negative or inverse relationship.

Duration gap the difference between a bond's Macaulay duration and its investor's investment horizon.

Dynamic pricing A pricing approach that charges different prices at different times. Specific examples include off-peak pricing, "surge" pricing, and "congestion" pricing.

Early repayment option May entitle the borrower to prepay all or part of the outstanding mortgage principal prior to maturity. This creates a risk from the lender's or investor's viewpoint because the cash flow amounts and timing cannot be known with certainty.

Earnings surprise The difference between reported EPS and expected EPS. Also referred to as *unexpected earnings.*

Economic indicators Economic statistics provided by government and established private organizations that contain information on an economy's recent past activity or its current or future position in the business cycle.

Economic infrastructure investments A category of infrastructure investments that support economic activity through transportation assets, information and communication technology assets, and utility and energy assets.

Economic stabilization Reduction of the magnitude of economic fluctuations.

Economic union Incorporates all aspects of a common market and in addition requires common economic institutions and coordination of economic policies among members.

Economies of scale A decline in costs per unit as output grows, generally resulting from having fixed costs in the cost structure that are spread over more units of output.

Economies of scope A decline in costs per unit as the number of product or business lines increases, generally resulting from having shared costs between the product lines.

Effective annual rate An interest rate with a periodicity of one.

Effective convexity An interest rate risk statistic that measures the non-linear/second-order effect of changes in the benchmark yield curve on a bond's price.

Effective duration The sensitivity of the bond's price to an instantaneous parallel shift in a benchmark yield curve—for example, the government par curve.

Efficient market A market in which asset prices reflect new information quickly and rationally. See also, *informationally efficient market.*

Either/or fee A custom fee arrangement whereby major investors are offered a structure where managers agree to charge *either* a lower management fee *or* a higher incentive fee, whichever is greater.

Electronic communications networks (ECNs) See *alternative trading systems* and *multilateral trading facilities.*

Embedded derivative A derivative within an underlying, such as a callable, putable, or convertible bond.

Embedded options Contingency provisions found in a bond's indenture representing rights that enable their holders to take advantage of interest rate movements. They can be exercised by the issuer, by the bondholder, or automatically depending on the course of interest rates.

Emotional biases Behavioral biases resulting from reasoning influenced by feelings; emotional biases stem from impulse or intuition.

Empirical duration Estimation of the price–yield relationship using historical bond market data in statistical models.

Employee stock ownership plan (ESOP) A type of employee benefit plan in which a company sets up a trust fund to receive contributions of newly issued shares or cash to buy existing shares. Contributions are tax deductible up to certain limits. Shares in the trust fund are allocated to individual employees based on relative pay or a formula.

Endowment bias An emotional bias in which people value an asset more when they hold rights to it than when they do not.

Enterprise risk management An overall assessment of a company's risk position. A centralized approach to risk management sometimes called firmwide risk management.

Enterprise value A measure of a company's total market value from which the value of cash and short-term investments have been subtracted.

Equal weighting An index weighting method in which an equal weight is assigned to each constituent security at inception.

Equity Ownership interest in an entity. A residual claim on the assets of an entity after more senior claims, such as debt, have been satisfied. Also known as *net assets*.

Equity swap A swap transaction in which at least one cash flow is tied to the return to an equity portfolio position, often an equity index.

Error term Represents the difference between the observed value of the independent variable and that expected from the true underlying population relation between the dependent and independent variable.

Estimated parameters In a simple linear regression, the estimated parameters are the intercept and slope of the fitted line.

Ether A programmable cryptocurrency created on the Ethereum blockchain in 2015 that allows for the execution of smart contracts.

Ethical principles Beliefs regarding what is good, acceptable, or obligatory behavior and what is bad, unacceptable, or forbidden behavior.

Ethics The study of moral principles or of making good choices. Ethics encompasses a set of moral principles and rules of conduct that provide guidance for our behavior.

Eurobonds A type of bond issued internationally, outside the jurisdiction of the country in whose currency the bond is denominated.

European options Options that may be exercised only at contract maturity.

European-style Said of an option contract that can only be exercised on the option's expiration date.

Event risk Risk that evolves around set dates, such as elections, new legislation, or other date-driven milestones, such as holidays or political anniversaries, known in advance. Example: Brexit referendum.

Ex-dividend date The first date that a share trades without (i.e., "ex") the right to receive the declared dividend for the period.

Excess kurtosis Degree of kurtosis (fatness of tails) relative to the kurtosis of the normal distribution.

Excess spread Surplus difference of yield remaining after payments to bondholders are made after expenses are made and losses are covered.

Exchange A rules-based, open access market venue where financial instruments are traded, with price and volume transparency accessible by issuers, investors, and their intermediaries.

Exchange-traded derivative (ETD) Futures, options, and other financial contracts available on exchanges.

Execution instructions Instructions that indicate how to fill an order.

Exercise The decision to transact the underlying by an option holder.

Exercise date The day that an option is exercised by its holder. For a call option, the day the strike price is paid and underlying is purchased. For a put option, when the strike price is received and the underlying is sold.

Exercise price The pre-agreed execution price specified in an option contract. Sometimes, this price is referred to as the strike price.

Exogenous risk A sudden or unanticipated risk that impacts either a country's cooperative stance, the ability of non-state actors to globalize, or both. Examples include sudden uprisings, invasions, or the aftermath of natural disasters.

Expansion The period of a business cycle after its lowest point and before its highest point.

Expansionary Tending to cause the real economy to grow.

Expansionary fiscal policy Fiscal policy aimed at achieving real economic growth.

Expected exposure (EE) The size of the investor's claim at the time of default.

Expected loss (EL) Default probability times loss severity given default.

Expected return on the portfolio Denoted as $(E\ (R_p))$. The weighted average of the expected returns (R_1 to R_n) on the component securities using their respective weights (w_1 to w_n).

Expected value of a random variable The probability-weighted average of the possible outcomes of a random variable.

Expert system A type of computer programming, often based on "if–then" rules, that attempts to simulate the knowledge base and analytical abilities of human experts in specific problem-solving contexts.

Export subsidy Paid by the government to the firm when it exports a unit of a good that is being subsidized.

Exposure at default (EAD) The size of the investor's claim at the time of default.

Extension risk The risk of later repayment of a mortgage-backed security than expected.

External credit enhancements Provisions or methods from a third party that allow a borrower improve their creditworthiness in a structured transaction.

External debt Sovereign debt owed to foreign creditors.

Extra dividend A dividend paid by a company that does not pay dividends on a regular schedule, or a dividend that supplements regular cash dividends with an extra payment.

Extraordinary general meetings (EGMs) Meetings besides an AGM of the corporate board and shareholders, typically held to deliberate and vote on urgent matters. Corporate charters and bylaws specify who can call an EGM and under what conditions.

Extreme value theory A branch of statistics that focuses primarily on extreme outcomes.

Face value The amount of principal on a bond, also known as par value.

Factoring arrangement When a company sells its accounts receivable to a lender (known as a factor) that assumes responsibility for the credit-granting and collection process.

Fair value A market-based measure of an investment based on observable or derived assumptions to determine a price that market participants would use to exchange an asset or liability in an orderly transaction at a specific time.

Fair value hedge Refers to a specific **hedge accounting** designation that applies when a derivative is deemed to offset the fluctuation in fair value of an asset or liability.

Fallen angels Formerly investment-grade-rated issuers whose bonds are downgraded to high yield due to credit deterioration.

Fat-Tailed Describes a distribution that has fatter tails than a normal distribution (also called leptokurtic).

Fed funds rate The US interbank lending rate on overnight borrowings of reserves.

Federal funds rate The US interbank lending rate on overnight borrowings of reserves. Also known as *Fed Funds rate*.

Fiat money Money that is not convertible into any other commodity.

Fiduciary call A combination of a purchased call option and investment in a risk-free bond with face value of the option's exercise price.

Fill or kill See *immediate or cancel order*.

Finance lease A type of lease which is more akin to the purchase or sale of the underlying asset.

Financial leverage The use of debt in the capital structure. Measured using ratios such as operating income to operating income less interest expense, total assets to total equity, or debt to equity.

Financial leverage ratio A measure of financial leverage calculated as average total assets divided by average total equity.

Financial risk The risk arising from a company's capital structure and, specifically, from the level of debt and debt-like obligations.

Fintech Technological innovation in the financial services industry, specifically with the design and delivery of financial services and products. It may also refer more broadly to companies involved in developing the new technologies and their applications, as well as the business sector that includes such companies.

Firm commitment A pre-determined amount (price and quantity) is agreed to be exchanged at settlement. Examples of firm commitments include forward contracts, futures contracts, and swaps.

First lien Also known as a priority lien, this investor protection grants a lender the right to take possession of property from a borrower which fails to repay debt.

First lien debt Debt secured by a pledge of certain assets that could include buildings, but it may also include property and equipment, licenses, patents, brands, etc.

First mortgage debt Debt secured by a pledge of a specific property.

Fiscal multiplier The ratio of a change in national income to a change in government spending.

Fiscal policy The use of taxes and government spending to affect the level of aggregate expenditures.

Fixed charge coverage A solvency ratio measuring the number of times interest and lease payments are covered by operating income, calculated as (EBIT + lease payments) divided by (interest payments + lease payments).

Fixed charge coverage ratio A measure of how well a company's earnings covers its fixed expenses, which may include debt payments, interest expense, and lease costs.

Fixed-income instruments Debt instruments such as loans or bonds.

Fixed-income securities Fixed-income instruments designed to be more easily tradeable than a loan, such as a bond.

Fixed-price call A contingency provision that grants an issuer the right to buy back a bond at a predetermined price in the future.

Fixed-rate payer The counterparty paying fixed cash flows in a swap contract. May also be referred to as the floating-rate receiver.

Flat price The full price of a bond minus accrued interest. Flat prices are usually quoted by bond dealers.

Float-adjusted market-capitalization weighting An index weighting method in which the weight assigned to each constituent security is determined by adjusting its market capitalization for its market float.

Floating-rate notes Notes on which interest payments are not fixed but instead vary from period to period depending on the current level of a reference interest rate. Also known as *floaters*.

Floating-rate payer The counterparty paying the variable cash flows in a swap contract. May also be referred to as the fixed-rate receiver.

Forecast object A variable on or related to an issuer's financial statements that an analyst makes a projection for. Examples include drivers of financial statements, financial statement lines, and summary measures like EBITDA.

Foreclosure Allows a lender to take possession of the property and ultimately sell the property to recover funds toward satisfying the outstanding debt obligation.

Foreign bonds A type of bond for which the issuer's domicile and jurisdiction of issuance are different.

Foreign currency reserves Holding by the central bank of non-domestic currency deposits and non-domestic bonds.

Foreign direct investments (FDI) Long-term investments in the productive capacity of a foreign country.

Foreign exchange gains (or losses) Gains (or losses) that occur when the exchange rate changes between the investor's currency and the currency that foreign securities are denominated in.

Forward contract A **derivative contract** for the future exchange of an **underlying** at a fixed price set at contract signing.

Forward price Represents the price agreed upon in a forward contract to be exchanged at the contract's maturity date, T. This price is shown in equations as $F_0(T)$.

Forward price-to-earnings ratio A P/E calculated on the basis of a forecast of EPS; a stock's current price divided by next year's expected earnings.

Forward rate agreement (FRA) An OTC derivatives contract in which counterparties agree to apply a specific interest rate to a future time period.

Founders class shares A way to entice early participation in startup funds whereby managers offer incentives that entitle investors to a lower fee structure and/or other favorable terms.

Framing bias An information-processing bias in which a person answers a question differently based on the way in which it is asked (framed).

Franchising A situation where an owner of an asset and associated intellectual property divests the asset and licenses intellectual property to a third-party operator (franchisee) in exchange for royalties. Franchisees operate under the constraints of a franchise agreement.

Free cash flow The actual cash that would be available to the company's investors after making all investments necessary to maintain the company as an ongoing enterprise (also referred to as free cash flow to the firm); the internally generated funds that can be distributed to the company's investors (e.g., shareholders and bondholders) without impairing the value of the company.

Free cash flow hypothesis The hypothesis that higher debt levels discipline managers by forcing them to make fixed debt service payments and by reducing the company's free cash flow.

Free float The portion of a listed company's equity securities that are not held by insiders, strategic investors, sponsors, founders, and so on, that are more freely available for trading.

Free trade areas One of the most prevalent forms of regional integration, in which all barriers to the flow of goods and services among members have been eliminated.

Free-cash-flow-to-equity models Valuation models based on discounting expected future free cash flow to equity.

Freemium business model A pricing approach that allows customers a certain level of usage or functionality at no charge. Those who wish to use more must pay.

Frequency table A representation of the frequency of occurrence of two discrete variables.

Full price The price of a bond including any accrued interest owed to the seller. It is the flat price plus accrued interest.

Fully amortizing loan A loan or bond with a payment schedule that calls for the complete repayment of principal over the instrument's time to maturity.

Fund investing In fund investing, the investor invests in assets indirectly by contributing capital to a fund as part of a group of investors. Fund investing is available for all major alternative investment types.

Fund of funds Funds that hold a portfolio of hedge funds; also called *funds of hedge funds*.

Fundamental analysis The examination of publicly available information and the formulation of forecasts to estimate the intrinsic value of assets.

Fundamental growth These strategies use fundamental analysis to identify companies expected to exhibit high growth and capital appreciation.

Fundamental long/short In this strategy, the hedge fund takes a long position in companies that are trading at inexpensive levels compared to their potential intrinsic value and shorts those that trade in the other direction, with the intention of reversing this trade to obtain alpha.

Fundamental value These strategies use fundamental analysis to identify undervalued and unloved companies for which there is a possibility that a corporate turnaround, with future revenue and cash flow growth, will result in higher valuations.

Fundamental weighting An index weighting method in which the weight assigned to each constituent security is based on its underlying company's size. It attempts to address the disadvantages of market-capitalization weighting by using measures that are independent of the constituent security's price.

Fungible Freely exchangeable, interchangeable, or substitutable with other things of the same type. Money and commodities are the most common examples.

Futures contract A variation of a forward contract that has essentially the same basic definition but with some additional features, such as a clearinghouse guarantee against credit losses, a daily settlement of gains and losses, and an organized electronic or floor trading facility.

Futures contract basis point value (BPV) The change in price of a futures contract given a 1 basis point (0.01%) change in yield.

Futures margin account An account held by an exchange clearinghouse for each derivatives counterparty. The funds in such an account are used to ensure that counterparties do not default on their contract obligation.

Futures price The pre-agreed price at which a futures contract buyer (seller) agrees to pay (receive) for the underlying at the maturity date of the futures contract.

FX swap The combination of a spot and a forward FX transaction.

G-spread Yield spread in basis points between a bond's yield-to-maturity and that of an actual or interpolated government bond. It represents the return for bearing risks relative to the government bond.

Game theory The set of tools decision makers use to incorporate responses by rival decision makers into their strategies.

Gamma A numerical measure of how sensitive an option's delta (the sensitivity of the derivative's price) is to a change in the value of the underlying.

Gate A provision that when implemented limits or restricts redemptions for a period of time.

General collateral repo Rather than involving a specific security, a repo that instead references a specific group of securities as eligible collateral (such as government bonds of a specific maturity).

General collateral repo rate The interest rate on a general collateral repo.

General obligation (GO) bonds Unsecured bonds issued by a non-sovereign government which are backed by the taxing authority of the issuer.

General obligation bonds Also known as GO bonds. Bonds issued by non-sovereign governments for general purposes and repaid from tax cash flows.

General partners (GPs) Private fund managers responsible for sourcing and deploying capital from limited partner investors over an investment life cycle and distributing returns to those investors over a finite investment holding period.

General partnership A business organizational form owned entirely by general partners.

Geophysical resource endowment Includes such factors as livable geography and climate as well as access to food and water, which are necessary for sustainable growth. Geophysical resource endowment is highly unequal among countries.

Geopolitics The study of how geography affects politics and international relations. These relations matter for investments because they contribute to important drivers of investment performance, including economic growth, business performance, market volatility, and transaction costs.

Gilts Bonds issued by the UK government.

Global depository receipt (GDR) A depository receipt that is issued outside of the company's home country and outside of the United States.

Global minimum-variance portfolio The portfolio on the minimum-variance frontier with the smallest variance of return.

Global registered share (GRS) A common share that is traded on different stock exchanges around the world in different currencies.

Globalization The process of interaction and integration among people, companies, and governments worldwide. It is marked by the spread of products, information, jobs, and culture across borders.

Gold standard With respect to a currency, if a currency is on the gold standard a given amount can be converted into a prespecified amount of gold.

Good-on-close An execution instruction specifying that an order can only be filled at the close of trading. Also called *market-on-close*.

Good-on-open An execution instruction specifying that an order can only be filled at the opening of trading.

Good-till-cancelled order An order specifying that it is valid until the entity placing the order has cancelled it (or, commonly, until some specified amount of time such as 60 days has elapsed, whichever comes sooner).

Goodwill An intangible asset that represents the excess of the purchase price of an acquired company over the value of the net identifiable assets acquired.

Governance tokens In permissionless networks, governance tokens serve as votes to determine how the particular network is run.

Government debt management Government policies that relate to the issuance of debt securities, typically handled by a treasurer or finance ministry.

Government equivalent yield Measures quoted using actual/actual day counts.

Grant date The day that terms of compensation are communicated by an issuer and accepted by an employee recipient.

Green bonds Bonds used to specifically finance environmental-related projects.

Greenfield investments New, "to-be-built" infrastructure projects and assets created to provide a specific essential service or to supply a public good.

Gross profit margin The ratio of gross profit to revenues.

Groupthink A behavioral bias that occurs when a team minimizes conflict and dissent in reaching and maintaining a consensus.

Growth cycle Refers to fluctuations in economic activity around the long-term potential trend growth level, focusing on how much actual economic activity is below or above trend growth in economic activity.

Growth option The option to make additional investments in a project at some future time if the financial results are strong. Also called an *expansion option*.

Growth rate cycle Refers to fluctuations in the growth rate of economic activity.

Haircut The difference between the market value of the security used as collateral and the value of the loan. Also called *repo margin*.

Halo effect An emotional bias that extends a favorable evaluation of some characteristics to other characteristics.

Hard commodities Traded natural resources, such as crude oil and metals, with markets often involving the physical delivery of the underlying upon settlement.

Hard hurdle rate Hurdle ratewhere the manager earns fees on annual returns in excess of the hurdle rate

Hard-bullet covered bonds Type of security where if payments do not occur according to the original schedule of a covered bond, a bond default is triggered and bond payments are accelerated.

Harmonic mean A type of weighted mean computed as the reciprocal of the arithmetic average of the reciprocals.

Hedge The **derivative contract** used in **hedging** an exposure.

Hedge accounting Accounting standard(s) that allow an issuer to offset a hedging instrument (usually a derivative) against a hedged transaction or balance sheet item to reduce financial statement volatility.

Hedge funds Private investment vehicles that may invest in public equities or publicly traded fixed-income assets, private capital, and/or real assets, but they are distinguished by their investment *approach* rather than by the investments themselves.

Hedge ratio The proportion of an underlying that will offset the risk associated with a derivative position.

Hedging The use of a derivative contract to offset or neutralize existing or anticipated exposure to an **underlying**.

Hegemony Countries that are regional or even global leaders and use their political or economic influence of others to control resources.

Held-to-maturity Debt (fixed-income) securities that a company intends to hold to maturity; these are presented at their original cost, updated for any amortisation of discounts or premiums.

Herding Clustered trading that may or may not be based on information.

Herfindahl-Hirschman Index (HHI) A measure of market concentration, calculated as the sum of the squares of competitor market shares. Antitrust regulators in some countries consider markets with an HHI between 1,500 and 2,500 moderately concentrated and consider markets with an HHI over 2,500 highly concentrated.

Heteroskedasticity Non-constant variance across all observations.

Hidden order An order that is exposed not to the public but only to the brokers or exchanges that receive it.

Hidden revenue business model Business models that provide services to users at no charge and generate revenues elsewhere.

High yield Bond issuers and issues rated BB+ (Ba1 on Moody's scale) or lower. Also known as speculative grade and junk.

High-water mark The highest value, net of fees, that a fund has reached in history. It reflects the highest cumulative return used to calculate an incentive fee.

Hindsight bias A type of cognitive bias that makes individuals misremember the past in ways that make them appear to have made better and more well-informed choices.

Holder-of-record date The date that a shareholder listed on the corporation's books will be deemed to have ownership of the shares for purposes of receiving an upcoming dividend.

Holding period return The single-period internal rate of return for a real estate property that includes property income and the change in property value over the period.

Home bias A preference for securities listed on the exchanges of one's home country.

Homogeneity of expectations The assumption that all investors have the same economic expectations and thus have the same expectations of prices, cash flows, and other investment characteristics.

Homoskedasticity Constant variance across all observations.

Horizon yield An investor's total rate of return on a fixed income instrument over their holding period, including reinvested coupon payments. It is an internal rate of return expressed as an annualized rate.

Hostile takeover When a potential acquirer seeks to acquire a company (the target) against the wishes of the target's board of directors. Typically, a tender offer is used to carry out the hostile takeover, against which a board might use a poison pill in its defense.

Household A person or a group of people living in the same residence, taken as a basic unit in economic analysis.

Human capital The present value of an individual's future expected labor income.

Hurdle rate Also called "preferred return." The minimum rate of return on investment that a fund must reach before a GP receives carried interest.

Hypothesis A proposed explanation or theory that can be tested.

Hypothesis testing The process of testing of hypotheses about one or more populations using statistical inference.

I-spread also known as interpolated spread, it is the yield spread for a bond over the standard swap rate in that currency of the same tenor.

Iceberg order An order in which the display size is less than the order's full size.

If-converted method A method for accounting for the effect of convertible securities on earnings per share (EPS) that specifies what EPS would have been if the convertible securities had been converted at the beginning of the period, taking account of the effects of conversion on net income and the weighted average number of shares outstanding.

Illusion of control bias A bias in which people tend to believe that they can control or influence outcomes when, in fact, they cannot.

Immediate or cancel order An order that is valid only upon receipt by the broker or exchange. If such an order cannot be filled in part or in whole upon receipt, it cancels immediately. Also called *fill or kill*.

Impact lag The lag associated with the result of actions affecting the economy with delay.

Implied forward rate An interest rate or yield over a future period implied by the current term structure of interest rates.

Import license Specifies the quantity of a good that can be imported into a country.

In-the-money Describes an option with a positive intrinsic value.

Income tax paid The actual amount paid for income taxes in the period; not a provision, but the actual cash outflow.

Income tax payable The income tax owed by the company on the basis of taxable income.

Increasing returns to scale When a production process leads to increases in output that are proportionately larger than the increase in inputs.

Incurrence test A financial ratio or other measurement taken prior to an action such as debt issuance, usually on a pro forma basis taking the action into account. Satisfaction of the test (e.g., leverage ratio below a certain value) is linked to covenants between the issuer and investors.

Indenture A written contract between a lender and borrower that specifies the terms of the loan, such as interest rate, interest payment schedule, or maturity.

Independent With reference to events, the property that the occurrence of one event does not affect the probability of another event occurring. With reference to two random variables X and Y, they are independent if and only if $P(X,Y) = P(X)P(Y)$.

Independent directors Members of a corporation's board of directors who do not have an employment or familial relationship with the company, nor do they have a relationship that would impair their independence such as an economic interest in a vendor or competitor of the company.

Independent variable An explanatory variable in a regression model.

Independently and identically distributed With respect to random variables, the property of random variables that are independent of each other but follow the identical probability distribution.

Index-linked bonds A bond whose coupon payments or principal repayment is linked to a specified index.

Indexing An investment strategy in which an investor constructs a portfolio to mirror the performance of a specified index.

Indicator variable A variable that takes on only one of two values, 0 or 1, based on a condition. In simple linear regression, the slope is the difference in the dependent variable for the two conditions. Also referred to as a *dummy variable*.

Indifference curve A curve representing all the combinations of two goods or attributes such that the consumer is entirely indifferent among them.

Indirect taxes Taxes such as taxes on spending, as opposed to direct taxes.

Inflation premium An extra return that compensates investors for expected inflation.

Inflation reports A type of economic publication put out by many central banks.

Inflation-linked bonds Debt instruments that link the principal and interest to inflation.

Information cascade The transmission of information from those participants who act first and whose decisions influence the decisions of others.

Information-motivated traders Traders that trade to profit from information that they believe allows them to predict future prices.

Informationally efficient market A market in which asset prices reflect new information quickly and rationally.

Infrastructure A type of real asset that is intended for public use and provides essential services. These assets are typically long-lived fixed assets, such as bridges and toll roads.

Initial coin offering (ICO) An unregulated process whereby companies raise capital by selling crypto-tokens to investors in exchange for fiat money or another agreed-upon cryptocurrency.

Initial margin The ratio of the price of collateral to the value of cash exchanged in a repo; a value over 1.0 or 100% indicates overcollateralization.

Initial margin requirement The margin requirement on the first day of a transaction as well as on any day in which additional margin funds must be deposited.

Initial public offering (IPO) The first issuance of common shares to the public by a formerly private corporation.

Inside directors Members of a corporation's board of directors who are not independent. Typically, inside directors are employees or founders (and their family) of the company.

Insolvency A situation in which an issuer's total liabilities exceed the market value of its assets.

Institution An established organization or practice in a society or culture. An institution can be a formal structure, such as a university, organization, or process backed by law; or it can be informal, such as a custom or behavioral pattern important to society. Institutions can, but need not be, formed by national governments. Examples of institutions include non-governmental organizations, charities, religious customs, family units, the media, political parties, and educational practice.

Intangible assets Assets without a physical form, such as patents and trademarks.

Interbank market The market of loans and deposits between banks for maturities ranging from overnight to one year.

Intercept The estimated value of the dependent variable when the independent variable is zero.

Interest coverage A solvency ratio calculated as EBIT divided by interest payments.

Interest coverage ratio A measure of an issuer's ability to service its debt, typically the ratio of operating income or EBIT to interest expense.

Interest rate A rate of return that reflects the relationship between differently dated cash flows; a discount rate.

Interest rate swap A swap in which the underlying is an interest rate. Can be viewed as a currency swap in which both currencies are the same and can be created as a combination of currency swaps.

Interest-indexed bond A type of index-linked bond for which changes in the index are captured with adjustments to interest payments.

Internal credit enhancements Provisions or methods a borrower initiates to improve their creditworthiness in a structured transaction, such as overcollateralization or excess spread.

internal rate of return The discount rate that makes net present value equal 0; the discount rate that makes the present value of an investment's costs (outflows) equal to the present value of the investment's benefits (inflows).

Internal rate of return (IRR) The uniform discount rate for a series of cash flows over n periods that returns a net present value of zero.

Internet of things The vast array of physical devices, home appliances, smart buildings, vehicles, and other items that are embedded with electronics, sensors, software, and network connections that enable the objects in the system to interact and share information.

Interquartile range The difference between the third and first quartiles of a dataset.

Intrinsic value The amount gained (per unit) by an option buyer if an option is exercised at any given point in time. May be referred to as the exercise value of the option.

Investment banks Financial intermediaries that provide advice to their mostly corporate clients and help them arrange transactions such as initial and seasoned securities offerings.

Investment grade Bond issuers and issues rated BBB- (Baa3 on Moody's scale).

Investment policy statement (IPS) A written planning document that describes a client's investment objectives and risk tolerance over a relevant time horizon, along with constraints that apply to the client's portfolio.

Issue rating A rating which seeks to capture the probability of default or expected loss of the issuer's senior unsecured bonds.

Issuer rating A rating which seeks to capture the credit risk of a specific financial obligation of an issuer which takes such factors as seniority into account.

J-curve effect Net income over a multiyear private investment holding period characterized by negative returns in an initial phase, followed by cash flow and income growth toward the end of the holding period.

Jackknife A resampling method that repeatedly draws samples by taking the original observed data sample and leaving out one observation at a time (without replacement) from the set.

January effect Calendar anomaly that stock market returns in January are significantly higher compared to the rest of the months of the year, with most of the abnormal returns reported during the first five trading days in January. Also called *turn-of-the-year effect.*

Joint probability function A function giving the probability of joint occurrences of values of stated random variables.

Judgmental sampling A procedure of selectively handpicking elements from the population based on a researcher's knowledge and professional judgment.

Junior debt Debt obligation with lower priority of payment than senior debt obligations.

Key rate duration Also known as partial duration, is a measure of a bond's sensitivity to a change in the benchmark yield at a specific maturity.

Keynesians Economists who believe that fiscal policy can have powerful effects on aggregate demand, output, and employment when there is substantial spare capacity in an economy.

Kurtosis The statistical measure that indicates the combined weight of the tails of a distribution relative to the rest of the distribution.

Lagging economic indicators Turning points that take place later than those of the overall economy; they are believed to have value in identifying the economy's past condition.

Law of one price A principle that states that if two investments have the same or equivalent future cash flows regardless of what will happen in the future, then these two investments should have the same current price.

Lead underwriter The lead investment bank in a syndicate of investment banks and broker–dealers involved in a securities underwriting.

Leading economic indicators Turning points that usually precede those of the overall economy; they are believed to have value for predicting the economy's future state, usually near-term.

Legal tender Something that must be accepted when offered in exchange for goods and services.

Lender of last resort An entity willing to lend money when no other entity is ready to do so.

Leptokurtic Describes a distribution that has fatter tails than a normal distribution (also called fat-tailed).

Lessee Tenant or property user that enters a lease with a property owner or lessor.

Lessor Property owner or manager that leases a property to a tenant or property user.

Level of significance The probability of a Type I error in testing a hypothesis.

Leverage A measure for identifying a potentially influential high-leverage point.

Leveraged buyout (LBO) A transaction in which a private acquiror uses equity and a high proportion of debt to acquire a public or private company in order to make changes to increase value over an investment period.

Leveraged loan Where private debt investor firms borrow money to make a direct loan to a borrower.

Leveraged loans Loans made to a borrower or issuer with relatively lower credit quality and/or higher leverage.

Liability-driven investing An investment industry term that generally encompasses asset allocation that is focused on funding an investor's liabilities in institutional contexts.

Licensing arrangements Rights to produce a product or have access to intangible assets using someone else's brand name in return for a royalty (often a percentage of revenues).

Lien A legal right or claim to property by a creditor.

Likelihood The probability of an observation, given a particular set of conditions.

Limit order Instructions to a broker or exchange to obtain the best price immediately available when filling an order, but in no event accept a price higher than a specified (limit) price when buying or accept a price lower than a specified (limit) price when selling.

Limit order book The book or list of limit orders to buy and sell that pertains to a security.

Limited company A business organizational form owned by shareholders or members with limited liability who elect a board of directors to appoint management. Generally, limited companies have indefinite life and easier transfer of ownership interests than limited partnerships.

Limited liability partnership (LLP) A business organizational form available in some jurisdictions owned entirely by limited partners with limited liability.

Limited partners (LPs) Outside investors in a private market fund who own a fractional interest in a limited, closed-end partnership managed by a general partner based on the investment commitment and other terms set out in a limited partner agreement.

Limited partnership Closed-end form of ownership frequently used in private market funds in which private market fund investors, or limited partners, commit capital that is invested, managed, and distributed by a private market fund manager, or general partner, over an investment holding period.

Limited partnership agreement (LPA) A legal document that outlines the rules of the partnership and establishes the framework that ultimately guides the fund's operations throughout its life.

lin-log model A functional form for transforming regression model data in which the dependent variable is linear but the independent variable is logarithmic.

Linear derivatives Firm commitment derivative contracts in which the contract's payoff/profit function is linear with respect to the price of the underlying.

Liquid market Said of a market in which traders can buy or sell with low total transaction costs when they want to trade.

Liquidity The extent to which a company is able to meet its short-term obligations using cash flows and those assets that can be readily transformed into cash.

Liquidity premium The compensation for liquidity risk that increases in proportion to the investment's illiquidity.

Liquidity ratios Financial ratios measuring the company's ability to meet its short-term obligations to creditors as they come due.

Liquidity risk The risk that an investment may not be readily sold at its true value.

Liquidity trap A condition in which the demand for money becomes infinitely elastic (horizontal demand curve) so that injections of money into the economy will not lower interest rates or affect real activity.

Load fund A mutual fund in which, in addition to the annual fee, a percentage fee is charged to invest in the fund and/or for redemptions from the fund.

Loan-to-value ratio (LTV) Ratio of the amount of the mortgage to the property's value. The lower the LTV, the higher the borrower's equity. From the lender's perspective, the higher the borrower's equity, the less likely the borrower is to default.

Loans Debt instruments agreed to between a borrower and lender, typically a bank.

Lockout or revolving period For an ABS with a non-amortizing collateral pool, such as credit card debt, is the period in which the cash proceeds from principal repayments are reinvested in additional loans with a principal equal to the principal repaid. During this period, there is no prepayment risk and potential default risk is generally limited. When the lockout period is over, principal repayments are used to pay off the outstanding principal on the ABS. Lockout period and revolving period are interchangeable.

Lockup period The minimum holding period before investors are allowed to make withdrawals or redeem shares from a fund. Its purpose is to allow the hedge fund manager the required time to implement and potentially realize a strategy's expected results.

log-lin model A functional form for transforming regression model data in which the dependent variable is logarithmic but the independent variable is linear.

log-log model A functional form for transforming regression model data in which both the dependent and independent variables are in logarithmic form.

Long A trading position in a **derivative contract** that gains value as the price of the **underlying** moves higher.

Long position A position in an asset or contract in which one owns the asset or has an exercisable right under the contract.

Long-run average total cost The curve describing average total cost when no costs are considered fixed.

Loss aversion The tendency of people to dislike losses more than they like comparable gains.

Loss given default (LGD) The amount a debtholder fails to recover if a default occurs, usually expressed as a percentage of par value.

Loss severity Portion of a bond's value (including unpaid interest) an investor loses in the event of default.

Loss-aversion bias A bias in which people tend to strongly prefer avoiding losses as opposed to achieving gains.

Low-cost producer A firm with lower production costs than its industry competitors.

M^2 A measure of what a portfolio would have returned if it had taken on the same total risk as the market index.

M^2 alpha Difference between the risk-adjusted performance of the portfolio and the performance of the benchmark.

Macaulay duration the present-value weighted average time to receipt of cash flows for fixed-income instrument, also the holding period needed to balance coupon reinvestment risk and price risk for a one-time instantaneous "parallel" shift in the yield curve once the bond purchase is settled. It is named after Frederick Macaulay, the Canadian economist who introduced the concept in 1938.

Machine learning (ML) Involves computer-based techniques that seek to extract knowledge from large amounts of data without making any assumptions about the data's underlying probability distribution. The goal of ML algorithms is to automate decision-making processes by generalizing, or "learning," from known examples to determine an underlying structure in the data.

Maintenance capital expenditures Investments in assets to keep them in operation or increase their efficiency without extending their useful lives.

Maintenance margin Minimum balance set below the initial margin that each contract buyer and seller must hold in the futures margin account from trade initiation until final settlement at maturity.

Maintenance margin requirement The margin requirement on any day other than the first day of a transaction.

Management buy-in A type of leveraged buyout where the current management team is replaced with the acquiring team involved in managing the company.

Management buyout A private sale to a strategic buyer that includes a company's existing management. The management team commits their own equity capital along with other investors as an incentive to grow the firm's cash flows and value.

Management guidance Management of public companies may publicly provide targets for earnings, revenues, and other measures (e.g., capital expenditures) for the next quarter, year, or longer term. Guidance can be detailed or rather directional and is often updated throughout the year. Initial guidance for next fiscal year might be provided during the fourth-quarter earnings call and updated for completed quarters, and new information provided at the first-, second-, and third-quarter earnings calls. Also known simply as *guidance*.

Margin call Request to a derivatives contract counterparty to immediately deposit funds to return the futures margin account balance to the initial margin.

Margin financing A financing arrangement whereby the prime broker lends shares, bonds, or derivatives and the hedge fund (or investment manager) deposits cash or other collateral into a margin account at the prime broker based on certain fractions of the investment positions.

Margin loan Money borrowed from a broker to purchase securities.

Marginal propensity to consume The proportion of an additional unit of disposable income that is consumed or spent; the change in consumption for a small change in income.

Marginal propensity to save The proportion of an additional unit of disposable income that is saved (not spent).

Mark to market (MTM) The practice in which a central clearing party assigns profits and losses to counterparties to derivative contracts. In exchange-traded markets, this practice takes place daily and is often referred to as daily settlement.

Market anomaly Change in the price or return of a security that cannot directly be linked to current relevant information known in the market or to the release of new information into the market.

Market bid–ask spread The difference between the best bid and the best offer.

Market discount rate The rate of return required by investors given the risk of the bond investment, also known as the required yield or required rate of return.

Market float The number of shares that are available to the investing public.

Market makers **Over-the-counter (OTC) dealers** who typically enter into offsetting bilateral transactions with one another to transfer risk to other parties.

Market model A regression model with the return on a stock as the dependent variable and the returns on a market index as the independent variable.

Market multiple models Valuation models based on share price multiples or enterprise value multiples.

Market neutral These strategies use quantitative, fundamental, and technical analysis to identify under- and overvalued equity securities. The hedge fund takes long positions in undervalued securities and short positions in overvalued securities, while seeking to maintain a market-neutral net position.

Market order Instructions to a broker or exchange to obtain the best price immediately available when filling an order.

Market reference rate (MRR) The interest rate underlying used in interest rate swaps. These rates typically match those of loans or other short-term obligations. Survey-based Libor rates used as reference rates in the past have been replaced by rates based on a daily average of observed market transaction rates. For example, the Secured Overnight Financing Rate (SOFR) is an overnight cash borrowing rate collateralized by US Treasuries. Other MRRs include the euro short-term rate (€STR) and the Sterling Overnight Index Average (SONIA).

Market risk Risk related to market movements, e.g., unexpected changes in share prices, interest rates, currency exchange rates, and commodity prices.

Market share A company's or product's revenue expressed as a percentage of its market size.

Market size Total sales for a good or service, which can be calculated on a global or more regional basis.

Market value The price at which an asset or security can currently be bought or sold in an open market.

Market-capitalization weighting An index weighting method in which the weight assigned to each constituent security is determined by dividing its market capitalization by the total market capitalization (sum of the market capitalization) of all securities in the index. Also called *value weighting*.

Market-on-close An execution instruction specifying that an order can only be filled at the close of trading.

Marketable limit order A buy limit order in which the limit price is placed above the best offer, or a sell limit order in which the limit price is placed below the best bid. Such orders generally will partially or completely fill right away.

Markowitz efficient frontier The graph of the set of portfolios offering the maximum expected return for their level of risk (standard deviation of return).

Master limited partnership (MLP) Has similar features to limited partnerships but is usually a more liquid investment that is often publicly traded.

Master repurchase agreement A legal document governing all repo trades between two parties.

Match funding Financing an asset with a source, such as a loan or bond, that is aligned with certain attributes of the asset, such as duration and the respective streams of income and financing costs.

Material (materiality) Refers to information that is decision-useful for a reasonable investor.

Matrix pricing An estimation process for financial instruments based on the prices of comparable instruments.

Maturity The date of a fixed-income instrument's final payment to investors.

Maturity premium An extra return that compensates investors for the increased sensitivity of the market value of debt to a change in market interest rates as maturity is extended.

Maturity structure of interest rates Also known as the term structure of interest rates, refers to the difference in interest rates or benchmark yields by time-to-maturity.

Mean absolute deviation With reference to a sample, the mean of the absolute values of deviations from the sample mean.

Mean square error (MSE) Calculated as the sum of squares error (SSE) divided by the degrees of freedom, which are the number of observations minus the number of independent variables minus one. Since simple linear regression has just one independent variable, the degrees of freedom calculation is the number of observations minus 2.

Mean square regression (MSR) Calculated as the sum of squares regression (SSR) divided by the number of independent variables in the regression model. In simple linear regression, there is only one independent variable, so MSR equals SSR.

Mean–variance analysis An approach to portfolio analysis using expected means, variances, and covariances of asset returns.

Measure of central tendency A quantitative measure that specifies where data are centered.

Measures of location Quantitative measures that describe the location or distribution of data. They include not only measures of central tendency but also other measures, such as percentiles.

Median The "middlemost" observation; i.e., in a set of observations that has been ranked from highest to lowest, the median will lie in the middle.

Meme coin A type of altcoin that is often inspired by a joke.

Mental accounting bias An information-processing bias in which people treat one sum of money differently from another equal-sized sum based on which mental account the money is assigned to.

Merger arbitrage Special situations investments related to business combinations in which investors seek to capitalize on price discrepancies of securities issued by the target company.

Mesokurtic Describes a distribution with kurtosis equal to that of the normal distribution, namely, kurtosis equal to three.

Mezzanine debt Refers to private credit subordinated to senior secured debt but senior to equity in the borrower's capital structure.

Mezzanine-stage financing Mezzanine venture capital that prepares a company to go public as it continues to expand capacity and enhance its growth trajectory. It represents the bridge financing needed to fund a private firm until it can execute an IPO or be sold.

Miner A validator of transactions on the blockchain that locks blocks of transactions into the blockchain and receives compensation for this process in the form of a digital asset.

Minimum efficient scale The smallest output that a firm can produce such that its long-run average total cost is minimized.

Minimum-variance portfolio The portfolio with the minimum variance for each given level of expected return.

Minority shareholder An individual or entity that owns less than a majority of the voting rights in a corporation.

Mode The most frequently occurring value in a distribution.

Modern portfolio theory (MPT) The analysis of rational portfolio choices based on the efficient use of risk.

Modified duration The first derivative of a bond's price with respect to its yield, this statistic is a measure of interest rate risk used to estimate the percentage price change for a given change in yield-to-maturity.

Monetarists Economists who believe that the rate of growth of the money supply is the primary determinant of the rate of inflation.

Monetary policy Actions taken by a nation's central bank to affect aggregate output and prices through changes in bank reserves, reserve requirements, or its target interest rate.

Monetary transmission mechanism The process whereby a central bank's interest rate gets transmitted through the economy and ultimately affects the rate of increase of prices.

Monetary union An economic union in which the members adopt a common currency.

Money convexity A measure that is used to complement modified duration to capture the second-order effect of yield changes on a bond's price, expressed in currency terms.

Money duration A measure of the price change of a fixed-income instrument in currency units from a change in yield-to-maturity. The money duration can be stated per 100 of par value or in terms of the actual position size. In the United States, money duration is commonly called "dollar duration."

Money market The market for short-term debt instruments (one-year maturity or less).

Money market securities Fixed-income securities with original maturities of one year or less.

Money-weighted return The internal rate of return on a portfolio, taking account of all cash flows.

Moneyness Expresses the relationship between an option's value and its exercise price across the full range of possible underlying prices.

Monopolistic competition Highly competitive form of imperfect competition; the competitive characteristic is a notably large number of firms, while the monopoly aspect is the result of product differentiation.

Monopoly In pure monopoly markets, there are no substitutes for the given product or service. There is a single seller, which exercises considerable power over pricing and output decisions.

Monte Carlo simulation A technique that uses the inverse transformation method for converting a randomly generated uniformly distributed number into a simulated value of a random variable of a desired distribution. Each key decision variable in a Monte Carlo simulation requires an assumed statistical distribution; this assumption facilitates incorporating non-normality, fat tails, and tail dependence as well as solving high-dimensionality problems.

Moral principles Beliefs regarding what is good, acceptable, or obligatory behavior and what is bad, unacceptable, or forbidden behavior.

Mortgage loan Agreement to finance real estate by the collateral of a specified property that obliges the borrower to make a predetermined series of payments to the lender.

Mortgage pass-through security Security created when mortgage lenders pool mortgages together and sell securities to investors. The cash flow from the mortgage pool––monthly payments of principal, interest, and prepayments––are "passed through" to the security holders.

Mortgage-backed securities (MBS) Debt obligations that represent claims to the cash flows from pools of mortgage loans, most commonly on residential property.

Multi-factor model A model that explains a variable in terms of the values of a set of factors.

Multi-market indexes Comprised of indexes from different countries, designed to represent multiple security markets.

Multilateral trading facilities See *alternative trading systems*.

Multilateralism The conduct of countries who participate in mutually beneficial trade relationships and extensive rules harmonization. Private firms are fully integrated into global supply chains with multiple trade partners. Examples of multilateral countries include Germany and Singapore.

Multiple of invested capital (MOIC) Also referred to as the multiple of money or total value to paid-in, this private market performance measure incorporates both the cumulative distributions received and the net asset value of a fund as a proportion of invested capital.

Multiple-price auction A debt securities auction in which bidders receive distinct prices based on their bids.

Multiplier models Valuation models based on share price multiples or enterprise value multiples.

Mutual fund A comingled investment pool in which investors in the fund each have a pro-rata claim on the income and value of the fund.

Nash equilibrium When two or more participants in a non-coop-erative game have no incentive to deviate from their respective equilibrium strategies given their opponent's strategies.

Nationalism The promotion of a country's own economic interests to the exclusion or detriment of the interests of other nations. Nationalism is marked by limited economic and financial cooperation. These actors may focus on national production and sales, limited cross-border investment and capital flows, and restricted currency exchange.

Natural language processing (NLP) A field of research within the field of text analytics and at the intersection of computer science, AI, and linguistics that focuses on developing computer programs to analyze and interpret human language.

Natural resources These include commodities (hard and soft), agricultural land (farmland), and timberland.

Negative externalities A cost to a third party because of the production or consumption of a good or service.

Negative pledge clause Limitations on investments, the disposal of assets, or issuance of debt senior to existing obligations. Negative covenants seek to ensure that an issuer maintains the ability to make interest and principal payments.

Net cash An issuer's total debt less cash and marketable securities. When the balance is negative it is referred to as net cash.

Net debt An issuer's total debt less cash and marketable securities. When the balance is positive it is referred to as net debt.

Net investment hedge Refers to a specific **hedge accounting** designation that applies when either a foreign currency bond or a derivative, such as an FX swap or forward, is used to offset the exchange rate risk of the equity of a foreign operation.

Net present value (NPV) The present value of an investment's cash inflows (benefits) minus the present value of its cash outflows (costs).

Net profit margin An indicator of profitability, calculated as net income divided by revenue; indicates how much of each dollar of revenues is left after all costs and expenses. Also called *profit margin* or *return on sales*.

Net tax rate The tax rate net of transfer payments.

Net working capital Working capital excluding short-term items unrelated to business operations, such as cash, marketable securities, and short-term debt.

Network effects A business model that enables users to contribute directly to a product, service, or online content.

Neural networks A type of computer program design based on how the human brain learns and processes information.

Neutral rate of interest The rate of interest that neither spurs on nor slows down the underlying economy.

No-load fund A mutual fund in which there is no fee for investing in the fund or for redeeming fund shares, although there is an annual fee based on a percentage of the fund's net asset value.

Node Each value on a binomial tree from which successive moves or outcomes branch.

Non-agency RMBS MBS backed by residential mortgages that are issued by private entities and not guaranteed by a federal agency or a GSE.

Non-amortizing loans Type of debt where there are no scheduled principal repayments.

Non-cooperative country A country with inconsistent and even arbitrary rules; restricted movement of goods, services, people, and capital across borders; retaliation; and limited technology exchange.

Non-cumulative preference shares Preference shares for which dividends that are not paid in the current or subsequent periods are forfeited permanently (instead of being accrued and paid at a later date).

Non-financial risks Risks that arise from sources other than changes in the external financial markets, such as changes in accounting rules, legal environment, or tax rates.

Non-fungible token (NFT) A unique cryptographic token on the blockchain that cannot be replicated and is used to represent ownership of physical assets, such as artwork, real estate, or other assets.

Non-linear derivatives Derivatives, such as options or other contingent claims, with payoff/profit profiles that are non-linear (asymmetric) with respect to the price of the underlying.

Non-participating preference shares Preference shares that do not entitle shareholders to share in the profits of the company. Instead, shareholders are only entitled to receive a fixed dividend payment and the par value of the shares in the event of liquidation.

Non-probability sampling A sampling plan dependent on factors other than probability considerations, such as a sampler's judgment or the convenience to access data.

Non-recourse loan Loan in which the lender does not have a claim against the borrower and thus can look only to the property to recover the outstanding mortgage balance.

Non-state actors Those that participate in global political, economic, or financial affairs but do not directly control national security or country resources. Examples of non-state actors are non-governmental organizations (NGOs), multinational companies, charities, and even influential individuals, such as business leaders or cultural icons.

Nonparametric test A test that is not concerned with a parameter or that makes minimal assumptions about the population from which a sample comes.

Nonsystematic risk Unique risk that is local or limited to a particular asset or industry that need not affect assets outside of that asset class.

Normal distribution A continuous, symmetric probability distribution that is completely described by its mean and its variance.

Normalized earnings The expected level of mid-cycle earnings for a company in the absence of any unusual or temporary factors that affect profitability (either positively or negatively).

Notching Ratings adjustment methodology where specific issues from the same borrower may be assigned different credit ratings.

Notice period The length of time (typically 30–90 days) in advance that investors may be required to notify a fund of their intent to redeem some or all of their investment. This allows a fund manager to liquidate a position in an orderly fashion without magnifying losses.

Novation process A process that substitutes the initial **swap execution facility (SEF)** contract with identical trades facing the **central counterparty (CCP)**. The CCP serves as **counterparty** for both financial intermediaries, eliminating bilateral **counterparty credit risk** and providing **clearing** and **settlement** services.

Null hypothesis The hypothesis that is tested.

Off-the-run Seasoned government bonds that are often less liquid.

Off-the-run securities Sovereign debt securities outstanding other than on-the-sun securities. Off-the-run securities are less liquid than on-the-run securities.

Offer The price at which a dealer or trader is willing to sell an asset, typically qualified by a maximum quantity (ask size).

Official interest rate An interest rate that a central bank sets and announces publicly; normally the rate at which it is willing to lend money to the commercial banks. Also called *official policy rate* or *policy rate.*

Official policy rate An interest rate that a central bank sets and announces publicly; normally the rate at which it is willing to lend money to the commercial banks.

Oligopoly Market structure with a relatively small number of firms supplying the market.

Omnichannel Refers to a company selling its products or services in multiple channels, such as in store and online.

On-the-run Most recently issued, and liquid, government bonds.

On-the-run securities The most recently issued and liquid sovereign debt securities.

Open interest The number of outstanding contracts.

Open market operations The purchase or sale of bonds by the national central bank to implement monetary policy. The bonds traded are usually sovereign bonds issued by the national government.

Open-end fund A mutual fund that accepts new investment money and issues additional shares at a value equal to the net asset value of the fund at the time of investment.

Operating cycle The length of time between a company's acquisition of goods or raw materials and the collection of cash from sales to customers.

Operating efficiency ratios Ratios that measure how efficiently a company performs day-to-day tasks, such as the collection of receivables and management of inventory.

Operating leases A type of lease which is more akin to the rental of the underlying asset.

Operating leverage The sensitivity of a firm's operating profit to a change in revenues, determined by the composition of fixed and variable operating costs.

Operating profit margin A profitability ratio calculated as operating income (i.e., income before interest and taxes) divided by revenue. Also called *operating margin.*

Operational deposits Bank deposits generated by clearing, custody, and cash management activities.

Operational independence A bank's ability to execute monetary policy and set interest rates in the way it thought would best meet the inflation target.

Operational risk The risk that arises from inadequate or failed people, systems, and internal policies, procedures, and processes, as well as from external events that are beyond the control of the organization but that affect its operations.

Operationally efficient Said of a market, a financial system, or an economy that has relatively low transaction costs.

Opportunistic real estate strategies Include major redevelopment, repurposing of assets, taking on large vacancies, or speculating on significant improvement in market conditions. These may be appealing for investors seeking higher returns and willing to accept additional risks from development, redevelopment, repositioning, and leasing.

Opportunity cost Reflects the foregone opportunity of investing in a different asset. It is typically denoted by the risk-free rate of interest, r.

Optimal capital structure The capital structure at which the value of the company is maximized.

Option A primary example of a **contingent claim**. A **derivative contract** that provides the buyer the right, but not the obligation, to buy or sell an **underlying**.

Option contract See *option.*

Option premium An amount that is paid upfront from the option buyer to the option seller. Reflects the value of the option buyer's right to exercise in the future.

Option-adjusted price The sum of a bond's flat price and value of an embedded option.

Option-adjusted spread or OAS for a bond is its Z-spread adjusted for the value of an embedded option.

Option-adjusted yield A yield measure for a bond adjusted for embedded options.

Order A specification of what instrument to trade, how much to trade, and whether to buy or sell.

Order precedence hierarchy With respect to the execution of orders to trade, a set of rules that determines which orders execute before other orders.

Order-driven markets A market (generally an auction market) that uses rules to arrange trades based on the orders that traders submit; in their pure form, such markets do not make use of dealers.

Ordinary shares Equity shares that are subordinate to all other types of equity (e.g., preferred equity). Also called *common stock* or *common shares.*

Organizational form A legal and tax classification of a business, specific to a jurisdiction, that determines the organization's legal identity, owner–manager relationship, owner liability, taxation, and access to financing.

Out-of-the-money Describes an option with zero intrinsic value because the option buyer would not rationally exercise the option. An example of such would be the case in which the price of the underlying is less than the option's exercise price for a call option.

Over-the-counter (OTC) Refers to derivative markets in which **derivative contracts** are created and traded between derivatives end users and **dealers**, or financial intermediaries, such as commercial banks or investment banks.

Overcollateralization Credit enhancement technique where collateral underlying the transaction exceeds the face value of the issued bonds.

Overconfidence bias A bias in which people demonstrate unwarranted faith in their own intuitive reasoning, judgments, and/or cognitive abilities.

Overfitting When a machine learning model learns the input and target dataset too precisely, making the system more likely to discover false relationships or unsubstantiated patterns that will lead to prediction errors.

P-value The smallest level of significance at which the null hypothesis can be rejected.

Par rate A yield-to-maturity that makes the present value of a bond's cash flows equal to par.

Par swap rate The fixed swap rate that equates the present value of all future expected floating cash flows to the present value of fixed cash flows.

Par value The amount of principal on a bond, also known as face value.

Parallel shift When all maturities along a yield curve increase or decrease in yield in the same direction by the same magnitude. A parallel shift in the yield curve is implicitly assumed in analytical duration and convexity.

Parameter A descriptive measure computed from or used to describe a population of data, conventionally represented by Greek letters.

Parametric test Any test (or procedure) concerned with parameters or whose validity depends on assumptions concerning the population generating the sample.

Pari passu clause A covenant or contract clause that ensures a debt obligation is treated the same as the borrower's other senior debt instruments and is not subordinated to similar obligations.

Partially amortizing bond A loan or bond with a payment schedule that calls for partial repayment of principle over the life of the bond, with the remaining principal paid at maturity.

Participating preference shares Preference shares that entitle shareholders to receive the standard preferred dividend plus the opportunity to receive an additional dividend if the company's profits exceed a pre-specified level.

Pass-through businesses Businesses that, by virtue of their organizational form and/or other legal and regulatory attributes, do not pay entity-level taxes on income or loss; income or loss is passed through to owners, who pay personal taxes.

Pass-through rate The coupon rate of a mortgage pass-through security that is received by the investor after administrative charges. It is lower than the weighted average mortgage rate earned on the underlying pool of mortgages because of administrative charges. The pass-through rate that the investor receives is said to be "net interest" or "net coupon."

Passive investment A buy-and-hold approach in which an investor does not make portfolio changes based on short-term expectations of changing market or security performance.

Payable date The day that the company actually mails out (or electronically transfers) a dividend payment.

Payment date The day that the company actually mails out (or electronically transfers) a dividend payment.

Payment-in-kind A bond feature whereby coupon payments can be fully or partially paid in the form of additional issuance or added to the principal amount.

Payments system The system for the transfer of money.

Pearson correlation A parametric measure of the relationship between two variables.

Pecking order theory The theory that managers consider how their actions might be interpreted by outsiders and thereby order their preferences for various forms of corporate financing. Forms of financing that are least visible to outsiders (e.g., internally generated funds) are most preferable to managers, and those that are most visible (e.g., equity issuance) are least preferable.

Penetration pricing A discount pricing approach used when a firm willingly sacrifices margins in order to build scale and market share.

Percentiles Values that divide a distribution into 100 equal parts.

Perfect competition A market structure in which the individual firm has virtually no impact on market price, because it is assumed to be a very small seller among a very large number of firms selling essentially identical products.

Performance evaluation The measurement and assessment of the outcomes of investment management decisions.

Performance fee Fee paid to the general partner from the limited partner(s) based on realized net profits.

Period costs Costs (e.g., executives' salaries) that cannot be directly matched with the timing of revenues and which are thus expensed immediately.

Periodicity Number of periods in a year, used for compound interest. The periodicity of a fixed-income instrument usually matches the frequency of its coupon payments.

Permanent differences Differences between tax and financial reporting of revenue (expenses) that will not be reversed at some future date. These result in a difference between the company's effective tax rate and statutory tax rate and do not result in a deferred tax item.

Permissioned networks Networks that are fully open only to select participants on a DLT network.

Permissionless networks Networks that are fully open to any user on a DLT network.

Perpetual bonds Bonds with no stated maturity date.

Perpetuity A perpetual annuity, or a set of never-ending level sequential cash flows, with the first cash flow occurring one period from now.

PESTLE analysis A framework for analyzing factors that influence an industry's economic outcomes.

Pet projects A capital investment that is pursued by management but is not economically justifiable by a disinterested party. Motivations for pet projects include self-dealing and vanity.

Physical risks Economic and financial losses from the increase in the severity and frequency of extreme weather due to climate change—for example, the loss of coastal real estate from a storm.

PIPE (private investment in public equity) A private offering to select investors with fewer disclosures and lower transaction costs that allows the issuer to raise capital more quickly and cost effectively.

Platykurtic Describes a distribution that has relatively less weight in the tails than the normal distribution (also called thin-tailed).

Pledge A legal right or claim to property by a creditor. Also called a lien.

Poison pill Officially known as a shareholder rights plan, a poison pill is a hostile-takeover defense adopted by boards of directors according to rules specified in the corporate charter. There are several types of poison pills. Generally, they allow shareholders, *excluding* the shareholder making the hostile bid and their affiliates, to buy newly issued shares at a discounted price. The share issuance would dilute the bidder's ownership percentage, rendering it impossible for the bidder to attain control.

Policy rate An interest rate that a central bank sets and announces publicly; normally the rate at which it is willing to lend money to the commercial banks.

Portfolio companies The individual companies owned by a private equity firm.

Portfolio investment flows Short-term investments in foreign assets, such as stocks or bonds.

Portfolio planning The process of creating a plan for building a portfolio that is expected to satisfy a client's investment objectives.

Position The quantity of an asset that an entity owns or owes.

Posterior probability An updated probability that reflects or comes after new information.

Power of a test The probability of correctly rejecting the null—that is, rejecting the null hypothesis when it is false.

Pre-funding period Allows the trust to acquire during a certain period of time after the close of the transaction.

Preference shares A type of equity interest which ranks above common shares with respect to the payment of dividends and the distribution of the company's net assets upon liquidation. They have characteristics of both debt and equity securities. Also called *preferred stock*.

Preferred stock See *preference shares*.

Premium In the case of bonds, premium refers to the amount by which a bond is priced above its face (par) value. In the case of an option, the amount paid for the option contract.

Prepayment option May entitle the borrower to prepay all or part of the outstanding mortgage principal prior to maturity. This creates a risk from the lender's or investor's viewpoint because the cash flow amounts and timing cannot be known with certainty.

Prepayment risk The risk that the some or all of a mortgage-backed security's principal is repaid at a different speed than expected, either in the form of contraction risk (or earlier repayment than expected) or extension risk (later repayment).

Present value models Valuation models that estimate the intrinsic value of a security as the present value of the future benefits expected to be received from the security. Also called *discounted cash flow models*.

Pretax margin A profitability ratio calculated as earnings before taxes divided by revenue.

Price discrimination A pricing approach that charges different prices to different customers based on their willingness to pay.

Price index Represents the average prices of a basket of goods and services.

Price limits Establish a band relative to the previous day's settlement price within which all trades must occur.

Price multiple A ratio that compares the share price with some sort of monetary flow or value to allow evaluation of the relative worth of a company's stock.

Price priority The principle that the highest priced buy orders and the lowest priced sell orders execute first.

Price return Measures *only* the price appreciation or percentage change in price of the securities in an index or portfolio.

Price return index An index that reflects *only* the price appreciation or percentage change in price of the constituent securities. Also called *price index*.

Price stability In economics, refers to an inflation rate that is low on average and not subject to wide fluctuation.

Price takers Producers that must accept whatever price the market dictates.

Price value of a basis point (PVBP) An estimate of the change in the full price of a bond given a 1 bp change in its yield-to-maturity. The PVBP is also called the "PV01," standing for the "price value of an 01" or "present value of an 01," where "01" means 1 bp. In the United States, it is commonly called the "DV01" for the "dollar value" of 1 bp.

Price weighting An index weighting method in which the weight assigned to each constituent security is determined by dividing its price by the sum of all the prices of the constituent securities.

Price-setting option The option to adjust prices when demand or supply varies from what is forecast.

Price-to-earnings ratio (P/E) The ratio of share price to earnings per share.

Pricing power A company's ability to set prices and other economic terms with customers without affecting its sales volumes.

Primary bond markets Fixed-income markets comprised of issuers issuing bonds to investors to raise capital, often intermediated by a third-party such as an investment bank.

Primary capital markets (primary markets) The market where securities are first sold and the issuers receive the proceeds.

Primary dealer Financial institution that is authorized to deal in new issues of sovereign bonds and that serves primarily as a trading counterparty of the office responsible for issuing sovereign bonds.

Primary market The market where securities are first sold and the issuers receive the proceeds.

Prime broker A broker that provides services that commonly include custody, administration, lending, short borrowing, and trading.

Prime loans Lending made to borrowers of high credit quality with strong employment and credit histories, a low DTI, substantial equity in the underlying property, and a first lien on the mortgaged property serving as the collateral for the loan.

Principal The amount that an issuer agrees to repay the debtholders on the maturity date.

Principal-agent relationship An arrangement in which one party (the agent) has authority to act for or on behalf of another party (the principal). Such an arrangement imposes a duty on the agent to act in the principal's best interest.

Prior probabilities Probabilities reflecting beliefs prior to the arrival of new information.

Priority of claims Priority of payment, with the most senior or highest ranking debt having the first claim on the cash flows and assets of the issuer.

Private capital Funding provided to companies that is not sourced from the public markets.

Private company A company, typically a limited company, that does not list its equity securities on an exchange.

Private debt Capital extended to companies through a loan or other form of debt.

Private debtholders Investors in an entity's non-securitized debt claims, such as a loan or lease. The most common type of private debtholder is a bank.

Private equity Equity investment capital raised from sources other than public markets and traditional institutions.

Private equity fund A hedge fund that seeks to buy, optimize, and ultimately sell portfolio companies to generate profits. See *venture capital fund*.

Private equity securities Securities that are not listed on public exchanges and have no active secondary market. They are issued primarily to institutional investors via non-public offerings, such as private placements.

Private investment in public equity (PIPE) An investment in the equity of a publicly traded firm that is made at a discount to the market value of the firm's shares.

Private limited company A type of limited company in many jurisdictions with pass-through taxation but restrictions on the number of shareholders or members and on the transfer of ownership interest.

Private placement A sale of debt or equity securities to a small group of investors on an unregulated basis. The terms of the offering are negotiated by the issuer and investors.

Probability of default (POD) The likelihood that a borrower fails to make full and timely payments of principal and interest according to debt terms, usually expressed in annual percentage terms.

Probability sampling A sampling plan that allows every member of the population to have an equal chance of being selected.

Probability tree diagram A diagram with branches emanating from nodes representing either mutually exclusive chance events or mutually exclusive decisions.

Production flexibility option The option to alter production when demand varies from what is forecast.

Profession An occupational group that has specific education, expert knowledge, and a framework of practice and behavior that underpins community trust, respect, and recognition.

Profit margin An indicator of profitability, calculated as net income divided by revenue; indicates how much of each dollar of revenues is left after all costs and expenses.

Profitability ratios Ratios that measure a company's ability to generate profitable sales from its resources (assets).

Prospectus Legal document in securitization that describes the structure of the transaction, including the priority and amount of payments to be made to the servicer, administrators, and the ABS holders, as well as the credit enhancements used in the securitization.

Protective put A strategy of purchasing an underlying asset and purchasing a put on the same asset.

Proxy contest When a shareholder or group of shareholders campaigns for certain matters they have submitted to a shareholder vote, often a slate of directors who oppose the incumbent board and management. The incumbent board and management simultaneously campaign for their side.

Proxy voting A form of casting a ballot in an election in which a voter authorizes a representative to vote on their behalf according to instructions. In corporate elections, proxy ballots are cast by shareholders that direct a representative, typically the corporate secretary, to enter their votes as instructed.

Public (listed) company A company with its equity securities traded on an exchange.

Public limited companies A type of limited company in many jurisdictions with entity-level taxation but no restrictions on the number of shareholders or transferability of ownership interest; the most suitable organizational form for a company that seeks to go public.

Public–private partnership A long-term contractual relationship between the public and private sectors for the purpose of having the private sector deliver a project or service traditionally provided by the public sector. Infrastructure is increasingly being financed privately through public–private partnerships by local, regional, and national governments.

Public–private partnership (PPP) An agreement between the public sector and the private sector to finance, build, and operate public infrastructure, such as hospitals and toll roads.

Pull on liquidity An action or event that accelerates cash outflows.

Purchase agreement Legal document in a securitization transaction that outlines the representations and warranties that the seller makes about the assets sold.

Pure discount bonds Bonds that do not pay interest during their life. They are issued at a discount to par value and redeemed at par. Also called zero-coupon bonds.

Put An option that gives the holder the right to sell an underlying asset to another party at a fixed price over a specific period of time.

Put option The right to sell an underlying.

Putable bonds Bonds that give the bondholder the right to sell the bond back to the issuer at a predetermined price on specified dates.

Put–call forward parity Describes the no-arbitrage condition in which at $t = 0$ the present value of the price of a long forward commitment plus the price of the long put must equal the price of the long call plus the price of the risk-free asset (with face value of the exercise price of both the call and the put).

Put–call parity Describes the no-arbitrage condition in which at $t = 0$ the price of the long underlying asset plus the price of the long put must equal the price of the long call plus the price of the risk-free asset (with face value of the exercise price of both the call and the put).

Quantile A value at or below which a stated fraction of the data lies. Also referred to as a fractile.

Quantitative easing An expansionary monetary policy based on aggressive open market purchase operations.

Quartiles Quantiles that divide a distribution into four equal parts.

Quick ratio A measure of liquidity that is the ratio of cash, marketable securities, and receivables to current liabilities.

Quintiles Quantiles that divide a distribution into five equal parts.

Quota rents Profits that foreign producers can earn by raising the price of their goods higher than they would without a quota.

Quotas Government policies that restrict the quantity of a good that can be imported into a country, generally for a specified period of time.

Quote-driven market A market in which dealers acting as principals facilitate trading.

Quoted margin Specified spread of a floating rate instrument over a market reference rate or benchmark.

Range The difference between the maximum and minimum values in a dataset.

Rapid amortization provisions Provisions in receivable ABS that may require early principal amortization if specific events occur. Such provisions are referred to as early amortization and are included to safeguard the credit quality of the issue, particularly during the revolving period.

Razor, razorblade pricing A pricing approach that combines a low price on a piece of equipment and high-margin pricing on repeat-purchase consumables.

Real assets Generally, these are tangible physical assets, such as real estate, infrastructure, and natural resources, but they also include such intangibles as patents, intellectual property, and goodwill. Real assets generate current or expected future cash flows and/or are considered a store of value.

Real estate Includes borrowed or ownership capital in buildings or land. Developed land includes commercial and industrial real estate, residential real estate, and infrastructure.

Real option A right, but not an obligation, for management to make a decision with respect to a capital investment that alters future cash flows from the original forecasted scenario.

Real risk-free interest rate The single-period interest rate for a completely risk-free security if no inflation were expected.

Rebalancing Adjusting the weights of the constituent securities in an index.

Rebalancing policy The set of rules that guide the process of restoring a portfolio's asset class weights to those specified in the strategic asset allocation.

Recapitalization Recapitalization via private equity describes the steps a firm takes to increase or introduce leverage to its portfolio company and pay itself a dividend out of the new capital structure.

Recognition lag The lag in government response to an economic problem resulting from the delay in confirming a change in the state of the economy.

Recourse loan Loan in which the lender has a claim against the borrower for the shortfall (deficiency) between the amount of the outstanding mortgage balance and the proceeds received from the sale of the property.

Recovery rate (RR) The percentage of an outstanding debt claim recovered when an issuer defaults

Redemption fee A fee charged to discourage redemptions and to offset the transaction costs for remaining investors in the fund.

Refinancing rate A type of central bank policy rate.

Regionalism In between the two extremes of bilateralism and multilateralism. In regionalism, a group of countries cooperate with one another. Both bilateralism and regionalism can be conducted at the exclusion of other groups. For example, regional blocs may agree to provide trade benefits to one another and increase barriers for those outside of that group.

Registered bonds Bonds for which ownership is recorded by either name or serial number.

Regression analysis Allows us to test hypotheses about the relationship between two variables, by quantifying the strength of the relationship between the two variables, and to use one variable to make predictions about the other variable.

Regression coefficients The collective term for the intercept and slope coefficients in the regression model.

Regret The feeling that an opportunity has been missed; typically, an expression of *hindsight bias.*

Regret-aversion bias An emotional bias in which people tend to avoid making decisions that will result in action out of fear that the decision will turn out poorly.

Relative dispersion The amount of dispersion relative to a reference value or benchmark.

Reopening Issuing bonds by increasing the size of an existing bond issue with a price significantly different from par.

Replication A strategy in which a derivative's cash flow stream may be recreated using a combination of long or short positions in an underlying asset and borrowing or lending cash.

Repo rate The interest rate on a repurchase agreement.

Representativeness bias A belief perseverance bias in which people tend to classify new information based on past experiences and classifications.

Repurchase agreement (Repo) A form of collateralized loan involving the sale of a security with a simultaneous agreement by the seller to buy back the same security from the purchaser at an agreed-on price and future date. The party who sells the security at the inception of the repurchase agreement and buys it back at maturity is borrowing money from the other party, and the security sold and subsequently repurchased represents the collateral.

Repurchase date The date when the party who sold the security at the inception of a repurchase agreement buys back the security from the cash lending counterparty.

Repurchase price The price at which the party who sold the security at the inception of the repurchase agreement buys back the security from the cash lending counterparty.

Required margin Also known as discount margin. The market-determined yield spread over or under the market reference rate such that a floating-rate loan is priced at par on a rate reset date following issuance.

Required rate of return The rate of return required by investors given the risk of the bond investment, also known as the market discount rate or required yield.

Required yield The rate of return required by investors given the risk of the bond investment, also known as the market discount rate of required rate of return.

Required yield spread The difference in yield-to-maturity between a bond and that of a government benchmark bond with the same or similar time-to-maturity.

Resampling A statistical method that repeatedly draws samples from the original observed data sample for the statistical inference of population parameters.

Reserve currency A currency held by global central banks in significant quantities and widely used to conduct international trade and financial transactions.

Reserve requirement The requirement for banks to hold reserves in proportion to the size of deposits.

Residual The amount of deviation of an observed value of the dependent variable from its estimated value based on the fitted regression line.

Restricted domestic currency A currency with limited convertibility into other currencies due to illiquidity.

Return on assets (ROA) A profitability ratio calculated as net income divided by average total assets; indicates a company's net profit generated per dollar invested in total assets.

Return on equity (ROE) A profitability ratio calculated as net income divided by average shareholders' equity.

Return on invested capital (ROIC) A measure of the profitability of a company relative to the amount of capital invested by the equityholders and debtholders.

Return on sales An indicator of profitability, calculated as net income divided by revenue; indicates how much of each dollar of revenues is left after all costs and expenses. Also referred to as *net profit margin.*

Return-generating model A model that can provide an estimate of the expected return of a security given certain parameters and estimates of the values of the independent variables in the model.

Revenue bonds Bonds issued by non-sovereign governments related to a government sponsored project expected to generate future cash flow as a primary source of repayment.

Reverse repurchase agreement A repurchase agreement viewed from the perspective of the cash lending counterparty.

Reverse stock split A reduction in the number of shares outstanding with a corresponding increase in share price but no change to the company's underlying fundamentals.

Revolving credit agreements The most reliable form of short-term bank borrowing facilities; they are in effect for multiple years (e.g., three to five years) and can have optional medium-term loan features. Also known as *revolvers.*

Rho The change in a given derivative instrument for a given small change in the risk-free interest rate, holding everything else constant. Rho measures the sensitivity of the option to the risk-free interest rate.

Ricardian equivalence An economic theory that implies that it makes no difference whether a government finances a deficit by increasing taxes or issuing debt.

Risk Exposure to uncertainty. The chance of a loss or adverse outcome as a result of an action, inaction, or external event.

Risk averse The assumption that an investor will choose the least risky alternative.

Risk aversion The dislike for risk such that compensation is required in terms of higher expected returns for assuming higher risk.

Risk budgeting The establishment of objectives for individuals, groups, or divisions of an organization that takes into account the allocation of an acceptable level of risk.

Risk exposure The state of being exposed or vulnerable to a risk. The extent to which an organization is sensitive to underlying risks.

Risk governance The top-down process and guidance that directs risk management activities to align with and support the overall enterprise.

Risk management The process of identifying the level of risk an organization wants, measuring the level of risk the organization currently has, taking actions that bring the actual level of risk to the desired level of risk, and monitoring the new actual level of risk so that it continues to be aligned with the desired level of risk.

Risk management framework The infrastructure, process, and analytics needed to support effective risk management in an organization.

Risk premium An extra return expected by investors for bearing some specified risk.

Risk shifting Actions to change the distribution of risk outcomes.

Risk tolerance The level of risk an investor is willing and able to bear.

Risk transfer Strategies implemented to mitigate the impact of specific risks by transferring them to an insurance company.

Risk-neutral pricing A no-arbitrage derivative value established separately from investor views on risk that uses underlying asset volatility and the risk-free rate to calculate the present value of future cash flows.

Risk-neutral probability The computed probability used in binomial option pricing by which the discounted weighted sum of expected values of the underlying equal the current option price. Specifically, this probability is computed using the risk-free rate and assumed up gross return and down gross return of the underlying.

Rollover risk The likelihood that a property owner will lose an existing tenant and forgo income until a new one is found.

Safety-first rules Rules for portfolio selection that focus on the risk that portfolio value or portfolio return will fall below some minimum acceptable level over some time horizon.

Sample correlation coefficient A standardized measure of how two variables in a sample move together. It is the ratio of the sample covariance to the product of the two variables' standard deviations.

Sample covariance A measure of how two variables in a sample move together.

Sample excess kurtosis A sample measure of the degree of a distribution's kurtosis in excess of the normal distribution's kurtosis.

Sample mean The sum of the sample observations divided by the sample size.

Sample skewness A sample measure of the degree of asymmetry of a distribution.

Sample standard deviation The positive square root of the sample variance.

Sample variance The sum of squared deviations around the mean divided by the degrees of freedom.

Sample-size neglect A type of representativeness bias in which financial market participants incorrectly assume that small sample sizes are representative of populations (or "real" data).

Sampling distribution The distribution of all distinct possible values that a statistic can assume when computed from samples of the same size randomly drawn from the same population.

Sampling error The difference between the observed value of a statistic and the estimate resulting from using subsets of the population.

Sampling plan The set of rules used to select a sample.

Saving deposits Bank deposits typically held for non-transactional purposes that often have a stated term.

Scatter plot A two-dimensional graphical plot of paired observations of values for the independent and dependent variables in a simple linear regression.

Scenario analysis A variation of the valuation process combining a base case with alternative outcomes, allowing the incorporation of more favorable or adverse scenarios in the valuation process.

Scraping An automated, large-scale, algorithm-driven approach that retrieves otherwise unstructured data available on websites and creates data in a more structured format.

Seasoned offering An offering in which an issuer sells additional units of a previously issued security.

Secondary bond markets Fixed-income markets comprised of investors trading existing bonds amongst themselves.

Secondary market The market where securities are traded among investors.

Secondary precedence rules Rules that determine how to rank orders placed at the same time.

Secondary sale Sale of a private company stake to another private equity firm or group of financial buyers.

Secondary-stage investments The second stage of development of an infrastructure asset. Secondary-stage investments involve existing infrastructure facilities or fully operational assets that do not require further investment or development over the investment horizon. These assets generate immediate cash flow and returns expected over the investment period.

Sector indexes Indexes that represent and track different economic sectors—such as consumer goods, energy, finance, health care, and technology—on either a national, regional, or global basis.

Secured With collateral; secured debt is backed by the cash flows of the issuer and the collateral as a secondary source of repayment.

Secured loans Loans collateralized by an asset of the borrower.

Security Evidence of equity or debt interest or in an entity or a related right, such as a derivative. Often standardized to conform to security exchange requirements.

Security characteristic line A plot of the excess return of a security on the excess return of the market.

Security market index A portfolio of securities representing a given security market, market segment, or asset class.

Security market line The graphical representation of the CAPM formula, showing the relationship between expected return and beta.

Security selection The process of selecting individual securities; typically, security selection has the objective of generating superior risk-adjusted returns relative to a portfolio's benchmark.

Security tokens Digitizes the ownership rights associated with publicly traded securities.

Segmenting A process of identifying and grouping customers by decision-useful attributes.

Self-attribution bias A bias in which people take too much credit for successes (*self-enhancing*) and assign responsibility to others for failures (*self-protecting*).

Self-control bias A bias in which people fail to act in pursuit of their long-term, overarching goals because of a lack of self-discipline.

Self-investment limits With respect to investment limitations applying to pension plans, restrictions on the percentage of assets that can be invested in securities issued by the pension plan sponsor.

Sell-side firm A broker/dealer that sells securities and provides independent investment research and recommendations to their clients (i.e., buy-side firms).

Semi-strong-form efficient market A market in which security prices reflect all publicly known and available information.

Semiannual bond basis yield Also known as a semiannual bond equivalent yield, it is an annualized interest rate with a periodicity of two.

Semiannual bond equivalent yield Also known as a semiannual bond basis yield, it is an annualized interest rate with a periodicity of two.

Senior debt A debt obligation with higher priority of payment than junior debt obligations.

Senior unsecured debt The highest-ranked debt in an issuer's capital structure which is a general obligation of the borrower.

Seniority Priority of payment of various debt obligations.

Sensitivity analysis A form of analysis used to determine the impact of a change in one or more key variables affecting investment returns or valuation.

Separately managed account (SMA) An investment portfolio managed exclusively for the benefit of an individual or institution.

Service period The time between the grant and vesting dates for an employee share-based award, usually measured in years.

Settlement The closing date at which the counterparties of a derivative contract exchange payment for the underlying as required by the contract.

Settlement price The price determined by an exchange's clearinghouse in the daily settlement of the mark-to-market process. The price reflects an average of the final futures trades of the day.

Share class Types of equity securities that have different voting rights—for example, an issuer may issue Class A shares that carry one vote per share and Class B shares that carry ten votes per share.

Share repurchase A transaction in which a company buys back its own shares. Unlike stock dividends and stock splits, share repurchases use corporate cash.

Shareholder activism A range of actions by a corporation's shareholders that are intended to result in some change in the corporation, typically a change in the board of directors, management, or business strategy.

Shareholder derivative lawsuit A legal action by a shareholder on behalf of a company, not the shareholder personally, against a third party. Often, the third party is a director or manager who the shareholder believes has harmed the company.

Shareholder engagement Shareholder engagement reflects active ownership by investors in which the investor seeks to influence a corporation's decisions on ESG matters, either through dialogue with corporate officers or votes at a shareholder assembly (in the case of equity).

Shareholder theory of corporate governance Espoused by Milton Friedman in his famous 1970 essay, the shareholder theory holds that the objective of a business is to increase profits and shareholder value.

Shareholders Hold a direct equity position in a firm, and both individual persons and financial institutions can be shareholders. The term comes from the individual or investment firm literally having a share of the company. It is most commonly used when talking about the rights and responsibilities that come with being an "owner" of a company, such as stewardship, voting, and engagement. This differentiates it from a situation where an individual or an investment firm lends money or invests in a bond (in other words, they are not an equityholder of a company). Because bond investors do not have a share and are not owners of a company, they cannot vote. Nonetheless, expectations around engagement are increasing for those who invest in loans and bonds as well, making the difference between the two terms more subtle.

Shares Units of ownership interest in a limited company.

Sharpe ratio The ratio of mean excess return to standard deviation (excess return).

Shelf registration A type of public offering that allows the issuer to file a single, all-encompassing offering circular that covers a series of bond issues.

Short A trading position in a **derivative contract** that gains value as the price of the **underlying** moves lower.

Short biased These strategies use quantitative, technical, and fundamental analysis to short overvalued equity securities with limited or no long-side exposures.

Short position A position in an asset or contract in which one has sold an asset one does not own, or in which a right under a contract can be exercised against oneself.

Short selling A transaction in which borrowed securities are sold with the intention to repurchase them at a lower price at a later date and return them to the lender.

Short-run average total cost The curve describing average total cost when some costs are considered fixed.

Shortfall risk The risk that portfolio value or portfolio return will fall below some minimum acceptable level over some time horizon.

Shutdown point The point at which average revenue is equal to the firm's average variable cost.

Side letter A side agreement created between the GP and specific LPs. These agreements exist *outside* the LPA. These agreements provide additional terms and conditions related to the investment agreement.

Signpost An indicator, market level, data piece, or event that signals a risk is becoming more or less likely. An analyst can think of signposts like a traffic light.

Simple linear regression (SLR) An approach for estimating the linear relationship between a dependent variable and a single independent variable by minimizing the sum of the squared deviations between the fitted line and the observed values.

Simple random sample A subset of a larger population created in such a way that each element of the population has an equal probability of being selected to the subset.

Simple random sampling The procedure of drawing a sample to satisfy the definition of a simple random sample.

Simple yield The sum of the coupon payments plus the straight-line amortized share of the gain or loss divided by the bond's flat price. Simple yields are used mostly to quote JGBs.

Simulation A technique for exploring how a target variable (e.g. portfolio returns) would perform in a hypothetical environment specified by the user, rather than a historical setting.

Simulation trial A complete pass through the steps of a simulation.

Single-price auction A debt securities auction in which all bidders pay the same price.

Sinking fund Provisions that reduce the credit risk of a bond issue by requiring the issuer to retire a portion of the bond's principal outstanding each year.

Situational influences External factors, such as environmental or cultural elements, that shape our behavior.

Skewed Not symmetrical.

Skewness A quantitative measure of skew (lack of symmetry); a synonym of skew. It is computed as the average cubed deviation from the mean standardized by dividing by the standard deviation cubed.

Slope coefficient The change in the estimated value of the dependent variable for a one-unit change in the value of the independent variable.

Small country A country that is a price taker in the world market for a product and cannot influence the world market price.

Smart beta Involves the use of simple, transparent, rules-based strategies as a basis for investment decisions.

Smart contracts Computer programs that are designed to self-execute on the basis of pre-specified terms and conditions agreed to by parties to a contract.

Social infrastructure investments A category of infrastructure investments that are directed toward human activities and include such assets as educational, health care, social housing, and correctional facilities, with the focus on providing, operating, and maintaining the asset infrastructure.

Soft commodities Standardized agricultural products, such as cattle and corn, with markets often involving the physical delivery of the underlying upon settlement.

Soft hurdle rate Hurdle rate where the fee is calculated on the entire return when the hurdle is exceeded. With a soft hurdle, GPs are able to catch up performance fees once the hurdle threshold is exceeded.

Soft power A means of influencing another country's decisions without force or coercion. Soft power can be built over time through actions, such as cultural programs, advertisement, travel grants, and university exchange.

Soft-bullet covered bonds Delay the bond default and payment acceleration of bond cash flows until a new final maturity date, which is usually up to a year after the original maturity date.

Solvency Refers to the condition in which firm value exceeds the face value of debt used to finance the firm's assets.

Solvency ratios Ratios that measure a company's ability to meet its long-term obligations.

Solvency risk The risk that an organization does not survive or succeed because it runs out of cash, even though it might otherwise be solvent.

Sophisticated investors Individuals or entities that are permitted in a jurisdiction to trade unregistered or, generally, less regulated securities, including shares of privately held companies; also called *accredited investors*.

Sovereign immunity A principle that limits legal recourse of lenders from forcing a sovereign borrower to declare bankruptcy or liquidate its assets to settle debt claims.

Spearman rank correlation coefficient A measure of correlation applied to ranked data.

Special dividend A dividend paid by a company that does not pay dividends on a regular schedule, or a dividend that supplements regular cash dividends with an extra payment.

Special purpose acquisition company A "blank check" company that exists solely for the purpose of acquiring an unspecified private company within a predetermined period or return capital to investors.

Special purpose entity (SPE) Also referred to as a special purpose vehicle (SPV), this legal entity is created for a specific economic purpose. In the case of a project SPV, the entity's sole purpose is to facilitate the construction, operation, and financing of an infrastructure asset over its contractual life.

Special purpose vehicle See *special purpose entity*.

Special situations An area of private capital investment which targets return by investing in stressed, distressed, or event-driven opportunities.

Split ratings Complex risks viewed very differently by rating agencies

Sponsored A type of depository receipt in which the foreign company whose shares are held by the depository has a direct involvement in the issuance of the receipts.

Spot curve Yields-to-maturity on a series of default-risk-free zero-coupon bonds.

Spot markets Markets in which specific assets are exchanged at current prices. Spot markets are often referred to as **cash markets**.

Spot prices The current prices prevailing in **spot markets**.

Spot rates Yields-to-maturity on default-risk-free zero-coupon bonds.

Spread The difference in yield-to-maturity between a bond and that of a another bond.

Spread risk Bond price risk arising from changes in the yield spread on credit-risky bonds; reflects changes in the market's assessment and/or pricing of credit migration (or downgrade) risk and market liquidity risk.

Spurious correlation Refers to: 1) correlation between two variables that reflects chance relationships in a particular dataset; 2) correlation induced by a calculation that mixes each of two variables with a third variable; and 3) correlation between two variables arising not from a direct relation between them but from their relation to a third variable.

Stablecoin A cryptocurrency that aims to maintain a stable value relative to a specified asset or to a pool or basket of assets.

Stackelberg model A prominent model of strategic decision making in which firms are assumed to make their decisions sequentially.

Staggered board A structure of board elections in which only part of the board is elected simultaneously—for example, only one-third of the board may be up for election each year, so the board can be replaced over three years, not in one year if all seats were elected annually. This structure fosters greater continuity of board members but is an obstacle for shareholders seeking to effect change.

Stakeholder theory of corporate governance An expansion of the shareholder theory of corporate governance under which the objective of a business is to maximize value for, and balance the interests of, a broad group of stakeholders, including shareholders, employees, society, and the non-human environment.

Stakeholders Any party with an interest, financial or non-financial, in an entity or its actions.

Standard deviation The positive square root of the variance; a measure of dispersion in the same units as the original data.

Standard error of the estimate A measure of the distance between the observed values of the dependent variable and those predicted from the estimated regression. The smaller this value, the better the fit of the model. Also known as the standard error of the regression and the root mean square error.

Standard error of the forecast Used to provide an interval estimate around the estimated regression line. It is necessary because the regression line does not describe the relationship between the dependent and independent variables perfectly.

Standard error of the slope coefficient Calculated for simple linear regression by dividing the standard error of the estimate by the square root of the variation of the independent variable.

Standardization The process of creating protocols for the production, sale, transport, or use of a product or service. Standardization occurs when relevant parties agree to follow these protocols together. It helps support expanded economic and financial activities, such as trade and capital flows that support higher economic growth and standards of living, across borders.

Standards of conduct Behaviors required by a group; established benchmarks that clarify or enhance a group's code of ethics.

Standing limit orders A limit order at a price below market and which therefore is waiting to trade.

State actors Typically national governments, political organizations, or country leaders that exert authority over a country's national security and resources. The South African President, Sultan of Brunei, Malaysia's Parliament, and the British Prime Minister are all examples of state actors.

Statement of cash flows A financial statement that details the movement of cash over a period. The statement is classified into operating, investing, and financing activities.

Static trade-off theory of capital structure A theory pertaining to a company's optimal capital structure; the optimal level of debt is found at the point where additional debt would cause the costs of financial distress to increase by a greater amount than the benefit of the additional tax shield.

Statistically significant A result indicating that the null hypothesis can be rejected; with reference to an estimated regression coefficient, frequently understood to mean a result indicating that the corresponding population regression coefficient is different from zero.

Status quo bias An emotional bias in which people do nothing (i.e., maintain the status quo) instead of making a change.

Statutory voting A common method of voting where each share represents one vote.

Step-up bonds Bonds for which the coupon, be it fixed or floating, increases by specified margins at specified dates.

Stock dividend A type of dividend in which a company distributes additional shares of its common stock to shareholders instead of cash.

Stock exchange An exchange in which equity securities are traded. See *exchanges*.

Stock split An increase in the number of shares outstanding with a consequent decrease in share price, but no change to the company's underlying fundamentals.

Stockholder overhang The downward pressure on the share price of stock as large blocks of shares are being sold on the open market.

Stop order An order in which a trader has specified a stop price condition. Also called *stop-loss order*.

Stop-loss order See *stop order*.

Stranded assets A resource that is no longer economically valuable owing to changes in demand, regulations, or availability of substitutes—for example, a newly discovered oil well that will not be brought into production.

Strategic asset allocation A long-term strategy that establishes target allocations for various asset classes and aims to optimize the balance between risk and reward by diversifying investments.

Stratified random sampling A procedure that first divides a population into subpopulations (strata) based on classification criteria and then randomly draws samples from each stratum in sizes proportional to that of each stratum in the population.

Street convention For yield measures on fixed-income instruments that assume payments are made on scheduled dates and ignore weekends and holidays.

Stress testing A specific type of scenario analysis that estimates losses in rare and extremely unfavorable combinations of events or scenarios.

Strong-form efficient market A market in which security prices reflect all public and private information.

Structural budget deficit Also known as the cyclically adjusted budget deficit. The deficit that would exist if the economy was at full employment (or full potential output).

Structural subordination Refers to the positioning of debt, which is issued by a legal entity, typically a holding company, which is separate and therefore one step removed from an operating company, which holds assets pledged under a security agreement to senior secured debtholders.

Structured notes A broad category of securities that incorporate the features of debt instruments and one or more embedded derivatives designed to achieve a particular issuer or investor objective.

Subordinated debt A class of unsecured debt that ranks below a firm's senior unsecured obligations.

Subordination A form of internal credit enhancement that relies on creating more than one bond tranche and ordering the claim priorities for ownership or interest in an asset between the tranches. The ordering of the claim priorities is called a senior/subordinated structure, where the tranches of highest seniority are called senior, followed by subordinated or junior tranches. Also called **credit tranching**.

Subprime loans Lending to borrowers with lower credit quality, high DTI, and/or are loans with higher LTV, and include loans that are secured by second liens otherwise subordinated to other loans.

Sum of squares error (SSE) A measure of the total deviation between observed and estimated values of the dependent variable. It is calculated by subtracting each estimated value $\hat{Y}_i$ from its corresponding observed value Y_i, squaring each of these differences, and then summing all of these squared differences.

Sum of squares regression (SSR) A measure of the explained variation in the dependent variable, calculated as the sum of the squared differences between the predicted value of the dependent variable, Y ^_i, based on the estimated regression line, and the mean of the dependent variable, Y¯.

Sum of squares total (SST) A measure of the total variation in the dependent variable in a simple linear regression. It is calculated by subtracting the mean of the observed values $\overline{Y}$ from each of the observed values Y_i, squaring each of these differences, and then summing all of these squared differences.

Sunk costs A cost that has already been incurred.

Supervised learning A type of machine learning in which the system attempts to learn to model relationships based on labeled training data.

Supervisory board In some jurisdictions, a corporation's board of directors is formally composed of a supervisory board and a management board. The supervisory board appoints and oversees the management board and often includes representatives of employees and other non-shareholder stakeholders.

Supply chain The sequence of processes involved in the creation and delivery of a physical product to the end customer, both within and external to a firm, regardless of whether those steps are performed by a single firm.

Supply shock A typically unexpected disturbance to supply.

Survivorship bias Relates to the inclusion of only current investment funds in a database. As such, the returns of funds that are no longer available in the marketplace (have been liquidated) are excluded from the database. Also see *backfill bias.*

Swap A firm commitment involving a periodic exchange of cash flows.

Swap contract An agreement between two parties to exchange a series of future cash flows.

Swap execution facility (SEF) A swap trading platform accessed by multiple **dealers**.

Swap rate The fixed rate to be paid by the fixed-rate payer specified in a swap contract.

Syndicate A group of lenders, typically made up of banks.

Synthetic protective put The combination of a synthetic long underlying position (i.e., a long forward and risk-free borrowing) and a purchased put on the underlying.

Systematic risk Risk that affects the entire market or economy; it cannot be avoided and is inherent in the overall market. Systematic risk is also known as *non-diversifiable* or *market risk.*

Systematic sampling A procedure of selecting every *k*th member until reaching a sample of the desired size. The sample that results from this procedure should be approximately random.

Systemic risk Refers to risks supervisory authorities believe are likely to have broad impact across the financial market infrastructure and affect a wide swath of market participants.

Tactical asset allocation A proactive strategy that adjusts asset class allocations within a portfolio based on short-term market trends, economic conditions, or valuation changes to capitalize on temporary market inefficiencies or opportunities to improve returns or manage risk more effectively.

Target capital structure Management's desired proportions of debt and equity financing, usually stated on a book value basis or indirectly using a financial leverage metric, such as net or gross debt to EBITDA or credit rating.

Target independent A bank's ability to determine the definition of inflation that they target, the rate of inflation that they target, and the horizon over which the target is to be achieved.

Target semideviation A measure of downside risk, calculated as the square root of the average of the squared deviations of observations below the target (also called *target downside deviation*).

Tariffs Taxes that a government levies on imported goods.

Tax base The amount at which an asset or liability is valued for tax purposes.

Tax expense An aggregate of an entity's income tax payable (or recoverable in the case of a tax benefit) and any changes in deferred tax assets and liabilities. It is essentially the income tax payable or recoverable if these had been determined based on accounting profit rather than taxable income.

Taxable income The portion of an entity's income that is subject to income taxes under the tax laws of its jurisdiction.

Taxable temporary differences Temporary differences that result in a taxable amount in a future period when determining the taxable profit as the balance sheet item is recovered or settled.

Technical analysis A form of security analysis that uses price and volume data, often displayed graphically, in decision making.

Tender offer A solicitation by a current or prospective shareholder to other shareholders to acquire a substantial percentage, including 100%, of shares at a specified price. This action is usually undertaken by a potential acquirer whose bid was rejected by the issuer's board of directors, prompting the potential acquirer to appeal directly to shareholders.

Tenor Remaining time-to-maturity for a fixed-income instrument.

Term repos Repos with a maturity longer than one day.

Term structure of interest rates Also known as the maturity structure of interest rates, refers to the difference in interest rates or benchmark yields by time-to-maturity.

Terminal stock value The expected value of a share at the end of the investment horizon—in effect, the expected selling price. Also called *terminal value.*

Terminal value The expected value of a share at the end of the investment horizon—in effect, the expected selling price.

Test of the mean of the differences A statistical test for differences based on paired observations drawn from samples that are dependent on each other.

Text analytics Involves the use of computer programs to analyze and derive meaning typically from large, unstructured text- or voice-based datasets, such as company filings, written reports, quarterly earnings calls, social media, email, internet postings, and surveys.

Thematic risks Known risks that evolve and expand over a period of time. Climate change, pattern migration, the rise of populist forces, and the ongoing threat of terrorism fall into this category.

Thin-tailed Describes a distribution that has relatively less weight in the tails than the normal distribution (also called platykurtic).

Tiered pricing A pricing approach that charges different prices to different buyers, commonly based on volume purchased.

Timberland investment management organizations Entities that support institutional investors by managing their investments in timberland by analyzing and acquiring suitable timberland holdings.

Time tranching Structure of a securitization that allows for the redistribution of "prepayment risk" among bond classes by creating bond classes of different expected maturities.

Time value The difference between an option's premium and its intrinsic value.

Time value decay The process by which the time value of an option declines toward zero as the option's expiration date is approached.

Time-weighted rate of return The compound rate of growth of one unit of currency invested in a portfolio during a stated measurement period; a measure of investment performance that is not sensitive to the timing and amount of withdrawals or additions to the portfolio.

Tokenization The process of representing ownership rights to physical assets on a blockchain or distributed ledger.

Top-down analysis An investment selection approach that begins with consideration of macroeconomic conditions and then evaluates markets and industries based upon such conditions.

Total probability rule for expected value A rule explaining the expected value of a random variable in terms of expected values of the random variable conditional on mutually exclusive and exhaustive scenarios.

Total return Measures the price appreciation, or percentage change in price of the securities in an index or portfolio, plus any income received over the period.

Total return index An index that reflects the price appreciation or percentage change in price of the constituent securities plus any income received since inception.

Total working capital The difference between current assets and current liabilities.

Tracking error The standard deviation of the differences between a portfolio's returns and its benchmark's returns; a synonym of active risk.

Tracking risk The standard deviation of the differences between a portfolio's returns and its benchmarks returns. Also called *tracking error.*

Trade creation When regional integration results in the replacement of higher cost domestic production by lower cost imports from other members.

Trade diversion When regional integration results in lower-cost imports from non-member countries being replaced with higher-cost imports from members.

Trade sale A portion or division of a private company sold via either direct sale or auction to a strategic buyer interested in increasing the scale and scope of an existing business.

Trade settlement date The date when the buyer and seller transfer consideration and securities.

Traditional investment markets Markets for traditional investments, which include all publicly traded debts and equities and shares in pooled investment vehicles that hold publicly traded debts and/or equities.

Tranches A grouping of securities within an issue with characteristics that vary from other tranches, such as different credit quality and seniority.

Transfer payments Welfare payments made through the social security system that exist to provide a basic minimum level of income for low-income households.

Transition risks Economic and financial losses from the transition to a lower-carbon economy in response to climate change—for example, the abandonment of an oil well that is no longer economical.

Treasury Inflation-Protected Securities (TIPS) US Treasury bonds with a principal that is adjusted for changes in the Consumer Price Index. TIPS are issued in 5-, 10-, and 30-year maturities.

Treynor ratio A measure of risk-adjusted performance that relates a portfolio's returns in excess of the risk-free rate to a portfolio's beta.

Trimmed mean A mean computed after excluding a stated small percentage of the lowest and highest observations.

Triparty repo A repurchase agreement in which the transacting parties agree to use a third-party agent that provides access to a larger collateral pool and multiple counterparties, as well as valuation and safekeeping of assets.

True yield Measures on fixed-income instruments use actual payment dates, accounting for weekends and holidays. The true yield on an instrument is always lower than the street convention yield.

Turn-of-the-year effect Calendar anomaly that stock market returns in January are significantly higher compared to the rest of the months of the year, with most of the abnormal returns reported during the first five trading days in January.

Two-fund separation theorem The theory that all investors regardless of taste, risk preferences, and initial wealth will hold a combination of two portfolios or funds: a risk-free asset and an optimal portfolio of risky assets.

Two-way table A table of the frequency distribution of observations classified on the basis of two discrete variables. Also known as *Contingency table.*

Two-week repo rate The interest rate on a two-week repurchase agreement; may be used as a policy rate by a central bank.

Type I error The error of rejecting a true null hypothesis; a false positive.

Type II error The error of not rejecting a false null hypothesis; false negative.

Uncommitted lines of credit Sources of bank credit that a bank can refuse to honor. Uncommitted credit lines are made up to a certain principal amount for a pre-determined maximum maturity, charging a market reference rate plus an issuer-specific spread on only the principal outstanding for the period of use.

Underfitted When a machine learning model treats true parameters as if they are noise and is unable to recognize relationships in the training data, making the model more likely to fail to fully discover patterns that underlie the data.

Underlying The asset referred to in a **derivative contract**.

Underwritten offering A type of securities issue mechanism in which the investment bank guarantees the sale of the securities at an offering price that is negotiated with the issuer. Also known as *firm commitment offering.*

Unearned revenue A liability account for money that has been collected for goods or services that have not yet been delivered; payment received in advance of providing a good or service. Also called *deferred revenue* or *deferred income.*

Unimodal A distribution with a single value that is most frequently occurring.

Unit economics The expression of revenues and costs on a per-unit basis.

Unitranche debt A hybrid or blended loan structure combining different tranches of secured and unsecured debt into a single loan with a single, blended interest rate.

Unsecured Without collateral; unsecured debt is backed only by cash flows of the issuer.

Unsponsored A type of depository receipt in which the foreign company whose shares are held by the depository has no involvement in the issuance of the receipts.

Unsupervised learning A type of machine learning in which the system tries to learn the structure of unlabeled data.

Utility tokens Tokens that provide services within a network, such as paying for services and network fees.

Validity instructions Instructions which indicate when the order may be filled.

Value added resellers Businesses that distribute a product and also handle more complex aspects of product installation, customization, service, or support.

Value at risk A money measure of the minimum value of losses expected during a specified time period at a given level of probability.

Value chain The systems and processes in a firm that create value for its customers.

Value proposition The product or service attributes valued by a firm's target customer that lead those customers to prefer that firm's offering.

Value-add real estate strategies Strategies that involve larger-scale redevelopment and repositioning of existing assets and that may allow the investor to earn a higher return compared with core-plus real estate strategies.

Value-based pricing Pricing set primarily by reference to the value of the product or service to customers.

VaR See *value at risk.*

Variance The expected value (the probability-weighted average) of squared deviations from a random variable's expected value.

Variance of a random variable The expected value (the probability-weighted average) of squared deviations from a random variable's expected value.

Variation margin The difference between current margin required and the current collateral price in a repurchase agreement.

Vega A measure of the sensitivity of an option's price to changes in the underlying's volatility.

Velocity The pace at which geopolitical risk impacts an investor portfolio.

Venture capital Private equity investment in a startup or early-stage company involving high risk and a high rate of failure.

Venture capital fund A hedge fund that seeks to buy, optimize, and ultimately sell portfolio companies to generate profits. See *private equity fund.*

Venture debt Private debt funding that provides venture capital backing to start-up or early-stage companies that may be generating little or negative cash flow.

Vest To become unconditionally entitled to.

Vesting date The day that an employee becomes unconditionally entitled to compensation.

Vintage year The year in which a private capital fund makes its first investment.

Volatility The standard deviation of the continuously compounded returns on the underlying asset.

Vote by proxy A mechanism that allows a designated party—such as another shareholder, a shareholder representative, or management—to vote on the shareholder's behalf.

Voting rights The power of shareholders to cast votes in corporate elections for directors and other matters submitted to a shareholder vote.

Warrant Debt feature or security granting the right to purchase additional common equity shares issued by the company at a predetermined price for a given period.

Waterfall structures These represent the distribution order for cash flows and risk to different tranches in a financing structure.

Weak-form efficient market hypothesis The belief that security prices fully reflect all past market data, which refers to all historical price and volume trading information.

Weighted average coupon rate (WAC) Rate calculated for a mortgage pass-through security by weighting the mortgage rate of each mortgage in the pool by the percentage of the outstanding mortgage balance relative to the outstanding amount of all the mortgages in the pool.

Weighted average maturity (WAM) Calculated for a mortgage pass-through security by weighting the remaining number of months to maturity of each mortgage in the pool by the outstanding mortgage balance relative to the outstanding amount of all the mortgages in the pool.

Weighted-average cost of capital (WACC) A weighted average of the after-tax required rates of return on a company's equity, debt, preferred stock, and other long-term financing sources, where the weights are the fraction of each source of financing in the company's current market value or management's target capital structure.

Winsorized mean A mean computed after assigning a stated percentage of the lowest values equal to one specified low value and a stated percentage of the highest values equal to one specified high value.

Write-off/liquidation Refers to a transaction that has not gone well, and the investment is likely to lose value. The private equity firm revises the value of its investment downward or liquidates the portfolio company.

Yield curve A graphical depiction of yields-to-maturity of bonds from the same issuer across maturities.

Yield spread The difference in yield-to-maturity between a bond and that of a another bond.

Yield-to-call An internal rate of return on a fixed-income instrument's cash flows assuming cash flows are received on scheduled dates and the bond is called at a certain call price and date.

Yield-to-maturity Internal rate of return on a fixed-income instrument's cash flows assuming all cash flows are received on their scheduled dates.

Yield-to-worst The lowest among a fixed-income instrument's yields-to-call and yield-to-maturity. A commonly cited yield measure for fixed-rate callable bonds.

Z-spread or zero-volatility spread is a constant yield spread for a bond over a government or swap curve.

Zero-coupon bonds Bonds that do not pay interest during their life. They are issued at a discount to par value and redeemed at par. Also called pure discount bond.